Lecture Notes in
Computer Science

Lecture Notes in Computer Science

Lecture Notes in Computer Science

Edited by G. Goos and J. Hartmanis

258

PARLE
Parallel Architectures
and Languages Europe

Volume I: Parallel Architectures
Eindhoven, The Netherlands, June 15–19, 1987
Proceedings

Edited by
J. W. de Bakker, A. J. Nijman and P. C. Treleaven

Springer-Verlag
Berlin Heidelberg New York London Paris Tokyo

CR Subject Classification (1987): C.1-4, D.1, D.3-4, F.1, F.3-4

ISBN 3-540-17943-7 Springer-Verlag Berlin Heidelberg New York
ISBN 0-387-17943-7 Springer-Verlag New York Berlin Heidelberg

Printing and binding: Druckhaus Beltz, Hemsbach/Bergstr.
2145/3140-543210

Preface

PARLE, the conference on Parallel Architectures and Languages Europe, was organized as a meeting place for researchers in the field of theory, design and applications of parallel computer systems. The initiative for the conference was taken by project 415 of ESPRIT (the European Strategic Programme for Research and Development in Information Technology). The scope of the conference covered central themes in the area of parallel architectures and languages including topics such as concurrent, object-oriented, logic and functional programming, MIMD and reduction machines, process theory, design and verification of parallel systems, performance evaluation, interconnection networks, systolic arrays, VLSI and RISC architectures, applications and special purpose architectures.

The scientific programme of PARLE consisted firstly of five invited lectures devoted to overviews of major recent research areas. Moreover, 44 papers were selected for presentation from 156 submitted ones. The program committee for PARLE was constituted as follows:

S. Abramsky (Imperial College)*
J.W. de Bakker (chairman,Amsterdam)*
J.P. Banâtre (Rennes)*
H. Barendregt (Nijmegen)*
W. Bibel (Munich)*
M. Broy (Passau)
W. Damm (Aachen)*
J. Gurd (Manchester)*
D. Harel (Weizmann and CMU)*
P. Henderson (Stirling)
L.O. Hertzberger (Amsterdam)*
T. Johnsson (Gøteborg)*
N.D. Jones (Copenhagen)
Ph. Jorrand (Grenoble)*
W. Kluge (Kiel)*

V.E. Kotov (Novosibirsk)
H.T. Kung (CMU)
H.W. Lawson (Linköping)*
G. Levi (Pisa).
D. May (INMOS)*
C. Moser (Orsay)
E.-R. Olderog (Kiel)*
W.P. de Roever (Eindhoven)
G. Roucairol (Bull)
G. Rozenberg (Leiden)*
L. Steels (Brussels)
J.-C. Syre (ECRC)*
P.C. Treleaven (chairman,
Univ.Coll.London)*
M. Vanneschi (Pisa)*

Members of the Program Committee who were present at the selection meeting are marked by a *.

We wish to extend our sincere thanks to the members of the Program Committee for their invaluable contributions to the shaping of the PARLE programme. We also express our gratitude to the PARLE referees for their assistance in this process.

The programme of PARLE furthermore comprised presentations on the subprojects which together constitute ESPRIT project 415. Parallel architectures based on a variety of programming styles (object-oriented, logic, functional, dataflow) were represented in these overviews.

The Proceedings of PARLE are collected in two volumes, the first one containing the papers in which the emphasis is more on Parallel Architectures, together with ESPRIT project 415 overviews, and the second one containing the papers which fall under the heading of Parallel Languages.

PARLE has received substantial sponsorship from the ESPRIT program, and from the companies which together form the consortium for ESPRIT project 415: AEG, West Germany; Nixdorf (Stollmann), West Germany; Bull, France; CSELT, Italy; GEC, UK; Philips, the Netherlands.

Philips Research Eindhoven was responsible for the local organization of PARLE. A special tribute is due to Frank Stoots for his skilful, cheerful and meticulous handling of all organizational details. Hans Oerlemans provided valuable help at crucial moments in the PARLE preparations. The Dutch National Concurrency Project assisted at various points in the organization. Technical support has been provided by the Centre for Mathematics and Computer Science, in particular by Ms. L. Vasmel-Kaarsemaker, and by University-College London.

Thanks to the contributions of all the above listed persons and institutions, we have been able to collect in these two volumes a wealth of material on the theme of PARLE. The editors would be amply rewarded for their efforts if these results were to prove instrumental for the further advancement of European research on Parallel Architectures and Languages.

March 1987   The Editors,

                                                  J.W. de Bakker
                                                  A.J. Nijman
                                                  P.C. Treleaven

Contents   Volume I

Contents Volume II

List of Referees

Alfons
Ambriova, V.
America, P.
Amjone, M.
Andersen, J.D.
Asirelli, P.
Aspetsberger, K.
Augustsson, L.
Baiardi, F.
Balbo, G.
Balsamo, S.
Bandman, O.L.
Barahona, P.M.
Barbuti, R.
Barringer, H.
Bayerl, S.
Beer, J.
Behr, P.
Benker, H.
Best, E.
Bistrov, A.V.
Bloedorn, H.
Bohm, A.P.W.
Brookes, S.
Bulyonkov, M.A.
Bush, V.J.
Capon, P.C.
Carlstedt, G.
Chassin de Kergommeaux, J. de
Cherkasova, L.A.
Cindio, F. de
Clausen, J.
Corsini, P.
Courcelle, B.
Cunningham, R.S.
Danvy, O.
Danulutto, M.
Dekkers, W.
Dencker, P.

Dill, D.L.
Dittrich, G.
Donatelli, L.
Duinker, W.
Eder, E.
Edwards, D.A.
Eekelen, M.C.J.D. van
Einarsson, B.
Emde Boas-Lubsen, G. van
Enjalbert, P.
Fagerstrom, J.
Fantechi, A.
Fehr, E.
Feijen, W.H.J.
Field, A.J.
Fischer, K.
Fjellborg, B.
Foley, J.F.
Francesco, N. de
Francoise, A.
Fronhofer, B.
Frosini, G.
Furbach, U.
Gamatie, B.
Gerth, R.
Glaser, H.W.
Goeman, H.J.M.
Goltz, U.
Graziano, F.
Groenewegen, L.
Grumberg, O.
Gruntz,
Hahn, W.
Halbwachs, N.
Hankin, C.L.
Hartel, P.H.
Harvills, P.
Hattem, M. van
Haverkort, B.R.H.M.

Held, A.J.

Holldobler, S.

Hommel, G.

Hooman, J.J.M.

HuBmann, H.

Janssens, D.

Jones, K.D.

Jonckers, V.

Josko, B.

Kaplan, S.

Keesmaat, N.W.

Kirkham, C.C.

Klint, P.

Klop, J.W.

Konrad, W.

Koymans, R.

Kramer, T.

Kreitz, C.

Kreowski, H.J.

Kroger, F.

Kuchcinski, K.

Kuchen, H.

Kucherov, G.A.

Kusche, K.D.

Laforenza, D.

Laurent, K.

Lange, O.

Lehmann, F.

Lelchuk, T.I.

Leoni, G.

Levin, D.Y.

Letz, R.

Lightner, J.M.

Lingas, A.

Lodi, E.

Loogen, R.

Lopriore, L.

Lotti, G.

Ljulyakov, A.V.

Main, M.

Maluzijnski, J.

Mancareua, P.

Marchuk, A.G.

Marcke, K. v.

Martinelli, E.

Marwedel, P.

Mazare, G.

Meijer, E.

Meinen, P.

Merceron, A.

Meurant, G.

Moiso, C.

Mooy, W.

Muntean, T.

Nepomnyashchy, V.A.

Nett, E.

Neugebauer, G.

Nickl, R.

Nicola, R. de

Nielsen, M.

Nocker, E.G.

Panzieri, F.

Paredis, J.

Park, D.

Pedreschi, D.

Pehrson, B.

Pepels, B.

Perrin, G.R.

Persson, M.

Peug, Z.

Philips, L.H.

Pinegger, T.

Plasmeyer, R.

Quinton, P.

Radig, B.

Rannov, R.

Ratiliffe, M.J.

Raynal, M.

Reisig, W.

Rezus, A.

Ribas, H.

Ricci, L.

Ringwood, G.A.

Robert, P.

Roscoe, A.W.

Rosenfeld, A.

Sadler, M.R.

Sardu, G.

Saubra, A.

Scheperes, J.

Schmeck, H.

Schnittgen, C.

Schneeberger, J.

Schumann, J.

Sedukhin, S.G.

Sestoft, P.

Seznec, A.

Simi, M.

Sleator, D.

Sofi, G.

Sondergaard, H.

Song, S.W.

Sralas, A.

Starreveld, A.G.

Stavridou, V.

Steen, M.R. van

Stoyan, H.

Swierstra, S.D.

Tanenbaum, A.

Tarini, F.

Taubner, D.

Tel, G.

Teugvald, E.

Thiagarajan, P.S.

Thorelli, L.E.

Tijgar, D.

Tomasi, A.

Tucci, S.

Vaglini, G.

Valkovsky, V.A.

Vautherin, J.

Vree, W.G.

Waning, E. van

Wanhammar, L.

Watson, I.

Westphal, H.

Yvon, J.

LEARNING TRANSLATION INVARIANT RECOGNITION
IN A MASSIVELY PARALLEL NETWORKS

Geoffrey E. Hinton
Computer Science Department
Carnegie-Mellon University
Pittsburgh PA 15213
U.S.A.

Abstract

One major goal of research on massively parallel networks of neuron-like processing elements is to discover efficient methods for recognizing patterns. Another goal is to discover general learning procedures that allow networks to construct the internal representations that are required for complex tasks. This paper describes a recently developed procedure that can learn to perform a recognition task. The network is trained on examples in which the input vector represents an instance of a pattern in a particular position and the required output vector represents its name. After prolonged training, the network develops canonical internal representations of the patterns and it uses these canonical representations to identify familiar patterns in novel positions.

1 Introduction

Most current models of human cognitive processes are based on logic. They assume that the formal manipulation of symbols is the essence of intelligence and they model cognitive processes by exploiting the sequential symbol processing abilities of conventional, serial computers (Newell, 1980). This approach has been very successful for modeling people's behavior when they are solving symbolic problems or playing intellectual games, and it has also had some success for expert systems which do not require much commonsense knowledge and do not involve complex interactions with the physical world. It has been much less successful for tasks like vision or commonsense reasoning that require rapid processing of large amounts of data or large amounts of stored knowledge.

An alternative approach that is much more compatible with fine-grained parallel computation is based on neural nets. It assumes that human abilities like perceptual interpretation, content-addressable memory, and commonsense reasoning are best understood by considering how computation might be organized in systems like the brain which consist of massive numbers of richly-interconnected but rather slow processing elements. Representations and search techniques which are efficient on serial machines are not necessarily suitable for massively parallel networks, particularly if the hardware is inhomogeneous and unreliable. The neural net approach has tended to emphasize learning from examples rather than programming. So far, it has been much less successful than the logic-based approach, partly because the ideas about representations and the procedures for learning them have been inadequate, and partly because it is very inefficient to simulate massively parallel networks with conventional computers.

The recent technological advances in VLSI and computer aided design mean that it is now much easier to build massively parallel machines and this has led to a new wave of interest in neural net models (Hinton and Anderson, 1981; Feldman and Ballard, 1982; Rumelhart, McClelland et. al., 1986). One very ambitious goal is to produce a general-purpose special-purpose chip (Parker, 1985). After learning, the chip would be special-purpose because the interactions between the processing elements would be specific to a particular task, with all the space and time efficiency which that implies. But before learning the chip would be general-purpose: The very same chip could learn any one of a large number of different tasks by being shown examples of input vectors and required output vectors from the relevant domain. We are still a long way from achieving this goal because the existing learning procedures are too slow, although one general-purpose special-purpose chip based on the Boltzmann machine learning procedure (Ackley, Hinton, and Sejnowski, 1985) has already been laid out (Alspector and Allen, 1987).

This paper describes a recent and powerful "connectionist" learning procedure called back-propagation (Rumelhart, Hinton, and Williams, 1986a, 1986b) and shows that it can overcome a major limitation of an earlier generation of learning procedures such as perceptrons (Rosenblatt, 1962) which were incapable of learning to recognize shapes that had been translated.

2 The network

The network consists of multiple layers of simple, neuron-like processing elements called "units" that interact using weighted connections. Each unit has a "state" or "activity level" that is determined by the input received from units in the layer below. The total input, x_j, received by unit j is defined to be

$$x_j = \sum_i y_i w_{ji} - \theta_j \qquad (1)$$

where y_i is the state of the i'th unit (which is in a lower layer), w_{ji} is the weight on the connection from the i'th to the j'th unit and θ_j is the threshold of the j'th unit. Thresholds can be eliminated by giving every unit an extra input line whose activity level is always 1. The weight on this input is the negative of the threshold, and it can be learned in just the same way as the other weights. The lowest layer contains the input units and an external input vector is supplied to the network by clamping the states of these units. The state of any other unit in the network is a monotonic non-linear function of its total input (see figure 1).

$$y_j = \frac{1}{1 + e^{-x_j}} \qquad (2)$$

All the network's long-term knowledge about the function it has learned to compute is encoded by the magnitudes of the weights on the connections. This paper does not address the issue of how to choose an appropriate architecture (i.e. the number of layers, the number of units per layer, and the connectivity between layers).

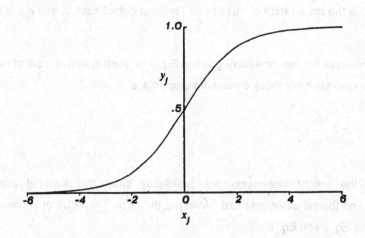

Figure 1: The non-linear transfer function defined in Eq. 2.

3 The learning procedure

Some learning procedures, like the perceptron convergence procedure (Rosenblatt, 1962), are only applicable if the actual or desired states of all the units in the network are already specified. This makes the learning task relatively easy, but it also rules out learning in networks that have intermediate layers between the input and the output. Other, more recent, learning procedures operate in networks that contain "hidden" units (Ackley, Hinton, and Sejnowski, 1985) whose desired states are not specified (either directly or indirectly) by the input or the desired output of the network. This makes learning much harder because the learning procedure must (implicitly) decide what the hidden units should represent. The learning procedure is therefore searching the space of possible representations. Since this is a very large space, it is not surprising that the learning is rather slow.

3.1 A simple LMS learning procedure

If the input units of a network are directly connected to the output units, there is a relatively simple procedure for finding the weights that give the Least Mean Square (LMS) error in the output vectors. The error, with a given set of weights, is defined as:

$$E = \frac{1}{2}\sum_{j,c}(y_{j,c}-d_{j,c})^2 \tag{3}$$

where $y_{j,c}$ is the actual state of output unit j in input-output case c, and $d_{j,c}$ is its desired state.

We can minimize the error measure given in Eq. 3 by starting with any set of weights and repeatedly changing each weight by an amount proportional to $\partial E/\partial w$.

$$\Delta w_{ji} = -\varepsilon\frac{\partial E}{\partial w_{ji}} \tag{4}$$

Provided the weight increments are sufficiently small this learning procedure is guaranteed to find the set of weights that minimizes the error. The value of $\partial E/\partial w$ is obtained by differentiating Eq. 3 and Eq. 1.

$$\frac{\partial E}{\partial w_{ji}} = \sum_c \frac{\partial E}{\partial y_j}\cdot\frac{dy_j}{dx_j}\cdot\frac{\partial x_j}{\partial w_{ji}} = \sum_c (y_j-d_j)\cdot\frac{dy_j}{dx_j}\cdot y_i \tag{5}$$

If the output units are linear, the term dy_j/dx_j is a constant. If the output units use the non-linear transfer function described in Eq. 2, dy_j/dx_j is equal to $y_j(1-y_j)$.

If we construct a multi-dimensional "weight-space" that has an axis for each weight and one extra axis (the "height") that corresponds to the error measure, we can interpret the simple LMS procedure geometrically. For each combination of weights, there is a height (the total error) and these heights form an error-surface. For networks with linear output units and no hidden units, the error surface always forms a concave-upward bowl whose horizontal cross-sections are ellipses and whose vertical cross-sections are parabolas. Since the bowl only has one minimum, gradient descent on the error-surface is guaranteed to find it. If the output units use the non-linear transfer function described in Eq. 2, the bowl is deformed. It still only has one minimum, so gradient descent still works, but the gradient tends to zero as we move far away from the minimum. So gradient descent can become very slow at points in weight-space where output or hidden units have incorrect activity levels near 1 or 0.

3.2 Back-propagation: A multilayer LMS procedure

In a multilayer network it is possible, using Eq. 5, to compute $\partial E/\partial w_{ji}$ for *all* the weights in the network provided we can compute $\partial E/\partial y_j$ for all the units that have modifiable incoming weights. In a system that has no hidden units, this is easy because the only relevant units are the output units, and for them $\partial E/\partial y_j$ is found by differentiating the error function in Eq. 3. But for hidden units, $\partial E/\partial y_j$ is harder to compute. The central idea of back-propagation is that these derivatives can be computed efficiently by starting with the output layer and working backwards through the layers. For each input-output case, c, we first use a forward pass, starting at the input units, to compute the activity levels of all the units in the network. Then we use a backward pass, starting at the output units, to compute $\partial E/\partial y_j$ for all the hidden units. For a hidden unit, j, in layer J the only way it can affect the error is via its effects on the units, k, in the next layer, K , (assuming units in one layer only send their outputs to units in the layer above). So we have

$$\frac{\partial E}{\partial y_j} = \sum_k \frac{\partial E}{\partial y_k} \cdot \frac{dy_k}{dx_k} \cdot \frac{\partial x_k}{\partial y_j} = \sum_k \frac{\partial E}{\partial y_k} \cdot \frac{dy_k}{dx_k} \cdot w_{kj} \qquad (6)$$

where the index c has been suppressed for clarity. So if $\partial E/\partial y_k$ is already known for all units in layer K, it is easy to compute the same quantity for units in layer J. The computation performed during the backward pass is very similar in form to the computation performed during the forward pass.

Back-propagation has been tried for a wide variety of tasks (Le Cun, 1985; Rumelhart,

Hinton and Williams, 1986b; Sejnowski and Rosenberg, 1986; Elman and Zipser, 1987; Plaut and Hinton, 1987). It rarely gets stuck in poor local minima, even though these can exist for networks with hidden units. A much more serious problem is the speed of convergence. High-dimensional weight spaces typically contain ravines with steep sides and a shallow gradient along the ravine. Acceleration methods can be used to speed convergence in such spaces. The idea of an acceleration method is to use the gradient to change the velocity of the current point in weight space rather than using it to directly determine the change in the position of the point. The method can be implemented by using the following weight update rule

$$\Delta w_{ji}(t) = -\varepsilon \frac{\partial E}{\partial w_{ji}} + \alpha \Delta w_{ji}(t-1) \tag{7}$$

where α is a coefficient between 0 and 1 that determines the amount of damping.

Gradient descent is still very slow for large networks, even using the acceleration method. More powerful techniques that use the second derivative would converge faster but would require more elaborate computations that would be much harder to implement directly in parallel hardware. So despite its impressive performance on relatively small problems, back-propagation is inadequate, in its current form, for larger tasks because the learning time scales poorly with the size of the task and the size of the network.

A second major issue with back-propagation concerns the way it generalizes. If the network must be shown all possible input vectors before it learns a function, it is little more than a table look-up device. We would like to be able to learn a function from many less examples than the complete set of possibilities. The assumption is that most of the functions we are interested in are highly structured. They contain regularities in the relationship between the input and output vectors, and the network should notice these regularities in the training examples and apply the same regularities to predict the correct output for the test cases.

4 Recognizing familiar shapes in novel positions

The task of recognizing familiar shapes in novel positions can be used as a test of the ability of a learning procedure to discover the regularities that underlie a set of examples. We use a very simple version of this task in which there is a one-dimensional binary image that is 12 pixels long. The shapes are all 6 pixels long and their first and last pixels always have value 1, so that they are easy to locate. The middle 4 pixels of a shape can take on values of either 1 or 0, so there are 16 possible shapes. Each image only contains one shape, and the background consists entirely of zeros. To eliminate end effects, there is wrap-around so that if a shape moves off one end of the image it reappears at the other end (see figure 3). The wrap-around also ensures that the group invariance theorem of Minsky and Papert (1969) is applicable, and this theorem can be used to prove that the task cannot be performed by a network with no hidden layers.

Since each of the 16 shapes can appear in 12 positions, there are 192 possible shape instances. 160 of these are used for training the network, and 32 are used for testing it to see if it generalizes correctly. There are two test instances, selected at random, for each shape.

The network has two hidden layers as shown in figure 2. The higher hidden layer acts as a narrow bandwidth bottleneck. Information about the identity of the shape must be squeezed through this layer in order to produce the correct answer. The aim of the simulation was to show that the network would develop canonical codes for shapes in this layer, and would use these same canonical codes for shapes in novel positions. The lower hidden layer consists of units that are needed to extract the canonical representation. Each unit in this layer receives connections from 6 adjacent input units, and sends outputs to all the units in the higher hidden layer.

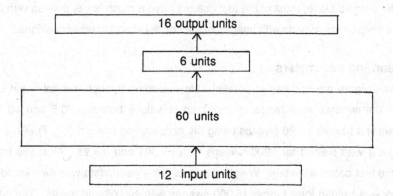

Figure 2: The architecture of the network. The activities of the input units in the bottom layer represent the image. The 60 units in the next layer up are each connected to 6 adjacent input units (with wrap-around) and to all the units in the layer above. The 6 units in the next layer up are all connected to all the output units which are in the top layer.

After extensive learning, the network performs perfectly on the training cases. To avoid requiring very large weights, the error of an output unit is defined to be zero if its activity is above 0.8 when it should be on or below 0.2 when it should be off. Otherwise the error is the square of the difference between the activity level and 0.8 or 0.2. After the network has learned to get the training cases correct, "weight-decay" is introduced -- each time the weights are updated, their magnitude is also decremented by 0.4%. This means that only weights that are doing useful work in reducing the error can survive. It forces the network to perform the task by exploiting strong regularities that apply to many cases, rather than using the accidental structure of individual cases. The weight-decay improves the generalization performance from 17/32 correct to 30/32 correct, where a "correct" answer is one for which the correct output unit is more active than any of the others.

Figure 3 shows the activity levels of the 16 output units for each of the 32 test cases. It also shows the activity levels of the 6 units in the higher hidden layer. Notice that the network has developed a canonical "description" for each shape so that the two novel instances of each shape receive very similar descriptions even though the network has not seen either instance before. This is what allows the network to generalize correctly. When presented with a novel image, the network converts it into a canonical description. It can do this because it has seen many other shapes in the same position, and so it knows how to produce canonical descriptions of the individual pieces of the image. The use of canonical descriptions is much more powerful than simply looking for correlations between the input and output. If we consider the images alone, most of the test images have a much larger overlap with images of some other shape than they do with images of the correct shape in other positions.

4.1 The learning parameters

All the weights are updated in parallel after sweeping through the entire set of training cases. All the weights were randomly initialized to values between −0.5 and +0.5 and the network was first trained for 20 sweeps using the acceleration method (Eq. 7) with $\varepsilon=.002$ and $\alpha=.5$. Then it was trained for 8000 sweeps with $\varepsilon=.004$ and $\alpha=.95$. After this training the errors on the test cases were tiny. Weight-decay of 0.4% per update was then introduced and the network was trained for a further 15,000 sweeps with $\varepsilon=.008$ and $\alpha=.98$. The parameters used were very conservative to ensure that there were no oscillations and that the weights were not accidentally driven to large values from which they could not recover. The training time could be reduced substantially by using an adaptive scheme for dynamically controlling the parameters. It could also be reduced by using a value for ε that is inversely proportional to the number of input lines that the unit receives. Nevertheless the learning would still be very slow.

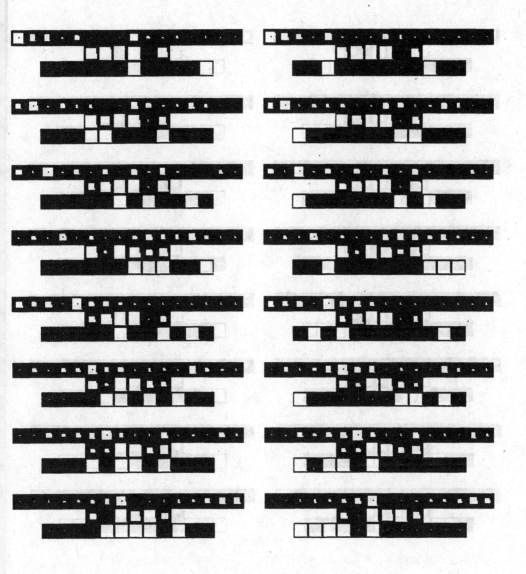

Figure 3a: The activity levels of some of the units for 16 of the 32 test cases. The bottom row of each group shows the input units (whose activity levels encode the image). The top row shows the output units and there is a small black dot on the correct answers. There are two different test cases, arranged side by side, for each shape. The middle row of each group shows the activity levels of the higher hidden layer. Notice that the two instances of each shape have very similar activity patterns in this layer. The lower hidden layer of 60 hidden units is not shown.

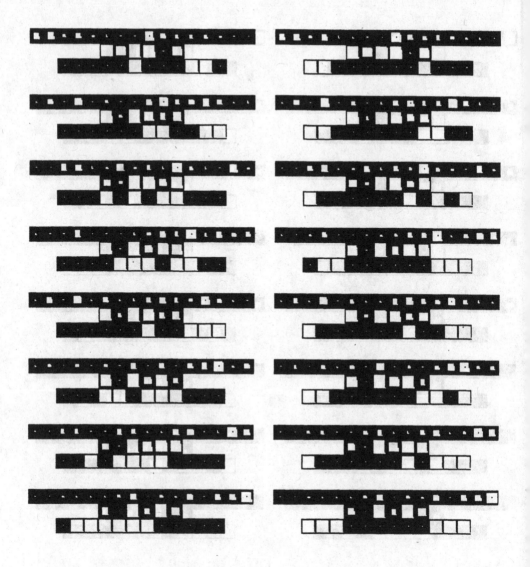

Figure 3b: The activity levels of some of the units for the remaining 16 test cases.

4.2 Some variations

Simulations in which the units in the lower hidden layer received inputs from the whole image did not generalize as well (20/32 correct), so the local connectivity is helpful in constraining the function that the network learns. Simulations that omitted the higher hidden layer (the narrow bandwidth channel) did not generalize nearly as well (4/32 correct).

A very different way of using back-propagation for shape recognition is described in Hinton (1987). It uses a network with recurrent connections that settles to a stable state when shown an image, and it incorporates a more elaborate mechanism for achieving invariance that includes an explicit representation of the position and orientation of the object in the image.

5 The future of back-propagation

One drawback of back-propagation is that it appears to require an external superviser to specify the desired states of the output units. It can be converted into an unsupervised procedure by using the input itself to do the supervision. Consider a multilayer "encoder" network in which the desired output vector is identical with the input vector. The network must learn to compute the identity mapping for all the input vectors in its training set. If the middle layer of the network contains fewer units than the input layer, the learning procedure must construct a compact, invertible code for each input vector. This code can then be used as the input to later stages of processing.

The use of self-supervised back-propagation to construct compact codes resembles the use of principal components analysis to perform dimensionality reduction, but it has the advantage that it allows the code to be a non-linear transform of the input vector. This form of back-propagation has been used successfully to compress images (Cottrell, personal communication, 1986) and to compress speech waves (Elman and Zipser, 1987). A variation of it has been used to extract the underlying degrees of freedom of simple shapes (Saund, 1986). It is also possible to use back-propagation to predict one part of the perceptual input from other parts. In domains with sequential structure, one portion of a sequence can be used as input and the next term in the sequence can be the desired output. This forces the network to extract features that are good predictors.

One promising technique for improving the way the learning time scales with the size of the task is to introduce modularity so that the interactions between the changes in different weights are reduced. For tasks like low-level vision, it is possible to specify in advance that each part of an image should be predictable from nearby parts. This allows a procedure like self-supervised back-propagation to be used in a local module which can learn independently and in parallel with other local modules. In addition to using this kind of innately specified modularity, it is clear that people solve complex tasks by making use of procedures and representations that they have already developed for solving simpler tasks. If back-propagation is to be effective for more realistic tasks than the toy examples that have been used so far, it probably needs to be developed in such a way that it too can exhibit this type of modularity.

6 Conclusions

There are now a number of different "connectionist" learning procedures which are capable of constructing interesting representations in the hidden units of a connectionist network. All of the existing procedures are very slow for large networks, and future progress will depend on finding faster procedures or finding ways of making the existing procedures scale better. Parallel hardware will probably be needed for this research because searching a very large space of possible representations is probably inherently expensive. If the research is successful it may lead to a new kind of chip that learns from examples rather than requiring explicit programming.

Acknowledgements

This research was supported by grant IST/8520359 from the National Science Foundation. The simulator for the learning procedure was developed by Kevin Lang and David Plaut. David Rumelhart provided helpful advice.

References

Ackley, D. H., Hinton, G. E., Sejnowski, T. J. (1985). A learning algorithm for Boltzmann machines. *Cognitive Science, 9*, 147-169.

Alspector, J. & Allen, R. B. (1987). A neuromorphic VLSI learning system. In P. Loseleben (Ed.), *Advanced Research in VLSI: Proceedings of the 1987 Stanford Conference..* Cambridge, Mass.: MIT Press.

Elman, J. L. and Zipser, D. (1987). *Discovering the hidden structure of speech* (Tech. Rep.). Institute for Cognitive Science Technical Report No. 8701. University of California, San Diego.,

Feldman, J. A. & Ballard, D. H. (1982). Connectionist models and their properties. *Cognitive Science, 6*, 205-254.

Hinton, G. E., & Anderson, J. A. (1981). *Parallel models of associative memory*. Hillsdale, NJ: Erlbaum.

Hinton, G. E. (1987). Learning to recognize shapes in a parallel network. In M. Imbert (Ed.), *Proceedings of the 1986 Fyssen Conference*. Oxford: Oxford University Press.

Le Cun, Y. (1985). A learning scheme for asymmetric threshold networks. *Proceedings of Cognitiva 85*. Paris, France.

Minsky, M. & Papert, S. (1969). *Perceptrons*. Cambridge, Mass: MIT Press.

Newell, A. (1980). Physical symbol systems. *Cognitive Science, 4*, 135-183.

Parker, D. B. (April 1985). *Learning-logic* (Tech. Rep.). TR-47, Sloan School of Management, MIT, Cambridge, Mass.,

Plaut, D. C., Nowlan, S. J., & Hinton, G. E. (June 1986). *Experiments on learning by back-propagation* (Tech. Rep. CMU-CS-86-126). Pittsburgh PA 15213: Carnegie-Mellon University,

Plaut, D. C. and Hinton, G. E. (1987). Learning sets of filters using back-propagation. *Computer Speech and Language*, .

Rosenblatt, F. (1962). *Principles of neurodynamics*. New York: Spartan Books.

Rumelhart, D. E., McClelland, J. L., & the PDP research group. (1986). *Parallel distributed processing: Explorations in the microstructure of cognition. Volume I.*. Cambridge, MA: Bradford Books.

Rumelhart, D. E., Hinton, G. E., & Williams, R. J. (1986). Learning internal representations by back-propagating errors. *Nature, 323*, 533-536.

Rumelhart, D. E., Hinton, G. E., & Williams, R. J. (1986). Learning internal representations by error propagation. In D. E. Rumelhart, J. L. McClelland, & the PDP research group (Eds.), *Parallel distributed processing: Explorations in the microstructure of cognition*. Cambridge, MA: Bradford Books.

Saund, E. (1986). Abstraction and representation of continuous variables in connectionist networks. *Proceedings of the Fifth National Conference on Artificial Intelligence*. Los Altos, California, Morgan Kauffman.

Sejnowski, T. J. & Rosenberg C. R. (1986). *NETtalk: A parallel network that learns to read aloud* Technical Report 86-01 . Department of Electrical Engineering and Computer Science, Johns Hopkins University, Baltimore, MD.,

TRACE THEORY AND SYSTOLIC COMPUTATIONS

Martin Rem
Dept. of Mathematics and Computing Science
Eindhoven University of Technology
P.O. Box 513, 5600 MB Eindhoven, Netherlands

0. Introduction

We discuss a class of concurrent computations, or special-purpose computing engines, that may be characterized by
 (i) they consist of regular arrangements of simple cells;
 (ii) the arrangement consumes streams of input values and produces streams of output values;
 (iii) the cells communicate with a fixed number of neighbor cells only;
 (iv) the communication behaviors of the cells are independent of the values communicated. Such arrangements are often referred to as systolic arrays [5]. Our computations, however, have a few other characteristics that are usually not found among systolic arrays:
 (v) synchronization of cells is by message passing only;
 (vi) each output value is produced as soon as all input values on which it depends have been consumed.

The formalism we use to discuss these computations is trace theory [4], [7], [8]. Section 1 is an introduction to trace theory, in which only those subjects are covered that are needed to understand the subsequent sections. Section 2, called Data Independence, addresses the question what it means that communication behaviors are independent of the values communicated. To express the simplicity of (the communication behaviors of) the cells we define in Section 3 the concept of conservative processes. The results of Sections 2 and 3 are assembled into a number of theorems that are used in Sections 4, 5, and 6. Each of these remaining sections discusses an illustrative example of a systolic computation: polynomial multiplication, cyclic encoding, and palindrome recognition.

1. Processes

This section is a trace-theoretic introduction to processes. A process is an abstraction of a mechanism, capturing the ways in which the mechanism can interact with its environment. A process is characterized by the set of events it can be involved in and by the possible orders in which these events can occur. Events are represented by *symbols*. Sets of symbols are called *alphabets* and finite-length sequences of symbols are called *traces*. The set of all traces with symbols from alphabet A is denoted by A^*.

A *process* is a pair $\langle A, X \rangle$, where A is an alphabet and X is a non-empty prefix-closed set of traces with symbols from A:

$$X \subseteq A^*$$
$$X \neq \phi$$
$$X = pref(X)$$

where $pref(X)$ denotes set X extended with all the prefixes of traces in X:

$$pref(X) = \{t \in A^* \mid (\exists u : u \in A^* : tu \in X)\}$$

For process T we let $\mathbf{a}T$ denote its alphabet and $\mathbf{t}T$ its set of traces: $T = \langle \mathbf{a}T, \mathbf{t}T \rangle$.
    An example of a process is

$$\langle \{a, b\}, \{\varepsilon, a, ab, aba, abab, \ldots\} \rangle$$

(ε denotes the empty trace.) We call this process $SEM_1(a, b)$. Its trace set consists of all finite alternations of a and b that do not start with b:

$$SEM_1(a, b) = \langle \{a, b\}, pref(\{ab\}^*) \rangle$$

where, for X a set of traces, X^* denotes the set of all finite concatenations of traces in X.
    The central operators of trace theory are projection and weaving. They are the formal counterparts of abstraction and composition respectively. The *projection* of trace t on alphabet A, denoted by $t{\restriction}A$, is obtained by removing from t all symbols that are not in A. We may write $t{\restriction}a$ for $t{\restriction}\{a\}$. We extend the definition of projection from traces to processes as follows:

$$T{\restriction}A = \langle \mathbf{a}T \cap A, \{t \mid (\exists u : u \in \mathbf{t}T : u{\restriction}A = t)\} \rangle$$

For example,

$$SEM_1(a, b){\restriction}a = \langle \{a\}, \{a\}^* \rangle$$

    The *weave* of processes T and U, denoted by $T \mathbf{w} U$, is defined by

$$T \mathbf{w} U = \langle \mathbf{a}T \cup \mathbf{a}U, \{t \in (\mathbf{a}T \cup \mathbf{a}U)^* \mid t{\restriction}\mathbf{a}T \in \mathbf{t}T \wedge t{\restriction}\mathbf{a}U \in \mathbf{t}U\} \rangle$$

For example,

$$SEM_1(a, b) \mathbf{w} SEM_1(b, a) = \langle \{a, b\}, \{\varepsilon\} \rangle$$

and

$$SEM_1(a, b) \mathbf{w} SEM_1(a, c) = \langle \{a, b, c\}, pref(\{abc, acb\}^*) \rangle$$

    Let $t \in \mathbf{t}T$. The *successor set* of t in T, denoted by $S(t, T)$, is defined by

$$S(t, T) = \{a \in \mathbf{a}T \mid ta \in \mathbf{t}T\}$$

For example,

$$S(\varepsilon, SEM_1(a,b)) = \{a\}$$

and

$$S(a, SEM_1(a,b) \text{ w } SEM_1(a,c)) = \{b,c\}$$

The successor set of t consists of all events the mechanism can be involed in after trace t has occurred. Projection, however, can cause the mechanism to refuse some, or all, of the events in the successor set. In the theory of CSP-processes [1],[3] such processes are called nondeterministic. (I would rather call them 'ill-behaved'.) For example, let

$$T = \langle\{a,b,x,y\}, \ \{\varepsilon, x, xa, y, yb\}\rangle$$

Then

$$T{\restriction}\{a,b\} = \langle\{a,b\}, \ \{\varepsilon, a, b\}\rangle$$

By projecting on $\{a,b\}$ symbols x and y have disappeared: they represent internal (non-observable) events. Although

$$S(\varepsilon, T{\restriction}\{a,b\}) = \{a,b\}$$

mechanism $T{\restriction}\{a,b\}$ may refuse to participate in event a (or b) because internal event y (or x) has already occurred. These types of refusals do not occur if we project on independent alphabets. Alphabet $A \subseteq aT$ is called *independent* when

$$(\forall t : t \in tT : \ S(t,T) \subseteq A \Rightarrow S(t,T) = S(t{\restriction}A, T{\restriction}A))$$

Alphabet $\{a,b\}$ in the example above is not independent:

$$S(y, T) = \{b\}$$

but

$$S(y{\restriction}\{a,b\}, T{\restriction}\{a,b\}) = S(\varepsilon, T{\restriction}\{a,b\}) = \{a,b\}$$

Refusals may also be caused by livelock. For example, let

$$T = \langle\{a,x\}, \ \{a,x\}^*\rangle$$

Then

$$T{\restriction}a = \langle\{a\}, \ \{a\}^*\rangle$$

If internal event x occurs every time it can be chosen, event a never occurs: it is refused forever. Alphabet $A \subseteq aT$ is called *livelockfree* when

$$(\forall t : t \in tT : (\exists n : n \geq 0 : (\forall u : u \in A^* \wedge tu \in tT : \ell(u) \leq n)))$$

where $\ell(u)$ denotes the length of trace u. In the example above alphabets $\{x\}$ and $\{a\}$ are not livelockfree.

Both types of refusals are avoided by projecting on transparent alphabets only. Alphabet $A \subseteq aT$ is called *transparent* when A is independent and $aT \backslash A$ (the complement of A within aT) is livelockfree. The importance of transparence is demonstrated by the following theorem [4].

Theorem 1.0 *Let T be a deterministic CSP-process and $A \subseteq aT$. Then CSP-process $T{\restriction}A$ is deterministic if and only if A is transparent.*

Consequently, if we project on transparent alphabets only, no refusals can occur and there is no need to resort to CSP-processes.

2. Data Independence

In this section the events are transmissions of values along channels. Each channel a has a non-empty set $V(a)$ of values that can be transmitted along it. The alphabets of our processes consist of pairs $\langle a, n \rangle$, where $n \in V(a)$. We consider processes such as

$$T_0 = \langle \{a, b\} \times Z \\ , pref\left(\{\langle a, n \rangle \langle b, 2 * n \rangle \mid n \in Z\}^*\right)\rangle$$

where Z stands for the set of integer numbers. For this process $V(a) = V(b) = Z$. Process T_0 may informally be described as one that doubles integer numbers.

$$T_1 = \langle \{a, b\} \times \{0, 1\} \\ , pref\left(\{\langle a, 0 \rangle, \ \langle a, 1 \rangle \langle b, 1 \rangle\}^*\right)\rangle$$

In this case $V(a) = V(b) = \{0, 1\}$. This process may be viewed as one that filters out zeroes and passes on ones. A process that separates zeroes and ones is

$$T_2 = \langle \{a, b, c\} \times \{0, 1\} \\ , pref\left(\{\langle a, 0 \rangle \langle b, 0 \rangle, \ \langle a, 1 \rangle \langle c, 1 \rangle\}^*\right)\rangle$$

A similar process is

$$T_3 = \langle (\{a\} \times \{0, 1\}) \cup (\{b\} \times \{\text{true}, \text{false}\}) \\ , pref\left(\{\langle a, 0 \rangle \langle b, \text{true} \rangle, \langle a, 1 \rangle \langle b, \text{false} \rangle\}^*\right)\rangle$$

A process that may be viewed as one that arbitrarily permutes two values is

$$T_4 = \langle \{a, b, c\} \times Z \\ , pref\left((\{\langle a, m \rangle \langle a, n \rangle \langle b, m \rangle \langle c, n \rangle \mid m \in Z \wedge n \in Z\} \\ \cup \{\langle a, m \rangle \langle a, n \rangle \langle b, n \rangle \langle c, m \rangle \mid m \in Z \wedge n \in Z\})^*\right)\rangle$$

If we are interested only in the channels along which the transmissions take place but not in the values transmitted, we replace each symbol $\langle a, n \rangle$ by its channel: $\gamma(\langle a, n \rangle) = a$. Function γ may, of course, be generalized from symbols to sets of symbols, (sets of) traces, and processes. For example

$$\gamma(T_0) = SEM_1(a, b)$$

and

$$\gamma(T_1) = \langle \{a, b\}, \ \{a, ab\}^* \rangle$$

Process T is called *data independent* when

$$(\forall t : t \in tT : \gamma(S(t, T)) = S(\gamma(t), \gamma(T)))$$

Set $\gamma(S(t,T))$ consists of all channels along which transmission can take place next. The condition above expresses that this set is independent of the values transmitted thus far. Processes T_0, T_3, and T_4 are data independent and the other two are not. For example,

$$\gamma(S(\langle a,0\rangle, T_1)) = \gamma(\{\langle a,0\rangle, \langle a,1\rangle\}) = \{a\}$$

but

$$S(\gamma(\langle a,0\rangle), \gamma(T_1)) = S(a, \gamma(T_1)) = \{a,b\}$$

In data independent processes we can separate the communication behavior and the computation of the values. (This is sometimes called 'separating data and control.') The *communication behavior* of process T is process $\gamma(T)$. Often the communication behavior is a rather simple process, but many properties, such as transparence, may already be concluded from it.

We shall specify communication behaviors by regular expressions. For example, we specify $\gamma(T_4)$ by the expression $(a\,;\,a\,;\,b\,;\,c)^*$. Notice that semicolons denote concatenation. If the regular expression generates language X the process specified is $\langle A, pref(X)\rangle$, where A is the set of all symbols that occur in the regular expression. This is a rather primitive way of specifying processes, but it suffices for most of the examples in this paper.

Let $A \subseteq \gamma(aT)$ and $t \in tT$. By $t{\restriction}A$ we mean $t{\restriction}(\cup a : a \in A : \{a\} \times V(a))$. This definition may be generalized from traces to processes. Then

$$\gamma(T{\restriction}A) = \gamma(T){\restriction}A$$

Data independence is closed under projection on transparent alphabets:

Theorem 2.0   *If T is data independent, $\gamma(aT)$ is finite, and $A \subseteq \gamma(aT)$ then*

$$A \text{ transparent} \Rightarrow T{\restriction}A \text{ data independent}$$

In order to maintain data independence under weaving we have to see to it that whenever a communication along some channel a can take place:

$$a \in \gamma(S(t{\restriction}aT, T)) \cap \gamma(S(t{\restriction}aU, U))$$

there is actually a transmissible value n:

$$\{\langle a,n\rangle \mid (t{\restriction}aT)\langle a,n\rangle \in tT\}$$
$$\cap\{\langle a,n\rangle \mid (t{\restriction}aU)\langle a,n\rangle \in tU\} \neq \phi \tag{2.0}$$

This is expressed by the following theorem.

Theorem 2.1   *Let T and U be data independent.*
Then

$$(\forall t : t \in t(T \text{ w } U) : \gamma(S(t{\restriction}aT, T) \cap S(t{\restriction}aU, U))$$
$$= \gamma(S(t{\restriction}aT, T)) \cap \gamma(S(t{\restriction}aU, U))) \tag{2.1}$$

f and only if

T w U *data independent and* $\gamma(T$ w $U) = \gamma(T)$ w $\gamma(U)$

In order to allow a simple check that (2.1) holds, we partition the channels of each process into *inputs*, *outputs*, and *signals*. We require
(i) for each signal a a set $V(a) = \{0\}$;
(ii) each input a (of process T) satisfies

$$(\forall t, n : t \in tT \wedge a \in \gamma(S(t,T)) \wedge n \in V(a)$$
$$: \langle a, n \rangle \in S(t,T))$$

.e., T does not restrict the values transmitted along its input channels. In processes T_0 through T_4 we can choose a to be an input and all other channels outputs. (We had this choice in mind in the informal descriptions of these processes.) When weaving we see to the observance of condition (2.1) by requiring that each symbol is an output of at most one of the processes in the weave.

We conclude this section with a—somewhat informal—discussion of a simple example. Its inclusion is meant to show how the computation of output values may be specified.

The example is a process to compute a cumulative sum. Its communication behavior is specified by $(a ; b)^*$. Channel a is an input, channel b is an output, and $V(a) = V(b) = \mathbb{Z}$. For $t \in tT$ and $0 \leq i < \ell(t{\restriction}a)$ we let $a(i,t)$ denote the value of the ith transmission along channel a in trace t:

$$a(i,t) = n$$
$$\equiv$$
$$(\exists u : t = u\langle a, n \rangle : \ell(u{\restriction}a) = i)$$

The values to be computed may then be specified by

$$b(i,t) = (\Sigma j : 0 \leq j \leq i : a(i,t))$$

or, dropping the reference to trace t,

$$b(i) = (\Sigma j : 0 \leq j \leq i : a(i))$$

for $i \geq 0$. Consequently,

$$b(0) = a(0) \tag{2.2}$$

and, for $i \geq 0$,

$$b(i + 1) = b(i) + a(i + 1) \tag{2.3}$$

We now describe how the output values are computed. To obtain a CSP-like [2] notation we add variables x and y (and assignments) to the communication behavior $(a\,;b)^*$. Our description of the computation is

$$y := 0\,;(a?\,x\,;b!\,(y+x)\,;y := y+x)^* \tag{2.4}$$

The symbols of the communication behavior have been changed into communication statements: as in CSP, each input is postfixed by a question mark and a variable, and each output is postfixed by an exclamation point and an expression. The effect of $b!\,(y+x)$ is that $\langle b, y+x \rangle$ is added to the trace thus far generated, establishing

$$b(\ell(t \restriction b)) = y + x$$

Statement $a?\,x$, similarly, establishes

$$a(\ell(t \restriction a)) = x$$

Step 0 of the repetition in (2.4) establishes $a(0) = x$, $b(0) = a(0)$ —as required by (2.2)—and $y = b(0)$. Consider, for $i \geq 0$, step $i+1$ of the repetition. We have initially $y = b(i)$. Statement $a?x$ establishes $a(i+1) = x$, statement $b!(y+x)$ establishes $b(i+1) = b(i) + a(i+1)$—as required by (2.3)—and $y := y + x$ establishes $y = b(i+1)$.

3. Conservative Processes

Communication behaviors are often rather simple processes. Checking whether alphabets are transparent is then not difficult. This is in particular the case if the communication behavior is a conservative process.

The successor set $S(t, T)$ consists of all symbols that may follow t. We now introduce the *after set* of t in T, which consists of all *traces* that may follow t:

$$after(t, T) = \{u \in aT^* \mid tu \in tT\}$$

for $t \in tT$. Process T is called *conservative* when

$$(\forall t, a, b:\ a \neq b \wedge ta \in tT \wedge tb \in tT$$
$$:\ tab \in tT \wedge tba \in tT$$
$$\wedge\ after(tab, T) = after(tba, T))$$

Conservatism expresses, informally speaking, that different events do not disable each other and that the order in which enabled events occur is immaterial.
We have

Theorem 3.0 *For conservative processes T each $A \subseteq aT$ is independent.*

Conservatism is closed under projection and weaving, as the next two theorems express.

Theorem 3.1 $\quad T$ *conservative* $\Rightarrow T {\restriction} A$ *conservative*

Theorem 3.2 $\quad T$ *and* U *conservative* $\Rightarrow T \mathbf{w} U$ *conservative*

The following theorem can be of help to demonstrate conservatism for some simple processes.

Theorem 3.3. *Let R and S be regular expressions consisting of symbols separated by semicolons. Then the process specified by $R \,;\, S^*$ is conservative. Moreover, each subset of its alphabet that contains a symbol occurring in S is transparent.*

For example, the process specified by

$$c \,;\, d \,;\, (a \,;\, a \,;\, b \,;\, c)^*$$

is conservative and every non-empty subset of $\{a, b, c\}$ is transparent.

A process may contain *subprocesses*. For reasons of simplicity we restrict ourselves in this paper to processes that have at most one subprocess. We always call the subprocess p. A subprocess has a *type*, which is again a process. If the subprocess has type U we let $p.U$ denote the process obtained from U by changing all symbols a into $p.a$, read 'p its a'. For example, if

$$U = \langle \{a, b\}, \{\varepsilon, a, ab\} \rangle$$

then

$$p.U = \langle \{p.a, p.b\}, \{\varepsilon, p.a, p.a \; p.b\} \rangle$$

Let process T with $\mathbf{a}T = A$ be specified by a regular expression and let its subprocess have type U. With S denoting the process specified by the regular expression, we require $\mathbf{a}S = A \cup \mathbf{a}p.U$. Then, by definition,

$$T = (S \mathbf{w} p.U){\restriction}A \tag{3.0}$$

For example, let p be of type $SEM_1(a, b)$ and let the regular expression be

$$b \,;\, (a \,;\, p.a \,;\, b \,;\, p.b)^* \tag{3.1}$$

Then $T = SEM_1(b, a)$. However, if p were of type $SEM_1(b, a)$ we would obtain

$$T = \langle \{a, b\}, \{\varepsilon, b, ba\} \rangle$$

The internal symbols in S represent the channels along which communications with p occur. Each such symbol $p.a$ is an (internal) input or output of S if the corresponding symbol a is an output or input, respectively, of p. This guarantees condition (2.1) for data independence of the weave in (3.0) to hold. Since (3.0) also contains a projection, we have to convince ourselves that A is transparent with respect to $S \mathbf{w} p.U$. For (3.1) this is guaranteed by Theorems 3.2 and 3.3.

An interesting case occurs when T is recursive, i.e., when it has a subprocess of type T. Then (3.0) becomes an equation in T:

$$T = (S \text{ w } p.T) \upharpoonright A$$

By definition process T is the least solution of this equation, where 'least' is meant with respect to the subset order for sets of traces. Phrased differently, process T is the least fixpoint of function f defined by

$$f(x) = (S \text{ w } p.x) \upharpoonright A \qquad (3.2)$$

which equals the following least upper bound [4]:

$$(\mathbf{LUB}\, i : i \geq 0 : f^i(\langle A, \{\varepsilon\}\rangle))$$

For example, if S is

$$(a\,;\,p.a\,;\,b\,;\,p.b)^* \qquad (3.3)$$

or

$$a\,;\,b\,;\,(p.a\,;\,a\,;\,b\,;\,p.b)^* \qquad (3.4)$$

we have $T = SEM_1(a,b)$. However, if S is

$$(a\,;\,p.a\,;\,p.b\,;\,b)^*$$

we find

$$T = \langle\{a,b\},\ \{\varepsilon, a\}\rangle$$

Theorem 3.4 *For conservative S the least fixpoint of f, as defined in (3.2), is conservative.*

For some processes, for example, those specified by regular expressions conforming to Theorem 3.3, it is sensible to talk about the duration between (external) events, or, more precisely, about the number of ordered internal events between successive external events. Let

$$T = (S \text{ w } p.U) \upharpoonright A$$

A sequence function

$$\sigma : aS \times \mathsf{N} \to \mathsf{N}$$

(N the set of natural numbers) is a function satisfying

$$(\forall t, a, b, :\ tab \in tS \land a \in aS \land b \in aS$$
$$:\ \sigma(a, \ell(t \upharpoonright a)) < \sigma(b, \ell(ta \upharpoonright b)))$$

We require that subprocess p has a corresponding sequence function σ', i.e., one that satisfies

$$(\forall a, i : a \in aU \wedge i \geq 0 : \sigma(p.a, i) = \sigma'(a, i))$$

If σ is a sequence function then so is $\sigma + m$ for all natural m.

The process specified by (3.3) has, for example, the following sequence function:

$$
\begin{aligned}
\sigma(a, i) &= 4 * i \\
\sigma(b, i) &= 4 * i + 2 \\
\sigma(p.a, i) &= 4 * i + 1 \\
\sigma(p.b, i) &= 4 * i + 3
\end{aligned}
\tag{3.5}
$$

This is an allowed sequence function, since $\sigma(p.a, i) = \sigma(a, i) + 1$, $\sigma(p.b, i) = \sigma(b, i) + 1$, and $\sigma + 1$ is a sequence function for p.

We say that process T has *constant response time* when there exists a sequence function σ for T such that

$$(\exists n : n \geq 1 : (\forall t, a, b : tab \in tT \wedge a \in aT \wedge b \in aT$$
$$: \sigma(b, \ell(ta\restriction b)) - \sigma(a, \ell(t\restriction a)) \leq n))$$

The process specified by (3.3) has constant response time: for σ as given in (3.5) the condition above holds for $n = 2$. The process specified by (3.4) does *not* have constant response time. A possible sequence function for that process is

$$
\begin{aligned}
\sigma(a, i) &= (i + 1)^2 - 1 \\
\sigma(b, i) &= (i + 1)^2 \\
\sigma(p.a, i) &= (i + 2)^2 - 2 \\
\sigma(p.b, i) &= (i + 2)^2 + 1
\end{aligned}
$$

We have now assembled all the theory we need to discuss a number of interesting examples. These are presented in the next three sections.

4. Polynomial Multiplication

Given is a polynomial q of degree M, $M \geq 0$. For $0 \leq i \leq M$ we let q_i denote the coefficient of x^i in q:

$$q = q_M * x^M + \cdots + q_1 * x + q_0$$

Polynomial q has to be multiplied by a polynomial r of degree N, $N \geq 0$, yielding a polynomial s of degree $M + N$, given by

$$s_{M+N-i} = (\Sigma j : \max(i - M, 0) \leq j \leq \min(i, N) : q_{M+j-i} * r_{N-j})$$

for $0 \leq i \leq M + N$.

The process that carries out the multiplication is to have input a and output b with $V(a) = V(b) = \mathbf{Z}$. Along input a the coefficients r_i are transmitted in order of decreasing indices, followed by zeroes:

$$a(i) = \begin{cases} r_{N-i} & \text{if } 0 \leq i \leq N \\ 0 & \text{if } i > N \end{cases} \qquad (4.0)$$

Along output b the coefficients of s are to be transmitted, followed by zeroes:

$$b(i) = \begin{cases} s_{M+N-i} & \text{if } 0 \leq i \leq M + N \\ 0 & \text{if } i > M + N \end{cases}$$

The communication behavior is $(a\,;\,b)^*$. In view of (4.0) we have for $0 \leq i \leq M + N$

$$b(i) = (\Sigma j : \max(i - M, 0) \leq j \leq \min(i, N) : q_{M+j-i} * a(j)) \qquad (4.1)$$

We design for $0 \leq k \leq M$ processes MUL_k, that have (external) communication behavior $(a\,;\,b)^*$ and, cf. (4.1),

$$b(i) = (\Sigma j : \max(i - k, 0) \leq j \leq \min(i, N) : q_{k+j-i} * a(j)) \qquad (4.2)$$

if $0 \leq i \leq k + N$, and $b(i) = 0$ if $i > k + N$. Then MUL_M is the process we are interested in.

Process MUL_0 is simple: (4.2) yields for $k = 0$

$$b(i) = \begin{cases} q_0 * a(i) & \text{if } 0 \leq i \leq N \\ 0 & \text{if } i > N \end{cases}$$

Since $a(i) = 0$ for $i > N$, this may be simplified to

$$b(i) = q_0 * a(i)$$

for $i \geq 0$. The computation of MUL_0 may be specified by

$$\boxed{(a?\,x\,;\,b!\,(q_0 * x))^*}$$

We now turn to MUL_k for $1 \leq k \leq M$. It has a subprocess of type MUL_{k-1}. Consequently,

$$p.a(i) = a(i) \qquad \text{for } i \geq 0 \qquad (4.3)$$

$$p.a(i) = a(i) \qquad \text{for } i \geq 0$$

$$p.b(i) = \begin{cases} (\Sigma j : \max(i - k + 1, 0) \leq j \leq \min(i, N) \\ \qquad : q_{k-1+j-i} * a(j)) & \text{if } 0 \leq i < k + N \\ 0 & \text{if } i \geq k + N \end{cases}$$

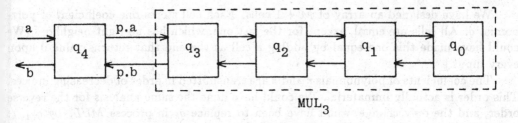

Fig. 1. Process MUL_4

By (4.2)

$$b(0) = q_k * a(0) \tag{4.6}$$

and for $0 \le i < k + N$

$$b(i + 1) = (\Sigma j : \max(i - k + 1, 0) \le j \le \min(i + 1, N) : q_{k-1+j-i} * a(j))$$

Hence, by (4.4),

$$b(i + 1) = \begin{cases} p.b(i) & \text{if } N \le i < k + N \\ p.b(i) + q_k * a(i + 1) & \text{if } 0 \le i < N \end{cases}$$

Since $a(i + 1) = 0$ for $i \ge N$, this may be simplified to

$$b(i + 1) = p.b(i) + q_k * a(i + 1)$$

for $0 \le i < k + N$. For $i \ge k + N$ we have $p.b(i) = 0$ and $a(i + 1) = 0$. Consequently,

$$b(i + 1) = p.b(i) + q_k * a(i + 1) \tag{4.7}$$

for $i \ge 0$.

Relations (4.3), (4.6), and (4.7) tell us how the output values may be computed. We choose

$$(a ; p.a ; b ; p.b)^* \tag{4.8}$$

as the communication behavior. Then $p.a(i)$ follows $a(i)$, as required by (4.3), $b(0)$ follows $a(0)$, as required by (4.6), and $b(i + 1)$ follows $p.b(i)$ and $a(i + 1)$, as required by (4.7). According to Theorem 3.3 alphabet $\{a, b\}$ is transparent. We have already shown that the process has constant response time and that, with S denoting the process specified by (4.8),

$$(S \text{ w } SEM_1(a, b)) \upharpoonright \{a, b\} = SEM_1(a, b)$$

Given (4.3), (4.6), and (4.7), it is now simple to specify the computation of the output values:

$$\boxed{y := 0 ; (a? x ; p.a! x ; b! (y + q_k * x) ; p.b? y)^*} \tag{4.9}$$

Process MUL_k consists of the process specified by (4.9), which uses value q_k, and MUL_{k-1} as a subprocess. Figure 1 shows process MUL_4, in which each process that uses value q_k is drawn as a rectangle with q_k in it.

We have designed an array of $M + 1$ cells. Each cell stores one coefficient of polynomial q. All cells are equal, except for the last one, which has no right neighbor. (We could have made this one equal by adding a cell at the end that returns value 0 upon every input.)

The coefficients of polynomials r and s are transmitted in order of decreasing indices. This order is actually immaterial. We could have done the same analysis for the reverse order, and the only change would have been to replace q_k in process MUL_k by q_{M-k}: the order in which the coefficients of q are distributed over the cells is reversed as well.

Our solution is independent of the degree of r. Process MUL_M will multiply polynomial q by polynomials of any degree. In order for the complete product to be produced at b, we have to require of the input only that the coefficients of r are followed by at least M zeroes. But afterwards we have $y = 0$ and a new polynomial may be input again! We have thus designed a systolic computation for repeatedly multiplying a fixed polynomial q by other polynomials. The only restriction on the input is that the coefficients of different polynomials are separated by (at least) M zeroes.

5. Cyclic Encoding

A nice application of polynomial multiplication is the encoding of messages, using a cyclic code. Given is a polynomial q of degree M with $M \geq 1$, $q_i \in \{0, 1\}$, and $q_M = 1$. Polynomial q is often called the generator polynomial of the cyclic code. Each message is a sequence $r_N r_{N-1} \ldots r_0$, where $r_i \in \{0, 1\}$ and $N \geq 0$. The message may be regarded as the coefficients of a polynomial r. The encoded message consists of the coefficients of polynomial

$$r * x^M \oplus t \tag{5.0}$$

of degree $M + N$, where t is the remainder polynomial after division of $r * x^M$ by q and $\oplus$ denotes addition modulo 2. More precisely, polynomial t is defined by

$$r * x^M = q * d \oplus t \tag{5.1}$$

where d is a polynomial of degree N and t has degree $M - 1$.

For example, if the generator polynomial is $x^4 + x + 1$ $(M = 4)$ and the message is 101110111, i.e., $r = x^8 + x^6 + x^5 + x^4 + x^2 + x + 1$, we find for (5.1)

$$x^{12} + x^{10} + x^9 + x^8 + x^6 + x^5 + x^4$$
$$=$$
$$(x^4 + x + 1) * (x^8 + x^6 + x^3 + x) \oplus (x^3 + x^2 + x)$$

The encoded message is, by (5.0), 1011101111110: the sequence 1110 of M check bits, corresponding to polynomial $x^3 + x^2 + x$, has been added to the message. A well-known example is the use of $x + 1$ as generator polynomial. It results in adding a parity bit.

On account of (5.1), polynomial (5.0), representing the encoded message, equals $q * d$. Our encoder, consequently, has to multiply polynomials q and d, a problem we have already solved in Section 4. Polynomial d is, of course, not given, but the amazing property—pointed out to me by F. W. Sijstermans of Philips Research—is that the coefficients of d may be determined as polynomial r is input.

By (5.1) we conclude

$$d_N = r_N \tag{5.2}$$

Notice that for $0 \le j \le N$

$$(q * d)_{M+j} = (r * x^M \oplus t)_{M+j} = (r * x^M)_{M+j} = r_j \tag{5.3}$$

Let q' be a polynomial of degree $M - 1$ such that

$$q = x^M \oplus q' \tag{5.4}$$

Then, for $0 \le j < N$,

$$
\begin{aligned}
d_j &= (x^M * d)_{M+j} \\
&= \{\text{by (5.4)}\} \quad ((q \oplus q') * d)_{M+j} \\
&= (q * d)_{M+j} \oplus (q' * d)_{M+j} \\
&= \{\text{by (5.3)}\} \quad r_j \oplus (q' * d)_{M+j}
\end{aligned} \tag{5.5}
$$

We introduce a subcomponent p of type MUL_{M-1} that computes $q' * d$. The output of p can be used to determine both d_j for $0 \le j < N$ and, as will turn out later, $b(i)$ for $N < i \le N + M$.

Our process has input a and output b. For $0 \le i \le N$

$$a(i) = r_{N-i} \tag{5.6}$$

and for $0 \le i \le M + N$

$$b(i) = (q * d)_{M+N-i}$$

The external communication behavior is

$$(a; b)^{N+1}; b^M$$

where S^N denotes N concatenations of S, for example

$$(a; b)^2 = (a; b; a; b)$$

We suggest to insert the internal communications as follows:

$$(a; p.a; b; p.b)^{N+1}; (p.a; b; p.b)^M$$

We have, according to the specification of MUL_{M-1},

$$p.a(i) = \begin{cases} d_{N-i} & \text{if } 0 \le i \le N \\ 0 & \text{if } N < i \le M + N \end{cases} \tag{5.7}$$

and

$$p.b(i) = \begin{cases} (q' * d)_{M+N-i-1} & \text{if } 0 \le i < M+N \\ 0 & \text{if } i = M+N \end{cases} \tag{5.8}$$

For $0 \le i \le N$ we have, by (5.3),

$$b(i) = (q * d)_{M+N-i} = r_{N-i} = a(i)$$

For $N \le i < M+N$ we find

$$\begin{aligned} b(i+1) &= (q * d)_{M+N-i-1} \\ &= \{\text{by } (5.4)\} \quad ((x^M \oplus q') * d)_{M+N-i-1} \\ &= (x^M * d)_{M+N-i-1} \oplus (q' * d)_{M+N-i-1} \\ &= \{M+N-i-1 \le M-1\} \ (q' * d)_{M+N-i-1} \\ &= \{\text{by } (5.8)\} \ p.b(i) \end{aligned}$$

Outputs $p.a(i)$ may be determined as follows.

$$\begin{aligned} p.a(0) &= \{\text{by } (5.7)\} \ d_N \\ &= \{\text{by } (5.2)\} \ r_N \\ &= \{\text{by } (5.6)\} \ a(0) \end{aligned}$$

For $0 \le i < N$ we derive

$$\begin{aligned} p.a(i+1) &= \{\text{by } (5.7)\} \ d_{N-i-1} \\ &= \{\text{by } (5.5)\} \ r_{N-i-1} \oplus (q' * d)_{M+N-i-1} \\ &= \{\text{by } (5.6) \text{ and } (5.8)\} \ a(i+1) \oplus p.b(i) \end{aligned}$$

Furthermore, $p.a(i) = 0$ for $N < i \le M+N$.

Summarizing, we have

$$b(i) = \begin{cases} a(i) & \text{if } 0 \le i \le N \\ p.b(i-1) & \text{if } N < i \le M+N \end{cases}$$

and

$$p.a(i) = \begin{cases} a(i) & \text{if } i = 0 \\ a(i) \oplus p.b(i-1) & \text{if } 1 \le i \le N \\ 0 & \text{if } N < i \le M+N \end{cases}$$

The computation of these output values may be specified as follows.

```
y := 0
; (a? x ; p.a! (x ⊕ y) ; b! x ; p.b? y)^{N+1}
; (p.a! 0 ; b! y ; p.b? y)^M
```

Since $p.b(M + N) = 0$, the last statement reestablishes $y = 0$. We have, therefore, simple way of changing the program into one that repeatedly encodes messages:

$$
\begin{aligned}
&y := 0 \\
&; ((a?\, x \; ; \; p.a!\, (x \oplus y) \; ; \; b!\, x \; ; \; p.b?\, y)^{N+1} \\
&\quad ; (p.a!\, 0 \; ; \; b!\, y \; ; \; p.b?\, y)^{M} \\
&)*
\end{aligned}
$$

Making the process independent of the message length requires a message-separator ignal. Calling that signal c, our solution becomes

$$
\begin{aligned}
&y := 0 \\
&; ((a?\, x \; ; \; p.a!\, (x \oplus y) \; ; \; b!\, x \; ; \; p.b?\, y)^{*} \\
&\quad ; c \; ; \; (p.a!\, 0 \; ; \; b!\, y \; ; \; p.b?\, y)^{M} \\
&)*
\end{aligned}
$$

By adding one cell to MUL_{M-1} (or one could say, by changing the first cell of MUL_M) we have obtained a systolic computation for encoding messages of varying lengths. Figure 2 shows a drawing of the process.

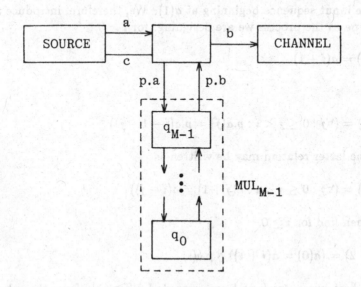

Fig. 2. Cyclic encoder

The communication behavior at the source side is $(a^{*} \; ; \; c)^{*}$: the messages are separated by signal c, and the value of M is immaterial to the source side transmissions.

6. Palindrome Recognition

In this section we discuss a recursive palindrome recogngizer. The object is to specify a process with external behavior $(b\,; a)^*$, where b is output and a is input, $V(b) = \{\text{true}, \text{false}\}$, and $V(a) = Z$. The value of output b has to indicate whether the sequence thus far received at input a is a palindrome. More precisely, for $i \geq 0$

$$b(i) = (\forall i : 0 \leq j < i : a(j) = a(i - 1 - j))$$

We have

$$b(0) = b(1) = \text{true} \tag{6.0}$$

and for $i \geq 0$

$$
\begin{aligned}
b(i+2) &= (\forall j : 0 \leq j < i + 2 : a(j) = a(i + 1 - j)) \\
&= (a(0) = a(i+1)) \\
&\quad \wedge (\forall j : 1 \leq j < i + 1 : a(j) = a(i + 1 - j)) \\
&\quad \wedge (a(i+1) = a(0)) \\
&= (a(0) = a(i+1)) \\
&\quad \wedge (\forall j : 0 \leq j < i : a(j+1) = a(i - j))
\end{aligned} \tag{6.1}
$$

The latter conjunct is again the outcome of a palindrome recognizer, but now one that pertains to the input sequence beginning at $a(1)$. We, therefore, introduce a subprocess of the same type as the process we are designing: for $i \geq 0$

$$p.a(i) = a(i+1) \tag{6.2}$$

and

$$p.b(i) = (\forall j : 0 \leq j < i : p.a(j) = p.a(i - 1 - j))$$

Using (6.2), the latter relation may be written as

$$p.b(i) = (\forall j : 0 \leq j < i : a(j+1) = a(i - j))$$

By (6.1) we then find for $i \geq 0$

$$b(i+2) = (a(0) = a(i+1)) \wedge p.b(i) \tag{6.3}$$

Since the first two outputs at b are computed differently from the subsequent ones, we suggest

$$b\,; a\,; b\,; (a\,; p.b\,; b\,; p.a)^* \tag{6.4}$$

s the communication behavior. Then $p.a(i)$ follows $a(i+1)$, cf. (6.2), and $b(i+2)$ follows $(i+1)$ and $p.b(i)$, as required by (6.3). By Theorem 3.3 alphabet $\{a, b\}$ is transparent. With S denoting the process specified by (6.4) we have

$$(S \text{ w } p.S) \upharpoonright \{a, b\} = SEM_1(b, a)$$

This shows that the process has the required external behavior. It also has constant response time. A sequence function is

$$\sigma(a, i) = 4 * i + 2$$
$$\sigma(b, i) = 4 * i$$
$$\sigma(p.a, i) = 4 * i + 9$$
$$\sigma(p.b, i) = 4 * i + 7$$

This is an allowed sequence function, since $\sigma + 7$ is a sequence function for p and

$$\sigma(p.a, i) = \sigma(a, i) + 7$$
$$\sigma(p.b, i) = \sigma(b, i) + 7$$

Given (6.0), (6.2), and (6.3), it is not difficult to extend (6.4) with the computation of the output values:

$$\boxed{\begin{array}{l} b! \text{ true } ; \ a? \, z \ ; \ b! \text{ true} \\ ; (a? \, x \ ; \ p.b? \, y \ ; \ b! \, ((z = x) \wedge y) \ ; \ p.a! \, x \end{array}}$$

Notice that $a? \, z$ establishes $a(0) = z$.)

We have designed an infinite array of cells. With the sequence function given above, subprocess p starts at moment $\sigma(p.b, 0)$, i.e., at moment 7. In general, cell k, for $k \geq 0$, starts at moment $7 * k$. Cell 0 produces the answers. For $i \geq 0$ answer $b(i)$ is produced at moment $\sigma(b, i) = 4 * i$. At that moment all cells k for which $7 * k \leq 4 * i$ have started: slightly over $i/2$ cells are required to produce answer $b(i)$.

7. Conclusion

Systolic arrays are often presented and explained by means of pictures. We have refrained from doing so. Of course, we showed a few pictures, but they were merely used as illustrations: in no way did our discussion rely on them.

We discussed systolic computations in terms of their input/output behaviors. This is a method for which the formalism of trace theory is very well-suited. We have isolated the concepts of data independence, transparence, and conservatism as central notions in the study of systolic computations. We are pleased with the nice way in which these concepts tie together. In contrast to what is customary, we did not describe the computations in terms of global states. As a matter of fact, we suspect that these solutions would not have been found then: in [9] the palindrome recognizer requires cells that are slightly more complicated (essentially, the combination of two of ours) to achieve that communication takes place with the neighbor cells only.

One of the reasons why we want each cell to have a fixed number of neighbor cells is to facilitate the realization of our computations as VLSI circuits. The main reason to have all synchronization be accomplished by message passing is that we would like these VLSI circuits to be delay-insensitive [10], which excludes the use of global clocks. The work by Alain J. Martin on compiling CSP-like programs into delay-insensitive VLSI circuits [6] shows that such realizations may be obtained by introducing handshaking protocols to implement the communication actions.

8. Acknowledgements

Acknowledgements are due to F. W. Sijstermans of Philips Research who pointed out to me the relation between cyclic encoding and polynomial multiplication. My solution for the latter is a slight variation of his.

I am very grateful to Gerard Zwaan, Anne Kaldewaij, and Tom Verhoeff for sharing with me their ideas on data independence, transparence, and conservatism. Many results presented in Sections 1, 2, and 3 are due to their prolific efforts. The discussions with them and with the other members of the Eindhoven VLSI Club have been a great help to me.

I thank Roland C. Backhouse and Jan L. A. van de Snepscheut for directing my attention to the problems of palindrome recognition and cyclic encoding.

California Institute of Technology is acknowledged for giving me the opportunity to prepare this paper during my visit of winter 1986-87.

The research described in this paper was in part sponsored by the Defense Advanced Research Projects Agency, ARPA Order number 3771, and was monitored by the Office of Naval Research under contract number N00014-79-C-0597.

9. References

[1] Brookes, S.D., Roscoe, A.W. An improved failures model for communicating processes. In: Seminar on Concurrency (S.D. Brookes, A.W. Roscoe, G. Winskel, eds.). Springer, Berlin, 1985 (Lecture Notes in Computer Science: 197), 281–305.

[2] Hoare, C.A.R. Communicating sequential processes. Comm. ACM **21** (1978), 666–677.

[3] Hoare, C.A.R. Communicating Sequential Processes. Prentice Hall, New York, 1985.

[4] Kaldewaij, A. A Formalism for Concurrent Processes. Doctoral Dissertation, Eindhoven University of Technology, Eindhoven, 1986.

[5] Kung, H.T. Let's design algorithms for VLSI systems. In: Proc. 1st Caltech Conference (C.L. Seitz, ed.). California Institute of Technology, Pasadena, 1979, 65–90.

[6] Martin, A.J. Compiling communicating processes into delay-insensitive VLSI circuits. Distributed Computing **1** (1986), 226–234.

[7] Rem, M. Concurrent computations and VLSI circuits. In: Control Flow and Data Flow: Concepts in Distributed Programs (M. Broy, ed.). Springer, Berlin, 1985, 399–437.

[8] Snepscheut, J.L.A. van de. Trace Theory and VLSI Design. Springer, Berlin, 1985 (Lecture Notes in Computer Science: 200).

[9] Snepscheut, J.L.A. van de, Swenker, J. On the design of some systolic algorithms. Note JAN 131, Groningen University, Groningen, 1986.

[10] Udding, J.T. A formal model for defining and classifying delay-insensitive circuits and systems. Distributed Computing 1 (1986), 197–204.

Boltzmann Machines and Their Applications

Emile H.L. Aarts and Jan H.M. Korst

Philips Research Laboratories
P.O. Box 80.000, 5600 JA Eindhoven, the Netherlands

Abstract

In this paper we present a formal model of the Boltzmann machine and a discussion of two different applications of the model, viz. (i) solving combinatorial optimization problems and (ii) carrying out learning tasks. Numerical results of computer simulations are presented to demonstrate the characteristic features of the Boltzmann machine.

Keywords: Boltzmann machines, simulated annealing, combinatorial optimization, learning.

1 Introduction

Many researchers believe that massive parallelism rather than raw speed of individual processors may provide the computational power required to carry out the increasingly complex calculations imposed by e.g. combinatorial optimization [3,13,15] and artificial intelligence [4,6,7]. A revolutionary development in the field of parallel computer architectures is based on the so-called connectionist models [5,6]. These models incorporate massive parallelism and the assumption that information can be represented by the strengths of the connections between individual computing elements.

The Boltzmann machine, introduced by Hinton *et al.* [4,6,11], is a novel approach to connectionist models using a distributed knowledge representation and a massively parallel network of simple stochastic computing elements. The computing elements are considered as logic units having two discrete states, viz. 'on' or 'off'. The units are connected to eachother. With each connection a connection strength is associated representing a quantitative measure of the hypothesis that the two connected units are both 'on'. A consensus function assigns to a configuration of the Boltzmann machine (determined by the states of the individual units) a real number which is a quantitative measure of the amount of consensus in the Boltzmann machine with respect to the set of underlying hypotheses. The state of an individual unit (if not externally forced) is determined by a stochastic function of the states of the units it is connected to and the associated connection strengths. Maximization of the consensus function corresponds to maximization of the amount of information contained within the Boltzmann machine.

Interest in the Boltzmann machine extends over a number of disciplines, i.e. future computer architectures [6,23], knowledge representation in intelligent systems [2,6,23,24], modelling of neural behaviour of the brain [11,21], and research on applications, e.g. pattern recognition [10,11,18,20,22] and combinatorial optimization [3,15]. Especially the research on recognition and synthesis of speech with a Boltzmann machine has recently shown a number of interesting achievements [18,20,22].

In this paper we discuss a formal model and two different applications of the Boltzmann machine. In §2 we present a graph-theoretical model of the structure of the Boltzmann machine and a stochastic state-transition mechanism that can be applied to maximize the consensus function. In §3 a model of the Boltzmann machine is presented that can be applied to solve combinatorial optimization problems. For two distinct 0-1 integer formulations of the traveling salesman problem (as an assignment problem and as a quadratic assignment problem) it is shown that near-optimal solutions can be obtained. This is done by mapping the corresponding 0-1 variables onto the computing elements of the Boltzmann machine and by setting the connection strengths so as to represent the cost function and the constraints of the optimization problem. In §4 we discuss the ability of a Boltzmann machine to learn. Learning takes place by examples. To this end a subset of the computing elements is selected. In the learning phase the connection strengths are adjusted such that the Boltzmann machine, when left completely free to set its states, tends to show on that subset of computing elements a number of patterns (given by the examples) with an a priory given probability distribution. After completion of the learning phase the Boltzmann machine is able to reproduce complete patterns if part of them are clamped into the given subset of computing elements by maximizing the consensus function. In this way a Boltzmann machine can not only reproduce given examples (memory) but also has associative and restricted inductive capabilities. The essential difference between the applications discussed in §3 and §4 is given by the fact that in the first application (solving combinatorial optimization problems) the Boltzmann machine adjusts the states of the units to a given set of connection strengths that is fixed in time, whereas in the second application (learning) the Boltzmann machine adjusts the values of the connection strengths to a given number of examples which fix the states of the units they are clamped into.

2 A Formal Model of the Boltzmann Machine

The model of the Boltzmann machine originates from the theory of neural networks as given by Hopfield [12] and was introduced by Hinton et al. [4,6,11] to cope with learning tasks. In this section we present a formal model of the Boltzmann machine based on a graph-theoretical formulation of the architectural structure of the network (§2.1), a description of the stochastic optimization algorithm that is applied to maximize the consensus function (§2.2) and a discussion of the implementation of parallelism (§2.3).

2.1 Structural Description

A Boltzmann machine consists of a (large) number of logical units, say N, that can be represented by an undirected graph $G = (V, E)$, where $V = \{v_0, \cdots, v_{N-1}\}$ denotes the set of vertices corresponding to the logical units, and $E \subseteq V \times V$ the set of edges corresponding to the connections between the units [2]. An edge $(v_i, v_j) \in E$ connects the vertices v_i and v_j. The set of edges includes all loops, i.e. $\{(v_i, v_i) \mid v_i \in V\} \subset E$. With each vertex v_i a number is associated denoting the state of the corresponding i-th logical unit, i.e. 0 or 1 corresponding to 'off' or 'on', respectively. A configuration k of the Boltzmann machine is uniquely defined by the states of all individual vertices. The state of vertex v_i in configuration k is denoted by $r_k(v_i)$. The configuration space $\mathcal{R}$ denotes the set of all possible configurations ($|\mathcal{R}| = 2^N$). An edge (v_i, v_j) is defined to be activated in a given configuration k if $r_k(v_i) \, r_k(v_j) = 1$. With each edge (v_i, v_j) a connection strength $s(v_i, v_j) \in \mathbf{R}$ is associated determining the strength of the connection between the vertices v_i and v_j. The connection strength $s(v_i, v_j)$ is considered as a quantitative measure of the desirability that the edge (v_i, v_j) is activated. If $s(v_i, v_j) \gg 0$ then it is considered very desirable that (v_i, v_j) is activated, if $s(v_i, v_j) \ll 0$ it is considered very undesirable. The consensus C_k of a configuration k denotes the overall desirability of all the activated edges in the given configuration and is defined as

$$C_k = \sum_{(v_i, v_j) \in E} s(v_i, v_j) \, r_k(v_i) \, r_k(v_j). \tag{1}$$

Next, a neighbourhood $\mathcal{R}_k \subset \mathcal{R}$ is defined as the set of configurations that can be obtained from a given configuration k by changing the state $(0 \to 1$ or vice versa) of one of the vertices. Thus, a neighbouring configuration $k^{(i)} \in \mathcal{R}_k$ obtained by changing the state of vertex v_i is given by

$$r_{k^{(i)}}(v_j) = \begin{cases} r_k(v_j) & j \neq i \\ 1 - r_k(v_j) & j = i. \end{cases} \tag{2}$$

The corresponding difference in the consensus $\Delta C_{kk^{(i)}}$ is given by

$$\Delta C_{kk^{(i)}} = C_{k^{(i)}} - C_k = (1 - 2 \, r_k(v_i))(\sum_{(v_i, v_j) \in E_{v_i}} s(v_i, v_j) \, r_k(v_j) + s(v_i, v_i)), \tag{3}$$

where E_{v_i} denotes the set of edges incident with vertex v_i. From eq. 3 it is apparent that the effect on the consensus by changing the state of vertex v_i is completely determined by the states of the vertices v_j that are connected to v_i and by the corresponding connection strengths. Consequently, the differences in consensus $\Delta C_{kk^{(i)}}$ can be computed locally, thus allowing parallel execution.

2.2 Consensus Maximization

Maximization of the consensus function is done by means of a parallel implementation of the simulated annealing [14] (or statistical cooling [1]) algorithm. Simulated annealing is a general randomization technique to solve combinatorial optimization problems. It is based on the ergodic theory of Markov chains (for a detailed description the reader is referred to [1,17]). In a similar way the concepts of Markov chains can be used to describe the transitions among the configurations within the Boltzmann machine required to maximize the consensus function of eq. 1. In this section we describe the sequential implementation of the simulated annealing algorithm, i.e. vertices are allowed to change their states one at a time. In the next section it is shown how this procedure can be extended to parallel implementations.

A Markov chain consists of a sequence of trials where the outcome of a trial depends probabilistically on the outcome of the previous trial. In the case of the Boltzmann machine a trial consists of two steps. Given a configuration k then firstly, a neighbouring configuration $k^{(i)}$ is generated and secondly, it is evaluated whether or not $k^{(i)}$ is accepted. If it is accepted the outcome of the trial is $k^{(i)}$, otherwise it is k. With this process a transition probability T_{kl} can be associated which defines the probability of obtaining configuration l as an outcome of a given trial provided the outcome of the previous trial is configuration k. Here, the transition probabilities T_{kl} are defined as follows:

$$T_{kl}(c) = \begin{cases} T_{kk^{(i)}}(c) & l = k^{(i)} \\ 1 - \sum_{j=0}^{N-1} T_{kk^{(j)}}(c) & l = k, \end{cases} \tag{4}$$

and

$$T_{kk^{(i)}}(c) = P_{kk^{(i)}}(c) B_{kk^{(i)}}(c), \tag{5}$$

where for a given value of the control parameter c $(c \in \mathbf{R}^+)$, $P_{kk^{(i)}}(c)$ denotes the generation probability, i.e. the probability of changing the state of vertex v_i given the configuration k, and $B_{kk^{(i)}}(c)$ denotes the acceptance probability, i.e. the probability of accepting the state transition of vertex v_i given the configuration k. In our applications the generation probability is chosen independent of c and k, and uniformly over all the N vertices, i.e.

$$P_{kk^{(i)}}(c) = N^{-1}. \tag{6}$$

The acceptance probability is chosen as

$$B_{kk(i)}(c) = \frac{1}{1 + e^{-\Delta C_{kk(i)}/c}},$$ (7)

where $\Delta C_{kk(i)}$ is given by eq. 3. From eq. 7 it is evident that the response of a vertex to a proposed change of its state is determined by its local connections (it only depends on $\Delta C_{kk(i)}$). Maximization of the consensus function takes place by starting off at an initial value of c with a (randomly) chosen initial configuration and subsequently generating a sequence of Markov chains according to eqs. 4-7. The value of c is lowered slowly in between subsequent Markov chains until it approaches 0. The Markov chains are generated by continuously trying to change the states of the individual vertices and applying the acceptance criterion of eq. 7. Eventually as c approaches 0 state transitions become more and more infrequent and finally the Boltzmann machine stabilizes in a configuration which is taken as the final solution.

It can be shown that for sufficiently long Markov chains and a fixed value of c equilibrium is achieved [1,17], in the sense that there exists a unique equilibrium vector $\pi(c) \in (0,1)^{|R|}$ whose components $\pi_k(c)$ determine the probability that the Boltzmann machine occurs in configuration k when equilibrium is achieved. The components take the form [1]

$$\pi_k(c) = \pi_0(c)\exp\left(\frac{C_k - C_{max}}{c}\right),$$ (8)

where C_{max} denotes the maximal value of the consensus of the Boltzmann machine for a given set of connection strengths, and π_0 a normalization constant such that $\sum_{k \in R} \pi_k(c) = 1$. From eq. 8 it is apparent that configurations corresponding to a higher consensus have a larger probability of occurring than configurations with a lower value of the consensus. This result plays an important role in the construction of the learning algorithm presented in §4. Furthermore, it can be shown that under the same asymptoticity conditions and for c approaching to 0 the final solution obtained by the simulated annealing algorithm is an optimal solution [1,17]. In practical implementations of the algorithm, however, the asymptoticity conditions are never attained and thus convergence to an optimal solution is not guaranteed anymore, i.e. the algorithm obtains a local optimum of the consensus function which is close (or even equal) to the maximal consensus. Consequently the algorithm is an approximation algorithm.

The quality of the final solution obtained by the algorithm is determined by the convergence of the algorithm which is governed by a set of parameters, known as the cooling schedule [17]. The parameters are: the start value of c, a decrement rule to lower the value of c, the length of the individual Markov chains and a stop criterion that justifies termination of the algorithm. The computer simulations presented in this paper (§3.3 and §4.3) are carried out with different cooling schedules and for the detailed choices of the parameters the reader is referred to [3] and [2], respectively.

2.3 Parallelism

As mentioned in the previous subsections vertices only require local information to calculate a (possible) state transition. Thus the generation of a Markov chain (§2.2) can be done in parallel. To discuss this subject we distinguish between synchronous and asynchronous parallelism.

Synchronous parallelism

A vertex only needs to know the states of its neighbouring vertices (i.e. the vertices to which it is connected) and the corresponding connection strengths to calculate a state transition. Consequently, vertices that are not connected to each other, are allowed to change their state in parallel.

Synchronous parallelism can be obtained by partitioning the set of vertices V into disjoint subsets $\{V_1, \cdots, V_m\}$, such that vertices in the same subset are not connected to each other. For synchronization reasons a clocking scheme is introduced. In each clock cycle a subset V_i is chosen (randomly) and the vertices of V_i are allowed to change their states simultaneously. For optimal exploitation of parallelism the number of subsets m should be as small as possible. The problem of finding such a partition of minimal size is known as the graph coloring problem. Due to the regular structure of the Boltzmann machine for most applications (see for instance §3 and §4) the problem of finding such a partition is easy.

The amount of parallelism that can be obtained in this way strongly depends on the connection pattern in a Boltzmann machine and it will be relatively small if the amount of connectivity is large. For instance in the case of the implementation of the traveling salesman problem with n cities on a Boltzmann machine (§3) a minimal partition of the n^2 vertices contains $2n$ subsets and consequently the efficiency compared to full parallelism equals $\frac{1}{2n}$ which is small for large n. Furthermore, using this mode of parallelism requires some form of global synchronization of the vertices, which one would like to avoid.

Asynchronous parallelism

Asynchronous parallelism is based on the assumption that *all* vertices can change their states in parallel. This may introduce errors in the calculation of the difference in consensus. If two neighbouring vertices v_i and v_j change their states in parallel, this may lead to an activation or deactivation of the connection (v_i, v_j) which is not accounted for in the evaluation of the differences in consensus $\Delta C_{kk(i)}$ and $\Delta C_{kk(j)}$. For example, suppose that both vertices v_i and v_j are 'off' and suppose that they both accept a state transition to 'on' (based on the information that they are both 'off'), then connection (v_i, v_j) is activated, whereas it is not accounted for in the calculation of the difference in consensus and therefore not in the acceptance criterion of eq. 7 (evidently the same holds for state transitions in the reverse order). This may lead to a decrement of the consensus, despite the fact that both vertices anticipated an increase of the consensus. However, the probability that these unaccounted (de-)activations occur, decreases during the optimization process. From the definition of the simulated annealing algorithm it can be shown [1,17,14] that the probability of a vertex to change its state decreases as the value of the control parameter decreases and eventually it approaches 0 as c approaches 0. Thus the probability that in the course of the optimization process two neighbouring vertices change their state simultaneously is negligible and the states obtained by erroneously accepted state transitions will be corrected. In this way asynchronous parallelism can be successfully exploited. Moreover, synchronization is no longer necessary.

The computer simulations presented in §3 and §4 are based on asynchronous parallelism and from the numerical results it is concluded that efficiencies up to 95 % can be obtained.

3 Solving Combinatorial Optimization Problems with a Boltzmann Machine

In [15] we show that many well-known combinatorial optimization problems can be implemented on a Boltzmann machine. Our approach is based on the observation that the structure of many combinatorial optimization problems can be directly mapped onto the structure of a Boltzmann machine by choosing the right connections and that the corresponding cost function can be transformed into the consensus function by choosing the right connection strengths. To illustrate this we briefly discuss hereinafter two approaches to implement the traveling salesman problem (TSP) on a Boltzmann machine. For a more detailed description the reader is referred to [3].

Our approaches are based on two different formulations of the TSP, viz. as an assignment problem and as a quadratic assignment problem. We conjecture that the approaches can be generalized to the complete class of assignment and quadratic assignment problems given by definition 2 and 3 of the next subsection.

3.1 The Traveling Salesman Problem

Among all existing combinatorial optimization problems the TSP is probably the best known. Many problems can be reduced to the TSP and for this reason the TSP serves as a good demonstrator to show the feasibility of implementing combinatorial optimization problems on a Boltzmann machine. We will give three possible formulations of the TSP [8].

Definition 1.
Let n be the number of cities and $D = (d_{ij})$ the distance matrix whose entries d_{ij} denote the length of the shortest path from city i to j, then the TSP is defined as the problem of finding a tour of minimal length visiting each of the n cities exactly once.

□

To construct a model of a Boltzmann machine that embodies the TSP it is useful to rewrite the TSP as a 0-1 integer problem. This can be done in two different ways: as an assignment problem (AP) and as a quadratic assignment problem (QAP).

Definition 2. (AP)
Let x_{ij} be a 0-1 variable indicating whether or not the tour goes directly from city i to city j or vice versa and d_{ij} the corresponding distance then the TSP can be formulated in terms of an AP as

minimize

$$\sum_{i,j=0}^{n-1} d_{ij} x_{ij} \tag{9}$$

subject to

$$\sum_{i=0}^{n-1} x_{ij} = 1 \quad (j = 0,\dots,n-1), \tag{10}$$

$$\sum_{j=0}^{n-1} x_{ij} = 1 \quad (i = 0,\dots,n-1), \tag{11}$$

$$X = (x_{ij}) \text{ is irreducible (no sub tours).} \tag{12}$$

□

Definition 3. (QAP)
Let x_{ip} and x_{jq} be 0-1 variables indicating whether or not the tour visits city i at the pth position and city j at the qth position in the tour and d_{ij} the corresponding distance then the TSP can be formulated in terms of a QAP as

minimize

$$\sum_{i,j,p,q=0}^{n-1} a_{ijpq} x_{ip} x_{jq} \tag{13}$$

subject to

$$\sum_{i=0}^{n-1} x_{ij} = 1 \quad (j = 0,\dots,n-1), \tag{14}$$

$$\sum_{j=0}^{n-1} x_{ij} = 1 \quad (i = 0, \ldots, n-1), \tag{15}$$

$$a_{ijpq} = d_{ij}t_{pq}, \tag{16}$$

where $T = (t_{pq})$ is a cyclic permutation matrix whose entries are given by

$$t_{pq} = \begin{cases} 1 & \text{if } q = (p+1) \bmod n \\ 0 & \text{otherwise.} \end{cases} \tag{17}$$

□

3.2   Implementing the TSP on a Boltzmann Machine

To implement the TSP on a Boltzmann machine we introduce an architecture corresponding to a grid of $n \times n$ vertices ($N = n^2$). The 0-1 variables x_{ij} correspond to the states of the vertices (see also figure 1). So, each configuration of the Boltzmann machine uniquely represents a value assignment to the 0-1 variables (including assignments not obeying the constraints given by eqs. 10-12 or eqs. 14-17). Vertices are mutually connected according to a given connection pattern using $O(n^3)$ edges. By assigning appropriate connection strengths to the edges it can be shown that the consensus function defined on the global configurations of the Boltzmann machine by eq. 1 has the following properties [3]:

(P1) a configuration corresponds to a local maximum of the consensus function if and only if it corresponds to a tour.

(P2) the shorter the tourlength of a given tour, the higher the consensus of the corresponding configuration.

From these two properties it follows that the consensus is maximal for configurations corresponding to an optimal tour and that near-optimal (with respect to the consensus) configurations correspond to near-optimal tours [3].

The AP and QAP formulations of the TSP give rise to different connection patterns. As an example we discuss the connection pattern for the QAP formulation. For convenience we redefine the set of vertices by $V = \{v_{00}, v_{01}, \cdots, v_{0(n-1)}, v_{10}, \cdots, v_{(n-1)(n-2)}, v_{(n-1)(n-1)}\}$, which reflects the grid structure (see figure 1a). The state of a vertex v_{ip} in configuration k, denoted by $r_k(v_{ip})$, corresponds to the value of the 0-1 variable x_{ip} and $s(v_{ip}, v_{jq})$ denotes the connection strength of the edge (v_{ip}, v_{jq}). Thus, the consensus function can be rewritten as

$$C_k = \sum_{(v_{ip}, v_{jq}) \in E} s(v_{ip}, v_{jq})\, r_k(v_{ip})\, r_k(v_{jq}). \tag{18}$$

Next, the set of edges is defined as the union of three disjoint subsets, viz.

- distance edges: $E_d = \{(v_{ip}, v_{jq}) \mid (i \neq j) \wedge (q = (p+1) \bmod n)\}$,

- inhibitory edges: $E_i = \{(v_{ip}, v_{jq}) \mid ((i = j) \wedge (p \neq q)) \vee ((i \neq j) \wedge (p = q))\}$, and

- bias edges: $E_b = \{(v_{ip}, v_{jq}) \mid (i = j) \wedge (p = q)\}$, where $i, j, p, q = 0, \ldots, n - 1$. Consequently the total number of edges equals $2n^3 - n^2$. The inhibitory edges must ensure that eventually (in the course of the consensus maximization) no row or column will have more than one vertex 'on'. The bias edges must ensure that eventually each row and column will have at least one vertex 'on'. Hence, the inhibitory and bias edges must ensure that the constraints given by eqs. 14-15 are satisfied. The connection strengths of the inhibitory and bias edges are chosen such that their contribution to the total consensus is identical for all tours.

Furthermore, the proposed connection pattern ensures that a distance edge (v_{ip}, v_{jq}) will only be activated if the tour goes directly from city i to city j. The connection strength of a distance edge (v_{ip}, v_{jq}) has a negative value proportional to the distance between the cities i and j. Hence, for a given tour the (negative) contribution of the distance edges to the total consensus is proportional to the corresponding tourlength. So, maximizing the consensus function is identical to minimizing eq. 13 subject to eqs. 14-17.

The consensus function C_k has the two properties P1 and P2 mentioned above if the connection strengths are chosen as follows [3]:

$$\forall (v_{ip}, v_{jq}) \in E_d : s(v_{ip}, v_{jq}) = -d_{ij}, \tag{19}$$

$$\forall (v_{ip}, v_{jq}) \in E_i : s(v_{ip}, v_{jq}) < -\min(\mu_i, \mu_j), \text{ and} \tag{20}$$

$$\forall (v_{ip}, v_{ip}) \in E_b : s(v_{ip}, v_{ip}) > \mu_i, \tag{21}$$

where

$$\mu_i = \max \{ d_{ik} + d_{il} \mid k, l = 0, \cdots, n - 1 \wedge (k \neq l) \}. \tag{22}$$

However, if the connection strengths are chosen according eqs. 19-22, relatively large amounts of computer time are required to obtain good final results [3]. This can be avoided if instead of eq. 22 μ_i is chosen as follows:

$$\mu_i = \sum_{k=0, k \neq i}^{n-1} \sum_{l=k, l \neq i}^{n-1} 2(d_{ik} + d_{il})/(n^2 - 3n + 2). \tag{23}$$

In this case property P1 only holds in the near-optimal regime provided the cities of the TSP are positioned sufficiently random.

For a more detailed discussion on the choices of the connection strengths the reader is referred to [3], where a description of the connection pattern for the AP formulation is given as well.

3.3 Computer Simulations

Computer simulations of the Boltzmann machine model for the AP and QAP are carried out for TSP instances with 10 and 30 cities. Figure 1 shows results obtained by the computer simulations for the AP model (figure 1a) and the QAP model (figure 1b). The corresponding tour is shown in figure 1c. The matrices of figs. 1a and 1b correspond to the final states of the vertices of the Boltzmann machine and denote the values of the 0-1 variables of the AP and QAP, respectively.

The simulated annealing algorithm is an approximation algorithm. Final solutions that are equal to optimal solutions are only obtained with probability one in the asymptotic case [1,17]. The quality of the final solutions obtained by the simulations is investigated by collecting statistics. Table 1 shows the results of a statistical analysis for the 10-city and the 30-city TSP taken from [13]. The samples were obtained by running the computer simulation programs M times for different values of the seed of the random generator used in the programs. The various quantities used in the table are defined as follows:

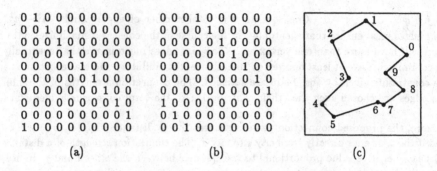

Figure 1: *Results of computer simulations for the AP model (a) and the QAP model (b) of a Boltzmann machine. The corresponding tour is shown in (c). The values of the entries of the matrices shown in (a) and (b) correspond to the final values of the 0-1 variables x_{ij} in the AP and the QAP formulation of the TSP, respectively. Note that the result for the AP formulation is unique whereas in the case of the QAP formulation there are $n = 10$ configurations corresponding to the same tour.*

$\bar{\ell}$: average tourlength,
σ : spreading in the tourlength,
$\ell_\vee$: smallest observed tourlength,
$\ell^\wedge$: largest observed tourlength,
M : sample size,
I : average number of iterations, and
ℓ_{min} : smallest known value of the tourlength.

The notion tourlength refers to the length of the final tour obtained by the simulations. As a result of the special choice of the connection strengths discussed above for the QAP model and in ref. [3] for the AP model the property P1 does not hold for the complete regime of values of the consensus function (it only holds in the near-optimal regime). Consequently, consensus maximization may yield a final solution that corresponds to a non-tour. If at the end of the consensus maximization a non-tour is obtained then the maximization algorithm is restarted. The average number of iterations required to obtain a tour is denoted by I.

We end this section with some remarks. In an important work Hopfield and Tank [13] recently introduced networks where the computing elements are linear analog neurons. They showed through computer simulations that near-optimal solutions for combinatorial optimization problems (e.g. (TSP)) could be obtained with these networks. Typical values obtained by Hopfield and Tank for the problem instances discussed above are 2.82 for the 10-city TSP and 5.65 for the 30-city TSP. The networks used by Hopfield and Tank are completely connected, i.e. each individual computing element is connected to all other elements (for a TSP with n cities $O(n^4)$ connections are required). The typical nature of the analog computing elements hampers the implementation of these networks on present-day massively parallel computer systems such as the distributed array processor (DAP) or the connection machine [9]. However, one should take into account that their approach is not designed for implementation on such computer systems but on special neural-network architectures using dedicated hardware. Furthermore, we remark that the typical analog nature of the computing elements, which Hopfield and Tank find to be essential for obtaining satisfactory results with their networks, is circumvented in our approach by the stochastic state-transition mechanism.

	10-city TSP		30-city TSP	
	AP	QAP	AP	QAP
$\bar{\ell}$	2.783	2.815	5.643	5.459
σ	0.097	0.141	0.434	0.312
$\ell_\vee$	2.675	2.675	4.769	4.929
$\ell^\wedge$	3.060	3.277	6.297	6.044
M	100	100	40	25
I	1.1	1.2	1.2	1.9
ℓ_{min}	2.675 [13]		4.299 [13]	

Table 1: *Numerical results obtained for the 10-city and the 30-city TSP (for explanation of the symbols see text).*

4   Learning in a Boltzmann Machine

In the previous section it is shown how the model of the Boltzmann machine can be used to solve combinatorial optimization problems. A special class of optimization problems is given by the set of classification problems [19]. For instance, let $\mathcal{N} = \{n_1,\ldots,n_k\}$ denote a set of k items (e.g. images) and m a partly distorted item (e.g. a corrupted image) then the problem is to find an item $n_i \in \mathcal{N}$ that is "closest to" m. Here the notion "closest to" can be defined in different ways depending on the metric defined on the set $\mathcal{N}$. In principle it should be possible to implement these problems on a Boltzmann machine. However, choosing the appropriate connections and their strengths is very difficult since different items may give rise to conflicting connection strengths. This major problem can be overcome by "learning" the Boltzmann machine the appropriate connection strengths. By applying a learning algorithm the connection strengths are adjusted over a number of iterations (learning cycles) to adapt themselves to a given set of learning examples (e.g. the set of items $\mathcal{N}$) that are subsequently clamped into a subset of the vertices of the Boltzmann machine (i.e. the environmental vertices). The learning algorithm discussed in this section starts off by setting all connection strengths equal to zero. Next, a sequence of learning cycles is completed, each cycle consisting of two phases. In the first phase learning examples are clamped subsequently into the environmental vertices (clamped situation) and for each learning example the Boltzmann machine is equilibrated using the current set of connection strengths (the meaning of equilibration is explained in §4.2). In the second phase all vertices are free to adjust their state (free-running situation) and again equilibration is carried out. Inbetween subsequent learning cycles the connection strengths are adjusted using statistical information obtained from the two situations of the previous learning cycle. This process is continued until the average change (over a number of learning cycles) of the connection strengths becomes zero. After completion of the learning algorithm the Boltzmann machine is able to complete a partial example (i.e. a situation where only a subset of the environmental vertices is clamped) by maximizing the consensus. In this way a Boltzmann machine can not only reproduce given examples but also has associative and restricted inductive capabilities.

Hereinafter we discuss the learning algorithm in more detail and present a number of examples to demonstrate the characteristic features of learning in a Boltzmann machine.

4.1 Extension of the Structural Description

To arrive at a formal description that is well suited for the formulation of a learning algorithm that can be used in a Boltzmann machine we add a few extensions to the structural description of §2.1. For this purpose the set of vertices is divided into three disjoint subsets, V_i, V_h and V_o, with $V = V_i \cup V_h \cup V_o$, where V_i, V_h and V_o denote the sets of input, hidden and output vertices, respectively. The union $V_i \cup V_o$ is denoted by V_{io}, the set of environmental vertices, and by definition we have $|V_{io}| = m$. An environmental configuration l is determined by the states of the vertices $v_i \in V_{io}$. The state of an environmental vertex v_i in an environmental configuration l is denoted by $q_l(v_i)$. The environmental configuration space $\mathcal{Q}$ denotes the set of all possible environmental configurations ($|\mathcal{Q}| = 2^m$). With each environmental configuration l a subspace $\mathcal{Q}_l$ can be associated:

$$\mathcal{Q}_l = \{k \in \mathcal{R} \mid \forall v_j \in V_{io} : r_k(v_j) = q_l(v_j)\}, \tag{24}$$

consisting of all configurations for which the states of the environmental vertices are given by l. The learning set $\mathcal{T}$ denotes the set of examples (environmental configurations) that can be clamped into the environmental vertices. Clearly we have $\mathcal{T} \subset \mathcal{Q}$. An input determines the states of the input vertices $v_j \in V_i$. The set of all possible inputs is denoted by $\mathcal{X}$. Similarly, an output is determined by the states of the output vertices $v_j \in V_o$. The set of all possible outputs is denoted by $\mathcal{Y}$. By definition, we have $\mathcal{Q} = \mathcal{X} \times \mathcal{Y}$.

4.2 A Learning Algorithm

The starting point of the learning algorithm presented in this subsection is given by the learning algorithm introduced by Hinton et al. [11,4]. The objective of the learning algorithm is to adjust the connection strengths such that the Boltzmann machine in the free-running situation tends to be with a large probability in environmental configurations that are used as examples in the clamped situation. To this end the probability distributions P and P' defined over the set of environmental configurations are used. P_l denotes the probability that the states of the environmental vertices are given by the environmental configuration l in the clamped situation. Similarly, P_l' denotes the probability that the states of the environmental vertices are given by l in the free-running situation. The probability distribution P is determined by the specific environmental configurations contained in the learning set and the frequency they are clamped into the environmental vertices. P_l is large if:[1] (i) l is contained in the learning set and (ii) l is frequently clamped into the environmental vertices. The probability distribution P' depends on the connection strengths $s(v_i, v_j)$ and as will be pointed out hereinafter P' can be related to the stochastic transition mechanism applied by the simulated annealing algorithm. The objective of the learning algorithm can be formulated as follows: *modify the connection strengths of the Boltzmann machine such that P' is close to P.* We then say that the Boltzmann machine has obtained an understanding of the learning set (e.g. if $P \approx P'$ the Boltzmann machine can obtain a correct output when only the input vertices are clamped).

An information-theoretic measure of the distance between the two probability distributions P and P' is given by the asymmetric divergence G, which is defined as [16]

$$G = \sum_{l \in \mathcal{Q}} P_l \ln \frac{P_l}{P_l'}. \tag{25}$$

The objective of the learning algorithm can be rephrased as: *minimize G by changing the connection strengths.*

Before we describe how G can be minimized we readdress the modelling of the state transitions of the individual vertices. In the learning algorithm the transitions of free-running vertices are modelled stochastically such that equilibrium is achieved, (see §2.2). In equilibrium the Boltzmann machine tends to be in configurations corresponding to large values of the consensus (see eq. 8). If equilibrium is achieved P'_l is given by

$$P'_l(c) = \sum_{k \in \mathcal{Q}_l} \pi_k(c), \tag{26}$$

where the $\pi_k(c)$ are the components of the equilibrium vector given by eq. 8. It can be shown [4] that the partial derivative of G with respect to $s(v_i, v_j)$ can be written as

$$\frac{\partial G}{\partial s(v_i, v_j)} = \frac{<p'_{ij}> - <p_{ij}>}{c}, \tag{27}$$

where $<p_{ij}>$ denotes the expectation of the probability that the edge (v_i, v_j) is activated in the clamped situation and $<p'_{ij}>$ denotes the expectation of the probability that (v_i, v_j) is activated in the free-running situation. Both expectations are defined under the condition that equilibrium is reached. To minimize G it suffices to collect statistics on $<p_{ij}>$ and $<p'_{ij}>$ and to change the connection strength proportionally to the difference between the expectations, i.e.

$$\Delta s(v_i, v_j) = \eta \left(<p_{ij}> - <p'_{ij}>\right), \tag{28}$$

where η denotes a constant.

The learning algorithm can be described as follows: the algorithm starts off with all connection strengths set to zero (tabula rasa). Next, a number of learning cycles is completed by changing repeatedly from the clamped situation to the free-running situation and collecting statistics on the expectations $<p_{ij}>$ and $<p'_{ij}>$. In between subsequent learning cycles the connection strengths are adjusted until G is minimal. In this way the environmental information from the learning set is distributed over and stored in the connection strengths. The learning algorithm consists of a number of learning cycles, that can be depicted schematically in pseudo-Pascal as follows:

PROCEDURE LEARNING_CYCLE;

```
begin

    for i := 1 to number_of_times do
    begin

        CHOOSE_EXAMPLE(according to P);
        EQUILIBRATE(hidden vertices);
        COLLECT_STATISTICS(< p_ij >);

    end;
    for i := 1 to number_of_times do
    begin

        RUN_FREE;
        EQUILIBRATE(all vertices);
        COLLECT_STATISTICS(< p'_ij >);

    end;
    ADJUST_CONNECTION_STRENGTHS;
end;
```

By definition environmental configurations l not included in the learning set T have a corresponding probability $P_l = 0$. Consequently, the asymmetric divergence G is not properly defined for

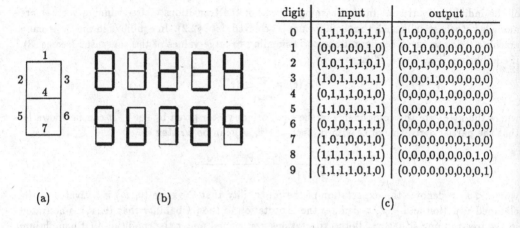

digit	input	output
0	(1,1,1,0,1,1,1)	(1,0,0,0,0,0,0,0,0,0)
1	(0,0,1,0,0,1,0)	(0,1,0,0,0,0,0,0,0,0)
2	(1,0,1,1,1,0,1)	(0,0,1,0,0,0,0,0,0,0)
3	(1,0,1,1,0,1,1)	(0,0,0,1,0,0,0,0,0,0)
4	(0,1,1,1,0,1,0)	(0,0,0,0,1,0,0,0,0,0)
5	(1,1,0,1,0,1,1)	(0,0,0,0,0,1,0,0,0,0)
6	(0,1,0,1,1,1,1)	(0,0,0,0,0,0,1,0,0,0)
7	(1,0,1,0,0,1,0)	(0,0,0,0,0,0,0,1,0,0)
8	(1,1,1,1,1,1,1)	(0,0,0,0,0,0,0,0,1,0)
9	(1,1,1,1,0,1,0)	(0,0,0,0,0,0,0,0,0,1)

(a)   (b)   (c)

Figure 2: *Schematic representation of the seven-segment display of the digits 0 - 9 (a) and (b), and the coded representation (c).*

these environmental configurations unless $P_l' = 0$, which can only be realized by infinitely large connection strengths due to the stochastic nature of the consensus optimization. To avoid this problem noise is introduced which allows the environmental vertices in the clamped situation to change their states with a small probability.

Equilibration is carried out by using the simulated annealing algorithm. Again a sequence of Markov chains is generated at descending values of c. However, in contrast to the consensus optimization described in §2.2, the value of c is not lowered until it approaches 0 but the algorithm is terminated at some finite value of $c > 0$ for which the acceptance ratio $\chi(c)$ is smaller than some fixed value χ_f (usually $\chi_f = 0.25$), where $\chi(c)$ equals the number of accepted transitions divided by the number of proposed transitions at a given value of c. In this way equilibration is rapidly achieved [2].

The results obtained by the learning algorithm during the learning phase can be tested by clamping an input into the input vertices. The set of inputs in the test is denoted by the test set. For a given input the consensus is maximized using the connection strengths obtained from the learning phase. Here, both the hidden and the output vertices are considered as free vertices, i.e. they are allowed to change their state during the consensus optimization. After optimization of the consensus the test can be completed by comparing the resulting output with the "expected" output. Consensus optimization is again carried out using the simulated annealing algorithm as described in §2.2. The number of vertices is discussed separately for each example.

4.3   Computer Simulations

In this section the learning behaviour of the Boltzmann machine is discussed by means of a number of simulation experiments. Simulations are carried out to illustrate the three characteristic functions of the Boltzmann machine mentioned above, e.g. memory, association and induction [1]. The simulations are based on a model of the Boltzmann machine in which

- all input vertices are mutually connected,
- all output vertices are mutually connected,

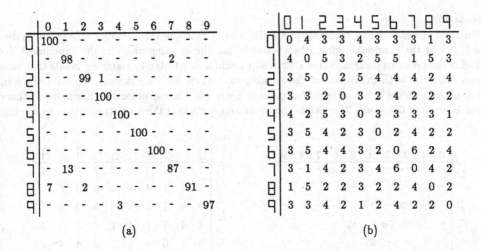

	0	1	2	3	4	5	6	7	8	9
0	100	-	-	-	-	-	-	-	-	-
1	-	98	-	-	-	-	-	2	-	-
2	-	-	99	1	-	-	-	-	-	-
3	-	-	-	100	-	-	-	-	-	-
4	-	-	-	-	100	-	-	-	-	-
5	-	-	-	-	-	100	-	-	-	-
6	-	-	-	-	-	-	100	-	-	-
7	-	13	-	-	-	-	-	87	-	-
8	7	-	2	-	-	-	-	-	91	-
9	-	-	-	-	3	-	-	-	-	97

	0	1	2	3	4	5	6	7	8	9
0	0	4	3	3	4	3	3	3	1	3
1	4	0	5	3	2	5	5	1	5	3
2	3	5	0	2	5	4	4	4	2	4
3	3	3	2	0	3	2	4	2	2	2
4	4	2	5	3	0	3	3	3	3	1
5	3	5	4	2	3	0	2	4	2	2
6	3	5	4	4	3	2	0	6	2	4
7	3	1	4	2	3	4	6	0	4	2
8	1	5	2	2	3	2	2	4	0	2
9	3	3	4	2	1	2	4	2	2	0

(a) (b)

Figure 3: *(a) Score matrix for the memory test,(b) Hamming-distance matrix for the inputs*

- all hidden vertices are connected to all input and output vertices, and
- all vertices are connected to themselves.

Memory

To demonstrate the capability of the Boltzmann machine to store information which can be retrieved afterwards, the following experiment is discussed. For the display of decimal digits the standard form is the seven-segment display (figure 2a and 2b). Each of the seven segments is a separate display (e.g. a LED or Liquid Cristal) that can be turned 'on' or 'off'. The display can be controlled by a binary seven-tuple where a 0 corresponds to 'off' and a 1 to 'on'. Thus, the digits 0 up to 9 can be coded by the inputs given in figure 2c.

The goal of the experiment is to learn the Boltzmann machine the codes corresponding to the 10 digits of figure 2c by using the learning algorithm described in §4.2. For this purpose a Boltzmann machine was modelled consisting of 7 input, 10 hidden and 10 output vertices. The learning set was given by the input-output combinations of figure 2c. During each learning cycle 20 randomly chosen learning examples were clamped into the environmental vertices. After a learning phase consisting of 870 learning cycles the results obtained in the learning phase were tested. During the test phase inputs given in figure 2c were used. Each input of the test set was clamped 100 times into the input vertices. The results of the test phase are shown in the score matrix given in figure 3a. For 972 of the 1000 inputs (97%) a correct output was retrieved. For the digits 0, 3, 4, 5 and 6 a full score was obtained. In the case of an incorrect retrieval (3%) it appears that the input corresponding to the retrieved output have a large "similarity" to the clamped input (1 and 7, 2 and 3, 0, 2 and 8, 4 and 9). A large similarity may be defined here as a small Hamming distance between the corresponding inputs. In the case of an incorrect retrieval the Hamming distance equals 1 or 2 (see the Hamming-distance matrix given in figure 3b). This suggests associative capabilities. Furthermore, from figure 3a it is observed that the score matrix is not symmetric. This feature can not be explained from simple external quantities such as the Hamming distance but is related to internal quantities of the Boltzmann machine, i.e. the maximal consensus and the connection strengths. This feature is also observed in the next paragraph.

Association

To illustrate the associative capabilities of a Boltzmann machine the following experiment is discussed. Using the connection strengths obtained from the learning phase of the experiment described in the previous paragraph, the Boltzmann machine was tested by clamping inputs that have a large similarity with the inputs of the learning set. Again each input was clamped 100 times. The results are shown in the score matrix given in figure 4a. The corresponding Hamming-distance matrix is given in figure 4b. The results clearly demonstrate that the outputs obtained by the test

	0	1	2	3	4	5	6	7	8	9
0	82	-	-	-	-	-	18	-	-	-
1	-	100	-	-	-	-	-	-	-	-
2	-	-	100	-	-	-	-	-	-	-
3	-	-	2	56	-	42	-	-	-	-
4	-	-	-	-	97	-	-	-	-	3
5	30	-	-	7	-	61	2	-	-	-
6	7	-	-	-	-	-	93	-	-	-
7	-	1	-	-	-	-	-	99	-	-
8	4	-	49	35	-	-	-	-	12	-
9	-	26	-	-	-	-	-	64	-	10

	0	1	2	3	4	5	6	7	8	9
0	1	5	4	4	5	2	2	4	2	4
1	5	1	4	4	3	6	6	2	6	4
2	4	4	1	3	4	5	5	3	3	3
3	4	4	3	1	4	1	3	3	3	3
4	5	3	6	4	1	2	2	4	4	2
5	2	4	5	3	4	1	3	3	3	3
6	2	4	5	5	4	3	1	5	3	5
7	4	2	5	3	4	3	5	1	5	3
8	2	4	1	1	4	3	3	3	1	3
9	2	2	5	3	2	3	5	1	3	1

(a)	(b)

Figure 4: *(a) Score matrix for the association test, (b) Hamming-distance matrix for the inputs.*

correspond to inputs of the learning set that have a large similarity with the tested inputs (i.e. a Hamming distance 1 or 2). Similar to the memory test different scores are observed for outputs whose corresponding inputs (in the learning set) have equal Hamming distances to the inputs used in the test. For instance the input corresponding to the 9-th row has a Hamming distance 1 to the inputs corresponding to the digits 2, 3 and 8. The scores, however, vary considerably for the corresponding outputs. Again, these features can only be explained from the associated internal quantities such as the connection strengths and the maximal consensus.

Induction

By induction we define the ability to discover an underlying pattern from a set of examples in such a way that afterwards inputs (not corresponding to or resembling the inputs of the learning set) can be classified according to this pattern. To illustrate that the Boltzmann machine exhibits restricted inductive capabilities the following experiment is discussed.

A Boltzmann machine is modelled consisting of 8 input, 12 hidden and 2 output vertices. The learning set consists of input-output combinations with an input of length 8 and an output of length 2. The output equals (1,0) if at least 2 successive components of the input equal 1, and (0,1) otherwise, e.g.

$$(1, 0, 1, 1, 0, 0, 1, 0) \rightarrow (1, 0)$$
$$(1, 0, 1, 0, 1, 0, 1, 0) \rightarrow (0, 1)$$

The goal of this experiment is to "learn" the Boltzmann machine to discover a '11'-pair in an input by using a learning set consisting of a subset of all the 256 possible environmental configurations.

By using another subset as test set the induction result can be tested. The learning set consisted of 60 learning examples, 30 having a '11'-pair and 30 not. The test set consisted of 40 inputs, 23 having a '11'-pair and 17 not. During each learning cycle 20 randomly chosen learning examples were clamped into the environmental vertices. After a learning phase of 560 learning cycles the results obtained by the learning was tested. Each input belonging to the test set was clamped twice. In 76% of the tests a correct classification was obtained (61 out of 80). To demonstrate the significance of this result it is compared with a result obtained by randomly choosing an output (0,1) or (1,0) with a probability of 0.5 to choose a correct output. In this way the probability of choosing 61 (out of 80) correct outputs equals 10^{-6}. The calculation is based on a binomial distribution. It, therefore, may be concluded that the degree to which the Boltzmann machine has "learned" the underlying '11'-pattern is significant. Moreover, it should be taken into account that recognition of a '11'-pair by a Boltzmann machine is a difficult task as it can not use the advantage of topological information, e.g. the human brain can discriminate a '11'-pair from a string of binary numbers by using visual information.

5 Conclusions

The model of Boltzmann machines combines typical features of neural networks and connectionist models. Salient features of the model are its massively parallel architecture of simple stochastic computing elements and the distribution of knowledge. It is concluded that Boltzmann machines can be effectively used to solve combinatorial optimization problems. For two distinct 0-1 integer formulations of the traveling salesman problem (as an assignment problem and as a quadratic assignment problem) it is shown that near-optimal solutions for these problems can be obtained by a network with $O(n^2)$ computing elements and $O(n^3)$ connections.

Furthermore, it is concluded that stochastic concepts can be successfully applied to the modelling of learning in parallel networks such as the Boltzmann machine. By "programming" the Boltzmann machine through a set of learning examples it exhibits memory, associative and inductive functions. Especially the latter two functions are interesting new features.

Asynchronous parallelism can be effectively exploited by the Boltzmann machine. Future research on the Boltzmann machine will have to concentrate on massively parallel hardware implementations. This is to a large extent an unexplored field of interest which will require considerable research efforts.

As an overall conclusion we state that the Boltzmann machine is promising for a number of complex computational tasks such as combinatorial optimization and learning. However, more analysis, large-scale simulations and practical experience are needed to judge the Boltzmann machine on its true merits.

References

[1] Aarts, E.H.L. and P.J.M. van Laarhoven, Statistical Cooling: A General Approach to Combinatorial Optimization Problems, *Philips Journ. Res.*, 40(1985)193.

[2] Aarts, E.H.L. and J.H.M. Korst, Simulation of Learning in Parallel Networks Based on the Boltzmann Machine, *Proc. 2nd Eur. Simul. Congr.*, Antwerp, September 1986, p. 391.

[3] Aarts, E.H.L. and J.H.M. Korst, Solving Traveling Salesman Problems with a Boltzmann Machine, *The European Journal of Operations Research*, to be submitted.

[4] Ackley, D.H., G.E. Hinton and T.J. Sejnowski, A Learning Algorithm for Boltzmann Machines, *Cognitive Science*, 9(1985)147.

[5] Feldman, J.A. and D.H. Ballard, Connectionist Models and Their Properties, *Cognitive Science*, 6(1982)205.

[6] Fahlman, S.E., G.E. Hinton and T.J. Sejnowski, Massively Parallel Architectures for AI: NETL, Thistle and Boltzmann Machines, *Proc. Nat. Conf. on AI, AAAI-83*, August 1983, p. 109.

[7] Fahlman, S.E and G.E. Hinton, Connectionist Architectures for Artificial Intelligence, *Computer*, January, 1987, p. 100.

[8] Garfinkel, R.S., Motivation and Modeling, in: E.L. Lawler, J.K. Lenstra, A.H.G. Rinnooy Kan and D.B. Shmoys (eds.), *The Traveling Salesman Problem*, Wiley, Chichester, 1985, p. 17.

[9] Hillis, W.D., *The Connection Machine*, MIT-press, Cambridge (MA), 1985.

[10] Hinton G.E. and T.J. Sejnowski, Optimal Perceptual Inference, *Proc. IEEE Conf. on Computer Vision and Pattern Recognition*, Washington DC, June 1983, p. 448.

[11] Hinton, G.E., T.J. Sejnowski and D.H. Ackley, Boltzmann Machines: Constraint Satisfaction Machines that Learn, *Tech. Rep.* CMU-CS-84-119, Carnegie-Mellon University, 1984.

[12] Hopfield, J.J., Neural Networks and Physical Systems with Emergent Collective Computational Abilities, *Proc. Nat. Academy Sciences*, USA, 79(1982)2554.

[13] Hopfield, J.J. and D.W. Tank, Neural Computation of Decisions in Optimization Problems, *Biological Cybernetics*, 52(1985)141.

[14] Kirkpatrick, S., C.D. Gelatt Jr. and M.P. Vecchi, Optimization by Simulated Annealing, *Science*, 220(1983)671.

[15] Korst, J.H.M. and E.H.L. Aarts, Solving Combinatorial Optimization Problems with Massively Parallel Computer Architectures Based on the Boltzmann Machine, *Operations Research*, to be submitted.

[16] Kullbach, S., *Information Theory and Statistics*, Wiley, New York, 1959.

[17] Laarhoven, P.J.M. van and E.H.L. Aarts, *Simulated Annealing: Theory and Applications*, Kluwer Academic Publishers, Dordrecht, The Netherlands, 1987, in press.

[18] Prager R.G. *et al.*, Boltzmann Machines for Speech Recognition, *Computer Speech and Language*, Vol. 1, 1986.

[19] *Proceedings NASI on Pattern Recognition: Theory and Applications*, P.A. DeVijver and J. Kittler (eds.), Springer, 1987 (and references therein).

[20] Sejnowski, T.J. and C.R. Rosenberg, NETtalk: A Parallel Network that Learns to Speak Aloud, John Hopkins University, *Technical Report*, JHU/EECS-86/01, 1986.

[21] Stevens, J.K., Reverse Engineering the Brain, *Byte*, 10(4)(1985)287.

[22] Traherne, J.F. *et al.*, Speech Processing with a Boltzmann Machine, *Proc. IEEE ICASSP-86*, Tokyo, 1986, p. 725.

[23] Treleaven, P.C., A.N. Refenes, K.J. Lees and S.C. McCabe, Computer Architectures for Artificial Intelligence, *Lecture Notes*, University of Reading, Reading, 1985.

[24] Waldrop, M.M., Artificial Intelligence in Parallel, *Science*, 225(1985)608.

COBWEB-2: Structured Specification of a Wafer-Scale Supercomputer

by

Paul Anderson*, Chris Hankin**, Paul Kelly**, Peter Osmon* and Malcolm Shute***.

* Computer Science Department, The City University, Northampton Square, London EC1 VOHB, UK.
** Department of Computing, Imperial College of Science and Technology, 180 Queen's Gate, London SW7 2BZ, UK.
*** Microelectronics Unit, Middlesex Polytechnic, Bounds Green Road, London N11 2NQ, UK.

1. Introduction

This paper describes the COBWEB-2 machine, with particular emphasis on the role of formal specification in the architecture's development.

COBWEB-2 aims to execute programs written in purely-functional programming languages (for example ALFL [Hudak & Kranz 83] and Miranda [Turner 85]). The project hopes to derive very high performance from a combination of powerful compiler optimisations and implementation using whole-wafer integration - thereby enjoying massive parallelism and, by avoiding chip-to-chip communications, high sequential speed.

The graph reduction approach to parallel evaluation of functional programs is shown to give particularly good utilisation of working elements in a fault-tolerant wafer-scale processor array.

The work presented here has its roots in the COBWEB-1 design, reported in [Hankin, Osmon & Shute 85], but differs in several radical respects. COBWEB-2 has substantially more random-access memory distributed through the wafer and a more subtle memory management system alleviates the program library access bottleneck. COBWEB-2 also has a new fault-tolerant communications mechanism, supplanting Catt's spiral, which was employed in COBWEB-1.

We start with a review of functional programming languages, compilation, and the run-time program representation - program graphs decorated with director strings and annotations to control parallel activity. An abstract machine executing this representation is defined, and used as the root of the specification-driven development of the architecture. The refinement of this specification has the structure represented below:

Normal-order reduction-based abstract
machine running the machine code.
|
Token-based specification,
showing structure sharing
|
Parallel graph-reduction abstract
machine.
|
Parallel abstract machine with eager
parameter distribution.
|
Engineering model, pool of virtual
reduction machines.
|
Distributed, copying, virtual memory
system with garbage collection.
|
Fault-tolerant, packet-switched
communications network.
|
Wafer-scale integration.

This development is mirrored in the structure of the paper as follows. After section 2 has introduced functional languages, showing how programs are compiled into the machine's run-time representation, section 3 introduces term-rewriting systems, and uses the notation to define a normal-order reducer for COBWEB-2's machine code. Section 4 describes an extension to the notation to describe graph-reduction, and this is used in section 5 to specify the parallel graph-reduction abstract machine which forms a specification for the engineering model. Section 6 describes the engineering model itself, and section 7 shows how this separates the implementation into independent aspects - virtual processor management, memory management, and inter-processor communications. Finally, section 8 discusses how wafer-scale integration makes the design feasible, and why it is particularly well-suited to a graph-reduction model of parallel computation.

2. Compilation and Program Representation

Functional, or applicative, programming languages concentrate on data inter-dependencies, making potential parallelism implicit. Their built-in determinacy avoids many parallel programming pitfalls, and their simple algebraic properties facilitate rigorous software development as well as sophisticated compilers.

Programming languages like Miranda [Turner 85], and ALFL [Hudak & Kranz 83] have "lazy" semantics - that is their semantics is based on call-by-name parameter passing. This contrasts with most current fast functional language implementations, such as [Cardelli 84], or [Hope 86], but is a considerable aid to program transformation.

The compilation technique of strictness analysis by abstract interpretation [Mycroft 81], [Burn, Hankin & Abramsky 85], is employed to deduce where a more "eager" parameter passing mechanism can be used without risking the triggering of unwanted computations. This is a principal source of parallelism in COBWEB-2.

Director Notation

In this paper, the director-string approach, first introduced in [Dijkstra 80] and [Kennaway & Sleep 81], is used as a unified framework to combine a combinator-based, variable-free program representation with annotation of apply-nodes in the original program. This notation can be substantially optimised, but provides a useful semantic link to quite low-level aspects of the machine's operation.

The director representation of a λ-expression has precisely the same structure as the original expression. The transformation can, intuitively, be regarded as annotating each apply-node in the expression with a marker showing which sub-expressions to route the parameter to.

There is a set of four directors:
- ^   send the parameter to both operator and operand
- /   send the parameter to the operator
- \   send the parameter to the operand
- -   destroy the parameter

Occurrences of parameters can be viewed as "holes" into which parameters are placed after being routed through the expression graph by the appropriate directors. "Holes" are written as "I", the identity combinator.

The annotation process is repeated for each parameter in turn, creating a string of director annotations on each apply node. For example, the Miranda definition

---

```
ray_trace_image image viewpoint
  = map (trace_ray image) (initial_rays viewpoint)
```

---

describes how the pixel intensities of an image can be computed by making a list of the rays from the viewpoint through each pixel, and tracing each ray backwards to its source, through refractions and reflections in the image database.

Translated into the λ-calculus, the program becomes
```
ray_trace_image = λ image viewpoint .
                    (map (trace_ray image)
                    (initial_rays viewpoint))
```
This can be clarified by showing the function applications explicitly as "@":

```
ray_trace_image = λ image viewpoint .
                    (@ (@ map (@ trace_ray image))
                    (@ initial_rays viewpoint))
```

After compilation to director form, each apply-node is annotated with directors:

```
ray_trace_image = (/\@ (\@ map (\@ trace_ray I))
                    (\@ initial_rays I))
```

Strictness Annotation

The lazy semantics of languages like Miranda and ALFL are based on a sequential interpretation of

```
(@ e1 e2)
```

in which e1 is evaluated first, and e2's evaluation is triggered only when (or if) e2 is actually used during e1's evaluation. This is "normal-order" evaluation. Its value is in not initiating infinite computations of unwanted values. Unfortunately, it is strictly sequential and often very inefficient.

To overcome this semantically-induced restriction, to purely-sequential program execution, abstract interpretation is used to discover where a less conservative strategy can safely be employed.

A context-sensitive strictness annotation appears on any apply-node

```
(@ e1 e2)
```

where the compiler can deduce that evaluation of e1 always results in evaluation of e2[1].

Additional parallelism is gained by annotating functions with the strictness of each of their parameters, so that a function passed to another function, as a parameter, can trigger parallel evaluation of its parameters when it, in turn, is applied. This is context-free strictness annotation [Hankin, Burn & Peyton Jones 86].

A context-sensitive strictness annotation appears as "#", before the "@" of an apply node. Context-free strictness is represented using a new combinator, P. Thus the annotated version of the example above is

```
ray_trace_image = (@ P
                    (\@ P (/\#@ (\#@ map (\#@ trace_ray I))
                    (\#@ initial_rays I))))
```

Here, the strictness analyser makes use of the definition of the functions "trace_ray" and "initial_rays" to infer that both are strict in all their parameters. It is not always the case that such an inference can be made, even when it holds.

---

[1] Throughout this paper, we discuss evaluation to "weak head normal form" [Peyton Jones 87]. Strictness analysis of programs with, for example, lazy lists, leads to strictness annotations for different degrees of evaluation.

3. A Normal-Order Reducer

The highest level specification of COBWEB-2 is given as a term-rewriting system [Klop 85], [Barendregt et al. 86]. This is simply a system of rules specifying, for each pattern appearing on the left-hand side, a substitution on the right. Beginning with an expression like the example above, substitution is repeated until no rule is applicable, whereupon the resulting term is the computation's result.

Normal order reduction is assumed.

Lower level specifications will break out of this purely-sequential reduction mechanism by using the strictness annotations. This causes no change to the semantics, since the annotations were only introduced by the compiler where their use would not compromise the program's meaning.

The specification of the top-level abstract machine is given in Figure 1 below:

$(@ (\backslash:D@ f x) a) \rightarrow (D@ f (@ x a))$

$(@ (/:D@ f x) a) \rightarrow (D@ (@ f a) x)$

$(@ (\hat{}:D@ f x) a) \rightarrow (D@ (@ f a)(@ x a))$

$(@ (-:D@ f x) a) \rightarrow (D@ f x)$

$(\#:D@ f x) \rightarrow (D@ f x)$

$(@ (@ P x) a) \rightarrow (@ x a)$

$(@ I a) \rightarrow a$

$(@ (@ K x) y) \rightarrow x$

$(@ Y f) \rightarrow (@ f (@ Y f))$

$(@ (@ (@ IF\ TRUE) y) z) \rightarrow y$

$(@ (@ (@ IF\ FALSE) y) z) \rightarrow z$

$(@ HD (@ (@ CONS x) y)) \rightarrow x$

$(@ TL (@ (@ CONS x) y)) \rightarrow y$

$(@ (@ PLUS x) y) \rightarrow x + y$ (when x, y values)

and similarly for the other operators, such as
MINUS, TIMES, DIVIDE, EQUAL, etc.

Figure 1. A Normal-Order Abstract Machine.

In the rules above, "d:D" denotes the string of directors headed by "d".

The Program Library

For the rules above, the initial program comprises just a single expression. An improvement in both clarity and efficiency is gained if function definitions in COBWEB-2 reside in a "library" - a data structure providing random access to all the definitions of the program's outermost level of lexical function nesting.

Use of the library is made by adding the following rule:

(name n)　　→　(lookup n)　(when n is a name).

---

4. Graph-Reduction Execution Model

The specification of COBWEB-2 given above fails to capture some important aspects of the computation, which, although not affecting the outcome, are needed if efficiency is to be achieved. As a preliminary to considering parallel activity, a specification is given of the reduction process in a form which shows how the graph representation of the program avoids unnecessary recomputation of parameter expressions.

The only addition to the notation above is a means of introducing names for new expressions. Subsequent use of an expression's name rather than its symbolic representation allows reduction of one occurrence of a subexpression to render reduction of other occurrences unnecessary. Names are related to brackets in a straightforward way:

    e1 = ...t...

where t is a name for e2, some expression, is precisely equivalent to writing

    e1 = ...(e2)...

except for the sharing property above. We shall thus write e1 as

    e1 = ...t... where t = e2.

This can be understood by considering all expressions to be composed of "tokens", every one with a different label. Expressions are directed graphs whose nodes are tokens, but which are written using the bracketted form wherever possible.

Figure 2 shows the modified notation, a graph-rewriting system, being used to specify a graph reduction abstract machine. The order of application of these rules is exactly as before - leftmost, outermost reducible expressions are reduced first.

Omitting two rules introduced in the next section, which generate parallel computation (marked with asterisks), gives a normal order reducer which is simply a graph-reduction version of figure 1.

Each rule should be read as *actually changing* the graph matching the LHS, while retaining the same name - the root token is overwritten.

The reader should notice that only tokens appearing as the root of the LHS are ever overwritten, and that tokens are only overwritten by an expression with the same meaning.

$t1 = (@ \ (\backslash:D@ \ f \ x) \ a) \rightarrow \quad t1 = (D@ \ f \ t2)$
$\text{where } t2 = @ \ x \ a$

$t1 = (@ \ (/:D@ \ f \ x) \ a) \rightarrow \quad t1 = (D@ \ t2 \ x)$
$\text{where } t2 = @ \ f \ a$

$t1 = (@ \ (\hat{}:D@ \ f \ x) \ a) \rightarrow \quad t1 = (D@ \ t2 \ t3)$
$\text{where } t2 = @ \ f \ a, \ t3 = @ \ x \ a$

$t1 = (@ \ (-:D@ \ f \ x) \ a) \rightarrow \quad t1 = (D@ \ f \ x)$

$t1 = (\# :D@ \ f \ x) \qquad \rightarrow \quad t1 = (D@ \ f \ <x>) \qquad \qquad *$

$t1 = (@ \ (@ \ P \ x) \ a) \quad \rightarrow \quad t1 = (\#@ \ x \ a) \qquad *$
$\text{equivalent to } t1 = (@ \ x \ <a>)$

$t1 = (@ \ I \ a) \qquad \rightarrow \quad t1 = a$

$t1 = (@ \ (@ \ K \ x) \ y) \quad \rightarrow \quad t1 = x$

$t1 = (@ \ Y \ f) \qquad \rightarrow \quad t1 = (@ \ f \ t1)^2$

$t1 = (@ \ (@ \ (@ \ IF \ TRUE) \ y) \ z) \rightarrow \quad t1 = y$

$t1 = (@ \ (@ \ (@ \ IF \ FALSE) \ y) \ z) \rightarrow \quad t1 = z$

$t1 = (@ \ HD \ (@ \ (@ \ CONS \ x) \ y)) \rightarrow \quad t1 = x$

$t1 = (@ \ TL \ (@ \ (@ \ CONS \ x) \ y)) \rightarrow \quad t1 = y$

$t1 = (@ \ (@ \ PLUS \ x) \ y) \rightarrow \quad t1 = x + y \qquad \text{(when x, y values)}$

and similarly for the other operators.

$t1 = (\text{name } n) \qquad \rightarrow \quad t1 = (\text{lookup } n) \quad \text{(when n is a name)}.$

Figure 2. A Parallel, Graph Reduction Abstract Machine.

5. Parallel Graph Reduction

We are now in a position to give a specification of the parallel graph reduction machine. Here, strictness annotations trigger parallel evaluation of the expression graph. Viewed as a definition of the machine code's semantics, this specification is more precise than those preceding, since incorrectly-annotated programs may fail to terminate under these rules.

---

[2] This is shown as the efficient, cyclic implementation. An alternative would be to write
$t1 = (@ \ Y \ f) \qquad \rightarrow \quad t1 = (@ \ f \ t2)$
$\text{where } t2 = (@ \ Y \ f)$

Parallel Graph-Rewriting

Parallel evaluation is represented in the graph-rewriting notation in a novel way. We retain the normal-order strategy used above for selecting reduction rules when several are applicable - left-most outermost first. The rule is generalised to a pool of reducible expressions ("redexes"). The expressions in the pool are subjected to reductions in parallel - i.e. in any order - but reduction rules are applied in normal-order to any one expression.

An expression joins the redex pool by appearing on the right-hand side of a rule, inside angle brackets. If the expression is already in the pool, this has no effect.

An expression leaves the redex pool when no rule is applicable to it.

The graph-rewriting system specifying parallel graph reduction in COBWEB-2 is given in figure 2, on the previous page.

6. The Engineering Model

Up to now, program execution on COBWEB-2 has been modelled by abstract machines, specified entirely in terms of the director-based programming language. Engineering models help to provide insight into the problems of implementing architectures. In general, a variety of engineering models can be conceived, all of them consistent with the formal model, but necessarily less general. The aim here is to define a particular notation and model which, while still some distance above the hardware, is sufficiently concrete to facilitate discussion of the key architectural issues. Two of these are interprocessor communications, and distribution of the library of function definitions.

Outline of the Model The model presumes an architecture consisting of a network of intercommunicating processors and a library of function definitions which are used as templates. An execution graph is presumed to be distributed across the communicating processors. The model describes in detail the transformation of this graph - this is what is meant by execution.

Evaluation is in normal order, modified as in the formal model to use strictness annotations. The engineering model is described in more detail in the following sections.

Function Definitions. These are named, directed, binary graphs. The branch nodes, called triples, correspond to the formal model's tokens and are described in the next section. The graphs may be self- or mutually-referential, as a result of recursive definitions. During execution, definition graphs behave as templates from which copies are made for consumption.

Triples. Triples are written

  (A[N] L R)

Each triple has a unique name, "N". "A" stands for the annotation string. The left and right children, "L" and "R", may be either

  a pointer to (i.e. name of) another triple.
  a constant.
  a placeholder for a pointer or constant, symbol □.

Annotations The varieties of annotations are:

  /,\,^,- : Directors.
  #   : Context-sensitive strictness annotation.

Constants The "child" fields of a triple may be occupied by constants such as integers or characters. Also considered constants are the machine's built-in operators, such as PLUS, etc, CONS, HD, TL, I, K and the context-free strictness annotation combinator P.

Function Applications These too are named, directed, binary graphs constructed from triples.

Execution Graph At the beginning of a computation the execution graph is simply a single function application. More generally, the application will have "matched" (see below) with a copy of the function definition it was pointing to, and execution will be in progress.

Matching A function application points to a specific function name. Matching is the name given in the COBWEB architecture to a look-up in the definition library of a function's name, for its definition. When the definition is supplied by the library, application and definition fuse together to form an execution graph.

The following example illustrates several aspects of program execution. The Miranda definitions

---

result = twice double 3

twice f x = f (f x)

double x = x + x

---

are compiled into annotated director graphs, which form the library

  result = ([result] ([r1] twice double) 3)

  twice = (^\[twice] □ (/\[t1] □ □))

  double = (^#[double] (\[d1] PLUS □) □)

Strictness annotations are omitted from "result" because the expressions concerned are all constants. Reduction of "result" proceeds as follows:

result = ([result*] ([r1] twice double) 3)

→   (match "twice")

result = ([result] ([r1*] (^\[twice] □ (/ \[t1] □ □)) double) 3)

→   (direct "double")

result = ([result*] (\[r1] double ([a] (/ \[t1] □ □) double)) 3)

→   (direct 3)

result = ([result] double* ([b] ([a] (/ \[t1] □ □) double)) 3)

→   (match "double")

result = ([result*]
        (^#[double] (\[d1] PLUS □) □)
        ([b] ([a] (/ \[t1] □ □) double) 3))

→   (direct [b])

result = (#[result*] ([c] (\[d1] PLUS □) b) b)
    where b = ([b] ([a] (/ \[t1] □ □) double) 3)

→   (spawn [b])

result = ([result] ([c*] (\[d1] PLUS □) b) b)
    where b = ([b*] ([a] (/ \[t1] □ □) double) 3)

→   (concurrently direct [b] and "double")

result = ([result] ([c*] PLUS b) b)
    where b = ([b*] (\[a] double □) 3)

→   (left * suspends; right * directs 3)

result = ([result] ([c*] PLUS b) b)
    where b = ([b*] double 3)

→   (match "double")

result = ([result] ([c*] PLUS b) b)
    where b = ([b*] (^#[double] (\[d1] PLUS □) □) 3)

→   (direct 3)

result = ([result] ([c*] PLUS b) b)
    where b = (#[b*] ([e] (\[d1] PLUS □) 3) 3)

→   (direct 3)

result = ([result] ([c*] PLUS b) b)
    where b = ([b*] ([e] PLUS 3) 3)

→   (add)

result = ([result] ([c*] PLUS 6) 6)

→   (add)

result = 12

An asterisk marks the name of the root triple of the left-most, outermost reducible sub-expression of each element of the redex pool. They can be regarded as marking the loci of computation. Initially, the redex pool contains only "result".

7. Interpreting the Engineering Model

The engineering model constitutes the interface between the formal specification of parallel program execution, and the design of the underlying hardware. This section presents the view of program execution from the hardware point of view.

A Pool of Virtual Processors For each element of the redex pool there is a virtual processor, responsible for retaining the location of an asterisk in the example above, and performing the graph transformations. This arbitrarily-large pool is simulated by a finite number of physical processors. Processor pool management entails allocating slots on real processors in suitable locations as virtual processors are spawned as a result of strictness annotations.

Each virtual processing element runs the same program, recognising patterns in the program graph, rewriting triples according to the rules used above, waiting for evaluation by other virtual processors, and spawning new ones. The virtual processors' operation is specified as a sequential program. The engineering model allows optimisation of common patterns of reduction by compiling functions expressed as program graphs into sequences of operations in the virtual processors' machine code.

A Distributed, Virtual Memory The operation of the virtual processor pool is supported by a memory management system, which presents each member of the processor pool with a uniform view of the whole of the library and program graph memory. The memory manager makes the entire multiprocessor's memory appear local to each processing element, if possible by making multiple, distributed copies of some data structures - notably immutable ones (see, for example, [Li & Hudak 86]). Writeable objects require more sophistication when deciding whether to copy. The memory manager is also responsible for garbage collection.

A Communications Mechanism The cooperative parallel reduction algorithm specified by the engineering model necessitates some communication between processing elements. This is manifest as access by separate processing elements to a data structure in the distributed virtual memory.

COBWEB-1's use of Catt's spiral [Aubusson & Catt 78] led to a one-dimensional packet addressing mechanism, with the result that the number of packet-forwarding "hops" involved in a communication is not easily predicted from its target address. If locality of communication is to be achieved, addresses must have a simple relationship to distance - addressing must have a *physical* significance.

8. Wafer-Scale Integration

Fabricating an entire multiprocessor on a single piece of silicon is a considerable technological challenge. There are serious problems - as witnessed by limited success of the approach to date. The physical design problems of package design, heat dissipation, power distribution etc. are not the concerns of this paper; the reader is referred instead to [Jesshope & Moore 86]. Of interest here is the presence of defects, with the consequent need for fault-tolerance, the need to keep wires short to speed point-to-point communications, and the necessity to design a tesselating rectangular array of largely identical devices to facilitate manufacture by wafer-stepping techniques.

The Importance of Wafer-Scale Integration

The need for very high speed inter-processor communication in a graph-reduction machine is the principle reason for looking at wafer-scale integration. Whereas a printed-circuit board design would require bit- or field-sequential transmission of packets between processing elements in order to satisfy pin-out constraints, neighbouring processing elements on a wafer can transfer packets in parallel. Moreover, such close proximity allows the link to operate at a far higher frequency.

Since parallel execution implies spatially-distributed data and processing power, communications bandwidth is crucial to the performance of a multiprocessor. Communications delay can be considered a time delay overhead incurred by the decision to evaluate an expression in parallel, arising from the communications involved in computing the value in a remote processor, and accessing a remotely-constructed result. Only when the communications overhead is exceeded by the time saved through parallel computation, can parallelism be exploited. Communications delay is thus a limit on the amount of parallelism applicable to a particular program.

A rather different reason for looking at WSI is that graph reduction appears to be a particularly efficient way of using a defect-ridden processor array, by efficiently making use of more working elements than a vector or array based algorithm.

The design described here is conservative in its expectations of the technology in the respects above. The paragraphs below describe how the design avoids long wiring, configures itself to avoid defective elements, whilst employing a grid array of identical devices and exploiting the technology's communications bandwidth potential. The reader should note that in this paper only a review of the wafer-scale technology aspects of COBWEB-2's design is presented.

Defects and Fault-Tolerance The unavoidable presence of manufacturing defects means that the cost of manufacturing a defect-free device rises exponentially with its size. By contrast, the semiconductor processing component of the cost of a board-level device rises linearly with the number of devices used. The discrepancy arises from the increase in discarded circuitry per defect as the area required to be defect free is increased.

To defeat this exponential cost growth, each processor on the COBWEB-2 wafer is designed to operate, provided it is intact, even if its neighbours are faulty. The processors are arranged on a grid, and can easily be fabricated using wafer-stepping.

The processors have highly-parallel links to their four nearest neighbours and are used to implement longer distance communications by message forwarding. This technique suffers another fundamental WSI problem: working processors which are isolated from the rest of the multiprocessor by failures in neighbouring processors cannot be used. Circuitry loss by this mechanism (measured as the "harvest", the ratio of useable devices to working ones) is minimal at a sufficiently high yield of working devices, but its onset is quite sudden and drastic below a threshold yield value dependent on the network's connectivity [Greene & El Gamal 84]. For a four-connected array (where each node is linked to its four nearest neighbours, as intended with COBWEB-2) the threshold is above a yield of 50% - but building a processing element of useful power with a yield of this order is next to impossible.

The solution employed in COBWEB-2 is to separate the communications function from the processing element, so that the communications device can work even if the processing element is faulty. The communications device is relatively simple, and can be fabricated using very conservative geometry with internal fault-tolerance to achieve a high yield.

Fault-Tolerant Packet Routing In a perfect two-dimensional grid, a packet is forwarded to a neighbour which is nearer to the packet's target. In a four-connected grid, a node usually has two neighbours nearer to a target - and each is equally far from the target. Therefore a degree of flexibility to route packets round defects and congestion is already available.

Provided a packet is always forwarded nearer its target, and nodes select incoming packets fairly, eventual arrival is guaranteed. We therefore forbid rerouting of a packet in a direction which takes it no nearer its target, if the obstruction is simply congestion.

This limited routing flexibility also ensures that packets always take one of the shortest paths.

If the preferred exits are blocked by defects, however, backtracking is the only alternative. Successful escape relies on dutifully following the obstacle's edge to the opposite side (see, for example, [Ansade et al. 86]).

Convex Wrapping As communications throughput is such a priority, backtracking is to be avoided if at all possible. A promising approach is to sacrifice those working nodes whose presence would present a problem. The nodes sacrificed are precisely those in concavities of a defect cluster's surface. Convexity of defective regions is guaranteed by sacrificing a communications and processing element pair if the following, locally-computable, condition holds:

(1) its neighbours include a representative of each of the "senses" (in a four-connected grid, North-South and East-West) which is defective or already sacrificed. That is, there exists no pair of working, opposite, neighbours.

(2) There exists a direction in which progress is blocked.

Condition (2) is redundant in a four-connected grid.

In a four-connected grid network, the sacrifice technique is inefficient since all convex shapes are rectangular. A much closer-fitting "envelope" can be used in an eight-connected grid.

Because the wafer is a finite grid, its edge is concave, and so requires special treatment. The technique is described in more detail in [Kelly & Shute 86].

Convex wrapping allows a simple routing element to achieve fault-tolerance with very little additional complexity. This benefit, together with the elimination of backtracking, must be weighed against the sacrifice of working circuitry.

The level of sacrifice involved has been the subject of simulation (reported in [Kelly & Shute 86]) assuming a Poisson defect distribution. At high yield, the "harvest" (the ratio of useable devices to working ones) is much higher than Catt's spiral achieves, but lower yields result in a collapse in harvest which the spiral avoids. Work on more realistic defect distributions is hoped to show a less drastic collapse.

Configuring the Communications Network. COBWEB-2 is designed to require no outside intervention during configuration; no fuses, for example, are used to control which elements are sacrificed, or to indicate which are faulty. Such techniques are avoided in order to simplify fabrication, and because reconfiguration can then occur in the field, in the event of in-service failures.

Testing and configuration are done during a start-up phase, every time the machine is turned on. An external microprocessor, which subsequently acts as a "front-end", is linked to a handful of processing elements around the wafer. It initiates the power-up sequence by testing those processing elements it can reach, until it finds a working one. This link is designated the test link, whilst the other working elements directly reachable by the front-end are used during program execution for input and output.

The test link is used to load the selected processing element with a test program, which is used to test neighbouring communications and processing elements. Working nodes are, in turn, loaded with test programs. In this way a parallel wave-front of testing proceeds across the surface of the wafer, gathering working/defective status information on each neighbour for each working node.

The sacrifice phase is preceded by the construction of a chain of working nodes around the wafer's edge, to avoid sacrificing the entire wafer as a concavity. Sacrifice itself is then very simple.

Next, each node determines its own Cartesian coordinates in a wave of messages originating at the test link. This allows the construction, in each working processing element's memory, of a set of pointers to free space and virtual processor slots. Thus the tags which are used to name tokens are guaranteed to refer only to processors known to be in working order.

Program loading starts by extracting free space and free processor slot tags. These provide the means for claiming and using resources in remote processing elements. The loader can build a map of the wafer's working device distribution, and use it to plan resource placement. Writing to remote processors' memory occurs as if the front-end were actually part of the network.

Improvements over COBWEB-1   The machine described by this paper improves on the related, earlier, COBWEB-1 design reported in [Hankin, Osmon & Shute 85], in several significant ways.

The use of a physical addressing mechanism, based on two-dimensional coordinates, removes searching from remote memory access - in contrast with COBWEB-1's associative one-dimensional addressing mechanism.

Access to the library is further improved by allowing multiple copies of definitions and other data structures to be made, and distributed around the network. This reduces both contention and communications path length. Often, copies of library definitions will exist in the local memory of all the processing elements using them.

9. Summary and Conclusion

Using an informal presentation of the specification techniques being used in COBWEB-2's design, this paper has described the machine and the principles of its operation.

An on-wafer communications network with a fault-tolerant packet routing mechanism has been described. These techniques, Cartesian routing with convex wrapping, are a substantial improvement on Catt's spiral (used in COBWEB-1). The use of the network to increase "harvest" without requiring very high yield processing elements provides the key to feasible wafer scale integration.

Future Work

The project is aimed at demonstrating feasibility and cost-effectiveness. Simulation of the communications network is in progress, and a simulator at the engineering model level of the design is under construction. The feasibility study also involves analysing the design's cost and relative performance benefits.

Correctness proofs linking semantics with term- and graph-rewriting specifications of abstract machines are in preparation. One of the project's main research themes is finding improved methods of specifying reduction order in graph rewriting systems, and alternative methods of specifying parallel reduction.

The performance of grid-topology package-switched communications networks, especially with respect to thrashing, is currently being investigated by simulation. This will lead to design of the packet-switching node, and analysis of its fault-tolerance efficiency.

Another major research topic is the compilation of director code. Of particular interest is compile-time control of process and data-structure placement to reduce communications delays.

Acknowledgements

The work reported in this paper has benefited from a long-term association with Rajiv Karia and his colleagues at GEC Hirst Research Centre.

The authors are partially funded by Alvey/SERC under contract GR/D/72914. One of the authors is partially funded by ESPRIT 415: Parallel Architectures and Languages for AIP - A VLSI Directed Approach.

References

[Ansade et al. 86]
Y. Ansade, R. Cornu-Emieux, B. Faure and G. Mazare "WSI Asynchronous Cells Network". Presented at IFIP Workshop on Wafer Scale Integration, Grenoble, France, 17-19 March 1986.

[Aubusson & Catt 78]
Russell Aubusson and Ivor Catt "Wafer-Scale Integration - A Fault-Tolerant Procedure." *IEEE Journal of Solid State Circuits*, Vol. SC-13, June 1978.

[Barendregt et al. 86]
H.P. Barendregt, M.C.J.D. van Eekelen and M.J. Plasmeijer "Specification of Reduction Strategies in Term Rewriting Systems." Preprint, Department of Computing Science, Nijmegen University, The Netherlands.

[Burn, Hankin & Abramsky 85]
Geoff Burn, Chris Hankin and Samson Abramsky "Strictness Analysis for Higher-Order Functions". Imperial College Department of Computing Report DoC 85/6, April 1985. To appear in *Science of Computer Programming*.

[Cardelli 84]
L. Cardelli "Compiling a Functional Language". *Proceedings of the ACM Conference on Lisp and Functional Programming*, Austin, Texas (1984).

[Dijkstra 80]
E.W. Dijkstra "A Mild Variant of Combinatory Logic". EWD735 (1980).

[Greene & El Gamal 84]
J.W. Greene and A. El Gamal "Configuration of VLSI Arrays in the Presence of Defects". *JACM*, Vol. 31, No. 4, October 1984, pp. 694-717.

[Hankin, Burn & Peyton Jones 86]
Chris Hankin, Geoff Burn and Simon Peyton Jones "A Safe Approach to Parallel Combinator Reduction" (Extended Abstract). *Proceedings ESOP 86 (European Symposium on Programming)*, Saarbrucken, Federal Republic of Germany, March 1986, Robinet B. and Wilhelm R. (eds.) Springer Verlag LNCS 213, pp. 99-110.

[Hankin, Osmon & Shute 85]
Chris Hankin, Peter Osmon and Malcolm Shute "COBWEB - A Combinator Reduction Architecture." *Functional Programming and Computer Architecture*, Nancy, France, September 1985. J.-P. Jouannaud (ed.), Springer Verlag LNCS 201 pp.99-112.

[Hope 86]
The FPM Hope Compiler. Department of Computing, Imperial College of Science and Technology, 180 Queen's Gate, London SW7 2BZ, United Kingdom.

67

[Hudak & Kranz 83]
   Paul Hudak and David Kranz "A Combinator-Based Compiler for a Functional Language".
   Principles of Programming Languages, 11th Annual Symposium, ACM SIGACT-SIGPLAN
   pp. 122-132 (Jan. 1984).

[Kelly & Shute 86]
   Paul Kelly and Malcolm Shute "Cartesian Routing and Fault Tolerance in Wafer-Scale
   Multi-computer." Presented at IFIP Workshop on Wafer Scale Integration, Grenoble,
   France, 17-19 March 1986.

[Kennaway & Sleep 81]
   J.R. Kennaway and M.R. Sleep "Director Strings as Combinators". University of East
   Anglia Report (1981).

[Klop 85]
   J.W. Klop *Term Rewriting Systems*. Notes provided for the seminar on reduction
   machines, Ustica, September 1985. Center for Mathematics and Computer Science,
   Amsterdam.

[Mycroft 81]
   Alan Mycroft *Abstract Interpretation and Optimising Transformations for Applicative Programs*. PhD. thesis, Department of Computer Science, University of Edinburgh, 1981.

[Peyton Jones 87]
   Simon L. Peyton Jones *Implementing Functional Languages using Graph Reduction*. To
   appear. Prentice-Hall (1987).

[Jesshope & Moore 86]
   C.R. Jesshope and W.R. Moore *Wafer-Scale Integration*, Adam Hilger Ltd. (1986).

[Turner 85]
   David Turner "Miranda: a Non-strict Functional Language with Polymorphic Types."
   Functional Programming and Computer Architecture, Nancy, France, September 1985. J.-P.
   Jouannaud (ed.), Springer Verlag LNCS 201 pp.1-16

A Novel Deadlock Free and Starvation Free Packet Switching Communication Processor

J.K. Annot and R.A.H. van Twist
Philips Research Laboratories
Eindhoven
The Netherlands

Abstract.
Deadlock and starvation are highly undesirable in packet switching networks. The communication processor presented in this paper was designed such that these phenomena can be proved not to occur. Deadlock is avoided using a new method called class climbing; fair usage of the classes and administration of the temporal order of arrival of the packets guarantee that no starvation can occur. The design is generally applicable in all types of networks, independent of topology or size. A planned VLSI implementation is briefly discussed.

1 Introduction.

Much research has been devoted to study the phenomena of deadlock and starvation in packet switching networks; see for example [2], [3], [4], [6], [7], [8], [9], [11], [12], [13], [14]. Much of this research concentrates on deadlock alone and remains on a theoretical level, without reporting any design based on the results; a recent exception is [4].

For the design of the communication processor[1] reported in this paper we tried to make use of known research results; it appeared to be rather problematic to extend these results to a design meeting all our sometimes conflicting requirements, such as:

- absence of deadlock;
- absence of starvation;
- independence of network topology or size;
- high data throughput;
- efficient usage and administration of buffer space;
- free routing, i.e. packets may be forwarded to the same destination via different routes;
- independent operation; especially no involvement of the outside world is allowed for the forwarding of packets not yet arrived at their destination;
- implementability in VLSI.

The design with which we eventually came up does meet the above requirements, but uses a new strategy to avoid deadlock; this strategy is called class climbing. A general and rather theoretical discussion of the problem of deadlock and the solution of class climbing can be found in [1]. In the current paper we concentrate on the actual design of the communication processor, i.e. we want to show how the theoretical result of our strategy to avoid deadlock is incorporated in a design which meets much more requirements than the bare 'it must be free from deadlock'. The order in which the details of the design are presented is guided by didactical considerations; therefore we first describe some simple aspects of the design and only halfway, starting with two intermezzi in Section 3, the more sophisticated parts concerning deadlock and starvation are discussed.

The structure of the rest of this paper is as follows. In Section 2 a general overview of the communication network is given. In Section 3 an algorithmic description of the communication processor is presented. In Section 4 we prove that the communication network is free from deadlock and starvation; above that, the strategy of class climbing is compared with strategies described in [13] and [2]. In Section 5 a planned VLSI implementation is discussed. Finally Section 6 presents some conclusions.

---

[1]This communication processor is part of the DOOM (Decentralized Object Oriented Machine) architecture researched by ESPRIT project 415-A [10].

Authors' present addresses: Jan Koen Annot, Philips Research Laboratories, WB 437, P.O.Box 80000, 5600 JA Eindhoven, The Netherlands (electronic mail: UUCP: (seismo!)mcvax!prle1!prle2!annot); Rob van Twist, Philips Research Laboratories, WB 435, P.O.Box 80000, 5600 JA Eindhoven, The Netherlands (electronic mail: UUCP: (seismo!)mcvax!prle1!prle2!twist).

2 System overview.

A general overview of a typical packet switching network using communication processors is given in Figure 1. Each communication processor uses one of its connections to communicate with its

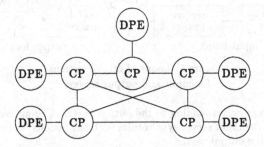

Figure 1. Typical packet switching network
consisting of five communication processors
connecting five data processing elements.

corresponding data processing element; all other connections can be used to communicate with other communication processors. The maximum number of connections of a communication processor is an implementation constant which does not have any influence on the design proper.

When a data processing element wants to send a message to another data processing element, the message is split up into a number of packets, each packet containing a part of the message contents and some routing information. The network of communication processors forwards the packets to their destination.

In Figure 2 two neighbouring communication processors are shown. The main parts of the com-

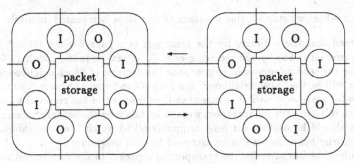

Figure 2. More detailed view
of two neighbouring communication processors.

munication processor are seen to be the packet storage and a number of input and output servers. The connection between neighbouring communication processors is bidirectional; one output and one input server at one side are connected to one input and one output server respectively at the other side; principally, by connecting only an input server at one side to an output server at the other side, a unidirectional connection could be established. The packet transport direction is always from an output server to an input server. The input and output servers of one communication processor operate quite independently, their only interaction being via the packet storage, to which they have mutually exclusive access.

The activities of the input and output servers consist of short infinitely repeated loops of atomic actions; each atomic action either accesses the packet storage or is a synchronization and communication action together with the complementary server at a neighbouring communication processor. Those loops of atomic actions are shown in Figure 3. The actions "reserve storage unit" and "store packet" access the packet storage corresponding to the input server; the action "retrieve packet"

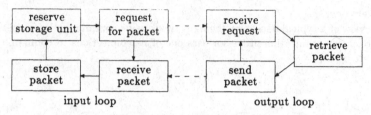

Figure 3. Loops of atomic actions
for input and output servers.

accesses the packet storage corresponding to the output server. The actions "request for packet" and "receive packet" of the input server synchronize with the actions "receive request" and "send packet" respectively of the output server.

The succession of events as far as such a pair of connected complementary servers is concerned can be deduced from Figure 3 to be as follows.

- Firstly, the input server reserves a storage unit in the packet storage of its communication processor and composes a corresponding request.
- Secondly, the input server sends the request to the output server of the neighbouring communication processor; this action is synchronized with the reception of that request by the output server.
- Thirdly, the output server retrieves from the packet storage of the sending communication processor a packet matching the request.
- Fourthly, the output server sends the packet to the input server, in synchronization with the reception of the packet by the input server.
- Fifthly, the input server stores the packet in the packet storage in the previously reserved storage unit.

Now we are back where we started; this sequence of five steps is repeated infinitely.

It can be observed that the initiative for the transport of a packet is not taken by the sending communication processor but by the receiving one. This can be found peculiar, but it is quite useful. It enables the sending processor to postpone the decision of which neighbouring communication processor will be the "next neighbour" if a packet can be sent to more than one neighbour; the decision can be postponed until it is sure that the input server has reserved a storage unit for the packet. If the initiative for the transport were to be taken by the sender, then for some packet at the sender it should be decided (at least temporarily) to which "next neighbour" to send it, without knowing whether or not it can be accepted by that neighbour.

The choice to allow the initiative for the transport of a packet to the receiver rather than to the sender has another consequence. It can occur that an output server receives from its neighbour a request for a packet at a moment that the corresponding packet storage has no packet matching the request. In such a case the output server is, for reasons of deadlock and starvation (see below), not allowed to wait infinitely long until a suitable packet arrives in the packet storage. Instead the output server then within bounded time must cancel the request from the input server: a special case of the action "send packet" in Figure 3. As a consequence the input server will perform a special case of the action "store packet": it will not fill but free the storage unit reserved previously.

For reasons of deadlock and starvation the implementation of the actions accessing the packet storage cannot be as simple as one would like. It can easily be shown that deadlock can occur if the action "reserve storage unit" would be allowed as long as the packet storage has at least one storage unit neither occupied by a packet nor reserved by some input server. Then it would be possible to fill the packet storage of two neighbouring communication processors with packets which all have the other communication processor as their only possible "next neighbour", thus obstructing any further progress of these two communication processors. This is an example of the classical Store-and-Forward deadlock [6], [8], [9].

3 Algorithmic description of the communication processor.

In this section we will describe the internals of the communication processor. We will do this by discussing the various data structures present in the communication processor and by presenting algorithms for the usage of these data structures to realize the wanted functionality of the communication processor. In two intermezzi we will explain the principles of class climbing and the used link protocol.

<u>Notation.</u> Some remarks about the used notation may be helpful. Firstly, an infix period (e.g. Reservable.j) is used as a common symbol for array indexing, field selection etc.; parenthesis pairs (e.g. match(a,b)) are used to denoté subroutines, possibly having side effects and possibly returning some result; of course parentheses are also used for grouping of sub-expressions.
Further, the usual guarded command language of [5] is extended with a parallel statement. In a parallel statement, of the form par <guarded command set> rap, all guarded lists with true guards are selected and they are executed in parallel. The parallel statement terminates when all guarded lists have terminated.
Above that, we sometimes use quantification to form guarded command sets. For example the notation ([] i: 0<i<=3: stuff.i) is used as a shorthand for stuff.1 [] stuff.2 [] stuff.3. Finally, as all communication processors have the same data structures, we sometimes add the name of a communication processor as a subscript to the name of a data structure (for example $rout_v$) to stress that we mean the data structure with that name present on that specific communication processor.

<u>Parallel-serial conversion.</u> The data traffic between connected complementary servers on neighbouring communication processors consists of requests sent from input server to output server and packets sent in the opposite direction; these opposite data streams alternate in time, so only a half duplex communication medium is needed per server pair. Let Nlinks be the number of links of each communication processor; we number the links and the corresponding input and output servers from 0 to Nlinks − 1. Input server j ($0 \leq j <$ Nlinks) has a shift register ireq.j to transmit requests from and a shift register ipack.j to receive packets in. Output server j receives requests in shift register oreq.j and transmits packets from shift register opack.j.
Transmission from $opack_v$.j may be destructive: communication processor v does not need the information in the packet after transmission. However, transmission from $ireq_v$.j must be nondestructive: the information in the request will be used again by communication processor v when administering the receipt of a packet in answer to the request. Therefore either ireq.j must be a circular shift register or some additional memory must be used to save the request.
Transmission from ireq.j or opack.j is started immediately after the value to be transmitted is assigned to the shift register. Receipt of a request in oreq.j or a packet in ipack.j is signaled by assigning true to the boolean Need_Packet.j or Packet_Delivery.j respectively; these booleans will be discussed much later.

<u>Packet storage.</u> Each communication processor has an amount of storage to buffer packets. Let memsize be the amount of packets that can be buffered. We denote the separate storage units by su.i ($1 \leq i \leq$ memsize); each storage unit can contain exactly one packet. Two small parts of each packet are defined to be interpreted by the communication processor; they are denoted by su.i.dest and su.i.class. The field su.i.dest contains the final destination of the packet. The field su.i.class is used to guarantee deadlock free communication; this will be explained later.

<u>Routing table.</u> Apart from a field indicating the final destination, a packet does not carry routing information with it. Each communication processor has a routing table containing for each possible destination a boolean vector indicating those output servers via which a packet with that destination may make its next hop. The routing table on communication processor v is denoted by $rout_v$; for destination d and output server j we have the boolean vector $rout_v$.d and the boolean $rout_v$.d.j such that

$rout_v$.d.j ≡ a packet with destination d, once arrived on v,
may make its next hop via output server j.

Temporal order administration. For each output server of the communication processor there is a data structure to administer the temporal order of arrival of those packets which may, according to the routing table, make their next hop via that output server. This data structure forms a double circularly linked list; for output server j of communication processor v it is denoted by $toa_v.j$ (toa standing for temporal order administration); the elements of the linked list are denoted by $toa_v.j.i.p$ ($0 \leq i \leq$ memsize, $p \in \{prev, next\}$). When the packet in storage unit $su_v.i$ may, according to the routing table, make its next hop via output server j and $toa_v.j.i.next = n$ and $toa_v.j.i.prev = p$, then

- $toa_v.j.n.prev = i$ and $toa_v.j.p.next = i$;
- if $n > 0$ then $su_v.n$ contains a packet which arrived in v after the packet in $su_v.i$ and which may also make its next hop via output server j; if $n=0$, then $su_v.i$ contains the youngest, i.e. last arrived packet which may make its next hop via output server j;
- if $p > 0$ then $su_v.p$ contains a packet which arrived in v before the packet in $su_v.i$ and which may also make its next hop via output server j; if $p=0$, then $su_v.i$ contains the oldest, i.e. first arrived packet which may make its next hop via output server j.

When a packet arrives in communication processor v and is stored in $su_v.i$, then the field $su_v.i.dest$ is used to index the routing table and the arrival of the packet is administered in parallel in the temporal order administration of all output servers indicated by the boolean vector $rout_v.(su_v.i.dest)$, according to the following algorithm.

```
add_to_toa(i)
|[ int d
 ; d := su.i.dest
 ; par ([] j
          : 0 <= j < Nlinks
          : rout.d.j
        -> |[ int youngest
            ; youngest := toa.j.0.prev
            ; toa.j.i.prev := youngest
            ; toa.j.i.next := 0
            ; toa.j.0.prev := i
            ; toa.j.youngest.next := i
           ]|
       )
   rap
]| .
```

When the packet in $su_v.i$ is transmitted to a neighbouring communication processor, then it is removed in parallel from the temporal order administration according to the following algorithm.

```
remove_from_toa(i)
|[ int d
 ; d := su.i.dest
 ; par ([] j
          : 0 <= j < Nlinks
          : rout.d.j
        -> |[ int n, p
            ; n := toa.j.i.next
            ; p := toa.j.i.prev
            ; toa.j.n.prev := p
            ; toa.j.p.next := n
           ]|
       )
   rap
]| .
```

The temporal order administration for output server j is used when a request is received from the neighbouring communication processor to which link j is connected. Then the linked list is followed to find the oldest packet, if any, matching the request. At this moment the matching operation between a request r and a packet p will be denoted by the boolean function match(r,p), which is true iff the matching succeeds; later on this matching will appear to be a very simple number comparison.

The algorithm to find the oldest packet matching the request is given below; when a packet is found, its nonzero index in the storage units su is given, otherwise zero is returned.

```
int find_packet(j, request)
|[ int try
; try := toa.j.0.next
; do try <> 0 and not match(request, su.try)
   -> try := toa.j.try.next
   od
; return try
]| .
```

Free list. Part of the temporal order administration for output server 0 is also used to maintain a singly linked list of free storage units. An additional variable freehead is used as the list header. The index of a free storage unit is obtained and removed from the free list by the following algorithm.

```
int obtain_su()
|[ int result
; result := freehead
; freehead := toa.0.result.next
; return result
]| .
```

When i is the last element of the free list, then toa.0.i.next = 0 and when the free list is empty, then freehead = 0. However, this need never be checked, as obtain_su() is only called when other administration guarantees that the free list is not empty.

A storage unit is appended to the free list by giving its index as an argument to the following algorithm.

```
free_su(i)
|[ toa.0.i.next := freehead
; freehead := i
]| .
```

Intermezzo I: class climbing. Before we proceed in describing the various data structures in the communication processor, we first present the principles of the strategies used in the communication processor to avoid deadlock and starvation. Later on, in Section 4, a more formal proof of the correctness of these principles will be given.

The main strategy used in the communication processor to avoid deadlock is what we call class climbing. This strategy is as follows. To each packet in the network a class is assigned; classes are numbered from 0 to Nclass − 1, where Nclass is the number of classes available; the same class can be assigned to different packets. The class of the packet in storage unit $su_y.i$ can be found in the field $su_y.i.class$. Further for each class an acyclic directed graph is superimposed on the physical communication network by assigning a direction to each of the physical links. The class of a packet is not changed as long as the packet travels according to the direction of the acyclic directed graph associated with its class. The class of a packet is incremented by one each time the packet makes a hop against the direction of the acyclic directed graph associated with its current class; hence the name class climbing. We assume that the packets injected into the network start in a low enough class and that the routing table is such that the class of a packet need never be incremented above Nclass − 1. This can be checked statically.

With "packet p is in state (v, c)" we mean that p has class c and is in communication processor v. Be $\vdash_c$ the relation corresponding to the acyclic directed graph associated with class c, then the relation $\vdash$ defined below gives all permitted state transitions of a packet:

$$(v_0, c_0) \vdash (v_1, c_1) \equiv \quad \{v_0, v_1\} \text{ is a physical link}$$
$$\wedge \quad c_0 \leq c_1 \leq c_0 + 1$$
$$\wedge \quad (c_0 = c_1 \equiv v_0 \vdash_{c_0} v_1).$$

Obviously the state transition graph is acyclic and this implies that we can find a non-unique function Number which maps all the states one to one to the numbers 1..Nstat (Nstat is the number of states), such that

$$(v_0, c_0) \vdash (v_1, c_1) \Rightarrow \text{Number}.(v_0, c_0) > \text{Number}.(v_1, c_1).$$

The inverse function of Number is called State. In Section 4 it will be proved that the communication network is free from starvation (implying that it is free from deadlock) by proving for each state (starting with state State.1 and then recursively for states State.2, ..., State.Nstat) that under certain conditions progress is guaranteed for each packet in that state.

For the principle of class climbing as described above there need not be any specific relation between the acyclic directed graphs associated with the various classes. In DOOM, however, there are only two different acyclic directed graphs and they are each other's opposite in the sense that they assign opposite directions to each of the physical links. One of these graphs is used for all even classes, the other one for all odd classes. This decision has an important consequence: we need only specify the acyclic directed graph for class 0 to know all the rest. Any packet traveling according to the direction of that basic graph has an even class or its class has just been incremented from odd to even; any packet traveling in the opposite direction has an odd class or its class has just been incremented from even to odd.

Intermezzo II: the link protocol. Now that we have discussed the principle of class climbing, we are able to proceed and present some more details of the protocol of exchanging requests and packets between neighbouring communication processors. The basic idea of the protocol is that the request, sent from an input server to an output server on the corresponding neighbouring communication processor, contains a class number c. The meaning of such a request is that the input server is ready to accept a packet of class c or higher. It is obvious that then the most general request is a request containing class number 0, meaning that any packet can be accepted. However, to avoid deadlock it is sometimes necessary to favour higher classes and send a request for higher class packets only; this will be the case when nearly all storage units of a communication processor are in use.

As explained above in DOOM the directions of the links according to the basic acyclic directed graph fully determine when packets have an even or odd class. We also decided that in DOOM it will be determined in exactly the same way whether a request will contain an even or odd class number: if an output server always sends packets of even class, then it will receive from its corresponding input server only requests with an even class number. This decision allows for a really simple realization of the above discussed boolean function match(r,p). When the class of the packet p is greater than or equal to the request r, then the matching succeeds; when the class of p is less than $r - 1$, then the matching fails; the only special case is when the class of p is equal to $r - 1$. In that special case the class of p is odd (even) and r is even (odd); then the class of p will certainly be incremented to r before p is transmitted, so the matching succeeds.

```
boolean match(r, p)
|[ return p.class >= r - 1 ]| .
```

Link direction table. Each communication processor has a boolean table Arrowhead.j ($0 \leq j <$ Nlinks) which gives for each of its links the direction of that link according to the basic acyclic directed graph. The following predicates hold.

Arrowhead$_v$.j $\equiv$ packets sent by v via output server j have odd class.

Arrowhead$_v$.j $\equiv$ packets received by v via input server j have even class.

Class administration. When none of the packets in the temporal order administration of an output server matches the request received by the output server, a special message called 'cancel' is sent instead of a normal packet. To avoid this as much as possible, the request always must have a class number as low as possible. A rather intricate administration is used to establish this. Here we only present the involved data structures and some invariants governing their behaviour; after the introduction of some additional data structures used to avoid starvation, we will present some algorithms which use all these data structures. In Section 4 we will show that our method corresponds to the 'optimal state controller' described in [13] and [2].

The class administration consists of an array of counters Cnt.i ($0 < i <$ Nclass), an array of booleans Reservable.i ($0 < i <$ Nclass) and a counter Reservable_zero. Before we can give the invariants governing the behaviour of the class administration, we need two definitions. Firstly, let cpc$_v$.i be the number of storage units of communication processor v reserved for or filled by packets of class i, $0 \le i <$ Nclass; cpc stands for 'count per class'. Secondly, let d.i for $0 \le i \le$ Nclass be recursively defined by

$$d.i = \begin{cases} 0 & \text{if } i = \text{Nclass} \\ 0 \underline{\max} (d.(i+1) - 1 + \text{cpc}.i) & \text{if } 0 \le i < \text{Nclass}. \end{cases}$$

Now the following predicates are invariantly true:

$$\begin{aligned} \text{Cnt.i} &= \text{d.i} && \text{for } 0 < i < \text{Nclass} \\ \text{Reservable.i} &\equiv \text{d.}(i+1) = 0 \wedge \text{cpc.i} = 0 && \text{for } 0 < i < \text{Nclass}. \\ \text{Reservable\_zero} &= \text{memsize} + 1 - \text{Nclass} - \text{d.1} - \text{cpc.0} \end{aligned}$$

Note that the values of cpc.i completely determine the values of the variables and that, conversely, from the values of the variables the values of cpc.i can be deduced as follows.

$$\begin{aligned} \text{cpc.(Nclass}-1) &= \begin{cases} 0 & \text{if Reservable.(Nclass}-1) \\ \text{Cnt.(Nclass}-1)+1 & \text{otherwise} \end{cases} \\ \text{cpc.i} &= \begin{cases} 0 & \text{if Reservable.i} \\ \text{Cnt.i} - \text{Cnt.}(i+1)+1 & \text{otherwise} \end{cases} \text{for } 0 < i < \text{Nclass}-1 \\ \text{cpc.0} &= \text{memsize}+1-\text{Nclass}-\text{Cnt.1}-\text{Reservable\_zero}. \end{aligned}$$

This means that thusfar the variables are nothing more than an intricate bookkeeping of the values of cpc.i. There is one thing more, however. In Section 4 it will be shown that for the network to be free from deadlock the predicate

d.0 $\le$ memsize $-$ Nclass

must be kept invariantly true; to check this invariant in terms of the cpc.i in which d.0 is defined is quite complex. But to check this invariant in terms of the introduced variables is quite straight-forward. According to the definition of d.0 the invariant is equivalent to

(memsize $-$ Nclass ≥ 0) $\wedge$ (memsize $+ 1 -$ Nclass $-$ d.1 $-$ cpc.0 ≥ 0).

The first inequality is a design constraint: Nclass and memsize must be chosen such that there is at least one storage unit per class. The second inequality is equivalent to

Reservable_zero ≥ 0

which is indeed simple to check. In Section 4, when comparing this administration with the 'optimal state controller' of [13] and [2], we will show

d.0 $\le$ memsize $-$ Nclass $\Rightarrow$ (Sum j: $0 \le j <$ Nclass: cpc.j) $\le$ memsize

so that the physical restriction of the memory size is met.

Now that we know that there is only one simple constraint on the value of Reservable_zero, two other benefits of this administration can easily be shown. Firstly, as long as Reservable_zero is positive, storage units can be reserved for class 0; such a reservation increments cpc.0, administered by simply decrementing Reservable_zero and nothing more. Secondly, when Reservable.i is true for certain i, $0 < i <$ Nclass, then a storage unit can be reserved for class i; this increments cpc.i, administered by making Reservable.i false and nothing more.

Other operations on this administration are a little bit more complex, as will be shown below; a typical example occurs when upon request for some class i a packet is transmitted with class j, i < j; this increments cpc.j and decrements cpc.i, possibly causing a lot of changes in the administration, but not touching the invariant Reservable_zero $\geq$ 0. This justifies the protocol in which upon request for class i a packet with a higher class than i may be transmitted.

Fairness administration for class 0. Above it was stated that requests must always have a class number as low as possible. However, to avoid starvation the communication processor must distribute all requests in a fair way over all its neighbours. That is why there is some fairness administration in each communication processor. This administration consists of two parts, one part for fair distribution of requests for class 0 and one part for all nonzero classes. The discussion of the second part is postponed for some time, we will first concentrate on the part for class 0.

For class zero a boolean array Fair_zero.j ($0 \leq j <$ Nlinks) and a round robin counter round_robin are used. The boolean Fair_zero.j is true if it is allowed to reserve a storage unit for class 0 for input server j. The following predicate is kept invariantly true:

$$(\underline{N} j: 0 \leq j < \text{Nlinks}: \text{Fair\_zero.j}) = \text{Reservable\_zero} \underline{\min} \text{Nlinks}.$$

This means that as long as Reservable_zero $\geq$ Nlinks, all booleans Fair_zero.j are true and there is no restriction to reserve storage units for class 0; only when Reservable_zero < Nlinks, some booleans Fair_zero.j are false and when in that case Reservable_zero is incremented, the counter round_robin is used to determine in a fair way which of the false booleans may be made true. The value of round_robin is always such that Fair_zero.round_robin is the last boolean made true in this way.

The following algorithms show how to adjust the fairness administration when Reservable_zero must be decremented (in behalf of some input server j given as an argument) or incremented.

```
decrement_Reservable_zero(j)
|[ Reservable_zero := Reservable_zero - 1
 ; if Reservable_zero >= Nlinks
   -> skip
   [] 0 <= Reservable_zero < Nlinks
   -> Fair_zero.j := false
   fi
]|
```

```
increment_Reservable_zero()
|[ if Reservable_zero >= Nlinks
   -> skip
   [] 0 <= Reservable_zero < Nlinks
   -> round_robin := (round_robin + 1) mod Nlinks
    ; do Fair_zero.round_robin
      -> round_robin := (round_robin + 1) mod Nlinks
      od
    ; Fair_zero.round_robin := true
   fi
 ; Reservable_zero := Reservable_zero + 1
]| .
```

Now we are ready to specify two other algorithms for the class administration. The first one is to administer that a storage unit reserved for or filled by a packet of class t is released. The second one is to administer that the class t0 for which a storage unit was reserved is exchanged for a possibly higher class t1. This can happen in two cases. The first case is when for an input server a storage unit was reserved of even (odd) class and the input server may according to the protocol only emit requests for odd (even) class. The second case is when a request for some class t0 was emitted and a packet of possibly higher class t1 is received.

```
release(t0)
|[ int i
; i := t0
; do i <> 0 and Cnt.i <> 0
   -> Cnt.i := Cnt.i - 1
   ; i := i - 1
  od
; if i = 0
   -> increment_Reservable_zero()
   [] i <> 0
   -> Reservable.i := true
   fi
]|

exchange(t0, t1)
|[ int i
; i := t1
; do i <> t0 and not Reservable.i
   -> Cnt.i := Cnt.i + 1
   ; i := i - 1
  od
; if i <> t0
   -> Reservable.i := false
   ; release(t0)
   [] i = t0
   -> skip
   fi
]| .
```

Both algorithms contain a loop that can be parallelized. For the loop in the routine release(t0) we can write:

```
   i := (Max j: j = 0 or (0 < j <= t0 and Cnt.j = 0): j)
; par ([] j
        : 0 < j < Nclass
        : i < j <= t0
        -> Cnt.j := Cnt.j - 1
      )
   rap .
```

and the loop in the routine exchange(t0, t1) can be transformed to:

```
   i := (Max j: j = t0 or (t0 < j <= t1 and Reservable.j): j)
; par ([] j
        : 0 < j < Nclass
        : i < j <= t1
        -> Cnt.j := Cnt.j + 1
      )
   rap
```

Fairness administration for non zero classes. The fairness administration for the non zero classes consists of a two dimensional boolean array Fair.i.j, $0 < i <$ Nclass, $0 \leq j <$ Nlinks. For each non zero class i there is always exactly one input server j for which Fair.i.j is true. The meaning of Fair.i.j being true is that only input server j has the right to reserve a storage unit for class i; of course input server j may only do that when the class administration allows this by making

Reservable.i true. After input server j has used its privilege, it must pass it to another input server by making Fair.i.j false and Fair.i.((j+1) mod Nlinks) true.

So we find the following algorithm to reserve a storage unit for input server j. Upon success the class for which the storage unit is reserved is returned; upon failure −1 is returned.

```
int reserve_storage_unit(j)
|[ int result
 ; if Fair_zero.j
   -> result := 0
    ; decrement_Reservable_zero(j)
   [] not Fair_zero.j and (E i: 0 < i < Nclass: Reservable.i and Fair.i.j)
   -> result := (Min i: 0 < i < Nclass and Reservable.i and Fair.i.j: i)
    ; Reservable.result := false
    ; Fair.result.j := false
    ; Fair.result.((j+1) mod Nlinks) := true
   [] not Fair_zero.j and not (E i: 0 < i < Nclass: Reservable.i and Fair.i.j)
   -> result := -1
   fi
 ; return result
]| .
```

Scheduler administration. The algorithms for different input and output servers of one communication processor cannot be executed fully in parallel. These algorithms use some shared data structures to which the servers have mutually exclusive access, so the algorithms must be sequentialized in a proper way. The communication processor has some administration to take care of this. It consists of three boolean arrays: Compose_Request.j, Need_Packet.j and Packet_Delivery.j, $(0 \le j < \text{Nlinks})$. The meaning of these booleans is as follows:

Compose_Request.j   ≡   for input server j
                        a request must be composed;

Need_Packet.j   ≡   output server j has received a request
                        and needs a packet matching the request;

Packet_Delivery.j   ≡   input server j has received a packet
                        and wants to deliver it to the packet storage.

This administration is scanned in an infinite loop by the so called scheduler, which executes the appropriate actions. Those actions are called store_packet(j), emit_request(j) and retrieve_packet(j) and will be discussed below. The scheduler can be considered as the 'main program' of the communication processor.

```
scheduler()
|[ int j
 ; j := 0
 ; do true
   -> if Packet_Delivery.j
      -> store_packet(j)
      [] not Packet_Delivery.j
      -> skip
      fi
    ; if Compose_Request.j
      -> emit_request(.j)
      [] not Compose_Request.j
      -> skip
      fi
    ; if Need_Packet.j
      -> retrieve_packet(j)
```

```
   [] not Need_Packet.j
      -> skip
      fi
    ; j := (j + 1) mod Nlinks
   od
]| .
```

As stated earlier, output server j indicates the receipt of a request in oreq.j by assigning true to Need_Packet.j and input server j signals the receipt of a packet in ipack.j by assigning true to Packet_Delivery.j. Those booleans are reset to false again by the actions retrieve_packet(j) and store_packet(j) respectively. The boolean Compose_Request.j is set to true by the action store_packet(j) and possibly reset to false by the action emit_request(j).

The action emit_request(j). When Compose_Request.j is true, the scheduler executes the routine emit_request(j) to compose an appropriate request for input server j. This is not always possible. When it succeeds, Compose_Request.j is made false; when it fails, Compose_Request.j is left true so that in the next cycle of the scheduler it is tried again. There are two cases in which emit_request(j) fails. The first case arises when the routine reserve_storage_unit(j) returns -1 indicating that nothing can be reserved at the moment. The second case arises when reserve_storage_unit(j) returns the maximum class number Nclass $- 1$ which is odd (even) where the boolean Arrowhead.j indicates that the request to be composed must be even (odd).

```
emit_request(j)
|[ int c
 ; c := reserve_storage_unit(j)
 ; if c <> -1
   -> if is_even(c) <=> Arrowhead.j
      -> ireq.j := c
       ; Compose_Request.j := false
      [] is_odd(c) <=> Arrowhead.j
      -> if c <> Nclass-1
         -> exchange(c, c+1)
          ; ireq.j := c+1
          ; Compose_Request.j := false
         [] c = Nclass-1
         -> release(j)
         fi
      fi
   [] c = -1
   -> skip
   fi
]| .
```

This routine can be optimized considerably by inserting all the tests of c directly in the algorithm for reserve_storage_unit(j); especially the complexity of exchange(c, c+1) can be drastically reduced then.

The action retrieve_packet(j). When Need_Packet.j is true, the scheduler executes the action retrieve_packet(j) to supply to output server j a packet matching the received request. First find_packet(j) is called to select a packet. If one is found, it is checked whether or not its class must be incremented; then the packet is supplied to output server j and finally some previously defined routines are executed to adjust all administration.

```
retrieve_packet(j)
|[ int i, request
 ; request := oreq.j
```

```
; i := find_packet(j, request)
; if i <> 0
  -> |[ int c
     ; c := su.i.class
     ; if is_odd(c) <=> is_odd(request)
       -> skip
       [] is_even(c) <=> is_odd(request)
       -> su.i.class := c+1
       fi
     ; opack.j := su.i
     ; release(c)
     ; remove_from_toa(i)
     ; free_su(i)
     ]|
  [] i = 0
  -> opack.j := cancel
  fi
; Need_Packet.j := false
]| .
```

The action store_packet(j). When Packet_Delivery.j is true, the scheduler executes the routine store_packet(j) to handle the packet received by input server j. When the received packet is a cancel packet, the reserved storage unit is released; otherwise the class administration is adjusted, a free storage unit is obtained from the free list to store the packet in and the temporal order administration is updated.

```
store_packet(j)
|[ if ipack.j = cancel
   -> release(ireq.j)
   [] ipack.j <> cancel
   -> exchange(ireq.j, ipack.j.class)
     ; |[ int i
        ; i := obtain_su()
        ; su.i := ipack.j
        ; add_to_toa(i)
        ]|
   fi
; Packet_Delivery.j := false
; Compose_Request.j := true
]| .
```

This finishes the algorithmic description of the communication processor. The question how to initialize all the data structures such that they reflect the initial, empty state of the communication processor is left undiscussed.

4 Deadlock and starvation.
In this section we will discuss some topics concerning deadlock and starvation. First we will compare the strategy of class climbing with the strategies described in [13] and [2]. Then we will show that the class administration method as described in Section 3 corresponds to the 'optimal state controller' described in [13] and [2]. Finally we will prove that the communication processor is free from deadlock and starvation.

Comparison of class climbing with other strategies. In [13] Toueg and Ullman present some algorithms for deadlock free communication in packet switching networks with fixed size packets. In [2] Bodlaender generalizes their results to networks with variable size packets and above that introduces the notion "count down", which is more general than the notions "forward count" and "backward count" used in [13]. A count down function is, roughly spoken, a function which assigns to each packet a nonnegative integer value; with each hop of the packet the assigned value is decremented by at least one. The strategy of class climbing presented in Section 3 can be seen as a generalization of the notion "count down". Taking into account the not relevant difference that the climbing goes up and the counting goes down, we can see the following resemblance between class climbing and counting down:

- packets start in a low enough class (with a high enough count) such that while traveling the class need never be incremented above the maximum (the count need never be decremented below the minimum);
- the higher the class (the lower the count) of a packet, the easier it can travel.

The important aspect where the class climbing is more general than counting down is: in class climbing the class of a packet need not be incremented with each hop, where in counting down the count of a packet must be decremented with each hop. This means that in class climbing a packet can often start in a class which is more favourable than the initial count which would have been assigned in counting down.

Comparison of class administration with the 'optimal state controller'. Now we will show that the class administration as described in Section 3 corresponds to the optimal state controllers described in [13] and [2]. First we need two definitions. Let $e.i$ for $0 \leq i \leq$ Nclass be defined by
$$e.i = \text{memsize} - \text{Nclass} + i - (\underline{\text{Sum}} \ j: 0 \leq j < i: cpc.j)$$
or recursively

$$e.i = \begin{cases} \text{memsize} - \text{Nclass} & \text{if } i = 0 \\ e.(i-1) + 1 - cpc.(i-1) & \text{if } 0 < i \leq \text{Nclass}. \end{cases}$$

Let the predicate $P.k$ for $0 \leq k \leq$ Nclass be defined by
$$P.k \equiv (\underline{A} \ i: 0 \leq i < k: e.i \geq 0) \wedge e.k \geq d.k.$$
Using the theorem
$$x \geq y \ \underline{\max} \ z \equiv x \geq y \wedge x \geq z,$$
of which the truth is easy to verify, and using the recursive definitions of $d.k$ and $e.(k+1)$ we find for $0 \leq k <$ Nclass:
$$e.k \geq d.k \equiv e.k \geq 0 \wedge e.(k+1) \geq d.(k+1).$$
Using this equivalence it is easy to see that
$$P.k \equiv P.(k+1)$$
for $0 \leq k <$ Nclass, so $P.0$ is equivalent to $P.$Nclass.

In Section 3 we described how to reserve a storage unit for a class as low as possible with as a single restriction that the predicate
$$d.0 \leq \text{memsize} - \text{Nclass}$$
must be kept invariantly true. We can write this as
$$d.0 \leq e.0.$$
This predicate is obviously equivalent to the predicate $P.0$. Above we showed that $P.0$ is equivalent to $P.$Nclass; as $d.$Nclass $= 0$, the predicate $P.$Nclass is equivalent to
$$(\underline{A} \ i: 0 \leq i \leq \text{Nclass}: e.i \geq 0).$$
The weakest precondition to keep this predicate invariantly true when reserving a storage unit for class c, i.e. when incrementing $cpc.c$ is
$$(\underline{A} \ i: c < i \leq \text{Nclass}: e.i - 1 \geq 0).$$
When in this precondition we write out $e.i$, we find the first formula below. In that formula we transform the terminology used by us to that used for the backward state controller in Section 2.4 of [13], by applying the six substitutions memsize:=b, Nclass:=k+1, j:=r, i:=j+1, c:=i and $cpc.r:=i_r$; this results in the second formula below.
$$(\underline{A} \ i: c < i \leq \text{Nclass}: i - 1 \geq (\underline{\text{Sum}} \ j: 0 \leq j < i: cpc.j) - \text{memsize} + \text{Nclass})$$
$$(\underline{A} \ j: i \leq j \leq k: j \geq (\underline{\text{Sum}} \ r: 0 \leq r \leq j: i_r) - b + k + 1).$$
The second formula is equivalent to the formula used in the backward state controller in Section 2.4 of [13].

By the way, the above discussion allows us to give the derivation promised in Section 3 of the implication

d.$0 \leq$ memsize $-$ Nclass $\Rightarrow$ ($\underline{\text{Sum}}$ j: $0 \leq j <$ Nclass: cpc.j) $\leq$ memsize.

This implication guarantees that the physical restriction of the memory size is met. Above we showed that the left hand side of this implication is equivalent to P.Nclass; on its turn P.Nclass implies e.Nclass ≥ 0, which is equivalent to the right hand side of the implication to be proved.

<u>Absence of deadlock and starvation.</u> Now we come to the proof that the communication network is free from deadlock and starvation. We need only prove the latter as it implies the former. We define the predicate Progress.(v,c) for each state (v,c) a packet can have.

Progress.(v,c) $\equiv$ there is guaranteed progress for each packet in state (v,c), i.e. all output servers of communication processor v via which the packet possibly can make its next hop always receive within finite time a request with class number at most $c + 1$.

In the proof we will use the notation Q.k ($0 \leq k \leq$ Nstat) as a shorthand for

($\underline{A}$ i: $1 \leq i \leq k$: Progress.(State.i)).

The property to be proved: the network is free from starvation, can now be formulated as Q.Nstat. We will prove this step by step, starting with Q.0 which is obviously true and successively proving Q.1,..., Q.Nstat, each time using Q.(k $-$ 1) to prove Q.k. This way we only need to prove for $1 \leq k \leq$ Nstat:

Q.(k $-$ 1) $\Rightarrow$ Progress.(State.k).

We cannot unconditionally prove this; below we will specify some consumption obligation that must be imposed upon the outside world to allow a complete proof. But first we will take a closer look at the predicate Q.k. According to the following reasoning Q.k implies for any state (v,c) with $1 \leq$ Number.(v, c) $\leq$ k that communication processor v will within finite time emit a request with class number at most c via each of its input servers j with Arrowhead$_v$.j $\equiv$ is_even(c). This means that v is ready to accept new packets in state (v,c).

- Consider the expression b defined by

  b = ($\underline{\text{Min}}$ i: $c < i \leq$ Nclass $\wedge$ d.i = 0: i);

  as d.Nclass = 0, the minimum is taken over a non-empty set and b is well defined. Further consider the predicate R.c defined by

  R.c $\equiv$ Reservable_zero = 0 $\wedge$ ($\underline{A}$ i: $0 < i \leq c$: $\neg$Reservable.i);

  this predicate holds iff no reservation is possible for any class at most c.

- When R.c holds, each of the possible actions which modify the class administration, if not invalidating R.c, either leaves b unchanged or increments b. To be precise:
  - reserve_storage_unit() leaves R.c and b unchanged; as R.c holds, reserve_storage_unit() will not reserve a storage unit for any class at most c.
  - release(t0) invalidates R.c iff t0 < b and otherwise leaves R.c and b unchanged.
  - exchange(t0,t1) with t0 $\leq$ t1 changes neither R.c nor b iff t0 $\leq$ t1 < b or b $\leq$ t0 $\leq$ t1 and increments b and/or invalidates R.c iff t0 < b $\leq$ t1.

- When R.c holds, within finite time one of the actions release(t0) with t0 < b or exchange(t0,t1) with t0 < b $\leq$ t1 will occur, each of which increments b and/or invalidates R.c. To prove this we distinguish three disjunct cases.
  - if b = 1 then c = 0 and d.1 = 0 and Reservable_zero = 0, so cpc.0 > 0.
  - if b > 1 and b = c + 1 then Reservable.c is false and d.(c + 1) = 0 so cpc.c > 0.
  - if b > c + 1 then d.(b $-$ 1) $\neq$ 0 and d.b = 0 so cpc.(b $-$ 1) $\geq$ 2.

  In all three cases there is a class t0 with c $\leq$ t0 < b such that cpc.t0 > 0. The progress predicate Q.k implies that within finite time either release(t0) will be executed or exchange(t0,t1) with t0 $\leq$ t1, eventually followed by release(t1); when in this last case exchange(t0,t1) leaves b and R.c unchanged, then t1 < b and release(t1) meets the requirements.

- As b cannot grow above Nclass, R.c will be invalidated within a finite number of the actions release(t0) with t0 < b or exchange(t0,t1) with t0 < b $\leq$ t1.

- Invalidation of R.c will allow reservation of a storage unit for some class at most c. The fairness administration is such that within a finite number of such reservations each input server j can do such a reservation; for each input server j with Arrowhead$_v$.j $\equiv$ is_even(c) this will result in a request with class number at most c to be emitted.

To formulate the consumption obligation to be imposed upon the outside world (i.e. upon the Data Processing Elements as shown in Figure 1), we define for each state (v,c) the predicate Consumption.(v,c):

Consumption.(v,c) ≡ there is guaranteed consumption for each packet in state (v,c) arrived at its destination, i.e. all output servers of communication processor v which are connected to the outside world and via which the packet possibly can make its next hop always receive within finite time a request with class number at most $c + 1$.

The consumption obligation imposed upon the outside world is formulated as:

($\underline{A}$ k: $1 \leq k \leq$ Nstat: Q.(k − 1) ⇒ Consumption.(State.k)).

In words we can describe this obligation as follows: the outside world must consume any packet which has reached its destination, but it need not do so unconditionally; to consume a packet from state State.k, it may use Q.(k − 1) as a presupposition. As shown above, Q.(k − 1) implies that within finite time the outside world will be ready to accept a packet in any state (v,c) with $1 \leq$ Number.$(v,c) < k$. This means that the outside world may refuse to consume a packet from state State.k until the network has accepted from the outside world a bounded amount of packets for states (v,c) with $1 \leq$ Number.$(v,c) < k$.

Now we are ready to finish the proof of Q.Nstat by proving as announced for $1 \leq k \leq$ Nstat:

Q.(k − 1) ⇒ Progress.(State.k).

Proof. Assume Q.(k − 1). The obligation imposed upon the outside world implies Consumption.(State.k).

Let State.k be (v_0,c_0), so k = Number.(v_0,c_0). Consider all output servers j_0 of communication processor v_0 via which a packet in state (v_0,c_0) can possibly make its next hop.

If output server j_0 is connected to the outside world, then Consumption.(State.k) implies that within finite time a request with class number at most c_0+1 will be received via output server j_0. If output server j_0 is connected to input server j_1 of neighbouring communication processor v_1, then there exists a class c_1 such that $(v_0,c_0) \vdash (v_1,c_1)$, implying $c_1 \leq c_0+1$, Arrowhead$_{v_1}.j_1 \equiv$ is_even(c_1) and k > Number.(v_1,c_1). Now Q.(k − 1) implies that communication processor v_1 will within finite time emit a request with class number at most c_1 via input server j_1 and this implies that communication processor v_0 will within finite time receive via output server j_0 a request with class number at most c_0+1.

Hence by definition Progress.(State.k). End of proof.

The above proof that the network of communication processors is free from deadlock and starvation is rather influenced by the algorithmic details of Section 3. A much more general approach of the deadlock problem in packet switching networks is presented in [1]; however, the starvation problem is not discussed there.

5 A VLSI implementation of the communication processor.

This section shows, on basis of a rough floor plan, how the communication processor fits on silicon. It is not the intention to give a complete and detailed working out of the implementation in VLSI, but to show where the important data structures can be found in the VLSI implementation, and how much the implementation costs.

The parameters of the communication processor under consideration have the following values: Nlinks = 9 (eight input and output servers for the links between neighbouring communication processors, and one input and output server for the link between the communication processor and the corresponding data processing element), Nclass = 16, memsize = 64 and the length of a packet is 256 bits of which 10 bits are used for the destination and 4 bits for the class. Figure 4 sketches a provisional floor plan of this communication processor. The ipack and opack shift registers of the input and output servers respectively fit very nicely around the 64 × 256 bit memory matrix of the packet storage su. Such a layout makes it possible to copy a packet from ipack to su or from su to opack within one memory cycle of the processor, which is very attractive with respect

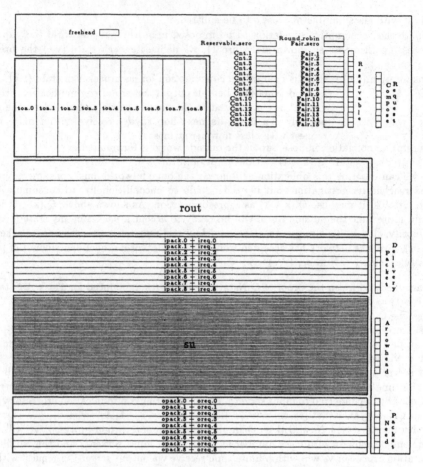

Figure 4. Floorplan of the communication processor.

to the delay and throughput of the packets and with that the performance of the processor. A substantial part of the chip is occupied by the routing table rout. This table, consisting of 1024 9-bit entries, is implemented as 4 memory matrices of 256×9 bit each which are addressed by the destination field of a packet stored in ipack, su or opack. The accessed 9-bit vector indicates via which output servers a packet can be forwarded, and with that determines which toa.j must be updated at the arrival and departure of a packet. Each toa.j implements a double linked list. Each cell toa.j.i of the double linked list contains fields next and prev. These fields can take any of the values i ($0 \leq i < 64$), so toa.j can be implemented as a 64×12 bit memory matrix.

In this layout it is assumed that the size of a cell of the shift registers ipack, ireq, opack and oreq is 4 times the size of a normal square memory cell from which su, rout and toa are constructed. The size of the registers described below are not scaled in the real proportions.

The variable freehead contains the address of the first free storage unit, and also refers to the first element of the free list implemented in toa.0. It can take any of the values i ($0 \leq i < 64$) and is implemented as a 6-bit register. The variables Cnt.i ($0 < i < 16$) and Reservable_zero are implemented as independently operating 6-bit up/down counters. Round_robin and Fair_zero are simple 9-bit registers (one bit per link). The remaining part of the buffer management administration deals with the classes 1 up to and including 15. The two dimensional boolean array Fair together with the boolean vector Reservable can be implemented as a 10×15 bit matrix of memory cells that can do some special operations such as bit_set, bit_reset and bit_match.

The variables Arrowhead, Compose_Request, Packet_Delivery and Need_Packet can be implemented as 9-bit registers.

The attentive reader has probably noticed that the VLSI implementation of the communication processor is very regular and mainly consists of memory cells. Also the absence of complex arithmetic and logic operations is remarkable. Because chip designers are good in building very dense memory cells it is plausible that this implementation is feasible. We think that the chip area of this communication processor implementation is roughly the same as the chip area of a 128 kbit static RAM chip.

6 Conclusions.

A design for a packet switching communication processor was presented. Detailed descriptions were given of the internal data structures and of the algorithms to use them. The design was proved to be free from deadlock and starvation. The method to avoid starvation is new and is called class climbing; it can be seen as a generalization of the notions "forward count" and "backward count" used in [13] and of the notion "count down" used in [2].
A short discussion of a planned VLSI implementation showed that the design can be integrated on a chip with the size of current 128 kbit static RAM chips.

References

[1] J.K. Annot, "Deadlock Freedom in Packet Switching Networks", Internal report no. 0157 of ESPRIT project 415-A, Philips Research Laboratories, Eindhoven, The Netherlands, November 1986.

[2] H.L. Bodlaender, "Deadlock-free packet switching networks with variable packet size", Techn. Rep. RUU-CS-85-25, Dept. of Computer Science, University of Utrecht, Utrecht, 1985. Extended abstract in Proceedings of NGI-SION 1986 Symposium Stimulerende Informatica, pp. 475-484, Utrecht, 1986.

[3] W.J. Dally and C.L. Seitz, "Deadlock-Free Message Routing in Multiprocessor Interconnection Networks", Dept. of Computer Science, California Institute of Technology, Technical Report 5206:TR:86, 1986.

[4] W.J. Dally and C.L. Seitz, "The Torus Routing Chip", Distributed Computing (1986) 1: 187-196.

[5] E.W. Dijkstra, "Guarded Commands, Nondeterminacy and Formal Derivation of Programs", Comm. ACM 18 (8) (1975) 453-457.

[6] D. Gelernter, "A DAG-Based Algorithm for Prevention of Store-and-Forward Deadlock in Packet Networks", IEEE Trans. Comput. (10)(1981) 709-715.

[7] K.D. Gunther, "Prevention of Deadlocks in Packet-Switched Data Transport Systems", IEEE Trans. Commun. 29 (4)(1981) 512-524.

[8] P.M. Merlin and P.J. Schweitzer, "Deadlock Avoidance in Store-and-Forward Networks - I: Store-and-Forward Deadlock", IEEE Trans. Commun. 28 (3)(1980) 345-354.

[9] P.M. Merlin and P.J. Schweitzer, "Deadlock Avoidance in Store-and-Forward Networks - II: Other Deadlock Types", IEEE Trans. Commun. 28 (3)(1980) 355-360.

[10] E.A.M. Odijk, "The Philips Object-Oriented Parallel Computer", J.V. Woods (ed.): Fifth Generation Computer Architecture (IFIP TC-10), North Holland, 1985.

[11] R.K. Shyamasundar, "A Simple Livelock-Free Algorithm for Packet Switching", Science of Computer Programming 4 (1984) 249-256, North-Holland.

[12] S. Toueg, "Deadlock- and Livelock-Free Packet Switching Networks", Proc. 12th ACM Symposium on Theory of Computing, Los Angeles, California, April 1980, pp. 94-99.

[13] S. Toueg and J.D. Ullman, "Deadlock-free Packet Switching Networks", SIAM J. Comput. 10 (1981) 594-611.

[14] W. Wimmer, "Using Barrier Graphs for Deadlock Prevention in Communication Processors", IEEE Trans. Commun. 32 (8)(1984) 897-901.

A Parallel Architecture for Signal Understanding through Inference on Uncertain Data

P.G. Bosco, E. Giachin, G. Giandonato, G. Martinengo, C. Rullent
CSELT Centro Studi e Laboratori Telecomunicazioni S.p.A
Via G. Reiss Romoli 274   10148 - TORINO - ITALY

Abstract

This paper describes an architecture for rule-based interpretation of uncertain data, which is currently under development at our labs. Inference on uncertain input facts is a central topic in AI, with application, e.g., to the syntactic-semantic layers of speech understanding systems. The severe requirements of real-time applications dictate a parallel approach to this problem. The description covers the main aspects related to parallelism and communication at the three levels which have interacted in the design of this architecture: the hardware machine, a higly-parallel homogeneous structure of processing element - memory pairs interconnected by a fast packet-switching network; the programming language, which is a dialect of Lisp augmented with asynchronous message passing primitives; the inferential algorithm, which unifies goal-driven and data-driven strategies under a score-guided search control. Rules are mapped into a set of processes which cooperate by exchanging, via the primitives and the network mentioned above, messages corresponding to succinct representations of intermediate deductions.

1. INTRODUCTION

This paper presents the current state of a CSELT research project which aims at designing and prototyping a highly-parallel architecture for real-time rule-based interpretation of uncertain data. According to the application-driven approach chosen since the early phase of the project, the work reported here was methodologically characterized by an effort of maximal integration among the three different levels involved in the conception of such a system: the hardware level, the programming language level and the algorithmic level. That resulted in a global architecture which, while preserving programmability, gives a solution specialized for the class of rule-based inference engines considered, to the problem of efficient communication, that is central to exploitation of parallelism. The solution is coherent among the above-mentioned levels: the dataflow-like nature of the parallel inferential algorithm is mirrored in the asynchronous semantics of the communication primitives defined at the language level and these are in turn supported through the buffered, packet-switched interconnection network at the physical level, so realizing an overall delay-insensitive behaviour, that is exactly the kind of optimal behaviour, only limited by the available bandwidth, required in VLSI-based highly-parallel structures.

This work is partially sponsored by European Economic Community under contracts for ESPRIT Projects N. 26 and N. 1219.

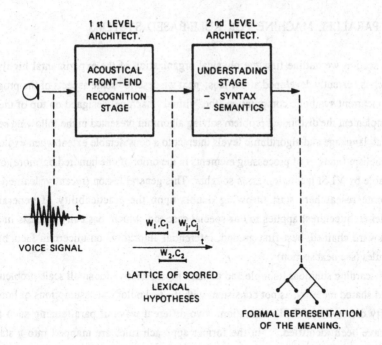

Fig. 1.   Global architecture of the experimental system for continuous
speech understanding

As a matter of fact we expect, on the basis of measures obtained in executing this kind of algorithms on sequential machines (tens of seconds on Symbolics 3600), that a high degree of parallelism, compatible with a VLSI orientation of the physical machine, will be needed to attain the goal of real-time performance required by the envisageable signal understanding applications (man-machine dialogue, artificial vision, ...).   The reason is the potentially very large size of the search space to be explored when, as in the case considered here, an additional source of nondeterminism is introduced by noise and/or use of imperfect (heuristic, probabilistic) knowledge in the previous processing stages.   This, as explained in section 3, rules out exaustive search and requires, in order to correctly identify and describe the event associated to the uncertain input data, a near optimal, score-guided, forward-backward control strategy.

In the next sections we describe the main features of the prototype under development, that we plan to test as second level architecture, see Fig.1, of an experimental continuous, natural speech understanding system; in this case input data of our architecture consist in a lattice of scored lexical hypoteses generated from the recognition stage described in [1] and rules embody knowledge about syntax of the natural language and semantics of the specific application domain.

2. A PARALLEL MACHINE FOR RULE-BASED SYSTEMS

In this section we outline first the physical organization of the experimental highly-parallel machine which is currently developed at our labs; next we describe some aspects of the programming system for concurrent symbolic computation (the "virtual" machine) designed on top of the physical machine to implement the distributed problem solving algorithm presented in the following section.

Physical, language and algorithmic levels interact to a considerable extent when exploitation of massive parallelism (number of processing elements in the order of one hundred or more) of the kind made affordable by VLSI technologies, is sought. This general lesson (recently learned to such a point that some researchers start throwing doubts upon the practicability of general-purpose highly-parallel architectures) applies in our special case too, which basically consists in a class of forward-backward chained, best-first guided, inferential algorithms on uncertain facts by a set of declarative rules (see next section).

After discarding solutions (simple and perhaps most effective for small scale problems) based on centralized shared memory, as not consistent with the technological assumptions of homogeneity and scalability dictated by VLSI orientation, two different ways of parallelizing such a class of algorithms have been identified. In the former approach rules are mapped into a static set of asyncronously communicating processes programmed in an extended version of Lisp; in the latter, not reported here and for which a dialect of Prolog is investigated, processes are dynamically created, being associated to hypoteses, i.e. to nodes of a search OR-tree.

It is a definite goal of our research to assess viability and relative merits of both approaches (roughly classifiable, at the language level, under the imperative/explicit and declarative/annotated parallelism paradigms respectively) by comparing their outcomes in a real and complex application, like the syntax-semantics processing of a speech understanding system.

2.1 Physical Architecture

The decision of taking an unbiased attitude towards the question of imperative/declarative parallelism implies that the underlying physical machine must be designed for maximal flexibility so as to efficiently realize a variety of execution mechanisms for different virtual machines. In other words we aim at providing the intermediate phase of our research programme with an efficient "hardware simulation" facility rather than designing in a single step the "ultimate" machine.

Basic design choices, however, are derived from the commonalities found in the computational models considered: for example, in both cases data structures representing partial, possibly incomplete hypotheses about input facts, are passed among processors and the problem arises of when and where to share information in order to avoid excessive copying. Moreover, to assure possibility of future-proof evolutions of the whole architecture, these choices are made consistently with the principles of locality, loose coupling and capability to tolerate long latency times, directly related to the

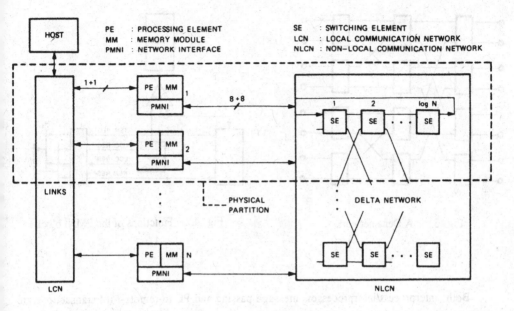

Fig. 2.   The physical machine

expected increase of disparity between on-chip and off-chip delays in VLSI-based computing structures (see e.g. [2] and [3] for excellent discussions on these principles).

Our machine, whose overall organization is shown in Fig. 2, belongs to the class of MIMD (Multiple Instructions Multiple Data streams) processors; it consist in a number, N, of computing nodes, each composed of a Processing Element (PE), built around a 32-bit Transputer device [4] and including a private memory that typically contains replicated code, of a Memory Module (MM) and of a PE+MM-to-Network Interface (PMNI). Nodes are interconnected via two distinct communication networks, the Local Communication Network (LCN) and the Non-Local Communication Network (NLCN). A Host computer is connected to the PE array for purposes such as loading programs, distributing input data, collecting solutions and monitoring.

MIMD architectures are usually classified in PE-to-PE or PE-to-MM organizations: interprocessor message passing and elementary (i.e. read, write, read/modify, ...) CPU-memory transactions being their basic communications mechanisms respectively. A better definition in our case could be PEMM-to-PEMM as MMs are organized in what can be called a "globally addressable physically distributed" scheme: i.e. the N pages in which the memory space is partitioned are equally distributed among the N PEs and each PE can address, for example when dereferencing a pointer, the remote MM of another node. The concept of global distributed storage was pioneered, though in a different context, by the CM* development and is used in an increasing number of contemporary works on higly-parallel architectures, most notably in Darlington's ALICE, Keller's Rediflow, BBN Butterfly and IBM RP3.

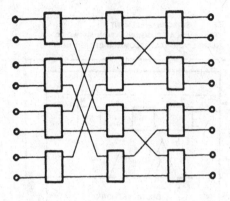

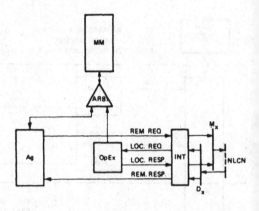

Fig. 3.   A Delta network

Fig. 4.   Functions of the PMNI block

Both interprocess/interprocessor message passing and PE-to-remote-MM transactions are supported by the packet-switched NLCN which is implemented, as detailed in the next subsection, by means of a number of Switching Elements (SE) arranged in a multistage Delta topology (Fig. 3). Notice that the two communication mechanisms above are indistinguishable at the network level and that it is possible to make them usefully coexist, for example when transmitting messages with pointers instead of long structured values (lists, vectors, ...) and then retrieving the needed elements on demand; the same technique (basically a "lazy fetch" strategy), here explained with reference to an imperative model, can be, invisibly, applied at the executor level for efficient transmission of parameters on activation of logical procedures in the declarative model.

To execute remote memory operations the processor, when issuing requests addressed to a non-local page (RemReq of Fig.4), behaves differently than in local accesses.   Namely, by cooperation with the local PMNI, it passes to the remote PMNI, via the NLCN, a packet which includes the type of the operation, the address of the object referred to, some additional parameters in case of complex operations, and the identity of the issuing agent: this because the PE is multi-tasked between a fixed and small number of executing agents (Ag of figure) to guarantee processor utilization in presence of long latencies to remote requests.   The important thing here is that a very fast context-switching property is required to achieve tolerance of latency times.   Basically this is, as explained in [3], the solution first implemented in the Denelcor HEP machine.   In this respect the choice of the Transputer as building block of the PE is essential to approximate the intended behaviour (context switching times in the order of 1 microsecond like those exhibited by this innovative device would not be achievable with more conventional microprocessors).

At the destination site request packets (LocReq of figure) are serviced by a memory handler (OpEx) which executes the operation and assembles the response packet (LocResp) the issuing agent is waiting for (RemResp).   Note that the whole mechanism is congenial to the so-called "intelligent memory" principle, i.e. to the inclusion of complex and fairly autonomous capabilities (such as following a chain of pointers, moving contiguous blocks of data, etc....) in the PMNI block.

The main role of the LCN, directly implemented by wiring in a fixed topology the Transputer links, is to support distributed load balancing strategies. These are required in the dynamic model to evenly distribute among PEs the work done in exploring a large, irregular search space. We expect to use here diffusion based strategies of the kind studied, for example, in [5], supplied with information about the priority of the leaves in the search tree to realize parallel best-first exploration. Recent work on related field, see [6], seems to show that even simple strategies on limited connectivity topologies are able to effectively balance the load if the time needed to expand a node is comparable to the time spent in transferring a problem.

Note that in this case the Transputer links are used for strictly near-neighbour communications, conveying a traffic totally different (continuous, long packets) from the traffic expected over the NLCN (random, short packets). This is the reason for keeping distinct, for the time being, the two networks; note that the interference between these two kinds of traffic should be considered even in long-term evolutions of the architecture described here, in which one can envisage the integration of PE, PMNI and of a communication element implementing on the same (static but with built-in through-routing capability) network the functions of both NLCN and LCN.

2.2 Hardware Aspects

The system is designed to be partitionable in such a way (see the dashed line in Fig. 2) as to have only one type of building block, a board containing 4 PE-MM pairs plus the corresponding slice of the NLCN. The equivalence in performance of all Delta topologies (which include SW-Banyan, Omega, Indirect Cube, etc...) when operating in asynchronous mode allows to choose the optimal topology with respect to a "wireability" criterion: in this way it is possible to interconnect, for example, 64 PEs on 16 boards with only 12 off-board unidirectional connections per board, each connection consisting, in our case, of 11 (8 data+ 3 control) wires.

The Delta network is built from $(N/2)\log N$ two inputs-two outputs SE; each SE corresponds to a single, custom-designed, 5.7 mm x 6.7 mm VLSI circuit of about 30000 transistors in 3 micron, double-metal, CMOS technology. The circuit buffers incoming variable-lenght packets in two 64 byte FIFO queues, automatically by-passed when empty; dialogue between ports is fully asynchronous and conforms to a simple four-phase handshaking protocol. An important feature of this circuit is the "cut-through" mechanism employed (the packet is transmitted as soon as possible; in contrast with "store and forward" techniques), making the network cross delay independent from the packet length. Additional functionalities are broadcasting and an error detection mechanism.

The target prototype is a 64/128 PE machine packaged in a standard 24 inch frame of 16/32 triple Eurocards, supervised by a MicroVax II host.

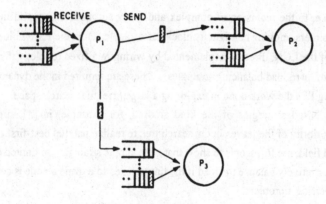

Fig. 5.   Computational Model

2.3 Computational Model

The computational model consist in a set of concurrent sequential Lisp processes statically
allocated on the PEs and cooperating through streams, i.e. ideally unbounded buffers into/from which
values (S-expressions) are sent and received (see fig.5). Each process is defined to have n input
buffers, each buffer corresponding to a message type. Inside buffers messages are queued according
to the value of a priority field specified by the sending process; this particular feature helps in realizing
the distributed best-first search algorithm described in the next section.

The syntax of the SEND primitive is:

(SEND <dest> <buff> < prior> < msg>)

where <dest> is the list of destination processes, <buff> is the buffer name, <prior> is an integer,
<msg> is a generic S-expression: both many-to-one and one-to-many interprocess communications
are supported.   SENDs are non-blocking operations: this is essential to achieve the data-flow like
behaviour mentioned in the introduction.

The syntax of the RECEIVE primitive is:

(RECEIVE <var>   (<buff-1>   <body-1>)
                          (<buff-2>   <body-2>)

.

[(<body-else >)])

where <var> is the name of the variable assigned to the received expression, <buff-1>, etc. are the names of the selected buffers, <body-1>, etc. are forms to be evaluated after receiving the corresponding message and <body-else> (optional) is the form to be evaluated if no message is present in the selected buffers.

The implementation scheme maps these user defined processes into Transputer processes synchronously communicating with run-time support processes that manage buffering and routing of messages. Other processes can be allocated to the host for supervisory or debug purposes. By combining slight variations of the above described primitives it is possible to define macro-operations such as remote read, remote procedure call, etc.

As one can see the extension is conceptually very simple and completely rests, unlike many other proposals on concurrent or parallel Lisps, upon the non functional, impure component of this language; our choice, while pragmatic in nature, has the advantage that the semantics of such a type of concurrency is well understood and their realization relatively straightforward.

2.4 Language Implementation

The extensions for concurrency control described above will be implemented by transporting LeLisp, a compiled Lisp system developed at INRIA by J. Chailloux [7], on the Transputer and suitably augmenting its run-time support.

Designed for efficiency, easy transport and large system construction, LeLisp includes an interpreter, a compiler, a set of debugging tools and full screen editors. It is derived from post MacLisp Lisps and offers compatibility with other Lisp dialects: in particular a full compatibility with Kernel Common Lisp (now under definition) is planned.

LeLisp base system is written in LLM3, an intermediate low-level language consisting of about 180 instructions: transport is obtained by mapping this intermediate language into the target machine language. For efficiency a direct translation of LLM3 instructions to the Transputer machine language is preferred, in order to manage with no intermediate layers the hardware resources. This requires the development of a macro-expander from LLM3 to Transputer code as well as an ad hoc assembler to obtain executable objects.

The run-time support consists of OCCAM (the native Transputer language) processes synchronously communicating with user-defined processes and performing the message buffering and routing functions required by the asynchronous computational model. These messages are in form of strings of bytes representing a linearization of the Lisp data structures to be transferred. Conversion in linearized form and viceversa is performed by the above described SEND and RECEIVE primitives, which act as an interface between user-defined and run-time support processes through the general LeLisp mechanism of "external function" call.

The generation of the final concurrent LeLisp object is carried out using the standard Transputer Development System (TDS) and will start from a base system consisting of a minimum Lisp environment, the run-time support and the I/O management. Enrichment of this base system with user-defined functions is performed during a run-time initialization phase by means of a machine-dependent linker-loader running on the Transputer. Down-loading of the Transputer array

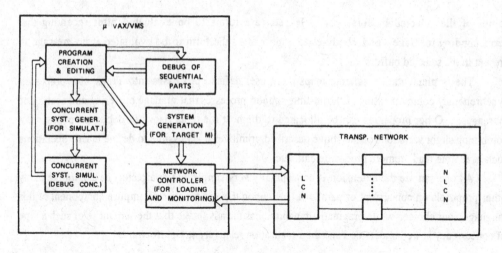

Fig. 6.   Software Development

is carried out by a LeLisp supervisor process, running on the host, which, through a TDS procedure and according to user descriptions, transfers to the network the related files.

Software development will be performed entirely on MicroVax (see fig. 6): creation and editing of programs and debug of sequential parts will use a version of LeLisp transported on MicroVax, while a simulation of concurrency through communicating VMS processes will allow the debugging of the whole concurrent system.   Then, as described above, using TDS the final system will be generated and loaded on the Transputer network, while monitoring facilities (i.e.tracing of messages) for controlling run-time behaviour of the whole system will be provided through interfacing the run-time support with a suitable process at the host level.

3. DISTRIBUTED PROBLEM SOLVING WITH UNCERTAIN DATA

Let us consider the problem of identifying an event on which only uncertain observations can be performed.   These observations can be simple measures (in a noisy environment) or even results of signal analysis performed on them using low level uncertain knowledge; normally scores giving the confidence degree on the observations can be easily obtained.   Events of this kind are also commonly characterized by a high number of observations, most of them in contrast with many of the others. Usually, only a small subset of observations is actually necessary to correctly identify the event; different subsets could exist that correspond to less probable events.   When analysis problems have to be solved on environments characterized by events of this kind, many difficulties arise, due to the high non-determinism of the input data; and control becomes a crucial point. In the past, the two requirements of task-specific, well-experimented control methods and of flexible knowledge-based approach to the problem have been addressed separately, and systems like HWIM [9] and Hearsay-II [10] (focusing respectively on the former and on the latter one) may be regarded as paradigmatic. Our proposal aims at integrating the two requirements, thus improving the trade-off between power and generality.

3.1 Problems in the Control

A Rule-Based System (RBS) is used to model the events we are interested to analyze. The RBS is supposed to be invertible, that is both forward and backward chaining can be performed. The RBS is faced with a high number of observations (called observed facts) and its task is to use the rule knowledge to identify the event that caused those observations and to extract from it the desired features. The RBS contains knowledge about the events that have to be identified. For example, in the case of speech understanding, supposing that a lower-level recognition system generates a lattice of word hypotheses, the RBS contains knowledge about the syntax of the language and the semantics of the application domain. The RBS is also provided with a working memory, or Rule-Based System Data Base, containing the facts and goals generated during the analysis.

The control of the problem solving activity performed by a RBS operating on highly non-deterministic input data is a central issue for the following reasons:

- the non-deterministic aspect of both input data and of the problem solving activity makes the search space very large. An exhaustive search is unreasonable: search must be guided by the scores of the observed facts. A quality factor is therefore assigned to solutions as well as to intermediate deduced facts, possibly starting from the scores of the observed facts that support them.

- the risk of incorrect identification of events must be considered: different subsets of the observed facts can lead to different, less probable identifications of the event. Since it is not possible to generate all the solutions and then select the best one (see previous point), problem solving has to be directed towards the best solution from the beginning. Moreover, optimality (that is finding first the best solution) would make an attractive additional feature.

Observed facts can be interdependent: they have complex descriptions pertaining to different aspects of the observation, on which knowledge can impose constraints not representable in the compositional part of the rules. Thus the rules are augmented with "constraint conditions" on these descriptions, expressed in turn by an associated set of rules or by procedural knowledge. Constraint propagation has to be performed in order to restrict the search space: when a goal has to be solved, it must be characterized by all of the possible constraints.

Our rule-based system control strategy is able to cope with the above mentioned problems and has the following features: 1) Step-by-step score-guided control of the deduction activity; 2) Complete integration between forward and backward problem solving activities. Integrating forward and backward activities has long proved to be an interesting idea [8], though it has not sufficiently analyzed in conjunction with a systematic score-guided search control; 3) Use of special structures called Deductive Instances as basic items managed by the control instead of using simple goals and facts; 4) Memory representation of such structures suitable to limit memory occupation, to permit constraint propagation and to allow distributed problem solving.

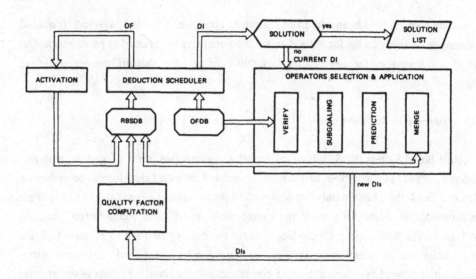

Fig. 7. Architecture of the RBS score-guided control strategy (RBSDB = rule-based system data base, OFDB = observed facts data base)

3.2 Deductive Process Instances

Let us consider the case of isolated backward search activity. Starting from a given goal, a solution is found through a sequence of simple deduction steps: decomposing a (sub)goal into subgoals, and solving a primitive subgoal against the observed facts. Then the single deductive process leading to the solution goes through a sequence of states called Deductive Instances (DIs). The whole deductive activity performed during the analysis can be seen as a search into an OR space of DIs. Of course the ORs are caused by different ways of decomposing a goal into subgoals (different rules involved) and by different observed facts used. In the case of forward search activity the ORs are given by different rules used to hypothesize new goals starting with the given facts. Two kinds of DIs, goal DIs and fact DIs, are present when the two strategies are integrated. Goal DIs are characterized by a current subgoal in addition to the top-level pursued goal.

Deductive Instances offer the following advantages:

- possibility of complete integration among forward and backward search activities: two DIs can be merged together obtaining a new DI; a fact DI can perform goal prediction, generating new goal DIs. The integrated forward-backward activity is described by five operators: ACTIVATION, PREDICTION, SUBGOALING, VERIFY, and MERGE (see fig.7). The first two perform a single forward activity, the third and fourth a single backward activity. MERGE can work both in forward and in backward, and is used when two DIs are joined.

- a step-by-step score-guided control of the deduction activity can be performed: at each step only the most promising DI (the DI with the highest quality factor) is selected by the control (see fig. 7). According to the characteristics of the selected DI a set of operators are applied on it. In this way a complete score-guided integration between the two strategies is obtained.

- the assignment of a quality factor (used as a priority) to a fact DI can take into consideration all the observed facts used to support the deduction of that fact (e.g. it could be an average of their scores). This is done also for goal DIs: the quality factor of a goal DI is determined on the basis of the observed facts that have been used till now to support the top-level goal of the DI. In other words the priority of a single subgoal depends on the context in which this subgoal has to be solved.

- at least for certain methods of assigning quality factors (for example, those proposed in [9]), the outlined integrated control strategy can reach optimality, a key factor to avoid incorrect identifications. Due to integration of the two search activities, optimality can be reached without loss of efficiency.

- when a proper memory representation for the DIs is chosen, the Rule-Based System Data Base (RBSDB, see fig.7) can be distributed on different processors, each of them performing a well defined part of the required problem solving activities. The remaining part of the paper will deal mainly with this point.

When the best DI has a worse score than the best observed fact in the Observed Facts Data Base (OFDB), the observed fact is extracted and inserted into the deductive environment using the ACTIVATION operator. It satisfies the primitive subgoals it is able to satisfy, generating new goal or fact DIs.

Derivation Trees are the standard structures that can be used to represent DIs. They are trees whose nodes are (sub)goals and facts, the leaves being observed facts or not yet solved subgoals. The maximum level of the tree depends on the depth of the corresponding deductive process. The use of such trees, however, causes an excessive waste of memory due to the number of nodes they are usually made of. Memory occupation is reduced by imposing appropriate limitations on the ways a deductive process can evolve and, consequently, on the structures a Derivation Tree can assume. Full integration between forward and backward activities is maintained. In this way a new DI can be represented by creating just one new one-level subtree that we call Physical Hypotesis, PH.

Usually many PHs have to be used to represent a given DI, but DIs share common parts: PHs are linked together to form AND-OR trees, and DIs are AND trees extracted from an AND-OR tree. Each PH corresponds exactly to one DI, in the sense that it includes all the information that is necessary for applying an operator. PHs are the actual active elements for the Scheduler. In the case of a fact DI, the representative PH is the root element of the AND tree, while in the case of a goal DI it is the leaf PH containing the description of the current subgoal of the goal DI. Further details on this point are beyond the scope of this paper; see fig. 8 for an example.

Since every DI directly corresponds to a PH, and every PH directly corresponds to a rule (in facts it represents a way of decomposing a goal into subgoal) , it follows that the Rule-Based System Data Base can be partitioned according to the rules of the system.

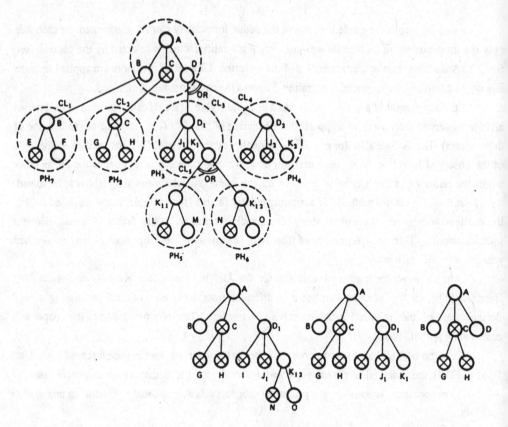

Fig. 8.   Physical Hypotheses and AND-OR trees a) An AND-OR tree representing 7 DIs
b) 3 extracted AND-trees corresponding to respectively PH6, PH3 and PH1

3.3 Distributed Problem Solvers

In the parallel system, the rules and the observed facts are distributed among N Distributed
Problem Solvers Elements (DPSEs). Each DPSE, mapped into a concurrent LeLisp process, has the
whole deductive capability of the centralized system, but can rely only on a subset of rules to
perform its deduction activity. The architecture of a DPSE is shown in fig. 9. Obviously the
various DPSEs must cooperate to carry on the overall analysis. The set of Physical Hypotheses
(PHs) generated during the analysis is then distributed accordingly: each PH corresponds to a
single rule, so it is created and managed by the DPSE which deals with that rule. At any time, given a
DI, there is just one DPSE that has a PH corresponding to that DI (i.e. a PH representing that DI
for the Scheduler).   So we can say that the DIs are distributed among the DPSEs.   On the other
hand, the nodes themselves of the AND tree constituting the DI are, in their turn, distributed
among the DPSEs.   The connections among the PHs used to form the AND-OR trees are called
Compositional Links, and connect PHs of different DPSEs.

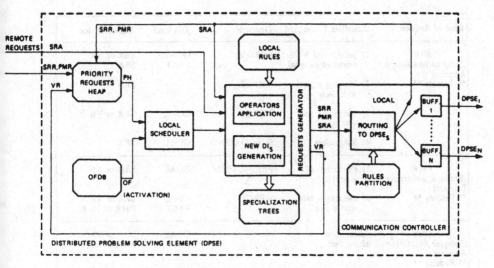

Fig. 9.   Architecture of a Distributed Problem Solving Element

Let PH1 and PH2 be two Physical Hypotheses referring to the same rule. PH1 is connected by a Specialization Link to PH2 if DI2 (corresponding to PH2) is more specific than DI1 (corresponding to PH1). That means that DI1 represents one of the previous states (DIs) of the deductive process leading to the state represented by DI2. Note that a deductive process leading to the state represented by DI2 is not a simple sequence of DIs (as in the case of separated forward and backward search strategies) but a graph of DIs, due to the merging of deductive processes. So when a new PH is generated it is always connected by a Specialization Link to a previously existing one managed by the same DPSE. Since many PHs can be connected to a given one, Specialization Trees are generated. They are created and managed by the corresponding DPSE and are the basic structures to be used when forward and backward search steps are merged.

3.4 Distributed Control

The DPSEs cooperate by exchanging message containing relevant information about the DI (more precisely, PH) they are treating. Table 1 illustrates the five different messages that a single Distributed Problem Solving Element (DPSE) has to deal with. The first three messages (Subgoal Resolution Request, SSR; Prediction-Merging Request, PMR; and Subgoal Resolution Answer, SRA) are usually remote messages, coming from other DPSEs. SRR and PMR represent respectively backward and forward activities. SRA simply informs a DPSE that a subgoal it has previously asked for solution has been solved; the involved activities consist only in creating a new PH (and then a new DI) representing the new deductive process instance. This message is not subjected to priority scheduling but is executed as soon as possible when the current scheduling cycle is terminated. The other two messages (Verify, VR; and Activation, ACT) are local.

Kind of Request	Activities Performed	Operator	DIs kind	Scheduled for
SRR (Subgoal Resolution Request) ** Remote **	1) Solution of a primitive subgoal	VERIFY	GOAL FACT	SRR or VR SRA
	2) Merging a goal with facts	MERGE	—	SRA
	3) Merging a goal with goals	MERGE	GOAL	SRR or VR
	4) Subgoaling	SUBGOALING	GOAL	SRR
PMR (Prediction-Merging Request) ** Remote **	1) Prediction of a goal	PREDICTION	GOAL	SRR or VR
	2) Merging a fact with a goal	MERGE	GOAL FACT	SRR or VR PMR or SRA
SRA (Subgoal Resolution Answer) ** Remote **	Acquisition of the fact	—	GOAL FACT	SRR or VR PMR or SRA
VR (Verify Request) ** Local **	Solution of a primitive Subgoal	VERIFY	GOAL FACT	SRR or VR PRM or SRA
ACT (Activation) ** Local **	Activation of an OF	ACTIVATION	GOAL FACT	SRR or VR PMR or SRA

Table 1. The messages exchanged between DPSEs and the associated activities

The first two requests are subjected to the Local Control Scheduler, together with the other two local messages, see fig.9. The interesting aspect is that each message refers directly to a fixed DI; then the scheduling allows the kind of score-guided control previously outlined. In fact it selects the message whose DI is characterized by the highest quality factor; the PH corresponding to that DI can be local or not. In this way, at any time, the best DI in absolute is always treated by one of the DPSEs.

The Local Scheduler is also faced with the ACTIVATION phase: when there is an observed fact (among those that can be used by this DPSE) with a better quality factor than that of the best DI among those in the Priority Requests Heap, that fact is used to try to solve the primitive subproblems of all the local PHs.

Each time a new PH (a DI) is created, a corresponding request is generated, according to Table 1. This request has the purpose of making this new DI visible by the Distributed Problem Solver. A Communication Controller generates the messages to be sent to the involved DPSEs. The knowledge about what DPSE can solve a subgoal (SRR requests), or what DPSE can predict a goal given a certain fact (PMR requests), is used to control the communication process and is based on the given partition of the rules among the DPSEs. In order to furtherly reduce the amount of communication, the communication buffers can be managed taking into account the values of the best quality factors of the DPSEs, i.e. those of the best DIs currently selected by the various

Local Schedulers.

The amount of communication among the DPSEs is relatively small compared with the activities performed at every request on the basis of local information. Another positive aspect is that messages are exchanged in an asynchronous way: when a message is sent, the sending process does not enter a waiting state but continues in its scheduling activity.

4. CONCLUSION

We have described an integrated parallel architecture (multiprocessor structure + concurrent programming language + distributed inferential algorithm) for rule-based interpretation of uncertain data.

The model presented here can be summarized as a parallel best-first search, driven by a unified, step-by-step score guided, forward-backward control strategy, carried out by a network of processes, statically allocated to the PEs and asyncronously communicating by streams of succinct representations (the PHs) of deduction paths (the DIs).

A possible drawback of this static, "processes as rules", model is that it may result in a poor utilization factor of the available processing resources (in contrast with the dynamic, "processes as hypoteses", model, mentioned in section 2, which is subject of current investigation). However this could be not a critical problem if a system-level parallelism (due to multiplexed input data) is guaranteed to exist in the final application, as could happen, for example, in multi-user telecommunication equipments for voice-based advanced services.

At the time of this writing, a first small-scale prototype multiprocessor is being built, mainly for basic software development. The switching element circuit, required for assembling the large scale final machine, has been completely designed. The parallel version of the inference engine has been implemented and is under testing on a distributed environment of networked machines.

Future directions of our work include, besides development of and experimentation with the prototype described in section 2, studies on possible evolutions of the physical machine by specialization and integration of its basic building blocks, analysis of the dynamic model in a parallel dialect of Prolog, following the approach of [11], applicability of the problem solving algorithm of section 3 to DAI (Distributed AI) problems.

5 REFERENCES

[1]   R. Pieraccini, F. Raineri, A. Giordana, P. Laface, A. Kaltenmeier, H. Mangold, "Algorithms for Speech Data-reduction and Recognition", Proceedings of the 1985 ESPRIT Technical Week, Brussels, Sept. 1985.

[2]   C. L. Seitz, "Concurrent VLSI Architectures", IEEE Trans. on Computers, Vol. C-33, No.12   Dec. 1984, pp. 1247-1265.

[3]   Arvind, R. A. Iannucci, "Two Fundamental Issues in Multiprocessing", Computation Structures Group Memo 226-3, Lab. for Comp. Science, MIT, Cambridge, Aug. 1985

[4]   C. Whitby-Strevens, "The Transputer", Proceedings of the 12th Annual Inter. Symp. on Computer Architeture, Boston, Mass., June 1985, pp. 292-300.

[5]   F. W. Burton, M. M. Huntbach, "Virtual Tree Architectures", IEEE Trans. on Computers,   Vol.C-33, No. 3, March 1984, pp. 278-280.

[6]   B. W. Wah, G. Li, C. F. Yu, "Multiprocessing of Combinatorial Search Problems", IEEE Computer, June 1985, pp.93-108.

[7]   J. Chailloux, M. Devin, J. Hullot, "LeLisp, a Portable and Efficient LISP System" Proc. of the 1984 ACM Symp. on LISP and Functional Programming, Austin, Texas, Aug. 1984,pp.113-122.

[8]   D.D.Corkill, V.R.Lesser, E.Hudlicka,"Unifying data-directed and goal-directed control an example and experiments", Proc. of the AAAI '82, Pittsburgh, PA, pp.143-147.

[9]   W. A. Woods, "Optimal Search Strategies for Speech Understanding Control", Artificial Intelligence 18, 1982, pp. 295-236.

[10]   L. D. Erman, F. Hayes-Roth, V. R. Lesser, D. Raj Reddy, "The Hearsay-II Speech Understanding System: Integrating Knowledge to Resolve Uncertainty", ACM Computing Survey 12, 1980, pp. 213-253.

[11]   G. Giandonato, G. Sofi, "Parallelizing Prolog-based Inference Engines", ESPRIT Project N. 26, Subtask T4.3 Techn. Rep., Sept. 1986.

AN AXIOMATIC APPROACH TO THE SPECIFICATION
OF DISTRIBUTED COMPUTER ARCHITECTURES*

W. Damm   and   G. Doehmen

Lehrstuhl für Informatik II, RWTH Aachen
Büchel 29 – 31, D-5100 Aachen, FRG

ABSTRACT

This paper presents two extensions to the axiomatic architecture description language AADL [11], which together allow for a modular and concise specification of multiprocessor architectures at levels of abstraction ranging from compiler/operating-system interface down to register-transfer-level. The specification method is illustrated by an AADL-definition of a top-level view of DOOM, a distributed object oriented machine, currently developed at Philips Research Labs., Eindhoven [19,20] within ESPRIT-project 415.

1   INTRODUCTION

ESPRIT project 415 explores alternative approaches of supporting advanced information processing by language-directed multiprocessor architectures. While the approaches differ in the computational model and the supported programming language, a number of key issues in the design of such architectures reappear (indeed: as could be expected). Commonly encountered problems include

- the extension of an originally sequential evaluation model to a parallel one (when are processes created how do they communicate?)
- the distribution of global OS-tasks as process-allocation and garbage collection
- the design of message handling components (what network topology? what low-level communication-concepts? how much work can/should be done by dedicated hardware components?)

Clearly it would be desirable if we could organize our designs in such a way, that common instances of problems can be identified and solved once. The complexity of the questions raised above forces us to look for ways of structuring the design, indeed to find levels of abstraction which provide just enough information to solve one (or perhaps: an interdependent class of) problem(s) at a time.

Structured designs and abstraction mechanism are now state of the art in "classical" sequential software-development. This holds only to a much more limited extent for the development of distributed software systems: while formal approaches to semantics, specification, and verification of such systems exist (see e.g. [21], [22], [17], for semantic models, [18], [14,15], [3], [23] for specification methods, and [6], [4] for verification methods), a satisfactory approach combining abstraction mechanisms with hierarchical design methods and the "right" semantic domain (based on partial orders, see below) is still lacking. The picture gets even worse, when we look at computer architecture design. While many architecture description languages (ADL's) have been proposed (see e.g. [2], [7,9] and the survey in [8]), even for the sequential (synchronous) case ADL's with a formal semantics are rare, and in general neither abstraction nor hierarchical design methods can be combined with existing ADL's because of their operational nature.

The topic of this paper is the introduction of an ADL providing these key ingredients:

- abstraction
- support for hierarchic design
- "right" semantic domain as a basis for formal verification
- applicable for synchronous and asynchronous systems
- applicable to levels of abstraction ranging from top-level specification (such as an abstract computational model underlying the supported programming language) down to register-transfer level.

It is in particular the necessity to incorporate hardware and possibly firmware subsystems in the formal specification method which distinguishes a general specification method for distributed systems from AADL. In computer architecture design, characteristics of hardware components may well influence higher-level design decisions. This entails both that a precise specification of the behaviour of hardware-components has to be part of the design (which could well serve additionally as input to VLSI design tools) and that in general a pure top-down approach is not feasible.

In AADL, the orientation towards architecture design becomes manifest in the following characteristics:

- The fundamental notion of the "state" of a computer architecture is explicitly visible (in contrast to e.g. [18], [13]).
- As most ADL's, AADL allows to mix structural and "functional"[1] specifications of the dynamic behaviour of an architecture by either specifying the information flow between (already defined) subsystems or explicitly specifying the state transformations possible in an architecture.
- In architecture design, semantic models which do not allow to distinguish between nondeterminism an concurrency (such as traces [17], branching time [15] and state-based approaches) are inapplicable, because they introduce observable states, which will never be visible in the hardware (which clearly does not "model" concurrency by interleaving but provides true concurrency). Indeed, already the notion of a global state in a distributed system is debatable, since it forces to order events in some global (time-) scale which are physically unrelated[2].

We thus will base the semantics of AADL on a partial order of events (as e.g. in [22]), by using Petri-Nets as an intermediate step in defining the semantics of AADL.

Chapter two of this paper introduces the key concepts of AADL.

Section 3, the main chapter of this paper, is intended to give a flavour of how AADL can be used as a tool in architecture design. We first discuss techniques of structuring the design and features of AADL pertinent to structuring techniques. These are then illustrated by deriving an AADL-specification of DOOM at a high level of abstraction, called POOL-machine, which is used as an intermediate architecture for code-generation.

Having gained some experience in the specification with AADL, the reader is confronted in section 4 with a short summary of the partial-order semantics of AADL.

2   SPECIFYING ASYNCHRONOUS ACTIONS IN AADL

The purpose of this section is to familiarize the reader with the key concepts of AADL for specifying the dynamic behaviour of an architecture.

AADL has been originally proposed as a means of introducing abstraction and hierarchic design methods into the design of microprogrammed single-processor architectures [11,10]. The treatment of asynchronous actions requires only a small extension of the previously introduced concepts. To make the paper self-contained, we summarize also the axiomatic specification style introduced in [10], but urge the reader to consult [11] to gain a deeper understanding.

The key for introducing abstraction into architecture-specification is the axiomatic style of specifying atomic actions of an architecture used in AADL.
Upon activation of an atomic action, it will transform the state of the architecture. The state-space is specified in the blockdiagram of the architecture using base types int, bool, bit, sequence <lb...up> bit and enumeration types, and as constructors arrays, lists, and (variant) records (for examples we refer to section 3). We consider the state-concept to be fundamental for architecture design; attempts to use pure functional methods in this context are in our opinion inadequate.
In contrast to most ADL's, the state transformation induced by activating an atomic action is not given operationally but, up to "syntactic sugar", by a pair of predicates: a state satisfying the precondition will be taken into a state satisfying the second predicate, the post-condition. Note that nothing is said (and thus specified) about how this state transformation is achieved. Fig. 1, which is taken from the top-level specification of DOOM, shows the "syntactic sugar" added to this pure axiomatic style to increase readability of specifications. The "pure" specification is (automatically) constructed from a set of effects, which are evaluated sequentially in the order first, main, and then, and in parallel within such an "evaluation state". Note again that this evaluation order is only introduced to ease the specification; it is externally invisible. Note also, that such a specification contains both a liveness property (... will be taken to a state satisfying ...) and a safety property (this is implicit by the semantics: nothing else will happen, e.g. no register may be changed unless explicitly specified).

The liveness-part entails, that we can only deal with terminating atomic actions, which sounds reasonable in theory but may be violated in "pathological" architectures (think of an uninterruptable memory-read operation with unbounded levels of indirect addressing).

```
    function answer (methods : seq <1..M> of bool) :

      trigger state = execute

      effects
        first
          increment stackpointer :
              pre true
              post stackpointer = NEXT(stackpointer')
        main
            move oldest message on stack :
                pre methods IN queue
                post stack[stackpointer].tag = mess
                    and stack[stackpointer].activation = GET methods FROM queue
                    and state = continue,

          If no such entry then wait for method activation message:
              pre not (methods IN queue)
              post answerstate = methods
                  and state = wait-for-meth-act
                  /* in this case the data-processor will stop normal execution until a
                      method-activation message he is waiting for arrives at the input-buffer */
        then
            delete stacked message from queue :
                pre methods IN queue
                post queue = DELETE methods FROM queue'

      semantics
        NEXT : extern,
        methods : seq <1..M> of bool IN queue : q-type =
            If empty(queue) => false,
                methods<head(queue).methodid> => true
                else methods IN tail(queue)
            fi : bool,
        GET methods : seq <1..M> of bool FROM queue : q-type =
            If empty(queue) => error,
                methods<head(queue).methodid> => head(queue)
                else GET methods FROM tail(queue)
            fi : meth-act-type,
        DELETE methods : seq <1..M> of bool FROM queue : q-type = ... : q-type

      instructionfields
          queue.opcode = codeof (answer),
          queue.meth = methods

    endfunction /* answer */
```

Fig. 1: A sample AADL operation specification

It is also important to observe, that the term "atomic action"[3] is not absolute but rather relative to the chosen level of abstraction, as an example, the "answer" operation of Fig. 1 is atomic at the specification level chosen in section 3 (it specifies the behaviour of a compiler-generated instruction which cannot be interrupted by another atomic action visible at this abstraction level), but will clearly be refined in subsequent design steps to some (interruptable) combination of lower-level atomic actions.

When specifying pre- and post conditions we allow the user to specify design dependent predicates and functions using a set of predefined primitives, which in particular include the canonical operations associated with AADL-data-types. The specification of user-specific extensions is done in a purely functional style following the keyword semantics. Types occurring in the definitions are defined in the blockdiagram of the architecture.

While in synchronous systems the activation of an operation is controlled by a clock and/or the presence of some encoding, in general the activation of an operation will depend on (local) conditions on the state, which may be (asynchronously) set or reset as a result of executing other operations. Such activation-conditions are specified in AADL following the keyword trigger. Typically triggers will be specified by propositional formulae: think of interrupt-requests becoming true, resources getting freed, new messages arriving – all these are sample instances of boolean conditions causing an action to get triggered. We expect this to be true for most operations in the envisaged context of architecture design. The verification of designs will be simplified if triggers are propositional.

A notable exception to this rule are operations which get activated by code (which could be specified as a trigger "memory[programcounter] = codeof(operation)". For obvious reasons we refer to such operations as "instructions" and treat their encoding information separately (by specifying it following the keyword instructionfields). Note that this information can be exploited by a compiler back-end.

A last concept (not shown in Fig 1) allows to specify conditions which are assumed to be true whenever an operation gets activated. Such conditions (which are specified following the keyword condition) will be checked while verifying designs whenever an operation gets activated (by generating appropriate assertions). In a hierarchical design, lower level implementations of a (higher-level) operation may assume that these conditions hold upon activation of the implementation of an operation. Care must be exercised when introducing conditions in the top-level specification of an architecture (as in section 3): in general the activation of top-level operations will depend on the "environment", i.e. the "user" of this top-level specification, thus such top-level conditions cannot be verified in the design. Instead, they formalize assumptions (or requirements) on the usage of top-level operations. As an example, the "user" of the specification shown in section 3 is the code-generator for POOL, thus conditions specified there must be ensured by the compiler.

3   DESIGNING ARCHITECTURES IN AADL: A CASE STUDY

This section is intended to give a flavour of how AADL can be used as a tool in architecture design. Though we illustrate our approach with examples taken from the design of DOOM, we stress generally applicable techniques and do not discuss at length aspects peculiar to DOOM.

3.1   Structuring the design

We view a computer architecture as a hierarchically ordered system of distinct architectural layers, which each encapsulate the capabilities of the architecture as seen at a particular level of abstraction. When designing such a system, we are confronted with the task to find such abstraction levels, or, equivalently interfaces. For the design of DOOM, four main abstraction levels have been suggested in [20], which seem to be similarly applicable in other designs of language-oriented multiprocessor-systems. The actual design will contain additional layers to close the bridge between adjacent main layers and down to the actual hardware components.

1. The top-level specification presents the compiler-writers view of the architecture. This is essentially an abstract-machine providing just what you need for "your" programming language. Examples of such levels are P-code for PASCAL, Warren's instruction set for PROLOG [24], or the FAM for Cardelli's implementation of ML [5]. For DOOM, it is a parallel stack machine extended with queues to support the parallel object-oriented language POOL. This POOL-machine hides from the compiler

   - the number of processing nodes: the compiler assumes that each process (which are called "objects" in POOL) has its own node;
   - the (topology of the) network: the compiler assumes, that it can directly send messages to any other known process;
   - finiteness of memory: the (first phase of the) compiler can directly store and send structured data;
   - distribution of code: the compiler assumes, that all code resides in a memory accessible from all nodes.

The following layers now gradually reveal more and more aspects of the architecture. As these aspects are revealed, the implementation will provide the more abstract view in terms of the now visible structures and operations. We refer the reader to [20] for a discussion of these implementation steps.

2. Reveal finite number of processors and code-distribution: necessitates scheduling capabilities to share nodes between many processors, process allocation routines, and code movement

3. Reveal finiteness of memory: necessitates memory management, garbage collection, message packating etc.

4. Reveal topology of network: necessitates communication processor to implement logically fully connected network (see [1]).

The role of AADL in such a design process is twofold:

- Because of its axiomatic style, AADL allows to cast our intuitive understanding of what we want to hide and what should be visible at a given level into an unambiguous, formal specification. It extends the typical interface definitions listing parameters of routines and global variables with a concise specification of the dynamic behaviour of the available services. Whatever property a higher level routine wants to use, it must be formally specified or derivable from the specification. This rigorous discipline is the prerequisite for a hierarchical verification of designs, as further discussed below.
- Anyone involved in the design of multiprocessor-systems is aware of the difficul-

ties in analyzing and establishing the well-behaviour of implemented subsystems. Even with disciplined ways of process-communication as in CSP [25], proving the correctness of distributed algorithms is a hard task. In architecture design, communication between concurrent processes is soon of the shared memory type, and at low levels not even semaphores have to be available. To directly prove, that a sequence of asynchronously activated hardware actions indeed e.g. passes a structured message from one node to some other node would be an impossible task. But once we have structured our design and provided AADL-specifications of its architectural layers, we can prove the correctness of the design in a hierarchical fashion. Indeed, it is then sufficient to establish the equivalence of a layer and its implementation using the primitives of the adjacent lower layer. Moreover, as will be shown in subsequent papers, proving the correctness of one implementation step can be split up into an automated proof of the liveness properties (assuming triggers are indeed propositional) and a modular prove of the safety properties. This constitutes a clear advantage over operational approaches using bisimulation equivalence.

3.2 Specifying one layer in AADL

We now pick out the POOL-machine layer of DOOM and show how to formally specify it in AADL. It must be emphasized that the aim of this section is <u>not</u> to give a <u>complete</u> specification but to illustrate how an intuitive understanding can be formalized in AADL. As we go on, we will in particular introduce those concepts of AADL which allow to specify <u>structural</u> refinements.

Fig. 2 is a graphical representation of the structural components of the POOL-machine as outlined in 3.1: there is some unbounded number of nodes, which all have access to a (thus shared) memory for code, and which all can directly communicate with each other. The transliteration of this picture into AADL follows.

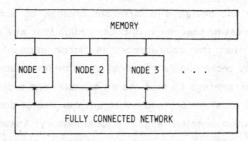

Fig. 2: top-level view of the POOL-machine

As mentioned in section 1, architectures can be described either by structural refinement or by explicit definition of the dynamic behaviour. The specification on the next page is an instance of a structural refinement step: it defines the POOL-machine in terms of certain sub-architectures (yet to be defined) and their interconnection. Two kinds of interconnection are feasible: communication via links using dedicated ports, or communication via shared memory.

```
architecture POOL-machine:

parameters
      mws : int /* size of memoryword */,
      ms  : int /* size of shared code memory */

subarchitectures
      node [i]   1 ≤ i
      /* each node i has inport[j] and outport[j] to communicate with node j ≠ i (see CP) */

links
      node[i].outport[j] connected with node[j].inport[i]   1 ≤ i ≠ j
      /* at this level we assume a fully connected network */

shared memory
      types
            instructionword = seq <1..mws> bit
      variables
            codememory : array [1..ms] of instructionword

endarchitecture
```

The specification of the link entails the existence of a unidirectional communication channel between outport[j] of node i and inport[i] of node j : any value loaded in node[i].outport[j] will (eventually) be available in inport[i] of node j . No assumption about the time taken for this communication is made. This concept is general enough to allow to specify communication in networks as well as transmission of signals over wires. Indeed, if we would like to specify chips at gate level, subarchitectures could describe standard cells (such as gate-layouts) and links would be used to specify their physical interconnection.

Declaring a "variable" as shared for subarchitectures as node[1], node[2],... entails that any operation of any node may access the shared variable and that concurrent accesses will be serialized in some arbitrary order[4]. Note that non-shared variables of a subarchitecture (declared locally in its specification) are not visible to operations declared in other subarchitectures and may thus only be changed locally.

A word about design parameters. Introducing these in the specification allows for later "tuning" by simulating the design with different choices of actual values. For the current level we just assume that mws is chosen such that any instruction fits into one memoryword and that the code-memory is "large enough". If desired, design constraints (imposed by technological reasons) could be introduced by requiring some inequalities between parameters to hold. As an example, one might decide to later on use 1 Megabit-chips as local memory and constrain the size of code memory to ensure that it can be distributed over the available local memory. Assuming then N as the envisioned number of nodes (and thus as an additional parameter of the design) it would be reasonable to require $ms \cdot mws \leq N \cdot 10^9$.

In designing language-directed multiprocessor-architectures, it is natural to releave the processor executing code as much from message handling as possible. While the exact distribution of message handling tasks will not be visible at this level, we already postulate a separate communication processor responsible for receiving and forwarding messages from and to other nodes. The next refinement step (see Fig. 3) specifies as well that the "data-processor"-part (which executes the code) will communicate with the communication processor using three shared variables: an input- and output-buffer for incoming and outgoing messages, and a destination register identifying the receiver-node for outgoing messages.

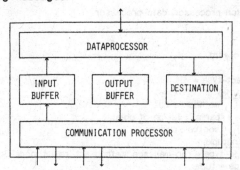

Fig. 3: The structure of a node.

At this point writing down the formal (AADL-) specification forces us to analyse the kind of messages we want to support, since we have to specify the class of values which can be stored in the buffer by defining a suitable type "message".

At this level, only messages which are induced from communication between user-defined processes and the creation of processes are visible. For the supported programming language POOL, these are

- method-activation messages: these ask another process (object) to execute a certain procedure (which are called "methods") with some actual parameters;
- result-messages: return the value computed after answering such a request to the sender of the request;
- process-creation messages: ask the processor to create a new process of a specified class.

Clearly similar messages will arise in any such design. E.g. in parallel graph-reduction of functional languages [12], [16] asking another processor to evaluate a particular serial combinator with some actual parameters corresponds to a combination of method-activation and process-creation messages, which will eventually be followed by a result message returning the computed value (i.e. pointer to some graph).

We will only formalize the message types as they are needed in subsequent examples and thus restrict our attention to method-activation-messages. In addition we want to be able to test the kind of message currently stored in a buffer or whether the buffer is free for new messages because the previous message has been processed, and thus introduce tags to distinguish these cases.

The specification shows, how variant records can be used to formalize the type of the buffer elements. The introduction of the tag no-message will be motivated below in connection with the specification of operations accessing the shared buffer.

We now turn to explicit definitions of the data-processor and the communication processor, and consider the data-processor first.

```
architecture node[i]

parameters
    pn : int /* maximal number of parameters per method */,
    M  : int /* maximal number of methods per object */

subarchitectures
    communication-processor, data-processor

shared memory
    types
        nodeno = int,
        object = ...,
        meth-act-type =
            tuple
                methodid : 1..M,
                parlist : list pn of object,
                source : nodeno
            endtuple,
        message-type = (no-message, method-act, result, node-act),
        message = tuple
                    case tag : message-type of
                        no-message : ( ),
                        method-act : (activation : meth-act-type),
                        result : (resultvalue : object),
                        node-act : (class : ...)
                    esac
                  endtuple
    variables
        input-buffer : message,
        output-buffer : message,
        destination : nodeno

endarchitecture  /* node[i] */  i ≥ 1
```

Consider the "life-cycle" of a typical process in an environment which has to provide synchronous message passing between processes. In POOL a process may at any time send a method-activation message to another known process. The sending process will be delayed, until the addressed process is willing to accept this message (which is indicated by executing an "answer"-statement) and has computed and returned the corresponding result. On the receiving side, if a process executes an answer-statement (and thus indicates that it is now willing to accept a method-activation message) but no such request is pending, then the process gets delayed until such a method-activation message arrives. In fact, the receiving process may selectively wait for particular methods and disregard method-activation messages for other methods.

The specification of primitives used in implementing synchronous computation uses directly the state diagram shown in Fig. 4 implied by the above discussion.

In the state diagram, c_1 denotes the condition, that a suitable method-activation message was pending when the answer-instruction was executed, while c_2 specifies, that the received method-activation message is one the processor is waiting for. Note that the process returns to its normal "execute" state by actions which are triggered by the arrival of certain kinds of messages, i.e. by asynchronous events. The operations of the Pool-machine thus fall into two categories, instructions and "message-handling"-routines, i.e. asynchronously activated actions. This again should be typical for such designs.

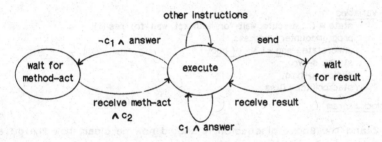

Fig. 4: the state diagram of a process

One more point has to be addressed: the treatment of "unwanted" method-activation messages. In DOOM a queuing strategy has been adopted: incoming meth-act-messages will always be "consumed" at the receiving node but put into a queue, if they are "unwanted". This assures at the same time a fair selection of such messages. We thus have to complete the state-diagram of Fig. 4 with arrows indicating that the activation of "receive meth-act" will keep the process in its current state if $\neg c_2$ holds. Note that arriving result-messages are always "wanted" (unless the compiler produced wrong code).

We now show how to cast this state-machine control mechanism into an AADL specification. First the storage structures of the data-processor will be defined. These include next to a run-time stack a queue for incoming "unwanted" method-activation messages, a variable "state" indicating the current state of the processor, a variable "answerstate" indicating which methods a process is waiting for if it is waiting for method-activation messages, and a programcounter pointing to the currently executed instruction in the shared code-memory.

The explicit definition of the data-processor will be completed by a specification of all operations, among them the answer-instruction shown in Fig. 1.

```
architecture data-processor:
blockdiagram
    parameters
        qs : int /* maximal size of queue */,
        ss : int /* maximal stack size */
    types
        address = 1..ms,
        q-type = list qs of meth-act-type,
        frametype = ...,
        stack-tag = (obj, fra, mess, addr, par),
        stackentry = tuple
                    case tag  : stack-tag of
                        obj  : (objectident : object),
                        fra  : (frame : frametype),
                        mess : (activation : meth-act-type),
                        addr : (memory address : address),
                        par  : (parameterlist : list pn of object)
                    esac
                endtuple,
        s-type = array [0..ss] of stackentry
```

```
variables
        state = (..., execute, wait-for-meth-act, wait-for-result),
        programcounter : address,
        anwerstate : seq <1..M> of bool,
        stack : s-type,
        queue : q-type,
        stackpointer : 0..ss
```

endblockdiagram

From section 2 and the above discussion it should now be clear, how the different types of operations of the data-processor become activated:

- "classical" instructions (not relating to communication aspects) will be triggered in state "execute" if the current instruction pointed to by the programcounter contains their code;
- "communication" instructions will be triggered similarly but may take the processor to another state;
- "message handling" operations will be triggered by new messages of the appropriate type (forwarded by the communication processor to the input-buffer) and will reset the data-processor into execute-state.

We will discuss a "matching pair" of type 2 and 3 operations.

Consider first the answer-instruction shown in Fig. 1. It contains as a parameter the set of methods the process is willing to execute (i.e. method-activation-messages for these methods are now "wanted"). Note that this parameter will be part of the encoding of the operation; the entry queue.meth = methods specifies, that the set of "wanted" methods is given by the "meth"-field of the instructionword (using the format for instructions accessing the queue).

As shown in Fig. 4, the state transition induced by activating "answer" will depend on c_1. Formally, c_1 is expressed using the (user-defined) binary predicate IN , which takes a set of "wanted" methods and checks whether a request for executing one of these methods is pending, i.e. whether a method-activation-message for such a method is stored in the queue. The predicate IN is defined recursively over the data-type list used in the specification of the queue: given that the queue is nonempty, it checks the head-method-activation. If its method-identifier is in the "wanted" set "methods", then the predicate is true, otherwise the tail of the list is checked recursively.

Now that we know how to check c_1, we can give a pre/post-specification of the intended state-transformation:

- if c_1 holds, then move the (oldest) wanted message on the stack (and continue by constructing a frame for this method call)[5], otherwise enter the "wait-for-method-activation-message" state and store the set of wanted methods in answerstate.

It should be straightforward for the interested reader to check, that GET indeed gets the oldest wanted message FROM the queue. The remaining transitions are "bookkeeping" actions: first increase the stackpointer, then delete the selected method-activation message from the queue.

In these specification we use the '-symbol to indicate the "old" value of a variable: e.g. stackpointer' refers to the value of the stackpointer in the state used to evaluate the precondition.

We now discuss the "dual" operation which receives method-activation message. This operation shares a resource (the input-buffer) with operations of the communication processor, thus a simple protocol will be specified which ensures, that the communication processor will not put a new message into the input-buffer unless the previous message has been received. We have already prepared this protocol by introducing an extra tag-value "no-message" (see the specification of node[i]), which will be set by a receiving action once it has consumed a message.

```
        function receive meth-act:

        trigger input-buffer.tag = method-act

        effects
            main
                put method-activation-message on queue:
                    pre not (state = wait-for-meth-act and
                             answerstate <input-buffer.activation.methodid>)
                    post queue = PUT input-buffer.activation ON queue',
                put method-activation-message on stack:
                    pre  state = wait-for-method-act and
                         answerstate <input-buffer.activation.methodid>
                    post stack[stackpointer].tag = mess
                         and stack[stackpointer].activation = input-buffer.activation
                         and state = continue

            then
                free buffer:
                    pre true
                    post input-buffer.tag = no-message

        semantics
            PUT act : meth-act-type ON queue : q-type =
                if size (queue) ≠ qs => append (queue, act)
                    else error
                fi : queue

        endfunction
```

The operation "receive meth-act" is "responsible" for method-activation messages and thus triggered whenever the tag of the input-buffer is set to "method-act". As shown in the state-diagram Fig. 4, the state-transition induced by activating this operation depends on whether condition c_2 is satisfied. c_2 can be formally expressed by state = wait-for-method-act (the process is waiting for a method-activation message) and answerstate <input-buffer.activation.methodid> (the method-identifier of the method-activation message is among the "wanted" ones).

The pre/post-style specification of the intended behaviour is then a straightforward transliteration of

- If c_2 is satisfied then put the message on top of the stack and trigger the construction of a matching frame, otherwise store the message in the queue.

Finally, to observe the protocol for buffer-access, the tag is set to "no-message" indicating that the communication-processor may now put a new message into the input-buffer.

To conclude the illustration of the specification method, we discuss the explicit definition of the communication processor.

At this level of abstraction, the communication processor simply moves the information from its inports to the input-buffer, and from the output-buffer to the outport specified by the destination register. Recall that the ports constitute the interface to the network. To guarantee that no message gets overwritten before it has been consumed, we again require, that a new message may be written into an outport only once the network has passed the "acknowledge" that the message has been consumed by the network.

Similarly, on the receiving side, we assume that the network will not destroy information in an inport before it has been consumed.

    function from outport to inport:
      trigger outport.status = busy and inport.status = available
      effects
        main
            transfer message:
              pre true
              post inport = outport
        then
          observe protocol:
            pre true
            post outport.status = available and inport.status = busy
    endfunction

Fig. 5: AADL-specification of link behaviour

To make our assumptions precise, we associate with each port p (as declared in the blockdiagram of the communication processor shown below) a (system defined) variable p.status which may take values busy, available. Specifying that port "outport" is connected with port "inport" induces implicitly a network operation with the AADL specification shown in Fig. 5.

In defining "his" protocol for the network, the user can make use of the status information of the ports and the fact that communication along a link obeys the above simple protocol.

Using these concepts, it is straightforward to specify the communication processor in AADL. Observe that the trigger of the operation now depends on both status information for the ports and the tag-value of the buffer, since for both protocols have to be observed to guarantee that no information is destroyed before it has been consumed.

    architecture communication-processor:
    blockdiagram
        inport[j], outport[j] : message | 1 ≤ j ≠ i
    endblockdiagram

```
operations
    function load input.buffer from inport[J]:
        trigger inport[J].status = busy and input-buffer.tag = no-message
        effects
            main
                transfer port values and set buffer-tag:
                    pre true
                    post input-buffer = inport[J]
            then
                free inport:
                    pre true
                    post inport[J].status = available
    endfunction | 1 ≤ J ≠ I

    function load outport[J] from output-buffer:
        trigger outport[J].status = available
            and outport-buffer.tag ≠ no-message
            and destination = J
        effects
            main
                transfer buffer value:
                    pre true
                    post outport[J] = output-buffer
            then
                observe protocols:
                    pre true
                    post outport[J].status = busy
                        and output-buffer.tag = no-message
    endfunction | 1 ≤ J ≠ I
endoperations
endarchitecture  /* communication-processor */
```

4   A SHORT SUMMARY OF THE NET SEMANTICS OF AADL

In this section we outline our approach to derive a formal semantics for AADL based
on a partial order of events. A full treatment will be given in a forthcoming paper.

Being taylored towards architecture description, AADL assumes only very low-level
constructs for expressing parallelism and communication.

- Parallelism in AADL is implicit: whenever trigger conditions of two operations are
  "simultaneously" true, the operations will be executed concurrently.

- Communication in AADL is implicit via shared variables, with the only restriction
  entailed by the division of an architecture into subarchitectures and the explicit
  use of linked ports. In particular no built-in primitives protecting access to
  shared resources are assumed, because they have to be realised explicitly at some
  level of the design. Recall that the only "assumption" we made was that concurrent accesses to shared resources will be serialized in some nondeterministic
  (unpredicatable) way. Note that a trigger condition of an operation trying to
  access a shared resource may become false while being delayed (unless a suitable

protocol Is part of the specification, which ensures that this will not happen!).

To give an adequate semantics to such a complex language without introducing any assumptions about the relative speed of operations we take a two step approach.

1. In step 1, we translate an AADL specification into a Petri-Net, which makes the parallelism in the specification explicit. In particular, for each trigger-condition of an operation there will be an entry-place to the transition modelling this operation in the net which will be marked iff the trigger condition is true. The translation will use data-flow analysis to make the dependencies in setting/resetting trigger-conditions explicit. Moreover, additional places ("semaphores") will be Introduced to serialize access to shared resources.

2. By playing the token game we thus have an explicit representation of the concurrency in the specification. The allowed sequence of markings of places will be constrained to fairly-implementable sequences. Given one sequence of markings and an initial set of local states (one for each subarchitecture) we can then construct a corresponding computation sequence by associating a state transformation with each step in the sequence of markings: given a marking m , execute all operations activated in this marking (according to the semantics defined in [10]) concurrently on the (set of local) state(s) valid in this marking. Note that no data conflicts will arise between a set of activated actions because of the introduced semaphore-places. The technique to join the resulting states into a set of local states has been employed previously in [10,11].

The term "fairly-implementable" will roughly correspond to weak eventual fairness with respect to an "allowed" set of trigger-places.

Each Petri-Net associated with an AADL-specification thus induces a set of configuration sequences with elements of the form (marking, set-of-local-states). Note that nondeterminism is only due to conflicts when accessing shared resources. In general, subsequent implementation steps should eliminate such conflicts (e.g. by introducing some scheduling mechanisms) and thus will eventually make the system completely deterministic. Care will be taken in the definition of the fairness constraint that schedules implementing the constraints can be defined.

CONCLUSION

We have guided the reader through several steps in formalizing the design of a language directed multiprocessor-architecture in AADL. In doing so, we hope to have demonstrated, how AADL helps as an abstraction tool, and that structural aspects as well as dynamic aspects of such a system can be naturally expressed in AADL.

Much foundational research on AADL remains to be done. As outlined, Petri-Nets provide an appropriate tool to define a formal operational semantics of AADL. (It should be emphasized, that a direct use of Petri-Nets in specifying architectures is inpractical because of the complexity of the generated nets.)

In a similar way, proving safety properties of specifications can be done using a Hoare-Style proof system for Petri-Nets while establishing liveness properties will be reduced to injecting firing sequences of (the Petri-Net associated with an) AADL-specification(s) into the firing-sequence of its refinement.
It is our aim that this research ultimately provides the theoretical foundation for advanced CAD-tools supporting architecture design.

ACKNOWLEDGEMENTS

The development of AADL has benefited from an intensive exchange of ideas with Subrata Dasgupta. In particular the trigger concept introduced in this paper to formalize the activation of asynchronous action reflects the approach suggested in [9].

We would also like to thank the members of ESPRIT subproject A , in particular Eddy Odijk, Wim Bronnenberg, and Hans Oerlemans for many hours of fruitful discussions.

* This work was partially supported by ESPRIT-project 415A.

FOOTNOTES

1 In the context of ADL's the term "functional" is used to denote an explicit behavioural description.
2 As an extreme example, consider two programs which do not communicate and which run on different nodes of a multiprocessor architecture.
3 We use "atomic action" and "operation" as synonyms.
4 Note that this does not imply, that a delayed operation will eventually be granted access to the shared variable. Any protocols regulating a disciplined access to shared variables would have to be explicitly specified in AADL, as shown in the specification of access to the "buffer". The serialization-assumption simply models the fact, that on the physical level race-conditions may occur which determine the order of accessing memory, which are unpredictable at the observed level.
5 The state "continue" triggers an operation constructing a frame.

REFERENCES

[1] Annot, J.K., and van Twist, R.
    Description of the communication processor of DOOM, Proceedings Conference on Parallel Architectures and Languages Europe, Lecture Notes in Computer Science, Springer-Verlag, June 1987

[2] Barbacci, M.R.,
    Structural and behavioural descriptions of digital systems, New Computer Architectures (eds. J. Tiberghien), International Lecture Series in Computer Science, 1984, pp. 140-223

[3] Bergstra, J.A., and Klop, J.W.,
    Algebra of Communicating Processes, Proceedings of the CWI Symposium Mathematics and Computer Science (eds. J.W. de Bakker, M. Hazewinkel and J.K. Lenstra), North-Holland, Amsterdam 1986

[4] Berthelot, G., and Terrat, R.,
    Petri Nets Theory for the Correctness of Protocols, Proceedings of the IFIP WG 6.1 Second International Workshop on Protocol Specification, Testing, and Verification (eds. C. Sunshine), North-Holland, 1982

[5] Cardelli, L.,
    ML under UNIX, Polymorphism Newsletter Vol. 1, No. 3, 1983

[6] Clarke, E.M., Emerson, E.A., and Sistla, A.P.,
    Automatic Verification of Finite-State Concurrent Systems Using Temporal Logic Specifications, ACM Transactions on Programming Languages and Systems, Vol. 8., No. 2, April 1986, pp. 244-263

[7] Dasgupta, S.,
The Design and Description of Computer Architectures, John Wiley & Sons, New York, 1984

[8] Dasgupta, S.,
Computer Design and Description Languages, Advances in Computers, Vol. 21, Academic Press, New York, 1982, pp. 91–154

[9] Dasgupta, S., and Heinanen, J.,
On the Axiomatic Specification of Computer Architectures, Proc. CHDL '85, North–Holland, 1985

[10] Damm, W.,
Automatic Generation of Simulation Tools: A Case Study in the Design of a Retargetable Firmware Development System, in: Advances in Microprocessing and Microprogramming, edts. B. Myhrhaug and D.R. Wilson, EUROMICRO, Elsevier Science Publishers B.V., North–Holland, 1984, pp. 165–176

[11] Damm, W., Döhmen, G., Merkel, K., and Sichelschmidt, M.,
The AADL/S*–Approach to Firmware Design Verification, IEEE Software Magazine, Vol. 3, No. 4, 1986, pp. 27–37

[12] Hudak, P., and Smith, L.,
Para–Functional Programming: A Paradigm for Programming Multiprocessor Systems, Proc. 13th POPL, 1986

[13] Klaeren, H.,
An Introduction into Algebraic Specifications, Springer–Verlag, 1986

[14] Lamport, L.,
Specifying Concurrent Program Modules, ACM Trans. Program. Lang. Systems, Vol. 5, 1983, pp. 190–222

[15] Lamport, L.,
"Sometime" is sometimes "not never", Proc. POPL '80, pp. 174–185

[16] Loogen, R.,
PAM – A parallel abstract reduction machine for the implementation of serial combinator systems, technical report, RWTH Aachen, 1987

[17] Manna, Z., and Pnueli, A.,
Temporal Verification of Concurrent Programs: The Temporal Framework, The Correctness Problem in Computer Science (eds. R.S. Boyer, J. Strother Moore), International Lecture Series in Computer Science, 1981, pp. 215–273

[18] Milner, R.,
A Calculus of Communicating Systems, Lecture Notes in Computer Science 92, Springer–Verlag, Berlin, 1980

[19] Odijk, E.A.M.,
The Philips Object–Oriented Parallel Computer, in: Fifth Generation Computer Architectures, edt. J.V. Woods, North–Holland, 1985

[20] Odijk, E.A.M., van Twist, R., Janssens, M., and Bronnenberg, W.,
The Architecture of DOOM, Proc. of the ESPRIT Summer School on Future Parallel Computers, Lecture Notes in Computer Science, Springer–Verlag, 1987

[21] Olderog, E.–R.,
Specification–oriented programming in TCSP, in: Logics and Models of Concurrent Systems (eds. K.R. Apt), NATO ASI Series, Series F: Computer and System Sciences. Vol. 13, Springer–Verlag, 1985

[22] Pinter, S.S., and Wolper, P.,
A Temporal Logic for Reasoning about Partially Ordered Computations, Proceedings of the Third Annual Symposium on Principles of Distributed Computing, 1984

[23] Reisig, W.,
Petrinetze, Springer–Verlag, Berlin, 1982

[24] Warren, D.H.D.,
An Abstract Prolog Instruction Set, SRI Technical Report, SRI International, Monto Park, CA, 1983

[25] Hoare, C.A.R.
Communicating Sequential Processes, Communications ACM, Vol. 21, 1978, pp. 666–677

Computing on a Systolic Screen: Hulls, Contours and Applications

Frank Dehne, Jörg-Rüdiger Sack and Nicola Santoro

School of Computer Science

Carleton University

Ottawa, Ontario

Canada K1S 5B6

1. INTRODUCTION

A *digitized plane* Π of size M is a rectangular array of lattice points (or pixels) with integer coordinates (i,j), where i,j$\in$\{1,..., $\sqrt{M}$ \}. A subset S$\subseteq \Pi$ is called an *image* (or digitized picture) on Π; its complement Π-S is denoted by S^c.

A *systolic screen* of size M is a $\sqrt{M}$ x $\sqrt{M}$ mesh-of-processors where each processing element P_{ij} represents the lattice point (i,j). A systolic screen is a natural tool for the representation of images on the digitized plane. An image S can be represented by a binary "color-register" C-Reg(i,j) at ach P_{ij}, where

$$C\text{-Reg (i,j)} := \begin{cases} 1, \text{ if } (i,j) \in S \\ 0 \text{ otherwise} \end{cases}$$

A set of (disjoint) images can be represented simultaneoulsly on a Systolic screen by assigning to the C-Registers a different integer value (color) for each image. The fundamental difference between the Systolic Screen and the Mesh-Connected Processor Array (MCPA) lies in the fact that the Screen is a mapping of the entire (digitized) plane while the MCPA (e.g., see [NS80,AK84,MS84,De85]) is a compact representation of the image only.

Mesh-of-processors (or Systolic Screen) have been already used to store images: The maximum size of an image typically ranges from 256x256 pixels in computer vision in an industrial environment to 4000x4000 pixels and larger for aerial photographs. A well known existing system is the MPP designed by NASA for analysing LANDSAT satellite data [Re84]. The MPP consists of 16,384 processing units organized in a 128x128 matrix with a local memory between 1K and 16K bits for each processing unit (to represent a subsquare of pixels).

Computing on a Systolic Screen has been the subject of recent investigations by Miller and Stout [SM84, MS85] they propose O($\sqrt{M}$) algorithm for the computation of the distance between two images and the computation of the extreme points (with respect to the convex hull), diameter, and smallest enclosing circle of an image as well as for convexity and separability testing and related problems on a Mesh-of-Processors of size $\sqrt{M}$x$\sqrt{M}$.

In this paper, we continue the study of computing in a Systolic Screen and present efficient solutions for the following problems:

1) computing *all* k^{th} m-contours of an image

2) computing *all* k^{th} retilinear convex hulls.

It is shown that both algorithms require $O(\sqrt{M})$ time on a Systolic Screen of size M, i.e. they are optimal. Furthermore, the solution to the first problem yields a new parallel solution to the *longest-common subsequence problem* (e.g. [Hi77, RT85]).

Before presenting the results, we will introduce some basic notation which will be employed throughout the paper (cf. [Ro79, Ki82]). The *4-neighborhood* of a pixel (x,y) is the set of its four horizontal and vertical 4-neighbors $(x\pm1, y)$ and $(x, y\pm1)$. The *8-neighborhood* (or neighbors) of (x,y) consists of its 4-neighbors together with its four diagonal neighbors $(x+1,y\pm1)$ and $(x-1,y\pm1)$. The *border* S^O of S is the set of all points of S which have neighbors in S^C. The *interior* of S, $S-S^O$, is denoted by $S^\bullet$.

Let p,q be two points in Π. A *[4-] path* from p to q is a sequence of points $p=p_0,...,p_r=q$ such that p_i is a [4-] neighbor of p_{i-1}, $1\le i\le r$. p and q are [4-] *connected* in S if there exists a [4-] path from p to q consisting entirely of points of S. With each pixel $p=(i,j)\in\Pi$ we associate its *cell* $<p> := [i-0.5, i+0.5] \times [j-0.5, j+0.5] \subseteq R^2$ and with each image $S \subseteq \Pi$ its region $<S> := \bigcup_{p\in S} <p>$.

2. DOMINANCE PROBLEMS

2.1 Determination of All K^{th} m-Contours

Given a digitized plane Π of size M and an image $S \subseteq \Pi$, a pixel $s=(i,j)\in\Pi$ *dominates* a pixel $s'=(i',j')\in\Pi$ (abbr. $s \geq s'$) if $i \geq i'$ and $j \geq j'$; and it is called *maximal* in S if there is no other $s'\in S$ which dominates it. The set MAX(S) of all maximal pixels of S (sorted by x-coordinate) is called the *1st m-contour* of S.

The definition of contour of S can be generalized to introduce the notion of the *K^{th} m-contour* of S, denoted by MAX(S,k), $k\in N$, as follows:

$$MAX (S, 1):= MAX (S)$$

$$MAX (S, k+1):= MAX (S - (MAX(S,1) \cup ... \cup MAX(S,k))).$$

Since in a digitized plane pixels with the same x- or y-coordinate may occur very often, the following restricted definition of dominance on a digitized plane is also useful: a pixel $s=(i,j)\in\Pi$ *strictly dominates* a pixel $s'=(i',j')\in\Pi$ (abbr. $s > s'$) if $i > i'$ and $j > j'$. The kth m-contour with respect to the strict dominance relation will be denoted by $MAX^*(S,k)$.

Assume that an image $S=\{s_1,...,s_n\}$ on a digitized plane Π of size M is stored in a Systolic Screen as described above. In addition to C-Reg(i,j), each P_{ij} contains a second register K-Reg(i,j). The K-Registers are used for storing the final result, i.e. all k^{th} m-contours, as follows:

for all P_{ij} for which $(i,j)\in S$ (K-Reg(i,j) $\leftarrow$ k)   <=> $(i,j)\in MAX(S,k)$.

In Figure 1 we present an algorithm to compute all k^{th} m-contours.

Theorem 1: Algorithm ALL-MAX computes all MAX(S,k) in time $O(\sqrt{M})$.

Proof: Each processor element (PE) representing a pixel $s \in S$ sends messages which proceed towards the lower left corner of the Systolic Screen to all PEs which are dominated. Thus, in the worst case these messages have to proceed from the upper right to the lower left corner of the mesh taking time $O(\sqrt{M})$. The correctness of the algorithm can be proved by an induction on |S|: For |S| =1 the algorithm obviously provides the correct result. Thus, assume |S|>1 and let $s' \in$ MAX(S,1) be a maximal element of S. We observe that during execution of algorithm ALL-MAX the final status of the registers of each PE is independent on the order in which the PEs are reached by messages originated at other PEs representing pixels $s \in S$. Thus, we obtain the same result by applying algorithm ALL-MAX to S-{s'} and then superimposing the messages originated at s'. With this we can easily prove that algorithm ALL-MAX applied to S provides the correct result. Figure 2 shows the possible cases which might occur, when the additional messages are superimposed. •

Algorithm ALL-MAX:

(1) All PEs P_{ij} initialize their K-Register

$$\text{K-Reg}(i,j) \quad \leftarrow \quad \text{C-Reg}(i,j) \ .$$

(2) All PEs with K-Reg = 1 send the contents of their K-Register to their lower and left neighbors, if they exist.

(3) For ease of description we set $v_u, v_r = 0$ if no value is received. All PEs, P_{ij}, which receive at least one value v_u and/or v_r from their upper and/or right neighbor, respectively, update their K-Register

$$\text{K-Reg}(i,j) \quad \leftarrow \quad \max \{\text{K-Reg}(i,j), \max\{v_u, v_r\} + \text{C-Reg}(i,j)\}$$

and send the new contents of their K-Register to their directly connected lower and left neighbors, if they exist.

(4) Step (3) is iterated until there is no more PE which has received at least one message.

Figure 1

Computation of all MAX(S,k)

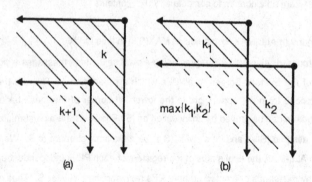

(a)   (b)

Figure 2

The algorithm for computing all MAX*(S,k), given in figure 3a, is essentially the same as the one for computing all MAX(S,k). However, we have to take into account that a pixel cannot dominate another pixel which has the same x- or y-coordinate. Thus when a PE receives a message it has to know whether this message has been passed on a direct horizontal or vertical line, yet. To provide the necessary information an additional bit b_1, b_b, respectively, is added to each message sent to a left, lower neighbor, respectively. A bit value 0 indicates that this message has been passed directly leftwards or downwards.

Algorithm **ALL-MAX***:

(1) All P_{ij} initialize their K-Registers

    K-Reg(i,j)   ←   C-Reg(i,j)

(2) All PEs with K-Reg = 1 send a message (K-Reg, 0) to their directly connected lower and left neighbors, if they exist.

(3) All PEs which receive at least one message (v_u, b_u) and/or (v_r, b_r) from their upper and right neighbor update their K-Reg and send a message (v_b, b_b) and (v_1, b_1) to their lower and left neighbor, respectively, as described in figure 3b.

(4) Step (3) is iterated until there is no more PE which has received at least one message.

Figure 3a

Computation of all MAX* (S,k)

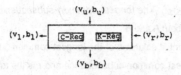

$b_u b_r$	$v_u > v_r$	$v_u = v_r$	$v_u < v_r$
* 0		[K-Reg]←max([K-Reg],v_r) b_1=0, b_b=1-[C-Reg]	
0 *		[K-Reg]←max([K-Reg],v_u) b_1=1-[C-Reg], b_b=0	
* 1		[K-Reg]←max([K-Reg],v_r+[C-Reg]) b_1=b_b=1-[C-Reg]	
1 *		[K-Reg]←max([K-Reg],v_u+[C-Reg]) b_1=b_b=1-[C-Reg]	
0 1	[K-Reg]← max([K-Reg],v_u] b_1=1-[C-Reg],b_b=0	[K-Reg]←max([K-Reg],v_r+[C-Reg]) b_1=b_b=1-[C-Reg]	
1 0	[K-Reg]←max([K-Reg],v_u+[C-Reg]) b_1=b_b=1-[C-Reg]		[K-Reg]← max([K-Reg],v_r) b_1=0,b_b=1-[C-Reg]
0 0		[K-Reg]←max([K-Reg],v_r,v_u) b_1=1-[C-Reg],b_b=0 | b_1=b_b=0	b_1=0, b_b=1-[C-Reg]
1 1		[K-Reg]←max([K-Reg],max(v_u,v_r)+[C-Reg]) b_1=b_b=1-[C-Reg]	

v_1=v_b=[K-Reg]

(* = no message)

Figure 3b

I/O Operations Performed by Each PE

Theorem 2: Algorithm ALL-MAX* computes all MAX*(S,k) in time O($\sqrt{M}$).

Proof: see [DSS86] •

The points of each kth m-contour computed by algorithm ALL-MAX* define a 4-path of pixels which we will refer to as the kth m-chain, denoted M-CHAIN(S,k), of S. We observe that upon termination of algorithm ALL-MAX*, the K-Registers of PEs of all pixels which lie on the Kth m-chain or below the kth m-chain and above the $(k+1)^{th}$ m-chain have value k. We refer to this set of pixels of S, with K-Register value equal to k, as the kth m-belt of S, and denote it by M-BELT(S,k).

Corollary 3: On a Systolic Screen of size M, all m-chains and m-belts of an image can be computed in time O($\sqrt{M}$).

2.2 The Longest Common Subsequence Problem

The proposed algorithm for parallel computation of all k^{th} m-contours yields a new parallel solution of the longest common subsequence problem which is defined as follows:

Given two strings A=A(1)...A(n) and B=B(1)...B(m), n≥m, over some finite alphabet Σ, a *substring* C of A is defined to be any string $C=C(1)\ldots C(r)$ for which there exists a monotone strictly increasing function $f:\{1,\ldots,r\} \to \{1,\ldots,n\}$ with $C(i)=A(f(i))$, for all $1\le i\le r$. The *longest common subsequence problem* is to find a string of maximum length which is a substring of both A and B.

A table of currently known sequential solutions of the longest common subsequence problem is given in figure 4 (p denotes the length of a longest common subsequence and r is the total number of ordered pairs (i,j) with $a_i=b_j$).

	Running Time	Worst-case behaviour
[HS77]	$O((r+n)\ \log\ n)$	$O(n^2\ \log\ n)$
[Hi77]	$O(p\ n)$	$O(n^2)$
[Hi77]	$O(p(m+1-p)\ \log\ n)$	$O(n^2\ \log\ n)$
[NKY82]	$O(n(m-p))$	$O(n^2)$

Figure 4

Sequential Solutions of the Longest Common

Subsequence Problem (from [RT85])

Hirschberg [Hi78] proved an $\Omega(n\ \log\ n)$ information theoretic lower bound for sequential solutions of the longest common subsequence problem. Recently, [RT85] introduced a parallel algorithm which computes a longest common subsequence in time O(n) using a one-dimensional systolic array of size m with a systolic stack of size n associated with each PE.

We will now give an O(n) time solution of the longest common subsequence problem on a Systolic Screen of size nxm such that all processing elements are of one type only (cf. [RT85]). Our solution has the additional advantage that it determines also *all* longest common subsequences in time O(n). The central idea which leads to this method is a transformation of the longest common subsequence problem to the Kth m-contour determination. This reduction was also used by Hirschberg in [Hi77].

Lemma 4:

(a) $A(i_1)\ldots A(i_r) = B(j_1)\ldots B(j_r)$ is a common subsequence of A and B if and only if $(i_1,j_1) < (i_2,j_2) < \ldots < (i_r,j_r)$.

(b) The length of a longest common subsequence is $k_{max} := \max\{k\in N/MAX^*\ (S_{A,B},k)\ne\varnothing\}$ with $S_{AB}:= \{(i,j)/\ A(i)=B(j)\}$.

Proof: see [Hi77] . •

An illustration of Lemma 4 is given in figure 5. The computation of a longest common subsequence of two strings A and B can be mapped into all m-contours problem with respect to the set S_{AB}.

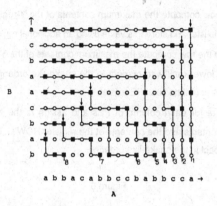

Figure 5

Before we consider the longest common subsequence problem we will first introduce the MAXBELOW searching procedure.

Given two sets P', P" of processors on a $\sqrt{n} \times \sqrt{n}$ subsquare of a Systolic Screen of size N each containing three registers X, Y, and Z (for positive numbers) then we define a procedure MAXBELOW (P', P", X, Y, Z) which results in the following:

$$(\forall p' \in P'): X(p') \leftarrow \max[\{Y(p") / p" \in P" \text{ and } Z(p") \leq Z(p') \} \cup \{ 0 \}]$$

with X(p) [Y(p), Z(p)] denoting the contents of the register X [Y, Z, respectively] contained in processor p.

Theorem 5: Procedure MAXBELOW (P',P",X,Y,Z) as described in figure 6 performs MAXBELOW search on a $\sqrt{n} \times \sqrt{n}$ submesh in time $O(\sqrt{n})$.

Procedure **MAXBELOW (P',P'',X,Y,Z):**

(1) Sort $P' \cup P''$ with respect to the contents of their register Z in snake-like ordering (cf. [TK77].

(2) Perform one shift procedure for each row of PEs and compute the following :
- For each PE in the row compute the maximum contents of the Y-registers of all PEs $p'' \in P''$ in the row (0 if no such PE exists) and store this value using an additional register ROWY.
- For each PE $p' \in P'$ in the row compute the maximum contents of the Y-registers of all PEs $p'' \in P''$ in the row which have lower rank with respect to the snake-like ordering computed in step (1) and store it into its X-register (0 if no such PE exists).

(3) Perform a shift procedure for each column of PEs and assign to the X-register of each $p' \in P'$ the maximum of its current contents and the contents of the register ROWY of all PEs in the column which have lower rank with respect to the snake-like ordering.

Figure 6

Theorem 6: Given two strings $A = A(1) \ldots A(n)$ and $B = B(1) \ldots B(m)$, $n \geq m$. Using a Mesh-of-Processors of size nxm the following problems can be solved in time $O(n)$:
(a) Computation of a longest common subsequence of A and B.
(b) Computation of _all_ longest common subsequences of A and B.

Proof: (a) see [DSS86]. (b) Given the set of all m-contours of S_{AB}. From Lemma 4 we know that each longest common subsequence is induced by a sequence $s_1, \ldots, s_r$ of points of S_{AB} such that $s_1 < \ldots < s_r$. The set of all such sequences is obtained by computing for each $s = (i,j) \in MAX^* (S_{AB}, k)$ its set of next dominances $ND(s) := \{ s' \in MAX^* (S_{AB},k-1)/s<s' \}$, $1 < k \leq k_{max}$. We observe that $ND(s) = \{ (i',j') \in MAX^* (S_{AB},k-1)/ i'>i$ and $j'>j \}$. Thus, it suffices to store for each $s=(i,j) \in MAX^* (S_{AB},k)$, $1 < k \leq_{max}$, the two values $i^* := \min \{i'>i/ (i',j') \in MAX^* (S_{AB},k-1) \}$ and $j^* := \min \{j'>j/ (i',j') \in MAX^* (S_{AB},k-1) \}$. This can be performed by a global MAXBELOW search procedure in time $O(n)$ as described above for each $[MAX^*(S_{AB},k), MAX^* (S_{AB},k-1)]$, $1 < k \leq k_{max}$, in parallel. •

3. DETERMINATION OF ALL K^{TH} RECTILINEAR CONVEX HULLS

Considerable attention has been given to finding estimators which identify the center of a set S and the depth of points with respect to S (see [Sh78], [OL81], [LP84]. For sets $S \subseteq E^2$ in the Euclidean plane Shamos (cf. [Sh78]) described a sequential $O(n^2)$ time algorithm for "peeling" S by iterating the following process: compute the convex hull (see [PS85] of S and remove its vertices from S, which is the two-dimensional analogous to the concept of the α–trimmed mean used in robust statistics (see [Sh78] p. 83 ff, [Hu72]). He also proved an $\Omega(n \log n)$ (sequential) lower bound for this problem. Subsequently Overmars and van Leeuwen [OL81] and Chazelle [Ch83] gave $O(n \log^2 n)$ and $O(n \log n)$, respectively, (sequential) solutions for this problem. Obviously all convex layers are a suitable representation of a set of point comparable with the sorted order in the one-dimensional case. Chazelle, Guibas and Lee [CGL83] demonstrated how to apply this structure to improve upon previous solutions of the halfplane range query problem.

This section will deal with the concept of "peeling" an image $S=\{s_1,\ldots,s_n\}$ of size M in a digitized plane, i.e. iterating on the following process: compute the *rectilinear* convex hull of S and remove its vertices from S.

On a Systolic Screen of size M we give an $O(\sqrt{M})$ parallel algorithm to peel an arbitrary image. We call S *rectilinear convex*, if the intersection of its region <S> and an arbitrary horizontal or vertical line in $<\Pi>$ consists of at most one line segment.

The intersection of all rectilinear convex images $S' \subseteq \Pi$ which contain S is called the *rectilinear convex hull* of S and denoted by HULL(S) : The rectilinear hull determination has been discussed in Sack [Sa84], Wood [Wo84], Monturo [Mo82]. The kth *rectilinear convex hull* HULL (S,k) and the kth *rectilinear convex belt* BELT (S,k) of S ($k \in N_0$) are defined as follows:

(a) HULL(S,O) $:= \Pi$

     HULL(S,1) $:=$ HULL(S)

     HULL(S,k+1) $:=$ HULL ((HULL(S,k) $\cap$ S) - HULL(S,k)^O)

(b) BELT(S,k) $:=$ HULL(S,k) - HULL(S,k+1)

See figure 7 for an illustration.

The maximum of all $k \in N_0$ such that HULL(S,k) $\neq \emptyset$ is called the *depth* of S and denoted by DEPTH(S).

For each pixel $s \in \Pi$ we define its depth DEPTH(s,S) in S:

DEPTH(s,S):=k $:<=>$ $s \in$ BELT(S,k).

Obviously, DEPTH(S) = max {DEPTH(s,S)/ $s \in \Pi$ }.

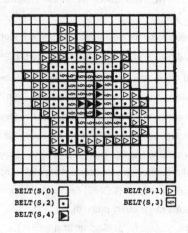

Figure 7
All BELT(S,k) of an Image S

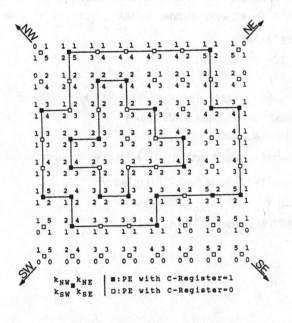

Figure 8

Given a pixel $s \in \Pi$. We define $k_{NE}(s,S):=k$ $[k_{SE}(s,S):=k, k_{SW}(s,S):=k, k_{NW}(s,S):=k]$ if $s \in M\text{-BELT}(S,k)$ with respect to the NE-direction [SE-direction, SW-direction, NE-direction, respectively], see figure 8 for an illustration.

Lemma 7:

(a) $(\forall s \in \Pi)$: $s \in \text{BELT}(S,k)$ $\iff$ $\min\{k_{NW}(s,S), k_{SW}(s,S), k_{NE}(s,S), k_{SE}(s,S)\} = k$

(b) $(\forall\ 0 \leq k \leq \text{DEPTH}(S))$: $\text{BELT}(S,k) = \{\ s \in \Pi/\min\{k_{NW}(s,S), k_{SW}(s,S),\ k_{NE}(s,S), k_{SE}(s,S)=k\}$

(c) $\text{DEPTH}(S) = \max \{\ \min\{k_{NW}(s,S), k_{SW}(s,S), k_{NE}(s,S), k_{SE}(s,S)\ \}\ /\ s \in \Pi\ \}$

This yields the following

Theorem 8: On a Systolic Screen of size M all k^{th} rectilinear convex hulls HULL(S,k), all rectilinear convex belts BELT(S,k) and the depth DEPTH(S) of an image S can be computed in time $O(\sqrt{M})$.

REFERENCES

[AG85] M.J. Atallah, M.T. Goodrich, EFFICIENT PARALLEL SOLUTIONS TO GEOMETRIC PROBLEMS, Report CSD-TR-504, Purdue Univ., March 1985

[AHU76] A.V. Aho, D.S. Hirschberg, J.D. Ullamn, BOUNDS ON THE COMPLEXITY OF THE LONGEST SUBSEQUENCE PROBLEM, J. ACM, Vol. 23, No. 1, 1976, pp 1-12

[AH85] M.J. Atallah, S.E. Hambrusch, SOLVING TREE PROBLEMS ON A MESH-CONNECTED PROCESSOR ARRAY, Report CSD-TR-518, Purdue Univ., West Lafayette, April 1985.

[AK84] M.J. Attalah, S.R. Kosaraju, GRAPH PROBLEMS ON A MESH-CONNECTED PROCESSOR ARRAY, J. ACM, Vol. 31, No. 3, July 1984, pp 649-667

[Ch83] B.M. Chazelle, OPTIMAL ALGORITHMS FOR COMPUTING DEPTHS AND LAYERS, Proc. 21st Allerton Conference on Communication Control and Computing, Oct. 1983, pp 427-436

[Ch84] B.M. Chazelle, COMPUTATIONAL GEOMETRY ON A SYSTOLIC CHIP, IEEE Trans. on Computers, Vol. C-33, No. 9, Sept. 1984, pp.774-785

[CGL83] B.Chazelle, L.J.Guibas, D.T./Lee, THE POWER OF GEOMETRIC DUALITY, Proc. 24th IEEE Symp. on Found. of Computer Science, Tucson, Ariz., 1983

[De85a] F. Dehne, SOLVING GEOMETRIC PROBLEMS ON MESH-CONNECTED AND ONE DIMENSIONAL PROCESSOR ARRAYS, in H. Noltemeier (ed.), Proceedings of the WG'85 International Workshop on Graphtheoretic Concepts in Computer Science, June 18-21, 1985, Linz: Trauner Verlag, 1985, pp 43-59

[De85b] F. Dehne, A ONE DIMENSIONAL SYSTOLIC ARRAY FOR THE LARGEST EMPTY RECTANGLE PROBLEM, Proc. of the 23rd Annual Allerton Conference on Communication, Control and Computing, Monticello, Illinois, October 2-4, 1985, pp 518-528

[De85c] F. Dehne, $O(N^{1/2})$ ALGORITHMS FOR THE MAXIMAL ELEMENTS AND ECDF SEARCHING PROBLEM ON A MESH-CONNECTED PARALLEL COMPUTER, Information Procesing Letters, Vol 22, No 6, May 1986, pp 303-306

[DL81] P.E. Danielson, S. Levialdi, COMPUTER ARCHITECTURE FOR PICTORIAL INFORMATION SYSTEMS, IEEE Computer, Nov. 1981

[DSS86] F. Dehne, J.-R. Sack, N. Santoro, COMPUTING ON A SYSTOLIC SECREEN: HULLS, CONTOURS AND APPLICATIONS, Tech. Rept. , School of Computer Science, Carleton University, Ottawa, July 1986.

[[Ha83] S.E. Hambrusch, VLSI ALGORITHMS FOR THE CONNECTED COMPONENT PROBLEM, SIAM J. COMPUT., Vol. 12, No. 2, May 1983, pp.354-365

[Hi77]   D.S. Hirschbeg, ALGORITHMS FOR THE LONGEST COMMON SUBSEQUENCE PROBLEM, J.ACM, Vol. 24, No. 4, 1977, pp 664-675

[Hi78]   D.S. Hirschberg, AN INFORMATION THEORETIC LOWER BOUND FOR THE LARGEST COMMON SUBSEQUENCE PROBLEM, Inform. Proc. Lett., Vol. 7, No. 1, 1978, pp 40-41

[Hu72]   P.J.Huber, ROBUST STATISTICS: A REVIEW, Ann. Math. Stat., Vol.43, No.4, 1972, pp 1041-1067

[HF83]   K. Hwang, K.S. Fu, INTEGRATED COMPUTER ARCHITECTURES FOR IMAGE PROCESSING AND DATABASE MANAGEMENT, IEEE Computer, Vol.16, pp.51-61, Jan. 1983

[HS77]   J.W. Hunt, T.G. Szymanski, A FAST ALGORITHM FOR COMPUTING LONGEST COMMON SUBSEQUENCES, C. ACM, Vol. 20, 1977, pp 350-353

[Ki82]   C.E. Kim, DIGITAL DISKS, Report CS-82-104, Computer Science Dept., Washington State University, Dec. 1982

[Kl79]   R.Klette, A PARALLEL COMPUTER FOR IMAGE PROCESSING, Elektronische Informationsverarbeitung und Kybernetik, EIK 15 (1979) 56/6, pp.237-263

[Le79]   C.E. Leiserson, SYSTOLIC PRIORITY QUEUES, Proc CALTECH Conference on VLSI, (ed. C. E. Leitz), California Institut of Technologies, Pasadana, CA, 1979

[[LP84]   D.T. Lee, F.P. Preparata, COMPUTATIONAL GEOMETRY - A SURVEY, IEEE Trans. on Computers, Vol. C-33, No. 12, Dec. 1984, pp 1072-1101

[LP85]   E. Lodi, L. Pagli, A VLSI ALGORITHM FOR A VISIBILITY PROBLEM, in Bertolazzi, Luccio (Ed.), 'VLSI: Algorithms an Architecures', North Holland, 1985

[Mi84]   P.L. Mills, THE SYSTOLIC PIXEL: A VISIBLE SURFACE ALGORITHM FOR VLSI, Computer Graphics Forum 3, North Holland 1984

[Mo70]   G.U. Montanari, ON LIMIT PROPERTIES IN DIGITIZATION SCHEMES, J. ACM 17, 1970, pp 348-360

[Mo82]   M.F. Montuno, A. Fournier FINDING THE X-Y CONVEX HULL OF A SET OF X-Y POLYGONS", Report, CSRG-148, University of Toronto, Toronto, Nov. 1982.

[MS84]   R. Miller, Q.F. Stout, COMPUTATIONAL GEOMETRY ON A MESH-CONNECTED COMPUTER, Proc. Int. Conf. on Parallel Processing, 1984

[MS85]   R. Miller, Q.F. Stout, GEOMETRIC ALGORITHMS FOR DIGITIZED PICTURES ON A MESH-CONNECTED COMPUTER, IEEE Trans. on Pattern Analysis and Machine Intelligence, Vol. PAMI-7, No. 2, March 1985, pp 216-228

[NKY82]   N. Nakatsu, Y. Kambayashi, S. Yajima, A LONGEST COMMON SUBSEQUENCE ALGORITHM SUITABLE FOR SIMILAR TEXT STRINGS, Acta Informatica 18 (1982), pp 171-179

[NS79]   D. Nassimi, S. Sahni, BITONIC SORT ON A MESH-CONNECTED PARALLEL COMPUTER, IEEE Trans. on Computers, Vol. C-28, No. 1, Jan. 1979, pp.2-7

[NS80]   D. Nassami, S. Sahni, FINDING CONNECTED COMPONENTS AND CONNECTED ONES ON A MESH-CONNECTED PARALLEL COMPUTER, SIAM J. COMPUT., Vol. 9, No. 4, Nov. 1980, pp.744-767

[NS81]   D. Nassimi, S. Sahni, DATA BROADCASTING IN SIMD COMPUTERS, IEEE Trans. on Computers, Vol. C-30, No. 2, Feb. 1981,pp 101-106

[OL81]   M.H. Overmars, J.V. Leeuwen, MAINTENANCE OF CONFIGURATIONS IN THE PLANE, Report RUU-CS-81-3, Dept. of Computer Science, Univ. of Utrecht, Feb. 1981

[Pr84]   F.P. Preparata, VLSI ALGORITHMS AND ARCHITECTURES, Proc. Mathematical Foundations of Computers Science, Praha 1984, Lecture Notes in Computer Science 176, Springer 1984, pp 149-161

[PS85]   F.P. Preparata, M.I. Shamos, COMPUTATIONAL GEOMETRY, Springer 1985

[Re84]   A.P. Reeves, SURVEY, PARALLEL COMPUTER ARCHITECTURES FOR IMAGE PROCESSING, Computer Vision, Graphics, and Image Processing 25, 1984, pp 68-88

[Ro79]   A. Rosenfeld, DIGITAL TOPOLOGY, Amer. Math. Monthly 86, 1979, pp 621-630

[RT85]   Y. Robert, M. Tchuente, A SYSTOLIC ARRAY FOR THE LONGEST COMMON SUBSEQUENCE PROBLEM, Inform. Proc. Lett., Vol. 21, Oct. 1985, pp 191-198

[Sa84]   J.-R. Sack, RECTILINEAR COMPUTATIONAL GEOMETRY, Technical Report SCS-TR-54, School of Computer Science, Carleton Univ., Ottawa, June 1984

[Sh76]   M.I. Shamos, GEOMETRY AND STATISTICS: PROBLEMS AT THE INTERFACE, in J.F. Traub (ed.), Algorithms and Complexity, Academic Press, New York 1976, pp.251-280

[Sh78]   M.I. Shamos, COMPUTATIONAL GEOMETRY, Ph.D. Thesis, Yale Univ., 1978

[SM84]   Q.F.Stout, R.Miller, MESH-CONNECTED COMPUTER ALGORITHMS FOR DETERMINATING GEOMETRIC PROPERTIES OF FIGURES, 7th Int. Conf. on Pattern Recognition, Montreal, Canada, July 30 - August 2, 1984

[Sn81] L. Snyder, OVERVIEW OF THE CHIP COMPUTER, in VLSI 81: Very Large Scale Integration (ed. J.P. Gray), Academic Press, London, 1981, pp.237-246

[Sn82] L. Snyder, INTRODUCTION TO THE CONFIGURABLE HIGHLY PARALLEL COMPUTER, IEEE Computer 15 (1), Jan. 1982, pp.47-65

[Sp85a] Th. Spindler, BILDVERARBEITUNG ALS WERKZUEG FÜR COMPUTATIONAL GEOMETRY PROBLEM?, Lecture presented at 3rd Workshop on Computational Geometry, Karlsruhe, March 1985

[Sp85b] Th. Spindler, private communication

[St83] Q.F. Stout, MESH-CONNECTED COMPUTERS WITH BROADCASTING, IEEE Trans. on Computers, Vol. C-32, No. 9, Sept. 1983, pp826-830

[TK77] C.D. Thompson and H.T. Kung, SORTING ON A MESH-CONNECTED PARALLEL COMPUTER, Comm. of the ACM, Vol. 20, No. 4, April 1977, pp. 263-270

[Ul84] J.D. Ullman, COMPUTATIONAL ASPECTS OF VLSI, Principles of Computer Science Series, Computer Science Press, 1984

[Un58] S.H.Unger, A COMPUTER ORIENTED TOWARDS SPACIAL INTERACTION, Proc. IRE, Vol.46, 1958, pp. 1744-1750

[Wo84] D. Wood, AN ISOTHETIC VIEW OF COMPUTATIONAL GEOMETRY, in Computational Geometry, (ed. G.T. Toussaint), North Holland, 1984, pp. 429-459

MULTIPROCESSOR SYSTEMS PROGRAMMING IN A HIGH-LEVEL DATA-FLOW LANGUAGE*

J.L. Gaudiot and L.T. Lee

Computer Research Institute
Department of Electrical Engineering - Systems
University of Southern California
Los Angeles, California
(213) 743-0249

Abstract

The data-flow model of computation is an attractive methodology for multiprocessor programming for it offers the potential for unlimited parallelism detection at no programmer's expense. It is here applied to a distributed architecture based on a commercially available microprocessor (the Inmos Transputer). In this project, we have integrated the high-level data driven principles of scheduling within the Transputer architecture so as to provide high programmability of our multicomputer system. A complete programming environment which translates a complex data-flow program graph into occam has been developed and is presented in this paper. We here describe in detail the mapping from the SISAL high-level constructs into the low-level mechanisms of the Transputer (synchronization, structure representation, etc.). The partitioning issues (granularity of the graph) are presented and several solutions based upon both data-flow analysis (communication costs) and program syntax (program structure) are proposed and have been implemented in our programming environment. Finally, we present and analyze graph allocation and optimization schemes to improve the performance of the resulting occam program.

I. INTRODUCTION

The programmability of the multiprocessors of the next generation is generally recognized to be the major issue to confront designers. Several methodologies for the safe and efficient programming of parallel architectures have been proposed in order to deal with these problems. These languages include concurrent PASCAL and ADA (Andrews, 1983). Among the constructs which enable the specification of parallelism, operations may authorize the execution in parallel of two or more processes. Similarly, processes may be synchronized on data dependencies by the introduction of shared variables. In order to ensure the proper ordering of the various updates to a specific cell of memory, the programmer must specify *critical sections* for the program which essentially lock out the access of some specific cells of memory until they have been safely updated by a single process.

As technology progresses, it will be possible to integrate very large numbers of processors in the same machine. The explicit parallelism specification is therefore a complicated problem with large multiprocessor systems since the number of tasks that must be kept concurrently ac-

---
*This material is based upon work supported in part by the National Science Foundation under Grant No. CCR-8603772 and by the USC Faculty Research and Innovation Fund

ive becomes very large. For instance, the Cray X-MP-4 contains up to 4 processors around a shared memory system but the upcoming Cray-3 will include 16 processors. This demonstrates the need for a new approach for the programming of large multiprocessor systems.

Backus (1978) has introduced functional languages as a way to unshackle the programmer from the structure of the machine. Indeed, instead of considering instructions which can modify memory cells, the functional model of computation assumes functions which are applied to values, producing result values. This model of execution does not have recourse to architectural notions. Moreover, the executability of an instruction is decided by the availability of its operands. This can be implemented in a distributed fashion, thereby obviating the need for the central program counter of the von Neumann paradigm.

Data-flow systems (Dennis, 1974) obey functional principles of execution. They implement a low level description of the execution mechanisms which govern a functional multicomputer architecture. In addition, high-level languages such as VAL (McGraw, 1982), Id (Arvind, Gostelow, and Plouffe, 1978), LAU (Syre et al., 1977), and HDFL (Gaudiot et al., 1985) have been proposed as a high level interface.

While this approach brings a solution to many multiprocessing problems (Arvind and Iannucci, 1983), several data-flow projects exploit the parallelism inherent in data-flow programming by the introduction of complex custom-made Processing Elements. We describe here a multiprocessor architecture based on off-the-shelf components which can be programmed under the data-flow model of computation. The research presented here demonstrates the applicability of the functional mode of execution to such a problem. We have chosen for this work the high-level functional language SISAL (Streams and Iterations in a Single Assignment Language) developed at the Lawrence Livermore National Laboratory by McGraw and Skedzielewski (1984). Note that this language has also been chosen for high-level language programming of the University of Manchester data-flow machine (Gurd et al., 1985).

The purpose of this paper is to demonstrate and describe in detail a methodology for multiprocessor systems programming. The schemes demonstrated are to be used as a testbed for future research in MIMD systems. The underlying architecture to which this effort has been applied as well as the integrated programming environment are described in section 2. The low level model of execution of the Inmos Transputer (the language occam) upon which the architecture is based, is presented in section 3.1. High-level language programmability is afforded by the data-flow language SISAL (sections 3.2 and 3.3.) The partitioning methods of the SISAL compiler output, as well as the translation mechanisms into occam are demonstrated in section 4. In section 5, we show the partitioning and optimization mechanisms which have been developed. The mapping mechanisms from SISAL high-level constructs are demonstrated in section 6, along with an illustrative example. Finally, some concluding remarks are drawn in section 7.

II. A MULTIPROCESSOR ARCHITECTURE
AND ITS PROGRAMMABILITY

This machine, called the TX16, has been described earlier in detail by Gaudiot *et al.* (1986). The elementary building block of the TX16 is the Transputer, manufactured by Inmos, Ltd. The Transputer is a new generation microprocessor which possesses not only a memory bus (data, address, and control) for communication with the outside, but also four serial links for transmission of data to and from the on-chip memory. Special on-chip interface circuitry allows the transmission of data packets between two Transputers connected by serial links. In addition (see Fig. 1), the processors are organized around a central memory system for transmission of large data structures. In this fashion, scalar data as well as synchronization messages can be sent over the serial interconnection links, while larger arrays can be exchanged and broadcast through the shared memory system.

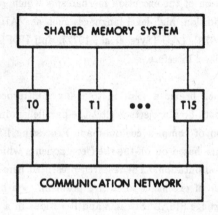

Fig. 1. The TX16

The TX16 can also be considered the elementary building block of a larger multiprocessor system. This architecture has also been described by Gaudiot *et al.* (1986), and takes the form of a hierarchical structure in which memory requests can be made at any level of the hierarchy. In other words, all the processors communicate through the interconnection network described above. This type of communication is made on a single level only. In addition, the shared memory system is built on the concept of *clusters* similar to the CM* (Gehringer *et al*, 1982). The TX16 is a cluster of processors. These can be further grouped into clusters of clusters at any level desired for the target architecture. As memory requests must be routed through more levels in the hierarchy, delays correspondingly increase. The effect of these penalties have been described in detail by Gaudiot and Dubois (1985) and their study is beyond the scope of this paper.

Since the number of processors which may ultimately be contained in this system is quite large, it appears that an explicit approach to parallelism specification by the programmer is quite unfeasible. The programmability afforded by functional principles of execution has therefore been adopted for the project. SISAL is the choice for our high-level language. Its output IF1 (Intermediate Form 1) is essentially a high-level data dependency graph which contains information concerning the structure of the original user's program. First, a high-level partitioning of the original program is made, based on the program structure as well as on heuristics. This creates processes which can be directly translated into occam constructs. The approach has been termed **occamflow** for it integrates principles of data-flow programming with the programming of a parallel architecture which supports the occam language.

III. PARALLEL PROGRAMMING LANGUAGES

We describe in this section both the high-level language (SISAL) and the low-level language (occam) which have been used in the course of this research. Particular attention is given in this section to the first step of the translation: the compilation of SISAL into an Intermediate Data-Flow Graph IF1. Note that we used for this purpose the Lawrence Livermore National Laboratory supplied SISAL compiler.

3.1. Occam

Occam (Inmos, 1984, May, 1983) is the programming language for the Transputer. Occam is directly related to CSP (Communicating Sequential Processes) as introduced by Hoare (1978). It allows the specification of processing modules and their intercommunication patterns. The basic construct in occam is the *process*. Communication is allowed between processes over *communication links* between processes. This model is evidently based upon communication by *message passing*. It allows the execution of a process when arguments have been received. This corresponds to *executability by data availability*.

An occam program can be represented as a graph where processes are nodes interconnected by links. Fig. 2. represents a simple occam program as well as its corresponding graphical representation.

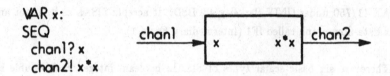

Fig. 2. A simple Occam program

There are three basic commands that can be invoked in occam: the *assignment state-*

ment , "*variable := expression*", the *input command*, " *channel ? variable*", and the *output command*, " *channel ! expression*". In addition to these simple constructs, there are some important keywords : the **VAR** keyword serves to declare the variables inside the process, an **indentation** indicates that the corresponding statements are part of the same process, the **SEQ** declaration signifies that the statements inside the process are to be executed sequentially, the **PAR** keyword indicates that the following processes are to be executed independently from each other, and the **ALT** construct is employed in cases where a subset of the input channels may be used to initiate computations within a process.

The synchronization between the occam processes is accomplished by the transmission and reception of data to and from the channels. When an output command is encountered in a process, the process is halted until another process has executed the corresponding input command. Note that the same would occur if the process with the input command was executed first. In other words, communication can occur between two processes only when they are *both ready to perform the I/O transfer*. For the input case, when an input command such as $C ? X$ is encountered, the process has to wait until the value X sent from the channel C is received.

It should be noted that the data-flow principles of execution can be directly supported by occam. The converse is not true, however, since it is possible to design unsafe occam programs which would have no corresponding part in the data-flow world. In a data-flow graph, a node corresponds to an operator, arcs are pointers for forwarding data tokens and control tokens (acknowledgement arcs), while the execution relies upon the availability of data. Alternatively, an occam process can describe the operation of a node of the data-flow graph. The function of the node is the main operation of the occam process. The input and output arcs of the node respectively correspond to the input and output channels of the occam process. At the same time, detection of data availability is achieved by the synchronization of occam channels. This mapping is made possible by the fact that both programming approaches rely upon the principles of *scheduling upon data availability*.

3.2. SISAL

SISAL (Streams and Iterations in a Single Assignment Language) is a high-level data-flow language which has been used in the course of this research. The compiler has been ported on a VAX 11/750 under UNIX Berkeley 4.2 BSD. It accepts SISAL as its input and produces a complex data-flow graph called IF1 (Intermediary Form 1).

There are six basic scalar types of SISAL: boolean, integer, real, double real, null and character. The data structure of SISAL consists of records, unions, arrays and streams. Each data type has its associated set of operations, while record, union, array and stream types are treated as mathematical sets of values just as the basic scalar types. Under the **forall** construct, these types can be used to support identification of concurrency for execution on a highly parallel processor.

Since SISAL is a single assignment language, it greatly facilitates the detection of parallelism in a program. A SISAL program comprises a set of functions. The input and output of the program is passed through a main program which is one of these functions. Fig. 3a. shows a SISAL function which adds two arrays. It will be used as an example throughout this paper.

3.3. Intermediate Form 1 (IF1)

An IF1 graph is produced by the SISAL compiler. It is a direct reflection of the original SISAL input. The IF1 graph corresponds to a combined graph of PSG (Program Structure Graph) and DFG (Data-Flow Graph). There are two kinds of nodes in IF1: compound nodes and simple nodes. A compound node can be considered as a control point which affects a sequence of actors in its controlled range. On the other hand, the simple node is the elementary processing actor; it consists of the information of its input and output arcs.

The PSG is a tree structure. It describes the relationships among the compound nodes and the simple nodes, according to the original user's program. The root and internal nodes of the tree are compound nodes, while leaves are all simple nodes. In addition to the compound nodes and simple nodes in IF1, we define a third kind of node, and call it *block node*. It is an internal node of the PSG. The block node is a dummy node which is created for the convenience of partitioning only.

Fig. 3b. is a combined graph of PSG and DFG. It corresponds to an IF1 description and describes the addition of two arrays. The corresponding SISAL program was shown in Fig. 3a. Solid lines in the graph represents the edges of the PSG and the dashed lines link the leaves to form a DFG.

```
type OneDim = array[integer];

function Aadd (A,B : OneDim ;
N : integer
returns        OneDim)

for i in 1,N
    c := A[i] + B [i] ;
    returns array of c
end for

end function
```

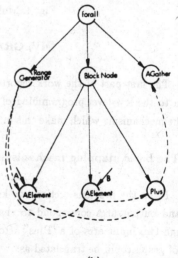

(a)   (b)

Fig. 3. Addition of two vectors

The iteration is controlled by the forall node. To process a multidimensional array, we can use multilevel forall nodes to control all successors. For instance, Fig. 4a. is a SISAL program which performs the multiplication of two N × N matrices, and its corresponding IF1 graph is shown in Fig. 4b.

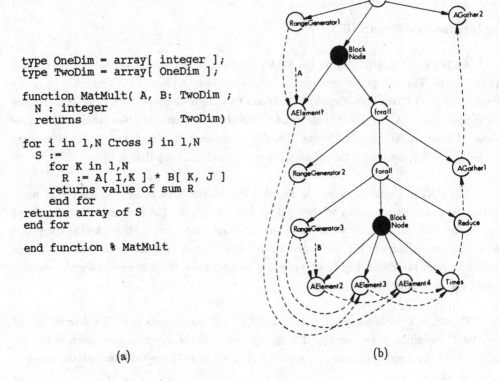

```
type OneDim = array[ integer ];
type TwoDim = array[ OneDim ];

function MatMult( A, B: TwoDim ;
  N : integer
  returns              TwoDim)

for i in 1,N Cross j in 1,N
  S :=
     for K in 1,N
       R := A[ I,K ] * B[ K, J ]
     returns value of sum R
     end for
returns array of S
end for

end function % MatMult
```

(a)   (b)

Fig. 4. Multiplication of two matrices

IV. GRAPH TRANSLATION

The first part of the work reported here is the application of functional principles of execution to the low-level programming of a multimicroprocessor system. We now describe in detail the mechanisms which make this mapping possible.

4.1. The basic mapping mechanisms

From the previous section, we know that a leaf of the PSG is an actor, and that its input and output arcs correspond to channels in occam. If two arguments x and y are passed through two input arcs of a "Plus" actor, to be the operands of this "Plus" operation, then this part of graph could be translated as:

```
C0001 ? x
C0002 ? y
```

The above discussion assumes that the addition actor is mapped into a single occam process. In this discussion, the "Plus" actor receives data x and y from the channels C0001 and C0002 respectively. After the actual operation has been completed, the sum of x and y is passed through the output of the process to the next process. This could be channel C0003. This action is translated into occam code:

$$C0003 \ ! \ x + y$$

If this result is to be sent to several actors, more than one channel should be created, and data will be sent out through all the channels that have been so declared. In summary, a simple add actor, if allowed its own occam process, will be translated by:

```
VAR  x,y :
SEQ
    PAR
        C0001 ? x
        C0002 ? y
    SEQ
        C0003 ! x+y
```

Note that the relatively complex notations will be needed for more involved program constructs and will be explained in the next section. In the above process, the operation of $x + y$ can be executed only after both values of x and y have been received. Thus, two channel input operations, " $C0001 \ ? \ x$ " and " $C0002 \ ? \ y$ ", can be performed either sequentially or in parallel. We chose in the original representation the parallel approach since it provides an additional speed-up by allowing the execution of some I/O operations before all operands have arrived.

Furthermore, if several actors are lumped together to form a group, this group could be mapped into a set of occam code, and some channels between the actors could be eliminated. For example, assume that we need to perform the function $(a+b) \times (c+d)$ in an occam process. The corresponding graph is shown in Fig. 5. The occam program is the process described by:

```
VAR  a,b,c,d :
SEQ
    PAR
        C0001 ? a
        C0002 ? b
        C0003 ? c
        C0004 ? d
    SEQ
        C0005 ! (a+b)*(c+d)
```

The input values of a, b, c, and d are received from the channels $C0001$, $C0002$, $C0003$, and $C0004$ respectively. As discussed above, these input operations can be performed either sequentially or in parallel. Note that the output value of $(a+b) \times (c+d)$ is sent out through the $C0005$ channel. This operation can be executed only after the values a, b, c and d have been received. In this process, no channel is needed to transfer the values from the outputs of these two "Plus" actors to the "Times" actor.

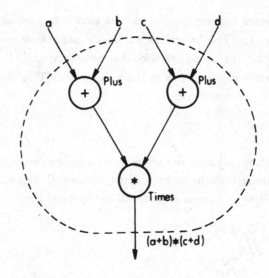

Fig. 5. A macro-actor

4.2. The translator environment

In order to execute a program in the TX16, the SISAL program should be translated into occam, the low level execution model of the Inmos Transputer.

Our translator can be logically divided into five phases: SISAL compilation, graph generation, basic partitioning, optimization, and occam code generation. Fig. 6. is an overview of a flowchart of the translator, depicting its passes instead of viewing the translator in terms of its five logical phases:

- **Pass 1** corresponds to the SISAL compilation phase. It translates the SISAL user program into IF1.

- **Pass 2** corresponds to the graph generation phase. It scans the IF1 description and generates a graph which consists of two subgraphs, the PSG (Program Structure Graph) and the DFG (Data-Flow Graph).

- **Pass 3** corresponds to the basic partitioning phase. Based on the PSG and DFG, it generates a partitioned data-flow graph (PDFG), a channel table and a communication cost matrix. Passes 2 and 3 could be combined by treating graph generation as part of the partitioning routine which scans IF1 and generates PSG and PDFG directly.

- **Passes 4 through N-1** correspond to the optimization phase. Each separate type of optimization may require several passes of re-partitioning. They also need a resource table (the number of PEs provided) to facilitate the work. A study of optimization will be discussed later.

- **Pass N** corresponds to the occam code generation phase. It traverses the PSG and PDFG, considers each partitioned group, eliminates the unnecessary channels, and generates the object occam code.

Passes 1 and 2 need no further explanation as they have been covered in detail in section 3. We will now describe the last pass (N) while the other passes will be described in detail in section 5.

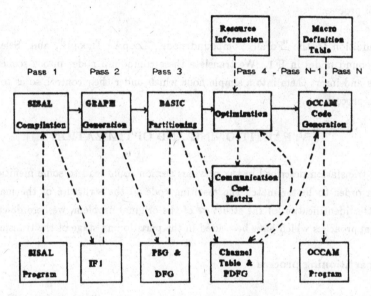

Fig. 6. The programming environment

4.3. Pass N: The translation step (Occam code generation)

The occam code generator uses the PDFG which has been produced by the previous passes. Each partitioned group corresponds to a process in the final occam program. A process will be executed in a Transputer, and all processes are allowed to execute in parallel. The data transfer between processes is performed through channels. Our occam code generator is processed in two steps: the macro instruction generation step and the macro expansion step.

In the first step, the PDFG is read to create a sequence of macro instructions. It references the channel table and takes the I/O information from the simple node as the arguments of the macro instruction. The format of a macro instruction is:

actor code , flag , partition number , arguments

The actor code is the identification of a simple node. The flag is set by the compound nodes, ancestors of the simple node which is being processed, to indicate the conditions under which this particular simple node is controlled. All simple nodes in the same partition have the same partition number. Each argument field contains two items. One of them is the argument and the other is an ID, which identifies the type of the argument and distinguishes the arguments from a channel, a literal, a function name, a vector or a scalar.

At the beginning of the second step, a macro table with definition of all actors is created. It reads the macro instruction, takes the actor code as an index to access the macro definition table, and applies the definition table to insert the arguments and expand the macro instruction to an occam process.

In addition to the "Forall" compound node, "LoopA", "LoopB", and "Select" are other major compound nodes in IF1. We translate these compound nodes into a sequence of occam instructions and insert them into a simple node which under their control, so as to form a complete occam process.

V. PARTITIONING AND OPTIMIZATION

The translation described in the previous section could lead to some inefficient code generation. In order to better match the resulting code to the structure of the machine and to make a better identification of the structure of the original problem, we here describe some optimization approaches which have been used in the partitioning stage of the translation.

5.1. The partitioning process

The goal of an effective partitioning is to increase the utilization of the PEs of the TX16, maximize the parallelism and minimize the communication costs.

To proceed with the partitioning step, the IF1 graph is translated into the PSG and DFG. A high level partitioning algorithm, based on the program structure and on heuristics which generates a PDFG (Partitioned Data-Flow Graph) can be described as follows:

1. Traverse the PSG, starting from T, the root of the PSG.
2. If T is a compound node or a block node with compound nodes as children, then go to step (3) to traverse this subtree until the tree is exhausted. Otherwise go to step (5).
3. If the current child of T is a simple node, then set this simple node in a separate partition, collect its input and output information and store the communication links (I/O channels in occam) of this partition into the channel table, and traverse the next child of T, if T has no other children then go to step (6), otherwise re-

peat this step until the child of T is not a simple node.

4. Set T = child of T, go to step (2).

5. Process the block node which contains only simple nodes : Set all the children of this block node in the same partition, collect the input and output information of this partition, and store the communication links of this partition.

6. With T = previous T, return to step (2).

This partitioning algorithm proceeds recursively: it traverses the PSG until the tree is exhausted. Applying this algorithm, a block node which contains only simple nodes will be grouped in a partition. The partition becomes a macro-actor which corresponds to an occam process, therefore the communication costs between each simple nodes of this macro-actor are eliminated. However, the degree of parallelism will be sacrificed, since the execution of this process should be sequential. Further optimization work will be discussed in the following sections. In addition to the PDFG, this procedure also creates a "Channel Table" which contains all the I/O links of a partitioned group. After partitioning, a communication cost between partitioned groups can be calculated by using the channel table and the communication cost matrix which is also generated by the partitioning procedure. We can optimize the PDFG by considering the communication costs, the load balancing as well as the degree of parallelism. In addition, the communication cost matrix can be used by the allocator for optimal task assignment.

5.2. Optimization techniques

Optimization operations such as constant folding, redundant-subexpression elimination, frequent reduction and strength reduction in the loop optimization have been done in the SISAL compilation phase of our system. The optimization strategies discussed here are mainly concerned with the minimization of communication costs as well as with the efficient implementation of array operations.

After the basic partitioning step, a communication cost matrix is generated. For the PDFG with n partitions, the communication cost matrix is a 2-dimensional $n \times n$ array, say A, with the property that $A(i,j)$ is the communication cost between processes i and j. The communication cost can be estimated to be the amount of data to be transmitted times the path length. The path length is given as $(0,1,2,\text{or } 3)$ in our mesh-interconnection network with 16 PE's.

In actuality, after the basic partitioning phase the communication cost matrix contains the data size only, while the path length will be determined after the allocation phase. In order to obtain the most efficient task assignment, two approaches have been used. These are described below.

5.2.1. Threshold method: When the number of PE's is much less than the number of partitions, a repartitioning technique will be helpful so as to reduce the number of partitions. Assuming that all PE's are completely connected, *i.e.*, the path length between different PE's is 1, we can then define a *threshold* value for repartitioning in order to allocate all the processes to the PE's and reduce the communication costs. In other words, the goal of the algorithm is to lump together those partition between which communication costs less than a specified value have been found. The algorithm of the threshold method is described below:

$$
\begin{aligned}
&Let\ D := n\ -\ 1\ ; \\
&S := \sum_{i=1}^{n-1} \sum_{j=i+1}^{n} \frac{A\,[i,j]}{D}\ ;\ \{\ determine\ the\ threshold\ value\ \} \\
&\{\ lump\ partition\ i\ and\ those\ partitions\ with\ communication\ costs > S\ together\ \} \\
&for\ i := 1\ to\ n\text{-}1\ do \\
&begin \\
&\quad for\ j := i+1\ to\ n\ do \\
&\quad if\ A[i,j] > S \\
&\quad\quad then\ partition\ i := (partition\ i)\ \cup\ (partition\ j)\ ; \\
&end\ ; \\
&\{\ lump\ two\ jointed\ partitions\ and\ eliminate\ one\ of\ them\ \} \\
&for\ i := 1\ to\ n\text{-}1\ do \\
&begin \\
&\quad for\ j := i + 1\ to\ n\ do \\
&\quad if\ (partition\ i) \cap (partition\ j) <> nil\ then \\
&\quad begin \\
&\quad\quad (partition\ i) := (partition\ i)\ \cup\ (partition\ j)\ ; \\
&\quad\quad (partition\ j) := nil\ ; \\
&\quad end\ ; \\
&end\ ; \\
&Calculate\ the\ communication\ costs\ between\ the\ new\ partitions\ ;
\end{aligned}
$$

In the algorithm, we have selected $D = n - 1$ to assure that the threshold value S will be in the range between the minimum and maximum value of A[i,j] (i,j $= 1,2,..,n$) and prevent from combining all partitions into a single partition. After repartitioning, if the number of partitions is still much greater than the number of available PE's, we may let $D = D - 1$ and repeat this procedure for further partitioning. Since the number of iterations of the loop in this algorithm is $\frac{(n+2)(n-1)}{2}$, the time complexity of the algorithm is $O(n^2)$, where n is the number of partitions.

5.2.2. Loop unrolling:

Loop unrolling is a very efficient optimization approach for array operations. This is particularly true in operations which are under the control of the IF1 "forall" pseudo-node.

In PDFG, a "forall" node contains three parts : index-generator, body and result-collector. If p PE's are available for loop unrolling, then the process of index-generator may generate p indices and propagate them through p independent channels simultaneously. The body and the result-collector parts of the "forall" node are grouped in the same partition and replicated p times. They are allocated to p separate processes and receive indices from the index-generator process through separate channels. In this case, the number of iterations is decreased from n to $\frac{n}{p}$, and p results can be created simultaneously. Thus, the speedup may approach p.

In this approach, we equally distribute the number of iterations to each unrolled body part of the loop. However, if p is large and the PE's are not complete-connected, the allocation of these unrolled processes will increase the communication costs depending on the type of the communication networks and the value p. An alternative approach that unequal distribution of the number of iterations to each unrolled body can be considered.

VI. AN EXAMPLE

As an illustration of the partitioning principles demonstrated in the previous sections, we show here a matrix multiplication as an example.

6.1. Translation

As we mentioned earlier, a SISAL program which performs the multiplication of two matrices was shown in Fig. 4a. After the SISAL compilation, the generated IF1 graph was shown in Fig. 4b. In Fig. 4b., actors "RangeGenerator1" and "RangeGenerator3", first children of nodes "forall1" and "forall3" respectively, broadcast index values i and k to the actors "AElement1" (Array Element select) and "AElement2 respectively. Once actors "AElement1" and "AElement2" receive the index values, they forward the pointers A[i,*] and B[k,*] to the actors "AElement3" and "AElement4". "AElement3" and "AElement4" are also waiting for the index values k and j which are sent from the actors "RangeGenerator3" and "RangeGenerator2", in order to generate elements A[i,k] and B[k,j] respectively. The "Times" actor receives two elements A[i,k] and B[k,j] and sends the product to the "Reduce" actor which accumulates the received data and forwards the result to actors "AGather1" as well as "AGather2" to form a two dimensional array.

Without further partitioning the above graph can be translated into an occam program which will not be shown here for simplification. Where actors "AElement2", "AElement3", "AElement4" and "Times" are in the same partition, actors "AGather1" and "AGather2" are grouped into the other partition. The remaining actors are in separate partitions. Each partition corresponds to an occam process and can be executed in parallel.

6.2. Performance evaluation

As discussed in section 3.1, a node of a data-flow graph can be directly mapped into an occam process. That is, an occam program can reflect the characteristics of an entire data-flow graph. However, describing a problem through a data-flow graph is not so easy, it requires a lot of efforts to analyze data dependencies, especially for large programs. In occamflow, it is easier and more natural for the user to develop a problem-oriented program. The effectiveness of occamflow is determined by the performance of the optimization work. The performance evaluations of our example are discussed below.

(i) *Repartitioning:* The main purpose of the repartitioning step is to match the number of the processes to the number of PE's with minimum reduction of the performance. In our example, after the basic partitioning the program of the matrix multiplication needs 7 processes in occam. If the threshold method is applied, the required processes are reduced to 5, and the communication costs among "RangeGenerator3" actor, "Reduce" actor, and "AElement2, AElement3, AElement4, Times" macro-actor are eliminated. For further repartitioning, the processes can reduced from 5 to 3 by lumping the macro-actor and the "AGather1,2" together.

The comparison of the communication costs, degree of parallelism and the execution time among these three cases are shown in Table. 6.1. From the table we can see that reduce the partitions will reduce the degree of parallelism and increase the execution time.

(ii) *Loop unrolling:* As described earlier, we expect that the speedup approaches p for a p-fold unrolling of a loop with small p. The execution time can be expressed as $T_{exe} = \lceil \frac{n}{p} \rceil T_{body-part} + T_{other-parts}$ where n is the number of the iterations and p is the number of the replications of the loop body. Table. 6.2 shows the loop unrolling case of Table 6.1. In both tables, we estimate the execution time by estimating the execution time of each actor as well as communication costs between processes. By comparing these two tables, it can be determined that increasing p and lumping the body-part of the loop will decrease the execution time. For instance, after the first repartitioning, we have 7 actors to be allocated, three of them are part of the loop body. The estimated execution time T_{11} is 8.01×10^4 cycles. If there are 16 PE's available, then 12 PE's can be used for loop unrolling, and $p = \frac{12}{3} = 4$. The execution time T_{21} is estimated as 2.02×10^4. This gives a speedup $\frac{T_{11}}{T_{21}} = \frac{8.01 \times 10^4}{2.02 \times 10^4} \simeq 4$.

VII. CONCLUSIONS

The overall goal of this project was to demonstrate a practical approach to provide high programmability to the user of a homogeneous, asynchronous MIMD architecture. For this purpose, we have chosen a functional high-level language interface (the high-level data-flow language SISAL) and have mapped it onto the low-level principles of execution of a commercially available microprocessor. The methodology developed in this work can be applied to many multiprocessor architectures because the programming environment is very modular. Program decomposition and allocation can be tailored to the target machine without modifying the initial stages of the mapping mechanisms. Note in addition that the final machine language need not necessarily be occam for the last processing box of the compiler set can be modified to fit the processor.

We have actually implemented in this paper the applicability of the data-flow principles of execution to a physically realizable multiprocessor architecture. A complete programming en-

149

vironment from high-level language to low-level principles of execution has been realized to illustrate the applicability of the data-flow approach to both low-level and high-level parallelism
specification in a multiprocessor system. We have directly implemented how the high-level
language constructs of SISAL would be mapped on the low-level mechanisms of occam and have
applied these results to an actual matrix operation problem.

We have studied several graph optimization schemes which will deliver higher performance at execution time. These include dynamic and static allocation approaches, partitioning
by communication cost thresholding as well as loop unrolling of parallel loop operations. The
performance of these methods has been evaluated and the throughput improvement notably
delivered by the latter approach has been shown to be substantial. Improvement by loop unrolling came at very low compiler cost because such vector operations are easily detectable in IF1.
Overall, the cost of compilation associated with all these schemes has been shown to be on the
order of the size of the graph or on the order of the square of the size of the graph.

Future research endeavors will include the definition of more sophisticated algorithms for
efficient allocation and partitioning of the programs. In addition, complex array handling
models such as presented by Gaudiot (1986) will be applied.

Acknowledgments: The authors would like to gratefully acknowledge the assistance of the
Computer Research Group at the Lawrence Livermore National Laboratory and particularly Dr.
James McGraw and Dr. Steve Skedzielewski. Professor Milos Ercegovac reviewed earlier drafts
of this paper and kindly provided helpful suggestions for improvement.

Table 6.1 Performance parameters without loop unrolling				
number of repartitioning	number of actors	total communication cost	degree of parallelism	estimated execution time (cycles)
1	7	$2(m+ml+mnl) = 2220$	4	$T_{11} = 8.01 \times 10^4$
2	5	$2(m+ml) = 220$	3	$T_{12} = 1.10 \times 10^5$
3	3	$2m = 20$	2	$T_{13} = 1.25 \times 10^5$

Table 6.2 Performance parametetrs with loop unrolling				
number of repartitioning	number of actors	total communication cost	degree of parallelism	estimated execution time (cycles)
1	16	$2(m+ml+mnl) = 2220$	13	$T_{21} = 2.02 \times 10^4$
2	16	$2(m+ml) = 220$	14	$T_{22} = 1.85 \times 10^4$
3	16	$2m = 20$	15	$T_{23} = 0.91 \times 10^4$

Note :

1. For the multiplication of an $m \times n$ matrix and an $n \times l$ matrix, assume that $m=n=l=10$ in the tables.
2. Assume 16 PE's are available

$$T_{11}=max([RangeGenerator\,1],[RangeGenerator\,2],[RangeGenerator\,3])+C_1+[AElement\,1]$$
$$+mnl(C_2+[Macro-actor\,1])+C_3+[Reduce]+C_4+[AGather\,1,2]=8.0\times10^4 cycles$$

$$T_{12}=max([RangeGenerator\,1],[RangeGenerator\,2])+C_1+[AElement\,1]$$
$$+mnl(C_2+[Macro-actor\,2])+C_3+[AGather\,1,2]=1.1\times10^5 cycles$$

$$T_{13}=[RangeGenerator\,1]+C_1+[AElement\,1]+mnl(C_2+[Macro-actor\,3])=1.25\times10^5 cycles$$

$$T_{21}=max([RangeGenerator\,1],[RangeGenerator\,2],[RangeGenerator\,3])+C_1+[AElement\,1]$$
$$+\lceil\frac{mnl}{4}\rceil(C_2+[Macro-actor\,1])+C_3+[Reduce]+C_4+[AGather\,1,2]=2.0\times10^4 cycles$$

$$T_{22}=max([RangeGenerator\,1],[RangeGenerator\,2])+C_1+[AElement\,1]$$
$$+\lceil\frac{mnl}{6}\rceil(C_2+[Macro-actor\,2])+C_3+[AGather\,1,2]=1.8\times10^4 cycles$$

$$T_{23}=[RangeGenerator\,1]+C_1+[AElement\,1]+\lceil\frac{mnl}{14}\rceil(C_2+[Macro-actor\,3])=0.9\times10^4 cycles$$

where [x] denotes the execution time of the actor x , and C_i's are the communication costs.
[Macro-actor1] = [AElement2,3,4,Times]
[Macro-actor2] = [RangeGenerator3,AElement2,3,4,Times,Reduce]
[Macro-actor3] = [RangeGenerator2,3,AElement2,3,4,Times,Reduce,AGather1,2]

REFERENCES

1] Andrews, G.R., *et al.*, "Concepts and Notations for Concurrent Programming," in *Computing Surveys*, Vol.15, No. 1, March 1983.

2] Arvind and Iannucci, R.A., "Two fundamental issues in multiprocessors: the data-flow solution," MIT Laboratory for Computer Science Technical Report MIT/LCS/TM-241, September 1983.

3] Arvind, Gostelow, K.P., and Plouffe, W., "An asynchronous programming language and computing machine," TR 114a, Department of Information and Computer Science, University of California, Irvine, December 1978.

4] Backus, J., "Can programming be liberated from the von Neumann style? A functional style and its algebra of programs," in *Comm. ACM 21*, 8 (Aug. 1978), pp. 613-641.

5] Dennis, J.B., "First version of a data flow procedure language," in *Programming Symp.: Proc. Colloque sur la Programmation* (Paris, France, Apr. 1974), B. Robinet, Ed., *Lecture notes in Computer Science*, vol. 19, Springer-Verlag, New York, 1974, pp. 362-376.

6] Gaudiot, J.L., Dubois, M., Lee, L.T., and Tohme, N., "The TX16: a highly programmable multimicroprocessor architecture," in *IEEE Micro*, October 1986.

7] Gaudiot, J.L, Vedder, R.W., Tucker, G.K, Finn, D., and Campbell, M.L., "A Distributed VLSI Architecture for Efficient Signal and Data Processing," in *IEEE Transactions on Computers, Special Issue on Distributed Computing Systems*, December 1985.

8] Gaudiot, J.L., "Methods for handling structures in data-flow systems," in *Proc. of the 12th International Symposium on Computer Architecture*, Boston, Massachusetts, June 1985.

9] Gaudiot, J.L., and Dubois, M., "Allocation and partitioning issues in a hierarchically structured multiprocessor system," USC CRI Technical Report, March 1985.

[10] Gehringer, E.F., *et al.*, "The Cm* Testbed," in *IEEE Computer*, October 1982.

[11] Gurd, J.R., Kirkham, C.C., and Watson, I., "The Manchester data-flow computer," in *Communications of the ACM, Vol. 28, Number 1*, January 1985, pp. 34-52.

[12] Hoare, C.A.R., "Communicating sequential processes," in *Communications of the ACM, Vol. 21, Number 8*, August 1978.

[13] Inmos, Ltd., "Occam Programming System: Reference Manual," Colorado Springs, CO, 1984

[14] May, D., "Occam," Inmos technical notes, 1983

[15] McGraw, J., and Skedzielewski, S., "SISAL: Streams and Iteration in a Single Assignment Language, Language Reference Manual, Version 1.2," Lawrence Livermore National Laboratory Technical Report M-146, March 1985.

[16] McGraw, J.R., "Data-flow computing: the VAL language," *ACM Transactions on Programming Languages and Systems 4*, 1 (1982), pp. 44-82.

[17] Syre, J.C., Comte, D., and Hifdi, N., "Pipelining, parallelism and asynchronism in the LAU system," in *Proc. 1977 Int. Conf. Parallel Processing*, Aug. 1977, pp. 87-92.

THE TWISTED CUBE

Peter A. J. Hilbers

Marion R. J. Koopman

Jan L. A. van de Snepscheut

Department of Mathematics and Computing Science

Groningen University, The Netherlands

0. Abstract

Properties that make the binary cube an attractive interconnection network for many-processor machines include expansibility, a simple routing-algorithm, and a diameter that grows logarithmically with the number of processors. In this paper we introduce an operation called *twist* that diverts two edges. By applying a twist to a number of judiciously chosen edges a cube is transformed into a so-called twisted cube. We show that the twisted cube has a diameter which is roughly half the diameter of the original cube, that a routing algorithm exists, albeit a more complex one, and that expansibility is retained.

1. Introduction

Efficiency considerations show that message-passing machines are more attractive than shared-storage machines; the greater the number of processors, the greater the advantage (cf. [2]). Message-passing machines are also simpler to design because of the separation of processor-storage communication and interprocessor communication. Again for efficiency reasons, it is preferable that each processor (or node) is connected through point-to-point channels (or edges), rather than through busses, to some other nodes to form a communications network. In order to be useful, the network should have a number of sometimes conflicting properties, including regular structure, expansibility, small diameter, and simple routing. The regularity and expansibility requirements are sometimes met by letting the network be the cartesian product of networks that satisfy these properties (cf. [2]). An extreme example hereof is the binary n-cube or hypercube, that we shall refer to as n-cube or cube. Although the simplicity of the construction may simplify the analysis of diameter and routing, we conjecture that it leads to too much symmetry: the networks obtained by the cartesian product contain too many similar routes and, therefore, have an unnecessarily large diameter. In this paper we show that, in the case of the cube, breaking the symmetry may roughly halve the diameter. In section 2 we introduce an operation called *twist* that diverts two edges. Application of a twist to a number of judiciously chosen edges transforms a cube into a twisted cube. In section 3 we give an inductive definition of a twisted cube. Next we present an algorithm for computing a shortest route between any two nodes, and we compute the diameter. In this paper we restrict ourselves to (twisted) cubes of odd dimension. Similar but not identical definitions and results exist for even dimension.

2. The twist operation

The twist is an operation defined on two edges that have no nodes in common. The operation consists of adding two new edges and removing the two edges to which it is applied. The new edges connect a node of one of the two edges to which the twist applies and a node of the other edge, and connect the remaining two nodes. Notice that two ways exist of twisting any two edges. If multiple edges between nodes are to be disallowed not every twist is feasible. Observe that a twist does not affect the number of edges incident to a node. As an example, a twist may be applied to a cube of dimension 3 yielding a twisted cube, as illustrated in figure 0.

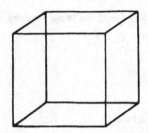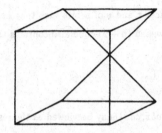

Figure 0. Cube and twisted cube.

It so happens that the particular twist chosen in the example yields a network whose diameter is 2, which is 1 less than the diameter of the original cube. Performing more twists does not reduce the diameter any further. If a different twist had been applied to the cube the diameter might have remained 3 or it might even have increased to 4. In the sequel we show that, for odd n, a twisted cube with 2^n nodes may be obtained whose diameter is $(n + 1)/2$. The number of twists performed is $(n - 1) \times 2^{n-4}$.

3. The twisted cube

In order to distinguish the nodes in a twisted n-cube each node is identified by a sequence of n bits. In a cube it is convenient to identify the nodes such that an edge is present between any two nodes that differ in one bit. In the twisted cube as constructed below an edge that results from a twist connects two nodes that differ in two adjacent bits, and two nodes that differ in one bit in the case of other edges.

Next we give an inductive definition of a twisted n-cube. Here, and in the sequel, n is an odd natural number. $\underline{P}x$ stands for the parity of bit sequence x, i.e. $\underline{P}x$ is the sum modulo 2 of the bits in x.

Definition

- $\{0,1\}$ is the edge of the twisted 1-cube.
- for any sequence x of n bits, and for any bits a, b, c, and d such that $a \neq c \wedge b \neq d$, the twisted $(n+2)$-cube contains edges

    $\{abx, cdx\}$ if $\underline{P}x = 0$, and

    $\{abx, adx\}$ if $\underline{P}x = 1$, and

    $\{abx, cbx\}$,

    and for any sequences x and y of n bits such that $\{x, y\}$ is an edge of the twisted n-cube, and for any bits a and b, the twisted $(n+2)$-cube also contains the edge

    $\{abx, aby\}$.

(End of definition)

Notice that the edges $\{abx, cdx\}$ may be viewed as the result of a twist.

From the above definition it follows that a twisted $(n+2)$-cube may be composed from 4 twisted n-cubes by adding 2^{n+2} edges. Of these added edges, 2^n edges correspond to those obtained by 2^{n-1} twists, whereas the other 3×2^n edges are non-twisted edges. The number of twists $t(n)$ performed on an n-cube to obtain a twisted n-cube is, therefore, given by

$t(1) = 0$

$t(n + 2) = 4 \times t(n) + 2^{n-1}$

from which we deduce

$t(n) = (n - 1) \times 2^{n-4}$.

Given a twisted $(n+2)$-cube, let $u \underline{c} v$ denote the presence of edge $\{u, v\}$. For bits a, b, c, and d and sequences x and y of n bits, we have the following four properties.

(0) $\underline{P}x = \underline{P}y \;\Rightarrow\; (abx \underline{c} cdx) = (aby \underline{c} cdy)$

(1) $\underline{P}x \neq \underline{P}y \wedge ab \neq cd \wedge \neg(abx \underline{c} cdx) \;\Rightarrow\; aby \underline{c} cdy$

(2) $a \neq c \wedge b \neq d \wedge \neg(abx \underline{c} adx) \;\Rightarrow\; abx \underline{c} cbx \wedge cbx \underline{c} adx$

(3) $a \neq c \wedge \neg(abx \underline{c} cdx) \;\Rightarrow\; abx \underline{c} cbx \wedge cbx \underline{c} cdx$

We conclude this section with two figures, thereby illustrating the above definitions. Figures 1 and 2 contain the twisted 3-cube and the twisted 5-cube respectively. Observe that the twisted 5-cube consists of four twisted 3-cubes, interconnected by an alternation of squares and twisted squares.

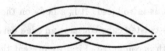

Figure 1. Another view of the twisted 3-cube.

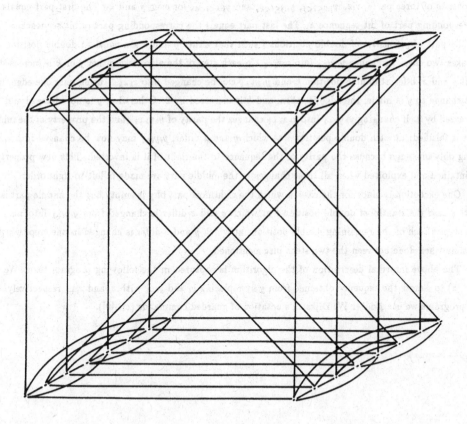

Figure 2. The twisted 5-cube.

4. Routing and diameter

In this section we discuss an algorithm for computing a path from node x to node z. Both x and z are sequences of n bits. We use x_i to denote the bit in sequence x that is preceded by i bits according to the construction given in the previous section.

In the algorithm below a variable y is introduced. It is a node on the path from x to z. Bits of y are changed one or two at a time only if the twisted cube contains an edge between the old and new value of y. It is in this sense that we say that a path is computed. First we present the algorithm informally. Next we give a formal description. Finally we compute the length of the path and the diameter of the twisted cube.

We say that y and z differ at double position i, for even i, $0 \leq i < n$, if either $i < n-1 \wedge y_i y_{i+1} \neq z_i z_{i+1}$ or $i = n-1 \wedge y_i \neq z_i$. The algorithm constucts a path from x via y to z by comparing the double positions in left-to-right order, and changing bits of y. Initially $x = y$ and upon termination $y = z$. Bit sequence y consists of three parts, viz. $y_{i:0 \leq i < j}$, $y_{i:j \leq i < k}$, and $y_{i:k \leq i < n}$, for even j and k. The first part equals the corresponding part of bit sequence z. The last part equals the corresponding part of bit sequence x. The middle part of y consists of double positions i such that either y and z are equal at double position i or it takes two edges to change $y_i y_{i+1}$ into $z_i z_{i+1}$. In each step of the algorithm either j or k is increased by 2. If y and z differ at double position k and $y_k y_{k+1}$ can be changed into $z_k z_{k+1}$ using only one edge, then this change to y is made, the edge is taken, and k is increased by 2. Otherwise, y is not changed and k is increased by 2. If changing $y_k y_{k+1}$ into $z_k z_{k+1}$ changes the parity of $y_k y_{k+1}$ then the property of the middle part is falsified: at each double position i at which y and z differ, $y_i y_{i+1}$ may now be changed into $z_i z_{i+1}$ using only one edge because the parity of the sequence to the right of it is inverted. This new property is maintained and exploited when all these changes to the middle part are made in left-to-right order.

One exception is made for the case in which the rightmost part of y is empty but the middle part isn't. In this case the rightmost double position l at which y and z differ is changed from $y_l y_{l+1}$ into $z_l z_{l+1}$ in two steps. Each of the remaining double positions at which y and z differ is changed in one step, which is possible when done between the two steps just mentioned.

The above informal description of the algorithm is captured in the following program text. We use $y(i : z)$ to denote the sequence obtained from y by replacing y_i and y_{i+1} with z_i and z_{i+1} respectively. For the programs we use Edsger W. Dijkstra's notation of guarded commands (cf. [0]).

$$j, k, d, q, y := 0, 0, 0, 0, x$$

$$; \underline{do} \; k \neq n - 1 \rightarrow$$

$$\qquad \underline{if} \; y_k y_{k+1} = z_k z_{k+1} \qquad\qquad\qquad \rightarrow skip$$

$$\qquad [\!] \; y \subseteq y(k : z) \;\wedge\; \underline{P} y_k y_{k+1} = \underline{P} z_k z_{k+1} \rightarrow y_k y_{k+1} := z_k z_{k+1}; \; d := d + 1$$

$$\qquad [\!] \; y \subseteq y(k : z) \;\wedge\; \underline{P} y_k y_{k+1} \neq \underline{P} z_k z_{k+1} \rightarrow y_k y_{k+1} := z_k z_{k+1}; \; d := d + 1; \; incj$$

$$\qquad [\!] \; y_k y_{k+1} \neq z_k z_{k+1} \;\wedge\; \neg(y \subseteq y(k : z)) \rightarrow q := q + 1$$

$$\qquad \underline{fi}$$

$$; \; k := k + 2$$

$$\underline{od}$$

$$; \underline{if} \; y_k \neq z_k \qquad\qquad \rightarrow y_k := z_k; \; d := d + 1; \; incj$$

$$\quad [\!] \; y_k = z_k \;\wedge\; q = 0 \rightarrow skip$$

$$\quad [\!] \; y_k = z_k \;\wedge\; q > 0 \rightarrow l := \underline{MAX}(i : j \leq i < k \;\wedge\; 2|i \;\wedge\; y_i y_{i+1} \neq z_i z_{i+1} : i)$$

$$\qquad\qquad\qquad\qquad ; \; y_l := 1 - y_l; \; d := d + 1; \; incj$$

$$\underline{fi}$$

where

$$incj = \underline{do} \; j \neq k \rightarrow \underline{if} \; y_j y_{j+1} = z_j z_{j+1} \rightarrow skip$$

$$\qquad\qquad\qquad\qquad [\!] \; y \subseteq y(j : z) \qquad \rightarrow y_j y_{j+1} := z_j z_{j+1}; \; q, d := q - 1, d + 1$$

$$\qquad\qquad\qquad\quad \underline{fi}$$

$$\qquad\qquad\qquad ; \; j := j + 2$$

$$\qquad\qquad \underline{od}$$

The outer loop maintains the following invariant.

$$P: \quad Q \;\wedge\; \underline{A}(i : j \leq i < k \;\wedge\; 2|i : \neg(y \subseteq y(i : z)))$$

The precondition of $incj$ is

$$Q \;\wedge\; \underline{A}(i : j \leq i < k \;\wedge\; 2|i : y_i y_{i+1} = z_i z_{i+1} \;\vee\; y \subseteq y(i : z))$$

and the postcondition of $incj$ is

$$Q \;\wedge\; j = k \; .$$

In each case Q is given by

$$Q: \quad 0 \leq j \leq k < n \;\wedge\; 2|j \;\wedge\; 2|k$$

$$\wedge \; d = \text{the number of edges constituting the path from } x \text{ to } y$$

$$\wedge \; \underline{A}(i : 0 \leq i < j : y_i = z_i) \;\wedge\; \underline{A}(i : k \leq i < n : x_i = y_i)$$

$$\wedge \; q = \underline{N}(i : j \leq i < k \;\wedge\; 2|i : y_i y_{i+1} \neq z_i z_{i+1}) \; .$$

The correctness of $incj$ is verified by choosing its precondition as an invariant of its loop.

The invariance of P in the outer loop requires some case analysis corresponding to the four alternatives in the program. The invariance of P in the first and last alternatives is straightforward. The invariance of P in the second alternative follows from property (0). The guard of the third alternative implies that, in this case, the assignment to y inverts the parity of the sequence $y_{i:k \leq i < n}$. Together with P and property (1) this implies the precondition of $incj$. From the postcondition of $incj$ we infer that P is maintained.

The loop terminates in a state satisfying $P \wedge k = n-1$. Three cases are then distinguished to complete the route to z. In the first case y_{n-1} is inverted. The presence of the corresponding edge follows from the definition of the twisted 1-cube. Together with P and property (1) this implies the precondition of $incj$. From the postcondition of $incj$ we infer $y = z$. In the second case $y = z$ follows from the guard. In the third case the parity of $y_l y_{l+1}$ is inverted using an edge whose presence follows from property (2) if $y_l = z_l$ or from property (3) if $y_l \neq z_l$. Again, the precondition of $incj$ is established. The operation $incj$ changes, among others, $y_l y_{l+1}$ into $z_l z_{l+1}$ using an edge whose presence follows from the same properties as mentioned before. The result $y = z$ follows from the postcondition of $incj$.

Next we concentrate on the length of the path from x to z. Upon termination this length equals d. Notice that $incj$ does not change $d + q$ and, therefore, it is easily seen that $d + q \leq k/2$ is an invariant of the outer loop. In the final part of the program $d + q$ may be increased by 1. Consequently, we have in any case $d + q \leq k/2 + 1$, hence $d \leq (n+1)/2$, upon termination. Observe that for various nodes x and z the equality $d = (n+1)/2$ holds, e.g. if x and z differ at every double position.

Finally we compute the diameter of the twisted cube, i.e. the smallest number such that for every pair of nodes a connecting path exists whose length is at most that number. We do so by showing that the above algorithm establishes for any x and z a shortest path. This implies that the diameter is $(n+1)/2$. From the construction of a twisted n-cube it follows that any edge connects two nodes y and z such that for some even i, $0 \leq i < n$, y and z differ at double-position i only. Hence any path between nodes x and z contains at least as many edges as double-positions at which x and z differ. In the routing algorithm presented above a path is established that contains exactly one edge per double-position at which x and z differ, with one notable exception. The exception is embodied by the last alternative in the sequence of three alternatives following the outer loop. If this case is selected $y_l y_{l+1} \neq z_l z_{l+1} \wedge \neg(y \subseteq y(l : z))$. Since in this case $\underline{A}(i : l+2 \leq i < n : y_i = z_i) \wedge \underline{P} x_{i:l+2 \leq i < n} = \underline{P} y_{i:l+2 \leq i < n}$ no ordering of the changes at double-positions from x via y to z exists that affects the parity of $y_{i:l+2 \leq i < n}$ and thereby the condition $y \subseteq y(l : z)$. Consequently, at least one extra step is needed, and the above algorithm generates exactly one extra step. As a result the algorithm establishes a shortest path between any two nodes.

5. Concluding remarks

In this paper we have presented the twisted cube. We encountered the twisted 3-cube in [2] where it is attributed to [1]. The construction of the twisted n-cube is believed to be new. It is shown that the twisted cube is expansible since four twisted cubes can be combined into a larger one. No expansible layout of the twisted cube exists, however, since the number of edges incident to a node increases as the size of the twisted cube increases, just like in the case of the cube.

159

The case of even n is very similar to the case of odd n that we have described here. The only difference is in the first of the three alternatives following the outer loop. Two steps may be needed there, rather than one, to correct the last two bits if their parity is not to change. Hence, this alternative becomes similar to the last of the three alternatives. As a result, the diameter is $(n-2)/2+2$, i.e. $n/2+1$, in the even case.

6. References

[0] Edsger W. Dijkstra
    A Discipline of Programming
    Prentice Hall, Englewood Cliffs, NJ, 1976

[1] W.D. Hillis
    The connection machine (computer architecture for the new wave)
    MIT AI Memo 646, Sept. 1981

[2] C.L. Seitz
    Concurrent VLSI Architectures
    IEEE Transactions on Computers, Vol. C-33(1984)1247-1265

An Implemented Method for Incremental Systolic Design

Chua-Huang Huang & Christian Lengauer
Department of Computer Sciences
The University of Texas at Austin
Austin, Texas 78712-1188, U.S.A.

Abstract

We present a mathematically rigorous and, at the same time, convenient method for systolic design and derive alternative systolic designs for one expository matrix computation problem: matrix multiplication. Each design is synthesized from a simple program and a proposed layout of processors. The synthesis derives (1) a systolic parallel execution, (2) channel connections for the proposed processor layout, and (3) an arrangement of data streams such that the systolic execution can begin. Our choices of alternative designs are governed by formal theorems. The synthesis method is implementable and is particularly effective if implemented with graphics capability. Our implementation on the Symbolics 3600 displays the resulting designs and simulated executions graphically on the screen. The method has also been successfully applied to other matrix computation problems.

1. Introduction

The development of programs need not immediately address implementation concerns. Instead, one can proceed in stages. One can first derive a program that conforms with the problem specification, and then derive an execution (or "trace") and provide an architecture. Programs do not contain concepts of execution but, from programs, executions can be derived for a variety of computer architectures. Such an approach bridges the gap between two separate concerns: correctness and efficiency. To keep the correctness proof simple, the program which is shown to solve the given problem should be simple. After correctness has been established, the program's execution can be complicated into a more desirable execution. The complicated execution must have exactly the input-output behavior established for the program.

This division of concerns can be of great help in program development. In the best of all worlds, where there is a proven, mechanical way to obtain efficient, complicated executions from simple programs, the programmer never has to go beyond the program in his understanding of the problem solution. In fact, he or she might even get help in constructing a suitable computer architecture without delving into the intricacies of program execution. We will provide a glimpse into such a world. We cannot deal with all programming problems, but the horizons of our world are expanding. Presently, it contains sorting problems [15] and matrix computation problems [9]. Our notion of efficiency is parallelism. Programs do not address the question of sequencing but may result in complicated, i.e., parallel executions.

For exposition, we will confine ourselves here to matrix computations - in fact, to just one matrix computation problem: matrix multiplication. We will present matrix multiplication programs and, automatically, derive parallel executions for them. We will then proceed to propose architectures that can perform these parallel executions. Our architectures will be systolic [11], i.e., they will be networks of processors that are connected in simple patterns and perform simple operations under global synchronization. We will only have to propose the layout of the processors. If it is suitable for our execution, the links of communication channels between processors and the layout and direction of the data travelling through the network can be synthesized automatically. After scrutiny of the resulting design, we might want to improve it by altering either the processor layout or the program. In our example, matrix multiplication, we will make one adjustment to the processor layout and then one adjustment to the program. Our search for alternative designs is guided by a number of theorems about our design method.

2. The Design Method

2.1. Programs

Our programs are expressed in a refinement language with the following features:

- The definition of a *refinement* consists of a refinement name with an optional list of formal parameters, separated by a colon from a refinement body. The following are the only three choices of a refinement body.
- The *null statement*, skip, does nothing.
- The *basic statement* is a statement that is not refined any further. For matrix multiplication, we will use a basic statement called the *inner product step* [11]. An inner product step accesses the elements $a_{i,k}$, $b_{k,j}$ and $c_{i,j}$ of three distinct matrices A, B, and C, respectively, and performs the operation

$$c_{i,j} := c_{i,j} + a_{i,k} * b_{k,j}$$

If variables A, B, and C are fixed, we can express the inner product step solely in terms of the matrix subscripts i, j, and k. We will use the notation $(i{:}j{:}k)$.

- The *composition S0;S1* of refinements $S0$ and $S1$ applies $S1$ to the results of $S0$. Each of $S0$ and $S1$ can be a refinement call (i.e., a refinement name, maybe, with an actual parameter list), a basic statement, or the null statement. Sequences of compositions $S0;S1;...;Sn$ are also permitted. Refinement calls may be recursive.

2.2. Traces

Following the conventional implementation of composition as sequential execution, a sequential execution is obtained from a refinement by replacing every semicolon with a right-pointing arrow. That is, program $S0;S1$ has trace $S0{\rightarrow}S1$. This implementation of composition is always safe, but may be overly restrictive. We can transform it into different executions with the same effect. Such transformations can relax sequencing and incorporate parallelism into executions. In certain cases we will execute program $S0;S1$ by trace $<S0\ S1>$ (angle brackets denote parallel execution). We call $<S0\ S1>$ a *parallel command*, and a trace with parallel commands a *parallel trace*.

We denote the length of a trace S by $|S|$ and define it as follows:

$$|stat| =_{def} 1 \qquad \text{for every basic statement stat}$$

$$|S0{\rightarrow}S1| =_{def} |S0| + |S1|$$

$$|<S0\ S1>| =_{def} \max(|S0|,|S1|)$$

The length of a trace serves as an estimate of the trace's execution time. Our estimate is rather crude. For more accurate estimates, the previous definitions can be adjusted accordingly.

2.3. Trace Transformations

Our intent is to shorten the length of a trace by a sequence of transformations. Each transformation must preserve the trace's effect. Trace transformations are justified by semantic relations that program components may or may not satisfy:

(1) A program component S that is *idempotent* can be executed once or any number of times consecutively with identical effect. Thus, $S{\rightarrow}S$ in a trace may be transformed to S, and vice versa. The idempotence of S is declared as: idem S.

(2) A program component S that is *neutral* has no effect other than that it may take time to execute. Thus, S may be omitted from or added to a trace. Neutrality implies idempotence. The neutrality of S is declared as: ntr S.

(3) Two program components $S0$ and $S1$ that are *commutative* can be executed in any order with identical effect. Thus, $S0{\rightarrow}S1$ in a trace may be transformed to $S1{\rightarrow}S0$. The commutativity of $S0$ and $S1$ is declared as: $S0$ com $S1$.

(4) Two program components $S0$ and $S1$ that are *independent* can be executed in parallel and in se-

quence with identical effect. Thus $S0 \rightarrow S1$ in a trace may be transformed to $<S0\ S1>$. Independence implies commutativity. The independence of $S0$ and $S1$ is declared as: $S0$ ind $S1$.

Semantic relations are made explicit by declarations that accompany the refinement program. The format of a semantic declaration is:

enabling predicate $\Rightarrow$ *semantic relation*

The enabling predicate is a condition on the parameters of the program components that are semantically related. Just like the correctness of refinements, the correctness of semantic declarations can be proved formally [14].

We will exploit semantic declarations for different programs in one and the same way. After having obtained a sequential trace, say l, from the program, we transform this trace into concurrency by exploiting the declared semantic relations according to the following pattern:

transform(l) = *remove-all-ntr*(*ravel-trans*(l))

Informally, *ravel-trans*(l) ravels all basic statements in l, one by one, from right to left to a parallel trace. First, the right-most basic statement is ravelled into the empty trace to form a single-statement parallel command. Then each of the remaining basic statements in l is ravelled into the parallel trace produced so far. Duplicate idempotent statements are discarded if possible. The ravelling process merges the basic statement with the right-most possible parallel command as permitted by the declared semantic relations; otherwise, it commutes the basic statement to the right-most possible position and forms another single-statement parallel command. Then *remove-all-ntr* removes all neutral basic statements. This transformation strategy is the heart of our method. It has been defined formally in the Boyer-Moore computational logic [1] and mechanically proved correct [9].

2.4. Architectures

A parallel trace specifies a partial order of basic statements without reference to a particular architecture. We will develop systolic arrays that can execute the parallel trace. We specify a systolic array with the help of four functions.

The first two functions are called *step* and *place*. The domain of both functions is the set of basic statements that occur in the parallel trace. *Step* determines when basic statements are to be executed, and *place* determines where basic statements are to be executed.[1]

Step maps basic statements to the integers. The intention is to count the parallel commands of the parallel trace in their order of execution. *Step* is derived from the parallel trace. The derivation of *step* must adhere to two conditions:

(S1) basic statements of the same parallel command must be mapped to the same integer,

(S2) basic statements of adjacent parallel commands must be mapped to consecutive integers.

We are free to choose an appropriate integer, fs, for the basic statements of the first parallel command. If *step* satisfies conditions (S1) and (S2), any two basic statements in the same parallel command must have identical step values. *Step* can be derived by solving a system of equations whose formulation is guided by conditions (S1) and (S2) (see the next section).

Place maps basic statements to an integer space of some dimension d. We assume that every point of that space is occupied by a processor. The intention is to assign basic statements to the processors. Processors that are not assigned a statement at some step simply forward the data on their input channels to the corresponding output channels during that step. Processors that are at no step assigned a statement need not be implemented. *Place* is not derived from the parallel trace but proposed separately. *Place* has to satisfy the following condition:

---

[1]In general, we must distinguish multiple occurrences of identical basic statements - by some sort of counter, say. However, we omit this trivial complication here. Matrix multiplication leads to traces whose basic statements are all distinct.

(P1) basic statements of the same parallel command must be assigned distinct points.
We have a simple condition that establishes whether our proposals for *place* satisfy (P1) (see the next section).

In programs, data are represented by variables. In systolic computations, data, i.e., variables travel between processors. A variable may be accessed by one processor at one step and by another processor at a later step. We have to specify a layout and flow of variables that provides each processor with the expected inputs at the steps at which it is supposed to execute its basic statement. At present, our method is confined to systolic arrays in which processors are only connected by unidirectional channels to processors that occupy neighboring points.[2] For designs with these characteristics, we can synthesize the input pattern and flow of data from *step* and *place*. To this end, we introduce two more functions: *pattern* and *flow*. The domain of both functions is the set of program variables. *Flow* specifies the direction of data movement, and *pattern* specifies the initial data layout.

Flow maps program variables to the same d-dimensional integer space as *place*. The intention is to indicate, for every processor in the network, which of its neighbors receive its output values at the next execution step, i.e., to which of its neighbors it must be connected by an outgoing channel. *Flow* is synthesized from *step* and *place* as follows: if variable v is accessed by distinct basic statements $s0$ and $s1$,

$$flow(v) =_{def} (place(s1) - place(s0))/(step(s1) - step(s0))$$

For variables v that are accessed by only one basic statement, we must provide the definition of *flow* explicitly. *Flow* is only well-defined if its images do not depend on the particular choice of pairs $s0$ and $s1$.

Pattern maps program variables to the same space as *place*. The intention is to lay out the input data for the various processors in an initial pattern such that the systolic execution can begin. (*Flow* describes the propagation of the data towards and through the network as the execution proceeds.) With constant fs being the arbitrary step value that we choose for the first parallel command, *pattern* is synthesized from *step*, *place*, and *flow* as follows: if variable v is accessed by basic statement s,

$$pattern(v) =_{def} place(s) - (step(s) - fs)*flow(v)$$

Pattern is only well-defined if its images do not depend on the particular choice of basic statement s. With *pattern* specifying the initial data layout, we can derive the data layout for successive steps of the systolic execution: the data layout after k steps is given by $pattern(v) + k*flow(v)$.

2.5. The Graphics System

We have implemented the transformation strategy and the computation of the previous functions in a graphics system on the Symbolics 3600. Our system can display two-dimensional processor layouts and simulate sequences of execution steps on them. At any fixed step, it displays the data layout and flow and indicates the active processors. The figures in this paper are hard-copies of images produced by our system.

3. Theorems for Linear Systolic Designs

A number of researchers have analyzed systolic designs with notions of linear algebra [7, 16, 17, 19, 20]. We shall do something similar here. In this section, we investigate a specific class of systolic designs: linear systolic designs. We defer the proofs of theorems to the appendix.

A systolic design is *linear* if it is specified by linear step and place functions. Linear systolic designs are particularly interesting because their data movement proceeds at a fixed rate in straight lines. We limit our

---

[2]Two points $(p_0,...,p_{d-1})$ and $(q_0,...,q_{d-1})$ of the d-dimensional integer space are *neighbors* if $0 \le |p_i - q_i| \le 1$, where $0 \le i < d$.

theoretical discussion to programs with only one type of basic statement.[3] Let us denote the basic statement by $s(x_0,x_1,...,x_{r-1})$. Also, we use $s[x_i'/x_i]$ to denote the substitution of x_i' for argument x_i in basic statement $s(x_0,x_1,...,x_{r-1})$.

Formally, a systolic design is linear, if *step* and *place* are described by the following linear equations:

(E1) $step(s(x_0,x_1,...,x_{r-1})) = \alpha_{0,0}x_0+\alpha_{0,1}x_1+...+\alpha_{0,r-1}x_{r-1}+\alpha_{0,r}$

(E2) $place(s(x_0,x_1,...,x_{r-1})) =$
$$(\alpha_{1,0}x_0+\alpha_{1,1}x_1+...+\alpha_{1,r-1}x_{r-1}+\alpha_{1,r}, ..., \alpha_{d,0}x_0+\alpha_{d,1}x_1+...+\alpha_{d,r-1}x_{r-1}+\alpha_{d,r})$$

where the range of *place* is the d-dimensional integer space. In a non-linear systolic design, equations (E1) and (E2) would be of a higher degree. We shall explain the derivation of *step* and discuss theorems about *place*, *flow*, and *pattern* that provide guidance in the choice of a place function.

Consider a non-empty parallel trace. The images of its individual basic statements under *step*, as defined in (E1), constitute a set of linear formulas. Take the image of the first basic statement in the parallel trace and equate it with a chosen number. Impose conditions (S1) and (S2) to derive equations for the other basic statements. The result is a set of linear equations in the variables $\alpha_{0,0}$, $\alpha_{0,1}$, ..., $\alpha_{0,r-1}$, and $\alpha_{0,r}$, whose solution determines *step*. However, the equations do not guarantee the existence of a unique solution. For example, if the parallel trace consists of only one statement, there are infinitely many solutions for *step*, all of which satisfy conditions (S1) and (S2). It is also possible that no solution exists at all.

While conditions (S1) and (S2) are, generally, sufficient to synthesize *step*, condition (P1) is not sufficient to synthesize *place*. We must propose *place* independently and test whether it satisfies (P1). The following theorem provides such a test.

Theorem 1: Let *step* be a linear step function for parallel trace t that satisfies (S1) and (S2). Let *place* be a linear place function for t. *Place* satisfies (P1) if the following equations have the zero vector as the unique solution:
$$\alpha_{0,0}u_0+\alpha_{0,1}u_1+...+\alpha_{0,r-1}u_{r-1}=0$$
$$\alpha_{1,0}u_0+\alpha_{1,1}u_1+...+\alpha_{1,r-1}u_{r-1}=0$$
$$...$$
$$\alpha_{d,0}u_0+\alpha_{d,1}u_1+...+\alpha_{d,r-1}u_{r-1}=0$$

where r is the number of arguments of basic statement s. In particular, if *place* maps to $r-1$ dimensions, i.e., $d=r-1$, *place* satisfies (P1) if the coefficient determinant of this previous system of equations is not zero.

Given a linear step function satisfying (S1) and (S2) and a linear place function satisfying (P1), we can compute *flow* and *pattern*. The computation of *flow* and *pattern* must be well-defined, that is, their result must not depend on the choice of basic statements. Matrix computation programs use subscripted variables. In our programming language, the variable subscripts appear as arguments of the program's basic statements. If the variable subscripts are determined by $r-1$ arguments of the r-argument statement, then the flow of the variable derived from *step* and *place* is well-defined. This property is stated in Theorem 2. In our programming example, matrix multiplication, matrix elements accessed by a basic statement are determined each by two of the statement's three arguments (Section 4).

Theorem 2: Let *step* be a linear step function for parallel trace t that satisfies (S1) and (S2). Let *place* be a linear place function for t that satisfies (P1). If the subscripts of variable v are determined by all but one of the r arguments of the basic statement, then *flow* is well-defined for variable v.

---

[3]This restriction is not as severe as it may seem. While matrix multiplication only requires single-type basic statements, we have been able to apply our theorems also to other programs that use basic statements of several types [10].

Given a parallel trace t which satisfies conditions (S1), (S2), and (P1), no two basic statements in t can be identical. If a variable's subscripts are determined by all r, not just $r-1$, arguments of a basic statement, this variable can be accessed by at most one basic statement. Therefore, we cannot derive its flow function, and have to provide that explicitly. In general, while the processor layout for a program with r-argument basic statements requires dimension $r-1$, the data layout requires dimension r. An example is matrix-vector multiplication [11].

Given a step function satisfying (S1) and (S2), a place function satisfying (P1), and a well-defined flow function, the derived pattern function is well-defined. This property is stated by Theorem 3.

Theorem 3: Let *step* be a linear step function for parallel trace t that satisfies (S1) and (S2). Let *place* be a linear place function for t that satisfies (P1). Let *flow*, derived from *step* and *place*, be well-defined. Then *pattern*, derived from *step*, *place*, and *flow*, is well-defined.

4. Systolic Designs of Matrix Multiplication

The problem is to multiply two distinct $n \times n$ matrices A and B and assign the product to a third $n \times n$ matrix C, such that

$$c_{i,j} = \sum_{k=0}^{n-1} (a_{i,k} * b_{k,j}) \qquad \text{for } 0 \le i \le n-1 \text{ and } 0 \le j \le n-1$$

With inner product steps, the following program is a simple solution to matrix multiplication; it is assumed that matrix C is initially everywhere zero:

> **for** i **from** 0 **to** $n-1$ **do**
>> **for** j **from** 0 **to** $n-1$ **do**
>>> **for** k **from** 0 **to** $n-1$ **do** $(i{:}j{:}k)$

Translated to our programming language, this program becomes:

	matrix-matrix(n):	product($n-1,n-1$)
	product($0,n$):	row($0,n,n$)
$\{i>0\}$	product(i,n):	product($i-1,n$); row(i,n,n)
	row($i,0,n$):	inner-product($i,0,n$)
$\{j>0\}$	row(i,j,n):	row($i,j-1,n$); inner-product(i,j,n)
	inner-product($i,j,0$):	$(i{:}j{:}0)$
$\{k>0\}$	inner-product(i,j,k):	inner-product($i,j,k-1$); $(i{:}j{:}k)$

The curly brackets on the left contain entry conditions on the formal parameters of the refinements. Our rather complex syntax has the advantage that each composition of two basic statements is represented explicitly by a semicolon. This will simplify the translation of the program into a sequential execution.

We consider matrices whose non-zero values are concentrated in a "band" around the diagonal. An inner product step $(i{:}j{:}k)$ containing off-band elements $a_{i,k}$ or $b_{k,j}$ does not change the value of $c_{i,j}$, i.e., is neutral. We exploit this neutrality. To identify off-band elements of the matrix, we must precisely describe the width of the band of non-zero elements around the diagonal. This *band width* is determined by two natural numbers: the largest distance p, of a potentially non-zero element in the upper triangle from the diagonal, and the largest distance, q, of a potentially non-zero element in the lower triangle from the diagonal. The *distance* of a matrix element from the diagonal is the absolute value of the difference of its two subscripts. In the following systolic designs, we fix the band widths of matrices A and B each to $p=1$ and $q=1$. As a result, the band width of matrix C is $p=2$ and $q=2$.

Only neutral inner product steps are idempotent. Since we exploit their neutrality, we do not exploit their idempotence.

On a parallel architecture that permits the sharing of variables, two inner product steps $(i0:j0:k0)$ and $(i1:j1:k1)$ are independent if their target variables $c_{i0,j0}$ and $c_{i1,j1}$ are distinct.[4] But we are interested in executions on particular, systolic architectures that do not permit the sharing of variables. Therefore, we must use a stronger independence criterion and require that $a_{i0,k0}$ and $a_{i1,k1}$ are distinct, $b_{k0,j0}$ and $b_{k1,j1}$ are distinct, and $c_{i0,j0}$ and $c_{i1,j1}$ are distinct. Recall that the three variables of an individual inner product step are distinct by assumption.

All inner product steps are commutative. This makes commutativity, per se, meaningless. We do not exploit commutativity in trace transformations unless it is a consequence of independence.

Therefore, we declare the following semantic relations of neutrality and independence for inner product steps:

(D1) $1 < k-i \lor 1 < i-k \lor 1 < j-k \lor 1 < k-j \Rightarrow \text{ntr } (i:j:k)$

(D2) $(i_0 \neq i_1 \lor j_0 \neq j_1) \land (i_0 \neq i_1 \lor k_0 \neq k_1) \land (j_0 \neq j_1 \lor k_0 \neq k_1) \Rightarrow (i_0:j_0:k_0) \text{ ind } (i_1:j_1:k_1)$

4.1. The First Design

Substituting ";" with "→" in the program to obtain a sequential trace, and then applying *transform* to the sequential trace, we derive a parallel trace. For example, the parallel trace for the multiplication of two 4×4 matrices (*matrix-matrix*(4)) expands to:

```
    <(0:0:0)>
→   <(0:0:1)  (0:1:0)  (1:0:0)>  →  <(0:1:1)  (1:0:1)  (1:1:0)>
→   <(0:2:1)  (1:1:1)  (2:0:1)>  →  <(1:1:2)  (1:2:1)  (2:1:1)>
→   <(1:2:2)  (2:1:2)  (2:2:1)>  →  <(1:3:2)  (2:2:2)  (3:1:2)>
→   <(2:2:3)  (2:3:2)  (3:2:2)>  →  <(2:3:3)  (3:2:3)  (3:3:2)>
→   <(3:3:3)>
```

This trace has length 10. In general, the length of the parallel trace is $3n-2$ and is independent of the band width. But the band width influences the width of the trace, i.e., the degree of concurrency.

The step function is derived from the parallel trace. Let the step function be a linear function:

$$step((i:j:k)) = \alpha_0 * i + \alpha_1 * j + \alpha_2 * k + \alpha_3$$

Recall that we are allowed to choose the step value of the first parallel command. We choose the value to make the constant term, α_3, 0. In this case, the step value of the first parallel command is 0. Applying the step function to the basic statements in the first two parallel commands of the above parallel trace, we obtain the following equations:

$$step((0:0:0)) = \alpha_3 = 0$$
$$step((0:0:1)) = \alpha_2 + \alpha_3 = 1$$
$$step((0:1:0)) = \alpha_1 + \alpha_3 = 1$$
$$step((1:0:0)) = \alpha_0 + \alpha_3 = 1$$

The solution to these equations is $\alpha_0 = \alpha_1 = \alpha_2 = 1$ and $\alpha_3 = 0$. The solution is consistent for the equations obtained by applying the step function to the rest of the basic statements. Therefore, the derived step function is:

$$step((i:j:k)) = i + j + k$$

The place function cannot be derived from the parallel trace but must be proposed separately. It seems promising to lay the processors out in a plane, i.e., in our method, on the two-dimensional integer lattice. Our first idea is to assign each basic statement to the point whose coordinates match the indices of the statement's target variable. This decision is rather arbitrary. At this stage, we do not have any information that might guide us in the choice of a processor layout. As we shall see later, other layouts are possible. Inner product step $(i:j:k)$ has target variable $c_{i,j}$. We propose:

---

[4] See the Independence Theorem of [13].

$$place((i{:}j{:}k)) =_{\text{def}} (i,j)$$

The dimension of *place* is two which is one less than the number of the arguments in $(i{:}j{:}k)$. By Theorem 1, *place* satisfies condition (P1), because the determinant constructed from the coefficients of *step* and *place* is not zero:

$$\begin{vmatrix} 1 & 1 & 1 \\ 1 & 0 & 0 \\ 0 & 1 & 0 \end{vmatrix} = 1$$

where the first row, (1 1 1), is constructed from *step*, the second row, (1 0 0), from the first dimension of *place*, and the third row, (0 1 0), from the second dimension of *place*.

Variable $a_{i,k}$ appears in basic statements $(i{:}j{:}k)$ and $(i{:}j+1{:}k)$, and these two statements are executed in consecutive steps. Therefore, we can derive the flow of $a_{i,k}$:

$$\begin{aligned} flow(a_{i,k}) &= place((i{:}j+1{:}k)) - place((i{:}j{:}k)) \\ &= (0,1) \end{aligned}$$

Similarly, we derive the flows of $b_{k,j}$ and $c_{i,j}$:

$$\begin{aligned} flow(b_{k,j}) &= place((i+1{:}j{:}k)) - place((i{:}j{:}k)) \\ &= (1,0) \end{aligned}$$

$$\begin{aligned} flow(c_{i,j}) &= place((i{:}j{:}k+1)) - place((i{:}j{:}k)) \\ &= (0,0) \end{aligned}$$

Variables $c_{i,j}$ stay stationary during the computation. By Theorem 2, *flow* is well-defined.

With functions *step*, *place*, and *flow*, we derive the initial data layout as follows:

$$\begin{aligned} pattern(a_{i,k}) &= place((i{:}j{:}k)) - step((i{:}j{:}k))*flow(a_{i,k}) \\ &= (i,-i-k) \end{aligned}$$

$$\begin{aligned} pattern(b_{k,j}) &= place((i{:}j{:}k)) - step((i{:}j{:}k))*flow(b_{k,j}) \\ &= (-j-k,j) \end{aligned}$$

$$\begin{aligned} pattern(c_{i,j}) &= place((i{:}j{:}k)) - step((i{:}j{:}k))*flow(c_{i,j}) \\ &= (i,j) \end{aligned}$$

By Theorem 3, *pattern* is well-defined.

The network of processors and the initial data layout, as produced by the graphics system, is depicted in Figure 1. Each dot represents an inner product step processor. Arrows represent the propagation of data. A variable name labelling an arrow indicates the location of that variable. If the arrow points to a processor, this variable is input to that processor at the current step of the systolic execution.

The processor layout of this design mirrors the band of matrix C. The number of processors depends on the size of the input. For matrices with large size, this design may require a large number of processors. We can improve this situation by proposing a different place function.

4.2. The Second Design

Let us assume that we will keep the band widths of the input matrices constant. That is, when increasing the size of the input, we never widen the matrices' bands. Under this assumption, we can derive for the same matrix multiplication program another design whose number of processors is constant. We must simply find a place function whose coordinates depend only on the band widths of the input matrices but not on their size. The band widths of the input matrices are determined by the differences of i and k and of j and k (see the enabling condition of our neutrality declaration). We choose our coordinates from these differences:

$$place((i:j:k)) =_{\text{def}} (i-k,j-k)$$

Again, other choices are possible. By Theorem 1, this place function also satisfies (P1):

$$\begin{vmatrix} 1 & 1 & 1 \\ 1 & 0 & -1 \\ 0 & 1 & -1 \end{vmatrix} = 3$$

With the new proposed function, we derive the following *flow* and *pattern*:

$$flow(a_{i,k}) = (0,1)$$
$$flow(b_{k,j}) = (1,0)$$
$$flow(c_{i,j}) = (-1,-1)$$

$$pattern(a_{i,k}) = (i-k,-i-2k)$$
$$pattern(b_{k,j}) = (-j-2k,j-k)$$
$$pattern(c_{i,j}) = (2i+j,i+2j)$$

Flow and *pattern* are, again, well-defined.

The network of processors and the initial data layout is depicted in Figure 2. This design is presented in [11]. The number of processors is $(p_A+q_A+1)*(p_B+q_B+1)$. It is independent of the size of the input.

After arriving at an improved processor layout, we now modify the program to improve execution speed. We could have proceeded in the converse order.

4.3. The Third Design

Recall that any two inner product steps are commutative. In Sect. 4.1, we decided not to declare this commutativity. A search reveals that a commutation in the definition of refinement *inner-product* yields the shortest trace:

$$inner\text{-}product(i,j,0): \qquad (i:j:0)$$
$$\{k>0\} \quad inner\text{-}product(i,j,k): \qquad (i:j:k); inner\text{-}product(i,j,k-1)$$

The parallel trace obtained for the multiplication of two 4×4 matrices (*matrix-matrix*(4)) expands to:

```
    <> → <>
 →  <(0:0:1)>
 →  <(0:0:0)  (0:1:1)  (1:0:1)  (1:1:2)>
 →  <(0:1:0)  (0:2:1)  (1:0:0)  (1:1:1)  (1:2:2)  (2:0:1)  (2:1:2)  (2:2:3)>
 →  <(1:1:0)  (1:2:1)  (1:3:2)  (2:1:1)  (2:2:2)  (2:3:3)  (3:1:2)  (3:2:3)>
 →  <(2:2:1)  (2:3:2)  (3:2:2)  (3:3:3)>
 →  <(3:3:2)>
 →  <> → <>
```

If we do not consider band width, i.e., do not exploit neutrality, this trace has the same length as previous trace: 10 or, in general, $3n-2$. But, contrary to the previous trace, a consideration of band width can shorten this trace: the leading and trailing empty parallel commands result from the elimination of neutral basic statements. Not counting the empty parallel commands, this trace has length 6 or, in general, $n+\min(p_A,q_B)+\min(q_A,p_B)$. Hence, for constant band width and large n, we achieve a speed-up by a factor of 3. The effect of the commutation in *inner-product* is that, in the execution, k is counted down, not up. Therefore, the derived step function contains a subtraction rather than an addition of k:

$$step((i:j:k)) = i+j-k$$

The step value of the first (non-empty) parallel command is -1 or, in general, $-\min(p_A,q_B)$. We keep the place function of the second design:

$$place((i:j:k)) = (i-k,j-k)$$

Again, we derive well-defined flow and pattern functions:

$$flow(a_{i,k}) = (0,1)$$
$$flow(b_{k,j}) = (1,0)$$
$$flow(c_{i,j}) = (1,1)$$

$$pattern(a_{i,k}) = (i-k, -i-\min(p_A,q_B))$$
$$pattern(b_{k,j}) = (-j-\min(p_A,q_B), j-k)$$
$$pattern(c_{i,j}) = (-j-\min(p_A,q_B), -i-\min(p_A,q_B))$$

Note that *pattern* depends on the band width because the value of the first step does.

The network of processors and the initial data layout (at the first inner product step) is depicted in Figure 3. This design is also presented in [23].

5. Evaluation

Let us review how we develop systolic executions and designs. We provide a program (in form of a refinement) and a processor layout (in form of a place function). Given to us are properties of the programming language (in form of semantic relations) and restrictions on the architecture (implicit in the requirements on *step*, *place*, *flow*, and *pattern*). From this information, we synthesize, via a sequential execution, a parallel execution of the program and, via a step function, the data layout and movement (in form of a flow function and a pattern function). We could also exchange what we propose and derive. For example, if we proposed the data movement, we could synthesize the data layout and the processor layout.

Our work is distinguished by the combination of three factors. Embedding systolic design into a general view of programming enables us to separate distinct concerns properly. The explicit formulation of a parallel execution provides a precise link between the two components proposed by the human in a systolic design: the program and the processor layout. Our insistence on formal rigor at every stage expedites the automation of a large part of the development. Theorems aid the human in his part of the development. The systolic design at which we arrive can be informally (graphically) conveyed to the human, but it also has a precise mathematical description.

These benefits are demonstrated by our graphics implementation. As a consequence of the isolation of different development stages (program, execution, architecture) in our method, we can quickly and easily change different parameters, one at a time, and obtain a clear display of the effect on the systolic design.

The pairing of a program with a processor layout makes the evaluation of a design particularly convenient: the program determines the execution speed (as the length of the parallel trace) and the processor layout determines the size of the design (as the number of processors). The density of the data layout is determined only by the pair but not by either component alone.[5] For example, our first and second designs of matrix multiplication are based on the same program but the densities of their data layouts differ. Similarly, our second and third designs have the same processor layout, but the densities of their data layouts differ.

At present, we use *transform* as a heuristic. Our initial definition of it removed neutral elements first, not last. In some cases, this version of *transform* leads to faster executions. We still abandoned it, because it also leads to more complicated step functions, and simplicity is important to us. *Transform* is just another variable in our method. So far, our specific transformation strategy has served us remarkably well [9, 10].

We are not very satisfied with the way in which we identified the commutation in the definition of *inner-product* that led to our third design for matrix multiplication. We also attempted commutations in the other refinements, *product* and *row*, but they lead to executions that are never shorter and sometimes longer. All we can

---

[5]In fact, it is given by the absolute value of the determinant derived from the coefficients of *step* and *place*. We have proved a theorem to that effect.

provide at this time is an implemented system that lets us conduct these searches conveniently. The fact that all statements of the matrix multiplication program are commutative is discouraging. It provides us with no information of what execution to pick.

To reach the first step of our parallel systolic execution, several steps of "soaking up" data may have to be taken. Similarly, after the last step of our execution, data remaining in the network may have to be "drained". After arriving at a particular design, we can compute the lengths of the soaking and draining phases from *step* and *place*. Soaking and draining influences the performance of the design.

We have applied our method of incremental systolic design to other problems like LU-decomposition [11] and polynomial evaluation [12]. Our method is particularly suitable for a search of different systolic designs for some fixed problem. An impressive example is our treatment of the Algebraic Path Problem. The Algebraic Path Problem subsumes many matrix computation problems, among them matrix inversion, transitive closure, and shortest paths. Its solutions are complicated systolic designs with seven different types of operations and different data items being reflected in different directions up to four times on their path through the processor array [21]. For variables whose flow is not constant over the entire execution, the well-definedness of *flow* and *pattern* is violated. However, we can cope with such cases in an incremental fashion. We can extend the parallel execution with statements that copy variables (whose direction of flow changes) to new variables (at the points of change). The flow of each of the resulting variables is then constant. We have obtained an algorithm by which the parallel execution can be successively enhanced with such reflection operations [10].

Programs lend themselves to a systolic implementation if they combine a few simple operations in a highly repetitive way. It is not easy to tell by looking at the program whether it permits a nice systolic implementation. We have not addressed this problem here. What we offer is a fast way to try. Our method works the better, the fewer types of basic operations need to be considered. Many different types of processors can cause an explosion in the number of semantic declarations. We expect our method to work best for problems in which the program does not reflect aspects of the systolic architecture. However, at least in the treatment of the Algebraic Path Problem, we were able to add operations imposed by the architecture at a later stage.

Our description of systolic designs does not explicitly address the propagation of synchronization signals as does, for instance, Snepscheut's systolic design for transitive closure [22]. We capture issues of synchronization, quite abstractly, in the parallel trace. They may be realized by synchronization signals or by some other means. For example, we think of our systolic designs as communicating an identification of the variable together with the variable's value. So far, all our examples have lead to systolic designs in which a processor can decide what operation to perform simply be inspecting the identifications of its input data.

Many researchers have investigated methods of systolic design in recent years (see the next section). All these methods require two kinds of input: one component that can be thought of as a program, and one component that gives some clue about the structure of the systolic array. In our approach both these inputs need not be cleverly chosen. Of the program, we require only that it solve the numerical problem at hand. For the place function, we can start with a simple proposition that looks promising. After evaluating the result of our inputs, we can make incremental variations. These variations may be random, or they may be carefully selected. In our matrix multiplication example, we adjusted each of the two inputs once.

6. Related Research

Chen [5, 6] chooses the inverse of our derivation. She supplies a "network", which is the analogue of our flow function, and an "abstract process structure" (a set of recurrence equations), which is the analogue of our refinement. Her informal derivation results in a "concrete structure", which is the analogue of our step and place functions. Chen does not spell out systolic executions, as we do with traces, and is, in general, less formal.

Like us, Moldovan and Fortes [19] require the input of a program, but their program must be augmented with "artificial" variables [18]. This augmentation is meant to specify parallelism and corresponds roughly to our semantic relations - except that semantic relations are properties of the programming language, not properties of individual programs. (The detection of parallelism receives more attention in another of their papers [8].) Systolic arrays are described by a space transformation which corresponds to our function *place* and a time transformation which corresponds to our function *step*. Moldovan and Fortes require the input of both transformations, while we only require the input of *place* (or even only part of *place*). Similarly to Chen, Moldovan and Fortes present an algorithm by which the space transformation can be derived from a set of proposed flow vectors. Mirankler and Winkler [17] employ the same space-time transformation as Moldovan but use a graph representation. Moldovan and Fortes propose guidelines for the derivation of some programs.

Chandy and Misra [4] propose an "invariant", which corresponds to our step function, and, with some additional assumptions, derive a systolic program from it. A program in their language, Unity [3], is a repeating multiple assignment statement. Chandy and Misra envision Unity as a tool in which programming solutions for many different architectures can be expressed with equal convenience. They equate the Unity programs that they derive with systolic executions and, indeed, with systolic architectures. An essential aspect of our synthesis method is that we distinguish the three concepts of a program, a trace, and an architecture.

Lam and Mostow [12] employ an implemented method of transformation similar to ours but, again, less precise. They require annotations to the Pascal-like program that give a clue about the processor layout ("in place" or "in parallel").

Cappello and Steiglitz [2] describe a method of systolic design by geometric transformation. They derive a first data flow scheme from a sequential program execution. The data flow scheme is expressed geometrically in space-time and is, usually, not well-suited for implementation. It is then improved by geometric transformations proposed by the human. As many other approaches in VLSI theory, this one aims at chip layout, not at programming. Our centerpiece, the parallel execution, is missing.

Systolic design spans several levels of abstraction, from a specification to a chip layout. The two ends of this spectrum are, at present, best understood. The front end is the refinement of a specification into an abstract program. Solutions to this end are offered by work in programming methodology. The back end is the refinement of an abstract systolic architecture into an optimized concrete one. Solutions to this end are offered by work in VLSI design. Our work provides a connection of both ends: it links an abstract program with an abstract systolic architecture.

Acknowledgements
This research was partially supported by Grant No. 26-7603-35 from the Lockheed Missiles & Space Corporation and by Grant No. DCR-8610427 of the National Science Foundation.

References
1. Boyer, R. S., and Moore, J S. *A Computational Logic*. ACM Monograph Series, Academic Press, 1979.

2. Cappello, P. R., and Steiglitz, K. Unifying VLSI Array Design with Linear Transformations of Space-time. In *Advances in Computing Research, Vol. 2: VLSI Theory*, F. P. Preparata, Ed., JAI Press Inc., 1984, pp. 23-65.

3. Chandy, M. Concurrent Programming for the Masses. Proc. 4th Ann. ACM Symp. on Principles of Distributed Computing, 1985, pp. 1-12.

4. Chandy, K. M., and Misra, J. "Systolic Algorithms as Programs". *Distributed Computing 1*, 3 (1986), 177-183.

5. Chen, M. C. Synthesizing Systolic Designs. YALEU/DCS/RR-374, Department of Computer Science, Yale University, Mar., 1985.

6. Chen, M. C. A Parallel Language and Its Compilation to Multiprocessor Machines or VLSI. Proc. 13th Ann. ACM Symp. on Principles of Programming Languages, 1986, pp. 131-139.

7. Delosme, J.-M., and Ipsen, I. Overview over SAGA and CONDENSE. Yale University, Jan., 1987.

8. Fortes, J. A. B., and Moldovan, D.I. "Parallelism Detection and Transformation Techniques for VLSI Algorithms". *Journal of Parallel and Distributed Computing 2*, 3 (Aug. 1985), 277-301.

9. Huang, C.-H., and Lengauer, C. The Derivation of Systolic Implementations of Programs. TR-86-10, Department of Computer Sciences, The University of Texas at Austin, Apr., 1986. Revised: Jan., 1987. To appear in *Acta Informatica*.

10. Huang, C.-H., and Lengauer, C. An Incremental, Mechanical Development of Systolic Solutions to the Algebraic Path Problem. TR-86-28, Department of Computer Sciences, The University of Texas at Austin, Dec., 1986.

11. Kung, H. T., and Leiserson, C. E. Algorithms for VLSI Processor Arrays. In *Introduction to VLSI Systems*, C. Mead and L. Conway, Eds., Addison-Wesley, 1980. Sect. 8.3.

12. Lam, M. S., and Mostow, J. "A Transformational Model of VLSI Systolic Design". *Computer 18*, 2 (Feb. 1985), 42-52.

13. Lengauer, C., and Hehner, E. C. R. "A Methodology for Programming with Concurrency: An Informal Presentation". *Science of Computer Programming 2*, 1 (Oct. 1982), 1-18.

14. Lengauer, C. "A Methodology for Programming with Concurrency: The Formalism". *Science of Computer Programming 2*, 1 (Oct. 1982), 19-52.

15. Lengauer, C., and Huang, C.-H. A Mechanically Certified Theorem about Optimal Concurrency of Sorting Networks. Proc. 13th Ann. ACM Symp. on Principles of Programming Languages, 1986, pp. 307-317.

16. Li, G.-H., and Wah, B. W. "The Design of Optimal Systolic Arrays". *IEEE Trans. on Computers C-34*, 1 (Jan. 1985), 66-77.

17. Miranker, W. L., and Winkler, A. "Spacetime Representations of Computational Structures". *Computing 32*, 2 (1984), 93-114.

18. Moldovan, D. I. "On the Design of Algorithms for VLSI Systolic Arrays". *Proc. IEEE 71*, 1 (Jan. 1983), 113-120.

19. Moldovan, D. I., and Fortes, J. A. B. "Partitioning and Mapping Algorithms into Fixed Size Systolic Arrays". *IEEE Trans. on Computers C-35*, 1 (Jan. 1986), 1-12.

20. Quinton, P. Automatic Synthesis of Systolic Arrays from Uniform Recurrent Equations. Proc. 11th Ann. Int. Symp. on Computer Architecture, 1984, pp. 208-214.

21. Rote, G. "A Systolic Array Algorithm for the Algebraic Path Problem (Shortest Paths; Matrix Inversion)". *Computing 34*, 3 (1985), 191-219.

22. van de Snepscheut, J. L. A. A Derivation of a Distributed Implementation of Warshall's Algorithm (JAN-113a). CS 8505, Dept. of Mathematics and Computing Science, University of Groningen, 1985.

23. Weiser, U., and Davis, A. A Wavefront Notation Tool for VLSI Array Design. In *VLSI Systems and Computations*, H. T. Kung, B. Sproull, and G. Steele, Eds., Computer Science Press, 1981, pp. 226-234.

Appendix: Proofs

We restate and prove Theorems 1, 2, and 3 of Section 3.

Theorem 1: Let *step* be a linear step function for parallel trace t that satisfies (S1) and (S2). Let *place* be a linear place function for t. *Place* satisfies (P1) if the following equations have the zero vector as the unique solution:

$$\alpha_{0,0}u_0+\alpha_{0,1}u_1+...+\alpha_{0,r-1}u_{r-1}=0$$
$$\alpha_{1,0}u_0+\alpha_{1,1}u_1+...+\alpha_{1,r-1}u_{r-1}=0$$
$$...$$
$$\alpha_{d,0}u_0+\alpha_{d,1}u_1+...+\alpha_{d,r-1}u_{r-1}=0$$

where r is the number of arguments of basic statement s.

Proof:

Place satisfies (P1)

$=$ {conditions (S1), (S2) and (P1)}

for all basic statements $s(x_0,x_1,...,x_{r-1})$ and $s(y_0,y_1,...,y_{r-1})$ in t,

$$s(x_0,x_1,...,x_{r-1})\neq s(y_0,y_1,...,y_{r-1}) \wedge step(s(x_0,x_1,...,x_{r-1}))=step(s(y_0,y_1,...,y_{r-1}))$$
$$\Rightarrow place(s(x_0,x_1,...,x_{r-1}))\neq place(s(y_0,y_1,...,y_{r-1}))$$

$=$ {*step* and *place* are linear, and equations (E1) and (E2)}

for all basic statements $s(x_0,x_1,...,x_{r-1})$ and $s(y_0,y_1,...,y_{r-1})$ in t,

$$s(x_0,x_1,...,x_{r-1})\neq s(y_0,y_1,...,y_{r-1})$$
$$\wedge\ \alpha_{0,0}x_0+\alpha_{0,1}x_1+...+\alpha_{0,r-1}x_{r-1}+\alpha_{0,r}=\alpha_{0,0}y_0+\alpha_{0,1}y_1+...+\alpha_{0,r-1}y_{r-1}+\alpha_{0,r}$$
$$\Rightarrow (\alpha_{1,0}x_0+\alpha_{1,1}x_1+...+\alpha_{1,r-1}x_{r-1}+\alpha_{1,r}, ..., \alpha_{d,0}x_0+\alpha_{d,1}x_1+...+\alpha_{d,r-1}x_{r-1}+\alpha_{d,r})$$
$$\neq (\alpha_{1,0}y_0+\alpha_{1,1}y_1+...+\alpha_{1,r-1}y_{r-1}+\alpha_{1,r}, ..., \alpha_{d,0}y_0+\alpha_{d,1}y_1+...+\alpha_{d,r-1}y_{r-1}+\alpha_{d,r})$$

$=$ {algebraic simplification}

for all basic statements $s(x_0,x_1,...,x_{r-1})$ and $s(y_0,y_1,...,y_{r-1})$ in t,

$$s(x_0,x_1,...,x_{r-1})\neq s(y_0,y_1,...,y_{r-1})$$
$$\wedge\ \alpha_{0,0}x_0+\alpha_{0,1}x_1+...+\alpha_{0,r-1}x_{r-1}+\alpha_{0,r}=\alpha_{0,0}y_0+\alpha_{0,1}y_1+...+\alpha_{0,r-1}y_{r-1}+\alpha_{0,r}$$
$$\Rightarrow \alpha_{1,0}x_0+\alpha_{1,1}x_1+...+\alpha_{1,r-1}x_{r-1}+\alpha_{1,r}\neq\alpha_{1,0}y_0+\alpha_{1,1}y_1+...+\alpha_{1,r-1}y_{r-1}+\alpha_{1,r}$$
$$\vee\ ...$$
$$\vee\ \alpha_{d,0}x_0+\alpha_{d,1}x_1+...+\alpha_{d,r-1}x_{r-1}+\alpha_{d,r}\neq\alpha_{d,0}y_0+\alpha_{d,1}y_1+...+\alpha_{d,r-1}y_{r-1}+\alpha_{d,r}$$

$=$ {algebraic simplification}

for all basic statements $s(x_0,x_1,...,x_{r-1})$ and $s(y_0,y_1,...,y_{r-1})$ in t,

$$s(x_0,x_1,...,x_{r-1})\neq s(y_0,y_1,...,y_{r-1})$$
$$\wedge\ \alpha_{0,0}(x_0-y_0)+\alpha_{0,1}(x_1-y_1)+...+\alpha_{0,r-1}(x_{r-1}-y_{r-1})=0$$
$$\Rightarrow \alpha_{1,0}(x_0-y_0)+\alpha_{1,1}(x_1-y_1)+...+\alpha_{1,r-1}(x_{r-1}-y_{r-1})\neq0$$
$$\vee\ ...$$
$$\vee\ \alpha_{d,0}(x_0-y_0)+\alpha_{d,1}(x_1-y_1)+...+\alpha_{d,r-1}(x_{r-1}-y_{r-1})\neq0$$

$=$ {predicate calculus}

for all basic statements $s(x_0,x_1,...,x_{r-1})$ and $s(y_0,y_1,...,y_{r-1})$ in t,

$$\alpha_{0,0}(x_0-y_0)+\alpha_{0,1}(x_1-y_1)+...+\alpha_{0,r-1}(x_{r-1}-y_{r-1})=0$$
$$\wedge\ \alpha_{1,0}(x_0-y_0)+\alpha_{1,1}(x_1-y_1)+...+\alpha_{1,r-1}(x_{r-1}-y_{r-1})=0$$
$$\wedge\ ...$$
$$\wedge\ \alpha_{d,0}(x_0-y_0)+\alpha_{d,1}(x_1-y_1)+...+\alpha_{d,r-1}(x_{r-1}-y_{r-1})=0$$

$$\Rightarrow \quad s(x_0, x_1, ..., x_{r-1}) = s(y_0, y_1, ..., y_{r-1})$$

$\Leftarrow$ {algebraic simplification}

$$\alpha_{0,0}u_0 + \alpha_{0,1}u_1 + ... + \alpha_{0,r-1}u_{r-1} = 0$$
$$\alpha_{1,0}u_0 + \alpha_{1,1}u_1 + ... + \alpha_{1,r-1}u_{r-1} = 0$$
$$...$$
$$\alpha_{d,0}u_0 + \alpha_{d,1}u_1 + ... + \alpha_{d,r-1}u_{r-1} = 0$$

have the zero vector as the unique solution.

(End of Proof)

Theorem 2: Let *step* be a linear step function for parallel trace t that satisfies (S1) and (S2). Let *place* be a linear place function for t that satisfies (P1). If the subscripts of variable v are determined by all but one of the r arguments of the basic statement, then *flow* is well-defined for variable v.

Proof: Let $s_x = s(x_0, ..., x_i, ..., x_{r-1})$, $s_{x'} = s_x[x_i'/x_i]$, $s_y = s_x[y_i/x_i]$, and $s_{y'} = s_x[y_i'/x_i]$. Let the subscripts of variable v be $x_0, ..., x_{i-1}, x_{i+1}, ...,$ and x_{r-1}, that is, the arguments of basic statement s_x, except the $(i+1)$-st one, x_i. Then, s_x, $s_{x'}$, s_y, and $s_{y'}$ all access variable $v_{x_0, ..., x_{i-1}, x_{i+1}, ..., x_{r-1}}$. Assuming $step(s_x) \neq step(s_{x'})$, and $step(s_y) \neq step(s_{y'})$, we can conclude:

flow is well-defined for variable $v_{x_0, ..., x_{i-1}, x_{i+1}, ..., x_{r-1}}$

= {well-definedness}

$$(place(s_x) - place(s_{x'}))/(step(s_x) - step(s_{x'})) = (place(s_y) - place(s_{y'}))/(step(s_y) - step(s_{y'}))$$

= {*step* and *place* are linear, and s_x, $s_{x'}$, s_y, and $s_{y'}$ have identical arguments in all positions but i}

$$(\alpha_{1,i}(x_i - x_i'), ..., \alpha_{d,i}(x_i - x_i'))/\alpha_{0,i}(x_i - x_i') = (\alpha_{1,i}(y_i - y_i'), ..., \alpha_{d,i}(y_i - y_i'))/\alpha_{0,i}(y_i - y_i')$$

= {algebraic simplification}

$$(\alpha_{1,i}/\alpha_{0,i}, ..., \alpha_{d,i}/\alpha_{0,i}) = (\alpha_{1,i}/\alpha_{0,i}, ..., \alpha_{d,i}/\alpha_{0,i})$$

= {algebraic simplification}

true

(End of Proof)

Theorem 3: Let *step* be a linear step function for parallel trace t that satisfies (S1) and (S2). Let *place* be a linear place function for t that satisfies (P1). Let *flow*, derived from *step* and *place*, be well-defined. Then *pattern*, derived from *step*, *place*, and *flow*, is well-defined.

Proof: If basic statements *s0* and *s1* are distinct and access variable v of identical subscripts:

pattern is well-defined for variable v

= {well-definedness}

$$place(s0) - (step(s0) - fs)*flow(v) = place(s1) - (step(s1) - fs)*flow(v)$$

= {algebraic simplification}

$$place(s0) - place(s1) = (step(s0) - step(s1))*flow(v)$$

= {definition of *flow*}

true

(End of Proof)

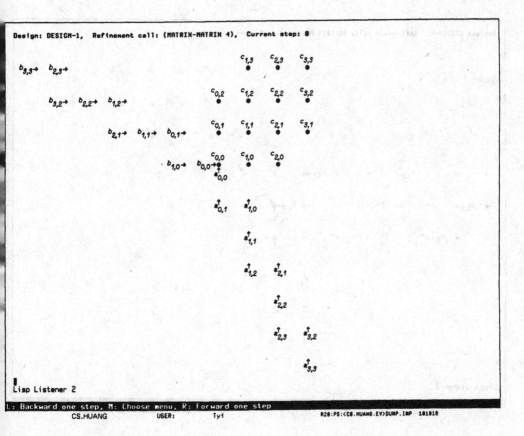

Figure 1. Matrix Multiplication -- The First Design

176

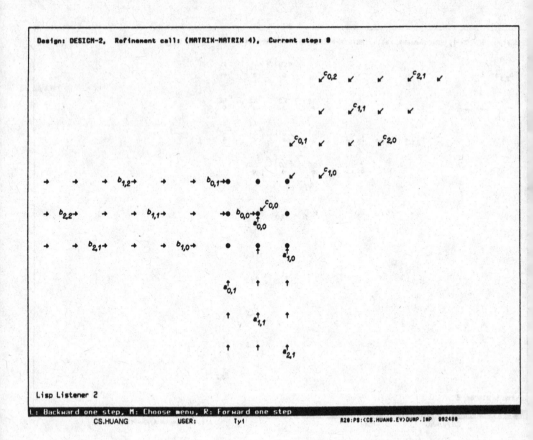

Figure 2. Matrix Multiplication -- The Second Design

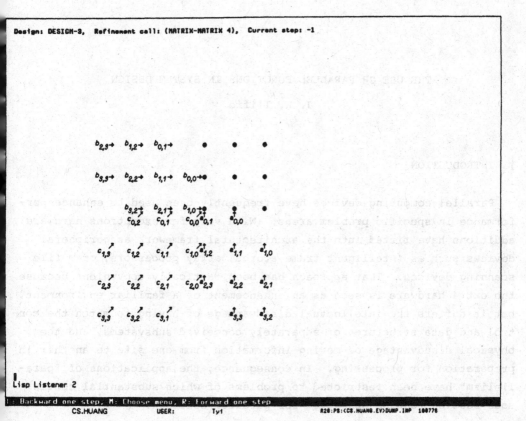

Figure 3. Matrix Multiplication -- The Third Design

THE USE OF PARALLEL FUNCTIONS IN SYSTEM DESIGN

J. K. Iliffe

1 INTRODUCTION

Parallel computing devices have frequently been used to enhance performance in specific problem areas. With very few exceptions hardware
additions have fitted into the architectural framework as peripheral
devices such as intelligent frame stores, array processors, or   file
scanning devices. That approach has been tactically convenient because
the extra hardware is seen as an enhancement of a familiar environment,
but it suffers the intellectual disadvantage of having to match the control and data structures of separately conceived subsystems, and the
physical disadvantage of moving information from one site to another in
preparation for processing. In consequence, the applications of "parallelism" have been restricted to problems of which substantial continuous sections can be scheduled for parallel solution.

If the parallel function is moved into the central computer the above
disadvantages are eliminated. Not only existing applications benefit:
many algorithms that invite frequent change from parallel to serial mode
of operation can be programmed without serious distortion. At the same
time consideration can be given to exploiting parallelism in the system
control functions themselves. That is obviously desirable, to capitalise
on an investment which is no longer optional. In this paper the extent
to which parallel functions can be used in system design is examined.

Confining attention for the moment to a single control stream, it is
clear that the "raw" function most readily provided is a multi-word transfer path to and from memory, together with an array of synchronised arithmetic or logical units performing whatever functions are found profitable
At first sight that prospect is unattractive. In operating systems it
might be claimed that relatively little time is spent in the system itsel
and that the need for mass movement or transformation of data has been
minimised. It must be recognised, however, that the control techniques
now in widespread use are the result of careful optimisation with respect
to a serialised view of computation and that here, as in other aspects of

nnovative design, it is advisable to step back and take a more funda-
ental view of requirements before reaching firm conclusions. It will
e seen here that potential applications can be grouped into "direct"
odifications to existing mechanisms, of which paging and cache memory
ontrol are prime examples, and "indirect" effects in which the existence
f parallel functions promotes a fresh analysis of system structure.
oremost in the second group are approaches to multiprocessor systems
nd to object management.

A configuration of M processors, each supporting parallel operations
n N-word data paths and accessing a shared main memory is assumed here.
he value of N will be determined in practice by the patterns of data
ccess occurring in applications. The value of M will depend on the
apacity of the network connecting processors and memory. The consequen-
es of moving from single to multiple control streams are notoriously
ifficult to predict. In general, however, the performance of the assem-
ly, given a certain memory bandwidth, is so strongly dependent on the
emands made by individual members that the first objective of design
ust be to minimise the number of transactions handled by the intercon-
ecting network (the $width$ of the data path is primarily determined by
). At the same time, effective application of M processors requires
he workload to be partitioned into a "pool" of at least M subtasks from
hich scheduling takes place. How that is done is a matter for program
esign, but it can be seen that memory traffic might be affected by the
tart-up phase of task initiation to a greater extent than in more con-
entional design. Here again attention to the details of single pro-
essor behaviour can be seen as the key to successful implementation
f multiprocessor systems.

The work to be described is in the line of array processor development
tretching from SOLOMON to DAP and MPP, in which application-specific
etails of array dimension, routing and function have been established.
t remains to be seen how they fit in with system requirements. The
econd line of development runs from the early Rice and Burroughs machines
o IBM System 38 and beyond, in which a form of high-precision software
ngineering based on the use of pointer elements has evolved. The third
rea of general interest is in the choice of data structures and control
rimitives to support the execution of high level language statements.
ncreasing use of parameter-matching calling mechanisms and dynamically
ssigned storage has drawn attention to the shortcomings of conventional
esign which cannot be dealt with satisfactorily merely by elaborating
he microprogram. It will be seen that the existence of parallel function

has a bearing on the RISC/CISC argument even though the source language
under discussion might not be overtly parallel. The main innovation lie
in harmonising general aims of system design that are often thought to
be in conflict. That means, amongst other things, that parallel operati
is seen as a natural extension of existing technology.

In order to proceed further it is necessary to present an idealised
model of the "system space". That will be outlined in Section 2. It is
then possible to present a practical realisation of the model as it appears in the author's Pointer-Number system (Section 3). In Section 4
the contribution of parallelism to the design of the PN Machine is assessed. Finally, conclusions are drawn, based on simulation studies, abo
the advantages gained from parallel function and the preferred dimension
routing paths and logical operations.

2 A MODEL OF SYSTEM SPACE

The following model is intended to provide a simple framework within
which a wide range of practical control and data structures can be repre
sented. Its interest lies not so much in the constructs themselves, whi
will be familiar to most designers, but in the points at which practical
systems depart from the ideal.

The elementary data values are bit-strings (numeric elements) and poi
ters. For practical purposes numeric values are manipulated in the preferred forms of word (16-bit), long (32-bit), and planar strings. It is
the last form which is important in the context of parallel operation:
the size of a plane is determined by the N-word parallel data path which
in the example of the next Section, implies 256-bit planes. For the
moment, however, it is assumed that the plane size remains to be chosen.

Pointers are subdivided into two groups: references to abstract objects (capabilities), and references to sequences of values in memory.
The latter correspond to conventional addresses with the additional attr
butes of *type* and *limit* specification: an address refers to a *sequence*
of elementary values of precisely determined length and type. In the
present context a sequence of planes is a key construct, but it is also
necessary to provide sequences of words for scalar processing, and seque
ces of "mixed" elements. The latter may contain both numeric and pointe
values,

An abstract pointer refers to a member of a class of objects. It therefore contains two indices, for the class and object respectively. In addition, it contains an encoded *rights* field which is used to decide the applicability of the characteristic functions of the class. As usual in such systems, certain classes and characteristic functions are built-in to the machine instruction set. That is trivially the case for numeric values. In addition the system supports the representation of files, tasks, errors, channels and storage segments with appropriate creation, update and interrogation functions. The built-in classes can be augmented by user-defined object managers in the following way. Firstly a request is made (to the system class manager) for a new class pointer:

$c = Class(name, size)$

where *name* is an identifier to be used for diagnostic purposes and *size* indicates the maximum size of the class. In due course the object manager will create representations of new elements, for which the system will provide object pointers:

$y = Object(c, rep)$

where *c* is the class identifier and *rep* is the object representation. The value of *y* will be retained for future reference and can be safely passed to potential users provided the class identifier is retained by the object manager. (The system class manager provides suitable functions for management of object rights and retrieval of representations.)

In such a system it is essential to provide an efficient means of controlling changes in accessibility. In practice, control is exercised at two levels. Firstly, since a mixed sequence defines an access list to any required precision, it is natural to map the "immediate access list", or as much of it as can conveniently be handled, into the processor registers. No object can be accessed without reference to one of the registers. (It will immediately be seen that an instant change of access list could be achieved by loading a "plane" of registers at once, though that is not the way the present implementation works.) Secondly, an environment must be defined in which properly authorised expansion of access domain can take place: as seen above, the class identifier *c* becomes accessible only in the object manager which provides characteristic functions of the class. In the model used here such an environment is provided by a system abstraction known as a *base*. A base is represented by a set of {name, value} pairs, and each control module is authorised to

access certain named elements of the base. Because a control module can
be obeyed concurrently by several tasks referring to several bases it is
advantageous to bind names to values dynamically (here again an opportun
ity for parallel operation can be seen, and in this case it is taken).
Transfers of control between modules occur in the same way, via specifie
entry points in named segments. Control modules constitute a class of
objects that can be created and destroyed like any others, subject to ob
vious restraints on usage.

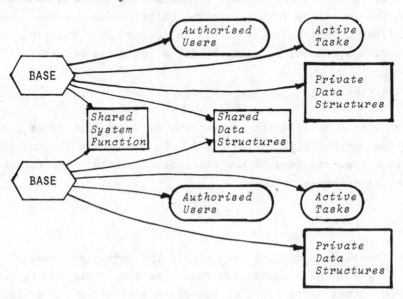

Figure 1: *The base or shared system environment*

The picture that evolves is illustrated in Figure 1. Although pointe
in the bases appear to refer directly to object representations it is to
be understood that the final connection is made via the system class man
ager. The picture is, of course, changing dynamically. Bases can be
created and destroyed, as can their constituents. The system retains
responsibility for object indices and their representations.

Change is brought about by the execution of tasks, eventually leading
to operations on data sequences. In the ideal model the entire system
space illustrated in Figure 1 would be represented in the shared memory,
and the M processors would schedule their activities by reference to a
list of (at least) M tasks ready for execution. The notion of a *local*
space is introduced to facilitate the isolation of parts of the structur
during processing. A function *Access(seg, m)* is provided to gain access
to a particular data segment *seg* in mode *m*; the function delivers the

dress of the corresponding sequence if it is available and blocks access
other tasks. Thereafter the sequence is accessed on a non-shared basis
the tasks requesting it, and can if necesary be shipped into a proce-
or to reduce access time without creating consistency problems. The
cal space also includes the activation records of incomplete procedures,
cally defined sequences, registers and task parameters (such as the
se pointer) as illustrated in Figure 2.

The total system space comprises those objects and sequences access-
le at any instant starting from the defined bases and tasks.

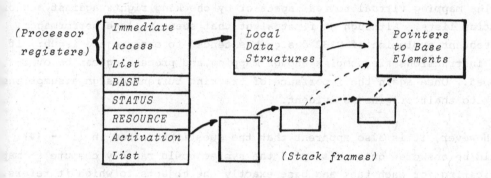

Figure 2: *The task or local (non-shared) environment*

The accuracy and speed with which a pointer-based design responds to
anges in system structure depend on the fact that all information rela-
ng to authorisation, accessibility and allocation can be retained in
e pointers themselves. The model outlined so far has not faced the
actical difficulties of allocating finite processing and storage capa-
ity to meet practically unbounded demand. The penalties are paid when
e structure changes in such a way as to invalidate some of the pointers.
at happens in various ways, of which the following are typical:

1)   Remapping physical space. This occurs, for example, if the base
        information is distributed across two storage levels, or if frag-
        mentation of primary memory prevents allocation of sequences.

2)   Index table management. The system is responsible for recycling
        index values in the classes it supports, and therefore needs to
        know which indices are currently in use. This is a variant of the

storage mapping problem.

(3)   Synchronisation. It is necessary to detect, once *Access* has suc-
        ceeded, when subsequent requests by other tasks to access the same
        segment can be granted.

(4)   Revocation and review of access status. It is sometimes necessary
        to revoke access rights to break deadlock, or to include additiona
        security checks to protect particularly sensitive data.

At hardware level the designer can recover the initiative by deferring
decisions to the time of use of the pointer, for example by referring to
tables mapping virtual to real space or by checking rights against author
isation lists. Although at first sight that seems to lose performance,
subsequent evolution of CISC design has tended to obscure the issue: if
the instructions are complex enough mapping and processing can be overlapped. Once again the importance of tracking current design assumptions
back to their origins is evident.

However, it is also apparent that the questions raised in (1) - (4)
could be answered quite easily if the system could rapidly compute a "map
indicating for each task and base exactly the objects to which it refers.
Normally the possibility of finding the map by scanning all pointer-bear
sequences is rejected because of the supposed overheads involved. But
that is precisely the point at which one can turn to parallel operations
for assistance. The combination of rapid data movement, parallel arithmetic and logic, and (as will be shown in Section 4) fast instruction
execution is enough to force a re-appraisal of control strategy. The mos
important elements from the point of view of performance are storage sequ
ences, but similar considerations apply to all index spaces.

The best-known commercial product following the above model is the IBM
System 38. The idea of a base appears as a "user profile". Pointers include both abstract or "system" references and byte addresses (limited
only by segment boundaries). The user has the option of "resolving" poin
ters, i.e. propagating rights into a pointer to gain speed, or of referring to the user profile to check authority at time of use. However, the
final mapping from virtual to real space is made via segment and page
tables. The system does not provide for user-defined object classes.

In System 38 the data space is entirely "mixed" in the sense of allowing both numeric and pointer values to be included in all data segments.

y scanning operation would need to cover the entire data space, but that
. avoided by not attempting to re-use object indices: provided the index
·ace is large enough it should last for the lifetime of the system. A
.milar approach was taken in the Intel iAPX432. In such designs pointers
·come large (128 bits) and carry a substantial retrieval and decoding
·erhead. It is possible that planar data paths would enable pointers to
· processed efficiently, but the need for large pointers can be avoided
·, as proposed here, indices can quickly be recycled in program space.
·at does not exclude the possibility of providing a large persistent-
·ject space using a distinct category of pointer.

The above considerations are quite foreign to the design of DAP, MPP,
·d other array processors. It might be that the search for numerical
·ccuracy and speed obviates consideration of program structure, and most
·nventional structuring techniques are certainly inconsistent with
·pid planar operation. That is not always true. In the following sec-
·ons it will be shown that parallel computation does not have to be
·rried out in an environment reminiscent of the early 1960's.

PARALLEL OPERATIONS IN THE POINTER-NUMBER MACHINE

To illustrate design issues more clearly some examples will be drawn
·rom the Pointer-Number Machine. Attention is focussed on a single mach-
·e within an assembly, especially on operations involving locally defi-
·d data sequences. As shown in the previous section data values must
· mapped into local (unshared) space prior to operating on them.

If parallel functions are to be widely used in system programming and
·anguage support it is essential to offer clear and efficient ways of
·xpressing parallelism without compromising the principles of abstraction
·d protection that have already been outlined. That is at variance with
·e view of array processors as microprogrammed engines onto which some
·rt of procedural interface can be grafted, though it is difficult to
·ay whether there is a significant performance penalty. The use of tag-
·d elements allows operations to be described at "register level" when
·ecessary, but the view of program space can extend from directly accessed
·egisters to abstract representation of classes of objects without loss of
·ecurity. Similarly, the control mechanism can range from a form of vert-
·al microprogram to complex high-level instruction execution without
·aving to resort to interpretive techniques. The PN Machine can be re-
·arded as a "sequence-processor" in the sense that some machines are seen

as list-processors; in the special case that sequences reduce to two elements the analogy would be quite close.

In the present context sequences of *planes* have a major part to play. To give specific examples planes are defined as 256-bit numeric strings, and they are processed either as 16 words of 16 bits or as 8 words of 32 bits. Hence "N" is either 16 or 8, and "M" is 1 for the time being. The other types of sequence are *word* and *mix*. It is possible to convert a pointer to a plane sequence (a "plane address") to a pointer to the same sequence viewed as words, but not conversely. It is never permitted to convert between a mix sequence and either of the other forms.

Table 1 summarises the elementary data types. The type is encoded as the tag of a mixed value (which occupies 36 bits of storage in total). Machine functions make the obvious checks on operands and abort with a "Tagcheck" error if not satisfied. Special functions are provided for address modification and limitation which ensure that the resulting address defines a sub-sequence of the original: a processor status flag signals "VA" (valid address) or "IA" accordingly. In the latter case the result is an escape Value which would lead to Tagcheck if used to access memory (see Table 2). Once tags are introduced there is considerable scope for adding to the complexity and possibly the power of the instruction set, for example by recognising numeric subtypes, by forcing dereferencing or coercion. In the present design the overriding concern has been to simplify the machine instruction set and to handle more complex types either in the compiler or in an efficient mechanism of instruction composition.

TABLE 1:   REGISTERS and MIXED ELEMENTS in the PN MACHINE

Type	Value
NUM	32-bit numeric string.
PTR	Either ADR or CTR or OBJ or ESC
ADR	Address {*type, limit, protect, location*} where *type* indicates plane, word or mix, *limit* gives length-1 of the sequence, *protect* indicates write-protect, and *location* gives the position in memory.
CTR	Control pointer {*segment, instr offset*}
OBJ	Object pointer {*class id, object id, rights*}
ESC	Escape value (see Table 2)

The escape codes play an important part in error management. With the exception of the Bound check indicator they are generated either by normal program action or by exception-handling procedures. It will be noticed that to create *any* tag value there must be a machine function to set each register field. The use of such a function is confined to the system class manager and exception handlers.

TABLE 2:   ESCAPE VALUES in the PN MACHINE

Null	Non-numeric code {*n*} assigned by program
Unass	Unassigned value (initial elementary value)
Fail	Internal exception (Tagcheck, Protection, etc)
Error	Programmed error code {*segment, error id*}
Var	Prolog variable {*n*}
Bound	Result of sequence bound check

The system recognises certain built-in object classes and provides characteristic functions for creating, deleting and assigning attributes. Additional object classes are introduced by the mechanism described in the preceding section. The system also provides characteristic functions for management of local space, for example the function *Plane(n)* delivers the address of a sequence of *n* planes, and similarly for *Word(n)*. The function *Mix(n)* delivers the address of a sequence of *n* unassigned values. It is thus possible to build arbitrary graph structures in local space, the nodes being mixed sequences and the leaves or terminals numeric.

TABLE 3:   INITIAL SYSTEM CLASSES in the PN MACHINE

Base	Operating environment of one or more tasks
Task	Task representation
File	Abstraction of file read/write head
SpDev	Special device or channel abstraction
Seg	Data segment (initially a plane sequence)
Mod	Control segment (compiled by system)
Class	Object class

It is now possible to give some examples of parallel operations. In what follows single lower-case letters are used to denote machine registers. The values they contain will be given by the context in which they are used. The usual control conventions are assumed. Unless otherwise specified arithmetic is carried out on 16-bit words (the least significant portion of a NUM element), in integer mode.

Consider first the formal correspondence between scalar and planar
arithmetic statements. In the interest of comprehensibility and ease
of transition from one to the other it is attractive to minimise their
differences. Scalar arithmetic involving registers x, y and z can be
expressed as, for example:

$x = y + z$

where it is understood that all registers contain NUM elements. The
analogous calculation for planes of 16 words is expressed by:

$[] \; x = y + z$

where it is now understood that all registers contain plane addresses.
Moreover, the addition involves only the *first* plane in each sequence.
The "[]" token signals the interpretation to be placed on the statement
that follows; it is convenient to imagine that the processor had acquired
planar registers and, as will be seen in the next Section, that is almost
the case.

In order to operate on a plane sequence it is necessary to modify the
plane address that points to it. Modification is denoted by the binary
infix prime operator '. A function to add two sequences a and b of equal
length and return their sum (ignoring overflow) can be written:

$add(a,b):$ $c = Plane(a \; limit + 1); x= c;$
$\qquad\qquad do \; \{ \; []x = a + b; \; a'1;b'1;x'1\} \; while \; VA;$
$\qquad\qquad return(c)$

Note that the statement "$a'1$" is short for "$a=a'1$" and similarly for
other binary operators.

Planar comparisons can also be used to evaluate conditions. A function comparing an argument plane a with the elements of a plane sequence
s, returning a pointer to the first matching plane, can be written:

$assoc(s,a): do \; \{ \; if(\; []s=a) \; return(s);s'1\} \; while \; VA; \; return(s)$

Note that if no match is found the IA condition is set.

Activity control is commonly exercised by using logical bitplanes, which indicate by a '1' the positions in a plane at which a result is to be stored. In the PN Machine greater emphasis is placed on *word*-activity, so that a logical mask of 16 bits is sufficient to determine whether or not assignment is to take place. For example, to exchange the first four words in each pair of corresponding planes of a and b:

> *exch(a,b):* *w= Plane(1); do {[]w=b; [$f000]b=a; [*]a=w;*
> *a'1;b'1} while VA; return*

where the activity mask is enclosed in the planar token; "[*]" adopts the last mask setting; "[]" implies full activity without changing the mask.

Planar translation along the word axis is achieved by parallel shift or scaling functions. Orthogonal translation assumes a cyclic routing path which allows all 16 words to be displaced a given distance. The displacement is expressed by following the register name by "[δ]" where is the distance to be shifted. For example, to add the reals in a plane sequence to give a real scalar result:

> *sum(s):* *x= Plane(1); do {[]x real + s; s'1} while VA;*
> *[$ff00]x real + x[8]; [$f000]x real + x[4]; [$c000]x real + x[2];*
> *return(x word 0.long)*

In the first part of the function planes are regarded as 8 real values and added in parallel; in the second part the 8 partial sums are accumulated by "folding" the workplane x. The value returned is extracted from as a "long" operand at position "0".

Finally, provision must be made for "broadcasting" data to a plane, which is a generalisation of writing to memory, and for the corresponding "read" operations. In each case there are two directions of transmission to choose from, which are referred to as *byrow* and *bycol*. A 16-bit word written *byrow* is copied into each of the 16 words of a storage plane; if written *bycol* the sign is replicated in word 0, the next bit in word 1, and so on to the least significant bit in word 15 of the plane. In planar expressions scalar values are implicitly broadcast *byrow* unless specified otherwise. For example, to make an 8*8 pattern of 2*2 squares of alternating 1's and 0's:

> *p =Plane(1); []p = $3333 % $3333 bycol*

where "%" denotes logical exclusive-or.

The corresponding "read" operations carry out logical-and of all 16 bits along one axis or the other, to give a 16-bit scalar value. It is also possible to select individual words or long-words from a plane sequence (as shown in the preceding example). It is not possible to select "words" in the orthogonal direction.

The parallel function of the PN Machine approximates to that of the DAP, except that reliance is placed on standard word-organised arithmetic rather than using bit-serial mode. The ability to perform planar logical operations is not affected. By defining function as a memory-memory transformation the internal structure of the planar ALU is left open to negotiation between logical design and compilation specialists. The main emphasis has been on making parallel functions readily and safely available, the only forethought required of the programmer being to organise data into plane sequences. The theoretical advantage of using planar functions in the example used here is a factor of eight or sixteen in performance: whether that is significant enough can only be decided by looking at potential applications.

4 APPLICATION OF PARALLEL FUNCTIONS AND DATA PATHS

The most important application of parallelism is perhaps the most obvious. Given that the system model demands a continuous supply of sequences of varying size, the high bandwidth of memory provides a means of dealing with fragmentation which, coupled with the large size of modern stores (relative to segment size) effectively eliminates the need for page tables and associated registers. In the PN Machine addresses contain physical location numbers, but if the underpinning provided by parallel operation were removed one would almost certainly revert to some form of virtual addressing.

The view of a single PN Machine given in Figure 3 shows that the memory bus is 288-bits wide, including 32 tag bits. Program structure is such that instructions and data can be strictly separated, and if necessary mixed and numeric data can be separated without giving rise to consistency problems. It is therefore possible to consider a wide range of cache memory control strategies, based on the "plane" as the unit of data transferred between the cache or buffer store and main memory. The particular use of planar transfers to and from I-O buffers has been used in several array machines. The performance of instruction cache stores can be inferred fairly easily from conventional system design.

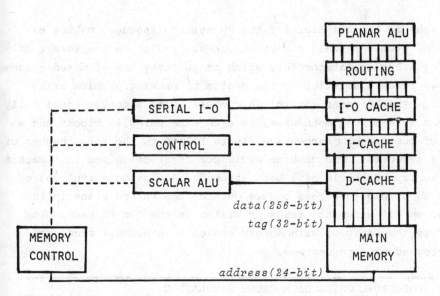

igure 3: *Main components of the PN Machine*

It is often asserted, without justification, that the implementation
f tag-dependent functions incurs significant loss of performance. In
act the use of tags can have the reverse effect, as the following argu-
ent shows.

It has been seen that in order to access memory an address must be
ormed in a register. The actual datum needed may be at any displacement
rom the start of the sequence, but there is far greater likelihood of
t being at the beginning than elsewhere. A cache mangement policy that
refetched and retained the first few planes of each accessible sequence
ould therefore stand a good chance of achieving high hit rates. More-
ver, the question of whether or not a datum could be found in the cache
ould be answered quickly by checking whether the displacement exceeded
he "first few planes" or not. Whenever a new address was formed a check
ould determine whether the data planes were in the cache: if not, a
emory fetch would be initiated and usually *completed before* the first
ead or write request from the processor. The mechanism is called a
orward-Looking cache control to distinguish it from alternatives that
ttempt to use past history ([1]). For a given cache size one would expect
o reduce the number of wait states forced on the processor.

Some preliminary results of simulation studies are given in Table 4.
hree sample programs have been chosen to illustrate a wide range of

behaviour: *comp* is the compiler for the PN system language, making extensive use of procedure call and stack access; *prolog* is the result of a test run of a Prolog interpreter, which makes heavy use of mixed sequences; and *pent* finds a solution to the pentomino packing problem using planar logic. The FL-cache control is compared with a conventional fully associative demand-driven mechanism, in each case using 16 blocks and a block size of one plane. Percentage figure relate to the total number of instructions executed. One machine cycle per instruction and four machine cycles per memory bus cycle have been assumed. An "associative" search occurs when an attempted access occurs outside the cached plane in the FL case, and on all attempted reads or writes in the non-FL case. The "miss rate" is the ratio of main memory cycles to processor reads and writes, expressed as a percentage.

TABLE 4: FORWARD-LOOKING DATA CACHE SIMULATION

16 plane (512 byte) cache memory

	compile		prolog		pent	
Total instr.	289K		455K		5.3M	
	FL	non-FL	FL	non-FL	FL	non-FL
Association	22.6%	62.3%	12.8%	30.0%	32.8%	52.9%
Miss rate	3. %	3. %	12. %	11. %	10. %	11. %
Wait states	2.2%	3.9%	2.1%	8.2%	3.5%	17.9%
Bus active	8.3%	8.0%	14.7%	13.6%	22.9%	25.7%

As expected, there is a reduction in wait states. The results of detailed study and interpretation will be presented elsewhere. The importance of such developments in the present context is that when the block transfer time is very short the gains from giving advanced warning become signficant. Moreover, if there is a likelihood of packaging tasks into small work-units in order to maintain activity in a multiprocessor system it is important to devise means of quickly reaching full speed. The combination of planar transfers and intelligent control of the cache content appears to offer an effective range of strategies.

It was noted earlier that it seemed attractive to load the registers in parallel at the start of a task, and possibly at procedure change. In the programs studied so far the average number of registers moved to or from the stack at once is between 2 and 3, so the idea of a "planar stack has been abandoned, at least for the present. If procedure calls were handled as task activations the strategy might change.

Index management provides a good example of the need to combine an

sentially serial mode of operation (scanning mix sequences) with para-
el operation on bitmaps. When an index is exhausted a task forces or
aits a recovery cycle, which involves scanning the pointers in each
sk and base and forming for each object class a map of the objects in
se. The free index lists can then be reconstructed by simple logical
erations. For storage the unit of allocation is a plane, so that a
mory of 1M planes would require a bitmap of 4K planes.

Parallel operations are used in the system to check authority, to bind
ntrol modules dynamically to base and task environments, to serach di-
ctories, to control scheduling, to search symbol tables, to test memory,
d on many other occasions. In most cases they replace more complex or
me-consuming algorithms based on scalar operands, but it is practically
possible to form a reliable estimate of their "value".

CONCLUSION

Introduction of any new facility incurs costs that must be weighed
ainst tangible advantages. In the system model outlined here the memory
s seen as a conventional interleaved array in which each word slice is
nhanced by additional buffer registers, processing elements, and data
aths. On the evidence of work to date there is no case for highly
pecialised functions on planar data. Most of the system operations
equire only elementary logic, arithmetic and comparison functions. In
omparison with DAP design there is little demand for vertical arithmetic
nd limited use of PE interconnections orthogonal to the word axis.
evertheless the resulting Active Memory Array can be seen as a replace-
ent for paged memory control system and an improvement on previous cache
emory subsystems.

In terms of return on investment, it can be argued that the best value
s obtained by improving generally useful facilities such as data movement
nd instruction composition rather than on specialised functions that, in
he system context, are used only a fraction of the time. The point can
e illustrated by considering the resolution of a Prolog goal such as:

:- $add(X,Y,Z)$

here X, Y and Z are permitted to be plane sequences and addition is ex-
ended to vectors. In the PN Machine the planar data paths assist not

only the vector calculation but also the management of the Prolog data structure, the Prolog interpreter, and the surrounding system. In a more specialised approach one would face the problem of scheduling access to three different machines: the "host", the Prolog engine, and the array processor.

With regard to the dimension of the array, the system functions do not operate on such large tables that massive parallelism is justifiable In the experimental studies a plane of 256 bits has been used, together with the tags on each word. That has some advantages from the coding point of view, and the expected pressure for larger planes has not mater ialised. The scale of parallelism is more likely to be determined by th applications, but even here the preferred approach is to increase M rather than N.

It is relatively easy to provide parallel function without parallel data paths. A microprogrammed version of the PN Machine was built by the author and P. Griffiths at Queen Mary College in 1985-86, using the AMD 29116 micromachine. It was used to show that a level of performance for scalar operations comparable with the Motorola MC68000 could be achieved without losing the ability to engineer precise program environments. The planar operations were implemented serially in microcode and required about thirty times the number of machine cycles of a truly parallel version. When the usage of parallel operations exceeds 5% the effect is noticeable. That was an instructive way of appreciating the value of parallelism in system design.

6 REFERENCE

[1]*J.K. Iliffe*, Patent Application Number 8626368 "A method of cache memory control", Patent Office, London (November 1986)

The translation of processes into circuits

Anne Kaldewaij

Department of Mathematics and Computing Science
Eindhoven University of Technology
P.O. Box 513, 5600 MB Eindhoven, The Netherlands

bstract

process is a pair $< A, X >$ in which A is a set of symbols (the alphabet) and X is a
on-empty prefix-closed subset of A^* (the trace set). A process may be viewed as the
ecification of a mechanism:

symbols correspond to events that may occur.

traces correspond to sequences of events that may be observed when the mechanism
is in operation.

 this paper we show how for a certain class of processes circuits can be derived that
ehave as prescribed by these processes. The circuits are delay-insensitive in the sense that
eir behaviour does not depend on delays in wires and switching elements.

vents may be initiated by a mechanism (active events) or by the environment of the
echanism (passive events). It is shown how active events can be transformed into pas-
ve events, and vice versa.

e show how the composition of processes corresponds to the composition of circuits.

Overview

 Section 1 we present the definition and most relevant properties of processes.

ection 2 addresses implementation aspects. The correspondence between events and tran-
itions on wires that are related to these events is discussed. A four phase handshaking
rotocol is explained, as well as the notions of active and passive.

 Section 3 we introduce the basic elements that will be used in the construction of cir-
uits.

ection 4 is devoted to an implementation of the process $SEM_1(a, b)$ in which a is active
nd b is passive.

 Section 5 we reconsider the notions of active and passive and we show how an imple-
entation of one kind can be transformed into an implementation of the other kind.

ection 6 discusses the compostion of circuits.

1 Processes

In this section we present the most relevant properties of processes. Readers familiar with trace theory as described in [2] may skip this section.

We assume the existence of a set of names, called Ω. Elements of Ω are called *symbols*. Subsets of Ω are called *alphabets*. The set of all finite-length sequences of elements of Ω is denoted by Ω^*. This includes the empty sequence ϵ. For an alphabet A, A^* is defined similarly. Elements of Ω^* are called *traces*. Subsets of Ω^* are called *trace sets*.

The *concatenation* of traces s and t is obtained by placing t to the right of s, and is denoted by st.

The *projection* of a trace t on an alphabet A, denoted by $t{\upharpoonright}A$, is obtained from t by removing the symbols that are not in A.

The projection of a trace set X on an alphabet A, denoted by $X{\upharpoonright}A$, is the trace set $\{t{\upharpoonright}A \mid t \in X\}$.

The length of a trace t is denoted by $l(t)$.

Trace s is called a *prefix* of t, denoted by $s \leqslant t$, if $(\mathbf{E}\,u : u \in \Omega^* : su = t)$.

The *prefix closure* of a trace set X, denoted by $pref(X)$, is the trace set consisting of all prefixes of elements of X: $pref(X) = \{s \in \Omega^* \mid (\mathbf{E}\,t : t \in X : s \leqslant t)\}$

Trace set X is called *prefix-closed* if $X = pref(X)$.

A *process* is a pair $<A,X>$ in which A is an alphabet and X is a non-empty prefix-closed subset of A^*. We call A the alphabet of the process and we call X the trace set of the process. If T is a process we denote its alphabet by $\mathbf{a}T$ and its trace set by $\mathbf{t}T$, i.e. $T = <\mathbf{a}T, \mathbf{t}T>$.

Let T be a process, then T specifies a mechanism in the following way.

The alphabet of T corresponds to the set of events the mechanism may be involved in.

With the mechanism in operation a so-called *trace thus far generated* is associated. Initially, this trace is the empty trace. On the occurrence of an event the trace thus far generated is extended with the symbol associated with that event. At any moment, the trace thus far generated belongs to the trace set of T.

Example 1.0

Consider a binary semaphore initialized at zero. We specify the semaphore by means of a process T. Possible events are

    a :   a V-operation on the semaphore
    b :   a P-operation on the semaphore

Hence, $\mathbf{a}T = \{a,b\}$.
Let $t \in \mathbf{t}T$. Since a P-operation can only take place if a corresponding V-operation has occurred, we have $l(t{\upharpoonright}a) - l(t{\upharpoonright}b) \geqslant 0$. From the fact that the semaphore is a binary semaphore we infer $l(t{\upharpoonright}a) - l(t{\upharpoonright}b) \leqslant 1$. These restrictions should hold for all t, $t \in \mathbf{t}T$,

nd their prefixes. Our specification becomes

$$T = <\{a,b\},\{t\in\{a,b\}^* \mid (\mathbf{A}\,s:s\leqslant t:0\leqslant l(s\restriction a)-l(s\restriction b)\leqslant 1)\}>$$

End of Example)

'inally, we define the following processes. For an alphabet A process $RUN(A)$ is defined by

$$RUN(A) = <A,A^*>$$

'or symbols a and b, and natural number k process $SEM_k(a,b)$ is defined by

$$SEM_k(a,b) = <\{a,b\},\{t\in\{a,b\}^* \mid (\mathbf{A}\,s:s\leqslant t:0\leqslant l(s\restriction a)-l(s\restriction b)\leqslant k)\}>$$

The first *composition operator* that we consider is called weaving.

Consider two mechanisms P and Q specified by processes T and U respectively. The behaviour of the *composite* of P and Q should be in accordance with the behaviour of each of the components:

if t is the trace thus far generated of the composite then $t\restriction\mathbf{a}T$ will be the trace thus far generated of P and $t\restriction\mathbf{a}U$ will be the trace thus far generated of Q. Hence, extension of the trace thus far generated with a common symbol of $\mathbf{a}T$ and $\mathbf{a}U$ is possible if and only if both P and Q agree upon that symbol. Extension with a non-common symbol depends on one of the components only.

n terms of processes this is captured in the following definition.

The *weave* of processes T and U, denoted by $T\,\mathbf{w}\,U$, is defined by

$$T\,\mathbf{w}\,U = <\mathbf{a}T\cup\mathbf{a}U,\{t\in(\mathbf{a}T\cup\mathbf{a}U)^* \mid t\restriction\mathbf{a}T\in tT \wedge t\restriction\mathbf{a}U\in tU\}>$$

Example 1.1

$SEM_1(a,b) = <\{a,b\},\{\epsilon,a,ab,aba,\cdots\}>$
$SEM_1(b,c) = <\{b,c\},\{\epsilon,b,bc,bcb,\cdots\}>$, hence,

$\quad t(SEM_1(a,b)\,\mathbf{w}\,SEM_1(b,c))$
$=\quad$ { definition of weaving }
$\quad \{t\in\{a,b,c\}^* \mid t\restriction\{a,b\}\in tSEM_1(a,b) \wedge t\restriction\{b,c\}\in tSEM_1(b,c)\}$
$=\quad$ { definition of SEM_1 }
$\quad \{\epsilon,a,ab,aba,abc,abac,abca,abacb,abcab,\cdots\}$

Since $t\restriction\{a,b\}\in tSEM_1(a,b)$ implies $0\leqslant l(t\restriction a)-l(t\restriction b)\leqslant 1$
and $t\restriction\{b,c\}\in tSEM_1(b,c)$ implies $0\leqslant l(t\restriction b)-l(t\restriction c)\leqslant 1$,
we have

$$0 \leqslant l(t \restriction a) - l(t \restriction c) \leqslant 2$$

(End of Example)

The weave of processes is viewed as the specification of the composite of the components they specify. Symbols that belong to more than one of the alphabets of the processes are called *internal* symbols.

The other symbols, i.e. those that belong to one of the alphabets only, are called *external* symbols. In the ultimate specification of a composite we want to specify a mechanism without any information about its internal structure. This leads to the following definition.

The *blend* of processes T and U, denoted by $T \mathbf{b} U$, is defined by

$$T \mathbf{b} U = (T \mathbf{w} U) \restriction (\mathbf{a}T \div \mathbf{a}U)$$

where $\div$ denotes symmetric set difference, i.e. $A \div B = (A \cup B) \setminus (A \cap B)$.

Processes may be represented by labeled directed graphs. The relation between processes and graphs is as follows.

Let T be a process. The equivalence relation $\underset{T}{\sim}$ on $\mathbf{t}T$ is defined by

$$s \underset{T}{\sim} t \equiv (\mathbf{A} u : u \in \mathbf{a}T^* : su \in \mathbf{t}T \equiv tu \in \mathbf{t}T)$$

The equivalence classes of $\underset{T}{\sim}$ are called the *states* of T. $[t]_T$ denotes, as usual, the equivalence class to which t belongs.
Whenever T is obvious, we omit T in $\underset{T}{\sim}$ and $[t]_T$.

Example 1.2

$SEM_1(a, b)$ has two states, viz. $[\epsilon]$ and $[a]$.

(End of Example)

If $[s] = [t]$ and $sa \in \mathbf{t}T$, we have, due to the definition of $\sim$ that $[sa] = [ta]$ as well. Hence, we have a relation R on the set of states, viz.

$$[s] R [t] \equiv (\mathbf{E} a : a \in \mathbf{a}T : [sa] = [t])$$

This relation can be represented by a directed labeled graph. The states of T are the nodes of the graph. If $[s] R [t]$ then there is an arc, labeled a, from $[s]$ to $[t]$ for each symbol $a \in \mathbf{a}T$ such that $[sa] = [t]$. State $[\epsilon]$ is called the initial state; in pictures of state graphs the initial state is drawn fat.

Figure 1.0 shows the state graph of $SEM_1(a,b)$.

A state graph of the weave of two processes can be constructed from the state graphs of these processes as follows.

Consider all pairs (α,β) where α is a state of T and β is a state of U. Take these pairs as nodes. There is a labeled arc from one node to an other node if and only if it is in agreement with both state graphs.

The initial state is the pair of the initial states of T and U. In the resulting graph one may remove all nodes that are not reachable from the initial node.

Example 1.3

The state graphs of $SEM_1(a,b)$ and $SEM_1(b,c)$ are shown in Figure 1.0 and Figure 1.1 respectively. Applying the method described above yields Figure 1.2, a state graph of $SEM_1(a,b) \mathbf{w} SEM_1(b,c)$.

Projection on $\{a,c\}$ yields Figure 1.3, the state graph of $SEM_2(a,c)$.

(End of Example)

Figure 1.0

Figure 1.1

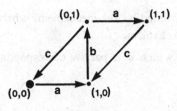

Figure 1.2

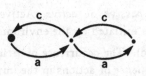

Figure 1.3

2 Implementation Aspects

Let T be a process. We wish to construct a circuit that behaves in accordance with T.

With symbol a we associate a pair (a_o, a_i) of boolean variables. One may associate an 'output wire' with a_o and an 'input wire' with a_i. The value true will correspond to a high voltage on the associated wire and the value false will correspond to a low voltage on the associated wire. If x is such a boolean variable then

$x\uparrow$ means $x := \text{true}$ ('set x to a high voltage')
$x\downarrow$ means $x := \text{false}$ ('set x to a low voltage')

Event a takes place when on the pair (a_o, a_i) a four-phase hand-shaking protocol takes place. Such a protocol is a sequence of transitions in such a way that any two successive transitions occur on different wires. This definition leaves room for two sequences: $a_i\uparrow; a_o\uparrow; a_i\downarrow; a_o\downarrow$ and $a_o\uparrow; a_i\uparrow; a_o\downarrow; a_i\downarrow$. Since a_i is an input, event a is initiated by the environment when the first sequence is used. When the second sequence is used the circuit initiates a.

For sequential programs we use the guarded command language with CSP-syntax (cf. [0]) :

[$\cdots$] instead of **if** $\cdots$ **fi**
*[$\cdots$] instead of **do** $\cdots$ **od**

Execution of an if-statement amounts to suspension of the program until one or more of the guards evaluate to true, after which a statement of which the guard is true is selected.

*[true $\rightarrow$ S] is abbreviated to *[S]   ('do S forever')
[$B \rightarrow$ **skip**] is abbreviated to [B]   ('wait until B')

For any boolean x
[x] may be interpreted as 'wait until x has a high voltage'.
[$\neg x$] may be interpreted as 'wait until x has a low voltage'.

We rephrase the notions explained above:

Events are either *passive* or *active*. Active events are initiated by the mechanism, whereas passive events are initiated by the environment of the mechanism.

Let a be a symbol. The occurrence of a in a process in which a is *passive* corresponds to the following sequence of actions in the implementation

[a_i] ; $a_o\uparrow$; [$\neg a_i$] ; $a_o\downarrow$ (a passive)

After execution of [a_i] ; $a_o\uparrow$ event a 'has happened'.
The environment of the implementation performs a by the sequence

$a_i\uparrow$; $[a_o]$; $a_i\downarrow$; $[\neg a_o]$ (environment of passive a)

The occurrence of a in a process in which a is *active* corresponds to

$a_o\uparrow$; $[a_i]$; $a_o\downarrow$; $[\neg a_i]$ (a active)

After execution of $a_o\uparrow$; $[a_i]$ event a 'has happened'.
The environment performs a by the sequence

$[a_o]$; $a_i\uparrow$; $[\neg a_o]$; $a_i\downarrow$ (environment of active a)

Apparently,

the pair (a_o,a_i) of a mechanism corresponds to the pair (a_i,a_o) of the environment. If (a_o,a_i) is active then (a_i,a_o) is passive and vice versa.

The transformation of symbol a into such a sequence is called *handshaking expansion*.

Example 2.0

Consider process $SEM_1(a,b)$, which is given by the program text $*[a;b]$.
If a is passive and b is active, handshaking expansion yields

$*[[a_i] ; a_o\uparrow ; [\neg a_i] ; a_o\downarrow ; b_o\uparrow ; [b_i] ; b_o\downarrow ; [\neg b_i]]$

If both a and b are active, we have

$*[a_o\uparrow ; [a_i] ; a_o\downarrow ; [\neg a_i] ; b_o\uparrow ; [b_i] ; b_o\downarrow ; [\neg b_i]]$

These programs express the behaviour of mechanisms with respect to a_i, a_o, b_i, and b_o.
In the next section we realize such a mechanism.

End of Example)

Basic Elements

A basic element has a single output and zero or more inputs. A basic element with output z is specified by means of two boolean expressions, B_0 and B_1 say, and is denoted as follows:

$B_0 \rightarrow z\uparrow$
$B_1 \rightarrow z\downarrow$

B_0 and B_1 are boolean expressions in the names of the element's inputs. In order to avoid conflicts on what value the output should be we require each element to satisfy the following rule of disjointness:

$$\neg B_0 \ \lor \ \neg B_1 \qquad \text{for all values of the inputs}$$

For the construction of our circuits we assume the existence of the following basic elements.

An *And-element* has two inputs and one output. If both inputs are true the output will be true, otherwise the output will be false. If x and y are inputs and z is output this is expressed by

$$x \land y \ \rightarrow \ z\uparrow$$
$$\neg x \lor \neg y \ \rightarrow \ z\downarrow$$

A *C-element* has two inputs and one output. If the inputs have the same value then the output will also receive that value, otherwise the output does not change its value. This is expressed by

$$x \land y \ \rightarrow \ z\uparrow$$
$$\neg x \land \neg y \ \rightarrow \ z\downarrow$$

An *Inverter* has one input and one output. The output receives as its value the negation of the value of the input. It is expressed by

$$x \ \rightarrow \ z\downarrow$$
$$\neg x \ \rightarrow \ z\uparrow$$

Figure 3.0 shows how these basic elements are represented in pictures of circuits.

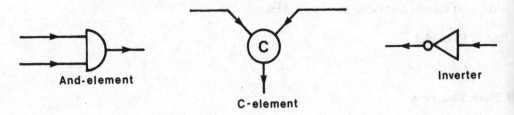

And-element

C-element

Inverter

Figure 3.0

An Inverter in front of an And-element or C-element is incorporated in that element, thus yielding a new basic element. The Inverter is drawn as a circle attached to the element. As an example, consider the specification

$$x \wedge \neg y \ \rightarrow \ z\uparrow$$
$$\neg x \wedge \ y \ \rightarrow \ z\downarrow$$

This denotes a C-element with
inputs x and $\neg y$, and output z.

The corresponding circuit is shown in Figure 3.1

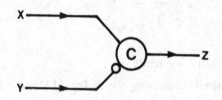

Figure 3.1

4 An implementation of $SEM_1(a,b)$

In this section we show an implementation of $SEM_1(a,b)$ where a is passive and b is active (cf. Example 2.0). Handshaking expansion yields

$$*[[a_i]'; a_o\uparrow ; [\neg a_i] ; a_o\downarrow ; b_o\uparrow ; [b_i] ; b_o\downarrow ; [\neg b_i]]$$

Initially we have $\neg a_o \wedge \neg a_i \wedge \neg b_o \wedge \neg b_i$. This state equals the state after $a_o\downarrow$. Hence, we need an additional variable, say x, to be able to trigger $b_o\uparrow$. Initially $\neg x$ holds. Since $x\uparrow$ should occur after $a_o\uparrow$ and before $a_o\downarrow$ we propose:

$$*[[a_i] ; a_o\uparrow ; x\uparrow ; [\neg a_i \wedge x] ; a_o\downarrow ; b_o\uparrow ; [b_i] ; x\downarrow ; [\neg x] ; b_o\downarrow ; [\neg b_i]]$$

We then have a unique state for every transition:

(0) $a_i \wedge \neg x \wedge \neg b_i \ \rightarrow \ a_o\uparrow$

         $\neg a_i \wedge \ . \ x \qquad\qquad \rightarrow \ a_o\downarrow$

(1) $a_o \ \rightarrow \ x\uparrow$

         $b_i \ \rightarrow \ x\downarrow$

(2) $\neg a_o \wedge x \ \rightarrow \ b_o\uparrow$

                 $\neg x \ \rightarrow \ b_o\downarrow$

Since in the period from $a_o\uparrow$ until $a_o\downarrow$ we have $\neg b_i$, we may transform (0) into

(0') $(\ a_i \wedge \neg x) \wedge \neg b_i \ \rightarrow \ a_o\uparrow$

         $(\neg a_i \wedge \ x) \vee \ b_i \ \rightarrow \ a_o\downarrow$

This is a combination of a C-element and an And-element :

$$a_i \wedge \neg x \ \rightarrow \ y\uparrow$$
$$\neg a_i \wedge \ x \ \rightarrow \ y\downarrow$$

$$y \wedge \neg b_i \rightarrow a_o\!\uparrow$$
$$\neg y \vee b_i \rightarrow a_o\!\downarrow$$

Initially $\neg y$ holds.

A similar reasoning yields for (1) and (2)

(1') $\neg b_i \wedge a_o \rightarrow x\!\uparrow$ a C-element
      $b_i \wedge \neg a_o \rightarrow x\!\downarrow$

(2') $\neg a_o \wedge x \rightarrow b_o\!\uparrow$ an And-element
      $a_o \vee \neg x \rightarrow b_o\!\downarrow$

The ultimate circuit is shown in Figure 4.0 . The fat dots denote so-called *internal forks*. As in [3], we assume that the propagation delay in a forked wire is short compared to the delays in the basic elements. These forks are needed due to the fact that some variables occur as input for distinct basic elements.

A slightly different circuit for $SEM_1(a,b)$ has been derived by R.R. Hoogerwoord (cf. [1]). He also constructed a prototype of this circuit.

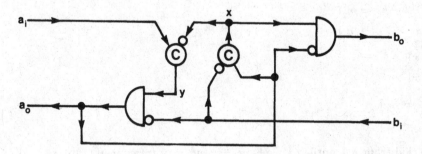

Figure 4.0

Active and Passive

Suppose we have a circuit corresponding to a process with passive a. We wish to connect an 'activator' (cf. Figure 5.0) to a_i and a_o such that its other two wires, p_i and p_o, yield an active version of a.

Action $p_o\uparrow$ is to be executed as soon as the original circuit is willing to acknowledge a_i. This yields

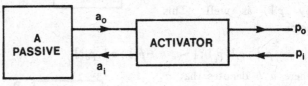

$$[a_i\uparrow : [a_o] : p_o\uparrow : [p_i] : a_i\downarrow : [\neg a_o] : p_o\downarrow : [\neg p_i]]$$

Figure 5.0

Notice that the 'return to zero phase' has been moved to the right. We have

$$\neg p_i \rightarrow a_i\uparrow \qquad \text{(an Inverter)}$$
$$p_i \rightarrow a_i\downarrow$$

and

$$a_o \rightarrow p_o\uparrow \qquad \text{(a wire)}$$
$$\neg a_o \rightarrow p_o\downarrow$$

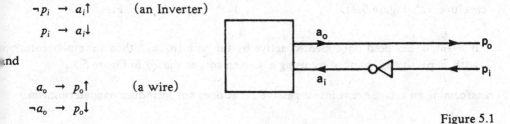

Figure 5.1

We conclude (cf. Figure 5.1)

> If event a has been implemented as passive, by the pair (a_o, a_i), then an implementation with a active is obtained by placing an Inverter in front of a_i.

Warning

Transforming a passive event into an active event in the way described above may introduce internal nondeterminism. If there is an (external) choice between two passive events then activation of these events will lead to an internal choice between them. (To implement a choice between two inputs a new basic element, an Arbiter element, is needed. A treatment of such an element falls beyond the scope of this note, we restrict ourselves to components that do not require the use of Arbiter-elements.)

(End of Warning)

Suppose event a has been implemented as an active event. We wish to connect a 'passivator' (cf. Figure 5.2) to a_i and a_o such that its other two wires, p_i and p_o, yield a passive version of a.

The original circuit may initiate a (by $a_o\!\uparrow$) as soon as that is possible. It is not acknowledged until the environment initiates a (by $p_i\!\uparrow$) as well. This yields

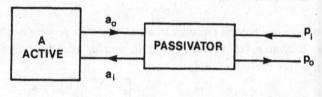

Figure 5.2

$$[\,[\,a_o \wedge p_i\,]\;;\,a_i\!\uparrow,p_o\!\uparrow\;;\,[\,\neg a_o \wedge \neg p_i\,]\;;\,a_i\!\downarrow,p_o\!\downarrow\,]$$

where $a\,,b$ denotes that a and b may occur in any order.

This gives rise to a C-element.

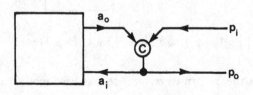

We conclude (cf. Figure 5.3)

Figure 5.3

If event a has been implemented active by the pair $(a_o\,,a_i)$ then an implementation with a passive is obtained by using a C-element as shown in Figure 5.3 .

(Transforming an active event into a passive event does not introduce nondeterminism.)

Consider the circuit shown in Figure 5.4 . It consists of a C-element and a part called M. The occurrence of event a corresponds to the sequence

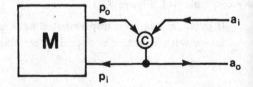

Figure 5.4

$$a_i\!\uparrow,p_o\!\uparrow\;;\,(a_o\!\uparrow\;;\,a_i\!\downarrow)\,,(p_i\!\uparrow\;;\,p_o\!\downarrow)\;;\,a_o\!\downarrow,p_i\!\downarrow$$

Projection on $\{a_o\,,a_i\}$ and $\{p_o\,,p_i\}$ yields respectively

$$a_i\!\uparrow\;;\,a_o\!\uparrow\;;\,a_i\!\downarrow\;;\,a_o\!\downarrow \qquad \text{(passive)}$$
$$p_o\!\uparrow\;;\,p_i\!\uparrow\;;\,p_o\!\downarrow\;;\,p_i\!\downarrow \qquad \text{(active)}$$

We conclude that removing the C-element transforms event a from passive into active. This transformation does not introduce nondeterminism.

In general we cannot transform an active event into a passive event by removing an Inverter. This is demonstrated by the following example.

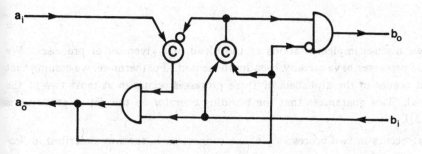

Figure 5.5

Example 5.0

In Section 4 we derived a circuit for $SEM_1(a,b)$ in which a is passive and b is active. Removing the inverters to which b_i is connected yields the circuit shown in Figure 5.5 .

After $a_i\uparrow$ nothing will happen until $b_i\uparrow$ has occurred. This is not a valid implementation of $SEM_1(a,b)$.

End of Example)

There is another remark on the difference between activators and passivators. In the next section we show how the composite of processes may be obtained by connecting wires that correspond to the same symbol. In view of the handshaking protocol we will connect events of different types only. If both implementations are active then a C-element is used (cf. Figure 5.6). Notice the symmetry of the connection (it is not known which of the implementations is turned into a passive one).

If both implementations are passive then a choice can be made (cf. Figure 5.7). This choice should be such that no nondeterminism is introduced.

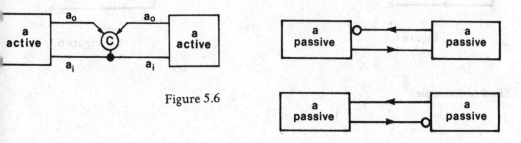

Figure 5.6

Figure 5.7

6 Composition

In this section we discuss implementations of the blend of a given set of processes. We assume that these processes have already been implemented. Furthermore, we assume that any symbol that occurs in the alphabets of these processes occurs in at most two of the processes involved. This guarantees that the blending operator on this set of processes is associative (cf. [2]).

Each symbol that occurs in two processes yields a connection in the way described in Section 5 :

If the events have different types the connection is straightforward. If the events are both active a passivator is used. If the events are both passive one of these is activated.

In the last case one of the events should allow activation, i.e. activation should not cause nondeterminism. Notice that activating may also be done by removing a passivator.

Finally, we may activate or passivate events.

Example 6.0

Process $RUN(a)$ is given by the program text $*[a]$.

With a passive, handshaking expansion yields $*[[a_i] ; a_o\uparrow ; [\neg a_i] ; a_o\downarrow]$ which is just a wire.

Process $RUN(a,b)$ equals the composite of processes $RUN(a)$ and $RUN(b)$. The method described above yields the circuit of Figure 6.0. An implementation with both a and b active is obtained by adding inverters, and is shown in Figure 6.1.

Figure 6.0   Figure 6.1

(End of Example)

Example 6.1

An implementation of $SEM_2(a,b)$ with a passive and b active can be obtained from implementations of $SEM_1(a,b)$ with a passive and b active.

The circuit is shown in Figure 6.2.

(End of Example)

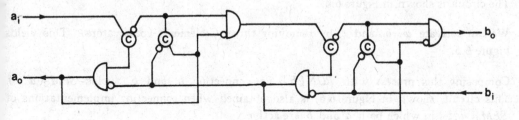

Figure 6.2

Example 6.2

We implement process $SEM_1(a,b) \mathbf{w} SEM_1(b,c)$ with a, b, and c passive.
This process is the blend of the processes
$SEM_1(p \cdot a, p \cdot b)$, $SEM_1(q \cdot a, q \cdot b)$,
and the process given by the program

$$[p \cdot a; a \mid p \cdot b, q \cdot a; b \mid q \cdot b; c]$$

The state graph of the weave
of these processes is shown
in Figure 6.3.

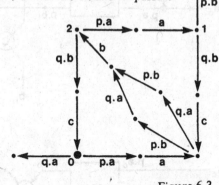

Figure 6.3

We assume that processes $SEM_1(p \cdot a, p \cdot b)$ and $SEM_1(q \cdot a, q \cdot b)$ have been implemented with all events active.

The state graph of Figure 6.3 shows two deadlock states. To avoid these we implement the program such that an alternative is executed if both subcomponent and environment initiate that alternative.

This yields the following expansions (output of a subcomponent is treated as input of the circuit corresponding to the command, and vice versa):

$$*[[\,p\cdot a_o \wedge a_i \;\rightarrow\; p\cdot a_i\!\uparrow, a_o\!\uparrow : [\neg p\cdot a_o \wedge \neg a_i] \;;\; p\cdot a_i\!\downarrow, a_o\!\downarrow\,]]$$

$$*[[\,p\cdot b_o \wedge q\cdot a_o \wedge b_i \;\rightarrow\; p\cdot b_i\!\uparrow, q\cdot a_i\!\uparrow, b_o\!\uparrow : [\neg p\cdot b_o \wedge \neg q\cdot a_o \wedge \neg b_i] \;;\; p\cdot b_i\!\downarrow, q\cdot a_i\!\downarrow, b_o\!\downarrow\,]]$$

$$*[[\,q\cdot b_o \wedge c_i \;\rightarrow\; q\cdot b_i\!\uparrow, c_o\!\uparrow : [\neg q\cdot b_o \wedge \neg c_i] \;;\; q\cdot b_i\!\downarrow, c_o\!\downarrow\,]]$$

The first and the last one give rise to a C-element (with forked output). The middle one yields two C-elements.

The circuit is shown in Figure 6.4.

We can activate a, b, and c by removing three C-elements (passivators). This yields Figure 6.5.

Composing this process with $RUN(b)$, i.e. connecting b_i and b_o yields $SEM_2(a,c)$. This circuit, shown in Figure 6.6, is also obtained when connecting implementations of $SEM_1(a,b)$ in which both a and b are active.

(End of Example)

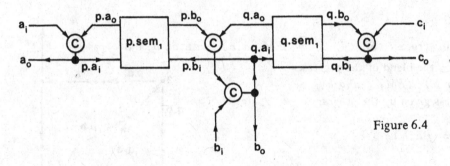

Figure 6.4

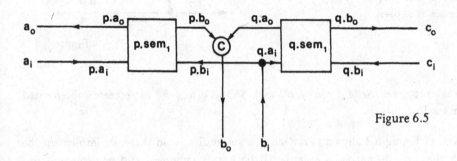

Figure 6.5

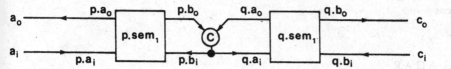

Figure 6.6

Final Remarks

We have shown how a certain class of processes can be implemented as delay-insensitive circuits. Nondeterminism did not play a role in the examples, due to the fact that we did not use Arbiter-elements. A treatment of these elements falls beyond the scope of this monograph. A typical process for which an Arbiter-element is needed is $SEM_1(a,\{b,c\})$ in which a, b, and c are passive.

A general method for the translation of programs into circuits has to be investigated. Since processes correspond to minimal deterministic state graphs, it is worthwhile to consider the translation from state graphs into circuits as well.

The concepts active and passive and the relations between these are very useful. The concepts 'input' and 'output' should be reserved for the description of processes on a higher level.

Acknowledgements

I gratefully acknowledge Alain J. Martin, who introduced me to the concepts that form the base of this paper. He visited the Eindhoven University during the summer of 1985. His suggestions and discussions inspired me very much.

References

[0]   Hoare, C.A.R.
       Communicating Sequential Processes.
       Communications of the ACM **21** (1978); pp. 666-677.

[1]   Hoogerwoord, R.R.
       Some reflections on the implementation of trace structures.
       Computing Science Notes CS86/3.
       Department of Mathematics and Computing Science.
       Eindhoven University of Technology, 1986.

[2]   Kaldewaij, A.
       A Formalism for Concurrent Processes.
       Ph.D.-thesis.
       Eindhoven University of Technology, 1986.

[3]   Martin, Alain J.
       The Design of a Self-Timed Circuit for Distributed Mutual Exclusion.
       Proceedings 1985 Chapel Hill Conference on VLSI; ed H. Fuchs.
       Computer Science Press, Rockville. 1985; pp. 247-260.

[4]   Rem, Martin
       Concurrent Computations and VLSI Circuits.
       Control Flow and Data Flow: Concepts of Distributed Programming;
       ed. M. Broy.
       Springer, Berlin, 1985; pp. 399-437.

as a characterization of the system behavior when using different mapping strategies. The sensitivity of the SUPRENUM architecture against various mapping strategies is discussed in chapter 6. We analyse the worst-/best-case behaviour of important process systems and work out the main criteria for good heuristics. Chapter 7 contains the sensitivity analysis for the Hypercube architecture. The rationale for adaptive routing is discussed in chapter 8.

2 A parallel programming paradigm of abstract machines

Our analysis is based on a fairly general programming paradigm which consists of a network of abstract machines (for detail see [MKLMS87]). The central abstract machine is called LAM – the Local memory Abstract Machine. LAM provides the following operations for entities called processes:

(I)   Processes are disjoint (no shared variables).

(II) Processes can create other processes and can terminate.

(III) Communication is done by asynchronous message passing between partners (processes which share some knowledge e.g. know each other).

LAM allows arbitrary communication and dynamic evolution.

In applications with regular networks more specific abstract machines can be defined by adding additional constraints. This will be explained by RLAM — the Ring Local memory Abstract Machine. RLAM is defined informally by (I) – (III) and

(IV) In RLAM every process has exactly two communication partners, called neighbors. Communication is restricted to neighbors only.

Similarly other topologies can be defined like tree, torus, hypercube and the totally interconnected abstract machines. These abstract machines have to be mapped onto real machines of a given connection structure, e.g. lattice, hypercube or butterfly.

The programming task can now be characterized as in figure 1. The problem is formulated in an

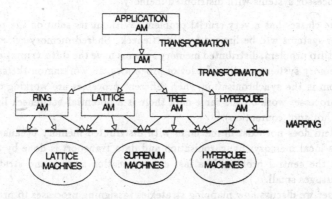

Figure 1: Transformation and mapping of the application to the real machine

application oriented abstract machine, then it is transformed (manually and/or automatically) to an specific abstract machine implementation. This machine will then be mapped onto the topology of the real machine (automatically by the operating system and/or by explicit mapping).

Mapping Strategies
in Message Based Multiprocessor Systems

O. Krämer, H. Mühlenbein

Gesellschaft für Mathematik und Datenverarbeitung mbH

Postfach 1240, D-5205 St. Augustin

Abstract

Machines with distributed memory have the mapping problem — assigning processes to processors. In this paper we define the mapping problem as an optimization problem and discuss the question, how far is an optimum solution from an average or random solution.

The term robustness is introduced and explained in detail with two examples, the SU-PRENUM and the Hypercube architecture. For the SUPRENUM architecture we show that a simple mapping strategy (optimal clustering of the processes) gives almost as good results as the optimal mapping. Optimal mapping is more important for the Hypercube architecture.

Mapping strategies are difficult to apply for inhomogeneous networks. For this networks adaptive routing seems promising.

1 Introduction

In the research for a new generation of computers a worldwide trend to parallel systems can be observed. The new machines make use of massive parallelism by the connection of some hundreds (or even thousands) of single processors to a "supercomputer".

The new machines can be divided into two classes, depending on their concept of memory access (see [Hock85]):

- multiprocessor systems with shared memory,

- multiprocessor systems with distributed memory.

Each of the classes has a very crucial problem. Without its solution the performance of the multiprocessor systems will be limited by a bottleneck. Shared memory systems have the **data synchronisation** problem, distributed memory systems have the **data transportation** problem.

Shared memory systems consist of a lot of processors, all working on the same memory. The central problem is the synchronisation when different processes are working on the same data. If too many processes work on the same data there is a potential bottleneck limiting the system performance (hot spot contention).

This problem does not exist in machines with distributed memory because each process can access only its local memory. Synchronisation and data transport is done by a message passing system. Now the central problem is a fast communication system and strategies to keep the amount of messages small.

In this paper we discuss how mapping strategies (assigning processes to processors) influence the amount of communication.

In chapter 2 we introduce a process model and the local memory abstract machine. In chapter 3 a mathematical model for the mapping problem is defined. Chapter 4 presents the three main approaches to solve the mapping problem: the topological mapping, a mathematical programming problem and an adaptive mapping strategy. In chapter 5 the term robustness is introduced

215

The program, running on a network of abstract or real machines, consists of independent processes, each communicating with partners. This program can be described by a process graph.

A process graph is given by a set of processes P and a neighbourship description K. It can be represented as digraph (P, K). An edge from process p to process q means that q is neighbour of p. So process p can send messages to his neighbour q.

A process structure is called

- **static**, if its number of nodes and the communication structure is fixed and known before runtime. The process–processor placement is done once at the program start and needs not to be changed during its run,

- **multi–phased**, if different communication structures are used during different phases of the computation (see figure 2),

- **dynamic**, if processes and communication links can be created during runtime. This model is more general and needs new concepts for process placement.

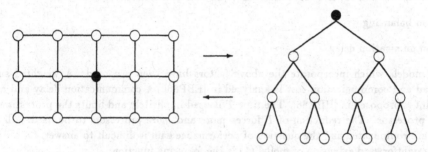

Figure 2: Multiphase computation

Some examples of multi-phased and dynamic networks are discussed in [HoMü86].

3 Mathematical Models for the Mapping Problem

Any distributed memory architecture can be described by the following model:

N set of processors
C communication cost
     $C_{m,n} :=$ cost per information unit from processor $m \rightarrow n$, $(m, n \in N)$
S size of storage for each processor, with $S = (S_1, \ldots, S_{|N|})$.

A static process structure is described similarly:

P set of processes
K communication amount,
     $K_{p,q} :=$ information units passed from process $p \rightarrow q$, $(p, q \in P)$
R amount of storage for each process with $R = (R_1, \ldots, R_{|P|})$

Common to the distributed architectures is the fact that the distances between pairs of processors are not equal. So the delay for sending a message depends on the locations of the sending and the receiving processor.

An optimal mapping is given by a function

$$\pi : P \rightarrow N$$

assigning each process to a processor, which minimizes the communication cost Γ_C

$$\Gamma_C^* = \min_{\pi} \Gamma_C = \min_{\pi} \sum_{p,q \in P} K_{p,q} \cdot C_{\pi(p),\pi(q)} \qquad (1)$$

s.t.

$$\forall n \in N : \sum_{\substack{p \in P \\ \pi(p)=n}} R_p \leq S_n$$

Γ_C describes the total communication cost, which is defined as the product of the communication amount between all pairs of processes (p, q) and the cost to transport this message between the assigned processes $(\pi(p), \pi(q))$. The assignment has to satisfy the constraint that the storage amount of all processes getting assigned to one processor may not exceed the available storage of this node.

The cost function (1) is a very simple measure and does not take into account

- load balancing

- communication delay.

Several models which incorporate the above factors have been proposed. A weighted sum of CPU-load and communication cost is analyzed in [EBP86]. A communication delay and a time constraint is proposed in [HHR86]. The time T is used implicitly and limits the processing time of each processor. The reduction of T forces more and more processors to be used. All these models are complicated and the question of performance gain is difficult to answer.

A straightforward extension of model (1) is the following function:

$$\Gamma = \min_{\pi} \left(\Gamma_C + \omega_L \Gamma_L + \omega_B \Gamma_B \right)$$

Γ_C as defined in (1)
Γ_L penalty for unbalanced CPU-load
Γ_B penalty for network bottlenecks

ω_L and ω_B are constants to balance the weights of the three criteria.
Γ_L can be defined as follows: let T_p be the execution time of process p and L_n the load of processor n, then

$$\Gamma_L = \frac{1}{|N|} \sum_{n \in N} (\overline{L} - L_n)^2 \qquad (2)$$

with

$$\overline{L} = \frac{\sum T_p}{|N|} \qquad L_n = \sum_{\substack{p \\ \pi(p)=n}} T_p$$

Γ_L is defined as the variance of the processor loads. Γ_B can be defined analogue.

We believe, however, that these complex models are of limited practical value. They need many parameters, which are seldom known a priori. Heuristics to solve this problem are difficult because three sometimes contradictory criteria influence the solution.

4 The Mapping Strategies

The strategies to solve the mapping problem can be divided into three methods:

- topological mapping,
- mapping by optimizing a cost function,
- adaptive mapping.

Given a machine model (N, C) and a process model (P, K), the following question will be called the **topological mapping** problem:

> Is there a mapping of the process system (P, K) on the machine structure (N, C) such that neighboring processes get assigned to neighboring processors ?

In this general formulation this problem is known to be equivalent to the graph isomorphism problem (see [Bokh81]). This is shown to be NP–complete, such that fast algorithms are not available.

Nevertheless many authors have examined this questions for regular graphs on specific machine architectures (for example [Snyd82] and [SaSc85]). This procedure is useful for the solution of the mapping problem for static process systems and can also be used to examine topological properties of LAMs.

In the case that a topological mapping is not possible, one has to develop fast suboptimal algorithms to get an acceptable solution.

To get a measure for the quality of a solution a mathematical model must be available which describes the communication behavior of the process system on the machine. Central in this **mathematical programming** formulations are the optimization criteria. They enable the algorithms to restrict their search area and lead them into the direction of local optima (heuristic search).

This procedure guarantees good solutions with low computational investments. A variety of heuristics have been developed in different areas where assignment problems arose ([ArRa80], [CHLE80], [ScGa85], [SAKA86]).

We will use the mathematical programming formulation of chapter 3 for the qualitative analysis of the mapping problem.

Both, the topological mapping and mapping as an optimization problem are *feed forward* techniques.

Systems with dynamic process creation need *feed back* strategies taking the actual system state into account. They have to adapt the processor selection to the actual load situation and assign a new process to a suitable processor.

Adaptive mapping can be implemented in a number of ways. In [NiSa86] a dynamic remapping strategy is analyzed and in [ScJo85] user directives are used.

5 Robustness

The tuple (process graph, processor graph) is called **robust**, when the communication costs do not differ significantly on different mapping strategies. If the tuple is robust, then we do not need to look for the optimum mapping.

In the **sensitivity analysis** we compare the results of the optimum mapping to "bad" mapping strategies. The evaluation is done by a comparison of the values of the objective functions of the mathematical model. This analysis can be used to get an answer to the question, how much expense should be invested in the development of mapping strategies.

As representative for the "bad" algorithms we take **random mapping**, which assigns each process to a randomly selected processor. This procedure is bad in the sense that it does not use information about the machine and the process structure. It is possible to find worse mappings, but to do this one has to use structural information. In other words it is as difficult to find a worst mapping than it is to find a best mapping.

In the next chapter we will make an **asymptotic sensitivity analysis** to get a more qualitative evaluation of mapping strategies. In this analysis we consider **graph families** (processor graph, process graph). A graph family is a graph with parameters, like a ring of length l, a $l \times l$ torus, etc.

We start with an important observation:

Lemma 1 *Any mapping strategy is optimal for any processor (process) structure if the process (processor) structure is completely connected.*

This lemma shows that mapping strategies are not very important if the graphs are very densely connected. Mapping strategies may be important for sparsely connected graphs. This will be investigated in the next two chapters.

6 Mapping strategies for SUPRENUM

SUPRENUM is a german supercomputer project. The architecture is described in [BGM86].

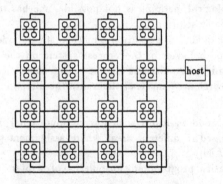

Figure 3: SUPRENUM architecture

The topology of a SUPRENUM multicomputer is shown in figure 3. It consists of $c_1 \times c_2$ clusters, where each cluster has d processors. The processors in a cluster are connected by a bus. The clusters are connected by row and column rings.

The estimation of the communication cost for this architecture is complicated because the communication media are shared. The communication cost is depending on the load of the communication medium, number of nodes and bus protocoll. A queuing network analysis of bus architectures has been done in [MBC83].

Such a complex model is unnecessary for our analysis. We will use a first order approximation taking three parameters into account.

We estimate the communication cost between processor m and processor n for a $(c \times c, d)$ configuration as follows:

$$C_{m,n} = \begin{cases} \varepsilon \approx 0 & m = n \\ d & m, n \text{ in the same cluster} \\ 2d + \alpha c & m, n \text{ in different clusters} \\ 2d + 2\alpha c & m, n \text{ in different rows/columns} \end{cases} \tag{3}$$

ε is the speed of the intraprocessor communication and α is the quotient of the speed of the intracluster bus and the intercluster ring.

The amount of communication K is application dependent. To keep the model simple we investigate regular and homogeneous communication structures (i.e. $K_{p,q} = const$, or $K_{p,q} = 0$).

Definition 1 *Let δ be the expected communication cost between two randomly selected processors.*

Lemma 2 *The communication cost δ for a $(c \times c, d)$ SUPRENUM architecture is given by:*

$$\delta = \frac{1}{c^2}((d-1) + 2(c-1)(2d+\alpha c) + (c-1)^2(2d+2\alpha c)) + \frac{\varepsilon}{c^2 d} \qquad (4)$$

Proof : Two randomly selected processors are with probability $1/c^2 d$ equal, with probability $(d-1)/c^2 d$ within a cluster, with probability $2(c-1)/c^2$ within a row/column and with probability $(c-1)^2/c^2$ on different rows/columns. If we weight the probabilities with the communication cost (3), we obtain (4). □

With $c \to \infty$ or $d \to \infty$, we obtain $\delta \to \infty$. This shows the limited communication bandwidth of this architecture. In the SUPRENUM architecture we have $\alpha \approx 10$ if a dual clusterbus is used, or $\alpha \approx 5$ otherwise.

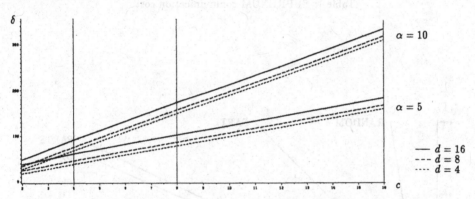

Figure 4: Expected communication cost δ for different SUPRENUM configurations

We compare the communication cost of four different mapping strategies:

OPT   Optimal mapping.
PART   Optimal partition of the process set into as many partitions as
               processors are available; the mapping is done randomly.
PARTS   Optimal partition of the process set into as many partitions as
               SUPRENUM clusters are available; optimal mapping within a cluster;
               the mapping of the partitions is done randomly.
RANDOM   Every process is mapped randomly.

Optimal partitioning minimizes the inter-partition communication.

Table 1 gives the communication cost for some standard process families. The costs are normalized, so that

$$K_{p,q} \cdot C_{\pi(p),\pi(q)} = d,$$

if the two communicating processes are on different processors in the same cluster. ε is assumed to be 0.

	Ring l	2-D Torus $l \times l$
OPT	$c^2d(d-1)+c^2(2d+\alpha c)$	$2cd(\sqrt{d}-1)l+2c(2d+\alpha c)l$
PART	$c^2d\delta$	$2c\sqrt{d}\delta l$
PARTS	$c^2d(d-1)+c^2\delta$	$2cd(\sqrt{d}-1)l+2c\delta l$
RANDOM	δl	$2\delta l^2$

	3-D Torus $l \times l \times l$	Binary Tree 2^l
OPT	$d^2l^2+2c(2d+\alpha c)l^2$	$c^2d(d-1)+(c^2-1)(2d+\alpha c)$
PARTS	$d^2l^2+2c\delta l^2$	$c^2d(d-1)+(c^2-1)\delta$
RANDOM	$3\delta l^3$	$(2^l-2)\delta$

Table 1: SUPRENUM communication cost

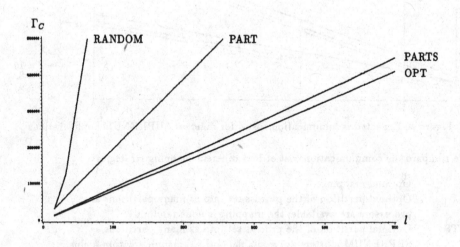

Figure 5: Communication cost for a 2-D torus on SUPRENUM

Proof : We take the 2-D torus as an example. The processors of a SUPRENUM cluster can be interpreted as a $\sqrt{d} \times \sqrt{d}$ grid. This makes it possible to arrange the SUPRENUM processors virtually in a torus of sidelength $c\sqrt{d}$.

The optimal partitioning of the process grid is the regular division into squares. Since $c^2 d$ processors are available, each dimension of the process grid has to be divided by $c\sqrt{d}$ cuts, each containing l communication paths. Each partition gets mapped onto one processor. Since ε is assumed to be 0, communication cost arise only between processes on different processors.

OPT: The mapping is done one-to-one between the partitions of the process-graph and the (virtual) SUPRENUM torus. $2c$ cuts lie on bounds between two neighboring SUPRENUM clusters while $2c(\sqrt{d}-1)$ cuts lie within the clusters. Multiplication of the communication cost (3) and the length l gives

$$\Gamma_C = 2c(\sqrt{d}-1) \cdot d \cdot l + 2c \cdot (2d + \alpha c) \cdot l$$

PART: Optimal partitioning gives $2c\sqrt{d} \cdot l$ paths between partitions. Because of random assignment of these partitions the paths have to be multiplied by the average communication cost

$$\Gamma_C = 2c\sqrt{d} \cdot \delta \cdot l$$

PARTS: The process torus is partitioned into c^2 clusters. $2c(\sqrt{d}-1)$ cuts, each consisting of l links can be handled within the clusters, while the other $2c$ cuts are mapped on random processor pairs, such that the following cost arise:

$$\Gamma_C = 2c(\sqrt{d}-1) \cdot d \cdot l + 2c \cdot \delta \cdot l$$

RANDOM: The 2-D torus of sidelength l contains $2l^2$ links. The processes get mapped randomly, that each link produces the mean communication cost δ

$$\Gamma_C = 2l^2 \cdot \delta$$

The proofs for the other process structures are similar. □

Figure 5 shows the communication cost for a 2-D torus on a $(4 \times 4, 16)$ SUPRENUM machine. We see that OPT and PARTS differ only slightly.

Table 1 shows that this is true for all considered process families. The cost for OPT and PARTS differ in the second term by a factor, the communication between two clusters $(2d + \alpha c)$ for OPT and δ for PARTS. The difference between these two functions increases with growing configuration size. It is about 17% for the average SUPRENUM configuration $(c = 4, d = 16, \alpha = 5)$ and about 41% for the large configuration $(c = 8, d = 16, \alpha = 5)$.

The communication cost for all mapping strategies lie between the values of OPT and RANDOM. OPT and RANDOM differ by a factor which is dependent on the problemsize l. For example the cost for the optimally mapped torus are in $\mathcal{O}(l)$ while the random mapping produces costs in $\mathcal{O}(l^2)$.

We believe however that the SUPRENUM architecture is fairly robust. Optimal mapping is not necessary, good partitioning is sufficient. The partitioning problem can be solved more easily and is discussed in [MüKr87]. A new partitioning algorithm for static process structures with inhomogeneous communication is described in [MGK87].

7 Mapping strategies for Hypercube Architectures

The mapping strategies considered so far for hypercubes concentrate on the topological mapping (see [SaSc85], [BrSc86]). We will analyse different mapping strategies with the cost function (1).

The communication cost $C_{m,n}$ between two processors (m,n) in a hypercube are given by their (hamming-) distance; i.e. a message has to be routed over $C_{m,n}$ communication links.

Let d be the dimension of the hypercube, i.e. the machine consists of 2^d processors.

Lemma 3 *The expected communication cost between two randomly selected processors is* $\delta = d/2$.

We are now able to compare mapping strategies:

OPT   Optimal mapping.
PART   Optimal partition of the process set into 2^d partitions;
              the mapping is done randomly.
RANDOM   Every process is mapped randomly.

PART and RANDOM need an operating system with a routing facility. The routing problem is discussed in the next chapter.

The communication cost for the standard process families are shown in table 2. The costs are normalized, that $K_{p,q} \cdot C_{\pi(p),\pi(q)} = 1$, if there is a link between $\pi(p)$ and $\pi(q)$.

	Ring	2-D Torus	3-D Torus	Binary Tree
	l	$l \times l$	$l \times l \times l$	2^l
OPT	2^d	$2^{(d/2)+1} l$	$3 \cdot 2^{(d/3)} l^2$	$2^d - 1$
PART	$\delta 2^d$	$\delta 2^{(d/2)+1} l$	$3\delta 2^{(d/3)} l^2$	$\delta(2^d - 1)$
RANDOM	δl	$2\delta l^2$	$3\delta l^3$	$\delta(2^l - 2)$

Table 2: Hypercube communication cost

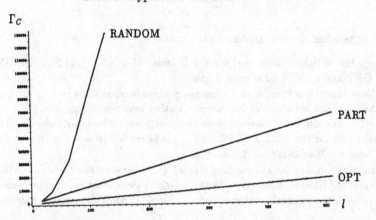

Figure 6: Communication cost for a 2-D torus on the Hypercube

Proof : We take the 2-D torus as an example. The optimal partitioning of the process grid is the regular division into squares. Since 2^d processors are available, each dimension of the process grid has to be divided by $2^{(d/2)}$ cuts, each containing l communication paths. Each partition gets mapped onto one processor. Since the communication cost for two processes on the same processor are assumed to be 0, communication cost arise only between processes on different processors.

OPT: The partitions can be mapped on the processors of the hypercube, that processes in neighboring partitions have a hamming distance of 1 (see [SaSc85]). There exist $2 \cdot 2^{(d/2)} \cdot l$ communication

paths between the partition, giving
$$\Gamma_C = 2^{(d/2)+1} \cdot l$$

PART: Optimal partitioning gives $2 \cdot 2^{(d/2)} \cdot l$ paths between partitions. Because of random assignment these paths have to be multiplied by the average communication cost δ

$$\Gamma_C = \delta \cdot 2^{(d/2)+1} l$$

RANDOM: The 2-D torus of sidelength l contains $2l^2$ links. Each link produces the mean communication cost $d/2$

$$\Gamma_C = d \cdot l^2$$

The proofs for the other process structures are similar. □

Figure 6 shows the functions for a 2-D torus on a Hypercubve of dimension 8.

In all cases the cost for OPT and PART differ by the factor of $\delta = d/2$. This gives 300% for a hypercube of dimension 8 with 256 nodes.

Thus the hypercube architecture is not very robust for the considered standard parallel processing tasks against different mapping strategies. This has also been conjectured in [HMSCP86].

8 Adaptive Routing

The above analysis was based on process networks with point-to-point connections. The basic performance parameter needed is δ, the average processor to processor communication cost.

Process networks with multicast and broadcast have to be handled differently. Ullman [Ullm84b] proposed a generalization of δ for these networks, the "flux". The flux of a network family is inversely proportional to the minimum time it takes to get the data from any set of processors out of that set. The extension of our analysis for this model is straightforward.

Inhomogeneous process networks have to be mapped with a different strategy, which does not try to optimize globally, but only locally. We illustrate this statement with an example. The inhomogeneous ring of figure 7 is to be mapped onto a 2×2 torus.

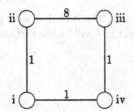

Figure 7: Inhomogeneous ring

We obtain an execution time $T = 8$ for a shift if we assume that CPU and IO overlap. If we can split the communication between process (ii) and (iii) into two independent communication streams, we get $T = 4$ when using two different communication links on the torus.

This example shows that the mapping problem consists of two assignment problems — process to processor and communication path to communication links. Of course this two problems are not independent.

Adaptive process to processor assignment needs process migration. Process migration is a very costly task, if the address space of the process has to be transported to the memory of another processor.

In contrast, adaptive routing is very inexpensive. In adaptive routing the assumption of a static mapping of the communication paths is abandoned. Every message between two processes can be transported by different communication links. Adaptive routing seems to be very promising in processor structures with a rich interconnection structure. A rich interconnection structure is characterized by many different routes between different processors and almost equal communication cost.

Randomized routing is a simple implementation of adaptive routing. It has been proven for hypercubes that random routing gives a nearly optimal communication time for many complex algorithms [Ullm84a]. In the previous chapter we have shown that this statement is not true for simple standard process families.

Adaptive routing for the SUPRENUM architecture is very simple to implement, because only the sending cluster has to decide, whether the row or column bus should be used.

We believe that with a growing number of applications a shift will occur from topological oriented process mapping done a priori to more general adaptive mapping strategies implemented in hardware or operating system. Path mapping (routing) is discussed in detail in [DaSe86].

9   Conclusion

Intricate process mapping strategies are very expensive. Therefore we have investigated the relation between the cost for the mapping and the advantage gained by the mapping.

We have shown that the process mapping can be broken into two subproblems: the process partitioning and the assignment problem. It turned out that for the SUPRENUM architecture a good partitioning of the process graph is sufficient. The partitioning problem is easier to solve than the assignment problem. In contrast the performance of point-to-point distributed architectures, like hypercubes depends more on a good assignment.

The mapping strategies have been analysed separately for different processor graph families (the normalization applied was architecture dependent). In the analysis, the average communication cost δ was used. If the absolute values of δ are given for different architectures it is easily possible to compare different architectures (e.g. a SUPRENUM configuration and a hypercube configuration with 256 processors).

Inhomogeneous process networks are difficult to deal with process mapping strategies. Adaptive routing is more easily to implement and will be the first step towards a more general purpose message-based parallel system.

References

[ArRa80]   R. K. Arora, S. P. Rana, *Heuristic Algorithms for Process Assignment in Distributed Computing Systems*, Information Processing Letters 11 (12/80) 199–203

[BGM86]   P. M. Behr, W. K. Giloi, H. Mühlenbein, *SUPRENUM: The German Supercomputer Project – Rationale and Concepts*, IEEE Internat. Conference on Parallel Processing (1986)

[Bokh81]   S. H. Bokhari, *On the Mapping Problem*, IEEE Transaction on Computers C-30 No. 3 (1981) 207–214

[BrSc86]   J. E. Brandenburg, D. E. Scott, *Embedding of Communication Trees and Grids into Hypercubes*, Intel iPSC User Group No. 1 (1986)

[CHLE80]   W. W. Chu, L. J. Holloway, M. T. Lan, K. Efe, *Task Allocation in Distributed Data Processing*, Computer (11/80) 57–69

[DaSe86]   W. J. Dally, Ch. L. Seitz, *The Torus Routing Chip*, Distributed Computing 1 (1986) 187–196

[EBP86]   A. K. Ezzat, R. D. Bergeron, J. L. Pokoski, *Task Allocation Heuristics for Distributed Computing Systems*, IEEE Int. Conf. on Distributed Systems (1986)

[HHR86]   C. E. Houstis, E. N. Houstis, J. R. Rice, *Partitioning PDE Computations: Methods and Performance Evaluation*, Report Purdue University (1986)

[HoMü86]   H. C. Hoppe, H. Mühlenbein, *Parallel Adaptive Full–Multigrid–Methods on Message-based Multiprocessors*, Parallel Computing 3 (1986) 269–287

[Hock85]   R. W. Hockney, *MIMD computing in the USA - 1984*, Parallel Computing 2 (1985) 119–136

[HMSCP86]   J. P. Hages, T. Mudge, Q. M. Stow, S. Colley, J. Palmer, *A Microprocessor based Hypercube Supercomputer*, IEEE Micro, Vol. 6, No. 5 (1986)

[MBC83]   M. A. Marsan, G. Balbo, G. Conte, *Comparative performance analysis of single bus multiprocessor architectures*, IEEE Trans. Computers, C-31 (1983) 1179–1191

[MGK87]   H. Mühlenbein, M. Gorges-Schleuter, O. Krämer, *New Solutions to the Mapping Problem of Parallel Systems — The Evolution Approach*, Parallel Computing, to be published (1987)

[MüKr87]   H. Mühlenbein, O. Krämer, *Parallel Solutions of the Graph Partitioning Problem*, to be published

[MKLMS87]   H. Mühlenbein, O. Krämer, F. Limburger, M. Mevenkamp, S. Streitz, *Design and Rationale for MUPPET — A Programming Environment for Message-Based Multiprocessors*, Journal of Parallel and Distr. Proc., to be published

[NiSa86]   D. Nicol, J. Saltz, *Dynamic Remapping of Parallel Computations with Varying Resource Demands*, ICASE Report 86-45, Nasa Langley (1986)

[SAKA86]   C. Saito, H. Amano, T. Kudoh, H. Aiso, *An adaptable cluster structure of $(SM)^2$ -II*, CONPAR 86, Aachen (9/86) 53–60

[SaSc85]   Y. Saad, M. H. Schultz, *Topological Properties of Hypercubes*, Research Report RR-389 Yale University (6/85)

[ScGa85]   K. Schwans, C. Gaimon, *Automatic Resource allocation for the CM* Multiprocessor*, 5th Distr. Comp. Conf. (1985)

[ScJo85]   K. Schwans, A. K. Jones, *Specifying Resource Allocation for Parallel Programs on the CM* Multiprocessor*, Ohio State University, OSU-CISRC-TR-85-10 (1985)

[Snyd82]   L. Snyder, *Introduction to the Configurable, Highly Parallel Computer*, Computer 15 (2/82) 47–56

[Ullm84a]   J. D. Ullman, *Computational aspects of VLSI*, Computer Science Press (1984)

[Ullm84b]   J. D. Ullman, *Some thoughts about Supercomputer Organization*, Proc. IEEE Compcon, San Francisco (1984) 424–431

HARDWARE MEMORY MANAGEMENT FOR LARGE KNOWLEDGE BASES.

S. H. Lavington*, M. Standring**, Y. J. Jiang*, C. J. Wang** and M. E. Waite*.
*Dept. of Computer Science, University of Essex, Colchester, CO4 3SQ.
**Dept. of Computer Science, University of Manchester, Manchester, M13 9PL.

Abstract

Large knowledge bases form an important applications area for parallel architectures.
The special problems of this domain concern the movement and protection of large
amounts of complex data in a hierarchy of storage devices and processing elements, in
a manner which is sympathetic to the logical structure of the information. This
structure is a reflection of the underlying knowledge representation formalism. An
analysis of candidate formalisms leads to the specification of a memory architecture
for large knowledge bases. The particular problems of paging are studied, and a
scheme for semantic caching is proposed. The design of a fast cache employing
highly-parallel pattern-directed searching is described. The performance of this
cache in a multi-level memory hierarchy is given.

1. Introduction

Most proposals for declarative architectures have concentrated on models of a
computational process which is central to the execution of a particular family of
languages. Examples are combinator reduction or the unification process. In order to
explore potential parallelism in such processes, simulations are performed on
computationally-intensive benchmarks which involve little data. Examples are
evaluation of a factorial or the four-queens problem. For these benchmarks, the
selection of things to unify or reduce is subservient to the central computation.
In contrast, data-intensive problems place more emphasis on the selection process
until, for applications involving very large knowledge bases, the selection mechanism
becomes a critical part of the architecture. The selection task is exacerbated if
parts of the knowledge base have to reside on secondary memory, and if the presence
of concurrent users requires some form of lock management in a shared memory.

The problem, then, is to devise a high-performance memory for large knowledge bases
that will offer an appropriate functional interface to one (or more) high-performance

declarative architectures. The memory design may have to take account of severe data-bandwidth differentials between units, and should be language-and applications-independent in its management of information.

In this paper we address the task which is considered central to the above problem, namely the design of memory-management hardware which will successfully integrate stores of widely differing access times. In section 2, we present the architectural background to the memory design. This includes a discussion of the functionality required by large knowledge bases. The importance of a top-down design which reflects the needs of knowledge-representation formalisms is stressed. Based on an analysis of candidate formalisms, we devise in Section 3 a format for memory organisation that is flexible enough to suit a range of languages and applications. We then derive a descriptor-based semantic caching scheme for the memory system. The design and performance of an associative hardware cache is presented in Section 5. Finally, we assess the results of using the caching scheme in a two-level knowledge base memory.

2. Architectural requirements

The overall requirements of memory management are simply stated: the movement and protection of information within a hierarchy of storage devices and processing elements should be organised in a manner which is sympathetic to the logical structure of such information. For large knowledge bases, the logical structure is a reflection of the underlying knowledge representation formalism. Such a formalism should be recognised by all sub-units in a total architecture.

The function of each sub-unit in an architecture is traditionally analysed into categories such as storage, processing, I/O, etc. In the case of knowledge bases, the functionality is not so clearly sub-divided. For example, Fahlman et al. (Ref 1) list transitive closure, set intersection, and various forms of pattern-directed search as good candidates for hardware assistance for general AI applications. If such functionality is to achieve its objectives of reducing the cost and complexity of software, it must be closely related to the knowledge representations being used - and hence closely related to memory design. It is therefore appropriate to consider increasing the functionality of the memory unit until it becomes a knowledge-manipulation engine (KME). The architectural concept of a KME, which has a formal basis in knowledge representations, is our starting point.

Memory functionality can also be discussed in engineering terms. By making the "memory" do more work, we reduce its output of non-essential data and hence reduce

the system bandwidth requirements. Examples would be a KME that can act as a pre-
unification filter delivering a set of potentially-unifiable instantiations, or as a
unit delivering function definitions in a graph-reduction machine. Such
functionality has been pursued on small quantites of data, for example in the
Intelligent Memory Unit of the GRIP project for graph reduction (Ref. 2), and in the
GAM chip developed at Strathclyde for transitive closure (Ref. 3). Increased
functionality should not be allowed to degrade the output of useful results to the
point where the destination processor(s) is/are kept waiting. It is therefore most
likely that the KME will employ parallel techniques.

From an engineering view, a good starting point for the design of a KME is the
identification of some appropriate operational unit(s) of stored information. The
task then becomes one of identifying such units at the right level of abstraction,
without getting too bemused by the implementation techniques employed for today's
languages on today's machines. A look at functional languages might suggest
applicative terms, perhaps represented as nodes and arcs in a graph, as appropriate
units of stored information – provided we acknowledge that the "memory" must play an
active part in a dynamic computation process. In contrast, logic languages might
suggest tuples, and more particularly logic clauses which include (pointers to)
variables and structures, as appropriate units. In the case of logic, it is noted
that semantic networks are a syntactic variant of FOPC, so that the handling of
graphs and graph-manipulation primitives might indeed be a possible starting point
for the design of a KME suitable for declarative languages. It is also worth noting
that graph/network paradigms occur in many areas of Computer Science. In order to be
independent of both languages and problem-domains, we focus first on knowledge
representation formalisms and their operational units of storage.

There are two practical observations which constrain our desire to build a truly
general-purpose memory. The first is that the knowledge-based systems' market place
requires an upgrade path from (relational) databases to logic databases. The second
observation is that, within modern declarative languages, the functional seems to be
less popular than the relational approach when it comes to implementing knowledge-
based systems. We admit to being influenced by these two factors in the analysis of
knowledge representations which follows.

3. Selecting the unit of Storage

Knowledge representations suitable for large systems must support a combination
of requirements drawn from AI and DBMS. These requirements include the need for:

a) formal semantics (eg. for reasoning in deductive systems);

b) expressive adequacy (eg. when used for Natural Language understanding);

c) domain-independence;

d) irreducibility (eg. allowing the co-existence of several user-views);

e) efficiency (including operational convenience).

Candidate representations include logic, production systems, frames and semantic nets. We select arguably the most promising formalism and examine the implications for low-level storage.

Semantic nets, which are built from simple 2-place predicates, seem to satisfy most of the requirements except for expressive adequacy. Attempts to make them more expressive usually result in loss of efficiency and a departure from first-order logic. However, it is shown in Reference 4 that by adding the ability to qualify each predicate and also to give it truth-values other than simply "true", we can greatly increase the expressive power without sacrificing efficiency or formality. The Qualified Binary Relationship Model (QBRM) is such a scheme. Its formal semantics and expressive power are analysed elsewhere (Reference 4). For now, we are only concerned with its low-level unit of information, which is:

$\langle$ L $\rangle\langle$ predicate name $\rangle\langle$ arg 1 $\rangle\langle$ arg 2 $\rangle\langle$ V $\rangle$ ...... eq. (1)

-where $\langle L\rangle$ is a unique Gödel number or label, and $\langle V\rangle$ is a truth-value from the set {true, false, undefined, ...}. The centre three fields, being the basic arc and two nodes of the semantic network, represent a well-formed formula. When this appears in its own right as a predicate, the mapping onto $\langle$ V $\rangle$ is the assignment function used in its interpretation; when the wff is used as a term in another expression, the gödel mapping onto $\langle$ L $\rangle$ is used as the assignment function in the wff's interpretation. $\langle$ L $\rangle$ gives the ability to represent and refer to sub-structures.

From a hardware viewpoint, the significant fact about the above unit of information is that it is of a fixed format - though the width of the centre fields may vary since these may contain lexemes. When performing pattern-directed searches over such semantic networks, the existence of lexemes creates problems if there is overlap between the allowable bit-patterns in the external lexical character set (eg. ASCII) and the internal bit-patterns used for labels and abstract (ie. non-lexical) nodes in the graph. The engineering solution is to use a common internal identifier (ID) space for _all_ nodes, arcs and labels in the graph, performing a separate translation between external lexemes and internal identifiers, when appropriate, prior to storing a predicate.

The existence of a system-wide internal identifier (ID) space has some of the characteristics of a large virtual address space in a conventional computer. In

particular, the ID space may be divided into non-overlapping segments. The ID format
is thus: $<$ segment $><$ count $>$, where can be used to distinguish the
following types of ID: lexical, abstract, gödelisation, existential variable, etc.
In addition, there is the possibility of user-defined types, for example when it is
desired to use the <count> bits for expression-encoding, in the spirit of schemes
such as superimposed codewords (Reference 5) or the PAM chip of the FAIM architecture
(Reference 6). (Such encoding conflicts with the generality and concept-locality of
semantic networks, but may be justified for certain applications).

Assuming appropriate ID-space segmentation, the format for the basic unit of stored
information in the extended semantic network representation becomes:
$$< ID_1 >< ID_2 >< ID_3 >< ID_4 >< V > \ldots. \quad \text{eq. (2)}$$
In practice the length of $< IDn >$ is a system constant. Our hardware described in
Section 5 allows the ID length to be defined at start-up time in the range 2 - 8
bytes. This permits small applications to be represented efficiently, whilst giving
a virtually infinite (and, if necessary, persistent) primitive object-space for very
large applications. The apparent symmetry of the first four fields is somewhat
misleading. The label field $< ID_1 >$ requires special dereferencing action, as
mentioned in Section 5. We also note that eq. (2) can be used to represent self-
referential knowledge and paradoxes; no special hardware action is proposed which
might constrain such use.

A KME should be language-and applications-independent. Before embodying the
information unit of eq. (2) into a hardware design, we should make sure that it can
be interfaced to a reasonable range of declarative languages. Languages which
require the representation of logic clauses as predicates map easily onto eq. (1) for
the special case of 2-place predicates. N-ary predicates can be modelled, with some
loss of search efficiency, in terms of these basic units by employing an order-break
(or case-frame) approach. In this connection it is interesting to note that the
average arity of Prolog predicates is about 2.8 (Reference 7). In another approach
to the representation of logic clauses, the logistic applicative formal system of
Schonfinkel can be taken as a starting point. This suggests a linear representation,
in which the basic unit of information is a triple consisting of a label, a term
(possibly a label), and a link to a tail substructure. This triple, which is
conceptually equivalent to a list cell, can be mapped onto a collapsed form of the
quintuple of eq. (1).

As for functional languages, we have studied simple Curry combinators. There are
interesting possibilities for representing SKI expressions as fixed-format tuples, in
a 5-field arrangement based on an extension of eq. (1). We also note that the ALICE

implementation of HOPE (Reference 8) has chosen a 6-field fixed format for packets, argument lists and "signal sets". Each field is four bytes wide. Clearly, some form of associative look-up on such objects, eg. to match packets with appropriate function definitions, to implement memo functions, and to pass results, could be a useful adjunct to the ALICE machine. The general aim would be to automate the movement and protection of logically-related "pages" of packets within a large (persistent) memory space. For rewrite architectures involving variable-sized packets (eg. FLAGSHIP?), memory management becomes more difficult. The problem is similar to that of handling tuples of arbitrary arity. For this, the existence of the gödel mapping < L > offers a useful mechanism for converting variable-length structures into fixed-length structures.

From the above observations, it is clear that some flexibility of storage format is required. We therefore generalise eq. (1) and propose a hardware KME whose main memory can be configured at start-up time to hold units of information with the following format:

$$< L >< T_1 >< T_2 > \ldots < T_n >< M_1 >< M_2 > \ldots < M_m > \ldots \text{ eq. (3)}$$

-where: $< L >$ is an optional label (gödelisation);

$< T_1 >< T_2 > \ldots < T_n >$ represent terms of a well-formed formula;

$< M_1 >< M_2 > \ldots < M_m >$ represent optional modifiers for the $< L >$

and $< T >$ fields.
Each tuple must be uniquely defined by the $< T >$ fields. In the implementation of Section 5, the width of the $< L >$ and $< T >$ fields is fixed to the internal identifier length; the total number of $< L >$, $< T >$ and $< M >$ fields must not exceed 15; the total length of the tuple must not exceed 63 bytes.

In advocating configurability, we assume that the functionality to be offered by such a memory is essentially semantics-free. This is not quite true, since the L, T and V fields have slightly different properties. From the memory management view, however, it is the terms $< T_1 >< T_2 > \ldots < T_n >$ of eq. (3) which specify the basic unit of information; on these we can define certain semantic-free operations such as pattern-directed (ie. associative) search, insert and delete. We note in passing that other graph operations such as transitive closure, path traversal, combining graphs, and breadth-first/depth-first navigation (ie. marker passing) can all be achieved by appropriate applications of search/insert/delete. In particular, search operations may be used to establish semantic vicinities, within which other more complex (or more problem-specific) operations may be performed. We concentate here on bulk memory management, the object of which is to prepare the way for complex functions such as unification or combinator reduction to take place quickly and locally. That such memory management is worthwhile is illustrated by measurements on two large Prolog programs, namely the geographical database of Chat-80 (Ref. 9) and a protein structure reasoning database (Ref. 10). These two were modelled in the knowledge representation of eq. (1), and queried via an appropriate logic language known as QULOG. It was found that, on average, 48% and 46% respectively of the total elapsed time for a query was spent on searching the database, prior to unification, etc.

The next section presents schemes for paging and protection in large knowledge bases, according to a technology-independent strategy.

4. Semantic Caching and Protection in a Multi-level Store

Paging in a multi-level store hierarchy has been traditionally approached from the viewpoint of physical locality of data, where the unit of paging is a physical data block. Architectures for large knowledge bases have been proposed which page physical blocks of information, such as DELTA [Ref. 11] and the FACT system [Ref. 3]. Both of these systems employ clustering, in the case of DELTA on relationship/attribute information, and in the case of FACT on higher level semantic information such as schemas and contexts. This clustering is necessary because information systems exhibit logical vicinity of reference rather than physical. Schweppe [Ref. 12] points out that physical clustering favours only one access path, which is unacceptable for a general-purpose knowledge store. Schweppe goes on to give examples of semantically related items that might be considered as the basis of a page unit. What is clearly desired is to page logically related information, where the exact logical relationship may vary dynamically. Such a system would aim to give similar cache benefits for a range of access paths and access patterns.

We now present a scheme which allows such semantic caching. Based on eq. (3), we consider knowledge representations which store well-formed formulae as:

$$< \text{term } 1 >< \text{term } 2 > \ldots < \text{term } n >,$$

where each term could in principle be a literal representing either a constant, a variable or a structure. We also assume the basic operations:

INSERT (term 1, term 2, ... term n)

DELETE (factor 1, factor 2, ... factor n)

SEARCH (factor 1, factor 2, ... factor n)

where a factor is either a term or a wild card. DELETE and SEARCH are essentially match specifications: any wff which matches the specification (wild card matches any value) is either removed or selected respectively. In general, more than one wff matches a specification and so we operate upon a set of wff. This concept of a set as an operational unit is important; some of the consequences for set processing are discussed later. A special literal "?", is used to denote a wild card. This means that the match specification can itself be regarded as a wff, termed a "set descriptor" since it denotes a <u>set</u> of wff. These sets are a good basis for logical paging for three reasons:-

a) All items within the sets are logically related, for example, by virtue of posessing common predicate names or referring to the same object, etc.

b) A set can be obtained for paging by merely issuing the appropriate SEARCH operation; no special commands are necessary.

c) Set descriptors are simple, and furthermore may be readily manipulated in a manner similar to tuples.

A semantic caching scheme can then be envisaged in which we page down sets of <u>logically</u> related wff into a faster store or cache, in a manner akin to conventional <u>physical</u> paging schemes. In addition, the set descriptors may be stored and manipulated within this faster level of storage.

When a SEARCH is issued, references to sets paged down can be detected by some elementary analysis. The case where the requested set has been paged down is trivial: if the requested set descriptor is found upon issuing a SEARCH to the fast store, then the set is selected from the fast store. More generally, the requested set may be wholly contained, partly contained, or wholly excluded from the set of paged sets. Let P_m be a paged set, and

$$(factor_{m1}, factor_{m2}, ..., factor_{mn}) \quad n>0$$

be its corresponding set descriptor. The contents of the fast store after several page operations may be expressed as

$$\{P_1, P_2, ..., P_m\} \quad m \geq 0.$$

If R represents the set of tuples requested by the SEARCH command, we can express the data locality constraints as follows:

wholly contained: $R \subseteq X$, $X \in \{P_1, P_2, ...P_m\}$ $m \geq 0$

partly contained: $(R \cap X) \neq \{\}$, $X \in \{P_1, P_2, ..., P_m\}$ $m \geq 0$

wholly excluded: $(R \cap X) = \{\}, \forall X \in \{P_1, P_2, ..., P_m\}$ $m \geq 0$

The second condition may be utilised to initiate processing on some results returned quickly from the fast store, but the main condition is that of whole containment, since this bypasses the need to access slow store. Examining the set descriptor for the requested set R:

$$(factor_1', factor_2', ..., factor_n') \quad n>1$$

and the set of set descriptors for $\{P_1, P_2, ..., P_m\}$ $m \geq 0$, namely

$$(factor_{11}, factor_{12}, ..., factor_{1n})$$

$$(factor_{21}, factor_{22}, ..., factor_{2n})$$

$$"\qquad\qquad "$$

$$(factor_{m1}, factor_{m2}, ..., factor_{mn})$$

(where factor can be ground or wild), then the request query can be selected solely
from the fast store iff:-

$$\exists P_j \ (1 \leq j \leq m) s.t. \ ((factor_{j1} = "?") \vee (factor_{j1} = factor_1')) \quad \wedge$$

$$((factor_{j2} = "?") \vee (factor_{j2} = factor_2')) \ \wedge$$

$$"\qquad\qquad "\qquad\qquad "$$

$$((factor_{jn} = "?") \vee (factor_{jn} = factor_n'))$$

If the paged set descriptors are stored in the fast cache, this condition can be
tested in a time independent of m by issuing a small number of SEARCHES to the fast
store, permuting factors from the requested set descriptor issued with the wild card
"?". If any of these returns a paged set descriptor, access to bulk store is
unnecessary and the SEARCH can be issued to the fast semantic cache. The overhead of
these select operations is small provided that $K >> 2^y$, where K is the
performance ratio of fast to slow stores (typically 10^3 to 10^5) and y is the
number of factors in the requested set descriptor which are not wild cards. y is
obviously application dependent. Initial results with a binary relationship model
[Ref. 13] have yielded median values of y=2n/3 where n is the number of fields.
Thus, y=2 in the case of 2-place predicates. for more advanced knowledge
representations which require the labelling (eg. gödelisation) facility of eq. (3),
the need to dereference a label introduces another class of search. For example,
when the Prolog protein structure program quoted earlier is modelled in the QBRM
formalism then on average 32% of all store requests are for a label dereference. As
is discussed later, the proposed hardware technique for dereferencing labels is
equivalent to a search with no wild cards. Overall, the search patterns for the QBRM
application are then simpler (ie. contain fewer wild cards) than those expected for
conventional binary relational models.

To assess the paging technique, typical sessions of user activity upon a binary
relational database storing information about historical documents were recorded.
Since the user activity consisted of random probings and browsing into different
areas of the database, it was felt that such a system would be a stringent test of
caching. The recorded sessions were input to a semantic caching simulator using
demand-paging of logical sets, and the following results obtained.

a) Average hit rate of 89% ie. only 11% of all SEARCHS needed bulk store access.

b) Cache sizes greater than 10% of the size of the total knowledge base seem unnecessary, whilst the hit rate starts to drop if the cache is constrained to be less than about 4% of the total knowledge base.

These initial results indicate that a semantic caching technique based on logical set descriptors looks promising. Further case-studies are in progress on large Prolog databases. We are also experimenting with prediction (pre-paging) and cache-replacement algorithms. The impact upon the performance of real stores is considered in Section 6.

As far as storage protection is concerned, the choice of logical units to lock in a concurrent-user environment is similar to the problem of choosing logical units to page. We propose using the same set descriptors as above for lock specifiers, thus allowing locks of varying granularity to be implemented in an applications-independent manner. Because the sets are logical (rather than physical), the phantom problem is eliminated. In practice, it is possible that a combination of pre-conflict locking and post-conflict ("optimistic") validation may be employed for concurrency control in ground databases; algorithms for such a scheme have been proposed (Ref. 17). For knowledge bases containing rules, it is necessary to ensure that access to all predicates in the condition-part of each invoked rule has the appropriate permission to procede. The manner in which rules are represented in the knowledge base can simplify the required checks.

A commit-buffer will be required for the proper administration of roll-back. Such a buffer is a good candidate for special hardware support in a KME. High-speed searching of a lock table to check for lock compatibility is also required; here again, special hardware assistance would be appropriate.

The fast store implied by semantic caching and the commit buffer required by a concurrency controller could possibly be contained within the same memory unit. At any rate, the implementation of both aspects of memory management requires a level of fast storage capable of supporting pattern-directed (ie. associative) storage. The implementation of such a store is now described.

5. Experimental hardware: the IFS

The functional requirements of Section 3 and the technology-independent management strategy of Section 4 together form the basis for a project called the Intelligent File Store (IFS). The aim of the IFS is to provide hardware support for large knowledge bases. Central to the IFS is an associative store for holding the graph-related structures of eqn. (3). Architectural options for this store included the local approach to association, as exemplified by the Connection Machine (Ref. 14), and the distributed approach as exemplified by the Boltzmann Machine (Ref. 15). In both these schemes, storage and processing capabilities are provided in the same physical network. Although reducing unnecessary information movement, this strategy seems bound to bring technological compromises in respect of ease of connectivity and cost per stored bit. In contrast, the IFS is based on what might be called the tuple approach. The units of eqn. (3) are held as position-independent entries in a large parallel-access associative store which provides search, insert and delete operations on large amounts of information of arbitrarily complex connectivity. Other processing tasks such as set intersection and transitive closure are performed in tailor-made sub-units, once responders have been extracted from the main store. Having chosen the tuple approach because of its flexibility, we can state its target capacity and speed. Hardware which meets the requirements is then described.

For simple queries on ground databases, it is assumed that say 10 searches of the store are required for each user-interaction. Thus, search times of up to 100 millisec per set of responders are sufficient to provide acceptable performance if there are no more than a few concurrent users. For deductive databases where the target is several hundred thousand unifications per second, the associative store can only expect to act as a pre-unification filter, delivering sets of potential unifiers. This emphasis on sets obviously has implications for the proof-mechanisation strategy and the management of search space. It holds out possibilities for implementing OR-parallelism and for avoiding some of the unnecessary unifications evident in one-at-a-time proof procedures. There are significant practical problems to be overcome before set-based resolution is fully exploited but, assuming the sets can be utilised by a (parallel) inference engine, the target rate of delivery of sets could be of the order of several thousand per second. In conclusion, the target performance for the fast (caching) section of a knowledge-base store is the completion of one pattern-directed search say every 200 microseconds. The size of the cache needs to be at least a few megabytes, as shown above.

In order to explore technical possibilities, a 4Mbyte associative cache has been built as part of the IFS project (Ref. 16). It is designed around the principle of hashing and the parallel searching of many RAM modules. Briefly, the total memory space is divided into say 512 logical hashing bins. The memory space is also divided into 64 physical modules, each equipped with a search engine. Each module stores a section of each hashing bin. During pattern-directed search, a hardware hasher produces an n-bit key ($0 \leq n \leq 9$) from the interrogand, depending on the number of wild cards. (For effiency reasons, the hardware may choose a different hashing strategy for the $< T >$ and $< M >$ fields of eq. (3)). A central controller then arranges for the appropriate hashing bin(s) to be searched by the 64 search engines operating in lock step. This gives a combined search rate of about 255 Mbytes/sec. This rate may be improved by using faster RAM – (the present design uses type 4164 chips). The store can be reconfigured by software according to eq. (3). Any combination of wild cards may be used in the search interrogand. The performance is as follows:

search with no fields unknown: 38 microsec.
search with one field unknown: 244 microsec. + 1 microsec. per responder
search with two fields unknown: 2 millisec. + 2 microsec. per responder
insert a predicate: 38 – 76 microsec.
delete a predicate: 4 – 38 microsec.

The times quoted are for a full store – ie. one logical hashing bin has become full. This typically represents 80% – 90% physical memory utilisation. There are in fact more physical bins than logical ones. Due to the strategy for the linear chaining of physical bins, the search times are in general faster for a partially-filled cache. For example, 244 microsec. becomes 146 microsec. for a half-filled store.

In the present implementation, there is no mechanism for ending a search early –for example if it is certain that a physical bin is only partly filled. The above search times are thus relatively independent of the format-options implied by eq. (3). The times are also independent of total cache capacity, since the addition of extra memory modules is exactly matched by the addition of extra search engines working in parallel. In the present implementation, the label-dereferencing required by eq. (3) is performed via firmware. In particular, the bit-pattern produced when allocating a label is made to include the hashing bits derived from the wff. This means that label-dereference becomes a parallel search with no wild cards.

As specified in Section 3, the cache actually holds information in the form of internal identifiers (IDs). In order to allocate, de-allocate and translate IDs, we have built a second hardware unit for the IFS called the Lexical Token Converter (LTC). The main section of the LTC is an associative look-up table for conversion to and from character strings.

The LTC allows lexemes of up to 120 characters and IDs (fixed at start-up time) in the range 2 - 8 bytes. Each lexeme is associated with a unique ID. Each ID is arranged to contain a certain number of bits which are a function of its hashed lexeme. This allows the more frequently-occurring translation ID-to-lexeme to be faster than the reverse translation. A scheme of hashing and parallel search engines somewhat similar to the cache is employed, except that LTC search times vary according to information distribution. The observed time-ranges are:

ID to lexeme : 10 - 87 microsecs.

lexeme to ID : 56 - 438 microsecs.

These times are seen to be compatible with those of the cache. The present LTC implementation contains 2Mbytes of 4164 DRAM chips arranged as eight parallel modules, each with a search engine. More modules can be added without affecting the speed. 2Mbytes provide space for about 100,000 lexemes.

In our experimental system the 4Mbyte cache and 2 Mbyte LTC communicate via a VME bus, which is connected via a DMA channel to a host processor - the whole forming an integrated hardware/software architecture simulation vehicle. Higher-level software accesses the associative cache and LTC through a semantics-free, model-independent IFS procedural interface. This consists of 17 commands. For example, pattern-directed search of the cache is initiated by calling procedure search (patt, resp.). The parameter "patt" is a pointer to an array containing the search pattern, which may contain wild cards. The set of responders is returned to an array pointed to by "resp".

The overall cost-per-bit of the (4+2) Mbytes of associative storage is about the same as the cost of purchasing 6Mbytes of conventional RAM for a VME bus. Other IFS sub-units will be attached to the VME bus in due course. For example, we have designed a hardware sorter to augment the functionality of the LTC. We are looking at the possibility of using GAM chips (Ref. 3) as the basis for a transitive closure sub-unit. A relational algebraic processor, performing such operations as set intersection, is being designed. Finally, there is the possibility of a VME bus link between the IFS store management system and a parallel Prolog engine being built by another team at Essex.

5. Performance and Conclusions

To assess the impact of semantic caching on the performance of practical knowledge base stores, detailed simulations were carried out on a hierarchical associative memory. This was composed of the 4Mbyte store of Section 5 acting as the fast cache for a modified disc with logic-per-head, searched on the fly. The actual disc used was a Kennedy 53160 Winchester, with seek times of 10 millisec. (track-to-track), 50 millisec. (average) and 80 millisec. (maximum). When employed for sample user-sessions on the historical database referred to earlier, the overall average search time for the disc alone was 309 millisec.; (the cache alone would have yielded 257 microsec.). When these two units were combined to form a hierarchical memory utilising the semantic caching scheme described in Section 3, the average search time dropped from 309 to between 140 and 180 millisec. (depending on user session) - a performance improvement of between 1.69 and 2.22. Based on the observed hit-rate of 89%, the theoretical improvement should be 2.53. The discrepancy arises because in practice the associative search times vary according to interrogand pattern.

In a fully-engineered version of an associative hierarchy, it is evident that the overall search times could be improved by a factor of about 2 by employing a higher performance disc. Some degree of request queueing, head-movement optimisation and track buffering might also be used, producing a further speed improvement. Thus, competitively-priced bulk associative stores with average search times in the range 60 - 100 millisec. are a practical proposition. This prediction is currently being investigated by incorporating onto the VME bus an intelligent disc controller for buffering the most-recently used tracks and driving a Fujitsu M2333 disc. This has seek times of 5 millisec (track-to-track), 20 millisec. (average) and 40 millisec. (maximum).

In conclusion, it has been shown that a general-purpose bulk storage system can be devised which, by reflecting the needs of knowledge representation formalisms, is suitable for use with a wide range of knowledge-based systems. Such a store may, for economic reasons, consist of a hierarchy of physical devices. A unifying management strategy is then necessary for paging and protection. We have presented semantic caching as such a scheme. A 4Mbyte associative store has been built which, when used as a semantic cache for spinning store, can give the desired rate of pattern-directed searches. It is intended that the results of such searches shall feed other sub-units within the IFS. These will provide specialist functions such as transitive closure and set-intersection.

Acknowledgements

The work described in this paper is part of the IFS project, a collaboration between ICL and the Universities of Essex and Manchester. It is supported by the Alvey Directorate under grant GR/D/45468 - IKBS/129. The authors would like to thank their colleagues in the team, and in particular M. Azmoodeh, R. Prasad and N. Sambanis.

References

1. S. E. Fahlman, G. E. Hinton and T. J. Sejnowski, "Massively parallel architectures for AI: NETL, THISTLE, and Boltzmann machines". Proc. National Conference on Artificial Intelligence (AAAI-83), Washington 1983, pages 109-113.

2. S. Peyton Jones, "Using Futurebus in a fifth-generation computer". Microprocessors and Microsystems, Vol. 10, no. 2, March 1986, pages 69-76.

3. D. R. McGregor and J. R. Malone, "An integrated high performance, hardware assisted, intelligent database system for large-scale knowledge bases", Proc. first Workshop on Architecture for Large Knowledge Bases, Manchester, May 1984. (Published by the Alvey Directorate, Millbank Tower, London, SW1P 4QU).

4. Y. J. Jiang and S. H. Lavington, "The qualified binary relationship model of information". Proc. fourth British National Conference on Databases, published by Cambridge University Press, July 1985, pages 61-79.

5. K. Ramamohanarao and J. Shepherd, "A superimposed codeword indexing scheme for very large Prolog databases". Proc. 3rd Int. Conf. on Logic Programming, London, July 1986, pages 569-576. (Springer-Verlag).

6. I. Robinson, "A Prolog processor based on a pattern matching memory device". Proc 3rd Int. Conf. on Logic Programming, London, July 1986, pages 172-179. (Springer-Verlag).

7. H. Matsumoto, "A static analysis of Prolog programs". University of Edinburgh, AI Applications Institute, report AIAI/PSG24/85, January 1985.

8. M. D. Cripps, A. J. Field and M. J. Reeve, "The design and implementation of ALICE: a parallel graph reduction machine". In: Functional Programming Languages, Tools and Architecture, ed. S. Eisenbach. Ellis Horwood, 1986.

9. F. C. N. Pereira and D. H. D. Warren, "An efficient easily adaptable system for interpreting natural language queries". American Journal of Computational Linguistics, Vol. 3, No. 3 - 4, July/December 1982.

10. C. J. Rawlings, W. R. Taylor, J. Nyakairu, J. Fox and M. J. E. Sternberg, "Using Prolog to represent and reason about protein structure". Proc. 3rd Int. Conf. on Logic Programming, London, July 1986, pages 536-543. (Springer-Verlag).

11. N. Miyazaki, T. Kakuta, S. Shibayama, H. Yokota and K. Muirakami, "An overview of relational database machine Delta". ICOTT Technical Report TR-074, 1984. (Published by ICOT, Tokyo 108, Japan).

12. H. Schweppe, "Some comments on semantical disk cache management for knowledge base systems". ICOT Technical Report TR-040, 1984. (Published by ICOT, Tokyo 108, Japan).

241

13. M. Azmoodeh, S. H. Lavington and M. Standring, "The semantic binary
    relationship model of information". Proc. third joint BCS/ACM symposium on
    R. and D. in Information Retrieval. Published by Cambridge University Press,
    July 1984, pages 133-151.

14. W. D. Hillis, "The Connection Machine". MIT Press 1985.

15. G. E. Hinton, T. Sejnowski and D. Ackley, "Boltzmann Machines: constraint
    satisfaction networks that learn". Report TR-CMU-CS-84119, Carnegie Mellon
    University, 1984.

16. M. Standring, S. H. Lavington and G. B. Rubner, "A 4Mbyte associative
    predicate store". Proc. first Workshop on Architectures for Large Knowledge
    Bases, Manchester, May 1984. (Published by the Alvey Directorate, Millbank
    Tower, London, SW1P 4QU).

17. W. N. Chin, "Concurrency control strategies for a database machine". M.Sc.
    thesis, University of Manchester, October 1984.

Transputer-Based Experiments with the ZAPP Architecture.

D.L.McBurney and M.R.Sleep

Declarative Systems Project,
University of East Anglia,
Norwich NR4 7TJ, England.

ABSTRACT.

We report experiments with a parallel architecture called ZAPP[2] simulated on several connected INMOS transputers. Besides the usual synthetic benchmarks (eg Nfib), our experiments covered a range of applications including matrix multiply, heuristic search and the 0-1 knapsack optimisation problem. Some of these applications cannot be adequately supported by the original ZAPP model. We report the modifications we made to ZAPP to accommodate them.

One experiment involved 40 transputers; we obtained a stopwatch speed of over *one million function calls per second*, corresponding to a *relative* speedup over a single simulated ZAPP element of 39.9, and a real performance improvement over a single transputer running the same algorithm directly programmed in OCCAM of more than 15. A similar experiment for matrix multiply confirmed that real improvements were obtained using ZAPP techniques.

Experiments with less structured problems, such as heuristic search and the 0-1 knapsack problem, revealed that the longer a problem took to solve using sequential implementation, the more likely it was to benefit from parallel solution using ZAPP techniques.

1.0   Introduction.

Exploring the potential of parallelism is receiving increasing attention [1,4,7]. There are a number of reasons for this interest:

a.   Some applications, such as speech and image processing, require large amounts of computational power which sequential computing cannot satisfy. In the field of general purpose computing, knowledge based applications will also need powerful engines if acceptable performance is required.

b.   Many problems have solutions which are most naturally expressed as static or dynamic networks of communicating processes. For example, control systems for industrial plants can be decomposed into a set of data collection processes, data integration and filtering processes, decision making processes, and effector processes (ie those which are responsible for realising the decisions made).

c.   Very Large Scale Integration technology enables us to produce large numbers of computing elements at low cost, perhaps on a single large chip or wafer.

1.1   Architecture Background: Good results have been obtained by careful machine-oriented programming of large SIMD (Single Instruction Multiple Data) machines for specific applications and the current generation of supercomputers is based on this experience.

The search for more general purpose MIMD (Multiple Instruction Multiple Data) parallel architectures has been less successful, particularly in achieving performance which would improve as the number of computing elements grows. Early experiments gave disappointing results, even after significant programming effort was deployed. Successful exploitation of parallelism has usually been associated with limiting both the degree of parallelism and the range of applications.

1.2   The Paradigm Approach: One difficulty in realising general purpose parallelism is that it is not in general sufficient to take a program designed for a sequential machine and recompile it for a parallel machine. Although progress has been made on automatic extraction of parallelism from sequential programs, it is in general necessary to re-think the problem in order to obtain an effective parallel solution.

Some rather abstract *paradigms* on which parallel solutions may be based have proved useful over a range of applications. Perhaps the simplest example is the *divide and conquer* paradigm, which is easy to understand and familiar to most programmers. In this paper we describe a parallel architecture (called ZAPP) for Divide and Conquer solutions, and report early experiments with a transputer-based implementation of ZAPP.

1.3   Plan of paper: Section 2 introduces the *process tree* interpretation of Divide and Conquer algorithms on which ZAPP is based. Section 3 describes the basic principle of ZAPP operation. Section 4 describes very briefly the OCCAM/Tranputer realisation of ZAPP we used in our experiments. Section 5 describes the experiments performed, and section 6 presents the experimental results. Section 7 contains the main conclusions.

2.0   The Divide and Conquer approach to parallelism.

A number of useful paradigms exist for obtaining parallel solutions to problems. These include pipelining, systolic networks, and parallel array processing. More recent paradigms include the *connection* paradigms of Hillis[6] and others. Here we will be concerned with the *Divide and Conquer* paradigm. This may be illustrated by the following function, which is written in a functional notation:

Nfib (n)= if n<2 then 1 else (Nfib (n-1))+ (Nfib (n-2))+1 fi

Operationally, this equation may be interpreted as a *rewrite rule*. For example Nfib(6) rewrites to (Nfib(5))+ (Nfib(4))+1. Parallel rewriting creates a number of sub-expressions which grows (initially exponentially) with time if all available sub-expressions are rewritten at each step.

Nfib is an example of the application of the *Divide and Conquer* paradigm for problem solving. This paradigm can be expressed by the D_C function defined as follows:

    def D_C (primitive,divide,combine,solve) = f
    where f(x)   =if primitive(x) then solve(x) else combine(map(f, divide(x))) fi

    x   is a problem description.
    primitive (x)   returns true if x can be solved directly, otherwise it returns false.

> solve (x) solves a primitive problem.
> divide (x) splits a non-primitive problem into a list of smaller ones.
> combine [s1...sk] combines a set of solutions of subproblems into a single solution.

For example, if we define:

> primitive(n) = if n<2 then true else false
> solve(n) =1
> divide(n) =[(n-1),(n-2)]
> combine(L) = if null (L) then 1 else ((head (L))+(combine (tail (L)))

we may write: Nfib= D_C (primitive,divide,combine,solve).

2.1 Process tree interpretation: Having abstracted the essence of the Divide and Conquer paradigm in the form of the D_C function, an obvious way of introducing parallelism is to implement (combine (map (f, divide(x)))) as a process which spawns a number of child processes, and is then *blocked* until all the results are available. The parent process combines the results and communicates the overall result to its parent. Thus the process of parallel reduction using the D_C function may be viewed as growing a process tree, which eventually shrinks to the overall result at the root.

In simple applications, communication occurs only between parent and child, and only at the beginning and end of a child's lifetime. A process tree for which this is so is called *simple*. Some of the applications examined below involve more interesting communication patterns.

3.0   The ZAPP Architecture.

ZAPP stands for Zero Assignment Parallel Processor, with Zero Assignment indicating the reduction aspects of the simple process tree model. The ZAPP architecture (first described in [2]) is a *virtual tree machine*, which is capable of dynamically mapping a process tree onto any fixed, strongly connected network of processors (called ZAPP elements). Communication is by message passing: there is no global memory. Each processor runs a ZAPP kernel which implements the Divide and Conquer function defined above.This is (with small modifications described below) the same for all applications. The user encodes a particular application by defining the four functions *primitive, solve, divide* and *combine*. The basic steps in applying a ZAPP to perform the calculation are:

(a) Initialise the ZAPP elements by broadcasting the user program to all the elements.
(b) Inject the data for the initial problem into a single element.
(c) Extract and report the final result from the ZAPP element chosen for (b) above.

3.1 Basic principles of the ZAPP architecture: The central notion is that each ZAPP element performs a sequential, depth first traversal of the process tree.Thus it visits the nodes in the process tree in the order which a sequential recursive implementation would. However, unlike a recursive implementation, ZAPP's depth-first traversal actually constructs descriptors of sibling processes. By the simple device of allowing other ZAPP elements to steal one or more of these siblings *from immediate neighbours* we introduce real parallelism. By immediate neighbours we mean ZAPP elements which are connected by a direct physical link.

Restricting offloading to immediate neighbours (the *single steal* rule) has the property that each communication between parent and child involves *at most* one physical link. On the other hand it can in principle lead to situations in which there are idle elements topologically distant from elements with much work. This occurs when very small process trees are run on large configurations: ZAPP works best for trees which are much larger than the physical configuration.

3.2   Space requirements: Because each ZAPP element traverses the process tree depth first, its space requirements are bounded above by $kD_{max}S_{max}$ where k is some constant, D_{max} is the maximum depth of the process tree, and S_{max} is the maximum number of siblings encountered. For the usual binary Divide and Conquer algorithm, S_{max} is 2. This analysis assumes that the siblings can be described in constant space, but this is not unreasonable for the applications examined so far. For example, in the matrix multiplication application sub-matrices can be described by two pairs of integers.

3.3   Communication requirements: When a sibling is moved from one ZAPP element to another, a full descriptor is communicated. In the case of eg matrix mutiplication this may mean copying large quantities of data because the basic ZAPP model does not support shared memory. However, the single steal rule prevents more than one physical link being involved in the communication. In short, ZAPP offloads problems by copying full descriptors, but *the single steal rule limits the consequences of this design decision.* In our experiments every ZAPP element is provided with a complete copy of the code and so code is copied just once, during the load phase.

3.4   Diffusion of work: If the offloaded task is primitive, then it is executed and its results are returned to its logical parent, which by the single steal rule must be on an immediately neighbouring element. If however the task is non trivial, then it is divided into subtasks which may subsequently be offloaded onto other ZAPP elements. If we assume that each non-primitive task divides into two or more sons and that one is offloaded to a neighbour, and the other retained and dealt with immediately, then the number of active tasks can initially grow exponentially with time given a rich enough topology.

The apparently very restrictive single steal rule, combined with task division, allows very large process trees to diffuse throughout the physical topology. Most of our experiments were run using full-interconnect topologies, and so do not shed much light on the importance of topology. However, we obtained encouraging results for a more restrictive topology involving 40 transputers.

3.5   Offloading stratgegy: The basic offloading strategy is that only idle processors may request work from neighbours, and that neighbours will agree to offloading whenever this is possible. However variations are possible: some element of look-ahead in requests may be desirable, and conversely a refusal to agree to offloading when the pool of outstanding work is running low may also be desirable. Through experiment, it seems that a good offloading strategy for a ZAPP element is to acquire new offloads only when the number of active tasks that it has falls below a small constant value .

3.6   *Comparison with idealised tree machine:* It might appear at first sight that the ideal architecture for executing simple process trees is a tree of physical processing elements large enough to support direct mapping of logical processes onto physical processors. However, for the following reasons this is not so

(a)   Interior nodes in the simple process tree are inactive during the lifetime of their offspring, and so on a tree machine, processor utilization can be exponentially bad.
(b)   The tree created by the solution of a particular problem is unlikely to match the shape or size of a particular tree machine.
(c)   The depth of the physical tree limits the size of problem that can be considered.

The ZAPP architecture described above allows great freedom in the *dynamic* mapping of the solution process tree onto the available processor network. This gives the ZAPP architecture major advantages over direct mapping of the process tree onto a physical tree of processors. In particular:

i.   No static scheduling is needed, all scheduling being done dynamically and automatically.
ii.   The logical process tree can be very much larger than the physical network.
iii.   ZAPP works for any connected topology.

The most obvious restrictions of ZAPP are:

A.   Every local memory must be large enough to accommodate single processor execution of the process tree. Note however that it is governed by the maximum depth of the tree, not its total size.
B.   It does not directly support shared memory.
C.   It supports only the very limited form of inter-process communication required to support simple process trees.

We recognise that many real problems are not solved by the simple process tree model underlying ZAPP. For this reason we examined two applications (knapsack problem, heuristic search) which require a more general model. Necessary modifications to accommodate these applications are described later.

4.0   OCCAM/Transputer realisation of ZAPP.

For our experiments we constructed a small variable-topology configuration from 5 Transputers, and encoded a ZAPP kernel in OCCAM. Each of the applications was programmed directly in OCCAM, and the programs so produced consisted of essentially two parts: one part effectively implemented the ZAPP architecture (the ZAPP kernel). The other part was an encoding of the particular application (essentially as OCCAM versions of the functions *primitive, divide, solve and combine* discussed in section 2).

4.1   *The ZAPP kernel:* The ZAPP kernel maintained the lists of tasks produced by the application part of the program, performed all interprocessor communications and controlled the transfer of work between processors.

The kernel evolved somewhat during our experiments. Some of these modifications can be seen simply as letting the kernel know the data structures necessary to describe a subproblem. A suitable high-level language would relieve this problem. Other minor modifications reflect different heuristics for deciding when a ZAPP element is willing to release a task in response to an offloading request from a neighbour.

For some applications, particularly those which required more sophisticated communication than is supported by simple process trees, more fundamental modifications to the kernel were required. These involved introducing some element of global communication.

We now consider various aspects of the OCCAM model used to represent the ZAPP kernel(s).

4.1.1 Task Sets: In our OCCAM model of the ZAPP architecture the tasks produced by the application part of the program can be in any one of three task sets called PENDING, FIXED and BLOCKED. Child tasks produced during the divide phase of the application are added to the PENDING set, which contains all the candidates for offloading. Once a task is scheduled on a given ZAPP element, it is moved to the FIXED set, which indicates that it is no longer a candidate for offloading. The BLOCKED set contains all those tasks which are unable to proceed until the results of some other tasks have been received.

4.1.2 Communication: All communication takes place between ZAPP kernels, and is done by passing messages between them. The ZAPP kernel maintains one message queue, one output buffer and one input buffer for each of its immediately neighbouring kernels. When a kernel wants to communicate with another kernel it adds its message to the appropriate queue.

4.1.2.1 Work Acquisition: When a kernel decides that it requires work, it sends messages to its neighbours asking them for tasks to perform. On receipt of a work request message the neighbours determine whether they have enough work of their own to offload some of it to the requesting kernel. If enough work is present then a task is offloaded from the PENDING set to the neighbour, otherwise a rejection message is sent back to the requesting kernel.

We have tried several rules for deciding when a kernel should acquire work and where it should acquire it from. The simplest rule used decides to request tasks from neighbours only when the kernel has no tasks which it can execute. Each neighbour is then asked in turn for a task. If the reply to the request is a rejection then the next neighbour is asked for a task, but if the reply is an offloaded task then it stops requesting tasks. The other heuristics tried are mainly variations of this basic type, which instead of waiting until no tasks are executable before requesting for work, start sending requests when the number of executable tasks falls below some small constant value, and only ask for work from neighbours which they have been told have offloadable tasks.

4.1.3 Structure of OCCAM Code: So far we have tried two designs for the structure of our OCCAM programs. In the first and simpler design, most of the OCCAM code for the ZAPP kernel and all of the code for the application is represented as a single OCCAM process. Each of the input and output buffers has its own OCCAM process. We will refer to this as the *simple structure*. The second design contains many more OCCAM processes than the first. The application part of the program exists in a single OCCAM process but the kernel is distributed over a number of other distinct OCCAM processes in addition to the buffering processes present in the simple structure. The second design is called the *complex structure*.

For the complex structure the kernel consists of a PENDING process, FIXED process, BLOCKED process, a message queue process for each of the neighbouring kernels, and as before input and output buffer processes. There is no control process as such, each process has its obligations and may call on other processes to help it fulfill them. The second design reveals parallelism within the kernel which could be exploited in any VLSI design of a ZAPP element.

5.0 Description of Experiments

In this section we describe the applications used for the experiments reported. The results are presented in section 6.

5.1 Divide and Conquer Addition: This experiment involves the creation of a tree of n processes by Divide and Conquer, and then counting the number of processes created. The only parameter required is an integer n, the number of processes to be created.

In this program the pending tasks on each processor are held in a de-queue, each processor develops its portion of the process tree in a depth first manner, so the last added pending task is the first removed and expanded. When a processor offloads work (effectively a portion of the tree to be expanded) it takes a task from the front of the pending de-queue. In this way the tree is distributed breadth first over the network of processors, but depth first on each individual processor.

The main value of this experiment (which was devised by Warren Burton) is in determining how well the basic ZAPP model distributes a well-balanced process tree.

5.2 Parallel Matrix Multiplication: This experiment uses the standard $O(n^3)$ method to multiply two nxn matrices A and B. If C is the result matrix then the value of each of its elements, c_{ij}, is calculated so:

$$c_{ij} = \sum_{k=1}^{n} a_{ik} b_{kj}$$

In our experiment, to allow the elements of C to be calculated in parallel, we divide the problem of calculating the elements of C into four problems of calculating the elements of the four sub matrices of C shown below.

$$C = \begin{bmatrix} C11 & C12 \\ C21 & C22 \end{bmatrix}$$

We then divide these sub matrices in a similar way until the problems are sufficiently trivial for the elements of C to be calculated. By dividing the problem in this way we avoid having to do any calculations when the results of the sub problems are combined.

For the matrix multiplication experiments the programs produced had the complex process structure described earlier. The pending tasks were held in a de-queue, and offloads taken off the front of the de-queue, whilst tasks for the resident application process were taken from the back of the de-queue.

Initially the matrices to be multiplied only exist on the processor with the seed task, but as tasks are offloaded, the elements of the matrices which will be required by the offloaded task are copied to the processor receiving the offload. Similarly when an offloaded task terminates, its results are copied back to the processor from which the offload came. As a result of this data copying a large amount of kernel to kernel communication takes place, making these experiments a good test of the ability of ZAPP and the transputer to handle large quantities of communication.

5.3 Backtracking Divide and Conquer Knapsack Algorithm:

The components of the 0-1 Knapsack problem are a Knapsack with weight capacity C and a set of n objects. Object i has a weight w_i and a profit p_i. Each object i has a variable x_i associated with it, x_i is assigned the value 1 if object i is in the knapsack, x_i is assigned 0 otherwise.

The objective is to obtain a filling of the knapsack which maximizes the total profit earned from the objects in the knapsack, but which has a total weight not exceeding some given value C. This may be stated as:

$$\text{Maximize} \sum_{i=1}^{n} p_i x_i$$

$$\text{Subject to} \sum_{i=1}^{n} w_i x_i <= C$$

and
$$x_i = 1 \text{ or } x_i = 0, p_i > 0, w_i > 0$$

There are many deterministic methods of solving this NP-complete problem. The method employed in the experiment is based on a backtracking algorithm described in [5]. We will first describe the sequential algorithm from which our parallel algorithm is derived, and then explain the changes made to produce the parallel version.

5.3.1 Method of Solution:

For a problem consisting of n objects we sort and number the objects 1..n so that

$$w_i / p_i <= w_{i+1} / p_{i+1}$$

Then we fill the knapsack adding the objects in order of increasing index, until we come to the first object, with index j say, which we cannot add to the contents of the knapsack without exceeding the weight limit C. Object j is left out of this filling of the knapsack, and then, provided that we can still achieve a filling of the knapsack which has a greater profit than the greatest profit already attained in a filling, we try to fill the remaining capacity of the knapsack by repeating the greedy fill procedure described above with the objects indexed j+1..n, again stopping to perform a bounding test every time we have to leave an object out.

This procedure stops either (a) when there are no more objects to consider (at which point we have found a filling with profit greater than any found previously, and which may be the optimal solution, so we record it), or (b) because the bound test could not be satisfied.

The next step is to backtrack to the last object that was added to the knapsack, with index k say, we remove it from the knapsack and then in the manner described above we greedily fill the remaining capacity with the objects indexed k+1..n, and start it off with a bounding test. When this filling process stops we repeat the backtrack and fill routine and continue to repeat it until there are no more objects to backtrack to.

When this process completes we will have found the optimal solution and recorded it.

5.3.2 Bounding Test:

The purpose of the bounding test is to prune search activities which cannot yield an optimal solution. Given a partially filled knapsack and a set of objects which have yet to be considered for inclusion in the knapsack, we calculate an upper bound for the total profit attainable from adding those objects to the current contents of the knapsack. We compare this estimate profit with the greatest profit yet attained in a filling of the knapsack. This value is called the *bounding value*. If the estimate is less than the bounding value then pruning may proceed.

The estimated profit is calculated by adding the objects in order, to the existing contents of the knapsack, until the next object to be considered, with index j say, cannot be added without exceeding the maximum weight C. The estimate is then the total of the profits of all the objects now in the knapsack and a component of the profit for object j, calculated as follows:

$$\text{component} = (w_j / (C - \text{total weight of contents})) * p_j$$

The estimate can be improved by making the observation that if the remaining capacity of the knapsack, before we start adding the objects to calculate the estimate, is less than the weight of the lightest of the objects remaining then the actually attainable profit is just the current profit of the contents of the knapsack. An extra refinement is possible when the profits of all the n objects in the problem are integer. On these occasions the calculated estimate can be rounded down to the nearest integer .

5.3.3 Conversion To Parallelised Form:

In a parallel version of the algorithm described we need to be able to expand many parts of the solution tree simultaneously. To do this we first of all adjust the sequential method of solution described so that we explicitly record the backtracks that have to be made (one every time we add and object to the knapsack) and maintain these task records in a stack. Then when we backtrack we simply pop a record off the stack.

Each of the task records in the task stack represent a problem of finding an optimal filling of the remaining capacity of a partially filled knapsack with a subset of the n objects. These tasks can be performed in parallel. In our ZAPP implementation the task records are maintained as the PENDING set.

The solution tree expanded by this parallel algorithm will not necessarily be the same as that expanded by the sequential algorithm. When a task is offloaded it gets expanded out of turn relative to the sequential algorithm, and this can lead to early pruning of the search tree. We should not therefore be suprised to find apparently anomalous speedups being achieved by the parallel algorithm.

Under these circumstances, we would like our parallel implementation to be as fast as a sequential one for every problem instance, and possibly considerably faster. To achieve this, our parallel implementation must appear to maintain the task records as a stack when tasks are required for execution on the same processor, and each processor in the network has to know what the best bounding value is.

5.3.4 Global Bound Updating: In our ZAPP implementation, the processes supported by a given kernel share a common local bound, implemented as shared memory. Global updating of the bounding value is achieved by making each ZAPP kernel communicate any improvements to its local bounding value to its neighbours at regular intervals. We experimented with a range of communication frequencies.

The introduction here of what is effectively communication between processes in the process tree, other than at their creation or termination, represents a major modification to the basic ZAPP design.

5.3.5 Offloading Strategy: The usual strategy for choosing which tasks to offload is to select the tasks which are the most computationally intensive, but the nature of this application makes it impossible to determine the amount of work involved in executing a task held in the PENDING set. We used uniform random choice for our experiments.

5.4 Parallel Heuristic Search: The fifteen puzzle consists of a small square frame capable of holding 16 square tiles in a 4 X 4 array, but actually containing only 15 numbered tiles, leaving one blank space. The problem is an example of least cost search, in which we have to search through a tree of legal moves of the tiles looking for the shortest sequence of moves which lead to the puzzle being in the goal state.

In the sequential A* algorithm [5] on which our parallel algorithm is based, a search tree is grown from the starting configuration. At each step a most promising node is chosen for expansion, on the basis of a heuristic function. For our experiments we used the 'Manhattan distance' as a basis for the heuristic function. This satisfies the lower bound requirement of A*.

5.4.1 Parallel Version: We introduced parallelism to the sequential algorithm described above by simultaneously expanding several nodes on the search frontier. The set of unexpanded nodes was represented by the tasks of the PENDING set which are maintained in a heap sorted on increasing cost, with the least cost node at the head of the heap. Offloads are taken from near the root of this heap.

The main drawback of this algorithm as it stands is that without some global control, many nodes which are not expanded by the sequential algorithm might be expanded by the parallel algorithm. As with the Knapsack problem, we introduced global control by simulating a broadcast mechanism between ZAPP elements. Every time a ZAPP kernel expands a certain number of nodes it communicates the value of its current least cost node to neighbouring kernels. Using this information the kernels can decide to either acquire extra nodes, with lower cost than their own nodes, from their neighbours or continue expanding the nodes they already have. In this way the search performed by the network of processors is restricted to approximately the same areas of the tree as are searched by a single processor.

5.5 Nfib Benchmark: A standard benchmarking value for functional languages is the number of function calls per second. This value can be measured using the Nfib function which has the nice property of returning as its result the number of times that the function was activated. Copying the definition given in section 3, the Nfib function is **Nfib (n) = if n < 2 then 1 else (Nfib(n-1))+(Nfib(n-2))+1 fi**

Note that this is a highly inefficient way of computing Nfib, just as Naive Reverse as used in benchmarking LISP or Prolog implementations is a highly inefficient way of reversing a list. However, Nfib does grow a large, unbalanced process tree and provides a measure of ZAPP's capability.

To gauge the overhead involved in simulating ZAPP using OCCAM, we wrote two single processor implementations of the Nfib function directly in OCCAM. One simulated recursion using a stack; the other by using an array of OCCAM processes, each one running a copy of the Nfib function.

Stacked Version: This single processor sequential version is simply an OCCAM conversion of a pascal implementation of the Nfib function, which uses a while loop and a stack to replace the explicit recursion.

Process Array: In this version recursion is modelled by using an array of n processes, n being the maximum depth of recursion required, each process executes the following Nfib procedure

```
PROC Nfib(CHAN from.parent, to.parent, to.child, from.child)=
  VAR n, res.1, res.2 :
  WHILE TRUE
    SEQ
      from.parent ? n
      IF
        n < 2
          to.parent ! 1
        TRUE
          SEQ
            to.child ! n - 1
            from.child ? res.1
            to.child ! n - 2
            from.child ? res.2
            to.parent ! res.1 + res.2 + 1:
```

The first process in the array is injected with the initial parameter n of the nfib function, the value returned by the first process is the nfib value of the given parameter.

6.0   Experimental Results.

Unless otherwise stated, all parallel runs involved 5 transputers. Most of the experiments measured *relative speedups*. That is, we compared the time taken to solve a given problem using all available transputers running ZAPP kernels with the time taken to solve the problem using just 1 ZAPP kernel running on a transputer. Relative speedups (RS) factor out the overhead of running the ZAPP kernels, and can show near-linear performance increases.

In some cases we also report *effective speedups*. In this case the single transputer runs are done with sequential algorithms directly encoded in OCCAM thus avoiding the overhead of running the ZAPP kernel. The effective speedup (ES) measures are more subjective than relative speedups because for example of the choice of sequential algorithm. However, the ES figures are interesting because where they are greater than 1 they show that some real benefit from parallelism can be obtained over a direct encoding of a sequential algorithm by running several simulated ZAPP elements.

6.1   *Divide and Conquer Addition:* Sample relative speedups (RS) measured using 5 ZAPP elements were:

No. Processes	RS
10	0.7755
100	1.0994
1000	2.6771
10000	4.5534
100000	4.9206

It can be seen that as the size of the process tree increases, the speedup approaches 5. This confirms the trend of the earlier single-processor simulation result reported in[3]. Note however that the process tree must be large for good speedups.

6.2   *Parallel Matrix Multiplication:* Both relative and effective speedups are reported for this

experiment. We were restricted by memory to matrices of size up to 32x32 on a configuration of 5 transputers. The effective speedup figures were obtained by comparing the time for 5 ZAPP elements with the time taken by a simple $O(n^3)$ program written in OCCAM running on a single transputer. The results are shown below (times are in seconds):

Matrix Size	Time for 1 Processor Tight Loops	Time for 1 ZAPP Standard MM	Time for 5 ZAPP Standard MM	Speedup Over Tight Loop Version	Speedup Over 1 ZAPP Version
n = 8	0.0377	0.0570	0.0208	1.81	2.74
n = 16	0.3040	0.4346	0.1036	2.93	4.19
n = 32	2.4457	3.2944	0.7188	3.40	4.58

The last two columns give the Effective and Relative Speedups. Note that as the matrix size increases, the relative speedup approaches 5, and that in all cases effective speedups >1 were obtained.

6.3 *Backtracking Divide and Conquer Knapsack Algorithm:* The problems generated ranged in size from 30 to 60 objects, and there were several problems of each size. For each of the problems the attributes of the objects were chosen from the same data set and the maximum weight C was half the total weight of all the objects. The data set used is shown below:

w_i = an integer chosen at random from the range 1..100. $p_i = w_i + 10$.

For this experiment, offloads were chosen at random from the list of pending task records. To see how different random selections of records would affect the performance of the program, we ran the ZAPP program five times with each problem, and computed an average figure for the relative speedup. The results of our experiments, presented in order of time for completion on a single ZAPP, were:

Time (1 ZAPP)	Rel. Speedup	No. Objects
0.0197	0.67	30
0.0251	0.88	40
0.0289	0.99	30
0.0462	1.11	30
0.0513	0.93	60
0.0645	1.47	30
0.0722	1.14	50
0.1414	1.66	50
0.1433	2.02	40
0.3671	2.9	30
0.6163	3.29	50
0.7565	3.62	30
0.958	3.57	40
1.1465	3.85	30
1.2413	3.42	60
1.9238	3.98	40
2.0526	3.94	50
2.1126	4.01	50
3.1282	4.42	30
3.7781	4.39	60
8.8229	4.71	40
9.7635	4.69	60
293.0407	5.01	60
338.5552	5.02	50

Times are in seconds.

6.3.1 *Discussion:* Our results show a relationship between the time taken to solve a problem on a single ZAPP element and the speedup obtained when solving it using 5 ZAPP elements. The speedup for simple problems is low: sometimes a slowdown, but as the problem complexity increases so too does the speedup with a five fold increase being achieved in some cases.

To highlight the relationship, note that if we exclude all problems which require less than 1 second to execute on a single ZAPP element, we obtain an average speedup approaching 5. We think that end users are unlikely to be very interested in performance for small problems, and that the larger problems (where we obtain our good speedups) are the interesting ones.

6.4 *Parallel Heuristic Search:* For our experiments with this program we generated ten problems and solved each on a single ZAPP element and on a configuration of four ZAPP elements. As with the matrix multiply experiment, the small amount of memory (64K) local to each of our transputers limited the size of problems that could be solved. Note the use of a configuration of four ZAPP elements instead of five, so that any speedups greater than 4 are superlinear.

To determine what effect the frequency of communicating least cost values has on the speedups obtained using the four Transputer ZAPP configuration, each problem was solved with a range of communication frequencies. For each ZAPP kernel the communication interval specifies the number of records that it has to search each time it communicates its least cost value to its neighbours: the larger the interval, the less frequent the communication.

The table below summarises the results obtained for the ten problems with the four most competitive communication intervals tried. Only very slight, if any, variations in speedup were found for most of the problems. Superlinear results are shown in bold face.

				SPEEDUP OVER 1 ZAPP			
Num. Records		Moves	Time On 1	Communication Interval			
Searched on 1		Required	In Seconds	15	20	25	30
1	75	28	0.1013	1.8588	1.7985	1.8670	1.8673
2	95	20	0.1502	1.5633	1.4921	1.4631	1.3091
3	263	24	0.4132	2.6489	2.6237	3.3656	**4.1621**
4	291	26	0.4627	2.9127	2.917	2.9534	3.0387
5	324	22	0.5207	**4.7262**	2.2374	1.6523	2.9267
6	325	28	0.5076	2.3143	3.0798	1.0387	1.0477
7	456	22	0.7207	**4.2788**	3.1409	2.9140	1.9670
8	562	24	0.8380	3.3397	3.7621	3.3365	3.1887
9	1282	28	1.9834	**4.2231**	3.4778	3.4864	3.0621
10	1970	28	2.5264	**4.8786**	**5.2039**	**8.6383**	**9.3178**
		Mean Speedup		3.2744	2.9733	3.0715	3.1887

6.4.1 *Discussion:* None of the communication frequencies tried consistently produces better speedups than any of the others, implying that the best frequency is problem dependent.

This program produces a number of anomalous (ie superlinear) results particularly with the shortest communication interval, where 4 out of the 10 results are superlinear. It also displays considerable non determinism on some sensitive problems with different speedups being produced for runs with the same problem and communication frequency. This is caused by slightly different timings of events in different runs resulting in different records being offloaded. The table below shows some examples of this behaviour.

Problem Number	Communication Frequency	Speedup Run 1	Speedup Run 2
9	15	4.2231	2.0123
9	25	3.4864	2.2269
10	25	8.6383	4.2952

6.5 *Nfib benchmark:* From the superlinear result encountered in the last section, we now turn to a standard benchmark much used in measuring performances of Functional Language implementations. This gives a basic measure of the rate at which ZAPP can grow a process tree.

For comparison purposes, we also ran two direct OCCAM versions on a single transputer which sidestepped the ZAPP simulation overhead. One simulated recursion using a stack, the other simulated recursion using a pipeline of processes, one for each depth of recursion.

Each of the programs was run with values of n ranging from 10 to 40. The table and graph show the results obtained

| PROGRAM | Function Calls Per Second | | | | | | |
	n = 10	n = 15	n = 20	n = 25	n = 30	n = 35	n = 40
ZAPP on 5 Transputers	26236	74811	112194	121067	122184	122305	122318
ZAPP on 1 Transputer	24618	24600	24594	24595	24595	24595	---------
Stack version	73691	73565	73549	73548	73548	73548	73548
Process Array	92252	94577	92500	78864	78828	76181	69390

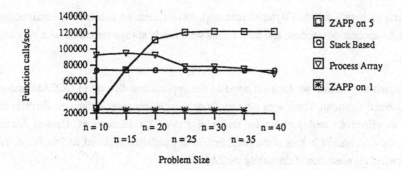

The row titled "ZAPP on 1 Transputer", gives the results obtained when the entire problem is solved on a single Transputer running the ZAPP software. This version was run with values of n up to 35.

The figures for the two sequential implementations are somewhat intriguing. For small problems, it is better to exploit INMOS's excellent support for processes on the transputer rather than manipulate stacks. For larger problems, this effect appears to vanish. Following discussions with INMOS and futher experiments we have confirmed that these differences are due to the difference in speeds of internal and external memory.

6.5.1 *Nfib on 40 transputers:* With the collaboration of INMOS we were able to run a short series of tests involving 40 transputers, using an ITEM300 product. The following table shows problem size (as indicated by the Nfib parameter n) against Function Calls per Second.

n	FCS_{40}	Relative SpeedUp
10	29422.	1.15
15	122334.	4.8
20	454256.	17.7
25	842816.	32.9
30	987811.	38.6
35	1017924.	39.8
40	1021125.	39.9

The 40 transputers were configured as a 4x10 wrap-around grid. Note the usual growth of speedup with problem size. The final problem (n=40) represents a very large process tree: Nfib(40)= 331160281. This problem took about 5.5 minutes to run on a 40-transputer ZAPP.

7.0   Conclusions.

a.   Throughout the applications studied, we saw strong evidence for the thesis that ZAPP 'buys speed' for suitable big problems. Most of our experiments were hampered by the small size of the configuration (just 5 transputers, each with only 64KBytes of memory). Nevertheless we consistently obtained good speedups across the applications studied, and poor results were nearly always associated with very small problems.

b.   For comparison purposes we encoded some of the applications directly in OCCAM, using a conventional sequential algorithm. These were run directly on a single transputer without the ZAPP kernel. The results (eg an effective speedup of 3.5 for multiplying two 32 x 32 matrices) showed that real performance benefit was obtained in spite of the small degrees of parallelism explored, and the fact that the parallel version carried the overheads of simulating the ZAPP kernel.

c.   We ran a short series of Nfib benchmarks on a 40 transputer INMOS ITEM 300 product. These produced an absolute speed of over one million function calls per second, corresponding to a relative speedup of 39.9.

Without further work, it is not possible to say how our results scale up for anything other than Nfib. However, we are encouraged to have observed some real benefit even with the low degrees of parallelism available for other experiments. Identifying suitable applications remains a topic for further work, as does extending language constructs beyond the D_C combinator which allows the programmer to introduce explicit parallelism. In particular, expression of broadcast notions required for the knapsack and heuristic search applications requires attention.

A more detailed version of this paper is available[9] from the authors.

8.0   Acknowledgements.

The first ZAPP kernel was designed by Warren Burton. Our transputer experiments would not have been possible without the close collaboration of INMOS, who provided us with five low-cost prototype boards and gave us access to a 40 transputer ITEM300 product on which we ran the last experiment reported. We would especially like to thank Richard Taylor, David May and Iann Barron of INMOS for their help and interest. Clifton Hughes of Logica suggested we run the process array version of the Nfib benchmark. Members of the Declarative Systems Project team at UEA made many useful comments and observations. We specially thank Anthony Clare for his careful reading of the final draft. The anonymous referees comments helped us improve this draft. The work was supported by an SERC grant.

REFERENCES.

[1]   VEGDAHL, S.R.
A Survey of Proposed Architectures for the Execution of Functional Languages.
IEEE Transactions on Computers, Vol. c-33, No.12, December 1984.

[2]   BURTON, F.W. and SLEEP, M.R.
Executing functional programs on a virtual tree of processors.
Proc.Conf.Functional Programming Languages and Computer Architecture, Portsmouth, New Hampshire, October 1982, pp.187-194.

[3]   KENNAWAY, J.R. and SLEEP, M.R.
The zero assignment parallel processor (ZAPP) project. In: D.A. Duce (Editor).
Distributed Computing Systems Programme, (Peter Peregrinus for IEE, 1984).

[4]   TRELEAVEN P.C., BROWNBRIDGE D.R. and HOPKINS R.P.
Data-Driven and Demand-Driven Computer Architecture.
ACM Computing Surveys **14**(1) 1982.

[5]   HOROWITZ, E. and SAHNI, S.
Fundamentals of Computer Algorithms.
Pitman 1978.

[6]   HILLIS W.D.
The Connection Machine.
AI Memo No.646, MIT Artificial Intelligence Laboratory.

[7]   KENNAWAY, J.R. and SLEEP, M.R.
Novel Architectures for Declarative Languages.
Software and Microsystems, Vol. 2, No. 3 (1983).

[8]
OCCAM Programming Manual
Prentice Hall International 1984

[9]   McBURNEY D. and SLEEP M.R.
Transputer based experiments with the ZAPP architecture.
University of East Anglia report no. SYS-C86-10. Oct. 1986.

SYNTHESIS OF SYSTOLIC ARRAYS FOR INDUCTIVE PROBLEMS

Catherine MONGENET (*), Guy-René PERRIN (**)
Centre de Recherche en Informatique de Nancy
Campus Scientifique
BP 239. 54506 Vandoeuvre-les-Nancy. FRANCE

Abstract :

We present a method for the synthesis of systolic arrays from a system of recurrent equations of a problem. The class of solved problems involves the inductive ones. For an inductive problem, the result sequence is calculated using its own elements : after its calculation, each element of this sequence is used as a data for other elements calculations. Therefore, the systolic arrays solutions are characterized by a 'reinjection' of each element of the result sequence in a data stream after its calculation.

This method is constructive. Therefore it is implemented in a software called SYSTOL.

Keywords : systolic arrays, synthesis.

This work is supported by the French Coordinated Research Program C^3

(*) Université Louis Pasteur, Département d'Informatique,
    7 rue René Descartes, 67084 STRASBOURG FRANCE.

(**) Université de Franche-Comté, Laboratoire d'Informatique,
     Route de Gray, 25030 BESANÇON FRANCE.

Introduction

The rapid advance in integrated-circuit technology involves a decrease in cost and an increase in number and complexity of the parts of a circuit. Hence, the design of special-purpose systems solving specific problems can be faced.

Systolic architectures presented by H.T. Kung ([KUN 79], [KUN 82], [MEC 80]) are special-purpose systems characterized by a regular structure of processing elements locally connected, through which data flow in a rythmic fashion. Because of their regular organization, they are consistent with VLSI technology limitations. Therefore a lot of researchers take an interest in systolic arrays ([MMU 87]). Among them, several are concerned with methods for designing systolic architectures ([CAS 83], [MOL 83], [QUI 83], [CHE 85], [DEI 85],[LIW 85], [FFW 85]). The subject of this article is precisely in this domain.

We present a software for the automatic synthesis of systolic arrays. This software, called SYSTOL, implements a constructive method ([MON 85], [MOP 85]) described in section 1. From a problem definition, SYSTOL automatically determines a set of systolic arrays solutions of this problem.

SYSTOL application is illustrated in section 2 with a two-dimensional inductive problem. The two-dimensional characteristic means that the result sequence is a double sequence of the form $(x_{ij})_{i \in I, \; j \in J}$ and that the systolic arrays are bidimensional. The inductive characteristic means that the result sequence is calculated using its own elements : after its calculation, an element of this sequence is used as a data for other elements calculations. In the systolic arrays solutions, this property imposes the reinjection of the element in a data stream after its calculation (see figure 4).

To conclude we give a comparison with other systolic array design approaches and try to present the originality of our method.

1. The SYSTOL' method

SYSTOL takes into account problems which can be defined by a system of recurrent equations of the form :

$$(1) \quad \begin{cases} x_{ij}^k = f(x_{ij}^{k-1}, d^1, \ldots, d^u) & i \in I, \ j \in J, \ 1 < k \leq ubk \ (i,j) \\[2ex] x_i^1 = v & v \in R \end{cases}$$

where f is the recurrence function,

$(x_{ij})_{i \in I, \ j \in J}$ is the double result sequence to be calculated,

I and J are intervals of Z,

k is the recurrence index,

ubk (i,j) is the affine function defining the upper bound of the recurrence index k,

$d^1, \ldots, d^u$ are data of the problem.

For a linear problem, the result sequence is a simple one of the form $(x_i)_{i \in I}$. In this paper, all the definitions are expressed for problems with double result sequence. The simplifications in the case of linear problems are evident.

One of the data d^q (q = 1...u) could be an item of the result sequence (x_{ij}). In this case, the problem is called an inductive one : each item of the result sequence depends on some others. In this article, we are interested in such inductive problems.

In this section, we illustrate the method with the following inductive linear problem. Given the factors sequence $(a_k)_{k=0 \ldots m-1}$, compute the sequence $(x_i)_{i=m \ldots n}$, n > m with

$$x_i = \sum_{k=0}^{m-1} a_k * x_{i+k-m}$$

where $x_0, x_1, \ldots, x_{m-1}$ are initial data. For visualization reasons, we suppose in the under figures that m = 4 and n = 8.

The system of recurrent equations of this problem is :

$$(2) \quad \begin{cases} x_i^k = x_i^{k-1} + a_k * x_{i+k-m} & m \leq i \leq n, \ 0 \leq k \leq m-1 \\[2ex] x_i^{-1} = 0 \end{cases}$$

with $x_0, \ldots, x_{m-1}$ given data.

From this system of equations, we can deduce an encoding called the **systolic specification** of the problem. The SYSTOL user must describe his problem by such a specification. From this specification, SYSTOL first determines a set of calculations orderings with regard to the time, which are called **time orderings**. Then it computes, from each time ordering, systolic arrays by allocating the calculations on a finite set of processing elements (or cells).

1.1 Systolic specification

This specification consists of :

- the convex domain $D \subset Z^n$ of all points corresponding to the elementary calculations of the problem (usually n is equal to 2 or 3, for linear and bidimensional arrays respectively). For n = 3,

$$D = \{ (i,j,k) \in Z^3 \mid i \in I, j \in J, 1 < k \leq ubk (i,j) \}$$

- the recurrence function f,

- the list of data items associated to each co-ordinate point (i,j,k) in D. This list is of the form $\{h_1,...,h_p\}$ where h_q (q = 1..p) is the function associated to the q-th data sequence of the problem which defines the element index used at the point (i,j,k) in D.

The h_q function is of the form $Z^n \rightarrow Z$ for a simple sequence $(x_i)_{i \in I}$, while it is of the form $Z^n \rightarrow Z^2$ for a double sequence $(x_{ij})_{i \in I, j \in J}$. To warrant a simple and correct propagation of data items along flows in the systolic array, we limit ourselves to problems where h_q functions define lines on D (every point of such a line uses the same data item).

For inductive problem, we have to associate a funtion h_q to the result sequence since its items are used as data.

Example : The systolic specification of the inductive problem defined by (2) is :
- the domain $D = \{ (i,k) \in Z^2 \mid m \leq i \leq n, 0 \leq k \leq m-1 \}$
- the recurrence function

$$\begin{aligned} f : \quad & R^3 & \rightarrow & \quad R \\ & (x^{k-1},a,x) & \rightarrow & \quad x^{k-1} + a * x \end{aligned}$$

where **x** is an item of the sequence $(x_i)_{i=0...n}$ used as data and **a** is an item of the factor sequence.
- the list of items used at a calculation point (i,k) in D. It consists of the function h_x (i,k) = i+k-m, related to the result sequence used as data and the function h_a (i,k) = k related to the factor sequence.

This specification is represented in the canonical basis of Z^2, noted (C.B.), in figure 1. The set of all points (i,k) in D, i constant, correspond to the recurrent calculation of one x_i. For i = 4, we have $x_4 = a_0x_0+a_1x_1+a_2x_2+a_3x_3$. The point (4,0) defines the first recurrence step : $x_4^0 = a_0x_0$, while the point (4,1) defines the second step : $x_4^1 = x_4^0 + a_1 x_1$. At the point $(4,3)$, the element x_4 is entirely calculated. For legibility, the recurrence function f is omitted in figure 1. To each point (i,k) in D, is associated the quantity $(a_k, x_{1+k-m}^{m-1}, x_1^{k-1}, x_1^k)$. This means that the point (i,k) in D defines the calculation x_1^k of the k-th recurrence step of x_1, using the result of the (k-1)-th step x_1^{k-1}, the entirely computed result x_{1+k-m}^{m-1} and the factor a_k.

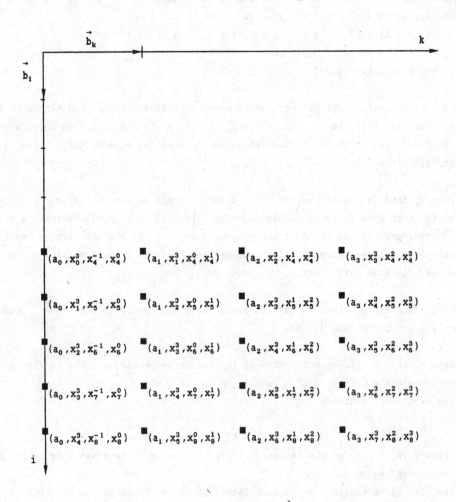

Figure 1. Representation of the problem (2) in the canonical basis

1.2. Determination of time orderings

The first objective of the method is to place points corresponding to elementary calculations in a space where one of the axes represents time. After that, it will be possible to determine systolic arrays by allocating elementary calculations to cells.

Analysing the way systolic arrays are working, we deduce an order relation between elementary calculation times.

This order relation is a *total* order on elementary calculations times associated to any given element x_{ij} of the result sequence : at a given time, at most one recurrence step x_{ij}^k can be computed for some i and j. This therefore conducts to choose the axis corresponding to the recurrence index k as **time axis**. We call **time-space (T.S.)** the space defined from the canonical basis of Z^n with this time axis. The elementary calculations considered in this time-space define the first time ordering.

Moreover, this order relation is a *partial* one on elementary calculation times associated to two different elements $x_{i1,j1}$ and $x_{i2,j2}$: at the same time, a recurrence step of each element, $x_{i1,j1}^{k1}$ and $x_{i2,j2}^{k2}$, can be simultaneously computed. We therefore deduce that it is possible to apply time-axis parallel **transformations**, so that we may obtain new time orderings. These transformations are affine to warrant the data regular organization in the deduced systolic arrays. They moreover minimize the displacement of the points of D along time axis to maintain an efficient parallel execution.

Notice that a time ordering may be not valid. We say that a time ordering is **valid if** :

- **(C1)** a data can not be used simultaneously by different elementary calculations.

- **(C2)** a result can not be used as data before the end of its calculation.

The first condition **(C1)** is justified by the following. If for some time ordering R, a simultaneous use of some data is made, then the corresponding arrays are semi-systolic with broadcasting (cf [KUN 82]). Such arrays are not easily expandable. So that the most interesting arrays are the pure systolic ones. This condition is defined by using the notion of **generating vectors**.

Definition 1 :

Let us consider a problem defined from p data sequences. Let h_q be the function related to the data sequence d_q (q = 1... p).

A generating vector related to the sequence d_q, denoted $\Phi_{dq} = (\varphi_i, \varphi_j, \varphi_k)_{c.B.}$, is a director vector of the line defined by the function h_q, such that GCD $(\varphi_i, \varphi_j, \varphi_k) = \pm 1$.

For inductive problem, an other generating vector is associated to the result sequence (x_{ij}). It is defined by using the function h_x related to (x_{ij}) then considered as a data sequence.

Remark : Each element x_{ij} of the result sequence is calculated by recurrence on any elementary calculation point (i,j,k) in D, where i and j are constant and k is variable. Therefore it is calculated on a line parallel to the recurrence axis (O b_k) in the canonical basis noted (b_i, b_j, b_k). This dependency is expressed by a trivial generating vector, related to the sequence (x_{ij}) considered as the result to be calculated. It is denoted Φ_0 with $\Phi_0 = (0,0,1)_{c.B.}$ for a double result sequence and $\Phi_0 = (0,1)_{c.B.}$ for a simple result sequence.

The second condition **(C2)** is defined by using **dependency vectors**. These vectors link the point corresponding to the last recurrence step of an item with the points using this item for their elementary calculations. All these vectors have the same origin and their extremity are aligned on a line defined by the function h_x related to the result sequence. Therefore they define an angular sector which is delimited by two vectors, called extreme vectors and noted Ψ_1 and Ψ_2. These two vectors are sufficient for the angular sector characterization.

Definition 2 :

Let us consider an inductive problem whose result sequence is (x_{ij}). Let h_x be the function related to the result sequence used as a data.

Let x_{i_0,j_0} be some result item. Its last recurrence step is computed at the point (i_0, j_0, k_0) in D where $k_0 = ubk (i_0, j_0)$. This item is used by all points of the line (L) defined by $h_x(i,j,k) = (i_0, j_0)$.

The **dependency vectors** are characterized by the two extreme vectors Ψ_1 and Ψ_2 of the form $(i-i_0, j-j_0, k-k_0)$ where (i,j,k) are the two intersection points of the line (L) and the domain edges.

For finding systolic arrays solutions, it is necessary to have conditions on dependency vectors. They must be identical for all items of a simple result sequence. They must define a finite set for a double result sequence. This places some restrictions on the problem equations (1), particulary on the bounds of the intervals I and J. These restrictions are detailed in [MON 86].

By applying transformations, SYSTOL can determine valid time orderings from the initial one. A transformation is applied to a time ordering if this ordering is not valid.

We therefore have the following formal definitions.

Definition 3 :

A time ordering in the time-space is given by

- the transition matrix P from the canonical basis (C.B.) of Z^n to the basis of the time-space (T.S.).
- the translation vector $V = \overrightarrow{O'O_{T.S.}}$ where O is the origin of the co-ordinate system related to the canonical basis and O' the origin of the time-space co-ordinate system.

Definition 4 :

Let R be a time ordering defined by P and V in the time-space. A **transformation** applied to the time ordering R, denoted T_R, is an affine application defined by :

$$T_R : \qquad R^3 \qquad \rightarrow \qquad R^3$$
$$(i,j,t)_{T.S.} \quad \rightarrow \quad (i,j,\alpha i + \beta j + \gamma t + \delta)_{T.S.}$$

where $\alpha, \beta, \gamma, \delta$ are integer constants depending on R, that is to say on the components of P and V.

The effective transformations applied in this method are described in detail in [MON 85]. We prove in [MON 85] the following theorem.

Theorem 1 :

Any time ordering R is defined in the time-space by

- a transition matrix P from the canonical basis to the time-space basis of the form :

$$P = \begin{pmatrix} 1 & 0 & 0 \\ 0 & 1 & 0 \\ b_1 & b_2 & b_3 \end{pmatrix}$$

with $b_3 \neq 0$

- a transition vector $V = (0,0,v)^t$

Its image by transformation T_R described in definition 4 is the time ordering defined by :

- the transition matrix

$$P' = \begin{pmatrix} 1 & 0 & 0 \\ 0 & 1 & 0 \\ \alpha+\gamma b_1 & \beta+\gamma b_2 & \gamma b_3 \end{pmatrix}$$

- the translation vector $V' = (0,0,\gamma v+\delta)^t$

SYSTOL uses this theorem to compute time orderings. Moreover the following definition allows to characterize the valid orderings.

Definition 5 :
  A time ordering is **valid** if :
  - any $\Phi_q = (\varphi_i, \varphi_j, \varphi_t)_{T.S.}$ (q = 1...p) is such that $\varphi_t \neq 0$
  - Ψ_1 and Ψ_2 of the form $(\psi_i, \psi_j, \psi_t)_{T.S.}$ are such that $\psi_t > 0$

Remark : in the particular case of a non-inductive problem, the second part of the validity condition is irrelevant.

  Lastly, we demonstrate in [MON 86] the following result.

Theorem 2 :
  Under the hypothesis that a transformation is applied on a time ordering only if this ordering is not valid, from a systolic specification, any sequence of applicable transformations is finite and the set of such sequences is finite.

  This theorem proves that the SYSTOL process which computes the valid time orderings is finite.

Example :
  From the systolic specification of the problem (2), SYSTOL computes the following results :
  - the generating vectors are $\Phi_o = (0,1)_{C.B.}$, $\Phi_x = (1,-1)_{C.B.}$ and $\Phi_a = (1,0)_{C.B.}$
  - the dependency vectors are characterized by $\Psi_1 = (4,-3)_{C.B.}$ and $\Psi_2 = (1,0)_{C.B.}$

  The initial time ordering is visualized in figure 2. For simplicity, only data are indicated. This ordering is not valid because $\Phi_a = (1,0)_{T.S.}$ (each item of the sequence (a_k) is broadcast) and $\Psi_1 = (4,-3)_{T.S.}$ and $\Psi_2 = (1,0)_{T.S.}$ are such that $\psi_t \leq 0$ (items of the result sequence are used before their calculation ends).

  By applying transformations, SYSTOL obtains a valid time ordering visualized in figure 3. SYSTOL does not search for other time orderings because they would not be efficient.

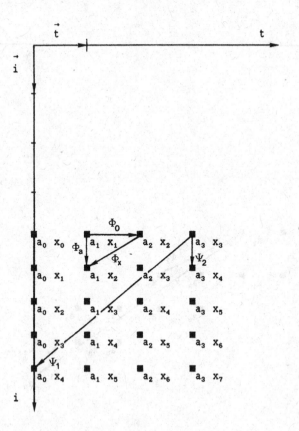

Figure 2. Initial time ordering

1.3. Computation of systolic arrays

After the determination of time orderings, the second step of SYSTOL is to compute systolic arrays associated to each valid time ordering.

This is realized, in the time-space, by projecting points associated to elementary calculations, relatively to a direction, called **allocation direction** and denoted ξ. This direction is an unimodular vector of integer co-ordinates (coordinates mutually prime) of Z^n, defined in the canonical basis. All the points of D belonging to the same line parallel to ξ, represent the calculations made on the same cell.

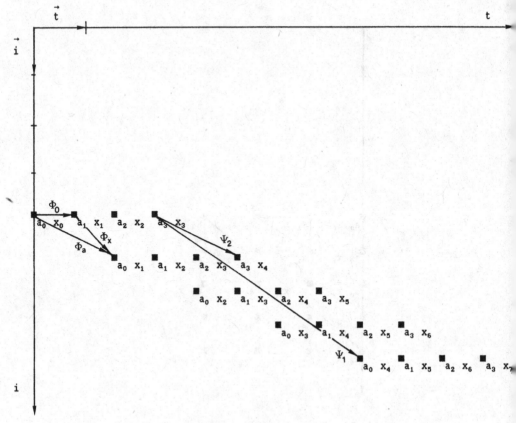

Figure 3. Valid time

For inductive problems, the only possible allocation directions must belong to the domain edges defined by ubk(i,j). This edge is a line in Z^2, a plane or two intersecting planes in Z^3. An other choice for ξ would not allow to find systolic arrays solutions (cf [MON 86]).

From this direction, SYSTOL determines the **allocation function** a of $D \subset Z^n$ in Z^{n-1} (with n = 2 or 3). This function indicates, for any point P of D, on which cell (referenced by $a(P)$) the calculation related to P is made. It is defined using mathematical results presented in [MON 85].

By applying the allocation function to the systolic specification to the generating vectors and to the dependency vectors, SYSTOL automatically computes the systolic arrays, i.e. the cells organization, the communication paths and the data organization on the paths. This process is detailed in [MON 85]. Its principal mechanisms are presented in the example mentionned below.

Example :

For the linear problem (2), the only possible allocation direction   choice is $\xi = (1, 0)_{C.B.}$. The allocation function is a $(i,k) = k$.

By considering the valid time ordering of figure 3, SYSTOL computes the systolic array visualized in figure 4. This array has 4 cells because a $(i,k) = k$ with $0 \leqslant k \leqslant 3$. The items of the sequence (a_k) stay in the cells because a $(\Phi_a) =$ a $(1,0)_{C.B.} = 0$.

The result sequence (x_i),
- first considered as the sequence to be calculated, moves from cell C to cell C + 1 because a $(\Phi_0) =$ a $(0,1)_{C.B.} = 1$.
- then is reinjected, at the end of the stream, on the same cell because a (Ψ_{min}) = a $(\Psi_2) =$ a $(1,0)_{C.B.} = 0$, where $\Psi_{min} = \Psi_i$ $(i = 1..2)$ such that ψ_t is minimal, $\Psi_1 = (4,5)_{T.S.}$ and $\Psi_2 = (1,2)_{T.S.}$. There is one "late cell" on this part of the stream because $\psi_t = 2$.
- finally considered as data sequence, moves from cell C to cell C - 1 because a $(\Phi_x) =$ a $(1,-1)_{C.B.} = -1$.
Because $\xi_t = 2$ $(\xi = (1, 2)_{T.S.})$, there is one space between data on the streams.

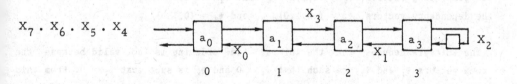

Figure 4. Systolic array solution of problems (2)

2. Example of a two-dimensional inductive problem

Consider the following problem. We want to compute a matrix X, for which each column (j) depends on the previous one (j-1), defined by :

$$(3) \quad x_{ij} = \sum_{k=0}^{n-i} x_{n-k, j-1} \quad 0 \leqslant i \leqslant n, \ 0 \leqslant j \leqslant n$$

where a column of index (-1) is a given data. Each element x_{ij} of column (j) is calculated by :

$$
\begin{cases}
x_{0,j} = x_{n,j-1} + x_{n-1,j-1} + \cdots + x_{2,j-1} + x_{1,j-1} + x_{0,j-1} \\
x_{1,j} = x_{n,j-1} + x_{n-1,j-1} + \cdots + x_{2,j-1} + x_{1,j-1} \\
x_{2,j} = x_{n,j-1} + x_{n-1,j-1} + \cdots + x_{2,j-1} \\
\\
\\
x_{n-1,j} = x_{n,j-1} + x_{n-1,j-1} \\
x_{n,j} = x_{n,j-1}
\end{cases}
$$

The recurrence definition of this problem is :

$$
(3') \quad
\begin{cases}
x_{ij}^{k} = x_{ij}^{k-1} + x_{n-k,\,j-1} \quad 0 \leq i \leq n,\ 0 \leq j \leq n,\ 0 \leq k \leq n-i \\
\\
x_{ij}^{-1} = 0
\end{cases}
$$

The systolic specification is defined by :
- the domain $D = \{\ (i,j,k) \in Z^3 \mid 0 \leq i \leq n,\ 0 \leq j \leq n,\ 0 \leq k \leq n-i\ \}$
- the recurrence function $f\ (x^{k-1}, x) = x^{k-1} + x$.
- the list of data used by any point of D. It is reduced to $h_x\ (i,j,k) = (n-k, j-1)$.

From this specification, SYSTOL computes :
- the generating vectors, $\Phi_0 = (0,0,1)_{c.B.}$ and $\Phi_x = (-1,0,0)_{c.B.}$
- the dependency vectors, $\Psi_1 = (-2,1,0)_{c.B.}$ and $\Psi_2 = (0,1,0)_{c.B.}$

The software deduces that the initial time ordering is not valid because the extreme vectors Ψ_1 and Ψ_2 are such that $\psi_t = 0$ and Φ_x is such that $\varphi_t = 0$. From this initial time ordering, SYSTOL determines the most efficient valid time ordering.

Since the angular sector of dependency vectors is the same for all the points in D, all vectors in the plane defined by ubk $(i,j) = k$, i.e. $i+k-n = 0$, are possible allocation directions.

By choosing $\xi = (0,1,0)_{c.B.}$, $\xi = (-1,0,1)_{c.B.}$ and $\xi = (-1,1,1)_{c.B.}$, SYSTOL successively computes the systolic arrays of figures 5, 6 and 7 respectively, with $n = 2$ for visualization reasons.

Notice that this problem could be defined by another equation :

$$
(4) \quad x_{ij} = \sum_{k=0}^{n-i} x_{i+k,j-1}
$$

273

This equation corresponds to the execution of calculations in the reverse order :

$$x_{ij} = x_{i,j-1} + x_{i+1,j-1} + \cdots + x_{n,j-1}$$

instead of

$$x_{ij} = x_{n,j-1} + x_{n-1,j-1} + \cdots + x_{1,j-1}$$

In this case, each dependency vector is of the form $(-k,1,i+2k-2)_{c.B.}$. They depend on index i, so that there is a set of angular sectors, one for each line (X_i). In any systolic array solution, every item of each line (X_i) has to be associated to the same stream, to warrant a static definition of the cell net. Therefore the only possible allocation direction is $\xi = (0,1,0)_{c.B.}$. By applying it on the most efficient valid time ordering, SYSTOL determines the systolic array presented figure 8.

3. Conclusion

The method presented here is a constructive one. Therefore it is possible to realize a software, called SYSTOL, which implements the method. There exist two other softwares for the design of systolic arrays : DIASTOL [QUG 84] which implements the method presented by P. Quinton [QUI 83] and ADVIS [MOL 84] realized by D. Moldovan.

The main difference between these two softwares and ours are the following. In the methods they implements, the description of the problem must define data dependencies. Therefore all systolic arrays computed by them belong to the same family, i.e. are characterized by the same orderings between dependent calculations. To obtain new systolic arrays, it is necessary to determine an other definition of the problem. It's a difficult task for the user, because it is not automated. In our method, the affine transformations applied to time orderings allow to determine systolic arrays belonging to different families.

Moreover our method allows to solve inductive problems, which are not treated in other methods. A new extension is studied ([MON 86]). By applying it, it will be possible to automatically determine heterogeneous systolic arrays, i.e. arrays which contain more then one type of cells. This extension will solve problems such as triangular system resolution, LU matrix decomposition, etc.

Finally, notice that SYSTOL automatically computes a set of systolic arrays solution of a given problem. The user can then choose the "best" one with respect to his application constraints : minimize execution time, minimize cells number, optimize parallelism rate, etc.

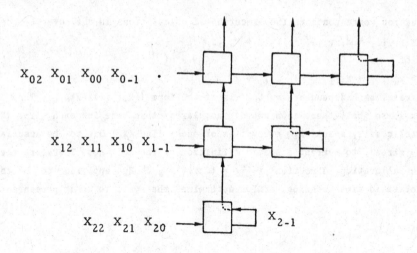

X_{02} X_{01} X_{00} X_{0-1} .

X_{12} X_{11} X_{10} X_{1-1}

X_{22} X_{21} X_{20} X_{2-1}

Figure 5

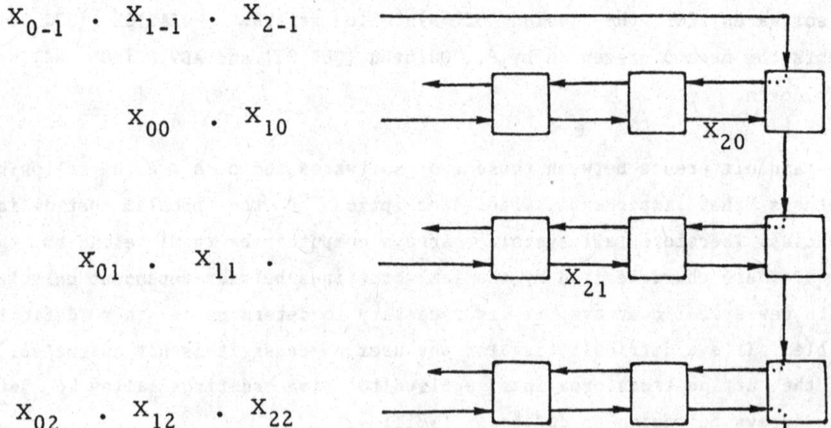

X_{0-1} . X_{1-1} . X_{2-1}

X_{00} . X_{10}
X_{20}

X_{01} . X_{11} .
X_{21}

X_{02} . X_{12} . X_{22}

Figure 6

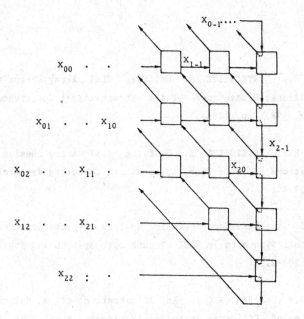

Figure 7

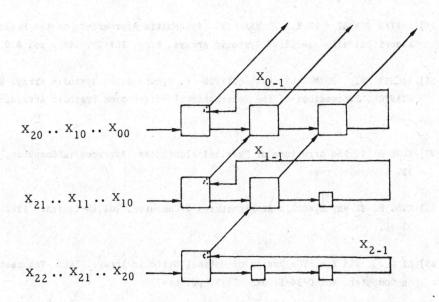

Figure 8

BIBLIOGRAPHY

[CAS 83] CAPPELLO P.R., STEIGLITZ K. Unifying VLSI Array Design with Geometric Transformations. Proceedings of the International Conference on Parallel Processing. 1983. pp. 448-457.

[CAS 84] CAPPELLO P.R., STEIGLITZ K. Unifying VLSI Array Design with Linear Transformations of Space-Time. Advances in Computing Research. JAI Press. 1984. pp 23-45.

[CHE 85] CHEN M.C. Synthesizing Systolic Designs. Proceedings of the Second International Symposium on VLSI Technology, Systems and Applications. May 1985. pp. 209-215.

[DEI 85] DELOSME J.M., IPSEN I.C.F. An Illustration of a Methodology for the Construction of Efficient Systolic Architectures in VLSI. Proceedings of the Second International symposium on VLSI technology, systems and applications. May 1985. pp. 268-273.

[FFW 85] FORTES J.A.B., FU K.S., WAH B.W. Systematic Approaches to the Design of Algorithmically Specified Systolic Arrays. Proc. ICASSP. 1985. pp. 8.9.1-4.

[GJQ 86] GACHET P., JOINNAULT B., QUINTON P. Synthesizing Systolic Arrays Using DIASTOL. Proceedings of the International Workshop on Systolic Arrays. July 1986.

[KUN 79] KUNG H. T. The Structure of Parallel Algorithms. Advances in Computer. Vol 19. Academic Press.

[KUN 82] KUNG H. T. Why Systolic Architectures ? Computer. Vol 15-1. jan. 1982. pp. 37-46.

[LIW 85] LI G.J., WAH B.W. The Design of Optimal Systolic Arrays. IEEE Transactions on Computer. Vol C-34-1. Jan. 1985. pp. 66-77.

[MEC 80] MEAD C., CONWAY L. Introduction to VLSI systems. Addison Wesley. 1980.

[MMU 87] MOORE W., McCABE A., URQUHART R. Systolic Arrays. Proceedings of the First International Workshop on Systolic Arrays. July 1986. Adam Hilger 1987.

[MOL 83] MOLDOVAN D.I. On the Design of Algorithms for VLSI Systolic Arrays. Proceedings of the IEEE. Vol 71-1. Jan. 1983. pp. 113-120.

[MOL 84] MOLDOVAN D.I. ADVIS : A Software Package for the Design of Systolic Arrays. Proceedings 1984 IEE ICCD : Vlsi in Computers. 1984. pp. 158-164.

[MON 85] MONGENET C. Une Méthode de Conception d'Algorithmes Systoliques, Résultats Théoriques et Réalisation. Thesis. Nancy. May 1985.

[MON 86] MONGENET C. Les Extensions du Système SYSTOL. CRIN Report. Nancy. Nov. 1986.

[MOP 85] MONGENET C., PERRIN G.R. Une Méthode de Conception Automatique de Réseaux Systoliques. Proceedings of the International Conference Future Trends in Computing, in Computer and Computing. Masson and Wiley. 1985. pp. 316-321.

[QUG 84] QUINTON P., GACHET P. Manuel d'utilisation de DIASTOL, version préliminaire. IRISA Report 233. Aug 1984.

[QUI 83] QUINTON P. The Systematic Design of Systolic Arrays. IRISA Research report 193. Apr. 1983.

[QUI 84] QUINTON P. Automatic Synthesis of Systolic Arrays from Uniform Recurrent Equations. Proceedings 11th Annual International Symposium on Computer Architecture. June 1984. pp. 208-214.

PRACTICAL PARALLELISM USING TRANSPUTER ARRAYS

D.J. Pritchard, C.R. Askew, D.B. Carpenter, I. Glendinning,
A.J.G. Hey, D.A. Nicole

Department of Physics, University of Southampton,
Southampton, United Kingdom SO9 5NH

ABSTRACT

This paper explores methods for extracting parallelism from
a wide variety of numerical applications. We
investigate communications overheads and load-balancing for
networks of transputers. After a discussion of some
practical strategies for constructing occam programs, two
case studies are analysed in detail.

1 Introduction

As part of ESPRIT project P1085 we are investigating a wide range
of computationally intensive applications in the physical and
engineering sciences, and developing techniques for efficient
implementation of such problems on large arrays of transputers. These
applications will be ultimately be coded for execution on one or more
of the supernode machines at present being built by the
collaboration. However, in this paper we report on our experience
gained using prototype components of the P1085 machine and other
multi-transputer machines, principally a Meiko Computing Surface.

The P1085 machines are clusters of "supernodes", each of which
consists of some 20 transputers linked by a switching network. The
supernodes are themselves connected by a large outer level switch to
produce a machine of initially some 300 transputers which can be
connected in any configuration. The supernode and outer layer
switches may be set so as to render the supernode structure invisible
to an application program. In many cases it will also be possible to

rearrange link configuration in part of the array without disturbing traffic on the rest of the network.

Depending on user requirements the transputers in the system may be equipped with 256k, 4M or 16M bytes of memory, in essentially any mix. Link-independent control and data transfers will be provided by an additional bus within each supernode, and utilisation of links and transputers may be monitored in real time. Distributed or concentrated disk storage can be supported on the network. The P1085 hardware will thus effectively support (*inter alia*) all algorithms described in this paper.

The problem of writing reliable and efficient software to exploit the concurrent operation of multi-processor arrays is greatly simplified when transputers are used, because their architecture directly implements the occam programming model. Occam achieves a natural synchronisation between a pair of concurrent processes communicating via a *channel*, each waiting for the other if necessary. INMOS serial links transparently implement channels between processes executing concurrently on different transputers, while channels between processes on the same transputer are implemented in local memory. Transputer compilers also exist for FORTRAN and C but, for the above reasons, most of our applications have been written in occam.

2 Methodologies for Practical Parallel Programming

In order to utilise efficiently the computational potential of a large number of processors, it is essential to identify the important parallel features of the application at the program design stage. These will have implications for the architecture of the target machine on which the application is to be run. In the case of the transputer supernode machine they will dictate the configuration and connectivity of the worker transputers.

We have found that the most commonly occurring types of parallelism in scientific and engineering applications fall into the following three broad classes:

- <u>Processor Farms</u>: Many scientific problems require repeated execution of the same program with different initial data (random number seeds, for example). Subsequent runs of the program do not require any knowledge of previous runs, so many runs could, in principle, be executed simultaneously. On most computers this option is not available, resulting, typically, in the submission of many different jobs consisting of the same program accessing different data, or running with different parameters. By contrast, this type of application can be run very efficiently on a multi-processor machine such as an array of transputers. Little or no communication is required between processors, except that after execution the results from each of the processors need to be collated and, perhaps, some sort of statistical analysis performed.

  The typical architecture for this type of application is a "farm" of processors receiving instructions from, and reporting back to, a controller. Each processor runs the same program (with data dependent branches) and has a complete, but different, set of data. Large amounts of storage are therefore required on each element. Because of the very limited communication requirements this method will be very efficient, but the memory costs may be significant.

- <u>Geometric Parallelism</u>: Many "physical" problems have an underlying regular geometrical structure, with spatially limited interactions (e.g. problems in field theory or hydrodynamics). This homogeneity allows the data to be distributed uniformly across the processor array, with each processor being responsible for a defined spatial area or volume. Neighbouring processors will have to exchange data at intervals, so that each has an accurate copy of not only the region for which it is responsible, but also the surrounding region within the range of possible interactions. The communication load will be proportional to the size of the boundary of the element, while the calculational load will be proportional to the volume of the element. This has already been shown to be an effective strategy for a wide range of problems on a conventional processor array [1].

  In contrast to the case of a Processor Farm, this type of "Geometric" Parallelism requires only a fraction of the total data on each processor. Each processor still has, however, an essentially complete copy of the whole program.

- Algorithmic Parallelism: The third most easily exploited type of parallelism is more fine-grained. Specific features of a problem that are capable of concurrent operation are identified and each processor implements a small part of the total algorithm. Clearly, the resulting structure will depend very much on the particular algorithm used in the application. A common feature of this approach is the construction of a number of "pipes" of processors, similar to those found in pipelined vector supercomputers such as the Cyber and Cray machines. Here, however, the pipes may be more general and capable of splitting and converging in a much more flexible way.

    In such a decomposition of the problem, the data now flows between the processing elements, severely increasing the communication load on each element, Indeed, without care, communication bandwidth overheads can become dominant and severely degrade the performance. An advantage of this type of decomposition, however, is that very little data space is required per processor, and in many of the problems that we have investigated all, or almost all, of the elements of the network need no memory other than the internal memory of each transputer (2K at present, but the new T8 transputers will have 4K).

- Hybrid Methods: The two distribution techniques described above distribute either the data or the code but not both. In the former case the communication overheads grow as the individual data areas shrink, eventually becoming dominant. In the latter case the communication load remains fixed as the code is further subdivided, but the computational work supported by that communication is reduced and again communication will eventually dominate. In both cases there is a limit to the number of processors that can be utilised efficiently.

    The solution to this dilemma is to incorporate both features into the distribution scheme. This will allow many more processors to be used before the communications limit is reached. This allows us to model a proposed multi-supernode machine in which individual supernodes can be programmed "algorithmically" in a manner suited to the individual application, but the inter-supernode connections will be of a more universal "geometric" nature.

The three main types of extractable parallelism discussed above should not be thought of as exclusive or exhaustive. Many applications will probably combine all three features, and there are probably other distributable features in particular cases.

3 Communications Overheads and Efficiency

The efficiency of an implementation of an algorithm on a multiprocessor machine has been defined by Fox in the following way [1]:

$$E = \frac{(\text{time on 1 processor})}{N \times (\text{time on N processors})}$$

To obtain a meaningful measure of efficiency of the distributed program, a processor merely performing host functions, such as maintaining a filestore, must be omitted from this counting. Thus, we must compare the performance of (control+1 worker) to that of (control+N workers).

The above expression implicitly assumes that the critical resources are the processors themselves. When, in the not too distant future, the cost of transputers is not significantly more than any other component, this formula may be less relevant. High efficiency of processor utilisation will not necessarily be the most cost-effective solution.

For a conventional multiprocessor array the timings can be split into two pieces: t_{calc} associated with the useful work to be done, and t_{comm} associated with the unproductive communications overhead. For a distributed program using either Farm or Geometric decompositions, if T_{calc} is the total work to be done, then the distributed $t_{calc} = T_{calc}/N$, so the efficiency becomes:

$$\frac{T_{calc}}{T_{calc} + T_{comm}}$$

where T_{comm} is the total communication in the array. Both of these quantities are easily estimated, but care must be taken to synchronise both ends of the communication channel, or to buffer the communication sufficiently to avoid dead time when the processor is neither calculating nor communicating.

For algorithmic decompositions the above is still true if the loads of each element are evenly balanced. In practice, this is difficult to achieve for realistic problems. These unbalanced loads are one of the main reasons for the relatively low efficiencies achieved with these decompositions.

For transputer arrays the analysis is more complicated. Each element of the array can <u>concurrently</u> perform calculation and up to 8 communications (2 in each direction). Communications are not completely free, however, since each communication channel has to be set up by the processor. We must therefore subdivide the communication time into two pieces

$$T_{comm} = T_{setup} + T_{overlap}$$

and the efficiency becomes

$$\frac{T_{calc}}{T_{setup} + MAX(T_{overlap}, T_{calc})}$$

We have measured the basic parameters from which T_{setup}, $T_{overlap}$ and T_{calc} can be calculated in any particular case.

T_{setup} ~ 2.6 microsecs per communication

$T_{overlap}$ ~ 1.95 microsecs per byte (T4 with 10 MHz link)
      1.18   (20 MHz)
      1.13   (T8 with 10 MHz link)
      0.57   (20 MHZ)

T_{calc} ~10-20 microsecs per flop (T4-20, internal RAM)
      0.66   (T8-20)

For both types of array, the ratio of basic floating-point performance to communication speed is crucial. In early versions of the Intel hypercube machine, the iPSC, the operating system overheads degraded the intrinsic communication bandwidth by more than a factor of 100, leading to much lower efficiencies for applications [2]. Even with the modified efficiency analysis for transputer arrays, it is still essential to ensure that there will be adequate bandwidth between processing nodes. For this reason we are investigating a variety of problems with very different communication requirements.

4 Practical Strategies for constructing occam programs

4.1 Multiplexers and Routing

A transputer has a limited number of links via which it can communicate with other transputers. Normally each link carries only two occam channels, one in each direction. Occam itself puts no restriction on how many channels can be connected to a given process, but a process with more than four input or output channels cannot be *PLACEd* directly on a single transputer. This limitation can be circumvented by multiplexing links, effectively putting more than one communication channel on some or all of the links. The "user process" on the transputer can then be written as if the number of tranputer links was unlimited, but its input and output channels are fed to a multiplexing process running concurrently on the same transputer, rather than being directly placed on links.

The implementation of multiplexers and demultiplexers in occam is straightforward: a multiplexer involves an ALT construct and a demultiplexer involves an IF or CASE statement on the packet tags. The choice of packet protocol is somewhat arbitrary, and depends on the required flexibility of the routing network.

Consider the following general problem. A common approach to distributing a program over a transputer array involves a number of similar "worker" processes connected in a regular network. The majority of communications involved in the computation will be relatively local - for example, there may only be nearest neighbour communications. However there will invariably be other, less frequent, communications needed to some central "host" or "controller" transputer. This extra processor has to be inserted physically somewhere into the basic regular array. An attractive scheme for communication between host and workers is to introduce a channel multiplexing scheme so that the logical network seems like a regular network of workers alone, each having an extra pair of occam channels connecting it directly to the host processor.

As a specific example, consider the case where the basic network is a two-dimensional lattice with periodic boundary conditions. One of the links of this lattice may be "cut", and the host processor inserted into this link (see figure 4.1).

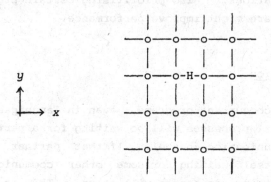

Figure 4.1 Insertion of Host into array

We have implemented a multiplexing system to achieve the desired effect for this case. The main criterion for the usefulness of this system is the speed of the frequent local (nearest neighbour) communications which must now occur via the multiplexing protocol. The test we used was a loop transferring data in the y-direction around the network. The timings for this loop on various packet sizes (in bytes) were

size	time/pkt	time/byte
1	0.26ms	260us
4	0.27ms	67us
64	0.41ms	6us
512	1.56ms	3us

Table 4.1 Routing Timings

The overhead for sending a packet, even to the nearest neighbour is around 0.25 milliseconds, rather than the microseconds one is accustomed to without the multiplexing protocol. Communications in the *x*-direction which actually have to be passed on across the host processor are slowed down by a further factor of 2.

There are various ways these timings could be improved. A large part of the overhead comes from having to wait for acknowledges, a problem which could be alleviated somewhat by introducing more buffering on the communications. Also prioritising certain processes in the multiplexing software might improve performance.

4.2 Deadlock and Termination

A common fault with concurrent programs, even in languages other than occam, is that several processes will be waiting for a partner at the other end of a communication channel. If that partner cannot proceed because it is itself waiting for some other communication, then a situation where nothing can happen will occur. This is called "deadlock". Sophisticated formal techniques exist for proving the absence of deadlock in occam programs, but have not yet reached the stage where these can be automated. Until that time we must rely on general rules and priciples derived, in the first instance, from experience as to what sort of structures work and which do not.

A related problem is the need for each process to terminate correctly - the absence of "livelock". Only in such a case is it possible for any overlying system control software to make reliable assumptions about the state of the user program. This will be especially important in situations where processes are being created and moved about dynamically.

The technique used to resolve these problems in the example of section 5.1 was to include a BOOLean value within each data packet, set to TRUE if the source intends sending more data (which it promises to do) and FALSE if there will definitely be no more data. The reader processes MUST continue to read until a FALSE is seen, and thereafter ignore that channel. Any process is free to initiate global termination by inserting a FALSE into its next packet, which will quickly spread throughout the network. Under these conditions the network will be deadlock-free, and can be terminated on demand by a variety of conditions.

4.3 Communication Overlapping

In order to exploit fully the novel features of the transputer it is necessary to arrange matters so that the maximum overlap between the calculational and communication parts of the program. This can be arranged by initiating input transfers as far in advance as possible, and making outputs as soon as possible. A typical structure might be:

```
PAR
    ...  input data for next time
    ...  do this cycle of calculation
    ...  output results from last time
```

4.4 Debugging

Traditional errors, such as divide-by-zero or array-bound-violation, can be dealt with in traditional ways. The development tools supplied by INMOS can be used to locate the exact source line on which the error occured, and traditional remedies applied. Within the P1085 project more sophisticated symbolic debugging tools are being developed.

Scheduling errors such as deadlock or failure to terminate are much harder to cure, as they usually reflect a fundamental flaw in the global design of the program. Insertion of communication buffers, for example, can have far-reaching implications for the synchronisation of the program and seriously affect the global behaviour. Often these effects are advantageous, but care must be taken nevertheless.

5. Examples

In this section we describe, in some detail, two examples of the application of the ideas described above to typical numerical problems The first, Laplace's equation in two dimensions, is not particularly complicated and serves to illustrate the basic concepts. The second, a Monte Carlo simulation of a lattice spin system, is somewhat more computationally intensive and more typical of real problems of interest to scientists.

5.1 Laplace's Equation

The problem to be studied (Laplace's equation in two dimensions) is a well studied problem from the point of view of the numerical analyst, but here we shall concentrate on the distribution techniques for an elementary algorithm, rather than the choice of the optimum algorithm. Mathematically, the problem is to solve the second order partial differential equation

$$[(d/dx)^2 +(d/dy)^2]f(x,y)=0$$

inside some given region, with f fixed on the boundary of that region.

We take the region to be a unit square, and approximate these equations with a set of finite-difference equations (whose merits are subject to the caveat described above).

$$f_{n,m} = (f_{n+1,m}+f_{n-1,m}+f_{n,m+1}+f_{n,m-1})/4$$

To solve these equation we can simply iterate them in the obvious way (Gauss-Jacobi relaxation, described in any standard text on numerical analysis). Each value on the grid is simultaneously replaced by the average of its 4 neighbours. The procedure is guaranteed to converge to the exact solution of the finite difference equations.

Four different occam programs were written to execute this simple algorithm. The first was a sequential program, against which the other distributed programs were later compared. The second implementation was a "geometric" program utilising the regularity of the data structure and the locality of the updating algorithm, splitting the 40 by 40 arrays of the sequential program into 4 separate 20 by 20 arrays. Next is an "algorithmic" version in which the same 4 processors were formed into pipelines, distributing the 4 floating-point operations as in figure 5.1. Finally a "hybrid" version containing both of these features was constructed.

We also included in the three distributed versions, parameters whereby the ratio between computation and communication could be varied, by repeated execution of the appropriate pieces of code.

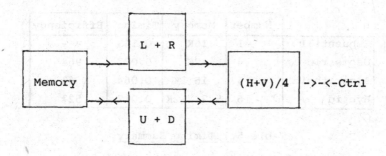

Figure 5.1 Algorithmic Network

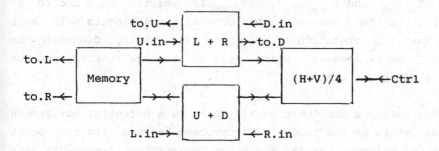

Figure 5.2 Hybrid network

To utilise the overlapped communications facility of the transputer effectively it is necessary to buffer the messages. Our experience suggests that the buffering process should be at high priority, so that a communication happens as soon as possible rather than waiting for its turn on the process queue. In this application the efficiency is reduced by 10% if the buffering process is not at high priority. In a more general case there will be many other processes competing for the processor's attention in addition to the buffers and we expect that the efficiency loss will therefore be increased. The buffers also improve the deadlock characteristics by introducing a higher degree of desynchronisation between processors. Finally, by transmitting only vectors (of length 40 or 20) the setup overheads are reduced.

	Number	Memory	Timing	Efficiency
Sequential	1	15K	0.143	---
Geometric	4	7K	0.037	96%
Algorithmic	4	15,2K	0.064	56%
Hybrid	16	5,2,2,2K	0.017	52%

Table 5.1 Timing Summary

In the purely geometric case we can, by adjusting the built-in work-load and communication-load parameters extract T_{calc} and T_{comm} (but not T_{setup} and $T_{overlap}$). T_{comm} is exactly what would be expected (set up the 4 channels, but overlap the 4 packets with each other). The interpretation of T_{calc} is less clear, depending on details of memory speeds: in this case an average performance of around 1/15 Mflop was achieved.

For the purely algorithmic case, there is a potential bottleneck at the final stage of the pipe. That process has two floating-point operations to perform, whereas the other two arithmetic elements have only one. Artificially doubling the work-load of the two lightly loaded processors, shows very little change in the performance. Thus we conclude that this load imbalance is therefore responsible for the major part of the efficiency loss.

5.2 2D spin systems

The physical problem we discus is a two-dimensional XY model [3]. This is a statistical system of "spins", each of which can be represented by an angle, A, defined at each site of a two-dimensional square lattice. In the simplest model the energy function for a single spin located at x is given by

$$E(x) = - \sum_{y} \{ \cos[A(x)-A(y)] \}$$

where the sum on y is over the four nearest neighbours of the spin under consideration. The Metropolis algorithm [4] uses this

"Hamiltonian" to generate a sequence of configurations with a Boltzman probability distribution. The quantities of interest are correlation functions of the spins sampled over this ensemble of configurations.

The algorithm starts from some arbitrarily chosen configuration of spins and repeatedly sweeps through the lattice, updating spins in turn. The candidate update for a spin takes the form

$$A(x) \rightarrow A(x)+dA(x)$$

where there is some freedom in the choice of $dA(x)$. Typically $dA(x)$ is taken to be a random number uniformly distributed in the range $-max$ to $+max$, with max adjusted to optimise the equilibration process. A given candidate update is then accepted or rejected according to the Metropolis criterion.

In principle the angles $A(x)$ are real numbers, but in practice they can be adequately represented by small integers stored as byte values. Calculation of the Hamiltonian can then be implemented efficiently by table look-up. It is also adequate to handle energy values as scaled integers instead of floating point values. With these economies the numerical work involved in a single update is modest and in fact the low computation/communication ratio makes this problem difficult to parallelise efficiently.

There are various ways to decompose this lattice geometrically onto an array of transputers. Two obvious possibilities are separation into square blocks, or separation into horizontal or vertical strips. We have written geometrically distributed programs exploiting both these decompositions, as well as the more trivial "processor farm" type of parallelism, which proves useful for small lattices which can not be conveniently subdivided. These decompositions tend to lead to very acceptable efficiencies (rarely less than about 70%) and are quite easy to program.

A typical algorithmically decomposed program involves one transputer on which the bulk of the data is stored. This transputer feeds data out to a collection of worker transputers all having only a limited storage capacity. In the program we describe here, none of the transputers in the array beside the store need any memory beyond their 2K internal RAM.

292

The main feature of the network is a short pipeline. This takes as input at one end a particular spin together with its nearest neighbours, and returns an updated spin at the other end. The network also has some provision for geometric replication in a simple chain

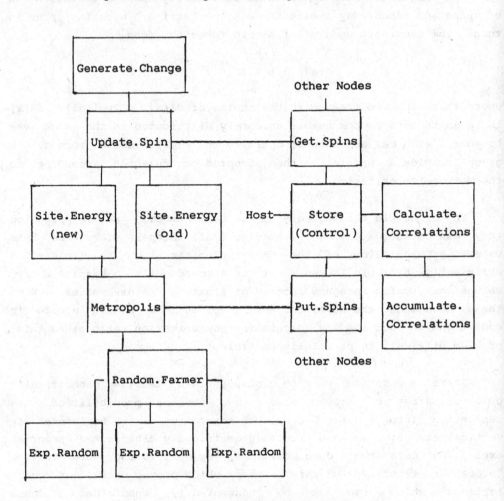

Figure 5.2 Algorithmic XY Network

The transputer network adopted is illustrated in figure 5.2. The boxes represent occam processes sitting on individual transputers, the connecting lines represent occam channels implemented on physical transputer links.

In the Metropolis pipe a substantial part of the total work goes into generating random numbers. These are required in *Generate.change*, and the three *Exponential.random* processes, which are replicated to create a "farm" of random number generators, to provide exponentially distributed random numbers fast enough to keep the rest of the pipeline busy.

In parallel with the updating process, correlation functions are calculated by the two processes *Calculate.correlations* and *Accumulate.correlations*. These are fed by *Store* with spins from a copy of the configuration taken every few complete update sweeps.

For the "geometric" program working on a 64 by 64 lattice, distributed over 16+1 transputers the effective updating rate was observed to be 12 microseconds per Metropolis update per spin (this includes measuring correlation functions every 5 sweeps). With a single worker (+ controller) the timing was 150 microseconds per update. This corresponds to an efficiency of about 75%.

For the "algorithmic" program the time for updating a single spin (in parallel with the computation of correlation functions) was about 36 microseconds. Comparing the algorithmic performance figure with the 1-worker case above yields an efficiency of around 30%. Put another way, the program running on 14 transputer runs just under 4 times as fast as the program running on a single transputer. This is not an enormous speedup factor, and reflects the fairly small amount of arithmetic involved in a single update.

6. Summary and Conclusions

In addition to the two studies described above, we have investigated a number of other applications with a wide variety of different demands on the calculation and communication capacities of processor arrays. Our principal conclusions can be summarised as follows:

- **Processor Farm parallelism:** Efficient and very easy to code. Each processor requires large amounts of memory.

- <u>Geometric parallelism</u>:   Efficient and easy to code. For a fixed data size the efficiency decreases as the number of processors increases.   The fixed number of links (4) makes it difficult to exploit 3D (or higher) geometries directly.

- <u>Algorithmic parallelism</u>:   Efficiency depends very much on balancing the loads of individual workers.   Coding requires more thought and care.

- <u>Hybrid parallelism</u>:   Probably necessary for large numbers of processors, but reasonable efficiencies and small memory sizes are still possible.

- <u>Network Topology</u>:   Whilst it is possible to implement algorithmic distributions of applications on fixed topology networks, the programming effort expended can be considerable, and, moreover, the efficiency obtained is certainly not as good as expected for a customised network.   The supernode switch should assist in designing such networks.

<u>References</u>

[1]   G.C. Fox, invited talk at Knoxville Hypercube Conference (1986)
[2]   A. Kolawa and S. Otto, CalTech Report (1986)
[3]   J. Tobochnik and G.V. Chester, Phys. Rev. <u>B20</u>, 3761 (1975)
[4]   N. Metropolis *et al.*, J. Chem. Phys. <u>21</u>, 1087 (1953)

SYSTOLIC ARRAY SYNTHESIS
by
Static Analysis of Program Dependencies

Sanjay V. Rajopadhye*
Computer and Info. Sci. Dept.
University of Oregon
Eugene, Or 97403

Richard M. Fujimoto[†]
Computer Science Department
University of Utah
Salt Lake City, Ut 84112

Abstract

We present a technique for synthesizing systolic arrays which have non-uniform data flow governed by control signals. The starting point for the synthesis is a *Recurrence Equation with Linear Dependencies* (RELD) which is a generalization of the simple recurrences encountered in mathematics. A large class of programs, including all (single and multiple) nested-loop programs can be described by such recurrences. In this paper we extend some of our earlier work [17] in two principal directions. Firstly, we describe a transformation called *multistage pipelining* and show that it yields recurrences that have *linear* conditional expressions governing the computation. Secondly, we discuss how it is possible to automatically derive control signals that govern the data flow by applying the same pipelining transformations to these *linear conditional expressions*. The approach is illustrated by deriving the Guibas-Kung-Thompson architecture for optimum string parenthesization.

1 Introduction

Systolic arrays are a class of parallel architectures consisting of regular interconnections of a very large number of simple processors, each one operating on a small part of the problem. They are typically designed to be used as back-end, special-purpose devices for computation-intensive processing. A number of such architectures have been proposed for solving problems such as matrix multiplication, L-U decomposition of matrices, solving a set of equations, convolution, dynamic programming, etc. (see [6,7,8] for an extensive bibliography).

Most of the early systolic arrays were designed in an *ad hoc*, case-by-case manner. Recently there has been a great deal of effort on developing unifying theories for automatically synthesizing such arrays [1,2,3,9,10,11,12,13,14,18,19]. The approach is to analyze the program dependency graph and transform it to one that represents a systolic array. The problem of synthesis can thus be viewed as a special case of the *graph-mapping* problem where the objective is to transform a given graph to an equivalent one that satisfies certain constraints. For systolic array synthesis there are two major constraints, namely *nearest-neighbor communication* and *constant-delay interconnections*.

---

*Supported by a University of Utah Graduate Research Fellowship
[†]Supported by an IBM faculty development grant.

The initial specification for the synthesis effort is typically a program consisting of a set of (say n) nested loops. The indices of each of the loops together with the range over which they vary define an n-dimensional domain in Z^n (Z denotes the set of integers). The computation in the loop body is performed at every point p in this domain, and the usage of variables within it defines the dependencies of the point p. For example, if the body contains a statement of the form. $a[i,j,k] := 2 * b[i, j+2, k-1]$ then the point $p = [i,j,k]^T$ depends on $q = [i, j+2, k-1]^T$. In this case, $p - q$ is a *constant* vector independent of p, namely $[0, -2, 1]^T$. Such a nested-loop program is equivalent to a recurrence equation defined on the same domain. In most of the earlier work cited above the underlying assumption is that the dependencies are uniquely characterized by a finite set, W of *constant vectors* in Z^n (as in the example above). The recurrence equations in this case are called Uniform Recurrence Equations (UREs), and the dependency graph can be shown to be a *lattice* in Z^n. Under these restrictions the problem of synthesizing a systolic array can be solved by determining an appropriate *affine* transformation (i.e., one that can be expressed as a translation, rotation and scaling) of the original lattice.

We have elsewhere argued [15,17] that this constraint of uniform dependencies is overly restrictive and a large number of interesting problems cannot be (very cleanly) expressed as UREs. We have proposed a new class where the dependencies of a point p are linear functions of p. Thus, for the simple example above, the body of the loop may contain a statement of the form $a[i,j,k] := 2 * b[i', j', k']$, where each of i', j' and k' are *linear* functions of i, j and k. The recurrence equations characterizing such computations are called Recurrence Equations with Linear Dependencies (RELDs). In an earlier paper [17] we have shown that simple systolic architectures (i.e., those that have uniform data flow) can be synthesized from RELDs by a two-step process consisting of an *affine transformation* (i.e., a timing function and an allocation function) along with *explicit pipelining*. The first step is very similar to the techniques used for UREs. However, it merely yields a target architecture — one whose data flow is neither spatially nor temporarally local. The second step, namely *explicit pipelining*, permits the dependencies to be localized, so that the architecture is systolic. A similar approach (called *broadcast removal*) has been described by Fortes and Moldovan [4] although they do not describe how a *timing function* (which is called a *linear schedule* there) can be derived.

In this paper we extend these results to permit the synthesis of systolic arrays with *time-dependent* data flow governed by *control signals*. To do so we propose a new class of recurrence equations, called Conditional Uniform Recurrence Equations (CUREs). In such recurrences the dependencies are *uniform* but the computation is governed by *conditional expressions*; this provides us with an intermediate representation. Synthesizing a systolic array now involves three steps. Firstly an *affine timing function* (ATF) is determined for the original RELD as in the earlier approach. We next perform *explicit pipelining* (a generalization of the earlier version) which yields a CURE. The final step involves mapping the CURE to a systolic array.

The rest of this paper is organized as follows. In the following section (Section 2 we formally define the various classes of recurrences that we shall use and develop some notation. Then, in Section 3 we shall briefly summarize the idea of *explicit pipelining* and develop one of our major results, namely *multistage pipelining*. We shall also describe how this yields a systematic procedure to derive a CURE from the original RELD. Then, in Section 4 we describe how to synthesize systolic arrays from CUREs. We shall show that this is similar to synthesizing one from UREs, except that there are additional constraints on the choice of timing and allocation functions. These constraints correspond to the requirement that control signals (which result directly from the introduction of *control dependencies*) must also have systolic interconnections. We illustrate the technique (in Section 5) by systematically deriving a well known systolic array for dynamic programming [6]. A satisfactory technique that can synthesize this architecture has not appeared in the literature.[1] The steps involved in the synthesis procedure may thus be described as follows.

1. Specify a RELD for the problem.

2. Determine a valid ATF $[\lambda_t, \alpha_t]$ for the RELD. Initially choose the optimal (i.e., the "fastest") ATF.

3. Pipeline the dependencies in the RELD, and derive the equivalent Conditional URE for the problem. If pipelining is not possible then go to step 2.

4. Pipeline the *conditional* expressions in the Conditional URE and derive the *control* dependencies. If pipelining is not possible go to step 2.

5. Determine an allocation function and derive the final architecture.

2 Recurrence Equations: UREs, RELDs and CUREs

Definition 1 A *Recurrence Equation* over a domain D is defined to be an equation of the form

$$f(p) = g(f(q_1), f(q_2) \ldots f(q_k))$$

where $p \in D$;
            $q_i \in D$ for $i = 1 \ldots k$;
and g is a single-valued function, strictly dependent on each of its arguments.

It should be immediately clear why such recurrences are an attractive starting point for synthesizing any class of *regular* architectures. The computation of the function f at any point in the domain involves applying the function g to exactly k arguments. The function g thus automatically defines the exactly what the functionality of the processor is to be. The relationship between p and the q_i's determines where the k arguments are going to come from. Based on this we have the following classes of recurrences.

Definition 2 A Recurrence Equation of the form defined above is called a Uniform Recurrence Equation (URE) iff
          $q_i = p - w_i$, for all i;
where w_i's are constant n-dimensional vectors.

Definition 3 A Recurrence Equation is said to have Linear Dependencies (called an RELD) if
          $q_i = A_i p - b_i$, for all i;
where A_i's are constant $n \times n$ matrices;
and b_i's are constant $n \times 1$ vectors;

---

[1]The techniques that do synthesize this array either require one to explicitly enumerate the dependencies (and do not give systematic techniques to derive the *affine transformations* [13]) or require an inductive analysis of the *entire* dependency graph [2]. Recently another technique has been presented [5], but that requires a somewhat awkward notation, and is less general than ours.

As mentioned above, most of the earlier work on systolic array synthesis has concentrated on UREs. Since the dependency structure of the *entire* computation is completely specified by a small set of constant dependency vectors, it is only necessary to analyze these vectors in order to synthesize a systolic array. If we assume that the computation of g takes unit time once its arguments are available (a reasonable assumption since g is a *strict* function), then the problem of synthesizing a systolic array can be solved by mapping the original URE to a *space-time* domain by affine transformations. Such a mapping must satisfy the following constraints.

- The *time* component of the (transformed) dependency vectors must be negative (i.e., causality must be satisfied).

- The *space* component of the transformed dependency vectors must correspond to nearest neighbor interconnections.

The time component of the mapping is called a *timing function*, and the space-component is the *allocation function*. When synthesizing systolic arrays from RELDs a similar approach is followed. However, we have shown [15,17] that merely using affine transformations alone is not enough. It is necessary to explicitly pipeline the dependencies of the RELD. Before we summarize those results we shall first introduce some notation.

Definition 4 A *Conditional Uniform Recurrence Equation* over a domain D is defined to be an equation of the form

$$f(p) = \begin{cases} g_1(f(p-w_{1,1}), f(p-w_{1,2})\ldots f(p-w_{1,k_1})) & \text{if } \theta_1 p > \pi_1 \\ g_2(f(p-w_{2,1}), f(p-w_{2,2})\ldots f(p-w_{2,k_2})) & \text{if } \theta_2 p > \pi_2 \\ \vdots \\ g_{k-1}(f(p-w_{k-1,1}), f(p-w_{k-1,2})\ldots f(p-w_{k-1,k_{k-1}})) & \text{if } \theta_{k-1} p > \pi_{k-1} \\ g_k(f(p-w_{k,1}), f(p-w_{k,2})\ldots f(p-w_{k,k_k})) & \text{otherwise} \end{cases}$$

where $p \in D$;
  θ_i's are constant vectors in Z^n;
  π_i's are scalar constants in Z;
  $w_{i,j}$'s are constant n-dimensional vectors (the set of all the dependency vectors $w_{i,j}$ is denoted by W)
and g_i's are single valued functions which are strictly dependent on each of their arguments.

In general, we may define CUREs where the condition is not just a single linear inequality, but a conjunction of a number of linear inequalities. Although the above definition uses only single linear conditional expressions, it can also be extended to the case where more than one such expression "guards" the function g_i. Since we are not interested in a non-deterministic recurrence, we shall also assume without loss of generality that in this latter case the conditional expressions are all mutually exclusive.

Note that a CURE is not exactly a recurrence equation since the computation that is performed at any point in the domain is not a *strict* function of all its arguments, but contains a set of conditional expressions. Also, the domain that we shall consider in the rest of this paper are *convex hulls* which may be viewed as being defined by a set of bounding planes. For CUREs, the domain is thus *implicitly* defined by the set of hyperplanes $[\theta_i, \pi_i]_{i=1...k}$.

3 Pipelining: Explicit and Multistage

There are two key ideas underlying the notion of explicit pipelining, which can be summarized as follows. Firstly, if more than one point in the domain depends on some other point, it is clear that one of them can *use* the value for its computation, and then *pass it on* to the other(s). Let p and p' be two points in D such that $A_j p + b_j = A_j p' + b_j = q$. Thus the computation of both $f(p)$ and $f(p')$ need $f(q)$ as their j^{th} arguments. Now, if we let $p - p' = \rho$, we may introduce a new function f' defined by $f'(p) = f'(p + \rho)$. It is straightforward to implement f' on any processor — it is simply an identity function that outputs the value it receives. However, by using f' we may transform the definition of f to be

$$f(p) = g(f(A_1 p + b_1), f(A_2 p + b_2), \ldots f'(p) \ldots f(A_k p + b_k))$$

Thus the linear dependency $[A_j, b_j]$ may be replaced by a uniform dependency ρ. In addition, for the above scenario to work correctly, the point that receives the value first, *must* be scheduled to be computed *before* the other point. This thus imposes a *partial order* on these points. We shall discuss these ideas formally as follows.

Definition 5 We define the jth *co-set* $C(p)$ of a point p in D (also referred to as the *inverse co-set* of the point $r = A_j p + b_j$) as the set of points in D which all depend on the same point as p for their j^{th} argument, i.e.,

$$C(p) = \{q \mid A_j q + b_j = A_j p + b_j\}$$

Remark 1 *There is a one-to-one correspondence between the* null *space of the dependency matrix* A_j, *and the* j^{th} *co-set of a point* p *in* D.

We assume that the dependency matrix A_j is nonsingular. The reason for this is that the equation $A_j x = 0$ will then have several (actually infinite) nontrivial solutions ρ, and hence the co-set of any point in the domain will contain at least two points.[2] Thus, it is advantageous to pipeline the value of $f(q)$, so that every point not only uses it as an argument for its computation, but also contributes in its propagation to other points. Let ρ_j be a *basis vector* for the *null* space of A_j. Then we can pipeline the jth dependency by replacing it with a *uniform* dependency ρ_j, and introducing an additional (identity) function at each point in the domain which gets its input from the value of the jth argument at $p + \rho$.

Note that since our domain is only the set of *lattice* points, the notion of a basis vector is slightly different from that in the vector space R^n over the reals. For example, in a one-dimensional subspace L of R^n, any vector l in L can be a basis vector, since any other member of L may be derived from

---

[2] The case when the dependency matrix A_j is singular requires a somewhat different treatment, and is beyond the scope of this paper. The interested reader is referred to [15](Chapter 4) for details

l as a (real) scalar multiple. However, in the lattice-point subset of R^n we want to choose as *basis vectors*.[3] only those vectors from which we can derive all the elements of the set by multiplying with *integers*. As a result there are only a finite number of basis vectors. For a one-dimensional set there are only two possible basis vectors (corresponding to the smallest positive and negative vectors in the space) and each one is the additive inverse of the other. For a higher dimensional set too, there are only a finite number of basis vectors.

Definition 6 A vector ρ is said to be *consistent* with an ATF $[\lambda_t, \alpha_t]$ iff $\lambda_t^T \cdot \rho < -1$. Similarly a set $\Gamma = \{\rho_i\}$ of vectors is consistent with an ATF $[\lambda_t, \alpha_t]$ iff each of the ρ_i's is consistent with $[\lambda_t, \alpha_t]$. We say that ρ (or Γ) is λ_t-consistent.

We also know that if the dot product of λ_t^T and ρ is zero then ρ is *parallel* to the timing function. Intuitively, we can say that if a vector ρ is consistent with an ATF $[\lambda_t, \alpha_t]$ then we can augment any RELD for which $[\lambda_t, \alpha_t]$ is a valid ATF by introducing a new dependency ρ, *and still retain* $[\lambda_t, \alpha_t]$ *as a valid ATF*. We thus have the following lemma and the subsequent remark.

Lemma 1 *If the null set* $null(A_j)$ *of a dependency matrix* A_j *is not parallel to the timing function* $[\lambda_t, \alpha_t]$ *then there exists a unique basis for* $null(A_j)$ *that is consistent with* $[\lambda_t, \alpha_t]$.

Remark 2 *A dependency* A_j *of a RELD which has* $[\lambda_t, \alpha_t]$ *as a valid ATF can be pipelined if the null space* $null(A_j)$ *of* A_j *has* λ_t-consistent basis vectors.

3.1 Multistage Pipelining

Based on the above discussion, we have a useful pipelining strategy [16] that enables us to derive (conditional) UREs from a given RELD, while preserving the ATF that had been determined for the RELD. The main condition for such a pipelining to exist is that

$$A_j(A_jp + b_j - p_\perp) = \rho'$$

where $p_\perp$ is the earliest scheduled point in $C(p)$. While such a class of transformations (called *simple pipelining*) is useful for a large number of computations, the above condition may not be always satisfied. It is not always the case that $p - q$ belongs to the null space of A_j. We shall now present another technique called *multistage pipelining*, where it will be possible to pipeline a particular dependency by sharing values that are required to be shared for *another dependency*. For the present we shall restrict our attention to the case where the rank of A_j is $n - 1$ (and thus its null space is a straight line with a basis vector, say ρ). The idea can be easily extended to the more general case (see [16] for details). Consider a point q in D and its jth inverse co-set. We know that for any point p in this set, the jth argument can be pipelined if somehow, the value of $f(q)$ can reach $p_\perp$ along a λ_t-consistent basis. In *simple* pipelining, the basic assumption was that this could be done, provided that the vector $p_\perp - q$ was a *constant* vector (independent of p).

---

[3]Strictly speaking, these are not basis vectors, since the lattice-point subset of R^n is no longer a vector space; however, the notion of a basis from which all elements of the set can be derived is a valid one.

There is however, an alternative way in which $p_\perp$ can receive the value of $f(q)$. Consider the th inverse co-set of q (corresponding to the dependency $[A_i, b_i]$). Clearly, if this dependency is pipelineable, then every point p' in this set $(C(p'))$ can get the value of $f(q)$ (albeit as its ith argument, not its jth one). However, if this set is "close to" $p_\perp$, then we can successfully pipeline the jth dependency too. The condition for *multistage pipelining* can thus be stated as follows.

$$\exists \rho_j' \mid \forall p \in D \quad A_i(p_\perp + \rho_j' - A_j p + b_j) = 0 \quad \wedge \quad A_i \text{ is pipelineable}$$

It can be shown that the point $p_\perp$ must lie on a domain boundary, say $\pi p = \theta$ (remember, that since the domain is a convex hull, every boundary is a hyperplane). If we adopt the convention (without any loss of generality) that $\pi p > \theta$ represents a point in the *interior* of the domain, we have the following function that achieves the pipelining operation.

$$f_j(p) = \begin{cases} f_j(p + \rho) & \text{if } \pi p = \theta \\ f_i(p) & \text{otherwise} \end{cases}$$

It is easy to see that this too is a *dummy* function in the sense that it sends its input value unchanged, but it is governed by a linear conditional expresion, and is thus a CURE. Moreover, since the new dependency introduced (i.e., the basis vector ρ) is λ_t-consistent the new CURE also has $[\lambda_t, \alpha_t]$ as a valid timing function.

4 Synthesizing Systolic Arrays from CUREs

Now that the original problem specification has been reduced to a CURE, and $[\lambda_t, \alpha_t]$, is a valid ATF for the CURE, the final step is to select an appropriate allocation function and synthesize the final architecture. By generalizing the previous results to the case when the dependency matrices have arbitrary ranks, we can show that the computation performed at any point in the domain consists of evaluating the k different pipelining functions, and also computing the value of the function g as follows.

$$f(p) = g(f_1(A_1 p + b_1), f_2(A_2 p + b_2) \ldots f_k(A_k p + b_k))$$

where, depending on the kind of pipelining used, each of the f_i's have the form of one of the following (note that in one case the value used is $f(p + \rho')$ while in the other it is $f_i(p + \rho')$ (where $i \neq j$).

$$f_j(p) = \begin{cases} f(p + \rho') & \text{if } \pi_1 p = \theta_1 \wedge \pi_2 p = \theta_2 \wedge \ldots \wedge \pi_r p = \theta_r \\ f_j(p + \rho_r) & \text{if } \pi_1 p = \theta_1 \wedge \pi_2 p = \theta_2 \wedge \ldots \wedge \pi_{r-1} p = \theta_{r-1} \\ f_j(p + \rho_{r-1}) & \text{if } \pi_1 p = \theta_1 \wedge \pi_2 p = \theta_2 \wedge \ldots \wedge \pi_{r-2} p = \theta_{r-2} \\ \vdots \\ f_j(p + \rho_2) & \text{if } \pi_1 p = \theta_1 \\ f_j(p + \rho_1) & \text{otherwise} \end{cases}$$

or

$$f_j(p) = \begin{cases} f_i(p + \rho') & \text{if } \pi_1 p = \theta_1 \wedge \pi_2 p = \theta_2 \wedge \ldots \wedge \pi_r p = \theta_r \\ f_j(p + \rho_r) & \text{if } \pi_1 p = \theta_1 \wedge \pi_2 p = \theta_2 \wedge \ldots \wedge \pi_{r-1} p = \theta_{r-1} \\ f_j(p + \rho_{r-1}) & \text{if } \pi_1 p = \theta_1 \wedge \pi_2 p = \theta_2 \wedge \ldots \wedge \pi_{r-2} p = \theta_{r-2} \\ \vdots & \\ f_j(p + \rho_2) & \text{if } \pi_1 p = \theta_1 \\ f_j(p + \rho_1) & \text{otherwise} \end{cases}$$

Thus, a naive architecture for the CURE would require that each processor be able to compute the function g as well as have the capability to evaluate the dot-products of vectors. In addition, it must have enough local memory to store the values of a set of vectors θ_i's (and also the π_i's). It must also know the value of p as the computation proceeds. Since we intend to use affine timing and allocation functions, there is a one-to-one correspondence between the point p in the original RELD and the point $[x, y, t]^T$ in the space-time domain. Thus each processor must be aware of its location in the final array (its space coordinates) and also the global clock value. Such a processor can hardly be considered systolic by any stretch of the imagination. In this section we shall propose a technique, very similar to the pipelining operation on the data dependencies, that permits us to achieve considerable optimization of this. The processor must still have the ability to compute each of the g_i's of the CURE. However, it is no longer necessary to compute the conditional expressions. These can be transmitted as *control signals*.

Consider any conditional expression $\theta_i p = \pi_i$ in the CURE. We view the computation of this condition as the evaluation of a *boolean function*. As with the pipelining of data dependencies, we would like to identify the set of points in D that "share" this result. This is exactly the entire hyperplane $\theta_i p = \pi_i$, which is a boundary of D. Thus assuming that some point p on this hyperplane has computed the value of $\theta_i p = \pi_i$ to be (the boolean value) *true* this result can be pipelined to its neighbor on the plane. This is exactly analogous to the pipelining operations for data dependencies. Since the value that is pipelined is boolean we refer to the new dependencies introduced as *control dependencies*, σ_i. Instead of being the basis vectors for the null space of the dependency matrices, these dependencies must satisfy the constraint that $\theta_i^T \sigma_i$ must be zero. Clearly, these control dependencies are not unique, and hence there is a *search space* of possible solutions. However, because of the requirement that the allocation function maps them to only *permissible* vectors (the nearest-neighbor interconnection constraint) the problem is restricted to only "small" values for these vectors.

5 Example: Optimal String Parenthesization

We shall now illustrate the entire procedure by synthesizing a systolic architecture for the optimal string parenthesization problem of optimally parenthesizing a string. This is a particular case of dynamic programming and has been discussed by Kung et al. [6]. The problem involves the computation of a cost function specified as follows. Given a string of n elements the minimum cost of parenthesizing substring i through j is given by the following.

$$c_{i,j} = \min_{i < k < j} (c_{i,k} + c_{k,j}) + w_{i,j} \qquad \text{where} \qquad c_{i,i+1} = w_{i,i+1}$$

Here, $c_{i,k}$ and $c_{k,j}$ are the optimal costs of parenthesizing two substrings, and $w_{i,j}$ is the (local) cost of the outermost pair of parentheses, once the substrings have been optimally parenthesized. A straightforward RELD that can be derived from the above definition (simply by introducing an additional parameter that serves as an "accumulation index") is as follows.

$$c(1, n) = f(1, n, 1)$$

where $f(i, j, k)$ is defined as

$$
f(i,j,k) = \begin{cases}
w_{i,j} & \text{if } j - i = 1 \\
w_{i,j} + \min \begin{pmatrix} f(i,j,k+1) \\ f(i,i+k,1) + f(i+k,j,1) \end{pmatrix} & \text{if } k = 1 \\
\infty & \text{if } k \geq j - i \\
\min \begin{pmatrix} f(i,j,k+1) \\ f(i,i+k,1) + f(i+k,j,1) \end{pmatrix} & \text{otherwise}
\end{cases}
$$

However this RELD does not admit an affine timing function (see [15] for a formal proof) and we shall use the following RELD as a starting point for the synthesis. The domain for this RELD is the convex hull bounded by $k > 0$, $j - i \geq 2k$, $i > 0$ and $j > 0$ as shown in Figure 1.

$$c(1, n) = f(1, n, 1)$$

where $f(i, j, k)$ is defined as

$$
f(i,j,k) = \begin{cases}
w_{i,j} & \text{if } j - i = 1 \\
w_{i,j} + \min \begin{pmatrix} f(i,i+k,1) + f(i+k,j,1) \\ f(i,j,k+1) \\ f(i,j-k,1) + f(j-k,j,1) \end{pmatrix} & \text{if } k = 1 \\
\infty & \text{if } 2*k > j - i \\
\min \begin{pmatrix} f(i,i+k,1) + f(i+k,j,1) \\ f(i,j,k+1) \\ f(i,j-k,1) + f(j-k,j,1) \end{pmatrix} & \text{otherwise}
\end{cases}
$$

5.1 Timing Function

The first step in the synthesis procedure is to determine an ATF, $[\lambda, \alpha]$ (denoted by $[[a, b, c], \alpha]$) for this RELD. Techniques for determining timing functions for RELDs are discussed elsewhere (see [15]). It can be shown that $[[a, b, c], \alpha]$ is a valid ATF if it satisfies the following inequalities (for all $[i, j, k]$ in the domain.

$$
\begin{aligned}
b(j - i - k) &> -c(k - 1) \\
ak &< c(k - 1) \\
c &< 0 \\
bk &> c(k - 1) \\
a(j - i - k) &< c(k - 1)
\end{aligned}
$$

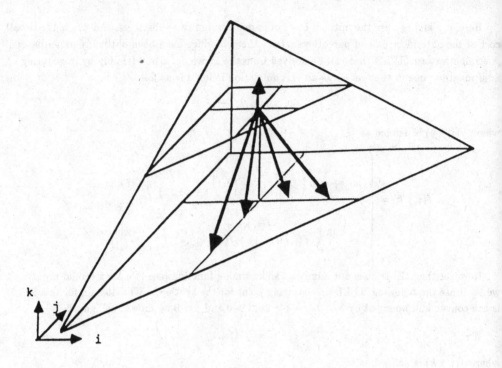

$$A_1 = \begin{bmatrix} 1 & 0 & 0 \\ 1 & 0 & 1 \\ 0 & 0 & 0 \end{bmatrix} b_1 = \begin{bmatrix} 0 \\ 0 \\ 1 \end{bmatrix}; A_2 = \begin{bmatrix} 1 & 0 & 1 \\ 0 & 1 & 0 \\ 0 & 0 & 0 \end{bmatrix} b_2 = \begin{bmatrix} 0 \\ 0 \\ 1 \end{bmatrix}; A_3 = \begin{bmatrix} 1 & 0 & 0 \\ 0 & 1 & 0 \\ 0 & 0 & 1 \end{bmatrix} b_3 = \begin{bmatrix} 0 \\ 0 \\ 1 \end{bmatrix};$$

$$A_4 = \begin{bmatrix} 1 & 0 & 0 \\ 0 & 1 & -1 \\ 0 & 0 & 0 \end{bmatrix} b_4 = \begin{bmatrix} 0 \\ 0 \\ 1 \end{bmatrix}; A_5 = \begin{bmatrix} 0 & 1 & -1 \\ 0 & 1 & 0 \\ 0 & 0 & 0 \end{bmatrix} b_5 = \begin{bmatrix} 0 \\ 0 \\ 1 \end{bmatrix};$$

Figure 1: Dependency Structure for the RELD for String Parenthesization

Since a, b and c are restricted to be integers, and $j - i \geq 2k$, these can be reduced to $c < 0$; $b \geq -c$ and $a \leq c$. The optimal ATF thus corresponds to the smallest integer (absolute-valued) solution to the above inequalities, and is given by $\lambda_{opt} = [-1, 1, -1]^T$ (with $\alpha_{opt} = 1$), i.e.,

$$t(i, j, k) \equiv j - i - k + 1$$

5.2 Pipelining the Data Dependencies

The next step in the synthesis procedure is to pipeline the linear dependencies. For this the null space of each of A_1, A_2, A_4 and A_5 must first be computed. It is easy to show that the rank of each of these matrices is 2, and hence their null spaces are all one-dimensional, specified by a single basis vector each, say ρ_1, ρ_2, ρ_4 and ρ_5, respectively. It is also a matter of straightforward linear algebra to solve the appropriate systems of equations and derive that ρ_1, ρ_2, ρ_4 and ρ_5 are respectively, $[0, m_1, 0]^T$, $[m_2, 0, m_2]^T$, $[0, m_4, m_4]^T$ and $[m_5, 0, 0]^T$.

However, the dot-product $\rho_2 \cdot \lambda$ is $[m_2, 0, -m_2]^T \cdot [-1, 1, -1]$ which is zero (similarly $\rho_4 \cdot \lambda$ is also zero). This means that it is *impossible* to obtain a λ-consistent basis for the null spaces of either A_2 or A_4. It is therefore necessary to choose another λ, for which the basis of the null spaces of A_i and A_j can be λ-consistent. It is seen that $[-2, 2, -1]$ satisfies this requirement, and hence a satisfactory ATF is the following[4].

$$t(i, j, k) \equiv 2(j - i) - k + 1$$

Now, λ-consistent basis vectors for each of the dependencies can be derived, and are $[0, -1, 0]^T$, $[1, 0, -1]^T$, $[0, -1, -1]^T$ and $[1, 0, 0]^T$.

The next step is to pipeline each of the dependencies of the RELD, either by using direct pipelining or through multistage pipelining. To recapitulate, for any linear dependency $[A_i, b_i]$, the condition for direct pipelining is that for any point $p \in D$ (i.e., for any $[i, j, k]^T$),

$$A_i \bullet ([i, j, k]^T - A_i \bullet [i, j, k]^T + b_i)$$

is a constant.

For each of the four dependencies that need to be pipelined, $A_i \cdot [i, j, k]^T + b_i$ is respectively $[i, i + k, 1]$, $[i + k, j, 1]$, $[i, j - k, 1]$ and $[j - k, j, 1]$, and consequently the value of $[i, j, k]^T - (A_i \cdot [i, j, k]^T + b_i)$ is $[0, j - i - k, k - 1]^T$, $[-k, 0, k - 1]^T$, $[0, k, k - 1]^T$ and $[i - j - k, 0, k - 1]^T$, respectively. Then, the values of $A_i(p - A_i p + b_i)$ for each of the four dependencies may be easily computed to be $[0, -k + 1, 0]^T$ for A_1, $[0, 0, 0]^T$ for A_2 $[0, 0, 0]^T$ for A_4 and $[-k + 1, 0, 0]^T$ for A_5. Thus, it is clear that only $[A_2, b_2]$ and $[A_4, b_4]$ can be directly pipelined by introducing a new pair of dependencies, ρ_2 and ρ_4 (along with the terminal dependencies $\rho'_2 = [1, 0, 0]^T$ and $\rho'_4 = [0, -1, 0]^T$), respectively.[5] Now, in order to decide exactly when the terminal dependencies come into play, it is necessary to determine the point at which the null space of A_2 (and correspondingly A_4) translated by $[i, j, k]^T$ intersects the domain boundary. This can be very easily seen to be the $k = 1$ boundary for both

---

[4]In fact, it can be shown that $[[-2, 2, -1]^T \mid -1]$ is the optimal ATF, which is also λ-consistent.
[5]Note that the terminal dependencies are also λ-consistent.

the null spaces and the corresponding intersection points are $[i + k - 1, j, 1]$ and $[i, j - k + 1, 1]$. Thus the auxiliary (pipelining) functions f_2 and f_4 that are introduced to achieve the pipelining are as follows.

$$f_2(i,j,k) = \begin{cases} f(i+1,j,k) & \text{if } k = 1 \\ f_2(i+1,j,k-1) & \text{otherwise} \end{cases} \quad \text{and} \quad f_4(i,j,k) = \begin{cases} f(i,j-1,k) & \text{if } k = 1 \\ f_4(i,j-1,k-1) & \text{otherwise} \end{cases}$$

It is also clear from the above discussion that $[A_1, b_1]$ and $[A_5, b_5]$ cannot be pipelined directly; if any pipelining is to be achieved, it must be multistage pipelining. In order to test for this it is necessary to determine the points where their null spaces (i.e., rays $[0, -1, 0]^T$ and $[1, 0, 0]^T$) translated by $[i, j, k]^T$ intersect the domain boundary. It is easy to see that the first boundary that a ray $\rho_1 = [0, -1, 0]^T$ passing through $[i, j, k]^T$ intersects is the $2k > j - i$ boundary (similarly a ray $\rho_5 = [0, -1, 0]^T$ passing through $[i, j, k]^T$ also intersects the same boundary). The exact point on the boundary that it meets may also be calculated to be $[i, i + 2k, k]$ (similarly ρ_5 meets the boundary at $[j - 2k, j, k]$).

To test for multistage pipelining of the dependency $[A_1, b_1]$ it must be the case that the difference Δ_1 between $[i, i + 2k, k]^T$ and $[i, i + k, k]^T$, i.e., $[0, k, k - 1]^T$ must satisfy the necessary condition for direct pipelining for either A_2 or A_4 with exactly the same terminal dependencies. This means that the following should hold.

$$A_2 \cdot \Delta_1 = \rho_2' \qquad \text{or} \qquad A_4 \cdot \Delta_1 = \rho_4'$$

Similarly, for the dependency $[A_5, b_5]$ it must be the case that $\Delta_5 = [j - 2k, j, k]^T - [j - k, j, 1]^T$ i.e., $[-k, 0, k - 1]^T$ must satisfy

$$A_2 \cdot \Delta_5 = \rho_2' \qquad \text{or} \qquad A_4 \cdot \Delta_5 = \rho_4'$$

It is a matter of straightforward algebra to ascertain that the following are satisfied.

$$A_4 \cdot \Delta_1 = \rho_4' \qquad \text{and} \qquad A_2 \cdot \Delta_5 = \rho_2'$$

Thus it is possible to pipeline $[A_1, b_1]$ by first pipelining along the dependency ρ_1, and then switching to a new dependency ρ_4 (and its corresponding function f_4). Similarly, $[A_5, b_5]$ can be completely pipelined by first pipelining along the dependency ρ_5, and then switching to a new dependency ρ_2 (and its corresponding function f_2). The original RELD is thus equivalent to the following CURE.

$$c(1, n) = f(1, n, 1)$$

where $f(i, j, k)$ is defined as

$$f(i,j,k) = \begin{cases} w_{i,j} & \text{if } j - i = 1 \\[2mm] w_{i,j} + \min \begin{pmatrix} f_1(i,i+k,1) + f_2(i+k,j,1) \\ f(i,j,k+1) \\ f_4(i,j-k,1) + f_5(j-k,j,1) \end{pmatrix} & \text{if } k = 1 \\[4mm] \infty & \text{if } 2 * k > j - i \\[4mm] \min \begin{pmatrix} f_1(i,i+k,1) + f_2(i+k,j,1) \\ f(i,j,k+1) \\ f_4(i,j-k,1) + f_5(j-k,j,1) \end{pmatrix} & \text{otherwise} \end{cases}$$

where

$$f_2(i,j,k) = \begin{cases} f(i+1,j,k) & \text{if } k=1 \\ f_2(i+1,j,k-1) & \text{otherwise} \end{cases} \qquad f_2(i,j,k) = \begin{cases} f(i,j-1,k) & \text{if } k=1 \\ f_2(i,j-1,k-1) & \text{otherwise} \end{cases}$$

and

$$f_1(i,j,k) = \begin{cases} f_4(i,j,k) & \text{if } 2k=j-i \\ f_1(i,j-1,k) & \text{otherwise} \end{cases} \qquad f_5(i,j,k) = \begin{cases} f_2(i,j,k) & \text{if } 2k=j-i \\ f_5(i+1,j,k) & \text{otherwise} \end{cases}$$

5.3 Determining the Control Dependencies and Allocation Function

The final step in the synthesis procedure is to choose an allocation function that satisfies the constraints of locality of interconnections, and if necessary, choose appropriate λ-consistent control dependencies σ_i. The allocation function must also map these control dependencies to neighboring processors. From the above CURE, it is clear that the various conditional expressions that need to be evaluated are the following

$$k = 1$$
$$j - i = 2k$$
$$j - i = 1$$

Note that the condition $2k > j - i$ has not been listed above, since it is really concerned with points that are *outside the domain*. The data dependencies of the CURE and the associated delays (derived from $\lambda \cdot \rho_i$) are as follows.

$$\begin{array}{lll} [0,-1,0] & \text{for } f_1 & \text{with a delay of 2 units} \\ [1,0,-1] & \text{for } f_2 & \text{with a delay of 1 unit} \\ [0,-1,-1] & \text{for } f_4 & \text{with a delay of 1 unit} \\ [1,0,0] & \text{for } f_5 & \text{with a delay of 2 units} \\ \text{and} \quad [0,0,1] & \text{for } f & \text{with a delay of 1 unit} \end{array}$$

The terminal dependencies are $[1,0,0]$ for f_2, and $[0,-1,0]$ for f_4. It is also clear that the value $w_{i,j}$ is a constant value, to be input from the external world, and that all the points in D need its value when $k = 1$. Thus, the most obvious choice for an allocation function is thus a simple vertical projection, i.e.,

$$[x,y] = a(i,j,k) \equiv [i,j]$$

With such an allocation function, the five dependencies above are mapped to $[0,-1]$, $[1,0]$, $[0,-1]$, $[1,0]$, and $[0,0]$, respectively. This means that each processor $[x,y]$ gets two values (corresponding to f_2 and f_5) from processor $[x+1,y]$ over lines of delay and 2 time units, respectively; it similarly receives two values (f_1 and f_4) from processor $[x,y-1]$ over lines of delay 1 and 2, respectively. The value corresponding to f remains in the processor (in an accumulator register) and is updated on every cycle. Thus the only remaining problem is to choose appropriate control dependencies for the three control planes $k = 1$, $j - i = 2k$ and $j - i = 1$, specified by $\pi_1 = [0,0,1]^{\mathsf{T}}$ $\pi_2 = [-1,1,-2]^{\mathsf{T}}$ and $\pi_3 = [-1,1,-1]^{\mathsf{T}}$, respectively. However, the third one intersects the domain

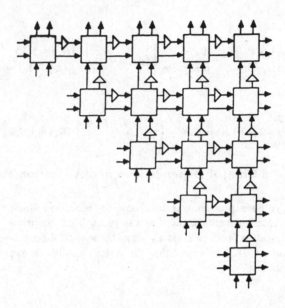

Figure 2: Final Architecture for Optimal String Parenthesization

at only one line $[i, i + 1, 1]$ and this line is mapped by the allocation function to the processors $[i, i+1]$.[6] As a result there is no need for a control signal. All the processors $[i, i+1]$ merely output the value $w_{i,i+1}$ at time instant $t = 1$. The important control dependencies are thus those corresponding to π_1 and π_2. These correspond to control signals σ_1 and σ_2 if $\pi_1 \cdot \sigma_1 = 0$ and $\pi_2 \cdot \sigma_2 = 0$. It is very straightforward to deduce that σ_1 should be $[c_i, c_j, 0]$ where c_i and c_j are arbitrary integers. The conditions of λ-consistency yield one constraint, namely $2(c_j - c_i)$ must be negative, and the constraint of locality of interconnections yields another constraint, namely that the vector $[c_i, c_j]$ must be one of the six permissible interconnection vectors $\{(\pm 1, 0), (0, \pm 1), (\pm 1, \pm 1)\}$. This yields only two possible values for σ_1, $[1, 0]$ and $[0, -1]$ and any one of them can be chosen (say the former). This corresponds to a vertical control signal that travels with a delay of two time units. For σ_2, the analysis is similar; $\sigma_2 \cdot \pi_2 = 0$ yields $\sigma_2 = [c_i, c_i + 2c_k, c_k]$, λ-consistency yields $3c_k < 0$. However, nearest-neighbor interconnection cannot be achieved, since the smallest (absolute) value for c_k that satisfies λ-consistency is -1, and that is not nearest-neighbor (any larger absolute value for c_k will correspond to an even more distant interconnection). If this last constraint is relaxed $\sigma_2 = [0, -2, -1]$ is a valid choice. This corresponds to a (horizontal) control signal that connects every alternate processor and travels at a speed of two processors every three time units.

The final architecture that this yields is shown in Figure 2 and is identical to the one developed by Guibas et al. [6], which is a well known systolic array and is considered by many to be a classic example of the intuitive *eureka* steps involved in systolic array design. One important point that needs to be mentioned here is that although the techniques presented in these two chapters have been developed in the context of *pure* systolic arrays (i.e., those that permit only nearest neighbor

---

[6]In fact this line is the only part of the domain that is mapped to this subset of the processors.

nterconnections) the same techniques are directly applicable when the architecture is not strictly systolic. As we have just seen, merely relaxing a few constraints achieves this result.

6 Conclusion

We have presented a technique for systematically deriving systolic architectures from a general class of recurrence equations. The principal contributions have been to propose two major steps for the synthesis process (in addition to determining a timing and allocation function). In the first step the dependencies are pipelined, so that results that are required by more than one points in the domain can be profitable shared by being *pipelined* among all the points that require them. We have presented a generalized theory for this process, and discussed how, under the most general case, this results in a recurrence equation that has uniform dependencies, but must perform a non-strict computation (governed by conditional expressions). We have also presented a technique whereby the computation of these conditional expressions may be optimized, thus yielding systolic arrays that have control signals governing the data-flow.

References

[1] Cappello, P.R. and Steiglitz, K. Unifying vlsi designs with linear transformations of space-time. *Advances in Computing Research*, (1984), 23–65.

[2] Chen, M.C. A parallel language and its compilation to multiprocessor machines or vlsi. In *Principles of Programming Languages*, ACM, 1986.

[3] Delosme, J.M. and Ipsen, I.C.F. An illustration of a methodology for the construction of efficient systolic architectures in vlsi. In *International Symposium on VLSI Technology, Systems and Applications*, Taipei, Taiwan, 1985, pp. 268–273.

[4] Fortes, J.A.B. and Moldovan, D. Data broadcasting in linearly scheduled array processors. In *Proceedings, 11th Annual Symposium on Computer Architecture*, 1984, pp. 224–231.

[5] Guerra, C. and Melhem, R. Synthesizing non-uniform systolic designs. In *Proceedings of the International Conference on Parallel Processing*, IEEE, August 1986, pp. 765–771.

[6] Guibas, L., Kung, H.T., and Thompson, C.D. Direct vlsi implementation of combinatorial algorithms. In *Proc. Conference on Very Large Scale Integration: Architecture, Design and Fabrication*, January 1979, pp. 509–525.

[7] Kung, H.T. Let's design algorithms for vlsi. In *Proc. Caltech Conference on VLSI*, January 1979.

[8] Kung, H.T. Why systolic architectures. *Computer 15*, 1 (January 1982), 37–46.

[9] Lam, M.S. and Mostow, J.A. A transformational model of vlsi systolic design. *IEEE Computer 18*, (February 1985), 42–52.

[10] Leiserson, C.E. and Saxe, J.B. Optimizing synchronous systems. *Journal of VLSI and Computer Systems 1*, (1983), 41–68.

[11] Li, G.J. and Wah, B.W. Design of optimal systolic arrays. *IEEE Transactions on Computers* *C-35*, 1 (1985), 66–77.

[12] Miranker, W.L. and Winkler, A. Space-time representation of computational structures. *Computing 32*, (1984), 93–114.

[13] Moldovan, D.I. On the design of algorithms for vlsi systolic arrays. *Proceedings of the IEEE 71*, 1 (January 1983), 113–120.

[14] Quinton, P. *The Systematic Design of Systolic Arrays.* Tech. Rep. 216, Institut National de Recherche en Informatique et en Automatique INRIA, July 1983.

[15] Rajopadhye, S.V. *Synthesis, Otimization and Verification of Systolic Architectures.* PhD thesis, University of Utah, Salt Lake City, Utah 84112, December 1986.

[16] Rajopadhye, S.V. and Fujimoto, R.M. *Synthesizing Systolic Arrays with Control Signals from Recurrence equations.* Tech. Rep. CIS-TR-86-12, University of Oregon, Computer and Information Science Department, December 1986.

[17] Rajopadhye, S.V., Purushothaman, S., and Fujimoto, R.M. On synthesizing systolic arrays from recurrence equations with linear dependencies. In *Proceedings, Sixth Conference on Foundations of Software Technology and Theoretical Computer Science*, Springer Verlag, New Delhi, India, December 1986. to appear.

[18] Ramakrishnan, I.V., Fussell, D.S., and Silberschatz, A. Mapping homogeneous graphs on linear arrays. *IEEE Transactions on Computers C-35*, (March 1985), 189–209.

[19] Weiser, U.C. and Davis, A.L. A wavefront notational tool for vlsi array design. In *VLSI Systems and Computations*, Carnegie Mellon University, October 1981, pp. 226–234.

specification of the algorithm using the Functional Parallel Programming language FP2, which is well suited to specify this pipelined approach for two reasons:
- there is a fixed number of communicating processes
- the internal behaviour of each process can be specified by using operations on data types

Based on the specification we prove liveness and termination properties of the corresponding network of FP2 processes. Moreover it is possible to "run" the specification, i.e. to specialize the general simulator and to simulate a specific discrete system, for example a digital circuit.

2. Pipelined event driven simulation of discrete systems

We start this section with a short review of the principles of simulation of discrete systems (see [2] for a more detailed presentation).

Discrete systems are generally described by a network of basic elements with inputs, outputs, possibly internal states, and a well-known functional and timing behaviour. For simplicity, it is assumed that each element has exactly one output and that the timing behaviour of the basic elements is rather elementary: only a fixed, element dependent delay time is considered in the model of the basic elements. The connections between elements are represented by variables with a given range of discrete or continuous values.

For simulation purposes the description of a system is split into a structural and a state part:
- The structure is described by a kind of directed graph where each node represents an element and an edge represents a connection between a node and a specific input of another node.
- The state (configuration) is the set of the states of all elements, where the state of an element is described by the values of its input, internal state, and output variables.

The pipelined simulation algorithm [1] is based on the event driven approach, which is standard for discrete simulation. Figure 1 illustrates the principle sequence of operations and the inherent parallelism.

Conceptually, operations on the same horizontal level may be performed in parallel, for example by separate processing units (PUs). This may lead to memory conflicts because of the need to share information between different PUs, e.g. the structure and state information and the event list (see [1]). One approach to resolve this

SPECIFICATION OF A PIPELINED EVENT DRIVEN SIMULATOR
USING FP2

Peter Schaefer *
Philippe Schnoebelen **

* AEG Aktiengesellschaft, Research Institute Berlin, FRG
Hollaenderstr. 31-34, D-1000 Berlin 51

** LIFIA-IMAG, Grenoble, France
BP68, 38402 St. Martin d'Heres Cedex

Abstract

The paper deals with the specification of a pipelined event driven
algorithm for discrete simulation using the Functional Parallel
Programming Language FP2. We start with a short review of the pipelined
event driven simulation algorithm and the main features of FP2. In the
main part, the FP2 specification procedure and a proof methodology for
liveness and correct termination of the specified network of processes are
described.

1. Introduction

Event driven simulation is the standard algorithm in simulation of discrete systems.
The simulated system is modeled by well-known basic elements and an interconnection
structure. The crucial point in event driven simulation is, that the simulation time
is advanced according to changes in the system - and not in fixed time steps. A
change of the state of the system is indicated by a so-called event, i.e. a change
of the value of a variable at a specific time instant. The simulation proceeds by
processing events - that means by evaluating elements - in increasing time order. At
any given time instant those and only those elements of the system are evaluated, to
which an event propagates. In general, these evaluations result in new events which
are to be processed subsequently.

A very efficient pipeline variant of this basic approach has been described in [1].
This pipelined algorithm is likely to be a kernel algorithm in a multi level
simulator [2], which is developed in ESPRIT project 415. This paper describes the

---

This research has been supported by ESPRIT Project 415: Parallel Architectures and
Languages for Advanced Information Processing - A VLSI-Directed Approach

problem is pipelining by identifying independent subtasks along the vertical line, dedicating one PU for each task and arranging the data flow between tasks in a pipelined fashion.

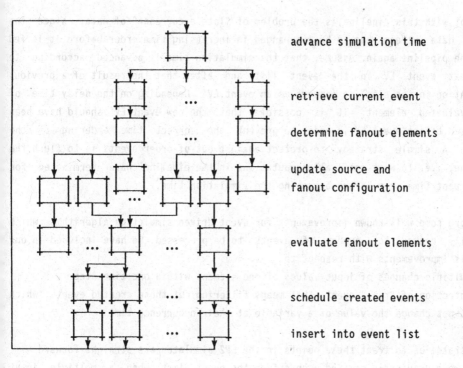

advance simulation time

retrieve current event

determine fanout elements

update source and
fanout configuration

evaluate fanout elements

schedule created events

insert into event list

Fig. 1: Structure of an event driven simulation algorithm, (similar to [1])

The basic subtasks of the pipeline are

- retrieving the next event from the event list (and recording results to an output device)
- determining from the structural description all elements of the system to which the event propagates (so-called fanout elements)
- updating the state of the source and all fanout elements of the event
- evaluating each fanout element using the internal state and the updated input values, i.e. computing new values of the internal state and the output variable according to the kind of the element
- scheduling created events for the insertion into the event list according to their occurrence time
- inserting scheduled events into the event list, delivering the next event to be processed, and advancing the simulation time, when there are no more events to be processed at the current simulation time.

These subtasks do not require to share information and each PU may proceed, while its result is being processed by the following PU. The PUs form a ring-shaped task pipeline, which performs on an input data stream of events and produces a data stream of events as output.

Inherent with this pipeline is the problem of "late occurrence" of data, since the output data stream has to be rearranged in increasing time order before it is fed into the pipeline again. Assume, that the simulation time is advanced according to the next event EV in the event list and after that the result of a previous computation in the pipeline appears as an event EV'. Depending on the delay time of the evaluated element, it is possible that the new event EV' should have been processed before event EV in order to prevent the correct time ordering of the events. A simple strategy to protect against out-of-order events is to flush the pipeline, i.e. to wait until all computations in the pipeline have terminated for the current time step before advancing the simulation time.

There are some well-known improvements for event driven simulation algorithms which basically reduce the number of events to be processed. We have included in our analysis improvements with respect to
- multiple changes of input values of one element within one time step
- detection of "real" event, that means filtering out those created events which do not change the value of a variable at their occurrence time.

The strategies to treat these points in the FP2 simulator are straight forward:
- remove previously created events from the event list when a multiple input change occurs
- check the current, the new and all "intermediate" values (the latter are contained in the event list) to detect whether an event really changes the value of a variable or not.

3. FP2 specification of the simulation algorithm

In this section it is described how the pipelined algorithm has been transformed into an FP2 program.

The aspects of FP2 seen as a programming language are recalled very shortly. For a more detailed discussion of these aspects we refer to [5] and [8]. In the main part of this section we present the methodology we adopted to specify the pipelined event driven simulator by using some parts of the program as examples.

3.1 Main features of FP2

FP2 is a Functional Parallel Programming language based on term rewriting. In FP2, one may define and use algebraic abstract data types, functions on these types, and communicating processes. All these objects can be polymorphic.

In FP2, a <u>type</u> is an algebra of terms built with a set of function names, the constructors of the type. A type can be polymorphic (or generic), that is to say parameterized by other types and functions. In FP2, a polymorphic type may require that its type and function parameters satisfy a given set of equations, then we say that the parameter types satisfy an equational property.

In FP2, a <u>process</u> is a non-deterministic state transition system defined by transition rules, which describe how the process may change its internal state and communicate with its environment.
The states of a process form an algebra of terms built with state constructors. An FP2 process owns typed connectors and uses them to communicate with the environment. The transmission of a value along a connector is a communication and a set of several communications occurring in the same transition form an event. (Do not confuse this FP2 event with an event in the simulator!)
The transition rules rewrite the internal state of the process. A rewriting step is a transition. A transition rule may contain communication terms, in which case the application of the rule causes communications to occur.

It is possible to combine FP2 processes to form a network of processes. In FP2, a network is just another process which happens to be defined in terms of smaller processes rather than just from scratch. It has connectors, state constructors and rules just like elementary processes. Out of the several process combining forms available in FP2, we shall only present the most important three and refer to [5] for more information.

Given P and Q two processes, it is possible to put them "in parallel"; the notion is P || Q. This operation is used for grouping several processes and consider them as a whole.

Given P a process and A and B two of its connectors, it is possible to connect A and B; the notion is P + A.B. Usually this is used in order to allow two different processes P and Q to communicate. They must be put in parallel first and then connectors A and B both belong to the parallel network P || Q even if they are issued from different components.

Given P a process and A one of its connectors, we may hide A; the notion is P - A.

Usually this is used when we have connected two connectors and do not want to connect them to other additional connectors. We may then abstract from these connectors which are there for "historical" reasons (they were necessary to connect the two previously distinct processes). This occurs so frequently that the shorthand P ++ A.B is used in place of P + A.B - A - B.

These operations are sufficient to combine processes in any way. In this paper we do not need anything more.

The way FP2 handles communication and concurrency is rather specific and this part of the language must be clearly understood to design correct programs.

The first point is the "instantaneous" communication in FP2. Let a process P have a rule "X : In(x) Out(x) ==> X", which is used to transmit along "Out" what is received along "In". The communications In(x) and Out(x) form an event in the rule and if the rule is applied, these two communications will take place in the same transition.
On the other hand, when two processes communicate, the communication is synchronized by "rendezvous", which means that the exchanged value is sent in the same moment it is received. Therefore if Q is another process with a rule "Y : In'(y) Out'(y) ==> Y" and if we connect P's "Out" with Q's "In'" then the communications along "Out" and "In'" being simultaneous by definition, it results that the communications along "In" and "Out'" are also simultaneously. Indeed, if we compute the rules of the network "P || Q + Out.In'" with the definitions of [5], we obtain (among others) the rule "XY : In(x) Out'(x) ==> XY" where "In" and "Out'" occur in the same event.

Another important feature of FP2 is the use of guards in communication terms. The terms of the event of a transition rule are patterns to be matched by the exchanged values. If a value is received, it must match the pattern of the rule and we have just seen that if it is sent, then it is received at the same moment. The consequence is that a rule can become non applicable simply because applying it would result in a communication that the environment does not accept at the moment (this behaviour is known in the literature both as "external nondeterminism" and "global nondeterminism"). A consequence is that we may define a process in a broader sense than requested by an informal specification, if we know that the environment restricts the process behaviour in the desired way, and we are still sure that the whole network cannot deadlock.

3.2. Programming methodology for FP2

In order to transform the informal algorithm of section 1 into an FP2 program, we first identified and specified the data types used in the algorithm. Then the different processes executing the different pipelined tasks were specified and lastly the functions which are used by the processes for their internal computations were defined. We shall now study more deeply these different points, mainly through examples from the simulation program.

This methodology has been used to translate the already existing pipelined (parallel) algorithm into FP2. We would like to emphasize that this is definitely not adapted to the task of writing a new algorithm. In that case, the decomposition of the problem must be considered first from a "parallelism" point of view (in a top-down way) and then a similar methodology can be used.

3.2.1 Specifying the general data types

We wanted to write a GENERIC event-driven simulator, able to simulate nearly any kind of networking activity. We assume that the simulated system is (roughly) a graph of nodes with only one output per node. Each node has an internal state and we require that a "transition function" is given for the nodes which returns the new internal state and the new output, when the kind of a node, its internal state, and its new inputs are given. The delays associated with the changes of internal state and output depend on the node.

From a top down point of view three structured data types are needed in the generic simulation algorithm, namely

- the event list
  - o similar to a "global clock", to store events resulting from an element evaluation and to deliver the next event that has to be processed according to the current simulation time.

- the system graph
  - o to store the structure of the system, essentially for each element of the system the set of all fanout elements

- the configuration
  - o to store the state of all elements, i.e. the values of all variables, of the system.

Let us consider, as an example, the definition of the data type SystemGraph.

Basically, each node in the network has one output feeding specific labeled input points of some other nodes. The structure of the system cannot be represented by a pure (directed) graph for the "edges" are not from node to node but from a node to a specific input point of a node. Thus we introduce a "Destination" type as an input point of a node.

```
type Destination
  cons des : Node,Input -> Destination
endtype
```

Now the structure of our system can be seen as a (bipartite) graph from Nodes to Destinations but as the only operation we apply on this graph is to fetch the Destinations fed by the output of a given node, we prefer to define this "graph" as a Table of Sets of Destinations, indexed by the Nodes and we introduce an auxiliary type "Fanout" for the Sets of Destinations :

```
type Fanout is Set[Destination]
```

```
type SystemGraph is Table[Node,Fanout]
```

Table and Set are two prefined generic types in FP2. Set[t] is defined only for types t which have an equality predicate. Table only requires an equality predicate for its first argument type (the index of the table) but not for the second (the values stored in the table).

"Node" and "Input" remain to be defined. The type Node can be seen as a tuple of values, the first one representing the unique identifier (of type Name) of the element, the second representing the kind of the element. The kind of the element gives the transition function of the element (by specifying the ElementType) and the time delays for the internal state and the output:

```
type Node
  cons node : Name, Kind -> Node
endtype
```

```
type Kind
  cons kd : Time, Time, ElementType -> Kind
endtype
```

The remaining data types ("Input", "Name", etc.) are some of the generic parameters of the program. The simulator will work with any instantiation of these types, for example, the instantiation given in table 1 will define a logic simulator for digital circuits. Please note, that a generic output parameter is not needed for the single output of an element.

generic parameters	meaning	specific data types for logic simulation
element type	type of the system's basic elements	AND, OR, XOR, ...
input	identifier to distinguish between the inputs of an element	string
internal state	value of the internal state of an element	not used with simple logic gates
name	identifier for an element	string
time	simulation and delay time	natural number
value	value of input or output variables of an element	boolean

Table 1: Fundamental data types and their instantiation for logic simulation

3.2.2. Specifying the basic processes

Each subtask of the pipeline algorithm is specified as a FP2 process. Then the discrete simulator is built by using the process operations described in 3.1, namely by putting all processors in parallel and connecting and hiding related connectors.

The functionality of the processes have already been roughly described in the informal presentation of the algorithm. In order to define a process, the possible orderings of communications with the environment must be considered. These possibilities are programmed by using different state names. We also have to consider which information must be retained in a given state for the process to perform its work, and this defines the arities of the state names. The computations done by the process are better executed by auxiliary functions which we introduce at first by using them in the definition of the process and which will be specified in detail later on. We shall now develop this sketch with two examples.

As a first example, let us consider the definition of GraphAccess (its job is to fetch the Destinations affected by the events). It receives the events from CurrentEventProcessor and transmits them to ConfigurationProcessor which must update the state of the source node (ConfigurationProcessor is the only process which knows the actual state of every element). For each received event, GraphAccess must also sequentially transmit to ConfigurationProcessor the fanout Destinations of the source node. Their state is updated (the input values are changing) and later on the elements represented by the nodes are evaluated.

When GraphAccess receives NullEvent along its GAin input connector (indicating that the pipeline has to be flushed!), it has nothing to store but just to pass NullEvent along its GAev output connector, which gives the rule:

$$X : GAin(NullEvent) \ GAev(NullEvent) ==> X$$

assuming that X is the initial state of the process.

Now, if it receives a non NullEvent, then it also transmits it, but must additionally get the fanout of the corresponding node and store it for future communications. We need a new state name to denote these situations where we still have to send fanout Destinations and we write the rule :

$$X : GAin(ev(n,s,t)) \ GAdest(ev(n,s,t)) ==> Y(Lookup(n,Graph))$$

Lookup is a standard function for the Table generic type. Note how the pattern term "ev(n,s,t)" in the GAin communication serves two purposes : it ensures that we receive a non-null event by filtering it out, but also it gives us access to the "node part" of the event through the variable n which can be used in the term "Lookup(n,Graph)"

When GraphAccess is in a Y state, it must sequentially send the Destinations it has stored through its GAdest connector, and return into state X when it has finished, ready for a new event to arrive :

$$Y(\{ \ \}) \qquad : \qquad \qquad ==> X$$
$$Y(\{d\} \ U \ f) : GAdest(d) ==> Y(f)$$

Together with some additional declarations for connectors, states, and variables this is the complete definition of the process GraphAccess.

Let us consider another example. The EventList process contains the buffer of events to be processed by the simulator. These events form two lists ordered w.r.t. time. Usually, EventList is in a state X(s,s') where s is the list currently processed and s' is the list of future events in which new events are inserted.

If it receives a new event along ELin with boolean flag b along ELflag, the new event is inserted :

$$X(s,s') : ELin(e) \ ELflag(b) ==> X(s,InsertEvent(e,s',b))$$

The Flag b is used as an indication of whether the event will change value of the corresponding variable or not and is used for "intelligent insertion" by InsertEvent.

If a NullEvent is received from EventScheduler we know that it has passed through the pipeline and that EventList will not receive any new event to be inserted. This is the condition for splitting the second list into two parts (if it is not empty):

X(nil,e.s) : ELin(NullEvent) ==> Y(SplitEvents(e.s))

We introduced a new Y state because SplitEvents returns a value of type Seq[Event] x Seq[Event]. We may "recover" from this by a rule without communication:

Y(s x s') : ==> X(s,s')

Now if the second list was empty, the arrival of NullEvent signals that the simulation is terminated. We just accept it and record the end of the simulation:

X(nil,nil) : ELin(NullEvent) ELend(Beep) ==> X(nil,nil)

To feed the pipeline with events EventList may always send the next event to be processed if the first list is non empty:

X(e.s,s') : ELout(e) ==> X(s,s')

If it is empty, a NullEvent is sent as a signal that the pipeline has to be flushed:

X(nil,s) : ELout(NullEvent) ==> X(nil,s).

With additional type and state declarations the definition of the process EventList is complete.

3.2.3 Defining the operations on data types

One basic idea in the programming methodology of FP2 is to describe the communication of processes by rules and the computation by auxiliary functions, i.e. operations on data types. Of course, there are fundamental operations on the generic data types, for example look up and insert for tables. In addition to these predefined functions, we use some specific operations in the specification of the basic processes, for example

- inserting an event into the event list

322

- partitioning of the event list for the execution of a time step
- updating the state of an element
- evaluating an element.

(Only the last operation is specific for a "real" simulator and is therefore not defined within the generic simulator.) There is no specific methodology for the definition of functions apart from the use of rewrite rules rather than imperative constructs. Consequently, the definition of functions is straight forward.

4. Analysis of the specification

Once we have specified the event driven simulator in FP2, it is possible to analyze it from a formal for each task point of view, but it is also possible to "run" it in the FP2 environment.
In this section, a general concept for the analysis of transition systems is developed and used to prove liveness and correct termination of the event driven simulator. We will stay on an informal level in order to present the basic ideas. A more formal treatment of this topic is given in [8]. The main purpose of this section is to show that the term rewriting aspects of FP2 considerably simplify such an analysis.

4.1 Deadlock-freeness of the simulator

The basic concepts for the analysis of transition systems are final and reachable states. Proving deadlock-freeness essentially means to prove that there are no final states or, in general, that final states are not reachable.

First we just recall basic definitions about transition systems and basic results about liveness analysis. These general concepts are adapted to the special case of FP2 where rewrite rules are used. A general treatment of transition systems can be found in [9].

4.1.1 Liveness of a transition system

A transition system is a transition relation on a set of states, which include a certain subset of initial states. A state which has no successor through the transition relation is a final state. A derivation is either an infinite sequence of consecutive (w.r.t. the transition relation) states beginning with an initial state or a finite sequence of states where the last state is a final state. The derivations are all the possible behaviours of the transition system. A state is reachable if there it is contained in a derivation, i.e. if it can be reached from an initial state through a finite number of transitions.

In FP2 a process is a transition system where states are ground terms and where the transition relation is defined by a set of transition rules, i.e. rewrite rules which rewrite the internal state of the process. We consider that a state term containing variables denotes a set of ground terms (its possible instantiations) which are the results of applying all possible ground substitutions to that state term.

A transition system is deadlock-free if it has no finite derivation, that is if no final state is reachable. This definition may be used to prove the liveness of a transition system by computing the set of final states and the set of reachable states of the transition system. In general this problem is undecidable, an important special case where it is decidable are systems with a finite set of states.

Now our problem is to determine which states of an FP2 process are final and which states are reachable.

4.1.2. Final states of an FP2 process

In FP2, a state is final if no transition rule can rewrite it (Have in mind, that a transition rule can rewrite all states matching the left-hand side of the rule). Thus we can determine whether a given state is final or not by trying to match it with the left-hand sides of the transition rules. There is no problem in checking all rules because there is always a finite number of rules, even if there is an infinite number of states. If the considered state does not match any left-hand part of the rules, then it is final.

Similarly, if a state term (i.e. possibly containing variables) matches the left-hand side of a rule then all its instantiations will match that same left-hand side, thus none of the states denoted by the state term is final. With these results, it becomes possible to deal with FP2 processes having an infinite number of states and an infinite transition relation.

As we prefer to remain at an informal level rather than being formal, let us consider, as an example, the EventList process used in our program:

```
proc EventList

states
X           : Seq[Event], Seq[Event]
Y           : Seq[Event] x Seq[Event]

rules
                                    ==> X(nil,nil)                      (init)
X(s,s')    : ELin(e) ELflag(b)      ==> X(s,InsertEvent(e,s',b))        (1)
X(e.s,s')  : ELout(e)               ==> X(s,s')                         (2)
X(nil,s)   : ELout(NullEvent)       ==> X(nil,s)                        (3)
X(nil,e.s) : ELin(NullEvent)        ==> Y(SplitEvents(e.s))             (4)
X(nil,nil) : ELin(NullEvent) ELend(Beep) ==> X(nil,nil)                (5)
Y(s x s')  :                        ==> X(s,s')                         (6)
```

It is clear that the left-hand sides of these six rules cover all possible cases for
the states of this process. Indeed EventList must be in an "X state", i.e. a state
of the form X(s,s') (with s and s' Sequences of Events) where rule 1 to 5 applies,
or in a "Y state", i.e. a state of the form Y(s x s') (with s x s' the cartesian
product of Sequences of Events) where rule 6 applies.

Matching a state term is done with respect to all possible decompositions of the
term into its several forms given by the initial algebra on state constructors.
Let us consider, as an example, the state X. The constructors of Seq are "nil" and a
binary "." operation. Rule 2 covers all X(nil,s) states and rule 3 covers all
X(e.s,s') states, so rules 2 and 3 together cover all X(s,s') states and therefore,
even if we remove rule 1, EventList has still no final states. Similarly, the
X(nil,s) states could be further split into X(nil,nil) and X(nil,e.s) states (from
rules 4 and 5) and we may remove rule 3 and still get no final state.

The problem of matching all rules is very similar to the well known problem of
deciding the completeness of equational specifications of algebraic data types,
where it also has to be proven that the equations cover all cases. The problem is
more difficult when we have to deal with equations whose left-hand sides are not
linear (i.e. they may contain several occurrences of a same variable), which is the
usual case in FP2 transition rules. An efficient algorithm to solve this problem is
presented in [4]. In the context of FP2, this algorithm may always be used to
compute the set of all final states of a process, and it is heavily used in [8].

4.1.3. Reachable states of an FP2 process

If there exist final states (i.e. states in which no rule is applicable), we may try to prove that they are not reachable. This is done by matching the final states against the right-hand sides of the rules. If a state cannot be unified with any rule then it cannot be reached through a transition. If furthermore it cannot be unified with any of the initial rules, then it is not reachable at all. Note that this is a sufficient but not necessary condition for reachability, but in our examples we shall always use this stronger condition for deciding non-reachability. Of course, we deal with general (i.e. decomposed) state terms, as we have done in 4.1.2. A state term with variables is not reachable (no one of its instantiations is reachable) if it cannot be unified with any right-hand side (including initial rules).

A problem in the determination of reachable states comes from the fact that right-hand sides of rules may contain non-constructor operations, as in rule 4 of our example. We do not want to do equational unification so we just replace these non-constructor terms with new variables. In our example, this implies to consider all Y(s x s') states as reachable states because we do not want to make any assumption about what could be the results of SplitEvents: as far as we are concerned it could be any cartesian product of Sequences of Events. Of course, this condition is again sufficient but not necessary, but anyway we accepted a stronger condition within our practical criterion for reachability.

With the results of the previous section, we obtain a very simple semi-decision procedure which can prove that a given FP2 process is deadlock-free
1. Try to verify that the left-hand sides of the rules cover all possible cases for the state of the process.
2. If some states are not covered, then try to verify that the corresponding state terms cannot be unified with any right-hand side of the rules.

This procedure can be used with the six processes composing our simulator and it is straightforward to see that none of them has any final state. Therefore they are trivially deadlock-free.

4.1.4. Liveness of a network

When we have proven that a given FP2 process is deadlock-free, this means that in any possible (i.e. reachable) state of the process there is a rule which is applicable. But that rule may contain communications and thus it is applicable only if the external environment of the process is willing to accept or transmit these specific communications. When we consider only one process, we do not make any assumption about the behaviour of its environment. Saying a process is deadlock-free means that it either may apply an internal rule (without communications) or is in a state where it accepts a communication with the environment.

If we put two deadlock-free processes in parallel and connect them, then the resulting network may have deadlocks. Indeed we cannot any more assume that the environment of one of the two processes is open to any communication because this environment is (partly) the other process.

In FP2, there is an easy solution to this problem because a network is equivalent to an elementary process. Indeed, this is the way the semantics of network expressions is given in [5]. What we "just" have to do is to compute the set of rules representing the network and to test it for liveness. In practice, it is not possible to use the definitions of [5] because this would rapidly give rise to an enormous number of rules. Informally, the solution is to compute a subset of the rules which is equivalent to the complete result from a behavioural point of view.

Doing that for the event-driven simulator, we obtain about 100 rules which have been mechanically tested for liveness with our prototype implementation of FP2 and which turned out to be deadlock-free.

4.2. Similar methods for similar results

The liveness analysis we have just done involved an ad-hoc treatment of the problem, where it appeared that the rewriting aspects of FP2 could be used to simplify the computations required by the proof. A general approach for proving temporal properties of FP2 processes would solve this liveness problem in a general framework but we have not enough space to develop it in this section. Such a general approach is presented in [8], where it is shown that the computations present in the (semi-) decision procedure of temporal logics (which are standardly used in this kind of problems) can benefit from the term rewriting aspects of FP2 to handle and represent infinite sets of states by a finite procedure.
In this section, we suggest how to solve other problems with similar ad-hoc treatments; and as all these solutions make heavy use of rewriting techniques, they are good illustrations of the point we want to stress.

4.2.1. Liveness of the pipeline

Once we know that the simulator will not deadlock, we may try to prove that it will do something that has to do with its simulation job. A possible result would be to prove that the pipeline will always be fed eventually. We may state this property informally as "Once EventList has received an event along ELin, then there will eventually be a communication along ELout". A possible way to prove this would be to build a modified network where EventList is not allowed to use its ELout connector any more (and where its initial state has been redefined to states which contain a non-empty list of events). This new EventList process is obtained from EventList simply by removing the rules of EventList which contain an ELout communication.
Now we may analyze the resulting network for liveness and if we prove that this modified network WILL ALWAYS DEADLOCK, then (remembering that the original network will never deadlock) this proves that, in the original network, at some time the ELout connector has to be used by EventList, and thus that the network satisfies the property we were interested in.

Let us note that proving that a network will always deadlock is different from proving that it may deadlock, and it cannot be simply done with the informal methods of section 4.1. because (in the case of the simulator process) it requires that some inductive reasoning be made.

4.2.2. Correct termination

Another property we may be interested in deals with "correct termination" of the simulator. We would like to prove that the simulator will stop when and only when there are no more events to be processed. By "will stop" we do not mean "will deadlock" because we have already seen that the simulator will not deadlock, we rather mean "will reach a state where the only possible action is to receive a new set of external inputs". In order to prove this property, we could describe with a finite set of terms the set of states of the whole network of processes where the event list is empty and where EventList has just sent a NullEvent value. These terms are obtained simply by looking at the rules obtained by the definition of networks following [5]: we just take all right-hand sides of rules (of the network) where EventList sends a NullEvent, then we may modify these terms in order to have the additional property that EventList contains an empty list of events (which is simply done by unification).
Once we have this set of states, we may compute the set of states which are reachable from these states. This is done by taking all right-hand sides of the rules instantiated by unifying their left-hand sides with a term of our set of states (this corresponds exactly to what is called "narrowing" in term rewriting

systems, but we apply it to a set of terms). Computing the set of states which are reachable from a given set of states corresponds to the "post" function of [9]; in FP2 it may be done by rewriting (or more precisely narrowing) and we have already used this in section 4.1.3.

It is then easy to see that the result are states where the applicable rules always involve only a communication of EventScheduler with the environment, which implies the property we are looking for: "once EventList is empty and the pipeline has been flushed, the simulator may only accept a communication which initiates a next simulation run". As before, this result is obtained because we may look at the rules of the compound network, where the interactions between the component processes have been taken into account.

[1] M. Abramovici, Y.H. Levendel, P.R. Menon: A Logic Simulation Machine, IEEE Trans. Computer-Aided Design of Integrated Circuits and Systems, 2 (1983), pp. 82-94

[2] E. Aposporidis, P. Mehring: Multilevel simulator for VLSI - an overview ESPRIT-Project 415, Subproject A, AEG, this volume

[3] D. Bert, R. Echahed: Design and implementation of a generic, logic and functional programming language, Proc. ESOP 86, Hrs. B.Robinet und R.Wilhelm, LNCS 213, (1986), pp. 119-132

[4] H. Comon: Sufficient completeness, term rewriting systems and anti-unification, Proc. 8th Int. Conf. on Automated Deduction, Oxford, July 1986 LNCS 230, pp. 128-140

[5] Ph. Jorrand, Term Rewriting as a Basis for the Design of a Functional and Parallel Programming Language. A case study : the Language FP2, Fundamentals of Artificial Intelligence, Hrs. W.Bibel und P.Jorrand, LNCS 232, (1987), pp. 221-276

[6] P. Schaefer, Ph. Schnoebelen: Specification of a pipelined event driven simulator ESPRIT-Project 415, Working Group on Semantics and Proof Techniques, Deliverable D2, 1986

[7] Ph. Schnoebelen, The semantics of concurrency in FP2 RR IMAG 558, LIFIA 30, Univ. Grenoble (1985)

[8] Ph. Schnoebelen, Rewriting techniques for the temporal analysis of communicating processes, this volume

[9] J. Sifakis: A unified approach for studying the properties of transition systems, Theoretical Computer Science, 18 (1982), pp. 227-258

A layered emulator for design evaluation of MIMD multiprocessors with shared memory

Per Stenström
Lars Philipson

Department of Computer Engineering
University of Lund
S-221 00 Lund, Sweden

Abstract

In the design and evaluation of new multiprocessor structures it is necessary to make experiments to explore the consequences of various decisions, e.g. the dynamic interaction between hardware, system software and executing parallel programs. When the target architecture is based on VLSI implementation, it is especially necessary to make the experiments prior to implementation.

An experimental system has been designed that can emulate a wide range of MIMD multiprocessor structures by implementing parts of the hardware functions by software. It consists of several layers of interacting hardware and software. The hardware for emulating the basic processing element contains two 32-bit processors, a floating point processor, 512 Kb RAM, local I/O and a special-purpose bus interface to support a set of communication primitives. A large number of such elements can be interconnected by a global bus.

Ada is one of the languages used for parallel application programs (Ada is a registered trademark of the US Government, AJPO).

1   Introduction

The aim of the present project is to study VLSI based design principles for MIMD multiprocessor computers (Flynn 1966, 1972) based on shared, virtual memory.

To test some of the initial design ideas, and early in the project get practical experience on the use of a multiprocessor computer with a parallel language, some preliminary studies were performed. These included the design of a small multiprocessor computer with a Pascal-based parallel language (Philipson et al. 1983, Ardo and Philipson, 1984).

As Ada was considered to be a potentially interesting language to implement on this type of processors, two preliminary studies of Ada implementation on multiprocessors were performed (Jones and Ardo 1982, Ardo 1984).

The new opportunities that VLSI implementation offers can be used to make new structures and mechanisms possible and efficient. Tradeoffs between hardware and software must be reexamined. An initial study along these lines focusing on virtual memory page replacement has been completed (Breidegard et al. 1984).

2 Architectures to be studied

2.1 System structure

The type of architecture to be studied has the following general characteristics (Philipson 1984): A number of processing elements (PEs) are connected to a global communication system. Each PE contains an execution unit, a part of the global memory and, if needed, some I/O. In each PE there is also the need for communication support and virtual memory mechanisms. The communication system handles processor-memory as well as processor-processor communication and I/O.

The memory is accessible from all the PEs, but physically distributed. Each PE contains an equal part of the global shared memory. By this subdividing into equal sized local memories, memory contention is reduced. This also makes it possible to reduce the amount of global communication, as memory references to the local part of the global memory can be handled locally. By applying a suitable allocation strategy with each PE, most memory accesses will be kept to local memory. One of the main considerations in the project is to find methods to reduce the need of global communication

In order to take best advantage of VLSI implementation, system partitioning becomes strategic due to the difference in speed between chip-level and board-level communication. As a quantitative base for the design considerations, the possibility of integrating one million transistors on one chip will be assumed. This will be used as base for the "budget" when it comes to partitioning the system. One of the issues in this context is the design of one or several *replicable VLSI building blocks*. Another aspect is that VLSI implementation opens possibilities for fast implementation of "smart" algorithms that can be used to reduce communication costs.

2.2 Dynamic resource management

One of the basic design principles has been to take advantage of the multiprocessor structure with distributed, shared memory by including extensive support for dynamic resource management.

The main resources to consider are *processors, storage* and *communication*. Consequently, mechanisms for demand paged *virtual memory*, dynamic *process allocation, communication cost reduction* etc should also be included.

- Dynamic storage and process allocation

- Mechanisms for dynamic allocation and reallocation based on run-time behaviour of the total system

- Run-time characteristics from previous executions of a program should also be used

- Special transactions of broadcast type for requests and acknowledgements of decentralized resource allocation

- Certain storage characteristics can be used to make allocation more efficient (write protected data and code can freely be copied etc.)

The actual allocation and reallocation mechanisms as well as the allocation policies will most likely be implemented in software. These algorithms will, however, need information about the run-time behaviour that must be collected by monitoring mechanisms in hardware.

Another type of information that can be used by these mechanisms is run-time behaviour characteristics from *previous* executions of the program.

2.3 Memory addressing

In a multiprocessor system with shared, virtual memory, the principles for memory addressing are crucial. Designing appropriate memory accessing schemes is probably the key to success for such a system.

The basic structure of the memory is an important part of the *programming model* of the multiprocessor. Languages such as Ada, containing visibility rules leading to cactus stack structures, impose specific requirements on the memory model.

We suggest a *decentralized* scheme for address decoding and translation, based on global virtual addresses and *associative address translation* (Philipson 1984). For each page of the memory, the corresponding virtual page address is stored in an accompanying associative memory word. The address translation table will then be limited to one address for each physical page of local memory. A preliminary study has shown that a solution based on precharged MOS logic (Mead and Conway 1980) can be used for this purpose and that the resulting area overhead is acceptable (Philipson 1984).

Conventional methods for address translation in computers with very large logical address space, which include several levels of address translation tables stored in (virtual) memory, address translation buffers holding the most recent translations, etc (Levy and Lipman 1982), do not work efficiently for the kind of decentralized global memory suggested here. Updating of such tables would be costly either in the communication system or in the PEs.

In summary, this means that system-wide virtual addresses will be the basis for memory access. All address decoding and translation will be done in a decentralized way, and the issuing PE will not know where the responding physical memory is located.

3 Layered architecture for an experimental system

In the design of multiprocessor systems with the kind of properties described in the previous sections there is a definite need for performing large scale experiments. The performance of the resulting system depends on an extremely complex interaction between components and mechanisms on several levels.

As there are no theories or general models to be used in such design evaluation, only experiments are left. The consequences of executing parallel programs on a number of processors with dynamic resource allocation are especially very little understood, when the dynamic properties of the programs are also taken into account.

The following are some of the design issues that must be based on experimental results.

- Evaluation of system structures
- Evaluation of mechanisms to be implemented in VLSI
- Performance studies of algorithms for dynamic resource management
- Interaction between mechanisms on different levels of the system as well as between hardware and software components

- Interaction between dynamic resource allocation mechanisms and dynamic properties of the application programs (program behaviour)

- Trade-off between hardware mechanisms and code generation, run-time system , etc, of parallel programming languages

The experience of *simulation* as a basis for such experiments has shown that not even supercomputers are suitable for handling models covering the interaction between mechanisms with time constants varying from fractions of a microsecond (memory access) to several seconds (program behaviour). Even if that had not been the case, the complexity of the necessary simulation software would most probably have been prohibitive (Stavenow and Philipson 1984). On the other hand, building dedicated prototype systems based on real hardware is not very useful because of the extremely limited room left to make experiments with different structures and hardware mechanisms.

We have found that the ideal solution is to build a system that can be used to *emulate* the range of structures and mechanisms needed to perform all relevant experiments. By emulation we mean that a basic hardware structure behaves like a *target hardware structure* partly by the execution of software on processors being parts of the hardware. The need for well defined interaction between all major hardware and software components, calls for a *layered structure* of the experimental system.

Trying to combine the favourable properties of all these approaches, we have chosen the following solution: An experimental system has been built from commercially available parts. By making appropriate use of microprocessors it is possible to implement different functional structures in software.

In this way the structure of the *emulated* PE will be defined entirely by the emulation software, within the constraints of the hardware. By adding a number of software oriented functions, the total system contains the following *nine layers* from top to bottom.

- Real-life application programs

- Parallel application language (Ada)

- Operating system

- Programming model

- "Software probes" for run-time measurements and statistics

- VLSI oriented hardware mechanisms emulated by software

- Real time kernel for system software implementation

- Board-level hardware

- Commercially available chips

The layered structure combined with the special-purpose hardware gives a special character to this approach, that differs from other recent multiprocessor emulation facilities (Arvind et al 1983, Pfister 1985).

4 Emulator hardware

4.1 System structure

An initial decision has been to map the structure of the experimental system as closely as possible to the logical system structure with processing elements and a global communication system. This is necessary if the parallelism and dynamic properties of the system are to be captured accurately enough.

A bus structure was chosen as the basis for the global communication system. This combines maximal flexibility and symmetry with simplicity and speed. It only provides one physical communication channel, but other logical communication schemes can be emulated on this basis.

Consequently, each processing element should be connected to the bus. Preferably all hardware for one processing element should be implemented on a single board. In order to make this possible, the engineering aspects had to be considered carefully.

4.2 Processing element

The main initial decision about the structure of the hardware for the processing element has been to use two microprocessors. The first of these, the execution CPU, corresponds directly to the execution unit on the logical level and the second, the communication CPU, is used to emulate the communication support and virtual memory mechanisms.

This design decision is crucial for the software structure. One of the main ideas behind the layered architecture of the system is that it should be possible to implement each layer independently from the others. Even if the execution processor will work only to a small fraction of its capacity because of the emulated environment, it would be almost impossible to mix the execution of its code with the very hardware oriented functions of the communication CPU without any interference.

The choice of what processors to use was based on a number of different criteria. For the execution CPU there is a need for large address space and basic mechanisms for virtual memory. When a page fault occurs it must be possible to make a context switch even in the middle of a machine instruction, and then return and re-execute the interrupted instruction. At the time when the decision was made, the NS32016 seemed a natural choice.

Having decided upon the execution CPU, the question for the communication CPU was mainly whether or not to use the same type of microprocessor. From the functional point of view the requirements on the communication CPU are much less. The advantage of having a single software development and support environment for both processors, however, led to the decision to use NS32016 also for the communication CPU. The resulting structure of the processing element is shown in figure 1 (Stenström 1986).

One of the main functions of the communication CPU is to emulate address translation mechanisms. Every memory reference made by the execution CPU must pass to the communication CPU to be processed according to a scheme that is part of the hardware emulation software. In order to perform this, and to make the interface between the two CPU:s extremely clear, the address, control and data bus of the execution CPU are connected to registers, which can be read by the communication CPU.

There is a separate mechanism that stops the execution CPU whenever it performs a memory reference. The execution CPU is reactivated when the communication CPU has handled the memory reference.

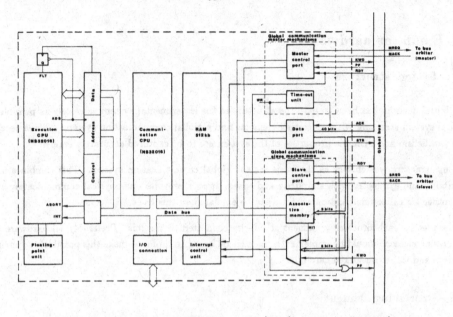

Figure 1: Hardware structure of the processing unit (from Stenström 1986)

The communication CPU thus completely controls the entire environment of the execution CPU. It can even cause interrupt and abort on the execution CPU.

To be able to perform floating point operations efficiently, a floating-point unit is included. As this will exclusively be used in application programs (executing on the execution CPU) it is connected to the execution CPU.

4.3 Memory and I/O

The memory is implemented as a single linear memory. The total amount of physical memory in each PE is 512 Kb RAM. This is also used for emulation of the associative memory of the virtual address translation 1. chanism and for the communication CPU software.

In order to keep all PEs identical there will not be any dedicated PEs for I/O. All PEs contain I/O-connections general enough to support a wide range of I/O-controllers. The corresponding I/O operations will be performed by the software in the communication CPU as parts of the operating system level. As the first example of this, a disk memory subsystem has been successfully integrated into the emulation environment.

4.4 Engineering aspects

In the design of the PE board, we have tried to maintain a high level of engineering ambition. One reason for this was the experience from several earlier projects of similar a kind which suffered from too little memory and I/O, too little flexibility or too little computing power. Another reason was the importance of keeping all the hardware for one PE on a single PC board. Part of this design was done during an initial study of the hardware for the processing element (Bergquist 1984).

The following are the most important engineering aspects of the experimental processor board.

- Powerful microprocessor technology using the NS32000 family with floating point processor

- 512 Kb RAM with ECC, based on 256 K DRAM chips

- Extensive use of programmable logic (PAL and PLA) in order to reduce the number of chips

- Multi-layer PC board in order to further reduce the size

- Two serial lines and three 8-bit parallel ports for I/O and diagnostics

- PROM-based bootstrap, host computer communication, downloading software etc

- LEDs indicating hardware and software status

Extensive use of *programmable logic* (PAL and PLA) together with commercially available high-density memory circuits resulted in smaller dimensions of the board.

The new style of using PAL and PLA has many advantages, besides higher circuit density. The hardware can be modified even after PC-board fabrication, which in some cases has shown to be of great importance. The use of programmable logic has been supported by special design tools. An optimizing finite-state machine compiler developed at our department, was used. Based on a state-transition graph, a series of synthesis and optimization steps are performed, including automatic state assignment. It would not have been possible to implement such complex state machines if this kind of tool had not been available.

The final board is shown in figure 2. The size is 233x250 mm and it is implemented as a six-layer PC board with power and ground occupying two of the layers. There are two 96-pin edge connectors on the rear side of the board. One contains the global bus and the other contains the I/O connections and the internal bus. The internal bus is also made available to make it possible to connect I/O controllers with DMA, e.g. disk controllers.

Figure 2: The final PE board containing two NS32016 CPUs, a floating point processor, 512 Kb RAM with ECC, 32 Kb EPROM, timer, interrupt controller, two serial lines, 32 parallel lines and the global bus control logic. In total the board contains more than 5 million MOS transistors.

5   Communication mechanisms

The layered structure of the system permits implementation of a wide range of global communication mechanisms. This will make it possible to make experiments with multiprocessor structures with different programming models and different VLSI based support mechanisms.

On the PE board this is reflected by a similarly layered communication structure, cf figure 3. The programming model may well permit a program executing on the execution CPU in one PE to access memory which is physically located in another PE.

The actual memory reference will, however, be handled by software in the communication CPU emulating parts of the hardware. In order to support the emulation and make it more efficient, each PE board contains a *bus interface* with a number of hardware mechanisms, cf figure 1. In figure 3 the different virtual communication channels associated with a global memory reference are shown.

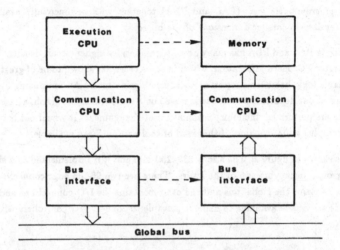

Figure 3: Communication structure for a global memory reference.

In every global bus transaction there is always one PE acting as the *master* with one or more PEs as *slaves*. The master is defined to be the PE which initiates the transaction and the other PEs directly involved in the transaction are the slaves. The global bus interface is accordingly divided into two parts, cf figure 1.

5.1   Bus interface

The bus interface consists of three parts: the first containing the control mechanisms needed when the PE is acting as master, the second one with the corresponding slave mechanisms, and the third, a common part for the data in both directions (cf figure 1). We will describe the operation of the bus interface by giving examples of some typical bus transactions.

By writing to a certain address in the master control port, a bus request is issued to a central arbitration unit. A bus acknowledge signal is sent in the opposite direction through the same port when the bus is available.

The bus contains 40 data bits and a small number of explicit control signals handled directly by the bus interface. The control signals needed for the emulated mechanisms are transmitted as data on the bus interface level. When the fifth byte is written to the data port the bus interface generates a strobe signal on the bus, indicating that valid data is now present.

In this situation all the other PEs are acting as potential slaves. Nine of the data lines on the bus are connected to an associative memory in each PE. This nine-bit vector is called a *key-word*. The bus interface will interrupt the communication CPU if the key-word on the bus matches any of the words stored in the associative memory. In this way many of the PEs will not be affected at all by a bus transaction that does not concern them. For certain addressing schemes this mechanism can be used to reduce the overhead caused by the address translation emulation. There is a specific control line by which the master can decide if this mechanism should be active during a certain bus cycle.

The master then waits for one of the following four possible conditions to occur: acknowledgement, page fault, retry or time-out. Retry means that a page is not resident but requested so that it will be accessible after a while. The first three conditions are detected by means of dedicated control signals that are common for each slave. Page fault is for example activated when every slave activates it (i.e. wired-AND). Retry is detected analogously. The time-out unit detects a lost answer within a preprogrammed time-out interval and will in this case interrupt the communication CPU.

The address might consist of several bus words sent to the slave. The bus interface of course provides also a means of sending a bus word in the opposite direction. A read operation might thus consist of an address sent from the master to the slave and the referenced datum as a bus word sent from the slave to the master. At the end of the bus cycle the master releases the bus by clearing the bus request signal.

One of the mechanisms in the bus interface has been designed specifically to support broadcast operations. This regards answers from every slave concerned in the broadcast operation. The slaves will use an additional bus arbitration unit, which selects one slave at a time for sending a reply, in order to carry out the operation within the same bus transaction.

5.2 Emulation of memory model and memory management

In order to implement virtual memory management a basic set of program modules will be needed on the communication CPU. We will refer to these as *emulation modules*. Figure 4 shows such a structure and the hardware mechanisms that interact with the emulated environment. The emulation modules depicted in the figure can be regarded as a basic structure in that they will be common to all computer structures that will be investigated in our project.

The main task of the communication CPU is to handle all memory references issued by the execution CPU (master mechanisms). Another task is to handle all memory references generated on other PEs incoming from the global bus (slave mechanisms).

The execution CPU interacts with the communication CPU and its software via registers. The mechanisms that handles local references will thus first decode the status signals in order to determine the type of reference. This will be done in a related emulation module called *Execution CPU decode*.

The address will then be checked by the emulation module *Page address translation*. The result from the address check could be that the referenced page is not present (i.e. a miss in the local memory), which leads to a *global memory operation*. This is taken care of by the emulation module *Master bus communication*.

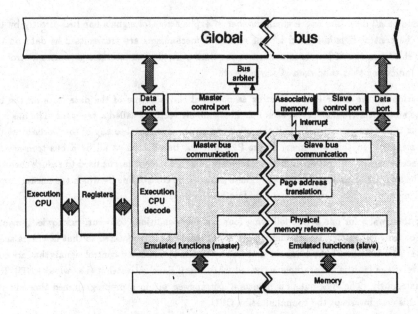

Figure 4: Basic structure of emulation modules involved in memory references

When a global memory operation is initiated, every processing element will (according to the decentralized address translation scheme) check the address, and if a hit has occurred carry it out. A miss means that either the page is not resident and has not been requested from the secondary storage (page fault) or that the page is not present but is already requested (retry).

Global references in the emulated environment will be handled by *Slave bus communication*. The address check and translation also in this case will be handled by the same emulation module that was used in the case of locally generated references.

The control flow concerned in a global memory operation is shown in figure 5. Before a bus transaction can take place, the master must gain control of the global bus (see circle 1 in figure 5).

When the bus is granted, part of the entire address is written on the bus (see circle 2). Those PEs that are interrupted due to hit in the associative memory will check the remaining bits of the bus word by means of the page address translation module. The result of the check (hit, retry or page fault) will be reported back to the master (see circle 3).

The next word to be transferred contains the remaining address bits (i.e. the page offset) and data in case of a write operation (see circle 4). In case of a read operation an additional bus word, containing the datum, must be sent from the slave to the master (see circle 5).

6 Performance evaluation

The possibility of emulation by means of software on the communication CPU enables us to build models of hardware mechanisms. The price of emulation is however paid by a considerable reduction in execution speed for the execution CPU.

339

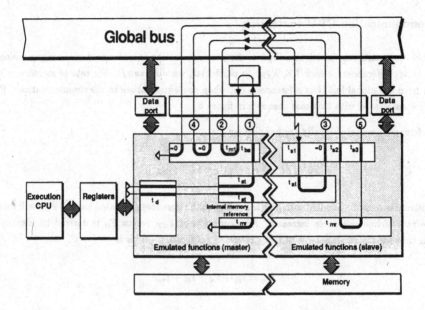

Figure 5: Control flow for memory operations

On the other hand we have the global bus with its simplicity. The price for this, however, is limited capacity compared to other interconnection structures. In order to get an idea of the limitations an initial performance evaluation of the experimental system has taken place.

The average execution time for each emulation module is denoted with a parameter, t_x, in figure 5. All parameters except t_{at} have been measured on an implementation made on the experimental system. They are listed in table 1 below.

Parameter	Measured value μs
Execution CPU decode, t_d	12
Physical memory reference, t_{mr}	1
First bus word reception, t_{s1}	34
Second bus word reception, t_{s2}	36
Third bus word reply, t_{s3}	24
Bus arbitration, t_{ba}	4
Address write operation, t_{m1}	3

Table 1: Measured average execution time for emulation modules according to figure 5

The parameters were measured in the following way. t_d and t_{mr} were measured on a program without address translation ($t_{at} = 0$). A strictly optimized bus protocol for global references according to the scheme given in figure 5 was developed in order to measure the other parameters.

For simplicity, it is assumed that the execution time for address translation, t_{at}, is independent of the result (i.e. hit, page fault or retry).

6.1 Communication CPU contention

We will use the emulation model described in the previous section in order to derive an expression of the rate of memory references for each PE, F_{EP}. In particular, we will examine the rate of memory references, incoming from the global bus (bus references), F_B, when contention arises in the communication CPU. The control flow associated with this case is shown in figure 5.

If only references generated locally are handled we get

$$F_{EP} = 1/(t_d + t_{at} + t_{mr})$$

As bus references must be handled with higher priority than references generated locally, F_{EP} will be reduced when the rate of bus references increases. An expression of F_{EP} versus F_B is derived by identifying the execution time for the management of a bus reference (cf figure 5). This is

$$t_{gw} = t_{s1} + t_{at} + t_{s2} + t_{mr}$$

in the case of a write operation ($t_{s3} = 0$) and

$$t_{gr} = t_{s1} + t_{at} + t_{s2} + t_{mr} + t_{s3}$$

in the case of a global read operation. This will reduce the entire rate of memory references according to

$$F_{EP} = \frac{1 - F_B(t_{s1} + t_{at} + t_{s2} + t_{mr})}{t_d + t_{at} + t_{mr}} \tag{1}$$

in case of a global write operation. The maximum value of F_{EP} corresponds to $F_B = t_{at} = 0$, which results in $F_{EP} = 77,000$ memory references/second (ref/s). The maximum value of F_B, before communication CPU contention, is in case of a read operation $F_B = 14,000$ ref/s and $F_B = 11,000$ ref/s in case of a bus write operation. Figure 6 shows F_{EP} versus F_B.

6.2 Bus contention

The next question is whether a rate such as $F_B \geq 11,000$ ref/s can be expected or not. Of course F_B is not unrelated to F_{EP}. In fact a reduction of F_{EP} will reduce F_B. In this section we will examine at what rate of memory references the bus contends.

Some of the locally generated references will not correspond to physical locations within the PE. In this case a miss in the page address translation will initiate a bus reference.

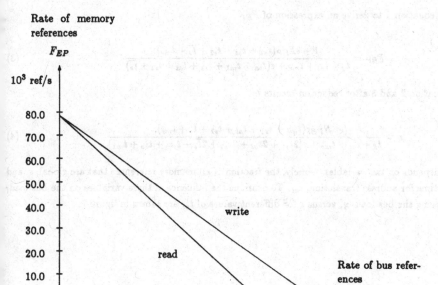

Figure 6: The diagram shows how the rate of memory references for each PE (F_{EP}) depends on the load of the communication CPU caused by management of memory references incoming from the global bus (F_B)

To derive an expression of the bus load, we need to know the rate of bus references and the time that every bus reference keeps the bus busy. The latter can easily be identified from figure 5 as $t_{m1} + t_{s1} + t_{at} + t_{s2} + \overline{t_s} + t_{mr}$, where $\overline{t_s}$ will be defined below. We also make the following assumptions.

- The rate of bus references that is generated by every PE is assumed to be proportional to the rate of memory references through $F_B = \epsilon F_{EP}$.

- Uniform distribution of global memory references over the PEs. This means that every PE will have to handle the same rate of bus references as it generates.

- The influence of bus operations other than memory read and write are neglected (for example broadcast operations).

- Equal amount of read and write operations. We thus define $\overline{t_s} = t_{s3}/2$.

- The system is dimensioned for $N_{PE} = 40$ PEs.

- Only the PE involved in the operation is interrupted, which means that the associative memory in the bus interface will perfectly filter only those bus references addressed to the PE.

The assumptions above lead to

$$\eta = N_{PE}\epsilon F_{EP}(t_{m1} + t_{s1} + t_{at} + t_{s2} + \overline{t_s} + t_{mr}) \qquad (2)$$

We now recall equation 1 to derive an expression of F_{EP}

$$F_{EP} = \frac{1 - \epsilon F_{EP}(t_{s1} + t_{at} + t_{s2} + \overline{t_s} + t_{mr})}{t_d + t_{at} + t_{mr} + \epsilon(t_{ba} + t_{m1} + t_{s1} + t_{at} + t_{s2} + \overline{t_s})} \quad (3)$$

Combining equation 2 and 3 after reduction results in

$$\eta = \frac{N_{PE}\epsilon(t_{m1} + t_{s1} + t_{at} + t_{s2} + \overline{t_s} + t_{mr})}{t_d + t_{at} + t_{mr} + \epsilon(2t_{s1} + 2t_{at} + 2t_{s2} + 2\overline{t_s} + t_{mr} + t_{ba} + t_{m1})} \quad (4)$$

The bus load depends on two variables, namely, the fraction of all memory references that are global, ϵ, and the execution time for address translation, t_{at}. To examine the influence of these variables on the bus load, a diagram showing the bus load, η, versus ϵ for different values of t_{at} are shown in figure 7.

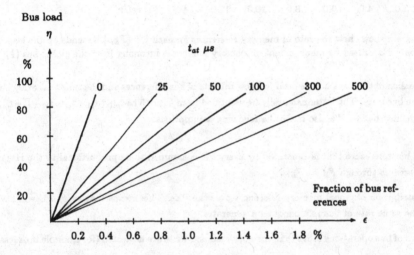

Figure 7: Bus load (η) versus fraction of bus references (ϵ) for different execution times of the page address translation algorithm (t_{at}).

Figure 7 shows that the bus will be saturated for unacceptable low values ϵ ($\epsilon > 1$ %). It is obvious that the rate of locally generated memory references has to be limited to avoid bus saturation.

For the kind of structures that our future work will be based on, we require that irregularity effects on the bus will not be introduced until $\epsilon \geq 10$ % (e.g. $\epsilon = 50$ %). Some experiments with address translation implementations have shown that $t_{at} = 100$ μs seems a realistical value. In this case the maximum rate of memory references will be $F_{EP} \approx 700$ ref/s according to equation 4.

7 Conclusion

We have shown that our experimental system constitutes a flexible tool for evaluation of VLSI based design principles for MIMD multiprocessors with shared memory with reasonable performance (700 memory references/PE/second).

The performance evaluation shows that the bus is the limiting resource, and that the rate of memory references has to be limited. The capacity of the communication CPU that is not used for emulation, however, will be utilized by operating system functions that logically is to execute on the execution CPU but due to performance will be migrated to the communication CPU.

A 38-processor version of the emulation system has been built. It is housed in a 19 inch cabinet together with a 80 Mb disk mainly for paging and a dedicated MicroVAX II for software development. The code is downloaded to the experimental system by means of a parallel communication channel.

For emulation of mechanisms according to figure 4, a real-time kernel for the communication CPU has been developed. Software development is based on Pascal and assembly language with symbolic debugging facilities. Some of the basic communication CPU mechanisms, such as handling the low level bus protocol, are included in the kernel. Other mechanisms can be added as user defined processes, coded in Pascal or assembly language. A common I/O system capable of handling terminal communication and a file system on the disk has been developed and successfully integrated with the emulation mechanisms of the communication CPU as a student project (Petersson 1987). It will be used as a basis for I/O operations on all the communication CPUs as well as on the application program level.

The first set of experiments that will be carried out on the system will be devoted to virtual memory and process management. For that purpose a kernel for the execution CPU has been developed. It can handle a set of processes distributed over several processing elements with static memory allocation in a system wide virtual address space. The application programs will be developed in Pascal and assembly code using the same tools as for the communication CPU.

In order to implement Ada on the experimental system, a retargetable Ada system has been acquired (Ardo and Philipson 1984). Based on that, an initial implementation of full Ada on the PE board level has been completed (Ardo 1987). This includes a time-sliced real-time kernel, a rudimentary operating system, a run-time system, a code generator and a linker. Work is now being done to define the support system so that Ada can be run on the execution CPU, and thus enable experiments on emulated structures.

8 Acknowledgements

The authors are indebted to the following persons who have implemented all the necessary software: Mats Brorsson, Peter Molin, Roland Petersson, Anders Svensson (system software), Anders Ardö, Kjell Persson, Joachim Roos and Peter Thulin (Ada). This research was sponsored by the Swedish National Board for Technical Development (STU) under contract numbers 80-3962, 83-3647 and 85-3899.

9 References

A. Ardo: "Experimental implementation of an Ada tasking runtime system on the multiprocessor computer Cm*", Proc Washington Ada Symp, March 1984.

A. Ardo and L. Philipson: "Implementation of a Pascal based parallel language on a multiprocessor computer", Software Pract and Exper, Vol 14(7), 643-657, 1984.

A. Ardo, L. Philipson: "Evaluation of commercially available retargetable and rehostable Ada systems", Proc 3rd Ada Europe/Ada TEC Conf, June 1984.

A. Ardo: "Experience acquiring and retargeting a portable Ada compiler", accepted for publ in Software Pract and Exper, 1987.

Arvind, M. L. Dertouzos and R. A. Iannucci: "A multiprocessor emulation facility", Laboratory for Computer Science, MIT (MIT/LCS/TR-302), 1983

F. Bergquist: "Prototype design of a processor module for an experimental multiprocessor computer", Technical report, Dep of Computer Engineering, University of Lund, April 1984.

B. Breidegard, B. Nilsson and L. Philipson: "VLSI implementation of a virtual memory paging algorithm", VLSI: Algorithms and Architectures, International workshop on parallel computing and VLSI, Amalfi, Italy, May 23-25, North-Holand, 1984.

M. Flynn: "Very High-Speed Computing Systems", Proceedings of the IEEE, vol. 54, No 12, pp. 1901-1909, December 1966.

M. Flynn: "Some Computer Organizations and Their Effectiveness", IEEE Trans. on Computers, Vol. C-21, No 9, pp. 948-960, September 1972.

A. Jones and A. Ardo: "Comparative Efficiency of Different Implementations of the Ada Rendezvous", Proceedings of the AdaTEC conference on Ada, October 1982, pp. 212-223.

H. M. Levy, P. H. Lipman: "Virtual Memory Management in the VAX/VMS Operating System", Computer, March, pp. 35-41, 1982.

C. A. Mead, L. Conway: "Introduction to VLSI Systems", Addison-Wesley 1980.

R. Petersson: "Implementation of an I/O-system in a multiprocessor environment", Technical Report, Dep of Computer Engineering, University of Lund, 1987.

G. Pfister: "An introduction to the IBM Research Parallel Processor Prototype (RP3)", Proc IEEE Int Conf on Comput Design, 114, 1985.

L. Philipson, B. Nilsson and B. Breidegard: "A communication structure for a multiprocessor computer with distributed global memory", Proc 10th Int Conf on Comput Arch, 334-340, 1983.

L. Philipson: VLSI based design principles for MIMD multiprocessor computers with distributed memory management. Proc of The 11th Annual Int Symp on Comp Arch, 319-327, 1984.

D. P. Siewiorek, G. B. Bell, A. Newell: "Computer structures: Principles and examples", McGraw-Hill, 1982

B. Stavenow, L. Philipson: "Performance simulation of a multiprocessor computer with virtual memory", Technical report, Dept. of Computer Engineering, University of Lund, 1984.

P. Stenström: "MUMS, Processing Element, Hardware Design", Technical report, Dept. of Computer Engineering, University of Lund, 1986.

The Alliant FX/Series:
A Language Driven Architecture for Parallel Processing
of Dusty Deck Fortran

Jack A. Test

Mat Myszewski

Richard C. Swift

Alliant Computer Systems Corporation
1 Monarch Drive
Littleton, Mass. 01460

Abstract

The Alliant FX/Series™ multiprocessor mini-supercomputers represent a major advance in commercial computing by bringing the benefits of vectorization and parallelism transparently to user applications. By providing compiler support for the automatic discovery of "concurrency" in existing Fortran programs, the FX/Series is often able to achieve time-to-solution speedups proportional to the number of processors applied to the problem. To achieve this computational performance advantage, the instruction set architecture supports scalar, floating point, vector, and concurrency instructions. The hardware architecture and operating system were designed and optimized to deliver both high throughput and computational performance to user programs.

Introduction

Alliant Computer Systems Corporation designs and manufactures high-performance, multiprocessor computer systems designed primarily for use in scientific and engineering applications. The machine architecture of these systems provides a tightly-coupled environment consisting of interactive processors (IPs) and computational-elements (CEs) with a coherent global memory system. Every IP and CE is a fully functional, independent processor. CEs support vector and floating point operations and can, through concurrency operations, participate together as a computational-complex (CE–Complex) in the execution of a single application.

FX/Series	Trademark of Alliant Computer Systems Corp.
FX/Fortran	Trademark of Alliant Computer Systems Corp.
Concentrix	Trademark of Alliant Computer Systems Corp.
UNIX	Trademark of Bell Laboratories

The FX/Fortran™ compiler is a state-of-the-art vectorizing and globally optimizing Fortran compiler that can also discover and exploit loop–level parallelism, known as Alliant concurrency, in existing codes. With this technology, the system can often realize application code speedups, without any reprogramming, proportional to the number of CEs applied. This automatic parallelization of Fortran "dusty-decks" can be extended with user directives to encompass concurrently called subroutines and loop transformations which cannot be easily detected automatically.

The Concentrix™ operating system is an enhanced and extended version of 4.2BSD Unix™ that supports multiple processors applied concurrently to separate applications as well as to single applications. This ability allows the architecture to achieve excellent interactive response while also executing computationally intensive applications.

This paper provides an overview of the FX/Series computer systems from both a hardware and software viewpoint. The hardware and instruction-set architecture is described, the major features of FX/Fortran and Concentrix are discussed, and the paper concludes with some performance results.

Machine Architecture

The Alliant computer architecture supports up to 20 processors working in parallel and connected to a coherent global physical memory. The processors fall into two classes: IPs and CEs. The IPs provide device support and non-compute-intensive user application support while the CEs provide high-performance computational power. Each CE can be dynamically "attached" to or "detached" from the concurrency control bus. The collection of "attached" CEs is known as the CE-Complex. A diagram of the full architecture is shown in Figure 1.

At the center of the architecture is the global physical memory system. The distributed memory bus (DMB) is a high speed, synchronous access bus that consists of two 72-bit-wide data paths (64 bits of data plus eight bits for single-bit error detection and correction and double-bit error detection), a 28-bit address bus, and a control bus. The data buses are bidirectional and driven by the memory and cache modules.

The memory module (MM) is field expandable in eight increments and supports the 256-Mb physical address space provided by the DMB. Four-way interleaving on each memory module permits any module to supply the full DMB bandwidth of 188 MB per second for sequential read accesses, and 80% of the bandwidth, or 150 MB per second, for sequential write accesses. Memory modules also monitor and test the parity of the address bus and can be dynamically reconfigured to bypass hard component failures.

The memory cache system is responsible for maintaining a coherent view of global physical memory on both IPs and CEs. There are two cache module types: the com-

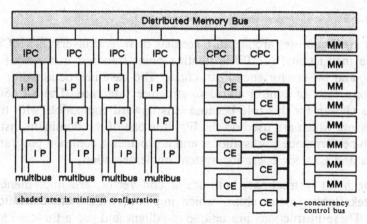

Figure 1: Alliant FX/8 System Architecture

utational processor cache (CPC) and the interactive processor cache (IPC). Each CPC is a two-way interleaved module that can interface up to four CEs to the DMB. When combined to support a full eight-CE complex, two CPCs provide a four-way interleaved 512Kb cache with a maximum bandwidth of 376Mb per second. Each IPC can interface up to three IPs to the DMB. When combined to support a full 12-IP configuration, four IPCs provide a 128Kb cache with maximum bandwidth of 188Mb per second.

The interactive processor module is a Multibus card containing a Motorola microprocessor, a virtual memory address translation unit, an I/O map, local parity-protected RAM, power-up EPROMs, and two serial ports. The IP interfaces to the global memory system via the IPC and to peripheral devices via the Multibus (IEEE 796 compatible). Direct memory access anywhere within the physical address space, including cross page transfers, is available to peripheral devices via the IPs I/O map.

The computational element is a Motorola 68020 instruction set compatible, microprogrammed, pipelined processor with integrated floating point, vector, and concurrency instruction sets. Each CE has a pipelined instruction unit, a pipelined floating point and vector unit, and a concurrency-control unit. The CE is designed to support up to five instructions in different execution stages simultaneously and can execute the industry standard Whetstone benchmark at 4800 KWhetstones single precision (32-bit) and 4100 KWhetstones double precision (64-bit). In vector mode, each CE executes floating point instructions at a peak rate of 11.8 million floating point operations per second (MFLOPs) for both single and double precision. A complex of eight CEs can approach a peak performance rate equal to eight times the performance of one CE.

Instruction Set

The Alliant instruction set architecture consists of several layers: (1) MC68020 compatible base instructions, (2) IEEE floating point standard instructions, (3) vector instructions, and (4) concurrency instructions. The base instructions implement integer operations, flow of control and data structure reference. The MC68020 instruction set was chosen for this role because it is upward compatible with the Motorola microprocessors which are used on the IPs, it is one of the dominant instruction sets used in high-performance workstations, and it provides a common programming base between IPs and CEs for operating system implementation.

The floating point instructions, both scalar and vector, are implemented with the 64-bit Weitek floating point chips, which implement IEEE standard floating point operations. These instructions are unique to Alliant and use a three address instruction format, where the destination and one of the sources are registers and the second source may either be a register or an operand in memory. This three address instruction format makes it easier for the compiler to generate tight code. The usual add, subtract, multiply, and divide are provided as well as square root, log, exp, sin, cos, and arctan. The divide and square root instructions are implemented in Alliant developed gate arrays.

The vector instructions apply a single operation to a set of data elements in memory or to one of eight vector registers. Each vector register contains 32 elements which can be 32-bit integers or 32- or 64-bit floating point numbers. Three data registers control vector operations:

> **Vector Length**: the number of elements to be processed by a vector instruction. If the length exceeds 32, a maximum of 32 elements are processed at one time. A special instruction, vcnt32, decrements this register by 32 and branches if the result is greater than zero. This makes it easy to construct loops that process vectors of arbitrary length.

> **Vector Increment**: the spacing between elements in a vector stored in memory (stride). This makes it as easy to access arrays by row as by column.

> **Vector mask**: each bit of this register specifies whether the corresponding element is to be operated on or skipped. This makes it easy to process conditional data.

In addition to a full complement of element-by-element integer, logical, shift, and floating point operations, the vector instruction set implements an extensive set of data editing operations. Data can be compressed or expanded either to or from a vector register, data can be selected from either of two vectors based on the bits of a mask value either element by element or by merging, and given a vector of indices, a vector can be gathered (loaded) from or scattered (stored) to a vector whose elements are at arbitrary locations. This is useful for applications that implement sparse data structures with index vectors. There is also a set of vector reduction instructions hat combine the elements of a vector into a single value: max, min, sum, product, polynomial, dot product, as well as logical operations.

The Cray-1 introduced the concept of vector chaining; that is, if one vector instruction is to use the result of a preceding instruction, it need only wait until the first result element is available to begin the second operation. This was implemented in hardware on that machine. The CE provides this capability by vector instructions that combine up to two vector operations with a vector memory reference. The "chaining" opportunity is detected at compile time and the combined instruction is used. The triadic (three operand) vector instructions combine a vector memory reference, a floating point multiply, and a floating point add or subtract.

The most important and unique class of Alliant instructions initiate and control concurrency, that is, the cooperation of several CEs on a single program. A single "concurrency-start" instruction can be used to begin a loop where each CE executes a different iteration. A "concurrency-repeat" instruction is used at the bottom of the loop to begin another iteration. When there are no more iterations, one of the CEs continues while the others become idle. Additional instructions support preemptive loop exit, control the synchronization that is necessary when data produced in one CE is to be used by another, and support the application of both vectors and concurrency to a single loop by splitting the vector into as many pieces as there are CEs.

Figure 2 illustrates the use of Alliant concurrency within a six iteration loop containing a data dependency. In the example, CE0 starts concurrency for the DO-loop and each CE immediately picks up a unique iteration to perform. As each CE completes an iteration it receives another iteration to perform until the loop limit is reached. The data dependency is handled through "concurrency-synchronization" instructions that coordinate CEs needing the value of a particular data item in order to proceed with a computation.

FX/Fortran Compiler

Automatic transformation of programs for vector and parallel execution on is achieved through the FX/Fortran compiler. During compilation, FX/Fortran automatically detects the potential for vector and parallel processing in standard Fortran programs and generates instructions that use the vectorization and concurrency features of the Alliant architecture. The compiler implements the ANSI Fortran-77[1] language standard, contains many of the proposed Fortran-8X[2] extensions, and performs scalar, vector, and concurrent optimizations.

Scalar optimizations performed by the compiler that are global and machine independent include common subexpression elimination, constant value propagation and folding, induction variable processing, invariant code motion, global register allocation, and dead code elimination. Scalar optimizations that are local and machine dependent include "peephole" code restructuring and instruction pipeline scheduling.

350

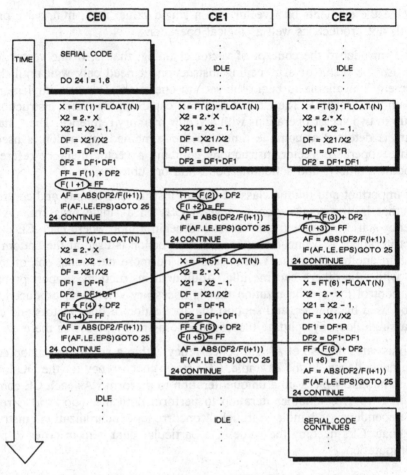

Figure 2: Concurrent Processing With Data Dependencies

Vector optimizations involve recognizing loop patterns with regular data references. Fortran arrays, for example, can be manipulated 32 elements at a time in vector mod, as compared with one element at a time in scalar mode. For loops that do not vectorize naturally, FX/Fortran utilizes techniques such as loop unrolling, loop rerolling, splitting loops, and merging loops in order to achieve partial vectorization.

Concurrent optimizations performed by the compiler utilize the CE–Complex in order to achieve linear speed improvements with the number of CEs participating. Any loop which can be vectorized can also be made concurrent by the compiler. Moreover, loops which cannot be vectorized, or do not improve much when vectorized, can often benefit from concurrency alone. Thus, minimally vectorizable loops that would run slowly on a conventional vector architecture can achieve speedups via concurrency on the FX/Series.

The compiler performs scalar, vector, and concurrent optimizations on the programs t compiles without requiring user intervention or reprogramming. The combination of these optimizations is typically more powerful than any single one. For example, register allocation can be applied in the presence of both vector and concurrent oops.

FX/Fortran utilizes three major hardware operational modes: scalar-concurrent, vector-concurrent, and concurrent-outer–vector-inner. In scalar-concurrent mode, each CE in the CE–Complex executes available loop iterations until the loop terminates. Where necessary, concurrency synchronizations are used to insure that the results of the concurrent loop are identical to the results of the scalar loop. Vector-concurrent mode is similar to scalar-concurrent except that each CE operates on up to 32 iterations of a loop using its vector hardware. With eight CEs simultaneously operating on a full vector of 32 elements, a vector length of up to 256 elements can be achieved in this mode. Concurrent-outer–vector-inner mode is used by the compiler in nested loops where the inner loop can be vectorized and the outer loop made concurrent. This mode of operation makes extremely efficient use of the Alliant architecture because it maps higher level parallelism inherent in a program directly onto the hardware.

At compile time, the programmer can control the optimization process at the program, subprogram, and loop levels, and recieves feedback on the optimizations the compiler performs. Messages notify the user of conditions that affect optimization, and summarize the degree of optimization attained for each routine. Optimization can then be modified by the programmer with directives that can be inserted as comments in the source code. For example, in run–time situations where vector lengths are very short, optimization of a loop could degrade performance. In this case, a directive could be used to suppress optimization. Directives also can be used to enable optimizations. For example, in a loop that contains an external subroutine or function call reference that inhibits optimization, the programmer can provide a "concurrent–call" directive that enables optimization by certifying that the subroutine or function call can be executed concurrently.

In general, the FX/Series machines achieve their best performance from loops that can be executed in both concurrent and vector modes. To this end, the compiler attempts to optimize both single loops and nested loops. Concurrent execution is also utilized for loops that cannot be effectively vectorized. Because concurrency can support loops containing data dependencies and other conditions that inhibit vector execution, the loop transformation performance of FX/Fortran exceeds the performance of compilers limited to vectorization alone, and this is one of its principal strengths.

Concentrix Operating System

Management of the hardware resources is the responsibility of the Concentrix Operating System which is an enhanced and extended version of 4.2BSD UNIX. Among the principal features of Concentrix are: multiple computing resource scheduling, mapped file I/O, demand-paged copy-on-write virtual memory, multiprocessing and multitasking, shared user memory, fast file system performance, and real-time support.

Concentrix maintains queues of ready-to-run jobs for three separate classes of computing resources: IPs, detached CEs, and the CE-Complex. Scheduling in Concentrix is centered around this computing resource classification, each IP and detached CE is scheduled independently while the CEs in the CE-Complex are scheduled as a unit. As each process is created, the image executed determines the type of computing resource on which the process can be scheduled. In particular, images that use vectorization and concurrency are schedulable only on CEs, other images are schedulable on IPs or CEs. At any given moment, every computing resource in the Alliant system is executing a different process. When a computing resource has no real work to do, it runs an "idle" system process.

At system boot time, Concentrix provides the ability to specify which CEs are to be members of the CE–Complex and which CEs are to always be scheduled independently. Moreover, under user–tunable scheduler control, the CEs comprising the CE-Complex can be dynamically "exploded" into independent detached CEs and "coalesced" back into CE-Complex form as the system is running. This ability balances the need for high system throughput with high speed single application execution.

In Concentrix, multiprocessing on detached CEs takes place in parallel with activity on the CE-Complex and IPs. In addition, the operating system supports multitasking which refers to the process of dividing a program into tasks that can be executed simultaneously on separate processors. Multitasking can be used to achieve high performance in applications where parallelism matches natural problem boundaries. Two forms of multitasking are provided by the Alliant system: process-level tasking and concurrent-loop-level tasking. Process-level tasking utilizes the "forking" properties of Unix to create separate processes that can be scheduled simultaneously on independent processors. In this form, tasks can synchronize and communicate via several mechanisms: advisory lock files, socket based interprocess communication, and by shared memory. Concurrent-loop-level tasking, in contrast, utilizes the CEs in the CE-Complex to carry out independent tasks all within a single Unix process environment.

Under Concentrix, every process is provided with a two-gigabyte demand-paged virtual address space. Copy-on-write semantics are used by the virtual memory system to support shared code and data between processes and for fast process creation. In addition, the operating system allows independent processes to share memory and utilize memory mapped files. Mapped file I/O is transparently available through FX/ Fortran for both sequential and random files, for example. For high–performance I/O, Concentrix provides the ability to "stripe" file systems across multiple disks. This capability supports both larger (multiple disk) file systems as well as multiple concurrent disk transfers.

To provide support for real-time applications, the Concentrix scheduler supports the assignment of dedicated computing resources to identified user processes. These processes can then use shared memory for synchronization and communication avoiding the use of Concentrix kernel services and assuring deterministic response.

In addition to those capabilities mentioned above, Concentrix supports a broad range of performance enhancements from high-bandwidth paging and swapping I/O to sophisticated network support software. As a final note, it is important to mention that Concentrix supports C, Pascal, and assembler in addition to FX/Fortran. While FX/Fortran can automatically transform programs for parallel and vector execution, the C programmer can explicitly use Alliant provided library routines to apply concurrency and vectorization within a C program.

Some Performance Results

There are several standard benchmarks which are often used to measure different aspects of a computer system's performance. One mentioned earlier, the Whetstone benchmark, gives a measure of the speed of a single processor on a non-vector code. By this measure, the Alliant CE is about equal to the VAX 8600 or four times a VAX 11/780. In contrast, the Linpack[4] benchmark is used to measure performance on a highly vectorizable code. This benchmark performs an LU decomposition (factorization) of a dense matrix. For a 100 by 100 double precision matrix, using vector-matrix basic linear algebra subroutines (BLAS), the FX/8 achieves the performance shown in Figure 3. This benchmark uses both vectorization on the inner loop and concurrency on an outer loop, and clearly demonstrates the benefits of concurrency.

The Livermore Loops[8] benchmark is designed to test system performance on a set of 24 kernels from a variety of numerical applications. Alliant's speed on this benchmark is 5.11 (average: dominated by fastest loop), 1.24 (harmonic mean: dominated by slowest loop), and 1.70 (median: not dominated by any single loop). Many of the kernels of this benchmark are single loops that are not well suited for either parallel or vector processing. In a complete application, these kernels would be nested inside of outer loops, providing an opportunity for parallel processing. In contrast to typical applications, therefore, this benchmark exercises few of the features of the Alliant system.

Complete applications that have nested loops and a mix of scalar, vector, and parallel code provide the best opportunites for measuring the performance of a computer architecture. To this end, a mechanical engineering benchmark consisting of 4000 lines of code was ported to the Alliant FX/8 system. Without any tuning, this benchmark executed in 3041 seconds. The time for the same benchmark on the Cray XMP is 740 seconds, or about four times the FX/8 speed. Neither machine was near its peak speed because of short vectors. For the Alliant, however, this benchmark did

VAX/VMS   Trademark of Digital Equiptment Corporation

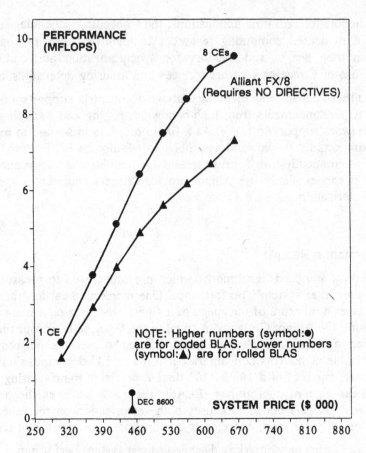

Figure 3: Reported Linpack Results

present an opportunity for high-level parallelism via the FX/Fortran concurrent call directive. With this additional modification, the time on the FX/8 dropped to 764 seconds, or nearly equal to the Cray XMP speed. The speedup is nearly linear for this application, with 8 CEs running six times the speed of a single CE. The vector operations, though short, are responsible for a speedup of two. The result is a code that runs 55 times the speed of a VAX 11/780, despite the fact that it is not well suited for a vector machine. This performance is typical of codes that have short vectors and an outer level of concurrency.

Another performance example[11] comes from The Analytical Sciences Corporation. In an image processing application, a multi-source sharpener running on four CEs ran 60 times the speed of the 11/780. This same example runs four times the speed of an FPS AP120B, despite the fact that the application was tuned for the array processor and no tuning whatever was done for the FX/8. Finally, an algorithm[10] developed at

Argonne National Laboratories for the Alliant architecture, illustrates the sort of performance improvements that can be achieved with some custom effort. In this benchmark, the Alliant system was able to solve 100 tridiagonal eigenvalue problems of order 150 in the time that it took to solve one problem on the VAX 11/780 using the standard algorithm.

These examples demonstrate the power of the FX/Fortran compiler and hardware architecture to reduce the time-to-solution for single applications. High performance is achieved transparently and often a small amount of additional tuning effort can yield very impressive results.

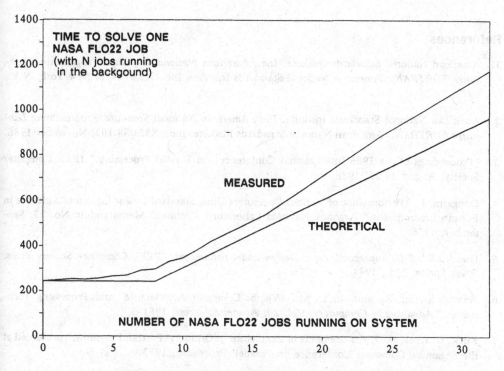

Figure 4: Measured Multi-User Performance on Alliant FX/8 With 8 CEs

It is also important to recognize that with detached CEs the system has great leverage in compute environments where the application mix is dynamic and consists of a large number of codes. In a throughput test, as shown in Figure 4, multiple copies of a NASA fluid dynamics code, FLO22, were run in the background while the time to execute an additional copy was measured. With up to seven copies running in the background, the eighth job takes only slightly longer than on an unloaded system. Thus the Alliant system can be used to achieve very high performance on single applications as well as to achieve high throughput for a large number of applications.

Summary

The Alliant FX/Series of computer systems, by combining innovative software and hardware technologies, has brought the benefits of concurrency to the computational marketplace. The machine architecture can support up to twenty processors working in parallel, the FX/Fortran compiler can automatically transform programs to take advantage of both vectorization and concurrency, and the Concentrix operating system can efficiently manage the machine resources to realize high application time-to-solution and all around job throughput. A number of benchmarks have shown the power and effectiveness of the FX/Series in a wide variety of applications.

References

1. American National Standards Institute, Inc., *American National Standard Programming Language FORTRAN*, American National Standards Institute, Inc., X3.9–1978, New York, N.Y., 1978.

2. American National Standards Institute, Inc., *American National Standard Programming Language FORTRAN*, American National Standards Institute, Inc., X3J3/S8.102, November 1986.

3. "Proceedings of the 1986 International Conference on Parallel Processing," IEEE Computer Society, August 19-22, 1986.

4. Dongarra, J., "Performance of Various Computers Using Standard Linear Equations Software in Fortran Environment," Argonne National Laboratory, Technical Memorandum No. 23, September, 1986.

5. Hwang, K., Ed., *Supercomputers: Design and Applications*, IEEE Computer Society Press, Silver Spring, Md., 1984.

6. Hwang, K., Su, S., and Ni, L. M., "Vector Computer Architecture and Processing Techniques," *Advances in Computers*, Vol. 20, Academic Press, 1981.

7. Kuck, D. J., et. al., "Measurements of Parallelism In Ordinary Fortran Programs," presented at the Sagamore Computer Conference on Parallel Processing, 1973.

8. McMahon, F. H., Lawrence Livermore National Laboratory, December, 1985.

9. Metcalf, M., *Fortran Optimization*, Academic Press Inc., 1982.

10. Sorensen, D. C., "Advanced Computing Research at Argonne National Laboratory," presented at the Alliant User Group Conference, September, 1986.

11. Stephenson, T., "Applications of the Alliant FX/8 and the Pixar 2D to Image Processing, Image Understanding, and Image Generation," presented at the Alliant User Group Conference, September, 1986.

EMULATING DIGITAL LOGIC USING TRANSPUTER NETWORKS
(VERY HIGH PARALLELISM = SIMPLICITY = PERFORMANCE)

P.H. Welch
Computing Laboratory
University of Kent at Canterbury, CT2 7NF, ENGLAND

ABSTRACT

Modern VLSI technology has changed the economic rules by which the balance between processing power, memory and communications is decided in computing systems. This will have a profound impact on the design rules for the controlling software. In particular, the criteria for judging efficiency of the algorithms will be somewhat different. This paper explores some of these implications through the development of highly parallel and highly distributable algorithms based on *occam* and *Transputer* networks. The major results reported are a new simplicity for software designs, a corresponding ability to reason (formally and informally) about their properties, the reusability of their components and some real performance figures which demonstrate their practicality. Some guidelines to assist in these designs are also given. As a vehicle for discussion, an interactive simulator is developed for checking the functional and timing characteristics of digital logic circuits of arbitrary complexity.

INTRODUCTION

The 'real world' consists of large numbers of autonomous structures operating concurrently and communicating (sometimes continually) in order to achieve common goals. It is not surprising that traditional sequential computing techniques — aimed at wringing optimum performance out of the traditional 'von Neumann' computer — eventually cease to be useful for realising systems above a certain level of complexity. The mis-match between target and implementation concepts is too great.

Occam [INMOS 83, May–Shepherd 85] is a simple programming language which allows us to express and reason about parallel (MIMD) designs with the same ease and fluency to which we are accustomed for sequential systems. Occam enforces some dramatic simplifications (such as not allowing parallel processes directly to share resources like data objects or communication channels) which sidestep many of the standard problems of concurrency. Occam communication is point-to-point, synchronised and unbuffered. However, broadcast, multiplexed, asynchronous or buffered communication may be obtained with minimal overhead by applying (reusable) software components to just those places where they are needed.

The simplicity of occam's concept of parallelism has two important consequences. Firstly, it allows us to be confident about designs with very high levels of concurrency (say > 100,000 parallel processes). Secondly, it permits very fast implementations. The INMOS Transputer [INMOS 84, May–Shepherd 85], which was itself designed concurrently with the occam language, imposes an overhead of about one micro-second when switching between parallel processes. Further, depending on the degree of parallelism in the occam design, the software may be distributed on to arbitrary size nets of Transputers. Since inter-Transputer links (like the occam communication channels that they implement) are point-to-point, the size of the network is never limited by the usual contention problems which arise from more normal methods of combining many processors (e.g. on a common bus). *With careful load-balancing and design*, performance can be improved linearly with the number of processors used. This paper makes a contribution to that care.

This situation compares favourably with the current state of Ada [AJPO 83] technology. Ada tasking is related to occam parallelism (both are derived from CSP [Hoare 85]), but is more complicated. It also violates certain principles of software engineering which makes it very difficult to use for describing highly parallel systems (although with rigorous discipline, this can be overcome to a certain extent — see [Welch 86, 87]). However, much work needs to be done to reduce the task switching overhead from, typically, one mille-second to something usable. Also, the distribution of a parallel system expressed as a single Ada program — essential for an integrated understanding of the whole design — on to multiple processors is still being researched.

EMULATING DIGITAL LOGIC

There exist many commercial packages [e.g. Cirrus 82, Tamsley-Dow 82] for simulating digital logic circuits so that their functional and timing characteristics can be checked before actual fabrication. Since the design of these packages have been optimised for conventional sequential execution, we do not believe that they are an appropriate starting point from which to try to extract parallelism. At best, some elements of SIMD and/or simple expression evaluation pipelining may be found. We wish to exploit more general forms of parallelism than these.

Further, because digital logic circuits are inherently such parallel systems, sequential simulations will need to manage complex data structures — necessarily in some global, persistent data space — in order to maintain the states of their various components. Also, there will have to be explicit means of scheduling the single execution thread of control around the components. These details are artifacts of the sequential implementation technique and obscure what is trying to be expressed.

In occam, every object in the system may be mapped on to an individual active process with its own local (private and, usually, very simple) state information. The parallel inter-object relationships are expressed directly and scheduling is automatic — the system designer is not concerned with the management of any global data-base to maintain the overall system.

There is one optimisation we lose with this direct approach. In a sequential implementation, advantage may be taken of the fact that the state of the whole system is available globally. For digital logic simulation, this enables us to work only on those parts of the circuit where we know logic levels are changing. In the parallel implementation we have built, we simulate 'real world' objects (e.g. gates) very closely and only have local information available (like the 'real' gates). So, just as gates are analog devices which continuously transform input signal levels into output signal levels (even when these levels are steady), our gate emulations will continuously operate on (digital samples of) input and output signals. Consequently, it might be argued that our models are inefficient in comparison to the standard ones. However, in the parallel world, the rules for judging efficiency are rather changed.

In [Dowsing 85], an attempt is made to recover this kind of optimisation through a central pool of information to which all gates report. We feel that the extra complexities, resources and restrictions needed to manage this are not worthwhile. We prefer to keep the designs simple and understandable. *In the distributed environment, it will not matter if we 'burn up' some MIPS.*

There is an analogy with earlier days of computing when memory resources were scarce. It used to be more important to conserve memory than organise clear data structures — great complexities, for instance, would be introduced to manage 'overlays'. Now that distributed processing power and communications are (becoming) abundant, we should stop being so concerned at optimising their use and seek new simplicity in our designs.

BASIC DIGITAL CYCLES

We concentrate on modelling the behaviour of real hardware components. Consider a *nand* gate with two input pins, *in.0* and *in.1*, and one output pin, *out* :−

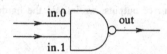

In our emulation, we shall be supplying an (infinite) stream of samples of the input signal levels and producing — at the same rate — an (infinite) stream of samples of the output signal. The pseudo-rate of sampling will be defined by the input data for the simulation and may be set to any value (e.g. one sample per nano-second).

In the models we have built, we allow only two sample values, *HIGH* and *LOW*. (The technique could easily be extended to allow a more continuous range of values — see the section on **EXTENSIONS**.) We do not need to develop 'multi-valued' logics to represent notions like 'rising' or 'falling' edges, 'spikes' or 'noise'. For simplicity, we have given ourselves the extravagance of 32-bit quantities to represent this two-valued logic :−

      VAL INT LOW IS #0000, HIGH IS ˜ LOW: −− this would be a DEF in occam 1

[The examples presented in this paper are expressed in *occam* 2 [INMOS 86], a strongly typed extension of *occam 1* which will be the new standard from early 1987. We assume the reader has encountered *occam 1*, which is sufficiently close for the details to be followed. In particular, the constructs supporting parallelism are identical.]

An (incorrect) model of the *nand* gate may now be given :−

```
PROC nand.2 (CHAN OF INT in.0, in.1, out)
  WHILE TRUE
    INT a.0, a.1:
    SEQ
      PAR
        in.0? a.0
        in.1? a.1
      out! ˜ (a.0 ∧ a.1)
```

The trouble with this model is that it captures no notion of time — it represents a gate with zero 'propagation delay'. Severe problems arise if we try to use such devices in circuits with feedback. Consider a simple *latch* :-

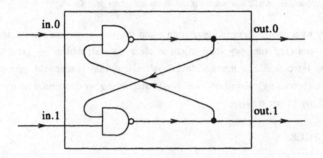

First though, there is another problem. The output from each *nand.2* gate needs to be 'broadcast' to two devices — the other *nand.2* gate and whatever is attached to the *latch* output. Rather than modify the *nand* gate to equip it with a pair of outputs, we imitate the hardware and introduce a process to represent the 'soldering' :-

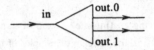

```
PROC delta.2 (CHAN OF INT in, out.0, out.1)
  WHILE TRUE
    INT a:
    SEQ
      in? a
      PAR
        out.0! a
        out.1! a
```

The latch circuit may now be drawn :-

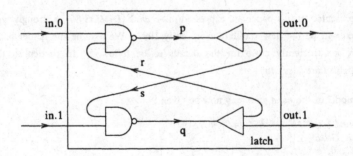

and implemented :-

```
PROC latch (CHAN OF INT in.0, in.1, out.0, out.1)
  CHAN OF INT p, q, r, s:
  PAR
    nand.2 (in.0, r, p)
    nand.2 (s, in.1, q)
    delta.2 (p, out.0, s)
    delta.2 (q, r, out.1)
```

Returning to the earlier problem, this circuit deadlocks immediately! There is no notion of delay in the *delta.2* or *nand.2* processes and so, because of the feedback, nothing can proceed.

The problem is solved by adding a 'propagation delay' to the model of the gate. A delay of one sample cycle may be introduced by 'double buffering' the internal logic of the gate :-

```
PROC nand.2 (CHAN OF INT in.0, in.1, out)
  INT a.0, a.1, b.0, b.1:
  SEQ
    b.0 := UNKNOWN
    b.1 := UNKNOWN
    WHILE TRUE
      SEQ
        PAR
          in.0? a.0
          in.1? a.1
          out! ~ (b.0 ∧ b.1)
        PAR
          in.0? b.0
          in.1? b.1
          out! ~ (a.0 ∧ a.1)
```

Note that we now input a 'slice' of sample signal levels and output a sample level in parallel — a more accurate model of the real gate. This illustrates a general principle of parallel design.

> When logic does not dictate the order in which things need to be done — *especially regarding input and output* — do not arbitrarily specify some sequence. Placing unnecessary sequential constraints on the way the system synchronises is the short-cut to deadlock.

Note that also on its first cycle, *nand.2* outputs some indeterminate value. *UNKNOWN* may be a constant set to *HIGH*, *LOW* or some other value — e.g. :-

```
VAL INT UNKNOWN IS #5555, KNOWN IS ~ UNKNOWN:
```

Alternatively, *UNKNOWN* may be set through some extra (VAL or even CHAN) parameter to *nand.2*.

A general method of allocating arbitrary (multiples of sample cycle) delays to any gate is given in the EXTENSIONS section. For the moment, all our gates will be modelled as above with a propagation delay of one sample cycle.

BUILDING LARGE CIRCUITS

First, we try to pin down some useful ideas :−

Definition: A device is *I/O-PAR* if it operates (or may be scheduled to operate) cyclically such that, once per cycle, it inputs a complete slice of values from every input channel *in parallel* with outputting a slice of values to every output channel.

Theorem A: any network constructed from *I/O-PAR* components — no matter how large or however much feedback there is in the network — will never deadlock and is also *I/O-PAR*.

'Proof':   the circuit will be self-synchronising around the parallel I/O operation in each device. We may imagine that, at any instant, there is either nothing on all the wires or there is precisely one item of information in flight along every wire. Physically, the circuit may be scheduled very differently with some nodes getting ahead of others — but they will eventually be held up through lack of input data and the rest of the circuit will catch up.

Definition: we call a device *I/O-SEQ* if it is not *I/O-PAR* but operates (or may be scheduled to operate) cyclically such that, once per cycle, it first inputs in parallel a complete slice of values from each input channel *and then* in parallel outputs a slice of values to each output channel.

Theorem B: any acyclic network constructed from *I/O-SEQ* components will never deadlock and is itself *I/O-SEQ*, but a cyclic network will deadlock.

'Proof':   clear.

Theorem C: any network constructed from *I/O-PAR* and *I/O-SEQ* components, such that there is (i) no sub-cycle consisting of just *I/O-SEQ* components and (ii) no direct connection from input to output via just *I/O-SEQ* components will never deadlock and is *I/O-PAR*.

'Proof':   because of theorems A and B, this reduces to showing that an *I/O-PAR* device followed by an *I/O-SEQ* device (or vice-versa) is still *I/O-PAR*. This is trivial.

Of course, the above definitions, theorems and proofs need a formal treatment based upon the techniques of CSP and the formal semantics of occam [Roscoe–Hoare 86]. This is outside the scope of this present paper which is to convey practical ideas, keep the reasoning informal and report on results. On the other hand, the insights provided even by such informal analysis are essential to understand how large systems may be built with impunity so that they faithfully reproduce the functional and timing characteristics of the real circuits. (These ideas will be formalised in a later paper.)

Clearly, the second version of *nand*.2 above is *I/O-PAR* and *delta*.2 is *I/O-SEQ*. By theorem C, the *latch* is *I/O-PAR* and does not deadlock. If the *I/O-SEQ* components merely copy input values to output, we may insert as many of them as we like into existing channels and the functional and timing characteristics will be unaltered. *I/O-SEQ* components introduce no notion of delay.

Any digital logic circuit that can be built from basic gates and wires can now be expressed trivially (although a little tediously) in occam. For instance, an 'edge-trigered JK flip-flop with clear' :−

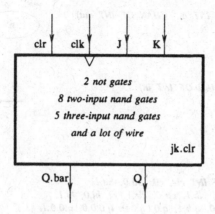

may be written :−

> PROC jk.clr (CHAN OF INT j, k, clr, clk, q, q.b)
>   ...

Within the body will be declared a *CHAN* for each length of wire in the circuit, followed by a *PAR* construct of instances of *delta.2* and *delta.3* processes (for the solder points) and *not*, *nand.2* and *nand.3* gates (which are implemented in the *I/O-PAR* style of the earlier *nand.2*).

Notice that, by theorem C, *jk.clr* is itself *I/O-PAR* (no input is directly connected to an output and there are no loops consisting just of bare wire) and it may be therefore be used as a component to construct higher level devices. Such hierarchical designs follow the way the real circuits are built. For instance, a 'two-bit counter' may be built from two *jk.clr*s and a constant *HIGH* signal source :−

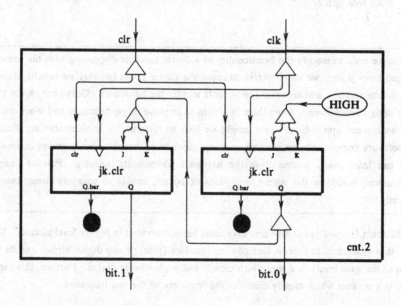

We have used two new basic devices, a constant generator and a 'black hole' for masking off unwanted outputs :–

```
PROC generate (VAL INT n,  CHAN OF INT out)
    WHILE TRUE
        out! n
```

```
PROC black.hole (CHAN OF INT in)
    WHILE TRUE
        INT any:
        in? any
```

Then :–

```
PROC cnt.2 (CHAN OF INT clr, clk, bit.0, bit.1)
    CHAN OF INT clk.0, clk.1, clr.0, clr.1, hi, hi.0, hi.1,
                q.b.0, q.b.1, q.0, q.0.0, q.0.0.0, q.0.0.1:
    PAR
        -- { split inputs
        delta.2 (clr, clr.0, clr.1)
        delta.2 (clk, clk.0, clk.1)
        -- }
        -- { jk 0
        generate (HIGH, hi)
        delta.2 (hi, hi.0, hi.1)
        jk.clr (hi.0, hi.1, clr.0, clk.0, q.0, q.b.0)
        delta.2 (q.0, q.0.0, bit.0)
        black.hole (q.b.0)
        -- }
        -- { jk 1
        delta.2 (q.0.0, q.0.0.0, q.0.0.1)
        jk.clr (q.0.0.0, q.0.0.1, clr.1, clk.1, bit.1, q.b.1)
        black.hole (q.b.1)
        -- }
```

When we need to modify the functionality of a device (such as dispensing with the second output from *jk.clr*), we much prefer to reuse the device intact (so that we inherit known characteristics) and add separate components to alter the behaviour. Only later, when the new design has matured, when there is a need to improve its performance and when there are widespread applications likely, might we look to integrate its implementation. Reuse of software components has obvious and urgently needed benefits, *but is seldom achieved*. We can learn many lessons from the hardware components industry. Parallel design techniques, based on the simple disciplines of occam, enable us to apply these lessons directly.

Again, by theorem C, *cnt.2* is *I/O-PAR* and may itself be incorporated in higher level circuits. We have a technique that enables us to express formally the interface (pins) of any digital circuit and its internal logic (down to the gate level) in a way which closely follows hardware design. Further, this expression will execute in a manner which closely emulates the behaviour of the real hardware.

TESTING THE CIRCUITS

An interactive *test.rig* for analysing such circuits may be built as follows :—

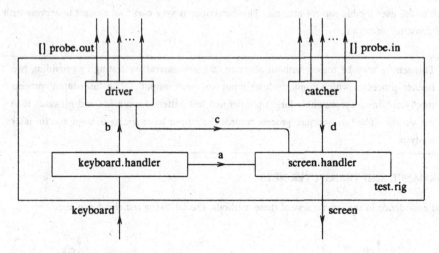

```
PROC test.rig (CHAN OF BYTE keyboard, screen, [] CHAN OF INT probe.out, probe.in)
    CHAN OF BYTE a:
    CHAN OF INT b, c, d:
    PAR
        keyboard.handler (keyboard, b, a)
        driver (b, c, probe.out)
        catcher (probe.in, d)
        screen.handler (a, c, d, screen)
```

The *driver* process generates a sequence of 'sample slices' of the test wave-form. Each component of the slice is output in parallel through the *probe.out* channels to the input pins of the circuit under test. The driver maintains a *count* of the number of slices sent — this *count* represents the 'real-time' base of the simulation. The particular wave-form it generates is determined by instructions received from the *keyboard.handler*. Constant or periodic signals may be programmed for each output line. The wave-form may be generated continuously or stepped through under user-control. If this wave-form is to be monitored on the screen, a copy is sent to the *screen.handler*. However, to save needless 'flicker' on the display, the *driver* only sends a copy of the wave-form slice when it changes, together with a 'time-stamp' (i.e. the value of its internal *count*).

Because the circuit under test is *I/O-PAR*, for each input 'wave-front' there is, in parallel, an output 'wave-front'. The *catcher* process inputs these fronts, maintains its own *count* (which will automatically keep in step with the *count* in *driver*) and forwards a copy of the front, with its *count* 'time-stamp', to the *screen-handler* when it changes (again to save 'flicker').

The *keyboard.handler* accepts key-strokes (or 'mouse'-input) from the user, interprets a human-oriented command language for specifying wave-forms, forwards appropriate 'echo' information to the *screen.handler* and transmits coded instructions to the *driver* process.

The *screen.handler* has to accept (*time.stamp*, *wave.front*) records from the *driver* and *catcher* and maintain a suitable display. [In our implementation, for which we only used a standard VDU, we simply output the *time.stamp* and *wave.form* logic levels numerically. To drive a more friendly (but expensive) graphical display, only this process needs to be modified.] The *screen.handler* also has to accept (at a higher priority) echoing information from the *keyboard.handler* and provide the necessary feedback to the user for his control actions. This behaviour is very easy and elegant to express with the *PRI ALT* construct of occam.

> This *test.rig* may be reused without alteration for non-interactive testing by providing two further processes which simulate 'user-input and user-output'. The 'user-input' process simply obtains a (presumably large) pre-defined test-pattern from a file and forwards it to the *test.rig*. The 'user-output' process records the output from *test.rig* to some file for later analysis.

PERFORMANCE AND TRANSPUTER NETS

To build confidence in the correctness of these methods, the following *test.circuit* was used :−

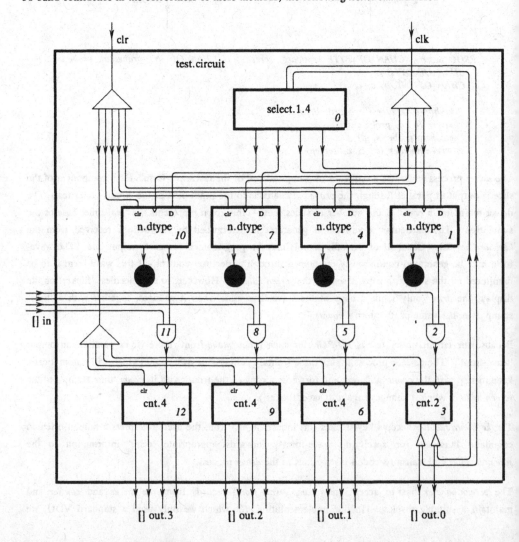

Each four-bit counter, *cnt.4*, contains 4 *jk.clr* and 2 *and* gates, making 62 gates overall. The *cnt.2* contains 30 gates. Each 'D-type negative edge with clear' device, *n.dtype*, contains 10 gates and the 'one-from-four selector', *select.1.4*, has 6 gates. In total, the circuit has 266 gates.

Each gate is a continuous parallel process in occam. Internally, these are transient parallel processes to handle *I/O* (and synchronise). In addition, there are the further *delta* processes (also with internal parallelism) to 'solder' channels together, as well as some *generates* and *black.holes*. The total number of parallel processes varies between 700 and 2000 during the simulation. Compared with some other technologies for expressing MIMD parallelism (e.g. semaphores, signals, monitors, Ada tasking, ...), these are high levels.

The simulation was tested with a pre-defined wave-form which exercised all its anticipated properties. The results were compared with those from a commercial HI-LO simulator [Cirrus 82]. The functional behaviour and circuit reaction times were identical from the two simulations.

The performance of the occam simulation on a VAX 11/750 (running single-user on 4.2 BSD UNIX†) was approximately 5 'wave-front' cycles per second. This was just bearable, given that the longest reaction time of this circuit was five cycles. However, for more complex circuits (e.g. > 100,000 gates) with much more lengthy test patterns, this route would become impractical — especially with other users on the machine!

Running under the INMOS Occam Programming System on a Stride 440 (a single-user 10 MHz M68000 workstation), performance increased to 8 cycles per second. Cross-compiled on to a single Transputer (a 15 MHz INMOS T414 processor running on a MEiKO MK014 "Local Host" board within a MEiKO "Computing Surface"), performance increased to 71 cycles per second — some 14 times faster than the VAX.

Our simulation techniques pay no regard to trying to keep down the levels of concurrency. This is what makes the algorithms so easy to develop — we just follow whatever is happening in the 'real-world'. The context switch between occam processes on the VAX (Stride) are approximately 60 (35) micro-seconds (respectively). To generate one wave-front about 1000 processes need to be scheduled — i.e. the VAX (Stride) manages one simulation process every 200 (125) micro-seconds, spending about 30% of its time in switching. The (15 MHz) Transputer spends only 14 micro-seconds for each process on our simulation. This implies a context switch overhead of about 7%, which is extremely (and comfortably) low considering the fine granularity of the parallel design being executed.

The performance of a single Transputer on this kind of simulation degrades linearly with the number of gates being simulated. Allowing for the extra *delta* processes, the method requires about 180 bytes of workspace per gate. Having 3M bytes of external RAM on the MEiKO Transputer board, there was sufficient room to run 60 copies of the simulation in parallel. The *test.rig* was also replicated, the keyboard input broadcast (through a *delta* process), the screen outputs gathered, checked for equality (which was, of course, logically unnecessary) and a single output stream sent to the terminal. Everything still worked and the cycle time dropped by a factor of 60 precisely. This was equivalent to a simulation of a circuit of 16,000 gates and required the management of 120,000 parallel processes.

† UNIX is a trademark of AT&T Bell Laboratories in the USA and other countries.

Going in the other direction, we configured the simulation to run on a network of Transputers. Because of the parallel design of the simulation, there is great flexibility as to how this can be done — almost any partition from everything on one Transputer down to one gate per Transputer is possible (although perhaps not sensible).

A minor technical problem needs to be overcome. The channel connectivity between the partition elements that are to be placed on individual Transputers exceeds the number of physical links supported by the Transputer (currently four — each one implementing a bi-directional pair of channels). For our simulation, where there is continuous synchronised data flow along *all* channels, it is trivial to insert extra processes to multiplex many channels on to the few hard links available — e.g. :−

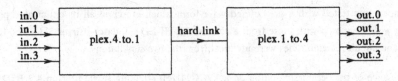

```
CHAN OF INT hard.link:
PAR
    plex.4.to.1 (in.0, in.1, in.2, in.3, hard.link)
    plex.1.to.4 (hard.link, out.0, out.1, out.2, out.3)
```

where :−

```
PROC plex.4.to.1 (CHAN OF INT in.0, in.1, in.2, in.3, out)
    WHILE TRUE
        INT x.0, x.1, x.2, x.3:
        SEQ
            PAR
                in.0? x.0
                in.1? x.1
                in.2? x.2
                in.3? x.3
            out! x0; x1; x.2; x.3


PROC plex.1.to.4 (CHAN OF INT in, out.0, out.1, out.2, out.3)
    WHILE TRUE
        INT x.0, x.1, x.2, x.3:
        SEQ
            in? x.0; x.1; x.2; x.3
            PAR
                out.0! x.0
                out.1! x.1
                out.2! x.2
                out.3! x.3
```

Clearly, the use of these two processes provides transparent *I/O-SEQ* buffers on the in.i/out.i channels. Consequently, they may be inserted anywhere into our simulation without affecting the functional or timing data obtained by the simulation.

At present, we only have a small "Computing Surface" with one other board (MEiKO Mk009) which contains four (15 MHz) T414 Transputers, each having 0.25M bytes of external RAM. We decided to place the *test.rig* on the original MK014 board and carve up the (computationally intensive) circuit into approximate quarters on the other four Transputers (the devices were partitioned $\{0, 1, 2, 3\}$, $\{4, 5, 6\}$, $\{7, 8, 9\}$ and $\{10, 11, 12\}$ — see the diagram of *test.circuit* for these device numbers).

For this, we needed 16 multiplexors. Compared with the total concurrency already being managed, this was no serious overhead. Indeed, testing the system modified to include the multiplexors on a single Transputer, performance only decreased from 71 to 68 cycles per second. After distribution to the five Transputers, performance increased to 317 cycles per second (which corresponds to about 90% of a 'perfect' linear speed-up).

The largest number of channels we had to multiplex on a single link was 4. That link, therefore had to carry 1268 cycles per second. Since we were using one word for the signal level, the link was carrying less than 5K bytes per second. Link capacity is currently about 500K bytes per second (and future Transputers will support 1.8M bytes per second), so we have an enormous margin on communications. Three of the Transputers (each managing 73 gates) were processor bound, a fourth (managing 47 gates) had some idle time and the fifth (just managing the *test.rig*) was more under-used.

If we distributed the simulation over more Transputers, performance would continue to increase so long as the capacity of the links was not exceeded (although we would need to introduce some DMA buffering — *a trivial process in occam* — as that limit was approached). About 20 gates could be managed on one Transputer using just its internal 2K bytes of fast static RAM. This will operate at about 1500 cycles per second (regardless of the number of logical inputs and outputs). If we had to multiplex 10 channels to one link, this will still only require a data flow of 60K bytes per second — about 10% of capacity. In fact, one gate *could* be managed per Transputer, producing about 30K cycles per second. 'Fan-in/fan-out' restrictions on the technology being simulated would probably mean that little multiplexing of channels would be needed. We would need to multiplex 4 channels to reach the current communication bandwidth of our links.

> Our design is very easy to balance on a Transputer network. We just have to distribute the gates per processor evenly and each Transputer will utilise its full processing power (currently 10 MIPS) with data always being available (and absorbable) on its links. Thus, a 100,000 gate system may, for instance, be distributed over 10 Transputers (giving about 2 cycles per second) or 1000 Transputers (giving about 200 cycles per second).

For other kinds of parallel design, where the pattern of communication is not so simple (e.g. where the network does not just consist of pure *I/O-PAR* or *I/O-SEQ* components), load balancing may not be so easy.

> In general, we must be careful to ensure that Transputers are not kept idle *either* because other Transputers have not yet computed their data *or* because they are generating so much data that the link bandwidth is exceeded. In this case, it is quite possible that adding further Transputers will actually slow down overall performance.

EXTENSIONS

Arbitrary length propagation delays — in multiples of the sample interval times — may be programmed into the behaviour of gates by maintaining a full 'cyclic buffer' of output values. The current 'double-buffering' described earlier represents a 'cyclic buffer' of length two. For simplicity and clarity, we separate the notions of computing the gate function and effecting the delay into two processes :—

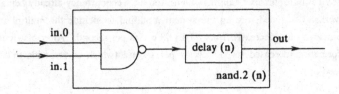

where :—

```
PROC delay (INT n, CHAN OF INT in, out)
    -- assume: n <= max.delay (some global constant)
    [max.delay] INT buffer:
    INT pointer:
    SEQ
        -- { initialise
        SEQ i = 0 FOR n
            buffer [i] := UNKNOWN
        pointer := 0
        -- }
        -- { main cycle
        WHILE TRUE
            INT x:
            SEQ
                PAR
                    in? x
                    out! buffer [pointer]
                buffer [pointer] := x
                pointer := (pointer + 1) \ n
        -- }
```

and where the gate process has the simple *I/O-SEQ* algorithm that was initially proposed (and labelled 'incorrect'). Notice that *delay* is *I/O-PAR* so that, overall, this new *nand.2(n)* is still *I/O-PAR*. Note also that, from the point of view of its environment, *nand.2(1)* is indistinguishable from the earlier *nand.2*.

We are extravagantly using an *INT* (i.e. 32 bits on a T414 Transputer, Stride or VAX) to represent just two logic levels. The boolean operators used in the computation of the gate functions act (in parallel) across every bit in the word. For very long pre-defined test patterns, advantage can be taken of this. Thirty-two independent wave-forms may be multiplexed on to separate bits in a word, passed through the simulation and de-multiplexed into thirty-two independent results. This will execute *at the same speed* as just a single simulation. Conventional sequential simulations, which 'optimise' by only computing those parts of the network where signal levels are changing, would find this difficult.

Alternatively, if we want to simulate finer detail, we could use a range of values (say 0..255) to represent sample levels of signal. Individual gates may be programmed to follow published response characteristics for particular devices to varying input signal levels (either through constant 'look-up' tables or, more crudely, by calculating minima or maxima). This would impose only a marginal increase in the memory and computational resources needed for each gate.

For interactive testing of the circuit, the user may wish to attach a 'probe' to any wire so as to inspect the signals being carried. The simulation needs to be equipped with special 'probe points', perhaps on every wire, to allow this :—

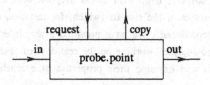

This *probe.point* is an *I/O-SEQ* device (with respect to the *in* and *out* channels) so as not to affect the timing characteristics of the circuit. There are two modes of behaviour. Normally, it just copies *in* data to *out*. However, if a *request* signal comes in (i.e. the user 'touched' this 'probe-point'), the *in* data is copied to *copy* as well as to *out*. A second *request* signal (i.e. the user 'removed' his 'probe') causes *probe.point* to revert to its normal mode. The *probe.point* listens for *request* or *in* data by means of a *PRI ALT* construct (with *request* having priority).

A similar technique lets the user cause a 'short' in the circuit. The simplest method is to extend the functionality of *probe.point* to respond to a second type of *request* signal that puts it in a mode where it transmits a constant value on *out* for every *in* data received. Such a capability is very useful in trying to diagnose faults in actual circuits or, at the design stage, for ensuring that dangerous outputs could not be produced should a fault occur.

Finally, we note that while it is quite trivial to express the circuit designs in occam, it is also very tedious. The numerous extra channels that have to be declared, because 'soldering' requires an active process, complicate the final code and mistakes can easily be made. For ease of use, it would not be hard to generate the code automatically from a higher level (perhaps graphical) description of the circuits. Similarly, the configuration information for distribution over Transputer nets, together with the necessary extra multiplexors/de-multiplexors, could be generated automatically following some interactive discussion with the tester (which might be limited to "how many gates per Transputer?"). Techniques will be reported in a later paper whereby the circuits may be built at run-time and without introducing a level of interpretation that would slow down the simulation.

CONCLUSIONS

We have demonstrated how the model of parallelism supported by occam allows us to emulate very directly the behaviour of certain 'real-world' objects (digital logic gates). We can then construct arbitrarily complex systems of these objects simply by following the way they are constructed in reality. Although we have reported here on one particular type of system, we believe that these techniques lead to 'object-oriented' design methods that have general application. Further, because the parallelism inherent in the system is retained in the design, the designs are very easy to distribute to multiple processors.

Traditional sequential methods for implementing such designs require extra layers of detail (global data-structures, scheduling, ...) that make both formal and informal reasoning about them very difficult. It is also very hard (probably impossible) to extract the parallelism back from the sequential code in order to take advantage of highly parallel hardware.

In the study reported here, we have shown how to emulate (very large) digital logic circuits. The system may be distributed on to as large a network of Transputers (up to the number of gates in the circuit) as the tester deems cost-effective, with linear improvement of performance. Functional behaviour and timing characteristics of the circuits (which, for instance, demonstrate the presence of 'race hazards') are faithfully reproduced. We have provided a user-interface which allows the tester many of the facilities of a 'logic analyser' working on the real devices. Future tools will allow the user interactively to design circuits and examine their properties at a much higher level (e.g. through graphical displays).

Finally, we note that no effort has been made to optimise on either memory (we use 32 bits for boolean logic), processing (no attempt is made to suspend the simulation of gates whose input signals are steady; no attempt is made to remove parallelism from the source code expression of the algorithm) or communications (no clever 'run-length encoding' tricks). We are convinced that for simplicity and confidence in design, the commitment to parallelism — at least in the prototype — should be total. With networks of Transputers, where memory, processing and communications resources can be equally balanced, such 'prototypes' make excellent 'production quality' systems.

ACKNOWLEDGEMENTS

These ideas were originally developed while the author was undertaking an Industrial Fellowship sponsored by the Royal Society and the SERC at GEC Avionics Limited (Rochester) [Welch 85]. I wish to thank, in particular, Keith Washington and Ian Roscow of the Automatic Test Equipment division (of GEC Avionics) for many useful discussions. The practical work was done at the University of Kent, which provided the "Computing Surface" and excellent support. Of course, many thanks are owed to the designers of the occam/Transputer concept for showing how elegantly and efficiently concurrent systems can be made to work.

REFERENCES

[AJPO 83]   Ada Joint Program Office: Ada Language Reference Manual; 1983.

[Cirrus 82]   Cirrus Computers Ltd.: *HI-LO 2 Users Manual*; 1982.

[Dowsing 85] D.Dowsing: *Simulating Hardware Structures in Occam*; Software & Microsystems, Vol. 4, No. 4, pp. 77-84; August, 1985.

[Hoare 83]   C.A.R.Hoare: *Communicating Sequential Processes*; Prentice-Hall, 1985.

[INMOS 83]   INMOS Ltd: *Occam Programming Language Manual*; Prentice-Hall, 1983.

[INMOS 84]   INMOS Ltd: *Transputer Reference Manual*; INMOS Ltd., 1000 Aztec West, Almondsbury, Bristol, BS12 4SQ; 1984.

[INMOS 86]   INMOS Ltd: *Occam 2 Programming Language Manual (Preliminary)*; INMOS Ltd., 1000 Aztec West, Almondsbury, Bristol, BS12 4SQ; 1986.

373

[May–Shepherd 85]   D.May and R.Shepherd: *Occam and the Transputer*; Concurrent Languages in Distributed Systems; North-Holland, 1985.

[Roscoe–Hoare 86]   A.W.Roscoe and C.A.R.Hoare: *The Laws of Occam Programming*: Technical Monograph PRG-53, Oxford University Computing Laboratory, Programming research group, 8-11 Keble Road, Oxford OX1 3QD; 1986.

[Tamsley–Dow 82]   J.Tamsley and P.Dow: *A Tutorial Guide to SPICE 2F.1*; Department of Computer Science, Edinburgh University; October, 1982.

[Welch 85]   P.H.Welch: *The Effect of New Real-Time Software Engineering Methodologies on Marconi Avionics — Final Report*; Royal Society/SERC Industrial Fellowship, reference number B/IF/43; July, 1985.

[Welch 86]   P.H.Welch: *A Structured Technique for Concurrent Systems Design in Ada*; Ada: Managing the Transition; Proceedings of the Ada-Europe International Conference, Edinburgh, May 1986, pp. 261-272; Cambridge University Press, 1986.

[Welch 87]   P.H.Welch: *Parallel Processes as Reusable Components*; Ada: Components, Libraries and Tools; Proceedings of the Ada-Europe International Conference, Stockholm, May 1987; Cambridge University Press, 1987.

A two-level approach to
logic plus functional programming integration

M. Bellia[+], P.G. Bosco[*], E. Giovannetti[*], G. Levi[+], C. Moiso[*], C. Palamidessi[+]

[*] CSELT - via Reiss Romoli 274 - 10148 Torino - Italy
[+] University of Pisa - Dipartimento di Informatica - corso Italia 40 - 56100 Pisa - Italy

1.   Introduction: the reasons for the integration

Logic programming and functional programming are the two most popular styles of declarative programming, and some debate went on in the past on the respective pros and cons of each of them with respect to the other. No wonder that an attitude to overcome this discussion by combining the two paradigms and thus the advantages of both (without their drawbacks) developed relatively soon.

Logic programming is characterized by two essential features: non-determinism, i.e. search-based computation, and logical variable, i.e. unification. The bidirectionality of unification, in contrast with the unidirectionality of pattern-matching, allows procedure invertibility and partially determined data-structures, and thus a more compact and flexible programming style. The central role of search (or *don't know* nondeterminism) in logic programming languages is connected with their being halfway between theorem provers and standard programming languages, which makes them particularly adequate for artificial intelligence applications, or as executable specification languages.

Functional languages share with logic languages the formal simplicity (function application as the only control construct) and the property of being based on a well-established mathematical theory, in this case (some kind of) lambda-calculus, which directly provides a clear semantics. Reduction is the key concept, which corresponds to the use of equalities as rewrite rules, in contrast with standard logic programming, where the equality is not explicitly present.

Apart from notational aspects, the other fundamental difference with the languages based on first-order logic is the presence of the notion of higher-order function, a powerful structuring concept which can be exploited in programming in the large, in program synthesis from specifications, etc.

In addition, functional languages offer a variety of other useful programming concepts, such as typing disciplines, outermost/innermost strategies, etc., which would be profitably included in an integrated system.

Several different approaches to the integration have been proposed. Roughly, they can be partitioned into two classes. On the one hand, the logic+functional languages, i.e. the logic languages enhanced with some limited functional features, essentially based on first-order logic with equality: they usually lack one of the very aspects which characterize functional programming, i.e. higher-order. On the other hand, the functional+logic approach, i.e. the functional languages augmented with logic capabilities, for example the ability to solve equations, to invert functions, etc.

For a survey of the most relevant proposals of both kinds see [Bellia85, Bellia86, Giovannetti86a].

The approach chosen in the Subproject D of ESPRIT Project 415, described in this paper, consists in splitting the problem into two levels. The upper level, or user interface, is a sort of superlanguage combining higher-order functional programming (i.e. lambda-calculus with a simple theory of types) with Horn clause logic. It is represented, for the time being, by the experimental language IDEAL [Bosco86a, Bosco86c]. This level is still subject to evolution, as it should eventually contain all the desirable features for this kind of language, w.r.t. different fields of applications. Some theoretical aspects still have to be deepened, in particular concerning a satisfactory definition and semantic characterization of the programming problems we want to be able to solve.

The lower level is a Prolog-like language augmented with directed equality, which is represented at the present stage of research by K-LEAF [Giovannetti86b, Bosco87b], an evolution and refinement of the language LEAF [Barbuti86]. It is a rather well assessed language, with a clear and original declarative semantics, and with a sound and complete operational semantics.

The upper level is mapped into this intermediate language by means of a transformation which removes the higher order by compiling it into first order (through a meta-interpretation). Moreover, in any implementation there will be a bottom level consisting of a control-flow imperative language close to the physical architecture (e.g. C-language in the present sequential prototype, maybe Occam in a future parallel architecture). Between this "machine-language" and the intermediate logic language further virtual machines could be introduced, corresponding e.g. to the elimination of nondeterminism in a mapping to a lower-level logic language, such as, for instance, Concurrent Prolog.

2. The Higher-Order Language

The user level is represented by the prototype higher-order (HO in the following) language IDEAL, for which an implementation on top of a standard Prolog environment is already available with a good efficiency.

The syntax for the functional component is, as usual, a sugared version of a *polymorphic lambda-calculus* with some form of universal types, in the style of MIRANDA [Turner85] or ML, while the logical component is basically the underlying first-order (FO in the following)

(Prolog-like) language.

The integration of the logic into the functional part is obtained, as at the intermediate FO level, by allowing function definitions to be heads of Horn clauses, functional terms to be arguments of predicates, and goals to be equations (to be solved). A program is therefore a set of possibly conditional function definitions, i.e. clauses of the form:

$$fname = \lambda X1.\lambda X2...\lambda Xn.term \ :- cond.$$

or equivalently

$$fname@X1@...@Xn = term :- cond.$$

where @ stands for the application. *Fname* is the name of the curried function being defined, and

Term is a term, not starting with λ, of a lambda-calculus equipped (sugared) with the *if-then-else* construct and a number of data constructors, tests and selectors, along with the related reduction rules. Recursive definitions are allowed with their usual meanings. The condition *cond* is a conjunction of literals, i.e., in general, a conjunction of equations between lambda-terms. Definitions by cases are also possible, with a straightforward extension of the pure lambda-notation:

$$fname@Dt1@...@Dtn = term :- cond.$$

where the *Dti* are data terms.

The usual *let, letrec, where, whererec* structuring constructs are permitted with their standard meanings corresponding to pure lambda-calculus expressions. The following example of functional program taken from [Turner85] is a good introduction to the syntax (the type information inferred by the system is listed after the ":" symbol).

Example 1.

```
foldr@Op@Z = g
  where    g@[] = Z,
           g@[A|X] = Op@A@(g@X).        :(A-->A-->A)-->A-->(list(A)-->A)
product = foldr@(*)@1.                  :list(int)-->int
sum = foldr@(+)@0.                      :list(int)-->int.
sum@[1,2,3]              ;term to be evaluated
:int            6        ;result
```

The user is allowed to define its own polymorphic data types, through a construct like the one suggested in [Turner85]:

$$typename(Typevar1,...,Typevarn) ::= \ constructor1(Typename11,...,Typename1n_1);$$

$$.............$$

$$constructorm(Typenamem1,...,Typenamemn_m)$$

which declares data objects of type *typename*, the structures being identified by *constructor1*, ...,*constructorm*, each of the appropriate argument types.

If the possibility of currying is to be coherently extended to predicates, these have to be considered as boolean-valued functions. The standard definition:

$p :- al,...,an$

has to be regarded as a short notation for:

$p = true :- al = true,...,an = true.$

With this extension of higher-order capabilities to predicates, definitions of predicate combinators and lexically scoped predicate definitions become possible, which greatly improves conciseness and modularization of logic programs, as is suggested by the following example.

Example 2.

```
comb@P@X@Y :- P@Z@X,P@Z@Y.        :(A-->B-->bool)-->A-->B-->bool
non-disjoint = comb@member
   where   member@X@[X|L] :-.
           member@X@[Y|L] :- member@X@L.   :list(A)-->list(A)-->bool

person ::= (a;b;c;d;...)                ;declares type person
brothers = comb@parent
   where   parent@a@b :-.
           parent@c@d :-.
           .....                        :person-->person-->bool
```

where *non-disjoint* is a predicate which succeeds when two lists are non disjoint, while *brothers* succeeds when its two arguments have a common parent.

The main program, or goal, is either the application of a function to arguments, i.e.

$?- f@tl @...@tn [= Result]$

or an existential logic-programming goal:

$?- p@tl @...tm [= true]$

or, more generally, an equation between lambda-terms

$?- tl =t2.$

As for the integration primitives, the construct *Term such_that Cond* has been introduced as a functional-flavoured version of the logic-programming conditional definition ...*Term ...:- Cond...* For example,

$k = g(X \ such\_that \ p(X)).$

is equivalent to:

$k = g(X) :- p(X).$

Moreover, a metalevel construct *bag* is available for producing, in formally one step, the possibly empty list of all the *Term* satisfying *Cond*. The following definition of *quicksort*, derived by a widely known functional program built on functional set-expressions, is an example of the use of *bag*, which enables a more abstract specification of the algorithm with respect to the way the list is scanned.

Example 3.

$[] ++ L = L$; definition of *append*

```
[X|U] ++ L = [X|U++L].                          :list(A)-->list(A)-->list(A)

gt@X@Y :- X > Y.                                :A-->A-->bool
lt@X@Y :- X < Y.                                :A-->A-->bool
gte@X@Y :- X >= Y.                              :A-->A-->bool
lte@X@Y :- X =< Y.                              :A-->A-->bool
inv(lt) = gte,
inv(gt) = lte.                                  :(A-->A-->bool)-->(B-->B-->bool)

qsort@p@[] = [],
qsort@p@[A|L] = qsort@p@bag(X,(member(X,L),p@X@A)) ++
                [A|qsort@p@bag(X,(member(X,L),inv(p)@X@A))]
                                        :(A-->A-->bool)-->list(A)-->list(A)
```

An example of the symmetrical possibility, i.e. the logic part "calling" the functional one, is the following goal, where the predicate *member* "calls" the function *map*, whose application occurs in one of the predicate arguments:

Example 4.

```
map([],F) = [],
map([X|L],F) = [F@X|map(L,F)]                   :list(A)-->(A-->B)-->list(B)

X such_that member(X,map([1,2,3],lambda(x,x+1)))   ;term to be evaluated

:int    2;
        3;
        4
```

the values 2,3,4 are "alternative" values which in a sequential environment are obtained by "backtracking".

Finally, to get the flavour of a more exciting field of application, consider the simple goal
        F@[1,1] = [1,1]
executed in the scope of the definitions of functions like reverse, append, the previous qsort. Among the possible solutions we can find

F = lambda x.x;   F = lambda x.[1,1];   F = reverse;   F = append@[];   F = qsort@lt

while the goal: F@[1,2] = [2,1]
would only yield the solutions

F = lambda x.[2,1];   F = reverse;   F = qsort@gt

HO programs, where functions and predicates are higher-order in the sense that they can take as arguments and deliver as results functions and predicates, are converted into "equivalent" L+F programs which are first-order in the usual logic sense (no quantification over predicates is allowed), e.g. K-LEAF programs (see next section). This merely amounts to considering the HO level as an object language described in the FO language used as a metalanguage. Terms of the object language, i.e. lambda-terms, are constants of the metalanguage. Reduction rules become FO equational axioms for the object structures in the metalanguage. "Equivalence" between the original program and its FO translation means that the transformation has to be sound and complete w.r.t. the class of solutions of equations we are interested in at the HO level. This strongly depends on the relation between the execution strategy of the lower level and the extension of the runtime core which is put at this same level to support the upper language. Some mappings from IDEAL to K-LEAF are complete (and sound) for a limited but meaningful class of programming (unification) problems, while for broader classes a complete mapping would involve a too large amount of interpretation with the related inefficiency. Enhancements of K-LEAF are presently being studied in order to be able to cope with this kind of problems efficiently.

3. The First-Order language

The lower level is a FO logic+equational programming language, i.e. a language based on HCL with equality. The term syntax is any *signature with constructors*, i.e. it is based on the distinction between constructors and functions, corresponding to the distinction, found in all the ordinary programming languages, between data structures and algorithms. Among the other distinctive features there are the allowing for partial functions and infinite objects, joined to a complete semantic characterization.

The concrete syntax of the first-order L+F programming system is basically the same as the language LEAF [Barbuti86]. The alphabet consists of a set C of data constructor symbols, a set F of function symbols, a set P of predicate symbols, a set V of variable symbols, and the special equality symbol $=$. The distinction between data constructor and function symbols leads to the distinction between *(general) terms* and *data terms*. The former are built both on C and F (and V), the latter are built on C (and V) only. The clauses of the language are defined in the usual way, with some constraints on the syntax of atoms.

A *head atom* is:

i) a *functional head* $f(d_1,...,d_n) = t$, where f is a function symbol, $d_1,...,d_n$ are data terms, t is a term, and the following two conditions are satisfied:

    1) *left-linearity*: multiple occurrences of the same variable in $(d_1,...,d_n)$ are not allowed

    2) *definite outputs*: all the variables occurring in t must also occur in $(d_1,...,d_n)$

ii) a *relational head* $p(d_1,...,d_n)$, where p is a predicate symbol and $d_1,...,d_n$ are data terms.

A *body atom* is:

i) an *equation* $t_1 = t_2$, where t_1 and t_2 are terms

ii) a *relational atom* $p(t_1,...,t_n)$, where p is a predicate symbol and $t_1,...,t_n$ are terms.

A *program* W is a set of definite clauses $\{C_1,..., C_m\}$ such that:

for each pair of equational heads $f(d'_1,...,d'_n) = t'$ and $f(d''_1,...,d''_n) = t''$,

$f(d'_1,...,d'_n)$ and $f(d''_1,...,d''_n)$ are not unifiable (*superposition free*).

The above syntax, unlike the earlier version of LEAF, is to be considered a sugared form of the actual underlying language which we called Kernel-LEAF, or K-LEAF, where all the equalities in the bodies and in the goal are *strict equalities*, denoted by the symbol $\equiv$, while equalities in the heads always are non-strict equalities, denoted by the usual symbol $=$.

In K-LEAF the heads of the clauses, either functional or relational, must be *left-linear*, and a user-language clause like $p(x,x) \leftarrow B_1,...,B_n$ is automatically transformed by the parser into the K-LEAF clause $p(x,y) \leftarrow x \equiv y, B_1,...,B_n$. This transformation cannot be used for functional heads, since it would cause the loss of the superposition-freedom. In the functional case the left-linearity constraint has been therefore introduced directly in the user-language

It is worth noting that equalities in the body, multiple occurrences of the same variable in (the argument-part of) a head or functional nestings in (the argument-part of) a head would introduce a not-semidecidable equality test on (possibly non terminating) subterms. Moreover, from the point of view of the declarative semantics developed in next subsection, this would violate the continuity requirement for the interpretations of functions and predicates.

The other constraints, i.e. definite outputs and superposition-freedom, have to do with confluence, i.e. with the requirement that function definitions actually define (univocal) functions.

The following set of clauses is a correct K-LEAF program:

Example 5.
```
.   samefringe(t1,t2) :-  fringe(t1) ≡ fringe(t2).
    fringe(t) = fringe1(t,nil).
    fringe1(leaf(x),continuation) = cons(x,continuation).
    fringe1(tree(tl,tr),continuation) = fringe1(tl,fringe1(tr,continuation)).
```

3.1. The model-theoretic semantics.

The natural setting for assigning meanings to possibly partial functions is found in the concept of algebraic CPO.

Let us briefly summarize the related notions. Let X be a set and let $\leq$ be an *order relation* on X. A set $D \subseteq X$ is a *chain* iff D is *totally ordered* with respect to $\leq$. $(X, \leq)$ is a Complete Partial Order (CPO) iff there exists a minimal element $\bot_X$ (bottom) and every chain D has a *least upper bound* $\bigsqcup D$. An element a is a *finite* (or *algebraic*) element iff there are not any infinite chains (from $\perp_X$) to a. $(X, \leq)$ is an *algebraic CPO* iff every element a is the least upper bound of the set of the *finite lower elements* (its finite approximations). Let $(X, \leq)$ and $(Y, \leq)$ be CPO's, and let f be a function from X to Y. f is *continuous* iff $f(\bigsqcup D) = \bigsqcup_{d \in D} f(d)$ holds for every chain D.

A simple algebraic CPO is the set $LL = \{ \perp_{LL}, true, false \}$, with the ordering $\perp_{LL} \leq true$ and $\perp_{LL} \leq false$. (three-valued boolean CPO). Note that all the elements of LL are algebraic. The formulae of the language will receive - from interpretations - truth-values in this CPO: we have therefore a three-valued logic, with "undefined" besides *true* and *false*.

Definition. Given a K-LEAF program W, an *interpretation* for W consists of an algebraic CPO $(X, \leq)$, and a meaning function $[\![ ]\!]_X$ which assigns to every constructor or function symbol a continuous function on X, and to every predicate symbol a continuous function from X to LL. The meaning of terms and atoms involves, as usual, the notion of *environment*. (that is a function $\rho : V \to X$) and is derived by imposing the structural compositionality, i.e.:

$$[\![v]\!]_{X,\rho} = v\rho \quad \text{for } v \in V.$$

$$[\![f(t_1,...,t_n)]\!]_{X,\rho} = [\![f]\!]_X ([\![t_1]\!]_{X,\rho}, ..., [\![t_n]\!]_{X,\rho}) \quad \text{for } f \in C \cup F, \ t_1,...,t_n \in T(V)$$

$$[\![p(t_1,...,t_n)]\!]_{X,\rho} = [\![p]\!]_X ([\![t_1]\!]_{X,\rho}, ..., [\![t_n]\!]_{X,\rho}) \quad \text{for } p \in P, \ t_1,...,t_n \in T(V)$$

The equality, i.e. the symbol = is interpreted as the identity eq_X on the CPO $(X, \leq)$, i.e.:

$$[\![t_1 = t_2]\!]_{X,\rho} = [\![t_1]\!]_{X,\rho} \ eq_X \ [\![t_2]\!]_{X,\rho} = \begin{cases} true & \text{if } [\![t_1]\!]_{X,\rho} \text{ and } [\![t_2]\!]_{X,\rho} \text{ are identical} \\ false & \text{otherwise} \end{cases}$$

Note that eq_X is non-strict and non-monotonic (and, therefore, non-continuous): for example, $\perp \ eq_X \ \perp = true$, while $\perp \ eq_X \ \xi = false$, for ξ different from $\perp$.

On the other hand the symbol $\equiv$, having to represent a sort of semidecidable test of equality, must be given a continuous interpretation. Hence the largest set on which strict equality can be true is the set of algebraic maximal elements. Maximality ensures that equal elements cannot become distinct by adding more information. Algebraicity guarantees that the comparison can be done in a finite time (by exploring a finite amount of information). A possible solution is the assignment of a fixed interpretation of $\equiv$ which satisfies this requirement, for example:

$$[\![t_1 \equiv t_2]\!]_{X,\rho} = \begin{cases} true & \text{if } [\![t_1]\!]_{X,\rho} \text{ and } [\![t_2]\!]_{X,\rho} \text{ are algebraic, maximal and identical} \\ false & \text{if } [\![t_1]\!]_{X,\rho} \text{ and } [\![t_2]\!]_{X,\rho} \text{ are algebraic and maximal, but not identical} \\ \perp_{LL} & \text{otherwise} \end{cases}$$

Alternatively, we can consider $\equiv$ as an ordinary predicate (whose interpretations must be continuous by definition) and axiomatize its *truth*, by adding to the program the clauses:

$$d(x_1, ..., x_m) \equiv d(y_1, ..., y_m) \leftarrow x_1 \equiv y_1, ..., x_m \equiv y_m \quad (m \geq 0)$$

for each constructor symbol d (this alternative will be the one choosen for implementing K-LEAF). Note that the two ways of defining $\equiv$ are equivalent, relatively to the set in which the value of strict-equality is *true*.

The meaning of non-atomic formulas is defined as follow:

$$[\![B_1,..., B_n]\!]_{X,\rho} = [\![B_1]\!]_{X,\rho} \text{ and } ... \text{ and } [\![B_n]\!]_{X,\rho}$$
$$[\![A \leftarrow B_1 ,..., B_n]\!]_{X,\rho} = [\![A]\!]_{X,\rho} \Leftarrow [\![B_1,..., B_n]\!]_{X,\rho}$$
$$[\![\leftarrow B_1 ,..., B_n]\!]_{X,\rho} = false \Leftarrow [\![B_1,..., B_n]\!]_{X,\rho}$$

where *and* and $\Leftarrow$ are continuous extensions of the standard conjunction and implication [Giovannetti86b].

Definitions . Let W be a set of Kernel or flat LEAF (program and goal) clauses. A *model* of W is any interpretation $M = ((X, \leq), [\![\,]\!])$ such that, for every clause cl in W and for every environment ρ, $[\![cl]\!]_{X,\rho} = true$. W is *consistent* if it has a model. A conjunction of atomic formulae, G, is true in M iff for every environment ρ $[\![G]\!]_{X,\rho} = true$. A conjunction of atomic formulae, G, is *valid* with respect to W, or is a *logical consequence* of W, iff it is true in every model of W.

A special class of interpretations is represented by Herbrand interpretations, which are based on a purely syntactical domain, the Herbrand universe. In our case the Herbrand universe is simply the set of the ground data terms, ground data partial terms and ground data infinite terms, i.e. the set of (possibly infinite) terms that can be built by means of the (constants and) constructors of the language and of the new constant $\perp$. Infinite terms may be defined in the standard way as infinite (finite-branching) trees. The ordering is the usual approximation order, which correctly gives to the above set the structure of an algebraic CPO [Giovannetti86b].

A *Herbrand model* for W is any Herbrand interpretation which is a model. In the following, HI will denote the set of Herbrand interpretations, while HM will denote the set of Herbrand models.

Let us point out the meaning of equality and strict equality on Herbrand interpretations. Equality simply is syntactic identity. To see the meaning of strict equality, note that in the CPO $(CU, \leq)$ maximal algebraic elements are the data terms which contain no occurrences of $\perp$. Hence strict equality is the syntactic identity only on the subset of the Herbrand Universe which is isomorphic to the ordinary "data-term" Herbrand Universe.

Consider the set of functions from a poset $(X, \leq)$ into a poset $(Y, \leq)$. This set is naturally ordered by the relation $g \leq g'$ iff $\forall x \in X \ g(x) \leq g'(x)$. The minimal function (Ω) is the function which maps every element of X in the bottom element of Y $(\forall x \in X \ \Omega(x) = \perp_Y)$.

This functional ordering induces an ordering on Herbrand interpretations:

for $I, I' \in HI$, $I \leq I'$ iff $\forall f \in F . \forall p \in P. \ [\![f]\!]_I \leq [\![f]\!]_{I'}$ and $[\![p]\!]_I \leq [\![p]\!]_{I'}$.

The interpretation I_0, which maps in Ω every function and predicate symbol, is the minimal element of HI. Also $(HI, \leq)$ is a CPO, as proved in [Giovannetti86b].

Herbrand models can be proved to keep, also in this kind of logics, the special role they have in standard logic. Namely, if W is a set of K-LEAF (program and goal) clauses, it is consistent iff it has a Herbrand model. Moreover, the lub of the Herbrand models of W is a Herbrand model, hence (if it is consistent) W has the *minimal Herbrand model*. Therefore a conjunction of ground atoms is valid in W iff it is true in the minimal Herbrand model of W.

It is possible to extend the standard transformation on Herbrand interpretations (used to define fixpoint semantics) so as to preserve monotonicity and continuity. Standard results still hold. Namely, the *least (minimal) fixed point* of the extended transformation T is equal to the minimal Herbrand model and can be effectively computed as the lub of the chain $I_0, T(I_0), T^2(I_0), \dots$.

3.2. The execution of K-LEAF programs

The computational methods that have been proposed for the execution of languages based on Horn clause logic with equality are, in general, linear refinements of resolution and completion (i.e. SLD-resolution and narrowing, respectively). Among them we find conditional narrowing [Dershowitz85, Fribourg85] and SLDE-resolution (i.e. SLD-resolution with syntactic unification replaced by a E-unification [Goguen86, Subrahmanyam86, Martelli87]).

The technique we have chosen in the project is *flat SLD-resolution*, i.e. SLD-resolution on *flattened* programs augmented with the clause $x=x$. The flattening tranformation consists in eliminating functional composition by recursively replacing a term $f(t1,...,tn)$ with a new variable v and adding the functional atom $f(t1,...,tn)=v$ to the body. The original idea, in the theorem-proving domain, probably traces back to [Brand75], while in the area of logic and functional programming it was first proposed in [Barbuti84, Tamaki84].

SLD-resolution on flat programs seems to be more adequate than narrowing, because:
- SLD-resolution was shown to be equivalent to "refined" narrowing [Bosco87a], with a considerable gain in efficiency with respect to "ordinary" narrowing (elimination of redundant solutions and, more generally, reduction of the search space);
- the full (relational + functional) language can be supported by a single inference mechanism;
- conditional equations can easily be handled, without need of extensions;
- sharing of subexpressions deriving from a common expression is obtained for free.

The flattening algorithm for K-LEAF is similar to the one described in [Barbuti86], with strict-equality atoms handled as ordinary predicates.

For instance, the K-LEAF program in Example 5 is flattened into:

```
samefringe(t1,t2) :-  fringe(t1)=v1, fringe(t2)=v2,v1 ≡ v2.
fringe(t) = v :- fringe1(t,nil)=v.
fringe1(leaf(x),continuation) = cons(x,continuation).
fringe1(tree(tl,tr),continuation) = v :- fringe1(tr,continuation)=v1,fringe1(tl,v1)=v2.
```

The flattening transformation is correct because an original K-LEAF program and its flat form have the same Herbrand models - where the notion of model for flattened programs is a trivial extension of the corresponding K-LEAF notion [Giovannetti86b].

An objection which has been raised to this approach concerns the presumed loss of the producer-consumer information contained in the functional notation. On the contrary, this information is still implicitly present in the flat form, and can be exploited by the selection strategy.

A selection rule corresponding in the unflattened program to an innermost rule can be easily implemented through the usual leftmost selection rule of Prolog [Bosco87a], provided the flat literals are put in the right order by the flattening procedure. This strategy has however a serious drawback in the unlimited possibility of resolving functional atoms with $x=x$, which results in a large amount of useless computation. The elimination of the reflexive clause causes the loss of completeness, unless functions are constrained to be everywhere defined, as in [Fribourg85]. The problem can be overcome by noting that the resolution of a functional atom $t=z$ with $x=x$ is only useful when the resolutions of the atoms in whose arguments z occurs, bind z to variables (i.e. they do not require a value for z). This is in general not the case, and it cannot be determined statically.

The detection of this situation requires an *outermost* strategy, analogous to lazy evaluation in functional programming, which reduces a functional atom only when its output variable would be bound to a non-variable term by resolution of a consumer atom. Resolution with $x=x$ can then be profitably applied to the functional atoms whose output variables do not occur elsewhere in the goal, and may therefore be implemented as an *elimination rule* (which can also be viewed as an explicit garbage collection step). Moreover, when, in the resolution of an atom, unification attempts to instantiate a variable produced by another (functional) atom, resolution of the current atom is suspended and resolution of the producer is tried instead. The suspended goal is resumed after (one step of) resolution of (all) the activated functional atom(s).

Example 6.
Consider the program (which is already in flat form):

     1) $p(x,y) :- q(x,x)$.

     2) $q(a,x)$.

     3) $f(b) = a$.

where a and b are constructors.

Let the goal be

     ?- $p(f(x),g(x))$.   flattened into: ?- $p(v1,v2),f(x)=v1,g(x)=v2$.

The only outermost atom is $p(v1,v2)$, which is resolved with (1):

     ?- $q(v1,v1),f(x)=v1,g(x)=v2$.

The functional atom $g(x)=v2$ can be eliminated, as the produced variable $v2$ does not appear elsewhere in the goal:

     ?- $q(v1,v1),f(x)=v1$.

Resolution of $q(v1,v1)$ is suspended, since (2) would bind the variable $v1$, produced by the other atom, to the non-variable term a. Resolution of the producer is executed instead: ?- $q(a,a)$.

Now resolution of $q(a,a)$ (i.e. $q(v1,v1)$ with $v1$ bound to a) with the clause (2) can be resumed. The goal thus succeeds with computed answer $\{x:=b\}$.

The strict-equality atoms can in principle be handled through their defining clauses like any other user-defined predicate. However, resolution with the $\equiv$-clauses can give rise to infinite branches of computation if atoms of the form $x \equiv y$, with x and y non-produced, are present. In this case the fake clause $x \equiv x$ is instead applied.

The outermost strategy, unlike the innermost case, cannot be implemented by means of a trivial compilation, because the atom selection order is not known statically, but can only be established at runtime. A more complex control of the computation than the one needed for Prolog is therefore required. While the selection order of the relational atoms is immaterial, the choice of the functional atoms to be resolved must be performed within the unification algorithm. The efficiency of the strategy is thus related to the efficiency in recognizing the produced variables and in finding their producers.

The complete definition of the outermost strategy is described in [Bosco87b] and in [Giovannetti86b], where it is proved correct and complete with respect to the declarative semantics.

As the design of an efficient sequential model is a preliminary step to any parallel implementation, we are now developing a K-LEAF abstract (sequential) machine. It consists in a modification of the Warren Abstract Machine (WAM) [Warren83] where, to implement the outermost strategy, the unification instructions are changed as follows:
- functional atoms are represented as terms stored in the heap;
- to represent produced variables, a new kind of term is introduced which links the variable to its producer;
- unification instructions collect all the (terms denoting the) functional atoms that produce the variables bound by the unification: these atoms are then resolved before body atoms.

Storing functional atoms as terms on the heap requires, to start their resolution, an efficient implementation of a meta-predicate similar to Prolog's *call* .

We have developed in C-Prolog a quite efficient "compiled-emulated" executor of K-LEAF where the unification instructions are emulated by Prolog predicates. Its natural evolution, planned for the next years, will be the implementation of the abstract parallel computational model described in [Giovannetti86b].

4. Mapping Higher-Order L+F to First-Order L+F

The approach consists in taking an HCL+E axiomatization of the higher order language and in trying to efficiently execute this axiomatization, possibly specialized to the particular computational needs required by the context of application. A technique for introducing HO curried functions in the logic programming framework was first proposed by Warren [Warren82]. He suggested to this end the definition and use of an *apply* predicate in Prolog programs. For example, the HO function *twice* would be written

apply(twice,X,twice(X)).

apply(twice(X),Y,R) :- apply(X,Y,R1), apply(X,R1,R).

To Warren's mind, the burden of building these clauses was to be left to the user. In our approach, on the other hand, they are automatically obtained by *partial evaluation* of the user-supplied function with respect to an axiomatization of lambda-calculus. This means that a procedure for deriving theorems from the axioms is used to reduce the application of a user function to a symbolic constant (i.e. to prove some universal properties of the function).

For example, with the function $\lambda(x,\lambda(y,x+y))$ we obtain:

(1) $\lambda(x,\lambda(y,x+y))@A => \lambda(y,A+y)$

and

(2) $\lambda(y,A+y)@B => A+B$

A "compiled" version of the function merely consists of the proved theorems (1) and (2). Observe that capital letters denote logical variables which are universally quantified when (1) and

(2) are asserted in a logic database. From a "functional" viewpoint, the term $\lambda(y,A+y)$, produced by the first application, is a *closure* where $\lambda(y,\_+y)$ is the text component (which could be substituted by a new constructor) while A is the environment component to be kept for further applications. At least for the sequential case, there is a strong analogy between the traditional implementation of functional programs with closures built on the heap, and the most standard computational model for logic programming, namely the Warren Abstract Machine (WAM) [Warren83], where the structure copying mechanism causes terms like the rightandside of (1) (an argument of the reduction relation) to be copied on the heap.

This approach was argued by Warren to be reasonably efficient in a Prolog environment equipped with the capability of indexing on the first argument of predicates, e.g. a standard WAM with *switch-on-term/constant/structure* instructions which, at every call of the *apply* predicate, perform a hashed search of the function definition. Optimized specific handling of *apply* could be obtained with a slight modification of the WAM: the function definition could be entered immediately through a fast indirect step, where the address of the function body to be executed is fetched in a special field of the function name which contains the index of that name in the scope of the *apply* predicate.

We merely reobtained in a logic programming framework what in the functional programming community is called *lambda-lifting* [Johnsson85], a technique used to find universal consequences of the reduction relation on a specific program. It basically consists in transforming a nested lambda-term into a set of *flat* rewrite rules, (or *super-combinators*): these rules are equivalent, with respect to reduction, to our *apply* clauses.

To produce by partial evaluation a "compiled" code like the one shown above, the interpreter of the HO language could be built, in principle, either in logic-programming style or in equational style. K-LEAF provides both alternatives. However, since for an interpreter of lambda-calculus the possibility of a leftmost strategy at the HO level must be guaranteed, the availability of a leftmost strategy already at the lower level allows a more compact and efficient axiomatization [O'Donnell85]. To this end, the so-called *micro-lambda-calculus* [Klop85] has been adopted, in this first experimental phase, as the equational theory to be "implemented" in (the equational part of) our FO language. A variant which seems to have the normalization property, derived by the idea in [Revesz85], could be the following:

$$\lambda X.X @ G = G \ :- \ \lambda var(X).$$
$$\lambda X.X @@ G = G \ :- \ \lambda var(X).$$
$$\lambda X.Y @ G = Y \ :- \ \lambda var(X), \lambda var(Y), X \neq Y.$$
$$\lambda X.Y @@ G = Y \ :- \ \lambda var(X), \lambda var(Y), X \neq Y.$$
$$\lambda X.E@F @ G = (\lambda X.E @ G)@(\lambda X.F @ G) \ :- \ \lambda var(X).$$
$$\lambda X.E@F @@ G = (\lambda X.E @ G)@(\lambda X.F @ G) \ :- \ \lambda var(X).$$
$$\lambda X. \lambda Y.B @ G = \lambda Y: (\lambda X.B @@ G) \ :- \ \lambda var(X), \lambda var(Y), X \neq Y, Y \notin varfree(G).$$

The compilation we could obtain by such a method looks like the following:

$$twice@X = twice1(X)$$
$$twice1(X)@Y = X@(X@Y)$$

or alternatively

$$twice@X = twice@'X$$
$$twice@'X@Y = X@(X@Y)$$

where @' is the "constructor" version of the function @, denoting the *closure*. These are correct K-LEAF programs.

4.1 Unification

If the general axiomatization of lambda-calculus is not kept at "run-time", and the compiled code is executed alone, unification at the FO level has a limited capability of solving equations in functional variables, which can only be instantiated to functional forms (functions) present in the original program. For example, if the simple definition $plus1@X = s(X)$ is added to the ones above, the execution of the goal $F@a=s(s(a))$ yields the substitution $F=twice@'plus1$; on the other hand, the solution $\lambda(x,s(s(x)))$ is not found out because this term does not belong to the Herbrand space of the "compiled" program.

This kind of invertibility can be achieved with a good efficiency, on the basis of the present K-LEAF implementation. The user interested in *synthesizing* programs should introduce a library of basic functions over which the search has to be performed. An external methodology could enforce the introduction in the library of second-order patterns which guarantee some correctness properties (well-typing in a broad sense). Suppose, for example, that a specification of an unknown recursive function F requires $F@3=6$. We could try to see whether, given a set of primitive functions, a particular recursive scheme s :

$$s(Arg,Test,End,F1,F2) = \underline{if} \ Test \ \underline{then} \ End$$
$$\underline{else} \ F1@s(F2@Arg,Test,End,F1,F2)$$

fits our I/O specification. This amounts to requesting the evaluation of the term

$$?\text{-} \ s(3,Test,End,F1,F2) = 6$$

which, in presence of a library of "fully" axiomatized integer functions like *plus*, *times*, etc., produces the solution

Test = eq0,   End = 0,   F1 = plus1,   F2 = sub1

corresponding to the function computing the sum from N downto 0, and the solution

Test = eq0,   End = 1,   F1 = times,   F2 = sub1

corresponding to the factorial function.

In conclusion, this approach amounts to translating the higher order program into the set of equations arising from the partial evaluation of an equational axiomatization of beta-reduction, and solutions of functional equations can be found only in lambda-terms already present in the program.

A natural generalization of the method consists in using the axiomatization itself and the FO-level inference method (roughly a form of narrowing) to obtain more general solutions for functional equations. In other words, equations between lambda-terms can be solved by executing a general E-unification algorithm on a particular equational theory for the lambda-calculus.

Because the problem of unification in lambda-calculus has been proven to be only semidecidable even in the typed case [Huet76,Goldfarb81], it does not follow that an algorithm which eventually finds unifiers, if they exist, is useless. Application domains like program transformation or program synthesis could supply sufficient edge conditions so as to make undecidabilty relatively irrelevant for the practical usage.

We have not taken into consideration specialized unification algorithms, like the one in [Huet76], recently chosen by [Miller86] in the integrated L+F language lambda-Prolog as the basic unification algorithm, to be used only when really needed. Our goal, at this stage of the research, rather consists in trying to identify one simple execution mechanism for both logic and functional programming.

In this perspective, our interest has concentrated on the *narrowing* technique, which can be efficiently supported by a resolution machine [Bosco87a]. Our present efforts are aimed at finding out which extra-features should be added to standard narrowing procedures in order to be able to deal with non-terminating systems like those for lambda-calculus, which do not satisfy the constraints of the language K-LEAF (non-superposition, distinction between functions and constructors, treatment of the occur-check). Recently [You86], narrowing has been proved complete for a class of non-terminating systems satisfying the "non-repetition" constraint, which means that a same rule cannot be indefinitely applied to E-equivalent terms. Unfortunately this result doesn't apply to lambda-calculus.

Some form of the so-called *narrowing-on-variables*, which is forbidden in standard algorithms, seems to be mandatory in the presence of rules like $f = c(f)$, if the execution of a goal like $?\text{-}X = c(X)$.must be able to produce the solution $X := f$. Following the idea suggested in [Holldöbler86], we are now experimenting with a modified narrowing algorithm where narrowing-on-variables is only tried on occur-check failure. More precisely, when a goal $t(...X...) = t(...f(..X..)...)$ fails for occur-check and $f(..X..)$ is no more narrowable, a rule of the form $l \rightarrow f(...)$ can be applied to narrow the variable X, and the goal becomes $t(...f(...)...) = t(...f(..X..)...)$. With this modification, the narrowing algorithm is able to solve equations like

$$F = z@F \qquad \text{(i.e. find a fixpoint of } z)$$
$$F := lambda(x,z@(x@x))@lambda(x,z@(x@x))$$
or $\qquad Y@f = f@(Y@f) \qquad \text{(i.e. find a general fixpoint combinator)}$
$$Y := lambda(z,lambda(x,z@(x@x))@lambda(x,z@(x@x)))$$

As a matter of fact, these solutions have been obtained by "driving" the narrowing process so as to narrow only the "interesting" subterms, and to disregard those which could lead to infinite failing computations.

One important source of infinite branches is the axiomatization of lambda-variables. If conditions of rules (declaring that the first arguments of lambda's must be lambda-variables) are evaluted before the narrowing step, (names of) lambda variables are actually generated, so introducing an infinite nondeterminism. This problem can be solved by a more complex narrowing strategy, where some conditions are carried over unresolved as constraints, and sometimes checked for satisfiability. In this case we may obtain solutions equipped with a set of satisfiable constraints. Of course falsity of constraints has to be computed as soon as possible. Some special meta-level primitives, hidden to the user, could be profitably embody some special cases of induction. Consider, for example, the $dif(X,X)$ test (where X is a logical variable), which yields *false* for every assignment of the variable X. The satisfiability test can be exemplified by the following Prolog clause

$dif(X,Y) = false :- var(X),var(Y),X==Y.$

where, in order to reduce the constraint as soon as possible, the special primitives *var* and $==$ are used, in a sound way.

4.2   Alfa and eta conversions

If we have an algorithm for confluent theories, eta-conversion does not pose particular problems. It can be added as a rewrite rule:

$\lambda(X,(M@X)) = M :- X \notin varfree(M)$.

As for alfa-conversion, in principle it could be introduced as a rewrite rule (actually an expansion rule)

$\lambda(X,B) = \lambda(Z,lambda(X,B)@Z) :- Z \notin varfree(B)$.

which executed by narrowing can prove alfa-equality with an infinite number of failing reductions (expansions). However, to cope with the alfa-equality in a "sensible" way, it is wise to embed it in the syntactic unification. The algorithm thus becomes a beta-eta-narrowing modulo alfa. If we represent syntactic equality by the term $eq(X,Y)$ the alfa-equality can be expressed as follows (but syntactic unification is implemented at a machine level):

eq(lambda(X,B),lambda(Y,B1)) = eq(lambda(X,B)@Z,lambda(Y,B1)@Z) :-

$$Z \notin varfree(B), Z \notin varfree(B1).$$

4.3 Impacts on the First-Order language

The scenario presented above, which has to be considered a research theme rather than a set of fully achieved results (in the sense that the completeness of the approach has not yet been proved), involves several assumptions on the underlying FO language. Some modifications and relaxations of constraints will be needed in K-LEAF, to make it able to directly support the kind of narrowing sketched above, necessary for a complete treatment of lambda-calculus. Among these features we recall: less strong distinction between functions and constructors, relaxation of the non-ambiguity constraint, introduction of the occur-check, strategies for carrying over unresolved constraints, ways of connecting with special algorithms for constraint satisfiability and (for more general purposes) with special unification algorithms.

4.4 Efficiency

So far the only figures about efficiency of functional programs compiled in a logical FO language are those obtained with the prototype language IDEAL, which is, as already mentioned, implemented in Prolog, following the original Warren's idea. We report here the timings (in seconds) relative to a simple benchmark (the computation of the list of permutations of a six-elements list) which exhibits a reasonable amount of closure construction, the distinctive feature for this kind of comparison. Three languages are compared, running on VAX780: Digital's Common Lisp and INRIA's LeLisp (with lexical scoping) both in their interpreted and compiled versions, and IDEAL, whose code is run by the C-Prolog interpreter and by Quintus Prolog.

```
map(F,[],C) = C,
map(F,[X|L],C) = [F@X|map(F,L,C)].
insert(A,[]) = [],
insert(A,[[]|L]) = [[A]],
insert(A,[L|L1]) = [[A|L]|map(lambda(E,[hd(L)|E],
                        insert(A,[tl(L)]),
                        insert(A,L1))].
perm([]) = [[]],
perm([A|L]) = insert(A,perm(L)).

perm([1,2,3,4,5,6]) = ?.
```

	Compiled	Interpreted
IDEAL (C-Prolog)		4.6
IDEAL (Quintus Prolog)	1.9	22
VAX Common Lisp	1.5	32
LeLisp	2.4	4.3

These figures, though having to be confirmed by a larger set of benchmarks, are quite encouraging. Similarly satisfactory results have been shown in [Heering86], where functional programs compiled into Prolog have been compared with the equational interpreter of [O'Donnel85].

5. Conclusions

Though the overall ESPRIT Project N.415 is on parallel architectures, and in this framework also the subproject D will produce as final result a parallel virtual machine, much of the work of the first two years concentrated, as scheduled, on the design of the L+F language, which was not in existence at the start. The result of the effort has been described in this paper, an can be judged quite satisfactory, even in comparison with what has been achieved elsewhere in the same domain.

While the choice of HO language as the user *ideal* language was mainly dictated by the need of powerful programming capabilities, the design of a new FO language to replace Prolog as intermediate compilation language was forced by the need of a semantic characterization, to start with, of the goals computable at the first order.

As regards parallelism, we are considering the applicability to the L+F language of the annotation scheme and computational model devised in [Giandonato86], and the mapping of these on the machine described in [Bosco87c].

Acknowledgement

This work has been partially sponsored by EEC under ESPRIT Project 415 "Parallel Architectures and Languages for Advanced Information Processing - a VLSI-directed approach".

References

[Barbuti84] **R. Barbuti, M. Bellia, G. Levi and M. Martelli**, On the integration of logic programming and functional programming, <u>Proc. 1984 Symp. on Logic Programming</u> (IEEE Comp. Society Press, 1985), 160-166.

[Barbuti86] **R. Barbuti, M. Bellia, G. Levi and M. Martelli**, LEAF: A language which integrates logic, equations and functions, in <u>Logic Programming: Functions, Relations and Equations,</u> D. DeGroot and G. Lindstrom, Eds. (Prentice-Hall, 1986), 201-238.

[Bellia85] **M. Bellia, E. Giovannetti, G. Levi and C. Moiso**, The relation between logic and functional languages, ESPRIT Project 415, First year report (1985).

[Bellia86] **M. Bellia and G. Levi**, The relation between logic and functional languages: A survey, <u>Journal of Logic Programming 3</u> (1986),217-236 .

[Bosco86a] **P.G. Bosco and E. Giovannetti**, IDEAL: An Ideal DEductive Applicative Language, <u>Proc. 1986 Symp. on Logic Programming</u> (IEEE Comp. Society Press, 1986), 89-94.

[Bosco86b] **P.G. Bosco, E. Giovannetti and C. Moiso**, A completeness result for a semantic unification algorithm based on conditional narrowing, to appear in <u>Proc. Foundations of Logic and Functional Programming</u> (Trento 15-19 December 1986).

[Bosco86c] **P.G. Bosco and E. Giovannetti**, A Prolog-compiled higher-order functional and logic language, to appear in <u>Proc. AIMSA '86</u> (North-Holland, 1986).

[Bosco87a] **P.G. Bosco, E. Giovannetti and C. Moiso**, Refined strategies for semantic unification, to appear in <u>Proc. TAPSOFT '87</u> (Springer-Verlag, 1987).

[Bosco87b] **P.G. Bosco, E. Giovannetti, G. Levi, C. Moiso and C. Palamidessi**, A complete semantic characterization of K-LEAF, a logic language with partial functions, submitted for publication (1987).

[Bosco87c] **P.G. Bosco, E. Giachin, G. Giandonato, G. Martinengo and C. Rullent**, A parallel architecture for signal understanding through inference on uncertain data, <u>these Proceedings</u>.

[Brand75] **D. Brand**, Proving theorems with the modification method, <u>SIAM J. Comput. 4</u> (1975), 412-430.

[Dershowitz85] **N. Dershowitz and D.A. Plaisted**, Logic Programming cum Applicative Programming, <u>Proc. 1985 Symp. on Logic Programming</u> (IEEE Comp. Society Press, 1985), 54-66.

[Fribourg85] **L. Fribourg**, SLOG: A logic programming language interpreter based on clausal superposition and rewriting, <u>Proc. 1985 Symp. on Logic Programming</u> (IEEE Comp. Society Press, 1985), 172-184.

[Giandonato86] **G. Giandonato and G. Sofi**, Parallelizing Prolog-based inference engines, ESPRIT Project 26, T4.3 Techn. Rep. (Sept. 1986).

[Giovannetti86a] **E. Giovannetti and C. Moiso**, Some aspects of the integration between logic programming and functional programming, to appear in <u>Proc. of AIMSA '86</u> (North-Holland).

[Giovannetti86b] **E.Giovannetti, G. Levi, C. Moiso and C. Palamidessi**, Kernel LEAF: an experimental logic plus functiona language - its syntax, semantics and computational model, ESPRIT Project 415, Second year report (1986).

[Goguen86] **J.A. Goguen and J. Meseguer**, Equality, types and generic modules for logic programming, in Logic Programming: Functions, Relations and Equations, D. DeGroot and G. Lindstrom, Eds. (Prentice-Hall, 1986), 295-364.

[Goldfarb81] **W. Goldfarb**, The undecidability of the second order unification problem, Theoretical Computer Science 13 (1981), 225-230.

[Heering86] **J. Heering and P. Klint**, The efficiency of the equation interpreter compared with the UNH Prolog interpreter, SIGPLAN Notices 21, n. 2 (ACM, 1986), 18-21.

[Holldöbler86] **S.Holldöbler**, A Unification Algorithm for Confluent Theories, Personal Communication (1986).

[Huet76] **G. Huet**, Resolution d'equations dans les langages d'ordre 1,2,...omega, These de Doctorat d'Etat, Universite' Paris VII (1976).

[Johnsson85] **T. Johnsson**, Lambda-lifting: Transforming Programs to Recursive Equations, Proc. of Int. Conf. of Functional Programming Lnguages and Architectures, LNCS 201(Springer-Verlag,1985), 190-203.

[Klop85] **J.W.Klop,** Term Rewriting Systems, Notes for the Summer Workshop on Reduction Machines (Ustica, 1985).

[Martelli87] **A. Martelli, C. Moiso and G.F. Rossi**, Lazy unification algorithms for canonical rewrite systems, to appear in Proc. of Colloquium on Resolution of Equations in Algebraic Structures, Lakeway, May 4-6 (Prentice-Hall).

[Miller86] **D. Miller and G. Nadathur**, Higher-Order Logic Programming, Proc. of Third Int. Conf on Logic Programming, LNCS 225 (Springer-Verlag,1986), 448-462.

[O'Donnell85] **M. O'Donnell**, Equational Logic as a Programming Language, (M.I.T. Press, 1985), 54-62.

[Revesz85] **G. Revesz**, Axioms for the theory of Lambda-conversion, SIAM J. COMP. vol.14, n.2 (May 1985), 373-382.

[Subrahmanyam86] **P.A. Subrahmanyam and J.-H. You**, FUNLOG: A computational model integrating logic programming and functional programming, in Logic Programming: Functions, Relations and Equations, D. DeGroot and G. Lindstrom, Eds. (Prentice-Hall, 1986), 157-198.

[Tamaki84] **H. Tamaki**, Semantics of a logic programming language with a reducibility predicate, Proc. 1984 Int. Symp. on Logic Programming (IEEE Comp. Society Press, 1984), 259-264.

[Turner85] **D.A. Turner**, MIRANDA: a non-strict functional language with polymorphic types, Proc. of Int. Conf. of Functional Programming Lnguages and Architectures, LNCS 201(Springer-Verlag,1985), 1-16.

[Warren82] **D. H. D. Warren**, Higher order extensions to Prolog. Are they needed?, Machine Intelligence 10 (Ellis Horwood, 1982), 441-454.

[Warren83] **D. H. D. Warren**, An Abstract Prolog Instruction Set, Technical Note 309, SRI International (Oct.1983).

[You86] **J.-H. You and P.A. Subrahmanyam**, E-unification algorithms for a class of confluent term rewriting systems, Proc. ICALP'86, LNCS 226 (Springer-Verlag, 1986), 454-463.

Overview of a Parallel Reduction Machine Project *

*D I Bevan, G L Burn and R J Karia ***

GEC Research Ltd
Hirst Research Centre
East Lane
Wembley
Middx. HA9 7PP
United Kingdom.

ABSTRACT

ESPRIT Project 415 has taken what are considered to be good programming language styles and is developing parallel architectures to support them. Here we describe the part of the project which is developing a distributed memory architecture for functional languages.

Designing parallel architectures for evaluating functional languages presents many challenging problems. Firstly a model for the parallel reduction of such languages must be found. An abstract interpretation has been developed which leads to a parallel reduction model. It can be implemented in a compiler so that programs can automatically be annotated with parallelism information.

The original COBWEB, a novel distributed memory architecture, is described, along with the conclusions we have drawn from our simulation work. We also briefly describe some of the architectural features of the architecture we are designing to support the parallel reduction model.

Many programming languages including functional ones require automatic storage allocation which has to be garbage collected. We present another piece of work from our project which has resulted in the discovery of a distributed reference counting garbage collection algorithm which has very low overheads.

Keywords : parallel reduction, functional languages, concurrent distributed garbage collection, combinators, COBWEB, evaluation transformers.

* Research partially funded by ESPRIT Project 415 : Parallel Architectures and Languages for AIP - A VLSI-Directed Approach.
** Electronic mail addresses of the latter two authors are geoff@gec-rl-hrc.co.uk and karia@gec-rl-hrc.co.uk respectively.

1. Introduction.

ESPRIT project 415 is investigating several styles of programming languages and architectures to support these languages. The project is taking a "languages first approach" to architectural design. Rather than designing a machine and then trying to implement a language on top of it, the project has chosen some styles of programming languages which are thought to be easier to program in and which are amenable to formal analysis, and is then investigating how to design parallel architectures to support them.

This paper deals with the parallel implementation of functional languages, work which is being completed by GEC Research Ltd at the Hirst Research Centre. We have found it especially interesting in this part of the project to see how much the language style influences architectural design.

The natural reduction model for the λ-calculus, upon which most functional languages are based is a sequential one. Therefore one of the first things we had to do was to see where we could obtain parallelism in the evaluation of functional languages. Our work on the abstract interpretation of functional languages has led us to a parallel reduction model which has the same feeling of naturalness as lazy evaluation does for sequential machines. This work is described in the second section of the paper.

While the work on the parallel reduction model was being completed, we investigated, using simulation, a novel distributed memory architecture for combinator reduction called COBWEB [Hankin, Osmon and Shute 1985]. Changes were made in the abstract machine to incorporate some of the early work on the analysis of functional languages for parallelism information. After a brief description of the architecture, a summary of our conclusions from this work is presented in the third section. We also give some indication of the constraints that a distributed memory architecture place on parallel reduction.

Finally, many languages, including functional ones, require automatic storage allocation and collection. This is a problem which is hard enough for sequential machines, but is even worse for distributed memory architectures. In section four a distributed reference counting garbage collection algorithm is outlined. It is more fully described in [Bevan 1987], a paper which also appears in this volume.

2. Parallelism in the Evaluation of Functional Programs.

There are two broad classes of ways we may choose to obtain parallelism in the evaluation of functional languages which have no explicit parallel constructs. A machine may employ *speculative parallel evaluation*, where all possible redexes in a graph are reduced in parallel, or it may use *conservative parallel evaluation*, where it only evaluates an expression if it knows it will need its value.

Speculative parallelism wastes machine resources by evaluating expressions which may eventually be discarded. For example, in the expression

    if condition then e_1 else e_2

the value of only one of e_1 and e_2 will be needed, depending on the truth of the *condition*. The problem is compounded in languages which allow the writing of expressions denoting infinite computations, for such computations may try and consume infinite amounts of resources.(*)

Because of the wastage of resources and the difficulties we foresaw in trying to garbage collect infinite processes, we decided to see if we could find out at compile-time when functions would definitely eventually need to reduce any of their arguments.

2.1. Determining Parallelism Information from Functional Programs.

By only ever evaluating the left-most outer-most redex and evaluating expressions only as far as head normal form, lazy evaluation ensures that no expression is evaluated more than is needed to produce the result of a calculation. While this is perfectly satisfactory for a sequential machine, it is hardly useful for a parallel machine for it only ever allows one expression to be evaluated at a time. The problem is that lazy evaluation is overly pessimistic about which expressions are going to be needed - it only knows that the left-most outer-most redex is needed.

Another way of looking at lazy evaluation is to notice that it never initiates a non-terminating computation unless the semantics of the original expression to be evaluated was undefined, that is, bottom. Our problem then reduces to ensuring that we do not initiate a non-terminating computation in evaluating a subexpression unless the semantics of the original expression is undefined. We will call this our *semantic criterion*.

By giving a different interpretation, an *abstract interpretation*, to the symbols in a programming language, we are sometimes able to find out information about a program without running it. An abstract interpretation for determining the definedness of functions in terms of the definedness of their arguments has been developed in a series of papers. Mycroft [Mycroft 1981] developed a strictness analysis for first-order functions

---

(*) An infinite computation does not necessarily mean no result is produced. When one has structured data types, a computation may produce a finite or unbounded amount of output as well as proceeding forever.

over atomic data types(*). This was extended in [Burn, Hankin and Abramsky 1986] to a strictness analysis for higher-order functions. Wadler [Wadler 1985] introduced an abstract domain for structured data types such as lists. All of these various strands were drawn together in [Burn 1986] where a framework for the abstract interpretation of functional languages was developed and applied to this problem.

Traditionally this abstract interpretation has been used to give a *strictness analysis* of functional programs, that is, finding if a function application is undefined when one of its arguments is undefined. However, this loses information, for it only tests the semantic criterion locally. By looking at the abstract interpretation in another way, we are able to determine more parallelism information, which leads to a natural model for the parallel evaluation of functional languages. We call the results of this analysis *evaluation transformers*, for they tell how much evaluation can be done to an argument of a function given that we can do a certain amount of evaluation of the function application.

The analysis can be completed by a compiler.

2.2. Evaluators.

We know that in some function applications, the argument will need more reduction than just to *head normal form (HNF)*. For example, an application of the function

$$length\ [] = 0$$
$$length\ x{:}xs = 1 + length\ xs$$

will eventually need to traverse the whole of the argument list, but will not need any of the values of elements of the list. The function

$$sumlist\ [] = 0$$
$$sumlist\ x{:}xs = x + sumlist\ xs$$

needs to traverse the whole of its argument list and also obtain the values of the elements of the list. We will call the process of recursively evaluating the second argument of *cons* until we reach *nil* (if we do, which will only happen if the list is finite), creating the *structure* of the list. There is a similar idea for all recursively defined types, such as integer binary trees which have type equation :

$$tree \cong 1 + num \times tree \times tree$$

or in a Miranda [Turner 1985](**) definition :

(*) An *atomic data type* is one which has a flat domain as its usual interpretation. Integers and booleans are two examples.

$$tree ::= \quad NIL\_TREE \mid NODE \; num \; tree \; tree$$

where the second and third arguments to the *NODE* constructor are recursively evaluated. Basically, evaluating the structure of an expression is unfolding the recursive part of the data type definition.

We will say that we can evaluate an expression using a particular *evaluator*, and call an evaluator which evaluates expressions to HNF ξ_1, an evaluator which evaluates the structure of a list ξ_2, and an evaluator which evaluates the structure of a list and every element of the list to HNF ξ_3. For completeness, the evaluator ξ_0 does no evaluation. The relationship between the evaluators is

$$\xi_3 > \xi_2 > \xi_1 > \xi_0$$

where the relationship > is read as *stronger than*, because the first evaluator does more evaluation than the second.

The abstract interpretation of [Wadler 1985], [Burn 1986] is able to detect situations when functions need to do more evaluation of their arguments than just to HNF. It can be used to determine *evaluation transformers* [Burn 1986], [Burn 1987] which will tell us which evaluator we may use for the argument in an application when given the evaluator we can use for the application.

2.3. A Model for the Parallel Evaluation of Functional Languages.

Just as lazy evaluation is the natural model for the sequential evaluation of functional languages, programs annotated with evaluation transformers lead to a natural model for their parallel evaluation.

One way of representing a functional program is as a graph [Wadsworth 1971] of binary apply nodes. Thus the application

$$f e_1 \cdots e_n$$

would be represented as :

(**) Miranda is a trademark of Research Software Ltd.

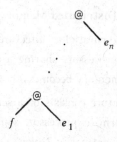

Left-most outer-most reduction is obtained by traversing the spine of the application, until the function f is reached. A copy of the body of f is made, substituting pointers to the arguments e_1 to e_m if f needs m arguments, and the root of this graph overwrites the the application node which points to e_m. Traversal of the spine begins again at this node. An excellent coverage of graph reduction is given in [Peyton Jones 1987].

Suppose we label the graph with evaluation transformers ET_1 to ET_n as in the diagram :

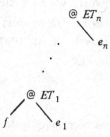

and that we are evaluating the expression with the evaluator ξ. Then the only thing that changes with the evaluation mechanism is that when traversing the spine of the graph, a task is initiated to evaluate each expression e_i with the evaluator $ET_i(\xi)$.

There are some important things to note about this evaluation mechanism. Any particular expression is being evaluated using left-most outer-most reduction. The evaluation mechanism is not some sort of parallel-innermost reduction strategy (i.e. a parallel version of call-by-value), for in the case that the f in the above example is a user-defined function, the evaluation of the expression e_i proceeds in parallel with the evaluation of the expression $f e_1 \cdots e_n$.

The abstract machine of [Clack and Peyton Jones 1986] solves the problems of synchronisation of processes evaluating pieces of the graph on a shared memory architecture when only the evaluator ξ_1 is being used. In [Karia 1987] an abstract distributed memory architecture is defined which fully supports the evaluation transformer model of parallel reduction. This is in the process of being further refined [Bevan et al 1987].

3. Parallel Graph Reduction and Distributed Memory Architectures.

For our purposes, we can divide parallel architectures into two broad classes. Shared memory architectures have many processors sharing a common memory. The problem with such architectures is that the memory becomes a bottle-neck in the system.

A distributed memory architecture consists of a series of *processing elements* (*PEs*), each containing, in its simplest form, a processor, some memory and communications capacity, connected together by a network. Given a suitable network, a distributed memory architecture in theory has no bounds to its extensibility. Because of this, we have chosen to develop a distributed memory architecture to support our parallel graph reduction model.

Concurrently with the work on the parallel reduction model, we have been investigating a particular computer architecture, the COBWEB, and the next section describes the results of that investigation.

Since finishing the simulation work, we have stepped back in order to determine more abstractly the essential features for the support of parallel graph reduction on a distributed memory architecture [Bevan et al 1987]. Two main findings of this investigation are summarised in section 3.2.

3.1. The COBWEB

One of the architectures that has been investigated in detail in our subproject is the COBWEB, a proposed architecture that exploits the potential of Wafer Scale Integration to support an SK1-combinator reduction model. A description of the architecture is given in [Shute and Osmon 1985] and an abstract machine for it is described in [Hankin, Osmon and Shute 1985].

In this section, a brief description of the architecture along with some discussion of the simulation results is given.

3.1.1. Overall Architecture

The COBWEB consists of a large matrix of identical processing elements on a wafer, each of which is capable of communicating and receiving tokens of machine code to and from its neighbours. The machine owes its name to the way in which the processing elements are interconnected. A bidirectional communications line originating from a central port in the two dimensional matrix of processors traverses through the processors in a spiral pattern and ends at the outermost processor, establishing a circumferential line for communication between processors. Bidirectional lines also traverse radially from the centre outwards through processors so that tokens can be communicated to an outer level in the web. The configuration is established dynamically by the processing elements on start up, avoiding any faulty processing elements and creating a spiral of all the good ones. This scheme was originally proposed in [Aubusson and Catt 1978], and ensures both fault tolerance and graceful degradation in the event of failing elements on the wafer. An example spiral configuration of processors is shown in Figure 3.1.1-1.

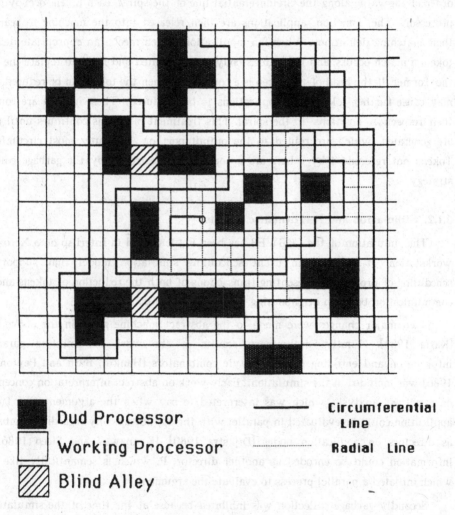

Dud Processor — Circumferential Line

Working Processor ⋯⋯ Radial Line

Blind Alley

Figure 3.1.1-1

A functional program is translated into combinators which can be represented as a graph. Tokens constitute the nodes of the combinator graph. The combinators used include the ones used in Turner's machine [Turner 1979] along with the **P** and **P'** combinators described in [Hankin, Burn and Peyton Jones 1986] for strict functions. Each token has an identifying tag by which it is addressed by other tokens. A program consists of two types of tokens - those that represent nodes in the function definitions and those that represent the function applications being reduced. Initially, the defining tokens are fed into the machine via the input port. By virtue of the communications logic in each processing element, they arrange themselves in ascending order of tag value along the circumferential line of the spiral, each token occupying one processor. The function applications are then released into the machine to search for their matching definitions. When an application token meets an appropriate definition token, a match occurs, and the latter's body is instantiated and made to replace the tag in the former. If the head of the token is a combinator then the token can be reduced, which may cause further tokens and applications to be produced. These in turn are routed to their respective positions in the spiral. This treatment of tokens continues until results are generated, which are routed to the output port on the outer most circumference. Tokens not referenced by others are automatically destroyed by the garbage collection strategy.

3.1.2. Simulation and Performance Results

The simulation of the COBWEB has been implemented in Interlisp on a Xerox 1108 workstation. It includes an event scheduling simulation model that supports the scheduling of processes representing transactions of both the reduction of tokens and their communication between neighbouring processing elements.

Two major changes were made to the abstract machine given in the above papers [Karia 1987]. Firstly, preliminary results of the work of detecting parallelism information and encoding it in SKI-style combinators [Hankin, Burn and Peyton Jones 1986] was included in the simulation. Early work on abstract interpretation concentrated on strictness analysis, which was interpreted to say when the argument in a function application could be evaluated in parallel with the application. By regarding combinators as directors on application nodes [Dijkstra 1980], [Kennaway and Sleep 1986], this information could be encoded as another director, **P**, which is semantically like **I**, but which initiated a parallel process to evaluate the argument.

Secondly garbage collection was inhibited because at the time of the simulation we had no suitable garbage collection algorithm for a distributed memory architecture. This situation has been solved in [Bevan 1987]. As well, deleting tokens in the middle of the contiguous chain of tokens merely increases the number of token hops, an overhead, whose price obscures the simulated time for the execution of a program.

In the realisation of the abstract machine in the simulation a third change was made in that square rather than hexagonal processors were used.

The simulation experiments were carried out on an "ideal" wafer, i.e. one without dud processing elements in order to determine the maximum possible performance.

We will not go into the simulation results in detail, for they are covered adequately elsewhere, for example [Karia 1987], but briefly discuss some of the lessons which we have learnt from the simulation.

One of the principal results of the simulation of a multiprocessor is its *speedup* factor, i.e. the ratio between the time taken to execute a program on a single processor to that taken on the whole system. This is the scheme adopted by a number of researchers investigating dataflow and reduction machines using simulation techniques, e.g. [Hudak 1985]. The move from a uniprocessor to a multiprocessor allows for parallelism at the cost of overheads in communication, which degrade the ideal performance, viz an n fold improvement (where n is the number of processors). For example a program that takes x time units to execute on a uniprocessor, would ideally take $\frac{x}{2}$ time units on two processors but in practice would take $\frac{x}{2} + y$, where y represents communication overheads. There are, of course, other factors that increase y, such as how much parallelism the algorithm has, memory management within each node, etc. but these are not as readily measurable as communication time. For a distributed memory reduction machine, communication time is dependent on the *access latency*, i.e. the time taken by an expression to access a subexpression whose value it needs. Consequently, simulation experiments are done to investigate schemes on the architecture to minimize access latency. As an example, one factor that influences access latency is the locality of reference in the program.

On COBWEB, the number of reductions done during program execution is merely a fraction of the number of hops. This implies that a fairly coarse grain of computation is required to balance communication overheads before benefiting from migrating work over the spiral. For example, our experiment with *pfac* 1 8(*), where *pfac* is the parallel factorial function defined by

$$
\begin{aligned}
pfac\ x\ y\ &=\ x\ \text{if}\quad x = y \\
&=\ x \times y\ \text{if}\ y - x = 1 \\
&=\ (pfac\ x\ z) \times (pfac\ (z + 1)\ y)\ \textbf{where}\ z = (x + y)/2
\end{aligned}
$$

showed that the grain for that program had to be large enough to be at least 6 times greater than the time for one hop. Hence, the need for a larger grain than SKI-combinators is one of the conclusions drawn from our simulation.

Since communication overheads dominate execution time, the machine's performance largely depends on how efficiently tokens are managed. The experiments that have been done with the simulator have been to identify what values of the variable parameters of COBWEB ensure efficient token management and minimal communication overheads. Unfortunately, the experiments show that suitable values for these parameters depend on the size of the program being executed. For example, the required ratio between ALU time and hop time varies with program size and so does the number of free tags required per cell to avoid tag requests. These, in addition to several other variable factors render the machine's performance is quite unpredictable and hence, no consistent measure of the speedup factor is obtainable. For this reason, the idea to run a suite of programs on the simulation was abandoned. Given the time taken to run a single experiment on the Xerox 1108 (typically 11 and 30 hours for *pfac* 1 8 and *pfac* 1 16 respectively), it was decided that the amount of useful information gained from trying a suite of programs would not be sufficient to justify carrying out such experiments. The results anticipated from such runs is the same as those seen with *pfac* .

One of COBWEB's features that distinguishes it from other distributed memory architectures is its unique addressing scheme. We have attempted to minimize access latency by defining a suitable routing algorithm for a spiral configuration and by providing an element of locality in the distribution of free tags. At present, the routing algorithm relies on the tags of tokens residing in each cell. The latter are constantly being shuffled, and hence, tokens are being sent through a maze of varying addresses to a moving destination. Also, the experiments have shown that radial lines are very poorly utilised. Perhaps allocating absolute addresses to the cells on a wafer would overcome a lot of the problems associated with routing tokens. Having absolute addresses would allow for a packet switching scheme for the routing of tokens as is done in some recently proposed point to point network multiprocessors, e.g. Cosmic cube [Seitz 1985]. It also overcomes the need for free tags, since the address space would be directly mapped onto memory locations or registers in cells. A third advantage of absolute addressing would be that resident tokens would not need to be maintained in a contiguous chain, i.e. gaps in the program are allowable. This does away with the need for pull tokens which are created to close the gaps in the spiral caused by the deletion of a token. A scheme for fault tolerant reconfiguration and token routing on a wafer with absolute address cells has been proposed [Anderson et al 1987].

The use of a spiral configuration makes COBWEB, in the best case (i.e. when there are no faulty cells) a two dimensional grid of processing elements. What is required of a network in a reduction multiprocessor is to diffuse work rapidly to all processors as it is generated, whilst maintaining locality of reference. The problem of locality of reference in functional programs has so far remained unanswered. However, topologies for multiprocessor systems have been proposed that have the diffusion property, e.g. doubly twisted torus, hypertree etc. These have been experimented with by other researchers in architectures for functional programming. For example, [Hudak 1984] shows how a doubly twisted torus diffuses work better than a complete interconnection of processors when experimenting with a simple diffusion heuristic.

In spite of the defects identified in COBWEB, it has several good features that can be well exploited in reduction architectures. For example, the use of variable sized tokens is a unique feature of COBWEB's abstract machine. The use of variable sized tokens eliminates the need to traverse graphs composed of binary apply nodes as in other proposed machines [Turner 1979], [Johnsson 1987], [Peyton-Jones, Clack and Salkild 1985]. Another favourable feature of COBWEB is the manner in which function definitions are maintained. Since tokens constituting a definition are spread over a number of processors, several tokens that are applications of a definition can concurrently traverse it in a pipelined fashion. This overcomes the need to hold several copies of the definition over the network of processors. Such a scheme is also employed in dataflow machines. Finally, COBWEB has been a very useful vehicle for research, since it incorporates numerous innovative approaches to reduction. Among the ideas generated from working with COBWEB are the refinement of the abstract machine to perform graph reduction and to evaluate programs in parallel (as opposed to normal order), the definition of a distributed reference count garbage collection scheme [Bevan 1987], and some ideas for the definition of an alternative reduction architecture which is described in [Bevan et al 1987].

At present, a collaborative project funded by the Alvey Committee in the UK is under way to investigate modifications to COBWEB's architecture to overcome the aforementioned problems in its original design [Anderson et al 1987].

3.2. Principles for the Design of a Distributed Memory Architecture.

COBWEB embodies many unique architectural features, and is very different to shared memory architectures for graph reduction. With this in mind, we decided to try and find out what features were essential features which had to be included in a distributed memory architecture for graph reduction [Bevan et al 1987].

There were two main conclusions. The first is that at the abstract machine level, programs must be represented as variable-sized tokens. Each token must be a *maximally unsharable* piece of the spine of the graph. This means that one does not have to traverse the spine over the network and also that sharing is not compromised. Interestingly these tokens correspond exactly to the tokens of COBWEB.

Secondly, the unit of work is to reduce an expression to head normal form. Because expressions are not allowed to be copied until they are in head normal form, this is a natural unit of computation; the root token of the result does not need to overwrite the root token of the original expression until it is in head normal form.

These ideas are incorporated into an abstract distributed memory architecture which supports our parallel reduction model in [Bevan et al 1987].

4. Distributed Reference Counting Garbage Collection.

One of the major problems with implementing languages which require some sort of automatic storage allocation is the recovery of storage when it is no longer needed. For an architecture which has several processors and memories, the problem is compounded because data structures may become spread over several memory modules. Reference counting garbage collection is attractive because memory is freed as soon as an object is no longer referenced, rather than having to stop the machine to do some sort of mark scan algorithm.

A major problem with reference counting garbage collection is that the natural way to think of it working is that whenever a reference to an object is duplicated, then the reference count of the object is incremented. Similarly, when a reference to an object is deleted, the reference count is decremented. This is not easily lifted to a distributed architecture because there is the problem that a decrement message may reach an object before an increment message, and so the object is deleted before it should be. A solution to this problem is to introduce a complex protocol such as in [Lerman and Maurer 1986].

The key point of our algorithm is that it only requires decrement messages to be sent, and so alleviates the need for complex protocols. Below we briefly outline the algorithm which is discussed in detail in [Bevan 1987].

4.1. The Basic Algorithm.

We assume that our machine consists of a number of PEs and that on each PE there are a number of objects. These objects may contain references to other objects (or indeed themselves), possibly on other nodes. At any time a reference may be deleted or a new object may be created and a reference to it created from an object already in existence. Similarly, at any time, a reference may be copied from one object to another. We require that no object be deleted if it is referenced and that objects be deleted when they are no longer referenced.

In order to achieve this, we associate with each reference a positive weight and with each object a reference count. The algorithm attempts to maintain the following invariant.

The reference count of an object is equal to the sum of the weights of the references to it.

This ensures that the reference count of an object is zero if and only if it is not referenced by another object. An object can thus be deleted if its reference count is zero. We consider the different possible operations on references separately.

When a new object is created with a reference from some object already in existence, the new object may be given an arbitrary reference count and the reference to it a weight equal to that reference count (see Figure 4.1-1(i)). This maintains the invariant.

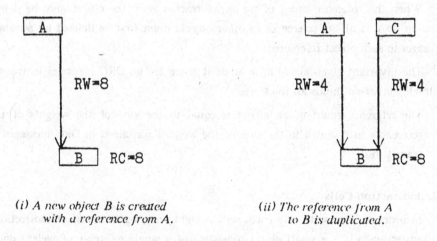

(i) A new object B is created   *(ii) The reference from A*
with a reference from A.   *to B is duplicated.*

Figure 4.1-1

When a reference is duplicated, its weight is split between the two resulting references in such a way that the sum of the weights of the resulting references is equal to the original weight of the initial reference (see Figure 4.1-1(ii)). This maintains the invariant without needing to communicate with the object referenced or to change its reference count.

When a reference to an object is deleted, the reference count of the object needs to be reduced by the weight of the reference. To achieve this, a message, known as a *decrement reference count (DRC)* message, is sent to the object. This message contains the weight of

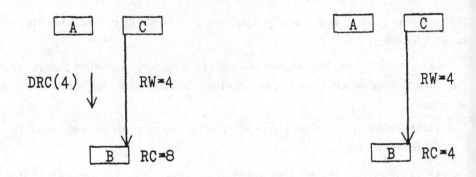

The reference from A to B is deleted.

Figure 4.1-2

the deleted reference. When an object receives a DRC message, it decrements its reference count by the weight contained in the message (see Figure 4.1-2). Thus the invariant is maintained.

When the reference count of an object reaches zero, the object may be deleted. In order to do this all its references to other objects must first be deleted by sending DRC messages to each object referenced.

The invariant given above now holds if there are no DRC messages in transit. The following invariant holds all the time.

The reference count of an object is equal to the sum of the weights of the references to it added to the sum of the weights contained in DRC messages in transit to it.

4.2. Indirection Cells

In order to cope with references with weight one, we make use of indirection cells. An indirection cell is a small object consisting of a single reference of weight one. Since the weight of the reference in an indirection cell is always one, its value need not be stored. When we wish to duplicate a reference with weight one we create an indirection cell containing a copy of the reference to be duplicated and having a maximum reference count. This indirection cell can be created on the same node as the object containing the reference to be duplicated, so no communication is necessary. Note that the reference count of the referenced object does not need to be changed. The reference to be duplicated is replaced with a reference to the indirection cell with maximum weight. This new reference can then be duplicated as normal (see figure 4.2-1).

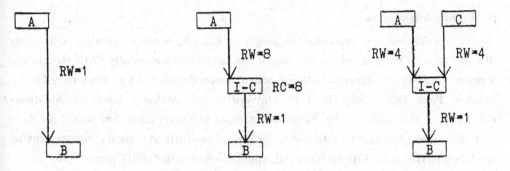

*Duplication of a reference with weight one
using an indirection cell*

Figure 4.2-1

4.3. Further Issues and Analysis of the Algorithm.

The paper [Bevan 1987] gives many more details and also shows how space overheads can be decreased by coding the refence information.

There are two ways in by which the performance of the algorithm can be measured, namely how many indirection cells an evaluator will have to go through in order to reach the object being referenced, and what the space overheads of recording the reference information are. Clearly the number of indirection cells is determined by how big the reference count and reference weight fields are. By taking into account the characteristics of the execution of functional programs, it is shown in [Bevan 1987] that the overheads are encouragingly small, typically between one and three bits per reference field for very good performance.

5. Conclusions and Further Work.

Two major breakthroughs have been made in this part of the project, namely the definition of a natural parallel reduction model and the discovery of a distributed reference counting garbage collection algorithm which has low overheads.

Using experience gained in looking at various parallel architectures for parallel graph reduction, and especially COBWEB, we have defined a distributed memory architecture which supports our parallel reduction model [Bevan et al 1987]. An emulation of our parallel reduction model could quite well be helpful in helping us understand how such a machine will work, and we need to now simulate our architecture.

410

6. Acknowledgements.

Our work has not proceeded in isolation, but has benefited greatly from many discussions with various people. We would like to single out especially Chris Hankin and Samson Abramsky of Imperial College London, Simon Peyton Jones of University College London, Peter Osmon of The City University and Malcolm Shute of Middlesex Polytechnic. The work on the distributed garbage collection algorithm would not have been done if we had not been forced to look more carefully at memory management by the Working Group on Architectures and Applications within ESPRIT project 415.

This work has been partially funded by ESPRIT Project 415 - Parallel Architectures and Languages for AIP : A VLSI-Directed Approach.

7. References.

[Anderson et al 1987]

Anderson, P., Hankin, C., Kelly, P., Osmon, P., and Shute, M., COBWEB-2 : Structured Specification of A Wafer-Scale Supercomputer, *In this volume*.

[Aubusson and Catt 1978]

Aubusson, R.C., and Catt, I., Wafer Scale Integration - A Fault-Tolerant Procedure, *IEEE Journal of Solid State Circuits*, Sc-13, 3, 1978.

[Bevan 1987]

Bevan, D.I., Distributed Garbage Collection Using Reference Counting, *In this volume*.

[Bevan et al 1987]

Bevan, D.I., Burn, G.L., Karia, R.J., and Robson, J.D., Design Principles of a Distributed Memory Architecture for Parallel Graph Reduction, Submitted to : *Third International Conference on Functional Programming Languages and Computer Architecture*, September 1987.

[Burn 1986]

Burn, G.L., *Abstract Interpretation and the Parallel Evaluation of Functional Languages*, PhD Thesis, Department of Computing, Imperial College of Science and Technology, University of London, 1986.

[Burn 1987]

Burn, G.L., Evaluation Transformers - A Model for the Parallel Evaluation of Functional Languages (Extended Abstract), Submitted to : *Third International Conference on Functional Programming Languages and Computer Architecture*, September 1987.

[Burn, Hankin and Abramsky 1986]

Burn, G.L., Hankin, C.L., and Abramsky, S., Strictness Analysis for Higher-Order Functions, *Science of Computer Programming*, 7, November 1986, pp.249-278.

[Clack and Peyton Jones 1986]

Clack, C., and Peyton Jones, S.L., The Four-Stroke Reduction Engine, *Proceedings of the 1986 ACM Conference on Lisp and Functional Programming*, Cambridge, Massachusetts, 4-6 August, 1986, pp. 220-232.

[Dijkstra 1980]

Dijkstra, E.W., *A Mild Variant of Combinatory Logic, EWD735, 1980.*

[Hankin, Burn and Peyton Jones, 1986]

Hankin, C.L., Burn, G.L., and Peyton Jones, S.L., A Safe Approach to Parallel Combinator Reduction (Extended Abstract), *Proceedings ESOP 86 (European Symposium on Programming)*, Saarbrucken, Federal Republic of Germany, March 1986, Robinet, B., and Wilhelm, R. (eds.), Springer-Verlag LNCS 213, pp. 99-110.

[Hankin, Burn and Peyton Jones, 1987]

Hankin, C.L., Burn, G.L., and Peyton Jones, S.L., A Safe Approach to Parallel Combinator Reduction, To be published in, *Theoretical Computer Science.*

[Hankin, Osmon and Shute 1985]

Hankin, C.L., Osmon, P.E., and Shute, M.J., COBWEB: A Combinator Reduction Architecture, in : *Proceedings of IFIP International Conference on Functional Programming Languages and Computer Architecture*, Nancy, France, 16-19 September, 1985, Jouannaud, J.-P. (ed.), Springer-Verlag LNCS 201, pp. 99-112.

[Hudak 1984]

Hudak P. and Goldberg B., Experiments in Diffused Combinator Reduction, *ACM Symposium on Lisp and Functional Programming*, Austin, Texas, USA, August 1984, pp 167-176.

[Hudak 1985]

Hudak P. and Goldberg, B., Distributed Execution of Functional Programs using Serial Combinators, *IEEE Transactions on Computers, Vol C-34* 10, October 1985.

[Johnsson 1987]

Johnsson, T., *Compiling Lazy Functional Languages*, PhD Thesis, Department of Computer Sciences, Chalmers University of Technology, 1987.

[Karia 1987]

Karia, R.J., *An Investigation of Combinator Reduction on Multiprocessor Architectures*, PhD Thesis, University of London, January 1987.

[Kennaway and Sleep 1986]

Kennaway, R., and Sleep, R., *Director Strings as Combinators*, University of East Anglia Technical Report, November 1986.

[Lerman and Maurer 1986]

Lerman, C.-W. and Maurer, D., A Protocol for Distributed Reference Counting, *Proceedings 1986 ACM Conference on Lisp and Functional Programming*, Cambridge, Massachusetts, August 4-6, 1986,

[Mycroft 1981]

Mycroft, A., *Abstract Interpretation and Optimising Transformations for Applicative Programs*, PhD. Thesis, University of Edinburgh, 1981.

[Peyton Jones 1987]

Peyton Jones, S.L., *Implementing Functional Languages Using Graph Reduction*, To be published in the Prentice-Hall International Series in Computer Science, 1987.

[Peyton Jones, Clack and Salkild 1985]

Peyton Jones, S.L., Clack, C. and Salkild, J., *GRIP - A Parallel Graph Reduction Machine*, Dept of Computer Science, University College, London, November 1985.

[Seitz 1985]

Seitz, C.L., The Cosmic Cube, *CACM 28, 1*, January 1985.

[Shute and Osmon 1985]

Shute, M.J., and Osmon, P.E., COBWEB - A reduction architecture, *International Workshop on Wafer-Scale Integration*, 10-12 July, 1985, Southampton University, United Kingdom.

[Turner 1979]

Turner, D.A., Another Algorithm For Bracket Abstraction, *The Journal of Symbolic Logic 44* 2, June 1979, pp. 267-270.

[Turner 1985]

Turner, D.A., Miranda: A non-strict functional language with polymorphic types, *Functional Programming Languages and Computer Architecture*, September 1985, Nancy, Jouannaud, J.-P., (ed.), Springer-Verlag LNCS 201, pp. 1-16.

[Wadler 1985]

Wadler, P., *Strictness Analysis on Non-Flat Domains (by Abstract Interpretation over Finite Domains)*, Draft Manuscript distributed via the FP mailboard, 10th November, 1985.

[Wadsworth 1971]

Wadsworth, C.P., *Semantics and Pragmatics of the Lambda Calculus (Chapter 4)*, PhD Thesis, University of Oxford, 1971.

AN OVERVIEW OF DDC: DELTA DRIVEN COMPUTER.

R. Gonzalez-Rubio, J. Rohmer, A. Bradier.
BULL SA CENTRE DE RECHERCHE
DSG/CRG/DMIA - PC 58 A 13
B.P. N° 3
68, Route de Versailles
78430 Louveciennes. France.

ABSTRACT

In this paper we present an overview of the DDC "Delta Driven Computer" and the state of this research project at the end of 1986.

DDC is a parallel inference computer, composed by a set of PCM (Processor, Communication Device, Memory) nodes interconnected. It is currently under design at BULL Research Center[*] .

From a conceptual point of view, DDC executes a language based on production rules, called VIM Virtual Inference Machine. This execution is made following the forward chaining strategy. Given a set of rules and a set of initial facts, the only mode of operation of the machine is the saturation (all conclusions are found).

VIM is an intermediate language; so, part of the project is the study of how to translate from a high level language to this intermediate language. The high level languages which we are thinking about are declarative ones (i.e. Logic Programming or Functional Programming).

The execution of VIM is possible by the DDEM Delta Driven Execution Model.The parallelism in the machine is achieved by distributing the facts among PCM nodes and by firing rules independently in each processor.

One goal of this project is to have a first prototype (including both hardware and software) at the end of 1987, so we try to prove that the parallelism handled by the model/machine has a valuable rate cost/performance.

[*] THIS WORK IS PARTIALLY SUPPORTED BY:
ESPRIT Project 415.

1 INTRODUCTION.

We present here the general ideas of DDC "Delta Driven Computer" and the state of this research project at the end of 1986.

DDC is a parallel inference multiprocessor computer, currently under design at BULL Research Center; early papers are just describing just part of our ideas [Gon 85], [Gon 86].

The architecture of DDC can be viewed as a multiprocessor system composed by a set of PCM (Processor, Communication device, Memory) nodes interconnected, in which there is no need to have a shared memory.

From a conceptual point of view, DDC executes a language based on production rules, called VIM (Virtual Inference Machine). This execution is made following the forward chaining strategy. Given a set of rules and a set of initial facts, the only mode of operation of the machine is the saturation (all conclusions are found).

VIM is an intermediate language; so, in the project, we study how to translate from a high level language to this intermediate language. The high level languages which we are thinking about are declarative ones (i.e. Logic Programming or Functional Programming).

The execution of VIM is possible with the DDEM (Delta Driven Execution Model). In this model the execution is driven by the facts deduced by the rules. We call these "new" facts the Delta.The parallel architecture we propose can support the DDEM.

The parallelism of the machine is achieved by distributing the facts among PCM nodes and by firing rules independently in each processor.

The implementation of DDEM is based on relational operations, so VIM rules are transformed into a program in DDCL (Delta Driven Computer Language).

One goal of this project is to have a running prototype (including both hardware and software) at the end of 1987. We had to take some decisions, and we made some restrictions to implement this prototype, but the ideas included it must prove that the parallelism handled by the model/machine has an interesting cost/performance rate.

In section 2 we give a general overview of the project DDC, the motivations for its architecture, and the key ideas concerning the different levels of languages . Section 3 presents the architecture and the DDEM mapped into it. Section 4 gives the current ideas of the first implementation. Section 5 gives some conclusions and an open for the future work.

2 A GENERAL OVERVIEW OF DDC.

2.1 MOTIVATIONS.

The basic motivations of the DDC project have been to design an efficient computer dedicated mainly to symbolic computation, to build "large" Artificial Intelligence (AI) applications.

Let us start by analyzing the situation in eighties. In one hand, the needs for high efficiency in AI are clear. It is commonly thought that they are from 100 Mlips to 1 Glips (see [Mot 84]).

But to reach such performances only with technological progress offered by Ultra Large Scale Integration is not possible. This is due to the von Neumann architecture model which is characterized by its sequential operations. Effectively, we know that the execution time of the instruction of a machine is bound by the propagation time of signals. Then predictions are that a processor's clock period cannot be smaller than 1 ns. Hence, the maximum performances are under the order of the Giga instructions per second [Lun 85]. Thus the only issue is to design parallel architectures.

On another hand, the requirement of AI machines is to maintain software costs as low as possible. This could be feasible by using a simple high level language where parallelism is hidden for the programmer.

Consequently, a prerequisite to the design of a specialized AI parallel architecture is an execution model well adapted to handle parallelism and symbolic processing.

Another prerequisite is that the architecture must not be dedicated to one particular language. Instead, it is enough opened to accommodate a variety of programming declarative styles, including:

- relational + deduction
- logic
- functional.

Typical applications for this architecture stem from relational databases, deductive databases, expert systems, simulation systems, etc..

2.2 AN INTERMEDIATE LANGUAGE APPROACH.

The language levels in DDC are:

- a high level language, which is issued of logic programming or functional programming. Currently we just work in the logic programming side.

- an intermediate language, which is the key of our approach. This language is based on production rules with a forward chaining (saturation) strategy. We call this language VIM.

- to execute the saturation the DDEM is provided. This model can be parallelized, as explained later. In fact a VIM program is translated into a program DDCL (Delta Driven Computer Language). DDC machine language is DDCL, and a program is executed following the DDEM.

The translation from a logic programming language into a VIM program is done following an algorithm called the Alexander Method, proposed by J. Rohmer [Roh 85].

In fact we define these three levels of language to get a better understanding of how the system works.

In the next sub-sections we describe the VIM language, to present how a computation takes place. Then, we examine the Alexander Method to show how a logic program is translated into a VIM program. We also present the DDEM, DDCL and the architecture of the machine.

We want to underline that what we present in the next sections are just the basic ideas of how to implement DDC, and at the end we consider how the machine can be used.

2.2.1 Virtual Inference Machine VIM.

The design of VIM is based on our background experience on production systems. [Pug 85]).

Basically, this language is composed of production rules [Pug 86], i.e. rules of the form:

$$h_1 \Rightarrow c_1, \ldots \ldots c_p$$
$$h_1, h_2 \Rightarrow c_1, \ldots \ldots c_p$$

Where the H_i and c_j are predicates of the form:

$$p(X_1, \ldots \ldots, X_n)$$

Where x_i is either an atom (constant) or a variable.

This means that functions (or trees) are not visible at this level.

We impose that variables in the conclusions must appear also in the hypotheses.

We can remark that the restrictions that we imposed to VIM are the same than these of Datalog (Logic database).

This means that if initially there exists a set of facts composed by constants, all the generated facts will also be composed by constants.

For implementation reasons we impose a maximum of 2 hypotheses in rules.

The only mode of operation of the machine is the saturation: Given a set of clauses and a set of initial facts "Find all possible conclusions".

The computation model is based on the notion of saturation of a rule-set by a set of facts. This notion corresponds to the generation of the semantic model associated to the logic program made of clauses. This model is indeed the Least Fixed Point of the set of clauses (rules and facts are just clauses in First Order Logic).

Example.

Consider the following rules:

```
father(X,Y) => ancestor(X,Y)
ancestor(X,Y),ancestor(Y,Z) => ancestor(X,Z)
```

Consider the set of initial facts:

```
father(1,2)
father(2,3)
father(3,4)
```

When a saturation takes place, all the ancestors are deduced.

```
ancestor(1,2)        ancestor(1,3)
ancestor(2,3)        ancestor(2,4)
ancestor(3,4)        ancestor(1,4)
```

The saturation stops when no more facts can be deduced. The termination of the saturation process was proved by J.M. Kerisit [Ker 86] in a Datalog framework.

The saturation process in the case of commutative rules can be executed in parallel.This means that the rules can be fired at the same time, as data are available.

We can describe the DDEM in an informal way at the VIM level. When a rule is applied, then eventually a fact or a set of facts is deduced, in our terminology a BΔ (read Black Delta). Only those facts which are not contained in the database are considered as new ones or in our terminology as a WΔ (read White Delta), and this WΔ is inserted in the database, then the rules can be tried again using just the WΔ as trigger.

Example:

Consider the set of facts and rules of the previous exemple:

We consider that the initial facts are WΔ:

The following facts can be deduced when the first rule is applied:

```
ancestor(1,2)        ancestor(2,3)
ancestor(3,4)
```

As they do not already exist, they are thus inserted into the database, and then they are considered as a WΔ.

Now the following facts can be deduced from the facts in the database and the WΔ are:

```
ancestor(1,3)          ancestor(2,4)
ancestor(3,1)
```

etc., until any more Δ is produced.

The rules have been triggered in parallel.

In some way VIM can be considered as a sub-set of Prolog, the Datalog part of Prolog, although the execution of VIM is different with respect to Prolog, but one big advantage is that VIM is really declarative. To illustrate this point consider this example.

The following set of clauses in Prolog loops

```
father(louis,jean).
ancestor(X,Y)  :- father(X,Y).
ancestor(X,Z)  :- ancestor(X,Y),ancestor(Y,Z).
```

with the query:

```
ancestor(X,Y)?
```

but if it executed in saturation with VIM rules it will stop.

2.2.2 The Alexander Method.

Forward chaining as in VIM exhibits an interesting property of simplicity. But forward chaining has the drawback of computing all possible solutions to all possible predicates included in the set of rules. For instance, if we want to know the ancestors of Jean, it is useless to start by computing all the ancestors of everybody (by saturating the database) and to select afterward just the ancestors of Jean.

The Alexander Method is an algorithm to tranform a set of VIM rules (to be executed in forward chaining) and a query (to be executed in backward chaining), into a new set of rules to be executed in forward chaining, that compute just the desired solutions. In some way, the Alexander Method permits to simulate backward chaining into forward chaining.

In an informal way the Alexander Method cuts a recursive goal in:

- one problem
- one or several solutions.

For instance, the goal (as the literal) `ancestor(W,jean)` is cut in:

- a new literal: `problem_ancestor(jean)` which can be interpreted as "The problem of finding the ancestor of Jean exists"
- literals like `solution_ancestor(louis,jean)` which can be interpreted as "Louis is a solution to the problem `problem_ancestor(jean)`".

To go from backward chaining to forward chaining, we need rules which handle `problem_ancestor` and `solution_ancestor` literals.

For instance:

```
problem_ancestor(X),q => r
```

can be read as "if there is the problem of finding the ancestors of x, and q is true, then ... "

and
```
a => solution_ancestor(W,X)
```

can be read as "if a is true then w is a solution ".

With these intuitive ideas in mind, let us process an example step by step:

Let's have as goal ancestor (W,jean) and the rules:

R1:   father(Y,X) => ancestor(Y,X)
R2:   father(Z,Y),ancestor(Y,X) => ancestor(Z,X)

R1 gives:

R1.1: `problem_ancestor(X),father(Y,X) => solution_ancestor(Y,X)`

"if there is the problem of finding the ancestors of x, and if y is the father of x, then solution is y"

R2 gives:

R2.1: `problem_ancestor(X),father(Z,Y),ancestor(Y,X) =>`
`                solution_ancestor(Z,X)`

"if there is the problem of finding the ancestors of x, and if z is the father of y, and if y i an ancestor of x, then a solution is z"

But this rule contains itself the goal ancestor(Y,X), thus it must itself be transformed This goal will itself be cut into two pieces, yielding two new rules R2.2 and R 2.3.

R2.2: `problem_ancestor(X),father(Z,Y) => problem_ancestor(Y)`

"if there is the problem of finding the ancestor of x, and if z is the father of y, then ther exists the problem of finding the ancestor of y, because y is an ancestor of x."

This rule generates a new problem_ancestor, which, through rule R1.1 for instance will generate news solution_ancestor.

R2.3: `solution_ancestor(Y,X) => solution_ancestor(Z,X)`

"the solution to the y problem are also solutions to the x problem".

In fact, rule R2.3 does not respect a restriction of VIM (predefined variables), since appears in conclusion and not in hypotheses. Thus, it is necessary to transmit th information z between rules R2.2 and R2.3. For that purpose, we create a new predicat named continuation.

The final version of R2.2 and R2.3 is now:

```
R2.2':problem_ancestor(X),father(Z,Y)=>
                    problem_ancestor(Y),continuation(Y,Z)
R2.3': solution_ancestor(Y,X),continuation(Y,Z)=>
                    solution_ancestor(Z,X)
```

The detailed algorithm of the Alexander Method was presented in [Roh 86].

2.2.3 Delta Driven Execution Model DDEM.

The DDEM is an algorithm to execute the saturation upon a logic database.

Considering a rule R_i containing the predicate r in the conclusion. Each time that a set of facts are deduced from the execution of the rule R_i, we call them a BΔ. This BΔ is compared with facts that already exist. If a fact exists, nothing happens. If it does not, then it is considered as a WΔ. Then this WΔ is inserted into the data base, and it is used to eventually fire rules with predicate r in hypotheses.

A VIM rule as

$$p,q \Rightarrow r$$

is transformed into:

```
WΔp,q_c => BΔr_1
WΔq,p_c => BΔr_2
```

where q_c and p_c are the current representation of q and p in the database
the BΔr is:

```
BΔr <- BΔr_1 Union BΔr_2
```

where <- is the assignation and Union is a set operation.

To eliminate the duplicates we consider that r_c means the current representation of r in the database

```
WΔr <- BΔr - r_c
```

where "-" is a set operation.

The insertion of WΔr into r_c is represented by:

```
r_c <- r_c Union WΔr
```

this WΔr can be tried in rules of the form:

```
WΔr,s => t
```

when any more $w\Delta$ is produced the logic database is saturated, and the work is finished. Let us apply this algorithm to an exemple.

Consider the following rules:

```
father(X,Y) => ancestor(X,Y)
father(X,Y),ancestor(Y,Z) => ancestor(X,Z)
```

Consider the initial facts:

father(1,2)   father(2,3)   father(3,4)

So the rules are transformed into:

R1: $W\Delta$father(X,Y) => $B\Delta$ancestor.$_0$(X,Y)

R2: $W\Delta$father(X,Y),ancestor$_c$(Y,Z) => $B\Delta$ancestor.$_1$(X,Z)

R3:   father$_c$(X,Y),$W\Delta$ancestor(Y,Z) => $B\Delta$ancestor.$_2$(X,Z)

then the saturation is executed as follows:

```
Init:
        ancestor_c <- empty
```
all initial facts are put in father$_c$
```
        father_c <- father(1,2),father(2,3),father(3,4)
```
also all initial facts are considered as $w\Delta$
```
        WΔfather <- father(1,2),father(2,3),father(3,4)
    Label 1:
        Apply WΔ to rules R1, R2, R3
        BΔancestor <-   BΔancestor.0
                        Union BΔancestor.1
                        Union BΔancestor.2
        WΔancestor <- BΔancestor - ancestor_c
        ancestor_c <- ancestor_c Union WΔancestor
        if  (WΔancestor is not empty) goto Label 1
```

Another way to represent what happens when saturation takes place is with an execution graph.

We can differentiate two types of process:

> - application of rules.
> - elimination of duplicates.

We can represent as a square block the application of a rule, and as a round block the elimination. See figure 2.1. In the figure a square block produces a $B\Delta r$, and a round block produces a $w\Delta r$. As many rules can produce conclusions on predicate r, all the outputs $B\Delta r$ go to the round block where elimination of r facts takes place.

The elimination process "transforms" a $B\Delta$ into a $w\Delta$ if the $B\Delta$ is not in the database.

Figure 2.2 shows the execution of a saturation in the form of a graph. Arrows represent the Δ productions. We can see that execution is driven for the Δ. We know that as far as wΔ are produced, the execution goes on but when there is no more wΔ produced, saturation stops.

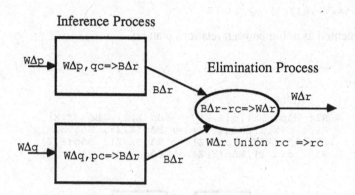

The DDEM process.

<<<<Figure 2.1>>>>

To represent what is happening in the elimination process, we define two operations; at this level they can be represented as rules. The first is the elimination:

$$BΔr - r_c => WΔr$$

The second is the insertion of the wΔ into the database:

$$WΔr \text{ Union } r_c => r_c$$

BΔr is the BΔ on r, r_c contains the facts on predicate r, wΔr is the wΔ on r.

This two rules are not VIM rules, they are needed for the DDEM. Their semantic is then different from VIM rules.

We can remark that a BΔ arrives at any time the operation $BΔ <- BΔ._1 \text{ Union } BΔ._2$ becomes implicit and it is unnecessary to add the suffix to distinguish BΔs.

One advantage of this model is that it is asynchronous, in the case of monotonic and commutative rules. This means that the order of Δ arrivals does not modify the final result.

2.2.4 Delta Driven Computer Language DDCL

To fill the gap between VIM code and machine language of each node we define another language called DDCL. The primitives of the language are mainly relational operations.

Some examples of rules:

```
p(X,'jean') => q(X)
```

can be implemented as a selection in the relation p.

```
p(X,Y),q(Y,Z) => r(X,Z)
```

can be implemented as a join beween relations p and q.

Rules

```
R1:  WΔp(X,Y),q(Y,Z)  => BΔp(X,Z),  BΔq(X,X)
R1': p(X,Y),WΔq(Y,Z)  => BΔp(X,Z),  BΔq(X,X)
R2:  WΔq(X,Y), p(Y,Z) => BΔq(X,Z),  BΔp(Z,Z)
R2': q(X,Y),WΔp(Y,Z)  => BΔq(X,Z),  BΔp(Z,Z)
```

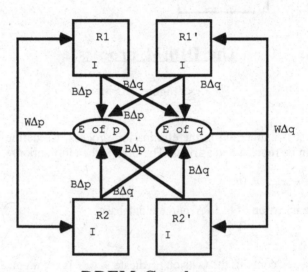

DDEM Graphe.

<<<<Figure 2.2>>>>

In section 3 we specify the reasons of this choice, and we present the execution of the primitives.

This transformation of rules VIM into relational operation is consistent with the defined properties of DDEM.

So we can consider that at DDCL level instead of predicates and facts the machine handles relations and tuples.

3 THE ARCHITECTURE AND DDEM.

3.1 THE ARCHITECTURE OF DDC.

DDC consists in a set of nodes linked by an interconnection system without shared memory. Figure 3.1 shows the DDC architecture. All nodes are identical, a P-C-M triple: Processor, Communication device and Memory.

The Processor has two parts:

- a general purpose microprocessor: Motorola 68020
- a special purpose custom VLSI chip called μSyC.

μSyC chip acts as a coprocessor of the 68020. This means that when a coprocessor code is detected by the 68020, it "calls" the coprocessor to execute a coprocessor instruction. Each instruction of the coprocessor is a complete relational operation, the whole algorithm is microprogrammed.

The Memory can be divided into three parts :

- fast static RAM on the CPU board - but not cache
- boards with large capacity
- a secondary storage.

The Communication Module.

This module is responsible for receiving and sending messages from and to the interconnection network.

3.2 DDEM INTO DDC.

The mapping strategy of DDEM into the DDC architecture is statically determined. We try to balance the load in the machine, keeping the communications as low as possible.

Here we detail how DDEM is mapped into DDC architecture without care about the initialization phase. So at a given time of a saturation we can consider that:

- facts are distributed along the pcm nodes
- all rules of DDEM level are copied on each node.

To be more precise:

- relations are distributed along the pcm nodes. According to a hash function h determined at compile time
- the DDCL code which "makes" the application of rules is copied on each node
- the code of the hash function, which serve to distribute relations is copied on each node.

As show on figure 3.2.

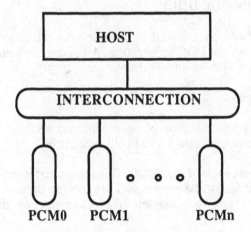

DDC Architecture.

<<<<Figure 3.1>>>>

A relation is distributed according to an hash code function applied to the value of one of their attributes. Relations can be "duplicated" in case of uses upon different attributes in rules.

In the case of "duplicate" relations they are distinguished by adding a suffix to the name of the relation.

The advantage of this mapping is that: the data go where they will be used, the locality is ensured by the hash function statically defined.

This is a commented example of a saturation following the DDEM:

Consider that DDC is composed of three nodes.

And the set of two VIM rules is :

R1: p(X,Y),q(Y,Z) => r(X,Z)
R2: p(X,Y),r(X,Z) => p(Y,Z)

The set of four initial facts:

p(aa,bb), q(cc,dd), q(bb,cc), r(aa,cc)

that must be stored as relations as follows: ·

At compilation it could be noticed that the p relation is used in R1 and R2 but in each one according to different attributes.

So, in the machine, instead of having p, there are two copies: $p_c._1$ and $p_c._2$.

$p_c._1(X,Y)$ to be used by R2 distributed according to values of its first argument.

$p_c._2(X,Y)$ to be used by R1 distributed according to values of its second argument.

For q there is just $q_c._1$ distributed according to values of its first argument.

For r there is just $r_c._1$.

In P.1 and P.2 are the same facts, but P.1 and P.2 are distributed in different ways.

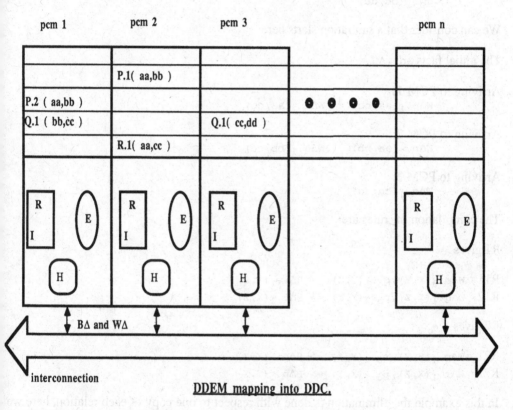

DDEM mapping into DDC.

<<<<Figure 3.2>>>>

So if we apply the hash function to values of arguments of the initial facts, we identify in which processor a tuple will be stored.

$$H(1,p._1(aa,bb)) = H(1,r._1(aa,cc)) = h(aa) = 1$$
$$H(2,p._2(aa,bb)) = H(1,q._1(bb,cc)) = h(bb) = 2$$
$$H(1,q._1(cc,dd)) = h(cc) = 3$$

where H is a function, with the arguments: the number of the attribute to apply the function and a tuple; h is the hash function which has as argument the value of the selected argument, and returns the identity of the destination node, and 1,2,3 are the node PCM number.

So in node PCM 1 there exists:

$$p_{c.1}(aa,bb) \qquad r_{c.1}(aa,cc)$$

In node PCM 2 there exists:

$$p_{c.2}(aa,bb) \qquad q_{c.1}(bb,cc)$$

In node PCM3 there exists:

$$q_{c.1}(cc,dd)$$

We can consider that a saturation starts here:

The initial facts are $w\Delta$:

Arriving to PCM 1:

$$W\Delta p._1(aa,bb) \qquad W\Delta r._1(aa,cc)$$

Arriving to PCM 2:

$$W\Delta p._2(aa,bb) \qquad W\Delta q._1(bb,cc)$$

Arriving to PCM 3:

$$W\Delta q._1(cc,dd)$$

The compilation of rules are:

R1 gives

R11 $W\Delta p._2(X,Y), q_{c.1}(Y,Z) \implies B\Delta r._1(X,Z)$
R12 $W\Delta q._1(Y,Z), p_{c.2}(X,Y) \implies B\Delta r._1(X,Z)$

R2 gives

R21 $W\Delta p._1(X,Y), r_{c.1}(X,Z) \implies B\Delta p._1(Y,Z)$
R22 $W\Delta r._1(X,Z), p_{c.1}(X,Y) \implies B\Delta p._1(Y,Z)$

In this example the elimination is done with respect to one copy of each relation, here we chose to execute the elimination taking as a reference the relation indice 1.

Elimination rules are:

R3: $B\Delta p._1(X,Y) - p_{c.1}(S,T) \implies W\Delta p._1(X,Y), W\Delta p._2(X,Y)$
R4: $B\Delta r._1(X,Y) - r_{c.1}(S,T) \implies W\Delta r._1(X,Y)$
We recall that in R3 and R4 the condition to produce something is $X \neq S$ or $Y \neq T$.

R5: $W\Delta p._1$ Union $p_{c.1} \implies p_{c.1}$
R6: $W\Delta r._1$ Union $r_{c.1} \implies r_{c.1}$

To each produced tuple of a B∆ one node the hash fonction h is applied, as shown before. Then each tuple is sent to just one processor.

In the elimination rules we can notice that in some cases one W∆ appears as conclusion (R4) and in other cases more than one W∆ appear. What happens is that each produced tuple, must be sent to one (i.e. R3) or more processors (i.e.R4) applying the hash function to different attributes.

Note that the processor who receives a tuple (a B∆) contains the part of the relation where the tuple (a B∆) can be "transformed" into a W∆.

Inside each node, the execution mechanism can be divided into basic cycles triggered according to delta arrivals. See figure 3.3.

> R   reception of W∆ or B∆ into a buffer
> P   production which is either an inference
>   W∆ produces a B∆ or nothing or an elimination
>   B∆ produces a W∆ or nothing
> T   transmission of either W∆ resulting from elimination or B∆ resulting
> from inference.

Let us see in details what happens in one node when a saturation starts.

At T0: data are distributed and "rules" installed.

At T0 + the time to recognize the W∆:

In node PCM1.

> Node state : facts = { $p_C.1(aa,bb)$, $r_C.1(aa,cc)$ }
>
> Production by W∆p.1(aa,bb) and R21
> of a B∆ containing {p (bb,cc)}.
> Transmission of this B∆ to node PCM 2
> because $H(1,B∆p.1(bb,cc))$ = h(bb) = 2
> Production by W∆r.1(aa,cc) and R22
> of a B∆ containing {p (bb,cc)}.
> Transmission of this B∆ to node PCM 2
> because $H(1,B∆p.1(bb,cc))$ = h(bb) = 2

Then this node waits for a W∆ or a B∆ or for the end of the saturation.

The work on the other nodes follows the same sequence, as far as there are ∆ in the input of a node.

We call this implementation of DDEM: scenario with elimination with respect to a single file, because the elimination is made taking as a reference one representation of the predicate. Another scenario where the elimination is made taking each "copy" as a reference is also under study.

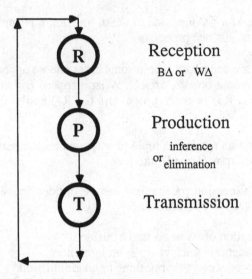

Reception
BΔ or WΔ

Production
inference
or elimination

Transmission

Execution mechanism in a node.

<<<<Figure 3.3>>>>

3.3 DDCL AND DATA REPRESENTATION.

As precised before, DDCL consists mainly in relational operations, most of them are executed following the principles of filtering by automata presented in [Gon 84], and the join algorithm LA-JOIN presented in [Bra 86].

Let us first describe how a selection can take place. Suppose that we make the selection on relation r of the tuples where the first attribut is equal to jean or paul or pierre. We build an automaton which recognizes jean or paul or pierre. Then each tuple of r is sent to the automaton which indicates if the tuple has to be kept or not.

The automaton representation can be more compact than the classical matrix.

The join of two files can be executed by making a selection of tuples of the first file then building an automaton to make a selection upon the second file.

3.3.1 The relational operations in DDC.

Here we consider just a join.

If we have the VIM rule:
R1: $p(X,Y)$, $q(Y,Z)$ => $r(X,Z)$

First it is transform in rules:
R11: $W\Delta p._2(X,Y)$, $q_{c}._1(Y,Z)$ => $B\Delta r._1(X,Z)$
R12: $W\Delta q._1(Y,Z)$, $p_{c}._2(X,Y)$ => $B\Delta r._1(X,Z)$

The current representation of $q_c._1$ will be stored as an automaton and pointers to the elements of the second attribute. The automaton is to recognize if a tuple of the WΔp.$_2$ can be joined to $q_c._1$. If that is the case a BΔ is produced. This BΔ contains tuples with the value of the first attribute and the different values of the second attribute of $q_c._1$. See figure 3.4.

The advantage of this solution is that with just a few comparaisons of characters of the WΔ against the automaton, a BΔ can be produced.

The same technique can be used to make other operations in DDC as pattern matching.

This solution is consistent with the DDEM because it is asynchronous. The locality of data is ensured by the hash code function. The WΔ only arrives to the node where the ith part of the join can take place.

$$WΔf(X,Y), \ ec(Y,Z) \ => \ BΔe(X,Z)$$

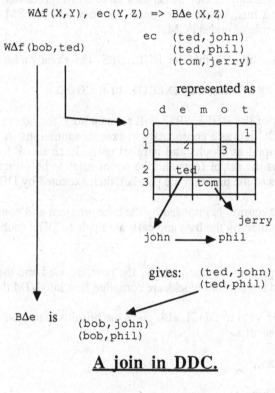

A join in DDC.

<<<<Figure 3.4>>>>

4 FIRST IMPLEMENTATION.

With all the ideas presented in section 2 and 3, we are implementing a first version of DDC.

Even if conceptually the DDEM seems to be a good solution to parallelism, compromises for the implementation must be taken and evaluated. So the aim of this first version is to gain experience, in parallel machines and particulary in the implementation of the DDEM. We hope to obtain a feedback to be able to propose improvements.

For this first version, we take an existing multiprocessor machine a BULL SPS7, and we concentrate our efforts in the software implementation of DDCL and the DDEM on this machine.

The BULL SPS7 is a multiprocessor which uses up to 8 PM (processor and local memory); they are attached to a bus, where a common memory lets the PM communicate. The modules PM play the role of nodes PCM.

The advantage of this solution is that the BULL SPS7 has already a lot of software.

4.1 FROM A USER PROGRAM TO EXECUTABLE CODE.

One of the processor of the BULL SPS7 will act as a host, the others constitute DDC. In this configuration DDC acts as a coprocessor to execute saturations. A program consists in sequential parts grouped as blocks and parallel parts. Each block for DDC describes a saturation, it contains the set of facts and the set of rules to be saturated. The user must indicate which blocks of the program are parallel, then executed by DDC.

The order of block execution is imposed by the user program and controlled by the host. Serial blocks are executed by the host and calls are made to DDC each time a saturation is needed.

Before execution, a program is compiled by the host, in one hand the sequential blocks, and on the other hand the parallel blocks are compiled first into VIM then into DDCL.

The transformation of VIM to DDCL also gives the primitives to load DDC, to initialize a saturation and to get results.

4.2 CURRENT WORK.

Currently we are working on:

- implementation of the first version
- optimisations of the compiler from high level language to VIM
- optimisations of the compiler from VIM to DDCL
- memory management problems
- planning the integration and test of the first version
- looking for applications
- performance prediction.

5 CONCLUSIONS.

We present in this paper the basis for the design of DDC, an AI parallel machine supporting DDEM, a suitable execution model where rules are executed in parallel with relational operators.

We describe all the levels, from the high level language until machine level, and how we can go from one level to another.

We are working on this first implementation as described in section 4.

Also we are active in the possible extensions of the system , as for instance:

- DDC as a coprocessor of a main -frame.
- introduction of predefined predicates.
- list and function processing.

Finally, we would like to thank the anonymous reviewers of the paper for their comments, also to: R. Lescoeur, J. M. Kerisit, and J. M. Pugin, F. Anceau, K. R. Apt and B. Bergsten; they are involved in the project and we benefit from their comments, ideas and suggestions. We are grateful to E. Pavillon for her help, improving the English of the paper, but if there are still some English faults we assume the responsability.

6 REFERENCES.

[Bra 86]   Bradier A.: "LA-JOIN: Un Algorithme de Jonction en Mémoire et sa Mise en Oeuvre sur le Filtre SCHUSS. II èmes Journées Bases de Données Avancées. Giens, Avril. 1986.

[Gon 84]   Gonzalez-Rubio R., Rohmer J., Terral D.: "The SCHUSS Filter: A Processor for Non-Numerical Data Processing". 11th Annual International Symposium on Computer Architecture. Ann Arbor. 1984.

[Gon 85]   Gonzalez-Rubio R., Rohmer J.: "From Data Bases to Artificial Intelligence : A Hardward Point of View". Nato Summer School, Les Arcs 1985.

[Gon 86]   Gonzalez-Rubio R., Bradier A., Rohmer J.: "DDC Delta Driven Computer. A Parallel Machine for Symbolic Processing". ESPRIT Summer School on Future Parallel Computers. University of Pisa. June.1986.

[Ker 86]   Kerisit J. M.: "Preuve de la Méthode d'Alexandre par une approche algébrique", BULL Rapport Interne, Mai1986.

[Lun 85]   Lunstrom S. F., Larsen R. L.: "Computer an Information Technology in the Year 2000- A projection". Computer, September 1985.

[Mot 84]   Moto-oka T., Stone H. S.: "Fifth Generation Computer Systems: A Japanese Project". Computer, March 1984.

[Pug 85]   Pugin J.M.: "BOUM: An Instantiation of the (PS)2 concept". 5èmes Journées Internationales Systèmes Experts. Avignon 1985.

[Pug 86]   Pugin J.M. : "VIM Language". Bull Internal Report 1986.

[Roh 85]   Rohmer J., Lescoeur R. : "The Alexander Method. A technique for the processing of recursive axioms in deductive databases". Bull Internal Report 1985.

[Roh 86]   Rohmer J., Lescoeur R., J. M. Kerisit: "The Alexander Method. A technique for the processing of recursive axioms in deductive databases". New Generation Computing, 4. 1986.

**Design and implementation
of a parallel inference machine for first order logic :
an overview***

Philippe Jorrand**

LIFIA
Laboratoire d'Informatique Fondamentale
et d'Intelligence Artificielle
Grenoble - France

ABSTRACT

Several approaches to parallel architectures and languages for advanced information processing are being investigated within ESPRIT Project 415. This overview presents one of these approaches, carrried out in one subproject of ESPRIT 415 ("Subproject F"), which aims at the design and implementation of a parallel inference machine.

- This machine, called LCM, for Logical Connection Machine, will be a highly parallel system for problem solving, mostly directed toward symbolic processing and artificial intelligence applications. It is based on the "connection method", which is a deductive inference technique for first order logic with significant possibilities for introducing parallelism.

- The design of such a complex system requires the use of formal means. The abstract specification of the LCM architecture reflects the parallel algorithmic description of the connection method and is expressed with FP2, a "Functional and Parallel Programming" language based on term rewriting techniques. Formal treatment and systematic transformations can be applied to FP2 programs.

- The actual implementation of the LCM requires a highly parallel multi-processor machine. Once such a machine is chosen, systematic transformations of FP2 programs can be applied for mapping the abstract process structure of the LCM specification onto the concrete processor structure of the machine.

This paper is an informal introduction to the bases of this work. It presents the main ideas and design decisions of the project through a series of simple examples.

Keywords : parallel inference, logic programming, connection method, parallel programming, communicating processes, FP2, parallel machines, program transformation.

* This research is partially funded by ESPRIT Project 415 : Parallel Architectures and Languages for Advanced Information Processing - A VLSI-Directed Approach.

** Address : LIFIA-IMAG, BP 68, 38402, SAINT MARTIN D'HERES Cedex, FRANCE

1. Introduction

At the basis of most artificial intelligence systems and applications there is some form of automated reasoning [BibJor86]. This is clearly the case, for example, in languages like Prolog and in knowledge based or expert systems. The work presented in this paper deals with one essential form of automated reasoning : the mechanization of deductive inference in first order logic.

Prolog is already an instance of such mechanized deductive inference. However, it suffers from several inherent limitations :

- Prolog covers only a very specific subset of first order logic, namely Horn clause logic.

- There is a meaning attached to the textual arrangement of clauses in a Prolog program which is irrelevant to the inference rules of first order logic.

- The resolution strategy used for Prolog is not complete.

- Prolog interpreters have poor performances on conventional computer architectures.

All these limitations stem from a unique source : sequential interpretation was an implicit, but ever present requirement at the root of the design of Prolog.

The hypothesis which is at the basis of the work presented in this paper is that all these limitations can be overcome by lifting the sequentiality requirement and aiming at a parallel inference machine for full first order logic. Research in that direction is currently quite active in a number of places, as shown in the impressive bibliography assembled by [BibAsp85].

There are three classes of problems to be solved in such a research project :

- An inference method must be chosen which shows significant possibilities for parallel organization.

- From the algorithmic description of the inference method, an abstract specification of the parallel machine architecture must de obtained.

- Given the abstract machine specification, it must be mapped onto a concrete machine structure.

In "Subproject F" of ESPRIT Project 415 the following design decisions have been made :

- The inference method is the connection method developed at the Technical University of Munich [Bib82,Bib83]. It gives its name to the machine : LCM, for "Logical Connection Machine".

- Parallel algorithms and parallel machine architectures are both described with the language FP2 developed at LIFIA in Grenoble [Jor86].

- Transformations can be applied to FP2 programs so that they become isomorphic to arbitrary machine structures. Rectangular grids and torus structures are being studied as targets for such transformations [MarA86].

This paper uses examples for showing the principles of the connection method and it gives hints to the possibilities it offers for parallel implementation. Then, the language FP2 is introduced and a simple program is shown which describes an abstract parallel machine applying the connection method to propositional calculus. Finally, the principles for transforming FP2 programs into specific parallel machine structures are briefly presented.

2. Connection method

The connection method is a complete proof calculus which allows to prove arbitrary valid formulae of full first order logic [Bib82,Bib83]. For the sake of simplicity, the basic principles of the connection method are first explained here in the case of propositional calculus. Furthermore, although the connection method can directly treat a non clausal formula like :

$$(A \vee B) \ \& \ (A \ \& \ C \rightarrow B) \ \& \ C \rightarrow B$$

it is explained here on the disjunctive normal form of that formula :

$$(\neg A \ \& \ \neg B) \vee (A \ \& \ C \ \& \ \neg B) \vee \neg C \vee B$$

This formula can be represented as a matrix with one column per clause :

$$
\begin{array}{cccc}
 & A & & \\
\neg A & C & & \\
\neg B & \neg B & \neg C & B
\end{array}
$$

A path through such a matrix (i.e. through the formula) is a sequence of literals, one from each clause, like $\neg A \ C \neg C \ B$ or $\neg B A \neg C \ B$. A pair of complementary literals, like $<C \neg C>$ or $<\neg B \ B>$, is called a connection. A path is said to be complementary if it contains at least one connection. Then, the connection method is based on the result that a formula is valid if and only if all its paths are complementary.

Thus, in principle, the connection method checks every path through the formula for complementarity. However, this computation can be greatly optimized by eliminating in one step all paths which contain the same subpath already known as complementary. This can be done in several different ways.

One possibility is to construct, in a stepwise fashion, subpaths of length 1, subpaths of length 2, subpaths of length 3, etc. : at step i, new subpaths of length j, where j=1..i, are constructed from overlaping subpaths of length j-1 obtained at step i-1 and, at each step, all complementary new subpaths are eliminated. If there remain no path of length n, where n is the number of clauses, the formula is valid. This approach already shows a way to introduce parallelism in the connection method : the elimination of complementary subpaths can be pipe-lined. In the next section an abstract description of it is given in the form of a triangular systolic array described in FP2.

Another possibility is to perform a deeper analysis of the matrix, using the notion of spanning set of pairs : a set of pairs of literals in the matrix is a spanning set if every path through the matrix contains at least one pair of the set. For example, $\{<A \ B>, <C \neg C>, <\neg B \neg C>\}$ is a spanning set of pairs for the above matrix, and so is $\{<\neg C \ B>\}$. The result on which the connection method relies can then be restated : a formula is valid if and only if there exist at least one spanning set of connections for it. In that case, the computation goes as follows : first construct the set of all connections of the matrix, then find a subset of them which constitute a spanning set. Here again, parallelism can be introduced for finding spanning sets.

But the logic of propositions treated so far is not really interesting for most applications in artificial intelligence. A useful inference method must deal with first order predicate logic. The above two approaches can be extended to work with first order predicate logic. However, since formulae now contain function symbols and quantified variables, the elimination of complementary subpaths in the first approach and the determination of spanning sets of connections in the second approach will have to rely on unification of first order literals rather than on the syntactic complementarity of propositional variables.

For example, using the spanning set approach, consider the following formula :

$$P(a) \ \& \ \forall x \, (P(x) \to P(fx)) \ \to \ \forall y \, P(fy)$$

Its disjunctive normal form is :

$$\neg P(a) \ \lor \ \exists x \, (P(x) \ \& \ \neg P(fx)) \ \lor \ \exists y \, P(fy)$$

The matrix representation of this formula is the following, where the connections are shown as lines between literals :

The set of connections now contains only pairs of complementary and unifiable literals : although the literals $\neg P(a)$ and $P(fy)$ have complementary predicate symbols, they do not form a connection. The substitution for the connection $<\neg P(a) \, P(x)>$ is $\{x<-a\}$ and the substitution for the connection $<\neg P(fx) \, P(fy)>$ is $\{x<-y\}$. Clearly, the unificiation processes for producing these substitutions are independent of each other and can operate in parallel : thus, as soon as the first step of constructing the set of connections, there is room for parallelism in the connection method applied to first order logic.

Then, a spanning set of connections must be found and, here again, unification must be applied to compute the most general substitution that is less general than the most general unifiers of the involved connections : if there exist such a "meet" in the lattice of unifiers, then the spanning set is unifiable and the formula is valid. In the example, this "meet" is $\{x<-a, y<-a\}$. However, this is a sufficient but not necessary condition which, alone, does not make the method complete, as the following formula shows :

$$P(a) \ \& \ \forall x \, (P(x) \to P(fx)) \ \to \ P(ffa)$$

The matrix representation of this formula is :

The individual unifiers of the connections are $\{x<-a\}$ and $\{x<-fa\}$, which have no "meet". But the formula is valid : intuitively, the universally quantified subformula has to be "used twice", once for deducing $P(fa)$ from $P(a)$ and a second time for deducing $P(ffa)$ from $P(fa)$.This must be reflected in the matrix representation of the formula. Since the validity of a formula is not changed when one of the clauses of its disjunctive normal form is repeated, the original matrix can be changed to :

There is now a unifiable spanning set of connections with substitution $\{x<-a, \ x'<-fa\}$. The connection method thus relies on the following result : a formula of first order predicate logic is valid if and only if there is a finite set of copies of its clauses which have a unifiable spanning set of connections. Since there are in general several possible candidate spanning sets, a form of "OR" parallelism can be employed for finding a unifiable one, whereas, in the computation of the "meet", it is a form of "AND" parallelism which can be used. A number of refinements to these essential steps of the connection method have also been developed [Asp85,AspBay85,Eder85].

438

3. Specifying and programming parallel machines in FP2

FP2 ("Functional and Parallel Programming") is a language for specifying and programming parallel machines [Jor84,Jor86,Schn85]. FP2 provides constructs based on term rewriting for describing abstract networks of communicating processes. Usually, in a description :

- A collection of elementary processes $P1, ..., Pn$ are described. The description of Pi defines the computation activity and the communication activity of Pi.

- A network P constructed with $P1, ..., Pn$ is described. The description of P defines the communication links among the Pi's and the communication links of P with its environment.

By a number of its properties, FP2 belongs to the family of languages like Occam [May84] or CCS [Mil80]. However, by its use of rewriting techniques, it is much more suited to formal manipulation than Occam [Per84,Rogé86,Schn86c] and much more suited to real programming than CCS [Huf86,SchnScha86].

In FP2, values are typed terms. Types are term algebras on sets of constructor names. Functions on these types can be defined through equations, which give an operational semantics built on pattern matching and term rewriting. For example, the types of integers and of sequences of integers are defined by the sets of their respective constructors given with their arities :

        type Nat is   *type Seq is*
            0   nil
         succ(Nat)   *cons(Nat,Seq)*
        end   *end*

Sequence *append* and *reverse* may then be defined as functions by rewrite rules :

    fct append is   *fct reverse is*
        append(nil,s) => s   reverse(nil) => nil
     append(cons(m,r),s) => cons(m,append(r,s)) reverse(cons(m,r)) =>
    end   append(reverse(r),cons(m,nil))
                                             end

Communicating processes are state transition systems. The transitions are labelled by events which are communication actions with the environment external to the process. A process has connectors which constitute its only means of comunication with its environment : the transmission of a value v along a connector C is a communication, denoted by $C(v)$. An event is a -possibly empty- set of communications which occur within one transition. The states of a process are terms built on a set of state constructors with an arity.

In the description of a process, the transitions that this process may perform are defined by transition rules : a transition rule is a rewrite rule for the state of that process, with a -possibly empty- event part. In addition to the transition rules, a process description also contains initial rules wich define the set of possible initial states of that process. For example, the process ADD is initially in state X, receives two integers along its connectors A and B, computes their sum, sends the result along connector C and goes back in state X for a new cycle :

        proc ADD is   => X
                    X : A(m) B(n)   => Y(m,n)
               Y(0,n) :   C(n)   => X
            Y(succ(m),n) :   => Y(m,succ(n))
        end

A sequence of transitions that ADD may perform, with the corresponding events, is :

X --{$A(3)$ $B(4)$}--> $Y(3,4)$ --{}--> $Y(2,5)$ --{}--> $Y(1,6)$ --{}--> $Y(0,7)$ --{$C(7)$}--> X

The labelled transition rules of a process define an operational semantics : at initialization, the process non-deterministically chooses one of its initial rules and enters the corresponding initial state. Then, a rule is a candidate for applicability if its left hand side matches the current state and it becomes applicable if the environment agrees with the communications of its event part (when candidate for applicability, rules with empty event part -internal rules- are always applicable). The process eventually chooses non-deterministically one of its applicable rules and applies it : the event of the rule occurs and the current state is rewritten.

A bounded $QUEUE$ of capacity k can be defined as a non-deterministic parameterized process which receives integers along W and sends them out in FIFO order along R.This example also shows that processes may apply user defined functions :

```
proc QUEUE [k] is
                                       =>  Q(nil,nil,k)
    Q(r,s,succ(l))        : W(m)       =>  Q(cons(m,r),s,l)
    Q(r,cons(n,s),l)      : R(n)       =>  Q(r,s,succ(l))
    Q(cons(m,r),nil,l)    :            =>  Q(nil,reverse(cons(m,r)),l)
end
```

It is possible to combine FP2 processes into networks of processes, by applying operators of a process operator algebra. The semantics of these operators associate with the constructed network an equivalent elementary process with connectors, state constructors, initial rules and transition rules labelled by events. Among the ten operators of [Jor86], the most basic three are :

- Parallel composition. If P and Q are two processes, then $P\|Q$ ("P in parallel with Q") is P and Q together considered as a single process. The connectors of $P\|Q$ are the connectors of P and the connectors of Q. A state of $P\|Q$ is a pair with a state of P and a state of Q. A transition of $P\|Q$ is a transition of P, or a transition of Q, or a transition of P together with a transition of Q where the event is the set union of the event in the transition of P and the event in the transition of Q.

- Connection. If P is a process, A and B two of its connectors, then $P+A.B$ ("A connected to B in P") is a process which has the same states and connectors as P. $P+A.B$ has all the transitions of P and, in addition, if P can perform the transition $s--\{A(v)B(v)...\}-->s'$, then $P+A.B$ can perform the transition $s--\{...\}-->s'$. In this transition, the value v transmitted along A and the value v transmitted along B are no longer exchanged with the environment but are exchanged among A and B. The rule of $P+A.B$ corresponding to the transition $s--\{...\}-->s'$ is obtained from the rule $S : A(t)B(u)...=> S'$ of P corresponding to the transition $s--\{A(v)B(v)...\}-->s'$ by computing $\sigma(S :...=>S')$ where σ is the most general unifier of t and u. This operator is also generalized to more than two connectors : $P+A.B.C$ contains a rule $\sigma(S :...=>S')$ if P contains a rule $S : A(t)B(u)C(w)...=> S'$, and σ is the most general unifier of t, u and w.

- Restriction. If P is a process and A one of its connectors, then $P-A$ ("A hidden in P") is the process P in which the connector A has been hidden : A thus becomes unable to communicate with the external environment of P. The transitions of $P-A$ are all the transitions of P which do not mention A. Of course, if A had been previously connected to a connector B, communications between A and B still remain possible, since the corresponding transitions, according to the semantics of the connection operator, do not mention A any longer. This property is used so often that the shorthand $P\pm A.B$ has been defined for $P+A.B-A-B$.

A first simple example of network construction uses the process NOP :

```
proc NOP is
                    =>  S
    S  :  U(x) V(x) =>  S
end
```

In this process, the same value is transmitted, in one event, on the two connectors U and V.

A process definition can be used as a template for a family of indexed processes : NOP_1 has the connectors U_1 and V_1, NOP_2 has the connectors U_2 and V_2, etc. Then, non-deterministic split of the flow of successive values communicated on U_1 into two sub-flows of values respectively communicated on V_2 and V_3 is accomplished by the network $SPLIT$:

$$proc\ SPLIT\ is\ NOP_1 \| NOP_2 \| NOP_3 + V_1.U_2 \pm V_1.U_3 - U_2$$

According to the semantics of process composition operators, this is equivalent to :

> **proc** SPLIT **is**
>
> | | | => SSS |
> |---|---|---|
> | SSS : | $U_1(x)\ V_2(x)$ | => SSS |
> | SSS : | $U_1(x)\ V_3(x)$ | => SSS |
>
> **end**

These rules do indeed reflect non-deterministic split. It should be noted that the "directions" of communications ("in" or "out") are not a-priori defined in FP2 processes : they are defined by the variable bindings established by unification when the connection operator is applied. As a consequence, the network $SPLIT$ can be used both ways : for non-deterministic split, but also for non-deterministic merge.

As another example, the flow on U_1 can also be synchronously duplicated on V_2 and V_3 :

$$proc\ DUP\ is\ NOP_1 \| NOP_2 \| NOP_3 \pm V_1.U_2\ .U_3$$

Connectors V_2 and V_3 of this network can be "plugged" into connectors A and B of ADD, so that twice the value of every integer communicated on U_1 is communicated on C :

$$proc\ TWICE\ is\ DUP \| ADD \pm V_2.A \pm V_3.B$$

The semantics of operators do indeed associate the following meaning to this definition :

> **proc** TWICE **is**
>
> | | | | => SSSX |
> |---|---|---|---|
> | SSSX | : $U1(x)$ | => | $SSSY(x,x)$ |
> | SSSY(0,n) | : $C(n)$ | => | SSSX |
> | SSSY(succ(m),n) | : | => | $SSSY(m, succ(n))$ |
>
> **end**

Network constructions can also be parameterized. A process $NETQ$ equivalent to the process $QUEUE$ defined earlier can be constructed as a chain of k identical buffers Q of capacity 1, using iterated versions of the process composition operators :

> **proc** Q **is**
>
> | | | => E |
> |---|---|---|
> | E | : $W(x)$ | => $F(x)$ |
> | F(x) | : $R(x)$ | => E |
>
> **end**

$$proc\ NETQ\ [k]\ is\quad \|\{Q_i \mid i=1..k\}\ \pm\{R_i.W_{i+1} \mid i=1..k\text{-}1\}$$

It is now possible to specify in FP2 an abstract parallel machine which applies (in quite a naive way) the connection method to propositional calculus. This machine implements a stepwise construction of subpaths of the matrix, while eliminating at each step all newly created complementary subpaths. This machine is a triangular systolic array, where all cells behave synchronously.

At each synchronous step, cells in row j construct new non complementary subpaths of length j from non complementary subpaths of length j-1 received from cells in row j-1. Not considering the special case of cells on the edges, each internal cell in row j is connected to 4 neighbours : North, and East in row j-1, West and South in row j+1. The connectors are named N,E,W and S.

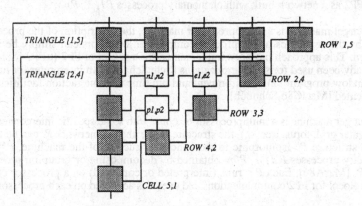

Upon completion of step i by an internal cell in row j, that cell contains the set *p1* of new non complementary subpaths of length j it has constructed during step i, and the set *p2* of all the non complementary subpaths of length j it had constructed previously, from step 1 to step i-1. Initially, *p1* and *p2* are empty. At step i+1, it sends the pair *(p1,p2)* along both of its *W* and *S* connectors to its West and South neighbours respectively. At the same time (i.e. in the same FP2 event), it receives the pairs *(n1,n2)* and *(e1,e2)* along its *N* and *E* connectors from its North and East neighbours respectively. Hence the FP2 specification of a *CELL* :

proc CELL is

$$Q(p1,p2) \quad : W(p1,p2) \; S(p1,p2) \qquad => Q(\emptyset,\emptyset)$$
$$N(n1,n2) \; E(e1,e2) \; => \; Q((n1*e1) \cup (n1*e2) \cup (n2*e1) , p1 \cup p2)$$

end

where "$\cup$" is set union and where "*" is a function for constructing sets of non complementary subpaths of length j from sets of non complementary subpaths of length j-1. For example :

$$\begin{Bmatrix} A\,B \\ A \neg C \\ \neg C\,B \end{Bmatrix} * \quad \{B\,C\} \;=\; \{A\,B\,C\}$$

Since $A \neg C$ and $B\,C$ do not overlap, they cannot form a subpath of length 3. The only possible subpaths are $A\,B\,C$ and $\neg C\,B\,C$: $\neg C\,B\,C$ is complementary (since $\neg C\,B$ and $B\,C$ are known to be non complementary, only their respective left and right extremities have to be compared for checking the complementarity of the newly formed subpath). The result is $\{A\,B\,C\}$.

Finally, the network structure of the systolic machine which *PROVE*s the validity of a propositional formula with this method is recursively defined as follows :

proc PROVE [k] is TRIANGLE [1,k]

proc TRIANGLE [i,j] is
  if j=1 then CELL$_{i,1}$
  if j>1 then ROW$_{i,j}$ || TRIANGLE [i+1,j-1] $\pm\{S_{i,l}.N_{i+1,l} , W_{i,l+1}.E_{i+1,l} \mid l=1..j \}$

proc ROW [i,j] is $\|\{CELL_{i,l} \mid l=1..j \}$

This and other parallel machine architectures for the connection method are being investigated for first order logic and will be described in FP2.

4. Implementation of the LCM

Abstract machines specified in FP2, like the LCM, can be simulated on monoprocessor sequential machines or mapped onto multiprocessor structures of actual parallel machines. Let P be a machine specified in FP2 as a network built with elementary processes $P1, ..., Pn$:

- If the target machine is a monoprocessor machine, the description of the process associated with P by the semantics of the process composition operators can simply be interpreted or compiled. This approach has been implemented for a subset of FP2 (μFP2 [Schn86a]) which has already been used for some applications [SchnScha86]. An interpreter for full FP2, with a multiwindow programming environment and run time user interaction facilities is also being implemented [MarJC86,Schn86b].

- If the target machine is a multiprocessor machine with some specific interconnection structure (rectangular grid, torus, tree, ...), the structure of the abstract network P can be translated into another structure P' isomorphic to the concrete structure of the machine. P' is built with elementary processes $P'1, ..., P'm$ obtained by decomposing or grouping processes $P1, ..., Pn$ of P [MarA86]. Each $P'i$ runs (interpreted or compiled) on a processor of the machine and a protocol for FP2 communications and events is activated on each processor.

With the monoprocessor implementation, FP2 abstract machines can be simulated. However, the actual parallel machine implementation will eventually be the only really interesting one for the LCM. There are two aspects to this problem :

- A specific target machine has to be chosen. The L-Machine [Buch85], with its adaptable interconnection structure and its L-Language for implementation, is a good candidate. The transputer, with Occam [May84], is another one and there are others. The choice of a particular machine will not be discussed here.

- The translation of FP2 specifications into networks of processes isomorphic to the machine interconnection structure must be done mechanically. This question is studied as FP2 to FP2 transformation [MarA86] : this is possible because FP2 programs (functions and processes described by rewrite rules) are quite well suited to formal manipulation.

This transformational approach is explained here in the case of rectangular grids of processors as machine structures : the problem is to tranform an FP2 program with an arbitrary network structure built on arbitrary processes, into an equivalent FP2 program with a network which is a rectangular grid of processes which all have exactly four bi-directional connections, one to each of their North, East, West and South neighbours. In a first approximation, three sub-problems can be isolated :

- The processes in the rectangular grid all have four connectors, although the processes in the initial FP2 network have an arbitrary number of connectors. Each process, or group of processes of the initial FP2 network must thus be transformed into one process with four connectors or into a sub-network composed of processes with four connectors each.

- The rectangular grid can be viewed a graph, where the vertices are the processes and the edges are the four connections of each process to its neighbours. This graph is planar, whereas the initial FP2 program, which can also be viewed as a graph, is not necessarily planar. A step in the transformation should thus map the initial FP2 network into a planar representation.

- Once there remain only processes with four connectors each and that the graph is planar, the network of these new processes or sub-networks must be placed on a rectangular grid. The difficulty there is that processes which were neighbours in the initial network will not be neighbours any longer. New processes thus have to be inserted, or existing processes have to be tranformed again, for the only purpose of transmitting communications among such processes which have been separated away.

In the first sub-problem, for obtaining processes with four connectors from processes with more than four connectors, one possibility is to decompose "too hairy" processes into several interconnected processes which have not more than four connectors each. There are several ways of doing this, as explained in [MarA86]. For example :

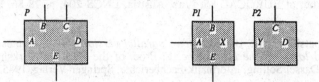

$P1$ has the same initial rules as P and every rule in P which does not mention C nor D is also in $P1$. Every rule in P which mentions C or D or both C and D is split into one rule in $P1$ and one rule in $P2$. For that, the rules in P are numbered. If rule number i has the following format :

$$(i) \quad Q : A(u) C(v) . ... \ => Q'$$

where u and v are arbitrary terms representing values, then $P1$ contains a rule :

$$Q : A(u) X(i,v) ... \ => Q'$$

where i is an integer number and $P2$, which always remains in state S, contains a rule :

$$S : Y(i,x) C(x) \quad => S$$

where x is a variable name. The semantics of the process composition operators state that the network $P1 \parallel P2 \pm X.Y$ is equivalent (syntactically !) to P.

Rather than decomposing into processes with less connectors, another possibility is to analyze the graph of the original network and partition it, or parts of it, into subgraphs which have at most four edges connecting them to the rest of the network. Then, each such subgraph can be replaced by the process that the semantics of process composition operators associate with it. This "composition" and the decomposition approaches can of course be combined.

The second sub-problem can be solved by creating a new process $CROSS$ at each point where two connectors of the initial network cross each other :

```
proc CROSS is
                    => S
    S :  N(x) S(x)  => S
    S :  E(x) W(x)  => S
end
```

Once again, the non planar network without the $CROSS$ processes and the planar network with the $CROSS$ processes have the same semantics, as defined by process composition operators.

Finally, there are algorithms for placing a planar network onto a grid. Such algorithms create "transparent processes" whose only purpose is to transmit communications among processes of the planar network which are assigned to distant positions on the grid. The goal is not only to minimize the "surface" covered by the network on the grid, but also to minimize the number of such transparent nodes. Even in the case of static networks considered here, this is a major difficulty, as shown by the study in [MarA86].

Aknowledgements. The research reported in this paper is partly conducted at LIFIA, under the responsibility of the author. But it would have never been as fruitful as it has become without the cooperation in ESPRIT Project 415 with the group led by Dr. Wolfgang Bibel at TUM and without all the care brought to it by Dr. Juergen Peters of Nixdorf Computer AG.

References

[Asp85] Aspetsberger K. *Substitution expressions : extracting solutions of non-Horn clause proofs.* In Proc. of EUROCAL 85, Linz, Austria, LNCS 204, p. 78-86, Springer-Verlag, 1985.

[AspBay85] Aspetsberger K., Bayerl S. *Two parallel versions of the connection method for propositional logic on the L-Machine.* In Proc. of the German Workshop on Artificial Intelligence, Dassel/Solling, Informatik-Fachberichte, Springer-Verlag, 1985.

[Bib82] Bibel W. *Automated theorem proving.* Vieweg Verlag, Braunschweig, 1982; second edition 1987.

[Bib83] Bibel W. *Matings in matrices.* CACM 26, p. 844-852, 1983.

[BibAsp85] Bibel W., Aspetsberger K. *A bibliography on parallel inference machines.* Journal of Symbolic Computation, Vol. 1 No. 1, p. 115-118, 1985.

[BibJor86] Bibel W., Jorrand Ph. (Ed.) *Fundamentals of artificial intelligence. An advanced course.* ACAI 85, LNCS 232, Springer-Verlag, 1986.

[Buch85] Buchberger B. *The L-Machine : an attempt at parallel hardware for symbolic computation.* In Proc. of AAEECC 3, Grenoble, France, LNCS 229, Springer-Verlag, 1985.

[Eder85] Eder E. *An implementation of a theorem prover based on the connection method.* In Proc. of AIMSA 84, Varna, Bulgaria, North-Holland, p. 121-128, 1985.

[Huf86] Hufflen JM. *Un exemple d'utilisation de FP2 : description d'une architecture parallèle et pipe-line pour l'unification.* RR LIFIA 43, Grenoble, 1986.

[Jor84] Jorrand Ph. *FP2 : Functional Parallel Programming based on term substitution.* In Proc.of AIMSA 84, Varna, Bulgaria, North-Holland, p. 95-112, 1984.

[Jor86] Jorrand Ph. *Term rewriting as a basis for the design of a functional and parallel programming language. A case study : the language FP2.* In ACAI 85, LNCS 232, Springer-Verlag, p. 221-276, 1986.

[MarA86] Marty A. *Placement d'un réseau de processus communicants décrit en FP2 sur une structure de grille en vue d'une implantation de ce langage.* RR LIFIA 49, Grenoble, 1986.

[MarJC86] Marty JC. *Un environnement de programmation pour le langage FP2.* RI LIFIA, Grenoble, 1986.

[May84] May D. *Occam programming manual.* Prentice-Hall International, 1984.

[Mil80] Milner R. *A calculus of communicating systems.* LNCS 92, Springer-Verlag, 1980.

[Per84] Pereira JM. *Processus communicants : un langage formel et ses modèles. Problèmes d'analyse.* Doctoral Thesis, LIFIA, INPG, Grenoble, 1984.

[Rogé86] Rogé S. *Comparaison des comportements de processus communicqnts. Application au langage FP2.* Doctoral Thesis, LIFIA, INPG, Grenoble, 1986

[Schn85] Schnoebelen Ph. *The semantics of concurrency in FP2.* In Working Group on Semantics, ESPRIT Project 415, 1985.

445

[Schn86a] Schnoebelen Ph. *μFP2 : a prototype interpreter for FP2*. RR LIFIA 41, Grenoble, 1986.

[Schn86b] Schnoebelen Ph. *About the implementation of FP2*. RR LIFIA 42, Grenoble, 1986.

[Schn86c] Schnoebelen Ph. *Rewriting techniques for the temporal analysis of communicating processes*. To appear, 1986.

[SchnScha86] Schnoebelen Ph., Schaefer P. *Specification of a pipe-lined event driven simulator*. To appear, 1986.

MULTI-LEVEL SIMULATOR FOR VLSI
- an overview - *

P. Mehring and E. Aposporidis

AEG Aktiengesellschaft, Berlin Research Institute
Hollaenderstraße 31-34, D-1000 Berlin 51

Abstract

Simulation is a key element in modern and future digital circuit design.
However, simulation becomes a bottleneck with increasing design complexity. There are mainly two ways to get out of this situation:
reduction of the simulation load through multi-level simulation and
acceleration of the simulation through exploitation of parallelism.

This paper deals with the development of a VLSI-Simulator which combines
both approaches to achieve optimal performance. It is an informal overview of the work of AEG and its subcontractor Technische Universität
Berlin carried out within ESPRIT Project 415.

1. Introduction

Within the frame work of ESPRIT 415, Philips and AEG are investigating the object-
oriented approach in a joint venture. The object-oriented approach is considered as
a natural evolution from current programming styles.

AEG's task is to develop one of the three demonstrators for the _machine, namely a
multi-level VLSI-simulator, together with its subcontractor Technische Universität
Berlin. The demonstrators are being developed in parallel with the architecture for
ensuring optimal design.

Powerful simulators are a key element in modern and future digital circuit design
environments. However, simulation becomes a bottleneck in the circuit design with
increasing design complexity.

There are mainly two ways to get out of this situation:

- Reduction of the simulation load through so-called multi-level simulation, i.e.
  using different modelling levels within a circuit and not only a basic level
  throughout, e.g. gate level or electrical level.

---

* This research has been supported by ESPRIT Project 415: Parallel Architectures
  and Languages for Advanced Information Processing - A VLSI-Directed Approach.

- Acceleration of the simulation through exploitation of parallelism on the different modelling levels and simulator levels.

The multi-level VLSI-simulator combines both approaches to achieve optimal performance.

2. Levels of abstraction in the design process

VLSI-circuits are very complex systems and can not be designed in one single step even with modern computer aided design techniques. There are four major design steps as shown in Figure 1.

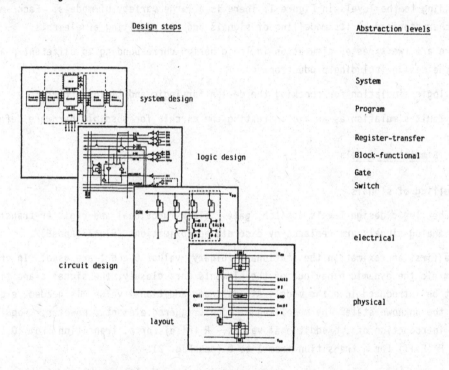

Figure 1: : Steps in the circuit design /Albe86/

The design starts with a global specification which is formulated at the highest possible level of abstraction and covers all system requirements. Then the detailed structure of the system is derived by breaking down this abstraction level step by step. In this process the designer tries to break down the problem into a number of interconnected subproblems. This process is repeated until solutions to all the subproblems are known or until well-known procedures are available which can be applied to solve these subproblems (top-down design).

At least eight levels of abstraction have become recognized (see Figure 1). Each abstraction level has a related notation for describing the system (i.e. the components, ways of combination and rules of behaviour).

In the following we focus on the logic design levels as these are the most important levels for multi-level simulation.

3. Principles of digital-circuit simulation

Simulation methods are characterized by the circuit model used and by the procedures for model handling. Models may represent different levels of abstraction corresponding to the levels in Figure 1. There is a large variety of models. Each model is characterized by its modelling of signals and its modelling of elements.

There are two types of simulation in logic design corresponding to different phases of the design including production:

- **logic simulation** for checking the design for logic and timing errors

- **fault simulation** as an aid in testing the circuit for possible hardware defects.

3.1 Simulation models

Modelling of signals

At the **logic design levels** (switch, gate, block-functional and register-transfer) the analog signals are replaced by discrete approximations /Blun77,Apos82/.

As a first approximation the stationary (binary) values 0 and 1 are used. In order to mimic the dynamic behaviour of the elements more closely, the signal transitions must be introduced into the model. At least one additional value is needed, e.g. U for the unknown state. The modelling of edge triggered elements, however, requires the introduction of two additional values - R (Rise) for a transition from 0 to 1 and F (Fall) for a transition from 1 to 0 (see Fig. 2).

Apart from these values, which serve to mimic the underlying analog signal, additional values or states are required to model particular technology or circuit specific characteristics. The following are commonly used:

- to model the high impedance condition of an element output (in general this refers to gate elements used in connection with busses) the additional value Z is used.

- to model MOS transistors as bidirectional switches at the "switch level" strength classes are added. They specify the type of connection between the voltage source and the node.

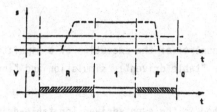

plus: U, X, Z,
strength classes

Figure 2: Modelling of circuit signals for a stochastic signal transition
s=signal, v=variable

Normally, these additional values are only used in those parts of the circuit where they apply (i.e. transmission gates, wired outputs and bus connections).

Modelling of elements

Modelling of circuit elements splits down into modelling of their logical behaviour and of their timing behaviour.

As an example we focus on the gate level, the basic level for the logic design. At this level the elements are gates, i.e. unidirectional basic elements with boolean logical functions.

In order to simplify the modelling of elements, the logical function is separated from the delay characteristics of the elements. Delays are represented by a delay element (DELAY) which is placed in series with the logic element (LOGIC) (Fig. 3).

The **logic** operation can be performed by an algorithm corresponding to the gate type or by a truth table (table look up-technique). As an example, the truth table of a NAND-gate for a tri-valued signal is shown in Figure 3.

The propagation **delay** of the circuit elements causes a delayed output reaction to a change at the input.

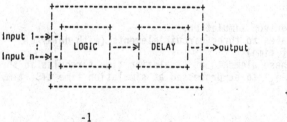

-1   -2

Figure 3: Modelling of circuit elements
- 1 Model of a gate
- 2 Truth table of a NAND-gate for a tri-valued signal

3.2 Simulation execution control

There are three basic methods for the control of the execution of a simulation: "compiled simulation", "event driven" (or "table driven") simulation and "interpretive simulation".

The most important execution control method is the **event-driven** (or **table-driven**) **simulation**. This method is applied in by far the greatest part of available simulators for digital circuits.

With this method "element calculations" are triggered by "events", i.e. changes of signal values. The "simulation time" is not incremented by fixed units of time but jumps from one event instant to the next. Moreover, only those elements are (re)-calculated which are immediately affected by an event, i.e. those of which at least one input signal has changed (selective trace).

An "event list" listing all future events (input-events as well as evaluated events) is used to keep track of the events.

The simulator fetches from the event list an event from the next time instant, enters the new variable values into the corresponding list and determines via the "connection list" those elements which are activated by this event. These elements are then calculated in sequence and resulting new events are entered into the event list (Fig. 4).

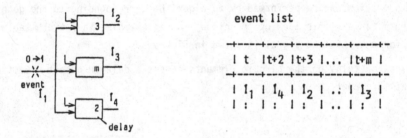

event list

Figure 4: Principle of event-driven simulation.
The event i_1 propagates to three circuit elements (with delay of 3, m and 2 units of time)
The evaluation of these elements at simulation time t results in three new events (i_2, i_3, i_4) to be processed at simulation time t+3, t+m, t+2

3.3 Fault simulation

Fault simulation serves in checking the quality of test patterns developed for a digital circuit. To this end the digital circuit is simulated assuming certain defects with their binary effects being injected into the circuit model. The results at the outputs are compared with the fault free case (good circuit).

The core of every fault simulation is, therefore, logic simulation for all fault configurations. It is to be determined how many of the assumed defects are detected and how many are not, and ultimately a "fault catalogue" is to be produced containing the detected faults.

The simplest fault simulation method is **single fault** simulation, in which every fault is simulated in a separate simulation run. This method is inefficient. A much more powerful approach is the so-called **concurrent** method, in which the whole set of faults is simulated concurrently. The basic idea here is to use the simulation of the good circuit as a reference for the faulty circuits. The faulty circuits execute explicitly only the changes to the reference behaviour; the rest is "borrowed" from the reference simulation.

3.4 Multi-level Simulation

Traditionally the design and simulation of a circuit is carried out on just one level, the gate level, using elementary logic operations such as AND, OR, etc.. However, simulation of VLSI-circuits at this level only is not efficient.

Because of reasons of time and cost multi-level methods have to be applied; i.e. simulation is accomplished at different levels of detail for the various parts of a circuit. This allows the cost of simulation to be considerably lowered compared to gate-level simulations.

With multi-level simulation a digital circuit is first of all partitioned into subcircuits and the subcircuits are modelled on different abstraction levels. These models are then translated or compiled into the corresponding simulator lists.

4. Exploitation of parallelism

The basic principle behind the organisation of parallel processing in the simulation of digital circuits is partitioning with regard to structure and time. There are three basic levels for the organisation of parallel processing plus special techniques on hardware level.

```
+-----------------+-------------------------------------------------------------+
! Level           ! Mechanisms                                                  !
+-----------------+-------------------------------------------------------------+
!                 !                                                             !
! Case            ! Partitioning of: fault set, stimuli set, variant set        !
!                 !                                                             !
! Circuit         ! Circuit partitioning, macro-pipelining, asynchron. proces.! !
!                 !                                                             !
! Algorithm       ! Algorithm partitioning, task pipelining, event handling     !
!                 !                                                             !
+-----------------+-------------------------------------------------------------+
!                 !                                                             !
! Hardware        ! Implementation parallelism                                  !
!                 !                                                             !
+-----------------+-------------------------------------------------------------+
```

4.1 Parallelism on the case level

On the case level, i.e. on the level of simulation jobs, there is a very important possibility for parallel processing for all of the types of variant simulation:

- the structure variants, such as with fault simulation and the simulation of design variants,

- the stimulus variants, such as, for example, with the simulation of instruction variants (e.g. addressing modes) of a processor.

The basis is that all the variants can be executed as single-case simulations independently from each other; i.e. in parallel.

Figure 5 illustrates the principle of variant simulation in the case of fault simulation. To this end the set of variants is divided into subsets which are then processed as parallel jobs.

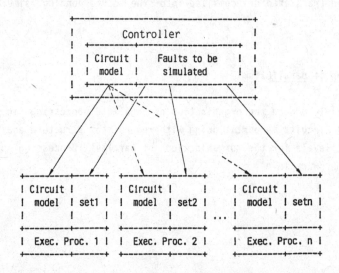

Figure 5: Principle of variant simulation in case of fault simulation

Because of cost reasons variant simulations have been done routinely only for fault simulation because fault simulation is indispensable for the analysis of testability and the preparation of test patterns.

Consistent use of VLSI technology and the cost savings which arise from this will also make the systematic testing of design variants economical.

4.2 Parallelism at the circuit level

At the circuit level, i.e. the level of individual circuit simulation, the basis for parallel processing is partitioning of the circuit into subcircuits. Modern design techniques (top down design) lend themselves automatically to a hierarchical partitioning of circuits into functional units.

On the highest partitioning level a combinatorial type of linking of functional units usually results. Such functional units can be treated independently from each other, i.e. each can be ascribed a "virtual simulator".

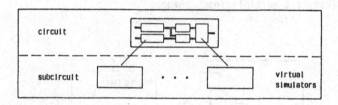

Figure 6 : Circuit partitioning

Circuit partitioning ascribing subcircuits to virtual simulators allows the exploitation, individually or in combination, of the following forms of parallel processing:

- Parallel processing of synchronous and asynchronous subcircuits between clock points,

- Macro-pipelining of the processing of subcircuits, and

- Asynchronous parallel processing of all subcircuits.

For asynchronous parallel processing of subcircuits there are two principally different strategies :

- Conflict-free strategy according to the principle of the so-called "delimited action" ("Worst case strategy") /Lein81/

- Strategy with conflicts according to the principle of the so-called "time warp" ("optimistic strategy") /Jeff85/.

As shown in /Lohn87/, the "time warp" principle is well suited for the object-oriented machine. This principle is also providing the basis for current experiments at the Cosmic Cube /Seit84/ within the framework of discrete simulations /Jeff85,Unge85/.

4.3 Parallel processing at the algorithm level

The algorithm level, i.e. the level of individual virtual simulation machines, offers very important and distinct options for parallel processing. It is the major level for exploitation of parallelism in today's "simulation machines".

In the following we concentrate on the event-driven algorithm.

Figure 7 illustrates the principle sequence of operations in the event-driven algorithm and the inherent parallelism /Abra83/. The "signals" are concurrently propagated along the different paths (vertical lines).

Conceptually all the operations on the same horizontal level may be performed in parallel. Note that different concurrent events may be propagated to the same element which may lead to a multiple input change.

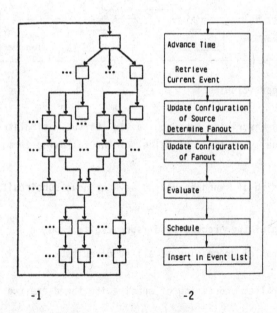

-1   -2

Figure 7 : Concurrency in Logic Simulation (event-driven algorithm) /Abra83/
- inherent parallelism
- principle sequence of operations

455

A very efficient and common approach is to map the sequence of operations onto a circular pipeline with a central event list.

4.4 Parallel processing at the hardware level

At the hardware level there is a whole bunch of options for exploitation of parallelism, e.g. through processor tailoring, parallel communication path, use of parallel table look up techniques for the evaluation of elements, data caching etc..

These are implementation details which heavily depend on the choice of methods and machine architecture. Both points are still under study.

5. Principle Features of the Simulator

The multi-level simulator covers the logic-design cycle, i.e. from register transfer level to functional level, gate level down to switch level with provisions for including the programming level and the electrical level and support for hardware-in-the-loop simulations. We expect that the lower level design cycles, namely the electrical and physical design cycle, will be largely automated in the near future.

The architecture exploits the inherent parallelism by use of the following principle techniques (Fig. 8):

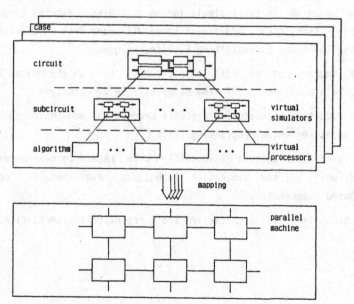

Figure 8 : Exploitation of parallelism

- Case partitioning with multi-case simulations, i.e. simulation of structure variants such as in fault simulation, design variants, stimuli variants.

- Functional circuit partitioning, i.e. partitioning of a whole circuit into sub-circuits (functional units.). Processing of subcircuits will be as far as possible asynchronous, e.g. using the so-called time-warp method.

- Algorithm partitioning primarily into pipelined tasks. How far multiple pipe-lines or a totally parallel approach are possible is yet to be determined.

The major question is how to match these techniques with the machine architecture for an optimal trade-off between node architecture and communication.

6. Goals of the Project

The fundamental goal in the development of the multi-level simulator is to gain precise insight into the different aspects of parallel machines in a sensible application, from architecture and programming to performance increase and cost effectiveness.

More detailed goals are:

- drastic simulation performance increase by use of multi-level simulation and massive parallel processing.

  We strive for a speed-up by a factor of more than 100 in logic simulation and a near linear speed-up in fault simulation on a 1000-node machine through paral-lel processing techniques. Additional speed will come from an advanced compute engine within the nodes by exploiting VLSI-technology.

- Significant improvement of cost effectiveness through the use of VLSI tech-nology for the simulation itself. The nodes will be of RISC-type.

- Substantial reduction of cost for software production and maintenance through use of the object-oriented programming style.

- Extensibility of architecture (especially with regard to maximum design com-plexity as well as new simulation techniques, e.g. symbolic processing or knowledge based components).

The goal is an open simulation architecture and a prototype implementation.

7. Present Status and Results

The main activities and results in the first half of the project, are:

- Development of a simplified experimental simulator (SILKE) and measurements
  with SILKE on a number of machines.

- First implementation of the experimental simulator in the parallel object-
  oriented language POOL on the POOL-simulator (SODOM).

- Specification of SILKE in FP2.

- Study of the above mentioned fundamental techniques of exploiting parallelism
  with prototype implementations /Apos86/.

7.1 Experimental Simulator

The experimental simulator is intended to serve as a vehicle for testing ideas,
mechanisms and machines. It was originally written in PASCAL and later on rewritten
in POOL, OCCAM and C. The basic version contains only the gate level; the first
multi-level version includes the register transfer level additionally. The implementation of the switch level as well as parallel versions (see later "circuit
partitioning") are underway.

The SILKE performance was measured on a number of complex instruction set machines
(VAXes, 68020, 80286) and RISC-type machines (TRANSPUTER, Fairchild CLIPPER). The
results support our option for a RISC-type compute engine.

7.2 Implementations in POOL

For checking the suitability of the object-oriented language (POOL-T) for parallel
logic simulation and the language constructs needed, three different experimental
approaches have been exercised:

- the **Circular Pipeline** as the "classical" approach for parallel processing
  at the algorithm level. This approach is similar to the pipeline in /Abra83/,
  see Fig. 7; it uses a central event list.

- in the "natural" **Gate/Object** approach each gate was modelled by one object.
  Objects communicate by sending event messages. An event is the tuple (value,
  time stamp). Each input of a gate is modelled by a FIFO-queue through which the
  time-ordered stream of event messages flows, i.e., each gate has his own event
  list.

This approach is the most natural one for object-oriented simulation and can be regarded as the extreme case of circuit partitioning, i.e., down to the gate level.

- the **Circuit Partitioning** approach using **Time Warp** synchronization performs parallel processing at the circuit level (see section 4.2, Fig. 6). This approach (which uses distributed event lists) is novel.

All these approaches implement the specification of SILKE. The underlying basic principles for simulation execution control are event-driven simulation with selective trace.

First measurements have indicated granularity problems. For solving the problems two different directions are performed: enhancements in the object-oriented language (POOL-2) and changes in the implementation of the simulator to achieve coarser granularity.

A detailed description of the implementations and the discussion of the results is given in /Lohn87/.

7.3 Specification in FP2

In connection with work of the Working-Groups in the project, a formal specification of SILKE in FP2 /Jorr86/ was done in collaboration with LIFIA, as reported in /Scha87/, this volume. The specification runs on the FP2-interpreter.

This specification serves as a basis for "benchmarking" the various programming styles in project ESPRIT 415 (object-oriented, functional, logic, data-flow) using SILKE as application example.

7.4 Exploitation of parallelism

In the field of exploiting parallelism (see section 4.) the following results were achieved.

Case partitioning

We successfully implemented a method for dynamic distribution of a fault-simulation task in a network. The implementation is based on a state-of-the-art fault simulator (DISIM fault simulator /Apos82/), as shown in Fig. 9.

The main component of the "parallel fault-simulator" is a SUPERVISOR which controls all "servers" and schedules them appropriately.

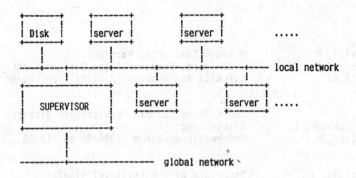

Figure 9: Initial implementation of the parallel fault-simulator

To give the SUPERVISOR dynamic control over the fault-simulations running on the servers, a special "fork on external request" was added to the DISIM fault-simulator. This external request is mapped onto an existing internal mechanism in the fault-simulator for splitting the actual fault-set in case of memory overflow.

The SUPERVISOR uses this mechanism for **dynamically splitting** the fault sets in the servers - as shown in Figure 6 - so that a nearly optimal load balancing of the servers is achieved.

Measurements with the parallel fault simulator are encouraging. As expected, the speed up is nearly linear with the number of processors, as long as the ratio between fault simulation and good circuit simulation per node is reasonable.

For giving insights into the dynamics of the various operations in the network, a special graphic monitor is developed.

Circuit partitioning

We implemented a prototype for a distributed (object-oriented) version of SILKE, in which the objects are subcircuits. Each subcircuit maintains a local clock and has its own processor. All processors run independently. Synchronization is by using a variant of Jefferson's "time-warp" algorithm /Jeff85/.

This work is in an early stage. The version is used as a testbed for testing the "time warp" method in combination with circuit partitioning.

Algorithm partitioning

We have designed a 3-stage pipeline for the algorithm level compute engine. The design is based on Fairchild CLIPPER, an advanced RISC-type processor. The pipeline is implemented using the novel cache features of CLIPPER.

This engine serves as as the basis for a DISIM-accelerator and for detailed pipeline design studies.

References

/Abra83/
Abramovici, M.   A Logic Simulation Machine;
Levendel, Y.H.   IEEE Trans. Computer-Aided Design of Integrated
Menon, P.R.   Circuits and Systems, 2 (1983), pp. 82-94

/Albe86/
Albert, I.   CAD-Systeme für die industrielle Rechner-
Müller-Schloer, C.   entwicklung;
Schwärtzel, H.   Informatik-Spektrum (1986)9, pp. 14-28

/Apos86/
Aposporidis, E.   Structure of a multi-level simulator
Daue, T.   exploiting maximal concurrency,
Mehring, P.   ESPRIT 415, Doc. No. AEG 008-86, April 1986

/Apos82/
Aposporidis, E.   Logik- und Fehlersimulation kundenspezifischer
Jud, W.   Schaltungen;
                        10. Intern. Kongress Mikroelektronik,
                        München, 9.-11. Nov. 1982, pp. 414-423

/Blun77/
Blunden, D.F.   Logic Simulation - Part 1;
Boyce, A.H.   The Marconi Review, Vol. XL, No. 206,
Taylor, G.   Third Quarter 1977, pp. 157-171

/Jeff85/
Jefferson, D.   Fast concurrent simulation using the time
Sowizral, H.   warp mechanism;
                        SCS Multiconference, San Diego, Jan. 85,
                        Part: Distributed Simulation, p. 63-69

/Jorr86/
Jorrand, P.   Term Rewriting as a Basis for the Design of a
                        Functional and Parallel Programming Language;
                        A case study: the Language FP2;
                        in Fundamentals of Artificial Intelligence,
                        LNCS 232, 1986

/Lein81/
Leinwand, S.M.   Process oriented Logic Simulation;
                        IEEE, 18th Design Automation Conference,
                        Paper 25.1, 1981, pp. 511-517

/Lohn87/
Lohnert, F.   Necessary Language Constructs for the Object-
                        oriented Language with Respect to Logic
                        Simulation
                        ESPRIT 415, Doc. No. AEG 001-87, Febr. 1987

/Scha87/
Schaefer, P.   Specification of a pipelined event driven
Schnoebelen, Ph.   simulator using FP2; this volume

/Seit84/
Seitz, C.L.   Concurrent VLSI Architectures;
                        IEEE Transactions on Computers, Vol. c-33,
                        No. 12, (December) 1984, pp. 1247-1265

/Unge85/
Unger, B.   A process oriented distributed simulation package;
Lomow, G.   SCS Multiconference; Part: Distributed Simulation,
Andrews, K.   January 1985, San Diego, S. 76-81

The DOOM system and its applications: A survey of Esprit 415 subproject A, Philips Research Laboratories

Eddy A.M. Odijk

Philips Research Laboratories

P.O.Box 80.000

5600 JA Eindhoven

The Netherlands

Abstract

This paper surveys the concepts of the Parallel Object-Oriented Language **POOL** and a highly parallel, general purpose computer system for execution of programs in this language: the **Decentralized Object-Oriented Machine, DOOM**. It reports on the approach to highly parallel computers and applications followed at Philips Research Laboratories, Eindhoven, as subproject A of Esprit project 415. The first sections present a short overview of the goals and premises of the subproject. In Section 3 the programming language POOL and its characteristics are introduced. Section 4 presents an abstract machine model for the execution of POOL programs. Section 5 describes the architecture of the DOOM-system. It is a collection of self contained computers, connected by a direct, packet-switching network. The resident operating system kernels facilitate the execution of a multitude of communicating objects, perform local management and cooperate to perform system wide resource management. In Section 6 we introduce the applications that are being designed to demonstrate the merits of the system. These symbolic applications will be shown to incorporate a high degree of parallelism. In the last section some conclusions will be drawn.

1   Introduction

In view of the increasing demand for processing power in many of today's scientific and engineering applications, parallel computers and computing have become a major issue in computer science and will acquire an important position in the computer industry soon. A multitude of research programs and projects has been launched with the same objective: to improve the performance of computer systems by designing them as a large number of concurrently operating processing elements, and with largely varying approaches to architectural and programming principles.

Central themes in parallel computer architecture are formed by the communication structure and processor support for new language features. Several shared memory systems have been proposed with busses or multi-staged switching networks as communication means. Another structure is provided by architectures that are based on message passing [21]. Unification in logic languages and garbage collection are just two examples of features that benefit from hardware support, [23] and [7].

Again, a variety of choices can been made when it comes to programming of parallel systems. The extension of sequential programming languages with primitives for parallelism and communication is one way. The model of functional and logic languages allows parallel execution as well. Since the parallelism is invisible for the programmer and is extracted by the implementation this is referred to as implicit parallelism. This approach is followed in [8]. Thirdly, explicit means for partitioning of programs, combined with high level mechanisms for communication and synchronization are offered by a number of parallel programming languages, e.g., Occam [15], POOL [1].

This paper presents a survey of an object-oriented approach to parallel computing. It presents the concepts of the Parallel Object-Oriented Language **POOL** and a highly parallel, general purpose computer system for execution of programs in this language: the **Decentralized Object-Oriented Machine** , **DOOM**. In POOL, a program is subdivided into a large number of so-called objects, which communicate by sending messages. The DOOM architecture contains many identical computers that are connected by means of a packet-switching network. Each computer supports the execution of a number of POOL-objects.

The approach described here, is carried out as subproject A of Esprit project 415, and contains the largest effort of the 6 subprojects. The partners involved are Philips Research Laboratories, Eindhoven, the Netherlands, and AEG-Aktiengesellschaft, Berlin, West-Germany. This paper surveys the work at Philips. In [16] a mixed level logic VLSI circuit simulator is presented. This program is one of three applications, designed to assess the potentials of POOL and the DOOM system. The results that are strived for at the end of this five years project are:

- A prototype Decentralized Object-Oriented Machine, DOOM, consisting of some 100 identical self-contained computers, each having a CPU, local memory and communications means, which are connected in a direct packet switching network. Each computer, called a node of the system, has a copy of the operating system kernel. This kernel performs local resource management, and cooperates with the other kernels for global operating system tasks. The prototype DOOM system is connected, as a satellite, to a host computer, where the programming environment resides. This setup was chosen for the prototype to postpone the programming effort on an environment to a development stage.

- A Parallel Object-Oriented Language, POOL, in which significant application programs can be programmed. The language provides the user with control of parallelism and granularity. It is important for the language to have clear semantics. Support for the verification of programs is desirable, and becomes even more important in a parallel environment. The design of a proof system forms therefore part of the effort.

- Two significant applications in the area of symbolic processing that demonstrate the performance increase through parallelism on DOOM. The first of these is a parallel theorem prover, applied to the verification of VLSI circuit designs. The second is a parallel version of the analytical component of the Rosetta natural language translation system [18]. Rosetta is currently being designed in the same (Computer Science) department at Philips Research.

While the emphasis of our approach is on symbolic processing, the VLSI circuit simulator of AEG and applications designed by others will demonstrate the applicability of DOOM for numerical applications.

Figure 1 pictorially represents the constituents of the prototype DOOM-system. From the above it follows that the new issues for the design of programming languages, application programs and computer systems, raised by the quest for massive parallelism, are approached in an integral and coherent manner. In our view this is essential to reach
all of the above goals.

This paper is structured as follows: the next section describes the starting points and initial choices of the project. Section 3 introduces the language POOL and discusses its characteristics. An Abstract POOL machine model is shown in Section 4, and is transformed into the model for DOOM. In making these transformations a number of design issues will be introduced. Section

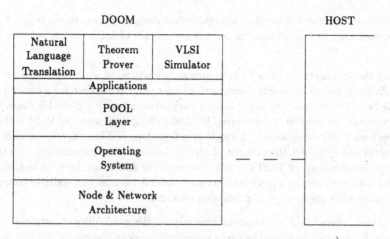

Figure 1: The components of DOOM

5 is dedicated to the DOOM system: its operating system and architecture. The sixth section introduces the applications that are designed to demonstrate the merits of the system. These symbolic applications will be shown to incorporate a high degree of parallelism. In the last section some conclusions will de drawn.

2 Starting points for DOOM

The DOOM system is being designed as a research vehicle to investigate the potentials and problems of the exploitation of parallelism and is aimed as a basis for an industrial development of a parallel computer system. Such systems have two important characteristics: first, they are meant to execute large application programs, which should be robust and well-structured, in order to facilitate team designs and proper software engineering, and secondly, cost/performance ratio is a prime design criterion. A number of conclusions have been drawn from these characteristics. On the program design level the available parallelism is best known and understood by the programmer. Languages with explicit means for structuring parallelism acknowledge this fact. Among such languages, we consider the object-oriented style as very promising.

In object-oriented languages the natural method for structuring and partitioning, combined with a message-passing mechanism for communication and synchronization, greatly relieve these aspects of the programming task. The subdivision of a system into so-called *objects*, which are integrated units of data and procedures, may yield coinciding notions for both information hiding and protection (essential for reliable and maintainable software) and concurrent execution. At this basic level of concurrency annotations can be introduced for control of computation granularity, and allocation or load-balancing strategies. The dynamic structures exhibited by many symbolic applications are matched in object-oriented languages by the mechanisms for dynamic creation of objects and for communication to other objects. Consequently, the object-oriented style eases the design of large and robust applications and facilitates team designs and proper software engineering. Its abstraction facilities relieve the user from being concerned with implementation details (until a post-design optimization, if he prefers to do so).

Individual objects in POOL and other parallel object-oriented languages behave as sequential, control-flow processes, and can be implemented with good efficiency on von Neumann type computers. No special computational support is required from the processor architecture (as e.g. in reduction and logic systems). The effort in architecture design is geared to the support of communication between the processing elements and the coexistence of many objects on every processing element.

Designing the architecture with a VLSI implementation in mind is considered important to improve the efficiency and to achieve the cost/performance ratio as required for a future commercial product. As Seitz [21] has pointed out, a loosely coupled structure is a desirable characteristic for a VLSI implementable parallel architecture. With shrinking dimensions of VLSI technology the building block may ultimately occupy a single or a few chips and have a very cost effective realization. The resulting systems then consist of identical elements, which complies with the relative design and replication costs of VLSI circuits. Extensibility and adaptability to the required performance is another favourable aspect, and is made possible because the available communication bandwidth scales with the number of processing elements.

As a contrast, shared memory organisations rely on the availability of very high bandwidth busses or switching networks as well as cache supported memory designs. Scalability and integration densities of such organisations lag behind the possibilities of loosely coupled systems. The absence of shared memory in the latter organisation should be reflected in the programming model. In fact, all variables in POOL programs are private to one of the objects. Beside compatibility with the architecture this has the advantage of protection as described above.

3 The programming language POOL

This section surveys the concepts of POOL-T. POOL is an acronym for "Parallel Object-Oriented Language", and denotes family of languages designed in the course of the DOOM project. The latest member POOL-T (T for target), defined in [1], was designed in 1985 as the language in which applications for the DOOM system will be expressed. In the sequel POOL and POOL-T will be used without distinction.

The effort in language design was directed at a language that exploits the ideas of object-oriented programming in order to make the programming of systems with a large amount of parallelism feasible. It was not meant as a tool for rapid prototyping (where the excellence of many existing object-oriented languages lies), but as a language to program large, well-designed systems in, with as many facilities for static checking as possible.

3.1 Introduction to POOL

The essence of object-oriented programming is the subdivision of a system into *objects*, which are integrated units of data and procedures. Objects are entities of a very dynamic nature: they can be created dynamically, the data they contain can be modified and they even have an internal activity of their own, as will be described later. The most important property of objects is that they form the units of abstraction and protection. An object can have *variables* (also called instance variables) to store its internal data in. A variable can contain (a reference to) an object. Changing (assigning to) a variable causes it to refer to a different object than before. The variables of an object cannot be accessed directly by other objects: there is a clear separation between the inside and outside of an object.

Objects may only interact by sending *messages* to each other. Each object explicitly states to which object it sends a certain message, and when it is prepared to accept one. Upon accepting a message, the object will execute one of its procedures and the object that is the result of this execution will be sent back to the sender. In object-oriented languages such a procedure is called a *method*. Note that the method executed by the object can access the object's variables. As the object has explicit control of its interaction with other objects, it can keep its internal data in a consistent state. Objects are never destroyed explicitly. However, when an object is only waiting for messages or its own activity has terminated, and furthermore no other object in the system has a reference to it, then it may be safely removed from the system executing the program.

Objects are entities of a semantic nature. On the syntactic level the corresponding notion is that of a **class**. A class is a description of the behaviour of a set of objects, the instances of the class. It describes the number and kind of their variables, and the methods that are executed in response to messages. Together these are called the *instance features* of a class. In POOL, a set of *standard classes* (e.g., Integer and Character) with a number of methods are already predefined.

Beside the methods attached to each instance of a class, there are also *routines*: procedural abstractions related to a class rather than to a specific object. They can be called by all instances of all classes in a program. A typical task for a routine is to create and initialize new objects of its class. The routines are also called *class features*.

POOL has a strong typing mechanism: with each variable a class is associated (its *type*); it may contain references to objects of that class only. With every expression in the language a class (again called its type) can be associated statically. A program is only considered valid if every expression is of the type as required by its context. Thus, many programming errors can be detected before the program is executed.

3.2   Parallelism in POOL-T

There are several ways to combine object-oriented languages with parallelism. In Smalltalk-80 [12] the traditional concept of a process is introduced, where several of these may execute in parallel, each acting in the same way as if it were an ordinary sequential object-oriented program. The same additional constructs are necessary as with traditional processes to get the concurrency under control. For example, in Smalltalk-80 synchronization and mutual exclusion are supported by semaphores.

A better approach to integration starts by associating a process with every object. By doing this, we also get a very natural model for a purely sequential execution, in which at any time only one object is active, by adhering to the following restrictions: (1) execution starts with only one active object, (2) the sender of a message always waits until the corresponding method has returned its answer (rendez-vous, synchronous message passing) and (3) an object is only active when answering a message.
Starting from such a sequential execution there are several possibilities to allow genuine parallelism, each one characterized by which of the above restrictions is relaxed. If we allow the sender of a message to go on with its own activities without waiting for result of the method, the receiver can start executing in parallel with the sender. By creating more objects and sending them messages, the number of concurrently active processes can be increased quickly. Let us call this principle *asynchronous message passing*. It is employed, for example, in the actor languages developed at MIT [13], and in the language of Lang [19].

Another possibility is to specify for each object a *body*, an activity of its own, which it executes without the need for a message to initiate it. In this case the moments when the object is willing to accept a message must be indicated explicitly. Because objects have a body, the concurrency need not come from the concurrent execution of a message sender and the processing of the message by the receiver, so in this situation the message passing may be restricted to be synchronous. This last approach has been taken in POOL-T. A rationale for this and other choices has been presented in [2]. For an example of a POOL-T program the reader is referred to [4].

3.3 Resulting characteristics of POOL-T

The object-oriented approach acknowledges the fact that the programmer is responsible for and has the best knowledge of the detection and use of parallelism in his application. To relieve his task, object-oriented languages supply the user with a natural method for structuring and partitioning combined with a message-passing mechanism for communication and synchronization. In POOL every data item, from a boolean to a complete database, is represented by an object. All these objects have the same general way of interacting with each other. An important benefit of this unification is the resulting simplification in the language.

The dynamic structures exhibited by many symbolic applications, for which the fifth generation parallel architectures are targeted, are matched in object-oriented languages by the mechanisms for dynamic creation of objects and for communication to other objects.

The subdivision of a system into objects yields coinciding notions for both information hiding and protection (essential for reliable and maintainable software) and concurrent execution. Security is further enhanced by the strong typing mechanism. A *unit* mechanism, not described here, is an important feature to further enhance abstraction and to improve reusability of program parts [1].

Until now some thirty programs of varying sizes have been written in POOL-T. A sequential implementation of POOL-T was designed early in the project and is available to third parties. This implementation allows us to execute programs, although it provides no information on the actual amount of parallelism. Evaluation of POOL-T characteristics is further supported by a characterization of the features of the DOOM system.

Some conclusions have been drawn. First, POOL-T tends to be verbose. Providing syntactic sugar for the creation and initialization of objects would alleviate this verbosity to great extent. Secondly, compared to the costs of communication in the present prototype design, the computational granularity of objects is rather small. This was not unexpected. On one hand, object-oriented programming leads to processes with a small grain-size when compared to "traditional" processes, while most of the available microprocessors are designed to support the latter. The directions are explored to reach a better balance. Provisions are made in the language which allow the implementation to detect objects which are known to only one other object and do not require a process of their own. Such objects can then be embedded in the other object resulting in a larger granularity. In the area of architectural support, more effective means to support context-switching and handling of messages are investigated. Solutions found in this area can only be implemented with new processor designs, based on VLSI technology.

A related issue is that of communication. The synchronous communication of POOL-T appears to be restrictive in a number of cases by requiring the programmer to take care to avoid situations of deadlock. Furthermore, with the increase of granularity as described above,the amount of available parallelism is reduced. These observations have led to reconsider this issue. Along the lines described here, a new language, POOL2, is presently being designed and evaluated on its implementability.

3.4 The computational model of POOL

Before proceeding to describe how POOL programs are executed, we now summarize the computational characteristics of POOL. The computational model consists of processes (objects) which internally show sequential control-flow, or imperative, behaviour. These processes can be dynamically created during program execution upon request by other objects. Thus many objects of each of the classes defined in the program can be alive and executing in parallel. Each process must have, in some way, access to the code of the class which specifies its behaviour. Each object maintains its own variables etc., and has no way (and no need) to directly access the data space of any other object.

Communication and synchronisation between objects in POOL-T are performed by synchronous message passing. The sending object is stalled while the message is being answered by another object. The parameters that are required for the method invocation by the receiver are specified in a send expression and form part of the message. The method will only be invoked by the destination object if this object executes an *answer* statement in which that method is named explicitly.

A sender can only send messages to objects to which it has a reference in one of its variables. If more than one message is sent to an object (by different sending objects), the first received message corresponding to a method in the answer statement will be invoked. If there is no such answerable message available, the object will be suspended until one arrives. An answer statement and a direct method call may occur within a method. In this way method invocations can be (recursively) nested and several instances of the local variables of the methods exist.

An object of a certain class is created explicitly and dynamically by means of a *new* expression. Explicit deletion of objects is not possible. However, in most POOL programs many objects will become inactive after a short while: they are awaiting forever for the arrival of messages. They will be implicitly removed from the system when they cannot be accessed any more.

4   An Abstract POOL machine

The computational model of POOL has been shown to consist of concurrently executing processes (objects) that communicate by passing messages. This model is reflected in the underlying hardware structure and operating system and the abstract model of this section. The architecture, classified as MIMD in Flynn's scheme [10], does not employ a shared memory structure for communication, but instead consists of a number of self-contained computers or nodes, i.e. processors with their private memory, which are connected through a network of communication channels.

4.1   Description of the APM

A structural diagram of the Abstract POOL Machine (APM for short) which closely resembles the computational model of Section 3.4 is depicted in figure 2. In this machine every object (or process) has its own node to supply it with processing power and memory. As the number of objects created during program execution is not known in advance the number of nodes in the APM is in principle unbounded. The code of the program to be executed is stored in a program code memory, which in this model is shared by the nodes. Each node only accesses that part of the code corresponding to its class definition. The means for communication between objects are provided by a fully connected network. Examining the characteristics of the APM, a number of remarks can be made. A node is *active*, i.e. it executes instructions of the object, when these belong to the object body or, alternatively, to a method it is answering. A node is *idle* after it has sent a message, but has not yet received an answer (sent via a return message), and when it has executed an answer statement, but no message is available. The amount of parallelism depends,

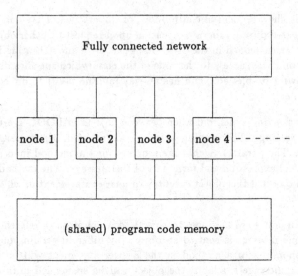

Figure 2: An abstract POOL machine

in this model, only on the degree in which it has been exploited at the algorithmic level.

Having treated the global structure of the abstract machine, the internal details of the node components should now be revealed. Again a structure diagram (of figure 3) supplies an overview of all parts and their interconnection. The operational heart is formed by the data processing part. It can be viewed as an ordinary Von Neumann type, control-driven, processor with an internal -hidden from this picture- alu and datapath, control section, and a set of registers.

The program counter is used in accessing the (common) program code memory, just as a stack pointer denotes the top-of-stack element in the private data stack of the node. The stack contains the data items of the node's object as well as the evaluation stack for the object execution. A LIFO behaviour of the stack is needed due to recursion and nested method answering allowed to the objects.

The other active element in the node is the communication part, which accepts any messages from the network, addressed to the object positioned at the node. The messages are placed in one of the queues, one-to-one corresponding with the method requested in the message. The queues are organised in a FIFO manner to guarantee fairness. As the number of queues corresponds to the number of methods defined in the class of the object, it is in principle unbounded. The heads of the queues are connected to the dataprocessor part, which has means to inspect the contents of the heading messages of all queues and to retrieve the head element of a specific queue. Not surprisingly, another -direct- connection exists from the communication part to the data processing part. This connection serves to receive the return messages, which should directly be communicated from the answering to the sending object. The connection from the dataprocessor part to the communication part serves to send both Pool-messages and return-messages.

Summarizing, the Abstract POOL Machine contains an unbounded number of processing nodes and method queues per node as well as a network of unbounded size. This model provides the ideal machine for the programmer, a proper abstraction for the POOL-compiler design, as well as a starting point for formal description and verification of the actual system design. A more detailed informal description of this so called Abstract POOL Machine (APM) has been presented in [7], its formalization in the axiomatic architecture description language AADL is given in this

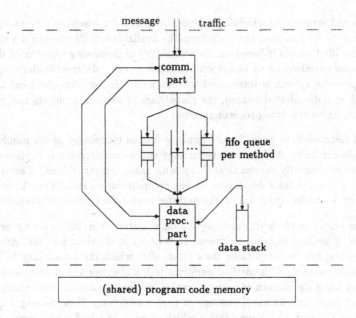

Figure 3: An abstract POOL node

volume [9].

The presented model is not appropriate, however, for efficient implementation of POOL programs. The number of objects in a POOL program would exceed by far the realizable number of processors. Arguments of flexibility, proper support for the POOL data types and operations upon them, as well as efficient use of the hardware lead to the conception of nodes as powerful as a personal computer, which have an OS to bridge the gap to the APM. The task of the OS, then, is to efficiently map a large dynamically changing computation graph of objects and their references onto the static (and smaller) network graph of computers. The nodes each execute the code of many objects and the network architecture provides a fast connection between any pair of nodes. This is the actual model of the DOOM system, that will be derived in the rest of this section.

4.2   Transforming the APM to DOOM

The Abstract POOL machine model can be transformed to a description of DOOM in three steps. In these steps the number of processors, the communications means and the number and size of memories, respectively, are bound to a fixed and finite constant. Performing these steps reveals the major issues for the system design.

The first parameter of the abstract machine to be bound is the number of processors in the system. The fixed number of processors must now accommodate a larger number of objects, resulting in these having to share parts of the nodes. Necessarily, each object retains its own data stack and method queues. Consequently the node model now contains multiple data stacks and sets of queues. Obviously, the dataprocessor and communication parts are the parts that can be shared. Doing so requires some extensions to these parts. The communication part must now be able to distinguish and handle the queues of a number of objects.

The consequences for the data processing part are more radical. First of all, it must be able to support the execution of multiple processes, e.g. by providing means for process switching. There must be a way and strategy to schedule the resident objects for execution. Secondly, the objects must, upon creation, be allocated to a node from the available set. This requires a strategy which in this, still simplified, model is based on the availability of processing capacity of the nodes and the costs of communication to an object on the same or on a different node, respectively. As a result, an operating system is introduced to each node. It performs the local task of object scheduling and, in a distributed fashion, the global task of allocating objects and maintaining a proper load balance on the data processing parts.

The second restriction, as posed by the implementation technology, is the number of connections that a node can have. With present technology and an architecture as explained in the next sections, a node can directly communicate only with some ten other ones. Therefore messages can, in general, not reach their destination in one communication step. They have to be passed on, in some way, by nodes which are on the path between their source and destination.

Two options exist : in the first, circuit switching, a static connection is set up between source and destination by putting switches at intermediate nodes in the right position. After this build-up phase the message is conveyed along the circuit, after which the circuit may be broken down or held for a next message. This method performs well under low and moderate traffic loads in the network and when the pattern of communication is relatively constant over time. The second method is called (store and forward) message or packet switching. Here, messages are forwarded to a next node on the path to the destination which stores it in a buffer and selects another node to pass it on to. In this method a communication channel or link is only occupied during the time needed for one step of the message. Therefore message switching lends itself better for high traffic loads, while it also accommodates fast changing patterns of communication. Having chosen this method for the DOOM system, the consequences for the systems architecture should now be discussed.

A new functional unit is placed between the, now more sparsely connected, network and the communication part (figure 4). First, it contains buffers to place the messages which have been received but should be passed on further. As these buffers are of finite size, messages potentially don't fit in this space. The usual solution is to split them into fixed size packets, which are treated separately in the network. For performance reasons, the size is usually chosen such that most messages fit within one packet. The second function of the new block is to select one of its outgoing links for forwarding packets to one of its neighbours. This function is called routing. For proper operation of the system this routing function should ensure the avoidance of deadlocks (possible due to the finite number of buffers) and take care of a proper balancing of the traffic on the various links. A last function which is required when packets do not necessarily arrive in sending order, is the reassembly of the original packet.

Since it is sparsely connected, the topology of the network now becomes of importance. A number of criteria can be applied for the selection of a suited topology to connect the nodes. Its degree (the maximum number of links per node) was mentioned above as being bound by technology. The diameter determines the maximum number of communication steps between any source and destination pair, which in turn influences the latency of answering a message. Other criteria deal with the reliability of operation, extensibility and the ease of mapping a computation graph onto the physical graph.

Now we are left with one still unbounded parameter. So far, an unbounded number of data stacks and queues, as well as a shared code memory have been assumed. Realistically, only one or two fixed size memories, spanning (part of) the reachable space of a processor, can be implemented. Our last transformation therefore assumes a single, fixed size and private memory. This memory serves to hold program code, the data stacks of the residing objects as well as their

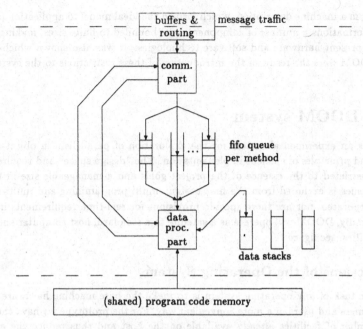

Figure 4: The APM after two transformations

queues. To exploit the available memory in a useful way, a function is added to the system: memory management. This function allocates pieces of memory to those elements who need it: queues that grow due to incoming messages, data stacks that become larger due to nested or even recursive answering of messages and finally pieces of program code that must be acquired (via the network) for the execution of a newly created object of a class, whose code is not present yet. The latter is caused by the fact that the memory is not large enough to contain the complete program code in addition to its other contents. Moreover, it would be wasteful to replicate unused code in all nodes of the system.

Now that memory has become a more or less scarce resource, it is essential to recycle those memory parts that are not used any longer. The regimes of memory (de)allocation by the above mentioned elements make it possible for the memory management function to do so. One other form of becoming unused is due to the fact that objects can become unaccessible for other objects. When this is the case and they are idly waiting for messages to arrive, they cannot contribute to the progress of the program. It is safe then to remove these objects from the node and regain their data and code space. The decision to do so is not a local one. It can only be taken if it has been shown that no object on any other node has a reference to the particular object. This task to collect inaccessible objects is called garbage collection.

Finishing the description of this last model, actually describing the DOOM architecture, the communication part has disappeared (due to the single memory); its function of putting arrived packets into the appropriate queue has been taken over by a local operating system process on the data processor. The unit connecting the node and the network, in the sequel called the Communication Processor, performs the packet switching function. Seen from the node perspective it is able to accept packets of data and deliver them at the node which houses the destination object.

In the previous transformation steps we have derived the global structure of the DOOM architecture from a machine description, which formed the ideal model to application programmers. In the transformations a number of components was bounded to finite sizes, making them implementable in present hardware and software technologies. It was also shown which issues in the design of DOOM were the result of the introduction of these restrictions to the systems architecture.

5   The DOOM system

DOOM is an experimental system for the exploration of parallelism in object-oriented programming and principles of efficient implementation. The "design space" and required manpower have been restricted to the essence of the project goals and a manageable size in two ways. A number of issues is excluded from the first design: multi-programming and multi-user facilities are not incorporated, nor are there specific provisions for real-time requirements in the present system. Secondly, DOOM will operate as a satellite to a standard, host computer and thereby use existing facilities, see figure 1.

5.1   Functions of the Operating System

The basic task of any operating system is to make the bare machine hardware available for the programmers and users in a more convenient way. For the prototype we have chosen to make use of a number of facilities already available on the host and thus reduce the effort. These facilities will be introduced later. The main target for the OS is: efficient execution of a POOL program. This task consists of a number of related aspects, such as (local and global) resource management, process management and communication handling. The comparison between the APM and DOOM shows how these tasks are related to the mapping of the first (unbounded in the number of processors, memories and communication means) onto the latter, which does have physical limitations. A number of issues will be described below.

Allocation of objects onto nodes

When an object is created, processor time and memory space must be assigned to it. In general, the object is "added" to a node where other objects already reside. The selection of a node must be done dynamically, due to the creation of objects during program execution, and should aim at an optimal use of resources. Conflicting criteria are: 1) load balancing, based on both processor and memory occupation, and 2) the low overhead of local compared to inter-node communication. According to the first, objects which can operate in parallel should be placed on different nodes. The second leads to keeping objects on the same node when they are interacting.

POOL programs can be annotated (by the user or by automated analysis) with directives as parameter for the new–instruction. Upon execution of this instruction the OS determines, on basis of this directive and by means of an appropriate algorithm, a "proposed allocation node". A request for allocation is then sent to that node, together with some information about the object to be created (e.g., its code-size). If the request is not accepted, another candidate has to be generated by the algorithm. Thus allocation of objects is a global OS task.

Garbage Collection

The basic garbage collection algorithm (GC) that is needed will be an on-the-fly mark and sweep algorithm of distributed garbage. The GC starts with marking all so called 'root objects', those objects that are *not* awaiting the arrival of messages (so root objects are not garbage). Then the GC recursively starts marking all objects, starting from these roots. Finally, all non-garbage objects will be marked. In the sweep phase all non-marked objects are collected. For a proper working of the GC it is necessary that references to objects (e.g. in variables) are traceable. There are several ways to accomplish this. One way is by means of a tagged memory, another way is using two stacks per object: one for references and one for other data. Architectural support for tagging in the presence of the 68020 data processor of the DOOM prototype was found to be possible. The small performance increase over the second scheme could not justify the expense.

Most traditional mark and sweep garbage collectors assume that no other processing is going on during a GC-phase. This is not acceptable for a multi-processor system, because at each moment only a fraction of the processors will be actually involved in GC and most processors would thus be idle. However, special care has to be taken in order to let GC go on in parallel with other processing. A special synchronisation problem that comes up with concurrent collection of distributed garbage is how to detect that a mark phase or sweep phase can start or has finished. A more detailed description can be found in [4].

A disadvantage of the mark and sweep method is that its overhead is in the order of the number of non-garbage objects. This means that ideally GC should only take place (be scheduled) if there is enough garbage. However, postponing garbage collection increases the chance of memory shortage and even node overflow.

Memory management

The memory of a DOOM node will be used to store three different types of items:

- Stacks: for each object residing on the node a dynamically extending and shrinking stack is needed.

- Message queues: for each method of each object residing on the node a dynamically extending and shrinking FIFO message queue is needed.

- Code blocks: in principle one code block per object is needed. However objects of the same class will share code blocks.

Obviously, these types of items exhibit quite different logical behaviours. More, their sizes differ and vary per object. Therefore a static split-up of a node's memory is out of the question. This holds also for memory management schemes requiring compaction.

For DOOM a two level memory management system has been designed, with a hardware supported paging system as the lower level. This paging system will *not* be used for extending the memory by means of a background store (like in most operating systems), but solely to obtain the desired flexibility of dynamic allocation of storage blocks. It supports the OS with sufficient virtually contiguous memory space to exploit, e.g., the logical behaviour of stacks and queues. The paging system implements a virtual memory split-up in fixed-size pages, which is an order of magnitude larger than the node's physical memory. The page sizes will be small, 128 bytes, and the paging system is supplied, as usual, with a page fault mechanism. Associative address translation can be implemented on megabit memories with a low penalty in chip area and access time. In the prototype system this behaviour will be emulated.

The so obtained large virtual memory is split up by the OS in fixed size segments. In this way, e.g., one segment can be reserved per data-stack. Increases and decreases in stack size, requiring allocation and deallocation of (physical) pageframes can be handled independently from the behaviour of other segments.

Communication

Two objects may or may not reside on the same node. As a result, the communication between objects is either internal (within a node, not involving the network) or external. This can only be determined at run-time, due to the dynamic creation and allocation.

In this section we consider inter-node communication. One of the main issues is the queuing or buffering of messages. In principle, POOL-messages are queued at the node where the destination object resides (destination buffering). In case of memory shortage, an escape mechanism is needed, which is capable of buffering the queued messages on other nodes (distributed buffering). The best node at which a message can be queued in an overflow situation is the node at which the sender of the message resides: because of the synchronous message passing mechanism, the sending object (having the sent message still on its stack) waits anyway until the message is consumed by the receiving object. A communication protocol which employs destination buffering under normal conditions, but switches to distributed buffering if necessary, has been designed.

The role of the host

At the beginning of this section, the task of the kernel has been confined to the execution of POOL programs. We now list the other facilities of the OS, which are offered by the host, a SUN workstation under the UNIX operating system:

1. The host offers the programming environment facilities (editing, printing, etc.).

2. The POOL compiler and linker will run on the host.

3. Via an extension to the POOL standard classes the filesystem facilities of UNIX can be used in POOL programs. This contains also a facility for creation of and communication with UNIX–shells. It gives POOL programs virtually the same "standard environment" that programs running on the host have.

4. The execution of a POOL program on the DOOM machine will be "supervised" by a program running on the host (the so called *executive*). This program takes care of (POOL) program start-up, (initial) code loading and monitor/debugging facilities.

It should be noted that only facilities 3 and 4 make use of the so called gateway connection between the host and the DOOM system.

5.2 The DOOM architecture

In this section the architecture of a DOOM node is presented, followed by an introduction of the network structure that connects these nodes. The node structure for the prototype system, is given in figure 5. It contains a data processor, memory subsystem, a gateway interface and a communication interface.

The *Data processor* (DP) executes the code of the objects which reside on the node.

As described, a DOOM node is able to execute many (presumably some 10 to 100) objects. The processor architecture must therefore support multi-processing. Efficient process switching is a first requirement. Presently available microprocessors are designed to support processes of coarse granularity and have not been optimized towards this aspect. For the prototype system, where the Motorola 68020 microprocessor will be used, this will lead to some performance degradation. Our experiments with RISC-type designs, that may be incorporated in future versions, have shown that feeding independent instruction streams through their, usually pipelined implementation, is in harmony with the DOOM concept and removes bypasses and interlocks from the implementation [7].

The *memory* must host the operating system and accommodate for the code, the stacks and the message queues of the residing objects. As discussed in the section on the OS, a paged virtual

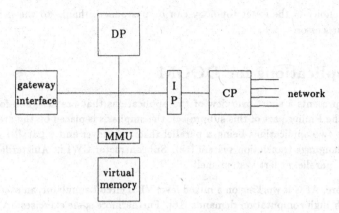

Figure 5: The structure of a DOOM node

memory scheme has been adopted to support memory management. This scheme is implemented on the prototype using the Motorola 68851 memory management unit.

The *gateway interface* is added to the prototype system to provide an interface between the host and every node in the system, employing an ethernet connection. This interface is available solely for the purpose of system diagnosis and performance evaluation.

The last component is the *communication interface*. It consists of a *communication processor* (CP), and an *interface processor* (IP). In order to avoid that interprocessor communication becomes the new bottleneck in parallel systems, hardware support is appropriate. We have taken it to the point where data packets, after transfer by the DP to the local CP, are injected by the CP into the network, passed on by other CPs on the path to the destination node and are handed over to the DP there. This provides a powerful and efficient mechanism for higher layers of the system, and in contrary to, e.g., the Cosmic Cube [21], avoids interruption of the intermediate DPs.

A major requirement of the packet switching CP is a deadlock and starvation free behaviour. Our solution, which is based on a new strategy called class climbing (see [3]), avoids restriction of the number of dynamically selectable alternative routes for a packet. The CP employs a number of independently operating channel servers which operate, in contrast to the usual approach, in a request driven manner. The servers share a common buffer pool to allow efficient use of this scarce resource. Supporting simulations have shown that the CP has a more than adequate bandwidth even with the employment of serial links of moderate frequency. Efforts in the area of queueing models have contributed further to our understanding. Aided by the models developed, it is possible to compare the behaviour of various networks and queueing characteristics for different parameters of packet consumptions by the DP. The interface processor serves the purpose of decoupling the production and the consumption rates of messages in both directions.

Another concern of the architecture is the design of a topology for the communication network. Criteria are, among others, the degree and diameter of the network, its properties with respect to fault-tolerance, its extensibility and its regularity. The latter is required to provide easy mappings of higher level functions onto the machine graph. A stronger form of regularity, vertex-transitivity, has been investigated [20]. Informally stated, every node of a network with this property has the same view of the network. The investigations of these graphs, also called homogeneous, have resulted in novel, high density, networks by the combination of cube networks (based on cartesian products) and chordal ring graphs. The resulting generalized chordal ring cubes yield a lower degree and diameter than (often used) toruses and hypercubes and have excellent fault tolerance properties. The choice of the exact topology can be postponed, thanks to the flexibility of the communication processor.

6 The applications for DOOM

This section presents a short overview of the applications that are designed for the DOOM system. Within the Philips part of this subproject, the emphasis is placed on the area of symbolic computation, the two applications being a parallel theorem prover and a parallel version of the Rosetta natural language translation system [18]. Subcontractor CWI in Amsterdam is involved in the design of a parallel expert system shell.

As stated before, AEG is working on a mixed level VLSI circuit simulator, an excellent example of a problem with high computation demands [16]. Furthermore some exercises are or have been done in cooperation with others, e.g., parallel algorithms for LU–decomposition and statistical cooling.

6.1 Theorem proving

We haven chosen for the theorem proving application in the field of AI since it incorporates many of the principles of knowledge based applications, (inference mechanisms, heuristics, etc.), but requires less effort: the representation of the domain knowledge is by mathematics, its acquisition is easy compared to other expert systems; the results of an expert system can only be validated by an expert in the field, whereas the results of a theorem prover can be validated by any mathematician.

The application will *not* be the parallelization of a presently existing theorem prover. We are working on a higher order typed logic, which is more expressive than first order logic and makes it easier to formulate heuristics. The logic of Martin-Löf's type-theory, or the logic used in De Bruijn's AUTOMATH are examples of such a logic, cf. [6,17]. A preliminary proposal for a language, called MENTHOL, is described in [14] and is presently being evaluated. In such a logic the typing can forbid many senseless deductions, and can be used to steer the heuristics as well. The higher order component of such a theory makes it easier to formulate short theorems and allows to regard proofs as objects. An important part of the theorem prover will be *heuristics*. They must guide the search for the proof. Most existing theorem provers have very universal heuristics, in order to let them perform good for many applications. In fact, this means that they perform equally *bad* for all applications. We prefer to include strong heuristics, which are dedicated to special parts of mathematics.

The obvious sources of parallelism (i.e., those that are the most discussed in the literature) are 'and'- and 'or'-parallelism. The small grain of parallelism of these forms is expected to prohibit their feasibility. Consideration of these forms of parallelism depends on a good control mechanism to keep it within bounds. We will investigate these control mechanisms.

A source of parallelism can be found in unification procedures, especially if terms become large or if these procedures require much processing, such as when we have to take into account several equalities, e.g., stemming from associativity or commutativity. Since unification works by comparing two (directed) graphs, we may get parallelism by splitting both graphs in parts.

We think that heuristics will become a large source of parallelism. First, there may be several different heuristics working in parallel, each influencing the search. This search is done by one or more processes parallel to the heuristics. Some of these heuristics have such an amount of work to do that they will be split up into several processes.

The effort has been structured such that a prototype theorem prover will be finished in the next year. This will serve as a vehicle for investigations and experiments w.r.t. the exploitation of parallelism, and will be structured such that we can add functionality and improve its power in the years after in an incremental way.

6.2 Natural language translation

Investigations in the area of natural language translation will, as far as linguistics are concerned, be based on the machine translation project Rosetta, also under design in our department, cf. [18]. The main task in this area is to parallelize a number of the components of the Rosetta system. The components that we plan to parallelize are the ones that use most of the CPU time in the sequential version: the analytical morphological component and the surface parser.

The parallel POOL-T algorithms will be implemented in such a way that they can be incorporated in the existing Pascal Rosetta system. Obviously, this is important for the demonstrability of this application. In the subsequent sections a description of the above mentioned components is given.

The analytical morphological component

The task of the morphological component is to analyse the words of an input sentence, that is: to detect stems in words by recognizing inflections, conjugations, derivations, and compounds. The result of the analytical morphological component is a sequence of sets of word derivations. Each set contains all possible derivations for a word of the sentence. The analysis of the words is done in three phases: First, in the segmentation phase, words are split in stems and affixes by means of segmentation rules. Then the affixes and the stem of each word are looked up in a dictionary. This yields the necessary syntactic and morphological information. In the last phase the information of the stem and the information of the affixes of a word are composed and it is checked whether the found stem and affixes match.

An obvious way of introducing parallelism in this algorithm is pipelining. For each word in the sentence an object is created. These objects are passed on by a pipeline of objects each performing one of the above transformations on the word. Furthermore, several words can be analyzed in parallel. To avoid that disk I/O (to the host) forms a bottleneck, we plan to store the complete dictionary in the main memory of DOOM (distributed over several nodes).

The surface parser

The function of the surface parser is to find all possible surface structures of an input sentence. The surface structures are the first syntactic parses of a sentence. The input data for the surface parser are the analysed words that result from the analytical morphological component. The surface parser uses a so-called surface grammar, that resembles a context-free grammar. Using this grammar the surface parser can construct all derivation trees of a sentence: the surface structures of that sentence.

The possibilities to parallelize the surface parser have been examined. In [22] it was pointed out that finding all possible surface structures for a sentence comes down to finding all possible derivation trees associated with an input string using a context-free grammar. The best known sequential algorithms solving this problem take $O(n^3)$ time, where n is the number of words in the sentence. Two parallel algorithms for parsing context-free languages have been constructed. These algorithms are both based on the Earley parser, cf.[5]. The first one is a mere parallelization, obtaining a time complexity of $O(n^2)$ using n processors. For the second algorithm the Earley parser was adapted such that there were less precedence constraints between the several actions. The time complexity of this algorithm is $O(n)$ if $O(n^2)$ processors are available, [22].

7 Conclusions

This paper has presented an overview of the goals, organization and effort in Esprit 415, subproject A. The work covers the entire range from applications to the underlying architecture to ensure a well balanced design, and a realistic proof of the exploitation of parallelism.

After the first two years of the project the design of the language as well as the parallel system (OS and architecture) have been finished. The characteristics of the parallel programming language POOL allow the design of large, well-designed programs, and provide a computational model which matches well with the proposed DOOM architecture. An evaluation of the language will lead to a number of improvements to be made in a next version. A sequential implementation has been made, allowing the applications programmers to evaluate their work in an early stage of the project.

The functions required from the OS have been analyzed and algorithms implementing these have been designed.

A first prototype of the architecture with less than ten nodes will be delivered by the end of 1987. This system will support a paged virtual memory system and contain the breadboard implementation of a novel packet-switching communication processor. The designs have been made with a future VLSI implementation in mind. The prototype system forms an intermediate, and not always optimal, stage to a final (few chip) implementation, where full advantage can be made of VLSI technology.

References

[1] Pierre America: *Definition of the Programming Language POOL-T*, Doc. No. 91, ESPRIT Project 415A, Philips Research Laboratories, Eindhoven, the Netherlands, 1986.

[2] Pierre America: *Rationale for the Design of POOL*, Doc. No. 53, ESPRIT Project 415A, Philips Research Laboratories, Eindhoven, the Netherlands, 1985.

[3] J.K. Annot, R.A.H. van Twist: *A Novel Deadlock free and Starvation free Packet Switching Communication Processor*, this volume.

[4] Lex Augusteijn: *Garbage Collection in a Distributed Environment*, this volume.

[5] A.V. Aho, J.D. Ullman: *The Theory of Parsing, Translation, and Compiling*, Vol 1, Prentice Hall, 1972.

[6] L.S. van Benthem Jutting: *Checking Landau's "Grundlagen" in the AUTOMATH system*, Mathematical Centre Tracts 83, (1979).

[7] W.J.H.J. Bronnenberg, M.D. Janssens, E.A.M. Odijk, R.A.H. van Twist, *The Architecture of DOOM*, Proceedings of the ESPRIT–415 Summerschool 1986, to appear in: Springer Lecture Notes in Computer Science.

[8] D.I. Bevan, G.L. Burn and R.J.Karia: *Overview of a Parallel Reduction Machine Project*, this volume.

[9] W. Damm, G. Döhmen : *An axiomatic Approach to the Specification of Distributed Computer Architectures*, this volume.

[10] M.J. Flynn: *Some Computer Organisations and their Effectiveness*, IEEE Trans. Comput. Vol C-21, 1972.

[11] K. Giloi : *Advanced Object-Oriented Architectures*, FGCS, Vol.1, No.3, Feb. 1985.

[12] A. Goldberg and D. Robson: *Smalltalk-80, The Language and its Implementation*, Addison-Wesley 1983.

[13] C. Hewitt: *Viewing Control Structures as Patterns of Message Passing*, Artificial Intelligence, Vol. 8, 1977, pp. 323-364.

[14] F.J. van der Linden: *Design of MENTHOL, a Language for the Theorem Proving Application*, Doc. No. 163, ESPRIT Project 415A, Philips Research Laboratories, Eindhoven, the Netherlands, September 1986.

[15] D. May: *Communicating Sequential Processes: Transputer and Occam*, Proceedings of the ESPRIT-415 Summerschool 1986, to appear in: Springer Lecture Notes in Computer Science.

[16] P. Mehring and E. Aposporides: *Multi-level Simulator for VLSI*, this volume.

[17] P. Martin-Löf: *An Intuitionistic Theory of Types: Predicative Part* , H.E. Rose (ed.): Logic Colloquium '73, pp. 73-118.

[18] S.P.J. Landsbergen: *Isomorphic Grammars and their use in the Rosetta Translation System*, Philips manuscript 12.950, Philips Research Laboratories, Eindhoven, The Netherlands, 1986.

[19] C. R. Lang Jr.: *The Extension of Object-Oriented Languages to a Homogeneous, Concurrent Architecture*, California Institute of Technology, Ph.D. thesis, 1982.

[20] E.A.M. Odijk, R.A.H. van Twist: *Networks for Parallel Computer Systems*, to appear in Proceedings of the Compeuro '87 conference.

[21] C.L. Seitz: *The Cosmic Cube*, Comm. ACM, Vol. 28, No. 1, January 1985.

[22] F.W. Sijstermans: *A Parallel Parser for Natural Language Processing*, Masters thesis, University of Technology Eindhoven, 1985.

[23] A. Goto, S. Uchida : *Toward a High Performance Inference Machine*, ICOT Technical report TR-201

Authors Index Volume I

This series reports new developments in computer science research and teaching – quickly, informally and at a high level. The type of material considered for publication includes preliminary drafts of original papers and monographs, technical reports of high quality and broad interest, advanced level lectures, reports of meetings, provided they are of exceptional interest and focused on a single topic. The timeliness of a manuscript is more important than its form which may be unfinished or tentative. If possible, a subject index should be included. Publication of Lecture Notes is intended as a service to the international computer science community, in that a commercial publisher, Springer-Verlag, can offer a wide distribution of documents which would otherwise have a restricted readership. Once published and copyrighted, they can be documented in the scientific literature.

Manuscripts

Manuscripts should be no less than 100 and preferably no more than 500 pages in length.
They are reproduced by a photographic process and therefore must be typed with extreme care. Symbols not on the typewriter should be inserted by hand in indelible black ink. Corrections to the typescript should be made by pasting in the new text or painting out errors with white correction fluid. Authors receive 75 free copies and are free to use the material in other publications. The typescript is reduced slightly in size during reproduction; best results will not be obtained unless the text on any one page is kept within the overall limit of 18 x 26.5 cm (7 x 10½ inches). On request, the publisher will supply special paper with the typing area outlined.
Manuscripts should be sent to Prof. G. Goos, GMD Forschungsstelle an der Universität Karlsruhe, Haid- und Neu-Str. 7, 7500 Karlsruhe 1, Germany, Prof. J. Hartmanis, Cornell University, Dept. of Computer-Science, Ithaca, NY/USA 14850, or directly to Springer-Verlag Heidelberg.

Springer-Verlag, Heidelberger Platz 3, D-1000 Berlin 33
Springer-Verlag, Tiergartenstraße 17, D-6900 Heidelberg 1
Springer-Verlag, 175 Fifth Avenue, New York, NY 10010/USA
Springer-Verlag, 37-3, Hongo 3-chome, Bunkyo-ku, Tokyo 113, Japan

ISBN 3-540-17943-7
ISBN 0-387-17943-7